Qualitative Research & Evaluation Methods

3

EDITION

To the faculty and learners of The Union Institute, Cincinnati, Ohio, for their friendship and scholarship, and their commitments to methodological eclecticism, interdisciplinary inquiry, integration of theory and practice, valuing both reflection and action, scholarship that is socially relevant and meaningful, individualized professional and personal development, lifelong learning, social justice and equity, human diversity and global community; a scholarly community governed by principles and processes rather than rules and regulations, and innovations in learning-centered, nontraditional doctoral education, including faculty meetings that are interesting and important, an indication of innovation of the highest order

Qualitative Research & Evaluation Methods

EDITION

Michael Quinn Patton

Sage Publications
International Educational and Professional Publisher
Thousand Oaks ▪ London ▪ New Delhi

For information:

Sage Publications, Inc.
2455 Teller Road
Thousand Oaks, California 91320
E-mail: order@sagepub.com

Sage Publications Ltd.
6 Bonhill Street
London EC2A 4PU
United Kingdom

Sage Publications India Pvt. Ltd.
M-32 Market
Greater Kailash I
New Delhi 110 048 India

Printed in the United States of America

Library of Congress Cataloging-in-Publication Data

Patton, Michael Quinn.
  Qualitative research and evaluation methods / by Michael Quinn
Patton.— 3rd ed.
    p. cm.
Rev. ed. of: Qualitative evaluation and research methods. 2nd ed. 1990.
Includes bibliographical references and index.
  ISBN 978-0-7619-1971-1
  1. Social sciences—Methodology. 2. Evaluation research (Social
action programs). I. Patton, Michael Quinn. Qualitative evaluation and
research methods. II. Title.
  H62.P3218 2001
  300'.7'23—dc21   2001005181

07 08 09 10 10 9 8 7

Acquiring Editor:	C. Deborah Laughton
Editorial Assistant:	Veronica Novak
Production Editor:	Diana E. Axelsen
Editorial Assistant:	Kathryn Journey
Copy Editor:	Kate Peterson
Typesetter/Designer:	Janelle LeMaster
Cover Designer:	Michelle Lee

Brief Contents

Detailed Contents

Preface

> The story is told that at the conclusion of a rigorous course in philosophy, one of the students lamented: "Professor, you have knocked a hole in everything I've ever believed in, but you have given me nothing to take its place."
>
> To which the philosopher replied: "You will recall that among the labors of Hercules he was required to clean out the Augean stables. He was not, let me point out, required to fill them."

While part of the task of this revision has been to clean out the qualitative Augean stables, the truly Herculean task has been deciding what to add. Unlike the professor who can be content with getting the stables cleaned, the author of a revision bears responsibility for restocking the stables with fresh nutrients and feed, a task made especially challenging because of the unprecedented blossoming of qualitative inquiry in recent years.

In doing this revision, I reviewed over a thousand new books on qualitative methods, program evaluation, case studies, monographs, and related works published in the last decade, as well as hundreds of articles scattered through scores of journals covering the full range of disciplines and professions. Two important new qualitative journals— *Qualitative Inquiry* and *Field Methods*—began publication, as did specialized qualitative journals in a number of professions (e.g., health, nursing, social work, organizational development) and some devoted to specific approaches (e.g., *Grounded Theory Review*). The *Handbook of Qualitative Research* was published (1994), as was a revision (2000), and the *Handbook of Methods in Cultural Anthropology* (1998) made its debut. Sophisticated new software programs have been developed to support qualitative analysis. Internet listservs have emerged to facilitate dialogue. The Herculean challenge has been analyzing this geometric growth to determine primary trends, patterns, and themes. The results of that analysis are reflected throughout this new edition.

The first edition of this book (1980), entitled *Qualitative Evaluation Methods*, focused on the variety of ways in which qualitative methods were being applied in the then still-emergent profession of program evaluation. (The American Evaluation Association was not established until 1984.) That edition appeared in the midst of the heated qualitative-quantitative debate about the relative value of different methods and alternative paradigms. The second edition (1990), entitled *Qualitative Evaluation and Research Methods,* was influenced by maturing of the paradigms debate. It included much more attention to the ways in which different theoretical and philosophical perspectives influenced qualitative inquiry, as well as the greater range of applications in evaluation as that profession blossomed. This latest edition involves yet another change of title, *Qualitative Research and Evaluation Methods,* reflecting the degree to which developments in qualitative inquiry during the last decade have been driven by a diversifying research agenda and scholarly dialogue, much of which has found its way into evaluation, to be sure.

The classic qualitative-quantitative debate has been largely resolved with recognition that a variety of methodological approaches are needed and credible, that mixed methods can be especially valuable, and that the challenge is to appropriately match methods to questions rather than adhering to some narrow methodological orthodoxy. With less need to establish the value of qualitative inquiry by debating those of quantitative and experimental persuasion, qualitative inquirers have turned their attention to each other, noticing that they are engaging in different kinds of qualitative inquiry from widely different perspectives. Qualitative methodologists and theorists have thus taken to debating each other. The upshot of all the developmental work in qualitative methods is that there is now as much variation among qualitative researchers as there is between qualitatively and quantitatively oriented scholars and evaluators. A primary purpose of this new edition is to sort out the major perspectives in that debate, portray the diversity of qualitative approaches now available, and examine the influences of this diversity on applications, especially but not exclusively in program evaluation, which has experienced a parallel flowering of diversity and attendant controversies about new directions.

⑤ Organization of This Edition

Chapter 1 provides a range of examples of qualitative findings. I begin by presenting a number of significant illustrations of the fruit of qualitative inquiry, in order to give a taste of what results from qualitative studies and help those new to such inquiry know where they are headed and what they are trying to produce. Chapter 2 reviews and adds to the primary strategic themes that define qualitative inquiry. Chapter 3 examines different qualitative approaches, including several that have emerged distinctly in the last decade. Chapter 4 presents a wide range of qualitative applications, many of them new, in evaluation, action research, and organizational, community, and international development. Chapters 5, 6, and 7 cover design and data gathering, offering guidance in purposeful sampling, mixed methods, fieldwork, observational approaches, and interviewing, with special attention directed to the skills and competencies needed to gather high-quality data. Chapter 8 provides direction and processes for analyzing qualitative data, always the most challenging aspect of this work. Finally, Chapter 9 deals with paradigms, politics, and ways of enhancing the credibility of qualitative inquiry. This chapter also presents what I consider to be the five distinct and competing frameworks for undertaking and judging the quality of qualitative studies: traditional scientific research criteria; social construction and constructivist criteria; artistic and evocative criteria; critical change criteria; and pragmatic, utility-oriented evaluation standards and principles. Along the way I've added, as is my wont, hundreds of new stories and examples. I've also created over 50 new exhibits that summarize and illuminate major points.

🖬 Acknowledgments

I began this preface by noting the Herculean task of revision given the enormous growth and increased diversity of qualitative inquiry. One task proved more than Herculean, and I could not complete it. I began to list the many colleagues and evaluation clients to whom I am indebted and who deserve acknowledgement for their contributions to my understanding and writing over the years. Now that I have reached this third edition and traveled many qualitative miles, the list of those to whom I am indebted is too long and the danger of leaving out important influences too great for me to include such traditional acknowledgements here. I can only refer the reader to the references and stories in the book as a starting point.

I must, however, acknowledge cartoonist Michael Cochran of Tupper Lake, New York, who drew the many new illustrations included here to lighten the reader's way along this journey. Our collaboration began at a Union Institute research methods seminar he took while pursuing his doctorate in professional psychology. His evaluation of the seminar included cartoons. I liked his wit and style, so I offered ideas for cartoons on qualitative inquiry and he turned them into art. Doing the cartoons, he told me, was a wonderful distraction from writing his dissertation. I'm grateful for his humor and talent.

The editorial and production staff at Sage Publications deserve special mention. Only fellow authors who have struggled with editors of limited vision and understanding can fully appreciate what it means to work with C. Deborah Laughton, an experienced and knowledgeable editor who not only knows qualitative methods and evaluation as deeply as any practitioner of these arts, but also has significantly shaped those fields by conceptualizing works that she saw a need for and then nurturing authors, which she does better than any editor I've ever known, to assure that those works came to fruition. That she is also a writer and designer has made our working together a genuine collaboration. Kate Peterson's skilled copyediting added appreciably to the final product as she made many suggestions for improving clarity and readability, and I came to trust and even rely on her unusual eye for detail. Janelle Lemaster's interior design work converted the raw manuscript into the carefully crafted book you now hold. Diana Axelsen pulled it all together as production editor to get the book launched on schedule. I came to count on not only her great management competence but also her good humor. Finally, in acknowledging the superb Sage production team, I should also reprise the preface to the first edition in which I noted that my initial foray into qualitative writing was due entirely to the persuasive powers of Sara Miller McCune, co-founder of Sage Publications, who had shepherded the first edition of *Utilization-Focused Evaluation* (1978) into print and, based on the perspective in that book, urged me during a trip to Minnesota in 1978 to write a qualitative companion. Her vision and follow-through have made Sage Publications the leading publisher of both evaluation and qualitative inquiry books.

With the reader's indulgence, and by way of further providing a historical context for this third edition, permit me to include an excerpt from that first preface so many years ago:

> As other authors know, there is no way to really recognize the contribution of one's family to a book like this, the writing of which was a struggle and matter of endurance for both family and author. While Sara Miller McCune was persuading me that the book should be written, Jeanne was persuading me that we could nurture together both a new book and a

newborn child. (Having been left out of that decision, the newborn child subsequently made it clear he didn't always agree.) The contribution of Jeanne to the book exemplifies why the personal and professional sometimes cannot and ought not be separated. Jeanne's reflections on her own evaluation fieldwork and interviewing experiences helped me clarify and break through some particularly difficult sections of the book. Her editorial advice was invaluable. Those were her tangible contributions; the intangibles she contributed are the things that made the book happen.

Those intangibles and Jeanne's ongoing support have remained the mainstay of my writing. Meanwhile, the newborn child referred to above, Quinn Campbell, has completed a master's degree in engineering, and his younger sister, Charmagne Campbell-Patton, is about to complete college. As this was being completed, their older brother, Brandon Patton, participated in a two-day workshop I conducted on qualitative methods in preparation for his first evaluation fieldwork, a sideline he has turned to as a way of supporting his real passion, writing and performing rock music. Thus have the years passed, love maturing and children growing, bringing forth the need to revise the old, celebrate the new, and clean out the qualitative Augean stables while restocking them with fresh nutrients. It is those nutrients that follow.

PART 1

Conceptual Issues in Qualitative Inquiry

- Psychometricians try to measure *it*.
  Experimentalists try to control *it*.
  Interviewers ask questions about *it*.
  Observers watch *it*.
  Participant observers do *it*.
  Statisticians count *it*.
  Evaluators value *it*.
  Qualitative inquirers find meaning in *it*.

- When in doubt, observe and ask questions.
  When certain, observe at length and ask many more questions.

- Gigo's law of deduction: Garbage in, garbage out.
  Halcolm's law of induction: No new experience, no new insight.

- Qualitative inquiry cultivates the most useful of all human capacities:
  The capacity to *learn*.

- Innovators are told: "Think outside the box."
  Qualitative scholars tell their students: "Study the box. Observe it. Inside. Outside. From inside to outside, and outside to inside. Where is it? How did it get there? What's around it? Who says it's a 'box'? What do they mean? Why does it matter? Or does it? What is *not* 'box'? Ask the box questions. Question others about the box. What's the perspective from inside? From outside? Study diagrams of the box. Find documents related to the box. What does *thinking* have to do with the box anyway? Understand *this* box. Study another box. And another. Understand *box*. Understand. Then you can think inside *and* outside the box. Perhaps. For awhile. Until it changes. Until you change. Until outside becomes inside —again. Then start over. Study the box."

- There is no burden of proof. There is only the world to experience and understand. Shed the burden of proof to lighten the load for the journey of experience.

—From Halcolm's *Laws of Inquiry*

1

The Nature of Qualitative Inquiry

The Fruit of Qualitative Methods

There once lived a man in a country with no fruit trees. A scholar, he spent a great deal of time reading. He often came across references to fruit. The descriptions enticed him to undertake a journey to experience fruit for himself.

He went to the marketplace and inquired where he could find the land of fruit. After much searching he located someone who knew the way. After a long and arduous journey, he came to the end of the directions and found himself at the entrance to a large apple orchard. It was springtime and the apple trees were in blossom.

The scholar entered the orchard and, expectantly, pulled off a blossom and put it in his mouth. He liked neither the texture of the flower nor its taste. He went quickly to another tree and sampled another blossom, and then another, and another. Each blossom, though quite beautiful, was distasteful to him. He left the orchard and returned to his home country, reporting to his fellow villagers that fruit was a much overrated food.

Being unable to recognize the difference between the spring blossom and the summer fruit, the scholar never realized that he had not experienced what he was looking for.

—From Halcolm's *Inquiry Parables*

EXHIBIT 1.1   Three Kinds of Qualitative Data

Interviews
  Open-ended questions and probes yield in-depth responses about people's experiences, perceptions, opinions, feelings, and knowledge. Data consist of verbatim quotations with sufficient context to be interpretable.

Observations
  Fieldwork descriptions of activities, behaviors, actions, conversations, interpersonal interactions, organizational or community processes, or any other aspect of observable human experience. Data consist of field notes: rich, detailed descriptions, including the context within which the observations were made.

Documents
  Written materials and other documents from organizational, clinical, or programs records; memoranda and correspondence; official publications and reports; personal diaries, letters, artistic works, photographs, and memorabilia; and written responses to open-ended surveys. Data consist of excerpts from documents captured in a way that records and preserves context.

Recognizing Qualitative Data

This book discusses how to collect, analyze, and use qualitative data. To begin, let's examine the fruit of qualitative methods. It is important to know what qualitative data and findings look like so that you will know what you are seeking. It will also be important to consider criteria for judging the quality of qualitative data. Apples come to market sorted by type (Red Delicious, Golden), purpose (e.g., cooking or eating), and quality. Likewise, qualitative studies vary by type, purpose, and quality.

Qualitative findings grow out of three kinds of data collection: (1) in-depth, open-ended interviews; (2) direct observation; and (3) written documents. *Interviews* yield direct quotations from people about their experiences, opinions, feelings, and knowledge. The data from *observations* consist of detailed descriptions of people's activities, behaviors, actions, and the full range of interpersonal interactions and organizational

processes that are part of observable human experience. *Document analysis* includes studying excerpts, quotations, or entire passages from organizational, clinical, or program records; memoranda and correspondence; official publications and reports; personal diaries; and open-ended written responses to questionnaires and surveys. (See Exhibit 1.1.)

The data for qualitative analysis typically come from fieldwork. During fieldwork, the researcher spends time in the setting under study—a program, an organization, a community, or wherever situations of importance to a study can be observed, people interviewed, and documents analyzed. The researcher makes firsthand observations of activities and interactions, sometimes engaging personally in those activities as a *participant observer*. For example, an evaluator might participate in all or part of the program under study, participating as a regular program member, client, or student. The qualitative researcher talks with people about their experiences and perceptions. More formal individual or group interviews may be conducted. Relevant records and documents are examined. Extensive field notes are collected through these observations, interviews, and document reviews. The voluminous raw data in these field notes are organized into readable narrative descriptions with major themes, categories, and illustrative case examples extracted through content analysis. The themes, patterns, understandings, and insights that emerge from fieldwork and subsequent analysis are the fruit of qualitative inquiry.

Qualitative findings may be presented alone or in combination with quantitative data. Research and evaluation studies employing multiple methods, including combinations of qualitative and quantitative data, are common. At the simplest level, a questionnaire or interview that asks both fixed-choice (closed) questions and open-ended questions is an example of how quantitative measurement and qualitative inquiry are often combined.

The quality of qualitative data depends to a great extent on the methodological skill, sensitivity, and integrity of the researcher. Systematic and rigorous observation involves far more than just being present and looking around. Skillful interviewing involves much more than just asking questions. Content analysis requires considerably more than just reading to see what's there. Generating useful and credible qualitative findings through observation, interviewing, and content analysis requires discipline, knowledge, training, practice, creativity, and hard work.

This chapter provides an overview of qualitative inquiry. Later chapters examine how to choose among the many options available within the broad range of qualitative methods, theoretical perspectives, and applications; how to design a qualitative study; how to use observational methods and conduct in-depth, open-ended interviews; and how to analyze qualitative data to generate findings.

🖫 Qualitative Findings: Themes, Patterns, Concepts, Insights, Understandings

N ewton and the apple. Freud and anxiety. Jung and dreams. Piaget and his children. Darwin and Galapagos tortoises. Marx and England's factories. Whyte and street corners. What are you obsessed with?

—Halcolm

Mary Field Belenky and her colleagues set out to study women's ways of knowing. They conducted extensive interviews with 135 women from diverse backgrounds probing how they thought about knowledge, authority, truth, themselves, life changes, and life in general. They worked as a team to group similar responses and stories together, informed partly by previous research but ultimately basing the analysis on their own collective sense of what categories best captured what they found in the narrative data. They argued with each other about which responses belonged in which categories. They created and abandoned categories. They looked for com-

Discovery of an early qualitative evaluation report

monalities and differences. They worked hard to honor the diverse points of view they found while also seeking patterns across stories, experiences, and perspectives. One theme emerged as particularly powerful: "Again and again women spoke of 'gaining voice' " (Belenky et al. 1986:16). Voice versus silence emerged as a central metaphor for informing variations in ways of knowing. After painstaking analysis, they ended up with the five categories of knowing summarized in Exhibit 1.2, a framework that became very influential in women's studies and represents one kind of fruit from qualitative inquiry.

EXHIBIT 1.2	Women's Ways of Knowing: An Example of Qualitative Findings

Silence: A position in which women experience themselves as mindless and voiceless and subject to the whims of external authority.

Received knowledge: Women conceive of themselves as capable of receiving, even reproducing knowledge from external authorities, but not capable of creating knowledge on their own.

Subjective knowledge: A perspective from which truth and knowledge are conceived as personal, private, and subjectively known or intuited.

Procedural knowledge: Women are invested in learning and apply objective procedures for obtaining and communicating knowledge.

Constructed knowledge: Women view all knowledge as contextual, experience themselves as creators of knowledge, and value both subjective and objective strategies for knowing.

SOURCE: Belenky et al. (1986:15).

One of the best-known and most influential books in organizational development and management is *In Search of Excellence: Lessons From America's Best-Run Companies.* Peters and Waterman (1982) based the book on case studies of 62 highly regarded companies. They visited companies, conducted extensive interviews, and studied corporate documents. From that massive amount of data they extracted eight attributes of excellence: (1) a bias for action; (2) close to the customer; (3) autonomy and entrepreneurship; (4) productivity through people; (5) hands-on, value-driven; (6) stick to the knitting; (7) simple form, lean staff; and (8) simultaneous loose-tight properties. Their book devotes a chapter to each theme with case examples and implications. Their research helped launch the quality movement that has now moved from the business world to not-for-profit organizations and government. This study also illustrates a common qualitative sampling strategy: studying a relatively small number of special cases that are successful at something and therefore a good source of lessons learned.

Stephen Covey (1990) used this same sampling approach in doing case studies of "highly effective people." He identified seven habits these people practice: (1) being proactive; (2) beginning with the end in mind; (3) putting first things first; (4) thinking win/win; (5) seeking first to understand, then seeking to be understood; (6) synergizing, or engaging in creative cooperation; and (7) self-renewal.

Both of these best-selling books, *In Search of Excellence* and *The 7 Habits of Highly Effective People,* distill a small number of important *lessons* from a huge amount of data based on outstanding exemplars. It is common in qualitative analysis for mounds of field notes and months of work to reduce to a small number of core themes. The quality of the insights generated is what matters, not the number of such insights. For example, in an evaluation of 34 programs aimed at people in poverty, we found a core theme that separated more effective from less effective programs: How people are treated affects how they treat others. If staff members are treated autocratically and insensitively by management, with suspicion and disrespect, staff will treat clients the same way. Contrariwise, responsiveness reinforces responsiveness, and empowerment breeds empowerment. These insights became the centerpiece of subsequent cross-project, collaborative organizational and staff development processes.

A different kind of qualitative finding is illustrated by Angela Browne's book *When Battered Women Kill* (1987). Browne conducted in-depth interviews with 42 women from 15 states who were charged with a crime in the death or serious injury of their mates. She was often the first to hear these women's stories. She used one couple's history and vignettes from nine others, representative of the entire sample, to illuminate the progression of an abusive relationship from romantic courtship to the onset of abuse through its escalation until it was ongoing and eventually provoked a homicide. Her work helped lead to legal recognition of battered women's syndrome as a legitimate defense, especially in offering insight into the common outsider's question: Why doesn't the woman just leave? An insider's perspective on the debilitating, destructive, and all-encompassing brutality of battering reveals that question for what it is: the facile judgment of one who hasn't been there. The effectiveness of Browne's careful, detailed, and straightforward descriptions and quotations lies in their capacity to take us inside the abusive relationship. Offering that inside perspective powers qualitative reporting.

Clark Moustakas (1995), a humanistic psychologist and phenomenologist, also gives us an insider's perspective: his own. An astute and dedicated observer of relationships, especially therapeutic relationships, he drew deeply on his own experiences and clinical cases to identify, distinguish, and elaborate three primary processes that contribute to the development of a relationship: "Being-In," "Being-For," and "Being-With."

• Being-In involves immersing oneself in another's world: listening deeply and attentively so as to enter into the other person's experience and perception. "I do not select, interpret, advise, or direct. . . . Being-In the world of the other is a way of going wide open, entering in as if for the first time, hearing just what is, leaving out my own thoughts, feelings, theories, biases. . . . I enter with the intention of understanding and accepting perceptions and not presenting my own view or reactions. . . . I only want to encourage and support the other person's expression, what and how it is, how it came to be, and where it is going." (Moustakas 1995: 82-83)

• Being-For involves taking a stand in support of the other person, being there *for* the other. "I am listening. I am also offering a position, and that position has an element of my being on that person's side, against all others who would minimize, deprecate, or deny this person's right to be and to grow. . . . I become an advocate of the person with reference to his or her frustrations and problems in dealing with others." (Moustakas 1995:83)

• Being-With involves being present as one's own person in relation to another person, bringing one's own knowledge and experience into the relationship. "This may involve disagreeing with the other's ways of interpreting or judging or presenting some aspect of the world. Being-With means listening and hearing the other's feelings, thoughts, objectives, but it also means offering my own perceptions and views. There is, in Being-With, a sense of joint enterprise —two people fully involved, struggling, exploring, sharing." (Moustakas 1995:84)

EXHIBIT 1.3   Coming–of–Age Paradigms

Dimensions of Comparison	Tribal Initiation	Modern Coming of Age
View of life passages	One-time transition from child to adult	Multiple passages over a lifetime journey
Territory	Tribal territory	Earth: Global community
Ancestry	Creation myth	Evolutionary story of humankind
Identity	Becoming a man or woman	Becoming a complete person
Approach	Standardized	Individualized
Outcome	Tribe-based identity	Personality identity: Sense of self
Message	You are first and foremost a member of the tribe	You are first and foremost a person in your own right

SOURCE: Patton (1999a:333, 335).

Qualitative findings often have this simple yet elegant and insightful character. This straightforward yet nuanced framework represents a creative synthesis of years of participant observation and personal inquiry. Through cases, dialogues, quotations, cases, and introspective reflections, Moustakas illuminates the process of moving from Being-In to Being-For and ultimately Being-With. His work exemplifies the contribution of phenomenological inquiry to humanistic psychology.

Still a different format for capturing and reporting qualitative findings is illustrated by my own inquiry into alternative coming-of-age approaches. I used the device of constructing ideal-typical alternative paradigms to compare and contrast what I learned (Patton 1997a). Exhibit 1.3 provides a sampling of contrasts between traditional tribe-centered initiations and modern youth-centered coming-of-age celebrations. These kinds of polar contrasts can sometimes set up a Hegelian dialectic of thesis and antithesis that leads to a new synthesis. In philosophy such contrasts derive from the ruminations of philosophers; in qualitative research such thematic contrasts emanate from and are grounded in fieldwork.

This quick sampling of the fruit of qualitative inquiry is meant, like a wine tasting, to demonstrate choices toward developing a more sophisticated palate, or like appetizers, as an opening to the fuller feast yet to come. The next section discusses some of the different research and evaluation purposes that affect what kind of fruit results from qualitative inquiry and how the quality of that fruit is judged.

Different Purposes of and Audiences for Qualitative Studies: Research, Evaluation, Dissertations, and Personal Inquiry

As the title of this book indicates, qualitative methods are used in both research and evaluation. But because the purposes of research and evaluation are different, the criteria for judging qualitative studies can vary depending on purpose. This point is important. It means one can't judge the appropriateness of the methods in any study or the quality of the resulting findings without knowing the study's purpose, agreed-on uses, and intended audiences. Evaluation and research typically have different purposes, expected uses, and intended users. Dissertations add yet another layer of complexity to this mix. Let's begin with evaluation.

Program evaluation is the systematic collection of information about the activities, characteristics, and outcomes of programs to make judgments about the program, improve program effectiveness, and/or inform decisions about future programming. Policies, organizations, and personnel can also be evaluated. Evaluative research, quite broadly, can include any effort to judge or enhance human effectiveness through systematic data-based inquiry. Human beings are engaged in all kinds of efforts to make the world a better place. These efforts include assessing needs, formulating policies, passing laws, delivering programs, managing people and resources, providing therapy, developing communities, changing organizational culture, educating students, intervening in conflicts, and solving problems. In these and other efforts to make the world a better place, the question of whether the people involved are accomplishing what they want to accomplish arises. When one examines and judges accomplishments and effectiveness, one is engaged in evaluation. When this examination of effectiveness is conducted systematically and empirically through careful data collection and thoughtful analysis, one is engaged in evaluation *research*.

Qualitative methods are often used in evaluations because they tell the *program's story* by capturing and communicating the *participants' stories.* Evaluation case studies have all the elements of a good story. They tell what happened, when, to whom, and with what consequences. Many examples in this book are drawn from program evaluation, policy analysis, and organizational development. The purpose of such studies is to gather information and generate findings that are useful. Understanding the program's and participants' stories is useful to the extent that they illuminate the processes and outcomes of the program for those who must make decisions about the program. In *Utilization-Focused Evaluation* (Patton 1997a), I presented a comprehensive approach to doing evaluations that are useful, practical, ethical, and accurate. The primary criterion for judging such evaluations is the extent to which intended users actually use the findings for decision making and program improvement. The methodological implication of this criterion is that the intended users must value the findings and find them credible. They must be interested in the stories, experiences, and perceptions of program participants beyond simply knowing how many came into the program, how many completed it, and how many did what afterward. Qualitative findings in evaluation illuminate the people behind the numbers and put faces on the statistics, not to make hearts bleed, though that may occur, but to deepen understanding.

Research, especially fundamental or basic research, differs from evaluation in that its primary purpose is to generate or test theory and contribute to knowledge for the sake of knowledge. Such knowledge, and the theories that undergird knowledge, may subsequently inform action and evaluation, but action is not the primary purpose of funda-

QUALIA

Neurologist V. S. Ramachandran studies unique cases of brain damage trying to find out how a young man can think his parents are imposters; why a woman with a stroke laughs uncontrollably; how a man with a stroke can be oblivious to being paralyzed on one side; why amputees have intense feeling, even pain, in missing limbs; and why an epilepsy patient has intense religious experiences. Beyond what can be measured in brain waves and electrical impulses, he strives to understand "qualia"— what humans subjectively add to the scientifically measurable aspects of experience. This involves inquiry into the greatest shared challenge for neuroscience, social sciences, and philosophy: understanding consciousness. Ramachandran postulates that consciousness may involve the capacity to process qualia and that that capacity resides in a specific brain location (Ramachandran and Blakeslee, 1998).

If Ramachandran is right, qualitative inquirers may need that part of the brain to be especially active, accessible, and responsive.

mental research. Qualitative inquiry is especially powerful as a source of *grounded theory*, theory that is inductively generated from fieldwork, that is, theory that emerges from the researcher's observations and interviews out in the real world rather than in the laboratory or the academy. The primary audiences for research are other researchers and scholars, as well as policymakers and others interested in understanding some phenomenon or problem of interest. The research training, methodological preferences, and scientific values of those who use research will affect how valuable and credible they find the empirical and theoretical fruit of qualitative studies.

Dissertations and graduate theses offer special insight into the importance of attention to audience. Savvy graduate students learn that to complete a degree program, the student's committee must approve the work. The particular understandings, values, preferences, and biases of committee members come into play in that approval process. The committee will, in essence, evaluate the student's contribution, including the quality of the methodological procedures followed and the analysis done. Qualitative dissertations, once quite rare, have become increasingly common as the criteria for judging qualitative contributions to knowledge have become better understood and accepted. But those criteria are not absolute or universally agreed on. As we shall see, there are many varieties of qualitative inquiry and multiple criteria for judging quality, many of which remain disputed.

While the preceding discussion of evaluation, research, and dissertations has emphasized taking into account external audiences and consumers of qualitative studies, it is also important to acknowledge that *you* may be the primary intended audience for your work. You may study something because *you* want to understand it. As my children grew to adulthood, I found myself asking questions about coming of age in modern society so I undertook a *personal inquiry* that became a book (Patton 1997a), but I didn't start out to write a book. I started out trying to understand my own experience and the experiences of my children. That is a form of qualitative inquiry. While doing interviews with recipients of MacArthur Foundation Fellowships (popularly called "Genius Awards"), I was told by a social scientist that her fieldwork was driven by her own search for understanding and that she disciplined herself to not even think about publication while engaged in interviewing and observing because she didn't want to have her inquiry affected by attention to external audiences. *She wanted to know because she wanted to know,* and she had made a series of career and professional decisions that allowed her to focus on her personal inquiry without being driven by the traditional academic admonition to "publish or perish." She didn't want to subject herself to or have her work influenced by external criteria and judgment.

In summary, all inquiry designs are affected by intended purpose and targeted audience, but purpose and audience deserve special emphasis in the case of qualitative studies, where the criteria for judging quality may be poorly understood or in dispute, even among qualitative methodologists. This book cannot resolve these debates, but it will illuminate the methodological options and their implications. (Chapter 9 discusses alternative criteria for judging the quality of qualitative studies.)

Making Methods Decisions

The implication of thinking about purpose and audience in designing studies is that methods, no less than knowledge, are dependent on context. No rigid rules can prescribe what data to gather to investigate a particular interest or problem. There is no recipe or formula in making methods decisions. Widely respected psychometrician Lee J. Cronbach has observed that designing a study is as much art as science. It is "an exercise of the dramatic imagination" (Cronbach 1982:239). In research as in art, there can be no single, ideal standard. Beauty no less than "truth" is in the eye of the beholder, and the beholders of research and evaluation can include a plethora of stakeholders: scholars, policymakers, funders, program managers, staff, program participants, journalists, critics, and the general public. Any given design inevitably reflects some imperfect interplay of resources, capabilities, purposes, possibilities, creativity, and personal judgments by the people involved.

Research, like diplomacy, is the art of the possible. Exhibit 1.4 provides a set of questions to consider in the design process, regardless of type of inquiry. With that background, we can turn to consideration of the relative strengths and weaknesses of qualitative and quantitative methods.

⌷ Methods Choices: Contrasting Qualitative and Quantitative Emphases

N ot everything that can be counted counts, and not everything that counts can be counted.

—Albert Einstein

EXHIBIT 1.4	Some Guiding Questions and Options for Methods Decisions

1. What are the purposes of the inquiry?
   Research: Contribution to knowledge
   Evaluation: Program improvement and decision making
   Dissertation: Demonstrate doctoral-level scholarship
   Personal inquiry: Find out for oneself

2. Who are the primary audiences for the findings?
   Scholars, researchers, academicians
   Program funders, administrators, staff, participants
   Doctoral committee
   Oneself, friends, family, lovers

3. What questions will guide the inquiry?
   Theory-derived, theory-testing, and/or theory-oriented questions
   Practical, applied, action-oriented questions and issues
   Academic degree or discipline/specialization priorities
   Matters of personal interest and concern, even passion

4. What data will answer or illuminate the inquiry questions?
   Qualitative: Interviews, field observations, documents
   Quantitative: Surveys, tests, experiments, secondary data
   Mixed methods: What kind of mix? Which methods are primary?

5. What resources are available to support the inquiry?
   Financial resources
   Time
   People resources
   Access, connections

6. What criteria will be used to judge the quality of the findings?
   Traditional research criteria: Rigor, validity, reliability, generalizability
   Evaluation standards: Utility, feasibility, propriety, accuracy
   Nontraditional criteria: Trustworthiness, diversity of perspectives, clarity of voice, credibility
   of the inquirer to primary users of the findings

Thinking about design alternatives and methods choices leads directly to consideration of the relative strengths and weaknesses of qualitative and quantitative data. The approach here is pragmatic. Some questions lend themselves to numerical answers; some don't. If you want to know how much people weigh, use a scale. If you want to know if they're obese, measure body fat in relation to height and weight and compare the results to population norms. If you want to know what their weight *means* to them, how it affects them, how they think about it, and what they do about it, you need to ask them questions, find out about their experiences, and hear their stories. A comprehensive and multifaceted understanding of weight in people's lives requires both their numbers and their stories. Doctors who look only at test results and don't also listen to their patients are making judgments with inadequate knowledge, and vice versa.

Qualitative methods facilitate study of issues in depth and detail. Approaching fieldwork without being constrained by predetermined categories of analysis contributes to the depth, openness, and detail of qualitative inquiry. Quantitative methods, on the other hand, require the use of standardized measures so that the varying perspectives and experiences of people can be fit into a limited number of predetermined response categories to which numbers are assigned.

The advantage of a quantitative approach is that it's possible to measure the reactions of a great many people to a limited set of questions, thus facilitating comparison and statistical aggregation of the data. This gives a broad, generalizable set of findings presented succinctly and parsimoniously. By contrast, qualitative methods typically produce a wealth of detailed information about a much smaller number of people and cases. This increases the depth of understanding of the cases and situations studied but reduces generalizability.

Validity in quantitative research depends on careful instrument construction to ensure that the instrument measures what it is supposed to measure. The instrument must then be administered in an appropriate, standardized manner according to prescribed procedures. The focus is on the measuring instrument—the test items, survey questions, or other measurement tools. In qualitative inquiry, **the researcher is the instrument.** The credibility of qualitative methods, therefore, hinges to a great extent on the skill, competence, and rigor of the person doing fieldwork—as well as things going on in a person's life that might prove

a distraction. Guba and Lincoln (1981) have commented on this aspect of qualitative research:

> Fatigue, shifts in knowledge, and cooptation, as well as variations resulting from differences in training, skill, and experience among different "instruments," easily occur. But this loss in rigor is more than offset by the flexibility, insight, and ability to build on tacit knowledge that is the peculiar province of the human instrument. (p. 113)

Because qualitative and quantitative methods involve differing strengths and weaknesses, they constitute alternative, but not mutually exclusive, strategies for research. Both qualitative and quantitative data can be collected in the same study. To further illustrate these contrasting approaches and provide concrete examples of the fruit of qualitative inquiry, the rest of this chapter presents select excerpts from actual studies.

Comparing Two Kinds of Data: An Example

The Technology for Literacy Center was a computer-based adult literacy program in Saint Paul, Minnesota. It operated out of a storefront facility in a lower-socioeconomic area of the city. In 1988, after three years of pilot operation, a major funding decision had to be made about whether to continue the program. Anticipating the funding decision, a year earlier local foundations and the public schools had supported a *summative evaluation* to determine the overall outcomes and cost-effectiveness of the center. The evaluation design included both quantitative and qualitative data.

The quantitative testing data showed great variation. The statistics on average achievement gains masked great differences among participants. The report concluded that although testing showed substantial achievement test gains for the treatment group versus the control group, the more important finding concerned the highly individualized nature of student progress. The report concluded, "The data on variation in achievement and instructional hours lead to a very dramatic, important and significant finding: *there is no average student at TLC"* (Patton and Stockdill 1987:33).

This finding highlights the kind of program or treatment situation where qualitative data are particularly helpful and appropriate. The Technology for Literacy Center has a highly individualized program in which learners proceed at their own pace based on specific needs and interest. The students come in at very different levels, with a range of goals, participate in widely varying ways, and make very different gains. Average gain scores and average hours of instruction provide a parsimonious overview of aggregate progress, but such statistical data do little to help funders understand what the individual variation means. To get at the meaning of the program for individual participants, the evaluation included case studies and qualitative data from interviews.

INDIVIDUAL CASE EXAMPLES

One case is the story of Barbara Jenkins, a 65-year-old Black grandmother who came to Minnesota after a childhood in the deep South. She works as a custodian and house cleaner and is proud of never having been on welfare. She is the primary breadwinner for a home with five children spanning three generations, including her oldest daughter's teenage children for whom she has cared since her daughter's unexpected

death from hepatitis. During the week she seldom gets more than three hours of sleep each night. At the time of the case study, she had spent 15 months in the program and progressed from not reading at all (second-grade level) to being a regular library user (and testing a grade level higher than where she began). She developed an interest in Black history and reported being particularly pleased at being able to read the Bible on her own. She described what it was like not being able to read:

> Where do you go for a job? You can't make out an application. You go to a doctor and you can't fill out the forms, and it's very embarrassing. You have to depend on other people to do things like this for you. Sometimes you don't even want to ask your own kids because it's just like you're depending too much on people, and sometimes they do it willingly, and sometimes you have to beg people to help....
>
> All the progress has made me feel lots better about myself because I can do some of the things I've been wanting to do and I couldn't do. It's made me feel more independent to do things myself instead of depending on other people to do them for me.

A second contrasting case tells the story of Sara Johnson, a 42-year-old Caucasian woman who dropped out of school in the 10th grade. She is a clerical office manager. She tested at 12th-grade level on entry to the program. After 56 hours of study over 17 days, she received her general equivalency diploma (GED), making her a high school graduate. She immediately entered college. She said that the decision to return for her GED was

> an affirmation, as not having a diploma had really hurt me for a long time.... It was always scary wondering if somebody actually found

out that I was not a graduate that they would fire me or they wouldn't accept me because I hadn't graduated. The hardest thing for me to do was tell my employer. He is very much into education and our company is education-oriented. So the hardest thing I ever had to do was tell him I was a high school dropout. I needed to tell because I needed time to go and take the test. He was just so understanding. I couldn't believe it. It was just wonderful. I thought he was going to be disappointed in me, and he thought it was wonderful that I was going back. He came to graduation.

These short excerpts from two contrasting cases illustrate the value of detailed, descriptive data in deepening our understanding of individual variation. Knowing that each woman progressed about one grade level on a standardized reading test is only a small part of a larger, much more complex picture. Yet, with over 500 people in the program, it would be overwhelming for funders and decision makers to attempt to make sense of 500 detailed case studies (about 5,000 double-spaced pages). Statistical data provide a succinct and parsimonious summary of major patterns, while select case studies provide depth, detail, and individual meaning.

OPEN-ENDED INTERVIEWS

Another instructive contrast is to compare closed-ended questionnaire results with responses to open-ended group interviews. Questionnaire responses to quantitative, standardized items indicated that 77% of the adult literacy students were "very happy" with the Technology for Literacy Center program; 74% reported learning "a great deal." These and similar results revealed a general pattern of satisfaction and progress. But what did the program mean to students in their own words?

To get the perspective of students, I conducted group interviews. "Groups are not just a convenient way to accumulate the individual knowledge of their members. They give rise synergistically to insights and solutions that would not come about without them" (Brown, Collins, and Duguid 1989: 40). In group interviews I asked students to describe the program's outcomes in personal terms. I asked, "What difference has what you are learning made in your lives?" Here are some responses.

I love the newspaper now, and actually read it. Yeah, I love to pick up the newspaper now. I used to hate it. Now I *love* the newspaper.

I can follow sewing directions. I make a grocery list now, so I'm a better shopper. I don't forget things.

Yeah, you don't know how embarrassing it is to go shopping and not be able to read the wife's grocery list. It's helped me out so much in the grocery store.

Helps me with my medicine. Now I can read the bottles and the directions! I was afraid to give the kids medicine before because I wasn't sure.

I don't get lost anymore. I can find my way around. I can make out directions, read the map. I work construction and we change locations a lot. Now I can find my way around. I don't get lost anymore!

Just getting a driver's license will be wonderful. I'm 50. If I don't get the GED, but if I can get a license . . . ! I can drive well, but I'm scared to death of the written test. Just getting a driver's license . . . , a driver's license.

Now I read outdoor magazines. I used to just read the titles of books—now I read the books!

I was always afraid to read at school and at church. I'm not afraid to read the Bible now at

Bible class. It's really important to me to be able to read the Bible.

I can fill out applications now. You have to know how to fill out an application in this world. I can look in the Yellow Pages. It used to be so embarrassing not to be able to fill out applications, not to be able to find things in the Yellow Pages. I feel so much better now. At least my application is filled out right, even if I don't get the job, at least my application is filled out right.

I'm learning just enough to keep ahead of my kids. My family is my motivation. Me and my family. Once you can read to your kids, it makes all the difference in the world. It helps you to want to read and to read more. When I can read myself, I can help them read so they can have a better life. The kids love it when I read to them.

These group interview excerpts provide some qualitative insights into the individual, personal experiences of adults learning to read. The questionnaire results (77% satisfied) provided data on statistically generalizable patterns, but the standardized questions only tap the surface of what it means for the program to have had "great perceived impact." The much smaller sample of open-ended interviews adds depth, detail, and meaning at a very personal level of experience. Another example will show that qualitative data can yield not only deeper understanding but also political action as the depth of participants' feelings is revealed.

The Power of Qualitative Data

In the early 1970s, the school system of Kalamazoo, Michigan, implemented a new accountability system. It was a complex system that included using standardized achievement tests administered in both fall and spring, criterion-referenced tests developed by teachers, performance objectives, teacher peer ratings, student ratings of teachers, parent ratings of teachers, principal ratings of teachers, and teacher self-ratings.

The Kalamazoo accountability system began to attract national attention. For example, the *American School Board Journal* reported in April 1974 that "Kalamazoo schools probably will have one of the most comprehensive computerized systems of personnel evaluation and accountability yet devised" (p. 40). In the first of a three-part series on Kalamazoo, the *American School Board Journal* asserted: "Take it from Kalamazoo: *a comprehensive, performance-based system of evaluation and accountability can work*" ("Kalamazoo Schools" 1974:32).

Not everyone agreed with that positive assessment, however. The Kalamazoo Education Association charged that teachers were being demoralized by the accountability system. Some school officials, on the other hand, argued that teachers did not want to be accountable. In the spring of 1976, the Kalamazoo Education Association, with assistance from the Michigan Education Association and the National Education Association, sponsored a survey of teachers to find out the teachers' perspective on the accountability program (Perrone and Patton 1976).

The education association officials were interested primarily in a questionnaire consisting of standardized items. One part of the closed-ended questionnaire provided teachers with a set of statements with which they could agree or disagree. The questionnaire results showed that teachers felt the accountability system was largely ineffective and inadequate. For example, 90% of the teachers disagreed with the school administration's published statement "The Kalamazoo accountability system is designed to personalize and individualize education"; 88% reported that the system does not assist teachers to become more effective; 90% responded that the accountability system has not improved educational planning in Kalamazoo; and 93% believed, "Accountability as practiced in Kalamazoo creates an undesirable atmosphere of anxiety among teachers." And 90% asserted, "The accountability system is mostly a public relations effort." Nor did teachers feel that the accountability system fairly reflected what they did as teachers, since 97% of them agreed, "Accountability as practiced in Kalamazoo places too much emphasis on things that can be quantified so that it misses the results of teaching that are not easily measured."

It is relatively clear from these statements that most teachers who responded to the questionnaire were negative about the accountability system. When school officials and school board members reviewed the questionnaire results, however, many of them immediately dismissed those results by arguing that they had never expected teachers to like the system, teachers didn't really want to be accountable, and the teachers' unions had told their teachers to respond negatively anyway. In short, many school officials and school board members dismissed the questionnaire results as biased, inaccurate, and the results of teacher union leaders telling teachers how to respond in order to discredit the school authorities.

The same questionnaire included two open-ended questions. The first was placed midway through the questionnaire, and the second came at the end of the questionnaire.

1. Please use this space to make any further comments or recommendations concerning any component of the accountability system.

2. Finally, we'd like you to use this space to add any additional comments you'd like to make about any part of the Kalamazoo accountability system.

A total of 373 teachers (70% of those who responded to the questionnaire) took the time to respond to one of these open-ended questions. All of the comments made by teachers were typed verbatim and included in the report. These open-ended data filled 101 pages. When the school officials and school board members rejected the questionnaire data, rather than argue with them about the meaningfulness of teacher responses to the standardized items, we asked them to turn to the pages of open-ended teacher comments and simply read at random what teachers said. Examples of the comments they read, and could read on virtually any page in the report, are reproduced below in six representative responses from the middle pages of the report.

Teacher Response No. 284: "I don't feel that fear is necessary in an accountability situation. The person at the head of a school system has to be human, not a machine. You just don't treat people like they are machines!

"The superintendent used fear in this system to get what he wanted. That's very hard to explain in a short space. It's something you have to live through to appreciate. He lied on many occasions and was very deceitful. Teachers need a situation where they feel comfortable. I'm not saying that accountability is not good. I am saying the one we have is lousy. It's hurting the students—the very ones we're supposed to be working for."

Teacher Response No. 257: "This system is creating an atmosphere of fear and intimidation. I can only speak for the school I am in, but people are tense, hostile and losing their humanity. Gone is the good will and team spirit of administration and staff and I believe this all begins at the top. One can work in these conditions but why, if it is to 'shape up' a few poor teachers. Instead, it's having disastrous results on the whole faculty community."

Teacher Response No. 244: "In order to fully understand the oppressive, stifling atmosphere in Kalamazoo you have to 'be in the trenches'—the classrooms. In 10 years of teaching, I have never ended a school year as depressed about 'education' as I have this year. If things do not improve in the next two years, I will leave education. The Kalamazoo accountability system must be viewed in its totality and not just the individual component parts of it. In toto, it is oppressive and stifling.

"In teaching government and history, students often asked what it was like to live in a dictatorship. I now know firsthand.

"The superintendent with his accountability model and his abrasive condescending manner has managed in three short years to destroy teacher morale and effective creative classroom teaching.

"Last evening my wife and I went to an end of the school year party. The atmosphere there was strange—little exuberance, laughter or release. People who in previous years laughed, sang and danced were unnaturally quiet and somber. Most people went home early. The key topic was the superintendent, the school board election, and a millage campaign. People are still tense and uncertain.

"While the school board does not 'pay us to be happy' it certainly must recognize that emotional stability is necessary for effective teaching to take place. The involuntary transfers, intimidation, coercion and top to bottom 'channelized' communication in Kalamazoo must qualify this school system for the list of 'least desirable' school systems in the nation."

Teacher Response No. 233: "I have taught in Kalamazoo for 15 years and under five superintendents. Until the present superintendent, I found working conditions to be enjoyable and

teachers and administration and the Board of Education all had a good working relationship. In the past 4 years—under the present superintendent—I find the atmosphere deteriorating to the point where teachers distrust each other and teachers do not trust administrators at all! We understand the position the administrators have been forced into and feel compassion for them—however—we still have no trust! Going to school each morning is no longer an enjoyable experience."

Teacher Response No. 261: "A teacher needs some checks and balances to function effectively; it would be ridiculous to think otherwise—if you are a concerned teacher. But in teaching you are not turning out neatly packaged little mechanical products all alike and endowed with the same qualities. This nonsensical accountability program we have here makes the superintendent look good to the community. But someone who is in the classroom dealing with all types of kids, some who cannot read, some who hardly ever come to school, some who are in and out of jail, this teacher can see that and the rigid accountability model that neglects the above mentioned problems is pure 'BULLSHIT!' "

Teacher Response No. 251: " 'Fear' is the word for 'accountability' as applied in our system. My teaching before 'Accountability' is the same as now. 'Accountability' is a political ploy to maintain power. Whatever good there may have been in it in the beginning has been destroyed by the awareness that each new educational 'system' has at its base a political motive. Students get screwed. . . . The bitterness and hatred in our system is incredible. What began as 'noble' has been destroyed. You wouldn't believe the new layers of administration that have been created just to keep this monster going.

"Our finest compliment around our state is that the other school systems know what is going on and are having none of it. Lucky people. Come down and *visit in hell* sometime."

Face Validity and Credibility

What was the impact of the qualitative data collected from teachers in Kalamazoo? You will recall that many of the school board members initially dismissed the standardized questionnaire responses as biased, rigged, and the predictable result of the union's campaign to discredit school officials. However, after reading through a few pages of the teachers' own personal comments, after hearing about teachers' experiences with the accountability system in their own words, the tenor of the discussion about the evaluation report changed. School board members could easily reject what they perceived as a "loaded" questionnaire. They could not so easily dismiss the anguish, fear, and depth of concern revealed in the teachers' own reflections. The teachers' words had face validity and credibility. Discussion of the evaluation results shifted from an attack on the measures used to the question: "What do you think we should do?"

During the summer of 1976, following discussion of the evaluation report, the superintendent "resigned." The new superintendent and school board in 1976-1977 used the evaluation report as a basis for starting fresh with teachers. A year later teacher association officials reported a new environment of teacher-administration cooperation in developing a mutually acceptable accountability system. The evaluation report did not directly cause these changes. Many other factors were involved in Kalamazoo at that time. However, the qualitative information in the evaluation report revealed the full scope and nature of teachers' feelings about what it was like to work in the atmosphere created by the accountability system. The depth of those feelings as expressed in the

> ### THROUGH THE EYES OF A CHILD
>
> *"I know of a small boy eight years old who sat alone on a park bench five or six hours every day for almost a week. He alternately played with the pigeons, watched the passing people, made patterns in the air with his feet and legs, or looked blankly into space. On the fourth day of his visit to this bench, a friend of mine asked this boy why he sat there every day. He replied that his mother brought him there in the mornings telling him to wait there while she looked for a job and a place for them to stay. There is no place else for him to go. When asked what he did all day he simply said that he watched and he waited. He watched the pigeons and the people. He made a game of guessing where each had to go. He said that mostly he just waited for his mother to come at the end of the day so they could wait together until the night shelter opened" (Boxill 1990:1).*

teachers' own words became part of the impetus for change in Kalamazoo.

The Purpose of Open-Ended Responses

The preceding example illustrates the difference between qualitative inquiry based on responses to open-ended questions and quantitative measurement based on scales composed of standardized questionnaire items. Quantitative measures are succinct, parsimonious, and easily aggregated for analysis; quantitative data are systematic, standardized, and easily presented in a short space. By contrast, the qualitative findings are longer, more detailed, and variable in content; analysis is difficult because responses are neither systematic nor standard-ized. Yet, the open-ended responses permit one to understand the world as seen by the respondents. The purpose of gathering re-sponses to open-ended questions is to en-able the researcher to understand and cap-ture the points of view of other people without predetermining those points of view through prior selection of question-naire categories. As Lofland (1971) put it: "To capture participants 'in their own terms' one must learn *their* categories for rendering explicable and coherent the flux of raw real-ity. That, indeed, is the first principle of qual-itative analysis" (p. 7, emphasis added).

Direct quotations are a basic source of raw data in qualitative inquiry, revealing respon-dents' depth of emotion, the ways they have organized their world, their thoughts about what is happening, their experiences, and their basic perceptions. The task for the qual-itative researcher is to provide a framework within which people can respond in a way that represents accurately and thoroughly their points of view about the world, or that part of the world about which they are talk-ing—for example, their experience with a particular program being evaluated. Too of-ten social scientists "enter the field with pre-conceptions that prevent them from allow-ing those studied to 'tell it as they see it' " (Denzin 1978b:10).

I have included the Kalamazoo evalua-tion findings as an illustration of qualita-tive inquiry because open-ended responses on questionnaires represent the most ele-mentary form of qualitative data. There are severe limitations to open-ended data col-lected in writing on questionnaires, limi-tations related to the writing skills of re-spondents, the impossibility of probing or extending responses, and the effort required of the person completing the questionnaire. Yet, even at this elementary level of inquiry, the depth and detail of feelings revealed in

the open-ended comments of the Kalama-zoo teachers illustrate the fruit of qualitative methods.

While the Kalamazoo example illustrates the most elementary form of qualitative in-quiry, namely, responses from open-ended questionnaire items, the major way in which qualitative researchers seek to understand the perceptions, feelings, and knowledge of people is through in-depth, intensive inter-viewing. The chapter on interviewing will discuss ways of gathering high-quality in-formation from people—data that reveal ex-periences with program activities and per-spectives on treatment impacts from the points of view of participants, staff, and oth-ers involved in and knowledgeable about the program or treatment being evaluated.

Inquiry by Observation

What people say is a major source of qual-itative data, whether what they say is ob-tained verbally through an interview or in written form through document analysis or survey responses. There are limitations, however, to how much can be learned from what people say. To understand fully the complexities of many situations, direct par-ticipation in and observation of the phenom-enon of interest may be the best research method. Howard S. Becker, one of the lead-ing practitioners of qualitative methods in the conduct of social science research, ar-gues that participant observation is the most comprehensive of all types of research strat-egies.

> The most complete form of the sociological da-tum, after all, is the form in which the partici-pant observer gathers it: an observation of some social event, the events which precede and follow it, and explanations of its meaning by participants and spectators, before, during, and after its occurrence. Such a datum gives us

Certain really discriminating people like nothing better than to relax on the beach with a good, in-depth, and detailed qualitative study in hand.

more information about the event under study than data gathered by any other sociological method. (Becker and Geer 1970:133)

Observational data, especially partici-pant observation, permit the evaluation re-searcher to understand a program or treatment to an extent not entirely possible using only the insights of others obtained through interviews. Of course, not everything can be directly observed or experienced, and participant observation is a highly labor-intensive—and, therefore, relatively expensive—research strategy. In a later chapter, strategies for using observational methods, including both participant and nonparticipant approaches, will be discussed at length. My purpose at this point is simply to give the reader another taste of the fruit of qualitative methods. Before discussing how to collect observational evaluation data, it is helpful to know what such data should look like.

The purpose of observational analysis is to take the reader into the setting that was observed. This means that observational data must have depth and detail. The data must be descriptive—sufficiently descriptive that the reader can understand what occurred and how it occurred. The observer's notes become the eyes, ears, and perceptual senses for the reader. The descriptions must be factual, accurate, and thorough without being cluttered by irrelevant minutiae and trivia. The basic criterion to apply to a recorded observation is the extent to which the observation permits the reader to enter the situation under study.

The observation that follows is meant to illustrate what such a descriptive account is like. This evaluation excerpt describes a two-hour observation of mothers discussing their child rearing in a parent education program. The purpose of the program, one of 22 such state-supported programs, was to increase the skills, knowledge, and confidence of parents. The program was also aimed at providing a support group for parents. In funding the program, legislators emphasized that they did not want parents to be told how to rear their children. Rather, the purpose of the parent education sessions was to increase the options available to par-

ents so that they could make conscious choices about their own parenting styles and increase their confidence about the choices they make. Parents were also to be treated with respect and to be recognized as the primary educators of their children—in other words, the early childhood educators were not to impose their expertise upon parents but, instead, to make clear that parents are the real experts about their own children.

Site visits were made to all programs, and parenting discussions were observed on each site visit. Descriptions of these sessions then became the primary data of the evaluation. In short, the evaluators were to be the eyes and ears of the legislature and the state program staff, permitting them to understand what was happening in various parent sessions throughout the state. Descriptive data about the sessions also provided a mirror for the staff who conducted those sessions, a way of looking at what they were doing to see if that was what they wanted to be doing.

What follows is a description from one such session. The criterion that should be applied in reading this description is the extent to which sufficient data are provided to take you, the reader, into the setting and permit you to make your own judgment about the nature and quality of parent education being provided.

OBSERVATION DATA ILLUSTRATED: A DISCUSSION FOR MOTHERS OF TWO-YEAR-OLDS

The group discussion component of this parent education program operates out of a small classroom in the basement of a church. The toddler center is directly overhead on the first floor so that noises made by the children these mothers have left upstairs can be heard during the discussion. The room is just large enough for the 12 mothers, one staff person, and me to sit along three sides of the room. The fourth side is used for a movie screen. Some mothers are smoking. (The staff person told me afterward that smoking had been negotiated and agreed on among the mothers.) The seats are padded folding chairs plus two couches. A few colorful posters with pictures of children playing decorate the walls. Small tables are available for holding coffee cups and ashtrays during the discussion. The back wall is lined with brochures on child care and child development, and a metal cabinet in the room holds additional program materials.

The session begins with mothers watching a 20-minute film about preschool children. The film forms the basis for getting discussion started about "what two-year-olds do." Louise, a part-time staff person in her early 30s who has two young children of her own, one a two-year-old, leads the discussion. Louise asks the mothers to begin by picking out from the film things that their own children do, and talking about the way some of the problems with children were handled in the film. For the most part, the mothers share happy, play activities their children like. "My Johnny loves the playground just like the kids in the film." "Yeah, mine could live on the playground."

The focus of the discussion turns quickly to what happens as children grow older, how they change and develop. Louise comments, "Don't worry about what kids do at a particular age. Like don't worry that your kid has to do a certain thing at age two or else he's behind in development or ahead of development. There's just a lot of variation in the ages at which kids do things."

The discussion is free flowing and, once begun, is not directed much by Louise. Mothers talk back and forth to each other, sharing experiences about their children. A mother will bring up a particular point and

other mothers will talk about their own experiences as they want to. For example, one of the topics is the problem a mother is having with her child urinating in the bathtub. Other mothers share their experiences with this problem, ways of handling it, and whether or not to be concerned about it. The crux of that discussion seems to be that it is not a big deal and not something that the mother ought to be terribly concerned about. It is important not to make it a big deal for the child; the child will outgrow it.

The discussion turns to things that two-year-olds can do around the house to help their mothers. This is followed by some discussion of the things that two-year-olds can't do and some of their frustrations in trying to do things. There is a good deal of laughing, sharing of funny stories about children, and sharing of frustrations about children. The atmosphere is informal and there is a good deal of intensity in listening. Mothers seem especially to pick up on things that they share in common about the problems they have with their children.

Another issue from another mother is the problem of her child pouring out her milk. She asks, "What does it mean?" This question elicits some suggestions about using water aprons and cups that don't spill and other mothers' similar problems, but the discussion is not focused and does not really come to much closure. The water apron suggestion brings up a question about whether or not a plastic bag is okay. The discussion turns to the safety problems with different kinds of plastic bags. About 20 minutes of discussion have now taken place. (At this point, one mother leaves because she hears her child crying upstairs.)

The discussion returns to giving children baths. Louise interjects, "Two-year-olds should not be left alone in the bathtub." With reference to the earlier discussion about urinating in the bathtub, a mother interjects that water with urine in it is probably better than the lake water her kids swim in. The mother with the child who urinates in the bathtub says again, "It really bugs me when he urinates in the tub." Louise responds, "It really is your problem, not his. If you can calm yourself down, he'll be okay."

At a lull in the discussion, Louise asks, "Did you agree with everything in the movie?" The mothers talk a bit about this and focus on an incident in the movie where one child bites another. Mothers share stories about problems they've had with their children biting. Louise interjects, "Biting can be dangerous. It is important to do something about biting." The discussion turns to what to do. One mother suggests biting the child back. Another mother suggests that kids will work it out themselves by biting each other back. Mothers get very agitated, more than one mother talks at a time. Louise asks them to "cool it," so that only one person talks at a time. (The mother who had left returns.)

The discussion about biting leads to a discussion about child conflict and fighting in general, for example, the problem of children hitting each other or hitting their mothers. Again, the question arises about what to do. One mother suggests that when her child hits her, she hits him back, or when her child bites her, she bites him back. Louise interjects, "Don't model behavior you don't like." She goes on to explain that her philosophy is that you should not do things as a model for children that you don't want them to do. She says that works best for her; however, other mothers may find other things that work better for them. Louise comments that hitting back or biting back is a technique suggested by Dreikurs. She says she disagrees with that technique, "but you all have to decide what works for you." (About 40 minutes have now passed since the film, and 7 of

the 11 mothers have participated, most of them actively. Four mothers have not participated.)

Another mother brings up a new problem. Her child is destroying her plants, dumping plants out, and tearing them up. "I really get mad." She says that the technique she has used for punishment is to isolate the child. Then she asks, "How long do you have to punish a two-year-old before it starts working?" This question is followed by intense discussion with several mothers making comments. (This discussion is reproduced in full to illustrate the type of discussion that occurred.)

Mother No. 2: "Maybe he needs his own plant. Sometimes it helps to let a child have his own plant to take care of and then he comes to appreciate plants."

Mother No. 3: "Maybe he likes to play in the dirt. Does he have his own sand or dirt to play in around the house?"

Mother No. 4: "Oatmeal is another good thing to play in."

Louise: "Rice is another thing that children like to play in and it's clean, good to use indoors."

Mother No. 5: "Some things to play in would be bad or dangerous. For example, powdered soap isn't a good thing to let kids play in."

Mother No. 2: "Can you put the plants where he can't get at them?"

Mother with problem: "I have too many plants, I can't put them all out of the way."

Louise: "Can you put the plants somewhere else or provide a place to play with dirt or rice?" (Mother with problem kind of shakes her head no. Louise goes on.) "Another thing is to tell the kid the plants are alive, to help him learn respect for living things. Tell him that those plants are alive and that it hurts them. Give him his own plant that he can get an investment in."

Mother with problem: "I'll try it."

Mother No. 2: "You've got to be fair about a two-year-old. You can't expect them not to touch things. It's not fair. I try hanging all my plants."

Louise: "Sometimes just moving a child bodily away from the thing you don't want him to do is the best technique."

Mother No. 4: "They'll outgrow it anyway."

Mother with problem: "Now he deliberately dumps them and I really get angry."

Louise: "Maybe he feels a rivalry with the plants if you have so many. Maybe he's trying to compete."

Mother No. 3: "Let him help with the plants. Do you ever let him help you take care of the plants?"

Mother No. 6: "Some plants are dangerous to help with."

Louise: "Some dangerous house plants are poison."

Louise reaches up and pulls down a brochure on plants that are dangerous and says she has brochures for everyone. Several people say that they want brochures and she goes to the cabinet to make them available. One mother who has not participated verbally up to this point specifically requests a brochure. This is followed by a discussion of child-proofing a house as a method of child rearing versus training the child not to touch things, but with less emphasis on child-proofing, that is, removing temptation versus teaching children to resist temptation. One parent suggests, in this context, that children be taught one valuable thing at a time. Several mothers give their points of view.

Louise: "The person who owns the house sets the rules. Two-year-olds can learn to be careful. But don't go around all day long saying, 'No, no.' "

The time had come for the discussion to end. The mothers stayed around for about 15 minutes, interacting informally and then going upstairs to get their children into their winter coats and hats for the trip home. They seemed to have enjoyed themselves and continued talking informally. One mother with whom Louise had disagreed about the issue of whether it was all right to bite or hit children back stopped to continue the discussion. Louise said:

> I hope you know that I respect your right to have your own views on things. I wasn't trying to tell you what to do. I just disagreed, but I definitely feel that everybody has a right to their own opinion. Part of the purpose of the group is for everyone to be able to come together and appreciate other points of view and understand what works for different people.

The mother said that she certainly didn't feel bad about the disagreement and she knew that some things that worked for other people didn't work for her and that she had her own ways but that she really enjoyed the group.

Louise cleaned up the room, and the session ended.

The Raw Data of Qualitative Inquiry

The description of this parenting session is aimed at permitting the reader to understand what occurred in the session. These data are descriptive. Pure description and

MAPPING EXPERIENCES: OUR OWN AS WELL AS THOSE OF OTHERS

Qualitative inquiry offers opportunities not only to learn about the experiences of others but also to examine the experiences that the inquirer brings to the inquiry, experiences that will, to some extent, affect what is studied and help shape, for better or worse, what is discovered. Approaches to qualitative inquiry such as autoethnography, heuristic inquiry, and critical reflexivity emphasize examining and understanding how who we are can shape what we see, hear, know, and learn during fieldwork and subsequent analysis. In that sense, qualitative inquiry can be thought of as mapping experiences, our own as well as those of others.

Imagine a map... drawn from your memory instead of from the atlas. It is made of strong places stitched together by the vivid threads of transforming journeys. It contains all the things you learned from the land and shows where you learned them. . . .

Think of this map as a living thing, not a chart but a tissue of stories that grows half-consciously with each experience. It tells where and who you are with respect to the earth, and in times of stress or disorientation it gives you the bearings you need in order to move on. We all carry such maps within us as sentient and reflective beings, and we depend upon them unthinkingly, as we do upon language or thought.... And it is part of wisdom, to consider this ecological aspect of our identity. (Tallmadge 1997:ix)

quotations are the raw data of qualitative inquiry.

The description is meant to take the reader into the setting. The data do not include judgments about whether what occurred was good or bad, appropriate or inappropriate, or any other interpretive judgments. The data simply describe what occurred. State legislators, program staff, parents, and others used this description, and descriptions like this from other program sites, to discuss what they wanted the programs to be and do. The descriptions helped them make explicit *their own* judgmental criteria.

In later chapters, guidance on interpreting qualitative data will be offered in depth.

People-Oriented Inquiry

Thus far, the examples of observation and interviewing in this chapter have been presented as separate and distinct from each other. In practice, they are often fully integrated approaches. Becoming a skilled observer is essential even if you concentrate primarily on interviewing because every face-to-face interview also involves and requires observation. The skilled interviewer is thus also a skilled observer, able to read nonverbal messages, sensitive to how the interview setting can affect what is said, and carefully attuned to the nuances of the interviewer-interviewee interaction and relationship.

Likewise, interviewing skills are essential for the observer because during fieldwork, you will need and want to talk with people, whether formally or informally. Participant observers gather a great deal of information through informal, naturally occurring conversations. Understanding that interviewing and observation are mutually reinforcing qualitative techniques is a bridge to understanding the fundamentally people-oriented nature of qualitative inquiry.

Sociologist John Lofland has suggested that there are four people-oriented mandates in collecting qualitative data. First, the qualitative methodologist must get close enough to the people and situation being studied to personally understand in depth the details of what goes on. Second, the qualitative methodologist must aim at capturing what actually takes place and what people actually say: the perceived facts. Third, qualitative data must include a great deal of pure description of people, activities, interactions, and settings. Fourth, qualitative data must include direct quotations from people, both what they speak and what they write down.

> The commitment to get close, to be factual, descriptive and quotive, constitutes a significant commitment to represent the participants in their own terms. This does not mean that one becomes an apologist for them, but rather that one faithfully depicts what goes on in their lives and what life is like for them, in such a way that one's audience is at least partially able to project themselves into the point of view of the people depicted. They can "take the role of the other" because the reporter has given them a living sense of day-to-day talk, day-to-day activities, day-to-day concerns and problems. . . .
>
> A major methodological consequence of these commitments is that the qualitative study of people in situ is a *process of discovery*. It is of necessity a process of learning what is happening. Since a major part of what is happening is provided by people in their own terms, one must find out about those terms rather than impose upon them a preconceived or outsider's scheme of what they are about. It is the observer's task to find out what is fundamental or central to the people or world under observation. (Lofland 1971:4)

The Fruit of Qualitative Methods Revisited

This chapter began with the parable of the man who traveled far in search of a widely proclaimed food called "fruit." When finally directed to a fruit tree, he confused the spring blossom of the tree with the fruit of the tree. Finding the blossom to be tasteless, he dismissed all he had heard about fruit as a hoax and went on his way. This chapter has described qualitative data so that the person in search of the fruits of qualitative methods will know what to look for—and know when the real thing has been attained. Exhibit 1.5 lists Internet resources for those who want to carry on this search for qualitative fruit in virtual space. To close this chapter, it may be instructive to consider two other short parables about the search for fruit.

While the first seeker after fruit arrived too early to experience the ripened delicacy and tasted only the blossom, a second seeker after fruit arrived at a tree that had been improperly cultivated, so that its fruit was shriveled and bitter. This bad fruit had been left to rot. Not knowing what good fruit looked like, he sampled the bad. "Well, I've seen and tasted fruit," he said, "and I can tell you for sure that it's terrible. I've had it with fruit. Forget it. This stuff is awful." He went on his way and his journey was wasted.

One can hope that such a foolish mistake is less likely today, because early in school students are taught the danger of generalizing from limited cases. Yet, rumors persist that some people continue to reject all qualitative data as worthless (and "rotten"), having experienced only bad samples produced with poor methods.

A third seeker after fruit arrived at the same tree that produced the shriveled and bitter fruit. He picked some of the rotting fruit and examined it. He took the fruit to a farmer who cultivated fruit trees with great

	Internet E-mail Discussion Groups (listservs) on
EXHIBIT 1.5	Qualitative Methods

1. QUALRS-L@listserv.uga.edu: Qualitative Research for the Human Sciences; to subscribe, send this message to listserv@listserv.uga.edu: subscribe QUALRS-L yourname

2. QUALNET@listserv.bc.edu: Qualitative Research in Management and Organization Studies; to subscribe, send this message to majordomo@listserv.bc.edu: subscribe qualnet

3. QUAL-L@scu.edu.au: Qualitative Research List, initiated by Penn State, but immediately attracted a broader audience; to subscribe, send this message to listproc@scu.edu.au: subscribe QUAL-L firstname lastname

Other resources for qualitative evaluation and research:

4. EVALTALK@bama.ua.edu: American Evaluation Association (AEA) Discussion List; to subscribe, send this message to listserv@bama.ua.edu: subscribe evaltalk ourname

   AEA home page with links to evaluation organizations, training programs, and Internet resources: www.eval.org

5. METHODS@cios.org: A list for social science research methods instructors; to subscribe, send this message to comserve@cios.org: join methods yourname

NOTE: Thanks to Judith Preissle, Aderhold Distinguished Professor, Social Foundations of Education, University of Georgia, for list subscription details. These sites and subscription details may change, and this list is not exhaustive. This list is meant to be suggestive of the qualitative resources available through the Internet. See Chapter 3, Exhibit 3.7; Chapter 4, Exhibit 4.9; and Chapter 8, Exhibit 8.3, for additional, more specialized qualitative resources through the Internet.

---

success. The farmer peeled away the rotten exterior and exposed what looked like a stone inside. The farmer told him how to plant this hard core, cultivate the resulting trees, and harvest the desired delicacy. The farmer also gave him a plump, ripe sample to taste. Once the seeker after fruit knew what fruit really was, and once he knew that the stonelike thing he held in his hand was a seed, all he had to do was plant it, tend properly the tree's growth, and work for the eventual harvest—the fruit. Though there was much work to be done and there were many things to be learned, the resulting high-quality fruit was worth the effort.

Between-Chapters Interlude

Top Ten Pieces of Advice to a Graduate Student Considering a Qualitative Dissertation

The following query was posted on an Internet listserv devoted to discussing qualitative inquiry:

I am a new graduate student thinking about doing a qualitative dissertation. I know you are all busy, but I would appreciate an answer to only one question.

If you could give just one bit of advice to a student considering qualitative research for a dissertation, what would it be?

The responses below came from different people. I've combined some responses, edited them (while trying to maintain the flavor of the postings), and arranged them for coherence.

Top Ten Responses

1. Be sure that a qualitative approach fits your research questions: questions about people's experiences; inquiry into the meanings people make of their experiences; studying a person in the context of her or his social/interpersonal environment; and research where not enough is known about a phenomenon for standardized instruments to have been developed (or even to be ready to be developed).

   (Chapter 2 will help with this by presenting the primary themes of qualitative inquiry.)

2. Study qualitative research. There are lots of different approaches and a lot to know. Study carefully a couple of the books that provide an overview of different approaches, then **go to the original sources** for the design and analysis details of the approach you decide to use.

(Chapter 3 covers different qualitative approaches.)

3. Find a dissertation adviser who will support your doing qualitative research. Otherwise, it can be a long, tough haul. A dissertation is a big commitment. There are other practical approaches to using qualitative methods that don't involve all the constraints of doing a dissertation, things like program evaluation, action research, and organizational development. You can still do lots of great qualitative work without doing a dissertation. But if you can find a supportive adviser and committee, then, by all means, go for it.

(Chapter 4 covers particularly appropriate practical applications of qualitative methods.)

4. Really work on design. Qualitative designs follow a completely different logic from quantitative research. Completely different. Are you listening? Completely different. Especially sampling. This is not the same as questionnaires and tests and experiments. You can combine designs, like quant and qual approaches, but that gets really complicated. Either way, you have to figure out what's unique about qualitative designs.

(Chapter 5 covers qualitative designs.)

5. Practice interviewing and observation skills. Practice! Practice! Practice! Do lots of interviews. Spend a lot of time doing practice fieldwork observations. Get feedback from someone who's really good at interviewing and observations. There's an amazing amount to learn. And it's not just head stuff. **Qualitative research takes skill.** Don't make the mistake of thinking it's easy. The better I get at it, the more I realize how bad I was when I started.

(Chapters 6 and 7 cover the skills of qualitative inquiry.)

6. Figure out analysis before you gather data. I've talked with lots of advanced grad students who rushed to collect data before they knew anything about analyzing it—and lived to regret it, big time. This is true for statistical data and quantitative data, but somehow people seem to think that qualitative data are easy to analyze. No way. That's a big-time NO WAY. And don't think that the new software will solve the problem. Another big-time NO WAY. You, that's YOU, still have to analyze the data.

(Chapter 8 covers analysis.)

7. Be sure that you're prepared to deal with the controversies of doing qualitative research. People on this listserv are constantly sharing stories about people who don't "get" qualitative research and put it down. Don't go into it naively. Understand the paradigms and politics.

(Chapter 9 deals with paradigms, politics, and ways of enhancing the credibility of qualitative inquiry.)

8. Do it because you want to and are convinced it's right for you. Don't do it be-

cause someone told you it would be easier. It's not. Try as hard as possible to pick/negotiate dissertation research questions that have to do with some passion/interest in your professional life. Qualitative research is time-consuming, intimate, and intense—you will need to find your questions interesting if you want to be at all sane during the process—and still sane at the end.

9. Find a good mentor or support group. Or both. In fact, find several of each. If you can, start a small group of peers in the same boat, so to speak, to talk about your research together on a regular basis—you can share knowledge, brainstorm, and problem solve, as well as share in each other's successes, all in a more relaxed environment that helps take some of the edge off the stress (for example, you might have potluck meals at different homes?). This can be tremendously liberating (even on a less than regular basis). Take care of yourself.

10. Prepare to be changed. Looking deeply at other people's lives will force you to look deeply at yourself.

    (See the discussions "Voice, Perspective, and Reflexivity" in Chapter 2 and "The Observer and What Is Observed: Unity and Separation" in Chapter 6.)

2

Strategic Themes in
Qualitative Inquiry

$\mathcal{G}$ rand strategy should guide tactical decisions. Within a grand strategy all manner of tactical errors may be made, and indeed, are inevitable, but can be corrected as long as the strategic vision remains true and focused. At least that's the theory. In practice . . . ? Try it and see.

—Halcolm

General Principles _____

Strategos is a Greek word meaning "the thinking and action of a general." What it means to be strategic is epitomized by that greatest of Greek generals, Alexander. He conducted his first independent military operation in northern Macedonia at age 16. He became the ruler of Macedonia after his father, Philip, was assassinated in 336 B.C. Two years later, he embarked on an invasion of Persia and conquest of the known world. In the Battle of Arbela, he decisively defeated Darius III, King of Kings of the Persian Empire, despite being outnumbered 5 to 1 (250,000 Persians against Alexander and fewer than 50,000 Greeks).

Alexander's military conquests are legend. What is less known and little appreciated is that his battlefield victories depended on in-depth knowledge of the psychology and culture of the ordinary people and military leaders in opposing armies. He included in his military intelligence information about the beliefs, worldview, motivations, and patterns of behavior of those he faced. Moreover, his conquests and subsequent rule were more economic and political in nature than military. He used what we would now understand to be psychological, sociological, and anthropological insights. He understood that lasting victory depended on the goodwill of and alliances with non-Greek peoples. He carefully studied the customs and conditions of people he conquered and adapted his policies—politically, economically, and culturally—to promote good conditions in each locale so that the people were reasonably well-disposed toward his rule (Garcia 1984).

In this approach, Alexander had to overcome the arrogance and ethnocentrism of his own training, culture, and Greek philosophy. Historian C. A. Robinson, Jr. explained that Alexander was brought up in Plato's theory that all non-Greeks were barbarians, enemies of the Greeks by nature, and Aristotle taught that all barbarians (non-Greeks) were slaves by nature. But

> Alexander had been able to test the smugness of the Greeks by actual contact with the barbarians, . . . and experience had apparently convinced him of the essential sameness of all people. (Robinson 1949:136)

In addition to being a great general and enlightened ruler, Alexander appears to have been an extraordinary ethnographer, a qualitative inquirer par excellence, using observations and firsthand experience to systematically study and understand the peoples he encountered and to challenge his own culture's prejudices.

And as Halcolm finished telling the story of Alexander the Great, he reminded those assembled that skills in observation and interviewing are life skills for experiencing the world. "One can say of qualitative inquiry what Marcel Proust said of art, 'Thanks to this, instead of seeing one world, our own, we see it multiplied. So many worlds are at our disposal.' "

—From Halcolm's *Historical Biographies*

The Purpose of a Strategic Framework

Perception is strong and sight weak. In strategy it is important to see distant things as if they were close and to take a distanced view of close things.

—Miyamoto Musashi (1584-1645),
Japanese warrior, strategist

D on't mistake a clear view for a short distance.

—Grand Canyon hiking advice

E verybody has a plan until they've been hit.

—Old boxing saying

A well-conceived strategy, by providing overall direction, provides a framework for decision making and action. It permits seemingly isolated tasks and activities to fit together, integrating separate efforts toward a common purpose. Specific study design and methods decisions are best made within an overall strategic framework. This chapter offers 12 major themes or principles of qualitative inquiry that, taken together, constitute a comprehensive and coherent strategic framework for qualitative inquiry, including fundamental assumptions and epistemological ideals. Exhibit 2.1 summarizes those themes in three basic categories: design strategies, data collection and fieldwork strategies, and analysis strategies.

🔳 Design Strategies for Qualitative Inquiry

Naturalistic Inquiry

An anthropologist studies initiation rites among the Gourma people of Burkina Faso in West Africa. A sociologist observes interactions among bowlers in their weekly league games. An evaluator participates fully in a leadership training program she is documenting. A naturalist studies bighorn sheep beneath Powell Plateau in the Grand Canyon. A policy analyst interviews people living in public housing in their homes. An agronomist observes farmers' spring planting practices in rural Minnesota. What do

these researchers have in common? They are in the field studying the real world as it unfolds.

Qualitative designs are naturalistic to the extent that the research takes place in real-world settings and the researcher does not attempt to manipulate the phenomenon of interest (e.g., a group, event, program, community, relationship, or interaction). The phenomenon of interest unfolds naturally in that it has no predetermined course established by and for the researcher such as would occur in a laboratory or other controlled setting. Observations take place in real-world settings and people are interviewed with open-ended questions in places and under conditions that are comfortable for and familiar to them.

Egon Guba (1978), in his classic treatise on naturalistic inquiry, identified two dimensions along which types of scientific inquiry can be described: (1) the extent to which the scientist manipulates some phenomenon in advance in order to study it and (2) the extent to which constraints are placed on outputs, that is, the extent to which *predetermined* categories or variables are used to describe the phenomenon under study. He then defined "naturalistic inquiry" as a "discovery-oriented" approach that minimizes investigator manipulation of the study setting and places no prior constraints on what the outcomes of the research will be. Naturalistic inquiry contrasts with controlled experimental designs where, ideally, the investigator controls study conditions

---

EXHIBIT 2.1 **Themes of Qualitative Inquiry**

Design Strategies

1. Naturalistic inquiry	Studying real-world situations as they unfold naturally; nonmanipulative and noncontrolling; openness to whatever emerges (lack of predetermined constraints on findings).
2. Emergent design flexibility	Openness to adapting inquiry as understanding deepens and/or situations change; the researcher avoids getting locked into rigid designs that eliminate responsiveness and pursues new paths of discovery as they emerge.
3. Purposeful sampling	Cases for study (e.g., people, organizations, communities, cultures, events, critical incidences) are selected because they are "information rich" and illuminative, that is, they offer useful manifestations of the phenomenon of interest; sampling, then, is aimed at insight about the phenomenon, not empirical generalization from a sample to a population.

Data Collection and Fieldwork Strategies

4. Qualitative data	Observations that yield detailed, thick description; inquiry in depth; interviews that capture direct quotations about people's personal perspectives and experiences; case studies; careful document review.
5. Personal experience and engagement	The researcher has direct contact with and gets close to the people, situation, and phenomenon under study; the researcher's personal experiences and insights are an important part of the inquiry and critical to understanding the phenomenon.
6. Empathic neutrality and mindfulness	An empathic stance in interviewing seeks vicarious understanding without judgment (neutrality) by showing openness, sensitivity, respect, awareness, and responsiveness; in observation it means being fully present (mindfulness).
7. Dynamic systems	Attention to process; assumes change as ongoing whether focus is on an individual, an organization, a community, or an entire culture; therefore, mindful of and attentive to system and situation dynamics.

---

by manipulating, changing, or holding constant external influences and where a very limited set of outcome variables is measured. Open-ended, conversation-like interviews as a form of naturalistic inquiry contrast with questionnaires that have predetermined response categories. It's the difference between asking, "Tell me about your experience in the program" and "How satisfied were you? Very, somewhat, little, not at all."

In the simplest form of controlled experimental inquiry, the researcher enters the program at two points in time, pretest and

Analysis Strategies

8. Unique case orientation	Assumes each case is special and unique; the first level of analysis is being true to, respecting, and capturing the details of the individual cases being studied; cross-case analysis follows from and depends on the quality of individual case studies.
9. Inductive analysis and creative synthesis	Immersion in the details and specifics of the data to discover important patterns, themes, and interrelationships; begins by exploring, then confirming; guided by analytical principles rather than rules; ends with a creative synthesis.
10. Holistic perspective	The whole phenomenon under study is understood as a complex system that is more than the sum of its parts; focus on complex interdependencies and system dynamics that cannot meaningfully be reduced to a few discrete variables and linear, cause-effect relationships.
11. Context sensitivity	Places findings in a social, historical, and temporal context; careful about, even dubious of, the possibility or meaningfulness of generalizations across time and space; emphasizes instead careful comparative case analyses and extrapolating patterns for possible transferability and adaptation in new settings.
12. Voice, perspective, and reflexivity	The qualitative analyst owns and is reflective about her or his own voice and perspective; a credible voice conveys authenticity and trustworthiness; complete objectivity being impossible and pure subjectivity undermining credibility, the researcher's focus becomes balance—understanding and depicting the world authentically in all its complexity while being self-analytical, politically aware, and reflexive in consciousness.

posttest, and compares the treatment group to some control group on a limited set of standardized measures. Such designs assume a single, identifiable, isolated, and measurable treatment. Moreover, such designs assume that, once introduced, the treatment remains relatively constant and unchanging.

While there are some narrow, carefully controlled, and standardized treatments that fit this description, in practice human interventions (programs) are often quite comprehensive, variable, and dynamic—

changing as practitioners learn what does and does not work, developing new approaches and realigning priorities. This, of course, creates considerable difficulty for controlled experimental designs that need specifiable, unchanging treatments to relate to specifiable, predetermined outcomes. Controlled experimental evaluation designs work best when it is possible to limit program adaptation and improvement so as not to interfere with the rigor of the research design.

By contrast, under real-world conditions where programs are subject to change and redirection, naturalistic inquiry replaces the fixed treatment/outcome emphasis of the controlled experiment with a dynamic, process orientation that documents actual operations and impacts of a process, program, or intervention over a period of time. The evaluator sets out to understand and document the day-to-day reality of participants in the program, making no attempt to manipulate, control, or eliminate situational variables or program developments, but accepting the complexity of a changing program reality. The data of the evaluation include whatever emerges as important to understanding what participants experience.

Natural experiments occur when the observer is present during a real-world change to document a phenomenon before and after the change. Durrenberger and Erem (1999) documented "a natural experiment in thought and structure" when, because of a change at a hospital they were studying, they were able to contrast two different structures of leadership in a union worksite. They had already documented the degree and nature of "union consciousness" before the change, so by repeating their observations after the change in a hospital structure, they were able to take advantage of a naturally occurring experiment. Natural experi-

ments can involve comparing two groups, one of which experiences some change while the other doesn't. What makes this naturalistic inquiry is that real-world participants direct the change, not the researcher, as in the laboratory.

However, the distinction is not as simple as being in the field versus being in the laboratory; rather, the degree to which a design is naturalistic falls along a continuum with completely open fieldwork on one end and completely controlled laboratory control on the other end, but with varying degrees of researcher control and manipulation between these end points. For example, the very presence of the researcher, asking questions, or as in the case of formative program evaluation, providing feedback, can be an intervention that reduces the natural unfolding of events. Unobtrusive observations are needed as an inquiry strategy when the inquirer wants to minimize data collection as an intervention. Nor are laboratory conditions found only in buildings. Field experiments are common in agriculture where researchers want to introduce a considerable amount of control, reduce variation in extraneous variables, and focus on a limited set of predetermined measures, as in crop fertilizer studies.

Let me conclude this discussion of naturalistic inquiry with two examples to illustrate variations in this design strategy. In evaluating a wilderness-based leadership training program, I participated fully in the 10-day wilderness experience, guided in my observations by nothing more than the sensitizing concept "leadership." The only "unnatural" elements of my participation were that (1) everyone knew I was taking notes to document what happened and (2) at the end of each day I conducted open-ended, conversational interviews with staff. While this constitutes a relatively pure naturalistic in-

Naturalistic Inquiry

Which way to the nude beach?

quiry strategy, my presence, note taking, and interviews must be presumed to have altered somewhat the way the program unfolded. I know, for example, that the debriefing questions I asked staff in the evenings got them thinking about things they were doing that led to some changes along the way in how they conducted the training.

The second example comes from the fieldwork of Beverly Strassmann among the Dogon people in the village of Sangui in the Sahel, about 120 miles south of Tombouctou in Mali, West Africa (Gladwell 2000). Her study focused on the Dogon tradition of having menstruating women stay in small, segregated adobe huts at the edge of the village. She observed the comings and goings of these women and obtained urine samples from them to be sure they were menstruating. The women only slept in the huts. During the day, they went about their normal ac-

tivities. For 736 consecutive nights, Strassmann kept track of all the women who used the hut. This allowed her to collect statistics on the frequency and length of menstruation among the Dogon women, but with a completely naturalistic inquiry strategy, illustrating how both quantitative and qualitative data can be collected within a naturalistic design strategy. There's no reason to believe that her presence over this long period changed the women's menstruation patterns.

Emergent Design Flexibility

In the wilderness leadership training program I evaluated, halfway through the 10-day experience the group I was with unexpectedly split into two subgroups. I had to make an in-the-field, on-the-spot decision about which group to follow and how to get interviews with the others at a later time.

Naturalistic inquiry designs cannot usually be completely specified in advance of fieldwork. While the design will specify an initial focus, plans for observations, and initial guiding interview questions, the naturalistic and inductive nature of the inquiry makes it both impossible and inappropriate to specify operational variables, state testable hypotheses, or finalize either instrumentation or sampling schemes. A naturalistic design unfolds or emerges as fieldwork unfolds.

Lincoln and Guba (1985) made an extensive comparison of the design characteristics of qualitative/naturalistic inquiry in contrast to quantitative/experimental methods. They concluded:

> What these considerations add up to is that the design of a naturalistic inquiry (whether research, evaluation, or policy analysis) *cannot* be given in advance; it must emerge, develop, unfold. . . . The call for an emergent design by naturalists is not simply an effort on their part to get around the "hard thinking" that is supposed to precede an inquiry; the desire to permit events to unfold is not merely a way of rationalizing what is at bottom "sloppy inquiry." The design specifications of the conventional paradigm form a procrustean bed of such a nature as to make it impossible for the naturalist to lie in it—not only uncomfortably, *but at all.* (p. 225)

Design flexibility stems from the open-ended nature of naturalistic inquiry as well as pragmatic considerations. Being open and pragmatic requires a high tolerance for ambiguity and uncertainty as well as trust in the ultimate value of what inductive analysis will yield. Such tolerance, openness, and trust create special problems for dissertation committees and funders of evaluation or research. How will they know what will result from the inquiry if the design is only partially specified? The answer is: They won't know with any certainty. All they can do is look at the results of similar qualitative inquiries, inspect the reasonableness of the overall strategies in the proposed design, and consider the capacity of the researcher to fruitfully undertake the proposed study.

As with other strategic themes of qualitative inquiry, the extent to which the design is specified in advance is a matter of degree. Doctoral students doing qualitative dissertations will usually be expected to present fairly detailed fieldwork proposals and interview schedules so that the approving doctoral committee can guide the student and be sure that the proposed work will lead to satisfying degree requirements. Many funders will fund only detailed proposals. As an ideal, however, the qualitative researcher needs considerable flexibility and openness. The fieldwork approach of anthropologist Brackette F. Williams represents the ideal of emergence in naturalistic inquiry.

Williams has focused on issues of cultural identity and social relationships. Her work has included in-depth study of ritual and symbolism in the construction of national identity in Guyana (1991), and the ways that race and class function in the national consciousness of the United States. In 1997, she received a five-year MacArthur Fellowship, which has allowed her to pursue a truly emergent, naturalistic design in her current fieldwork on the phenomenon of killing in America. I had the opportunity to interview her about her work and am including several excerpts from that interview[1] throughout this chapter to illustrate actual scholarly implementation of some of the strategic ideals of qualitative inquiry. Here she describes the necessity of an open-ended approach to her fieldwork because her topic is broad and she needs to follow wherever the phenomenon takes her.

> I'm tracking something—killing—that's moving very rapidly in the culture. Every time I talk to someone, there's another set of data, another thing to look at. Anything that happens in America can be relevant, and that's the exhausting part of it. It never shuts off. You listen to the radio. You watch television. You pass a billboard with an advertisement on it. There's no such thing as something irrelevant when you're studying something like this or maybe just studying the society that you're in. You don't always know exactly how it's going to be relevant, but somehow it just strikes you and you say to yourself: I should document the date of when I saw this and where it was and what was said because it's data.
>
> I don't follow every possible lead people give me. But generally, it is a matter in some sense of opportunity sampling, of serendipity, whatever you want to call it. I key into things that turn out to be very important six months later.
>
> I do impromptu interviews. I don't have some target number of interviews in mind or predetermined questions. It depends on the person and the situation. Airports, for example, are a good place for impromptu interviews with people. So sometimes, instead of using airport time to write, I interview people about the death penalty or about killing or about death in their life. It's called *opportunity sampling*. I begin with a general description. You're such and such an age. You come from such and such a place and, by the way, what do you think about all this killing? And I sort of launch into a conversation. Sometimes the interview goes on for a couple of hours and sometimes, maybe 10 or 15 minutes. I just say, "You wouldn't mind if I record this, would you?" If they say no, I take notes.
>
> I did a lot of that kind of impromptu interviewing in the first year to formulate a proto-col of questions and issues to pursue. It was general sampling to get a sense of what I wanted to know. At other times, it's just to get a general opinion from John Q. Public about a question that I've gotten all kinds of official responses to, but I want to know what people in general think. In an airport, I may get an opportunity to talk to 5 or 10 people. If I have several stops, I may get 15 or 20 by the time I come home.
>
> I fashion the research as I want to fashion it based on what I think this week as opposed to what I thought last week. I don't follow some proposal. I don't have in mind that this has to be a book that's going to have to come out a certain way. I'm following where the data take me, where my questions take me.

Few qualitative studies are as fully emergent and open-ended as the fieldwork of Williams. Her work exemplifies the ideal of *emergent design flexibility.*

Purposeful Sampling

In 1940, eminent sociologist Kingsley Davis published what was to become a classic case study, the story of Anna, a baby kept in nearly total isolation from the time of her birth until she was discovered at age six. She had been deprived of human contact, had acquired no language skills, and had received only enough care to keep her barely alive. This single case, horrifying as was the abuse and neglect, offered a natural experiment to study socialization effects and the relative contributions of nature and nurture to human development. In 1947, Davis published an update on Anna and a comparison case of socialization isolation, the story of Isabelle. These two cases offered considerable insight into the question of how long a human being could remain isolated before "the capacity for full cultural acquisition" was permanently damaged (Davis 1940,

1947). The cases of Anna and Isabelle are extreme examples of purposeful case sampling.

Unusual clinical cases in medicine and psychology, instructive precisely because they are unusual, offer many examples of purposeful sampling. Neurologist Oliver Sacks (1985) presents a number of such cases in his widely read and influential book *The Man Who Mistook His Wife for a Hat,* the very title of which hints at the uniqueness of the cases examined. While one cannot generalize from single cases or very small samples, one can learn from them—and learn a great deal, often opening up new territory for further research, as was the case with Piaget's detailed and insightful observations of his own two children.

Perhaps nowhere is the difference between quantitative and qualitative methods better captured than in the different strategies, logics, and purposes that distinguish statistical probability sampling from qualitative purposeful sampling. Qualitative inquiry typically focuses on relatively small samples, even single cases ($N = 1$) such as Anna or Isabelle, selected *purposefully* to permit inquiry into and understanding of a phenomenon *in depth.* Quantitative methods typically depend on larger samples selected randomly in order to generalize with confidence from the sample to the population that it represents. Not only are the techniques for sample selection different, but the very logic of each approach is distinct because the purpose of each strategy is different.

The logic and power of probability sampling derive from its purpose: generalization. The logic and power of purposeful sampling derive from the emphasis on in-depth understanding. This leads to selecting *information-rich cases* for study in depth. Information-rich cases are those from

which one can learn a great deal about issues of central importance to the purpose of the research, thus the term *purposeful* sampling. For example, if the purpose of an evaluation is to increase the effectiveness of a program in reaching lower-socioeconomic groups, one may learn a great deal more by focusing in depth on understanding the needs, interests, and incentives of a small number of carefully selected poor families than by gathering standardized information from a large, statistically significant sample. The cases sampled can be individual people, families, organizations, cultures, incidents, or activities, to mention examples. But regardless of the kind of unit of analysis (e.g., an athlete or a sports team, a teacher or a classroom), the purpose of purposeful sampling is to select information-rich cases whose study will illuminate the questions under study.

Chapter 5 will review several different strategies for purposefully selecting information-rich cases. In my interview with her, Brackette F. Williams offered an example of an information-rich case from her ongoing study of killing in America.

I've been tracking information on a serial killer—someone who has just been identified as a "serial killer" in Louisiana—who's killing young Black men, shooting them up with drugs and taking one of their tennis shoes, sometimes both. Now, I'm interested in the fact that as society more and more identifies young Black men as sort of the quintessential bad guys, this serial killer picks a bad guy. For contrast, look at serial killers who picked women at a certain period of time, about 15-20 years ago, because they wore, in his estimation, a size 13. Now, track our obsession with obesity. How a serial killer picks his victims can tell you something important about what's going on in society.

🔄 Data Collection and Fieldwork: Strategies for Qualitative Inquiry

Qualitative Data

Qualitative data consist of quotations, observations, and excerpts from documents. The first chapter provided several examples of qualitative data. Deciding whether to use naturalistic inquiry or an experimental approach is a design issue. This is different from deciding what kind of data to collect (qualitative, quantitative, or some combination), although design and data alternatives are clearly related. Qualitative data can be collected in experimental designs where participants have been randomly divided into treatment and control groups. Likewise, some quantitative data may be collected in naturalistic inquiry approaches. Nevertheless, controlled experimental designs predominantly aim for statistical analyses of quantitative data, while qualitative data are the primary focus in naturalistic inquiry. This relationship between design and measurement will be explored at greater length in the chapter on design.

Qualitative data describe. They take us, as readers, into the time and place of the observation so that we know what it was like to have been there. They capture and communicate someone else's experience of the world in his or her own words. Qualitative data tell a story. In the excerpt below, from my interview with her, Williams tells the story of checking out a childhood memory. This story gives us insight into the nature of her naturalistic inquiry and open-ended interviewing, shows how a critical incident can be a purposeful sample, and, in the story itself, offers something of the flavor of qualitative data.

I was down in Texas interviewing last March, thinking about my research and interviewing people, and there was a childhood memory that I had of an electrocution of a man that was the son of a woman who lived across the field from us. Now a rumor about this had always been in the back of my mind. Whenever I'd hear about a death penalty case over the years, I would think about this man having been electrocuted. I thought he was electrocuted because he raped this White woman. So I'm sitting in my cousin's kitchen after I had done some of these interviews and another woman, an older woman who was a relative of hers, came in and the conversation goes around. I happen to mention this memory of mine. I asked, "Is that just something that I concocted out of having read a book or something, but it never happened?" She answered, "Oh, no, it happened. You only have one part of the story wrong. He didn't rape her. He looked at her."

You know, you read about these things in history books and then all of a sudden, it's like a part of a world that you existed in. These things happened around you and yet somehow there was so much of a distance, you couldn't touch it. I knew about this man all my life, but in all the reading and all the history books, I couldn't touch that. *Doing this project the way I'm doing it allows me to touch things that otherwise I would never touch.*

Direct Personal Experience and Engagement: Going Into the Field

The preceding quotation from Williams exemplifies the personal nature of qualitative fieldwork. Getting close to her subject matter, including using her own experiences, both from childhood and day-to-day in her adult life, illustrates the all-encompassing and ultimately personal nature of in-depth qualitative inquiry. Traditionally, social scientists have been warned to stay distant from those they studied to maintain "objectivity." But that kind of detachment can limit one's openness to and understanding of the very nature of what one is studying, especially where meaning-making and emotion are part of the phenomenon. Look closely at what Williams says about the effects of immersing herself personally in her fieldwork, even while visiting relatives: "Doing this project the way I'm doing it allows me to touch things that otherwise I would never touch."

Fieldwork is the central activity of qualitative inquiry. "Going into the field" means having direct and personal contact with people under study in their own environments —getting close to the people and situations being studied to personally understand the realities and minutiae of daily life, for example, life as experienced by participants in a welfare-to-work program. The inquirer gets close to the people under study through physical proximity for a period of time as well as through development of closeness in the social sense of shared experience, empathy, and confidentiality. That many quantitative methodologists fail to ground their findings in personal qualitative understanding poses what sociologist John Lofland (1971) called a major contradiction between their public insistence on the adequacy of statistical portrayals of other humans and their personal everyday dealings with and judgments about other human beings.

> In everyday life, statistical sociologists, like everyone else, assume that they do not know or understand very well people they do not see or associate with very much. They assume that knowing and understanding other people require that one see them reasonably often and in a variety of situations relative to a variety of issues. Moreover, statistical sociologists, like

> other people, assume that in order to know or understand others one is well-advised to give some conscious attention to that effort in face-to-face contacts. They assume, too, that the internal world of sociology—or any other social world—is not understandable unless one has been part of it in a face-to- face fashion for quite a period of time. How utterly paradoxical, then, for these same persons to turn around and make, by implication, precisely the opposite claim about people they have never encountered face-to-face—those people appearing as numbers in their tables and as correlations in their matrices! (Lofland 1971:3)

Qualitative inquiry means going into the field—into the real world of programs, organizations, neighborhoods, street corners—and getting close enough to the people and circumstances there to capture what is happening. To immerse oneself in naturally occurring complexity involves what qualitative methodologist Norman Denzin (1978a) has called "the studied commitment to actively enter the worlds of interacting individuals" (pp. 8-9). This makes possible description and understanding of *both* externally observable behaviors *and* internal states (worldview, opinions, values, attitudes, and symbolic constructs). Given the qualitative emphasis on striving for depth of understanding, in context, attitude surveys and psychological tests are inadequate for revealing inner perspectives. "The inner perspective assumes that understanding can only be achieved by actively participating in the life of the observed and gaining insight by means of introspection" (Bruyn 1963:226).

Actively participating in the life of the observed means going where the action is, getting one's hands dirty, participating where possible in actual program activities, and getting to know program staff and participants on a personal level—in other words, getting personally engaged so as to use all of one's senses and capacities, including the capacity to experience affect no less than cognition. Such engagement stands in sharp contrast to the professional comportment of some in the field, for example, supposedly objective evaluators, who purposely project an image of being cool, calm, external, and detached. Such detachment is presumed to reduce bias. However, qualitative methodologists question the necessity and utility of distance and detachment, asserting that without empathy and sympathetic introspection derived from personal encounters, the observer cannot fully understand human behavior. Understanding comes from trying to put oneself in the other person's shoes, from trying to discern how others think, act, and feel.

In a classic study, educational evaluator Edna Shapiro (1973) studied young children in classrooms in the national Follow Through program using both quantitative and qualitative methods. It was her closeness to the children in those classrooms that allowed her to see that something was happening that was not captured by standardized tests. She could see differences in children, observe their responses to diverse situations, and capture the varying meanings they attached to common events. She could feel their tension in the testing situation and their spontaneity in the more natural classroom setting. Had she worked solely with data collected by others or only at a distance, she would never have discovered the crucial differences in the classroom settings she studied—differences that actually allowed her to evaluate the innovative program in a meaningful and relevant way. Where standardized tests showed no differences between classrooms using different approaches, her direct observations documented important and significant program impacts.

It is important to note that the admonition to get close to the data is in no way meant to deny the usefulness of quantitative methods. Rather, it means that statistical portrayals must always be interpreted and given human meaning. I once interviewed an evaluator of federal health programs who expressed frustration at trying to make sense out of statistical data from over 80 projects after site visit funds had been cut out of the evaluation: "There's no way to evaluate something that's just data. You know, you have to go look."

Going into the field and having personal contact with program participants is not the only legitimate way to understand human behavior. For certain questions and for situations involving large groups, distance is inevitable, perhaps even helpful, but to get at deeper meanings and preserve context, face-to-face interaction is both necessary and desirable. This returns us to a recurrent theme of this book: matching research methods to the purpose of a study, the questions being asked, and the resources available.

In thinking about the issue of closeness to the people and situations being studied, it is useful to remember that many major contributions to our understanding of the world have come from scientists' personal experiences. One finds many instances where closeness to sources of data made key insights possible— Piaget's closeness to his children, Freud's proximity to and empathy with his patients, Darwin's closeness to nature, and even Newton's intimate encounter with an apple. In short, closeness does not make bias and loss of perspective inevitable; distance is no guarantee of objectivity.

Empathic Neutrality

If, as the previous section has discussed, naturalistic inquiry involves fieldwork that puts one in close contact with people and their problems, what is to be the researcher's cognitive and emotional stance toward those people and problems? No universal prescription can capture the range of possibilities, for the answer will depend on the situation, the nature of the inquiry, and the perspective of the researcher. But thinking strategically, I offer the phrase "empathic neutrality" as a point of departure. It suggests that there is a middle ground between becoming too involved, which can cloud judgment, and remaining too distant, which can reduce understanding. What is empathic neutrality? Consider this anecdote by way of illustration.

Pragmatist philosopher William James, also a scholar of anatomy and psychology, had a great capacity for empathy, as displayed in his classic study *The Varieties of Religious Experience* ([1902] 1999). Editor Clifton Fadiman (1985:305) recounts that while he was teaching at Radcliffe, Gertrude Stein took a course from him in which, having attended the opera and then partied into the wee hours the night before an exam, she wrote, "Dear Professor James, I am so sorry but I do not feel a bit like writing an examination paper today." James is said to have written back: "Dear Miss Stein, I understand perfectly. I often feel like that myself." Had he added, but the exam is still due, instead of ordinary sympathy he would have displayed extraordinary empathic neutrality.

Methodologists and philosophers of science debate what the researcher's stance should be vis-à-vis the people being studied. Critics of qualitative inquiry have charged that the approach is too *subjective,* in large part because the researcher is the instrument of both data collection and data interpretation and because a qualitative strategy includes having personal contact with and getting close to the people and situation under study. From the perspective of advocates

of a supposedly value-free social science, subjectivity is the very antithesis of scientific inquiry.

Objectivity has been considered the strength of the scientific method. The primary methods for achieving objectivity in science have been conducting blind experiments and quantification. "Objective tests" gather data through instruments that, in principle, are not dependent on human skill, perception, or even presence. Yet, it is clear that tests and questionnaires are designed by human beings and therefore are subject to the intrusion of the researcher's biases by the very questions asked. Unconscious bias in the skillful manipulation of statistics to prove a hypothesis in which the researcher believes is hardly absent from hypothetical-deductive inquiry.

Part of the difficulty in thinking about the fieldwork stance of the qualitative inquirer is that the terms *objectivity* and *subjectivity* have become so loaded with negative connotations and subject to acrimonious debate (e.g., Scriven 1972a; Borman and Goetz 1986; Krenz and Sax 1986; Guba 1991) that neither term any longer provides useful guidance. These terms have been politicized beyond utility. To claim the mantle of "objectivity" in the postmodern age is to expose oneself as embarrassingly naive. The ideals of absolute objectivity and value-free science are impossible to attain in practice and are of questionable desirability in the first place since they ignore the intrinsically social nature and human purposes of research. On the other hand, *subjectivity* has such negative connotations in the public mind that to admit being subjective may undermine one's credibility with audiences unsophisticated about phenomenological assumptions and nuances. In short, the terms *objectivity* and *subjectivity* have become ideological ammunition in the methodological paradigms debate. My pragmatic solution is to avoid using either word and to stay out of futile debates about subjectivity versus objectivity. Qualitative research in recent years has moved toward preferring such language as *trustworthiness* and *authenticity*. Evaluators aim for "balance," "fairness," and "completeness" (Patton 1997a:282). Chapter 9 will discuss these terms and the stances they imply at greater length. At this point, I simply want to note the strategic nature of the issue of inquirer stance and add empathic neutrality to the emerging lexicon that attempts to supersede the hot button term *objective* and the epithet *subjective*.

Any research strategy ultimately needs credibility to be useful. No credible research strategy advocates biased distortion of data to serve the researcher's vested interests and prejudices. Both qualitative/naturalistic inquiry and quantitative/experimental inquiry seek honest, meaningful, credible, and empirically supported findings. Any credible research strategy requires that the investigator adopt a stance of *neutrality* with regard to the phenomenon under study. This simply means that the investigator does not set out to prove a particular perspective or manipulate the data to arrive at predisposed truths. The neutral investigator enters the research arena with no ax to grind, no theory to prove (to test but not to prove), and no predetermined results to support. Rather, the investigator's commitment is to understand the world as it unfolds, be true to complexities and multiple perspectives as they emerge, and be balanced in reporting both confirmatory and disconfirming evidence with regard to any conclusions offered.

Neutrality is not an easily attainable stance, so all credible research strategies include techniques for helping the investigator become aware of and deal with selective perception, personal biases, and theoretical predispositions. Qualitative inquiry, because the human being is the instrument of data collection, requires that the investigator carefully reflect on, deal with, and report potential sources of bias and error. Systematic data collection procedures, rigorous training, multiple data sources, triangulation, external reviews, and other techniques to be discussed in this book are aimed at producing high-quality qualitative data that are credible, trustworthy, authentic, balanced about the phenomenon under study, and fair to the people studied.

The livelihood of evaluators and researchers depends on their integrity and credibility. Independence and neutrality, then, are serious issues.

However, neutrality does not mean detachment. It is on this point that qualitative inquiry makes a special contribution. Qualitative inquiry depends on, uses, and enhances the researcher's direct experiences in the world and insights about those experiences. This includes learning through *empathy*.

Empathy and Insight

⎰he idea of acquiring an "inside" understanding—the actors' definitions of the situation—is a powerful central concept for understanding the purpose of qualitative inquiry.

—Thomas A. Schwandt (2000:102)

Empathy develops from personal contact with the people interviewed and observed during fieldwork. Empathy involves being able to take and understand the stance, position, feelings, experiences, and worldview of others. Put metaphorically, empathy is "like being able to imagine a life for a spider, a maker's life, or just some aliveness in its wide abdomen and delicate spinnerets so you take it outside in two paper cups instead of stepping on it" (Dunn 2000:62). Empathy combines cognitive understanding with affective connection, and in that sense differs from sympathy, which is primarily emotional (Wispé 1986).

The value of empathy is emphasized in the phenomenological doctrine of *Verstehen* that undergirds much qualitative inquiry. *Verstehen* means "understanding" and refers to the unique human capacity to make sense of the world. This capacity has profound implications for how one studies human beings. The *Verstehen* doctrine presumes that since human beings have a unique type of consciousness, as distinct from other forms of life, the study of human beings will be different from the study of other forms of life and nonhuman phenomena. The capacity for empathy, then, is one of the major assets available for human inquiry into human affairs.

The *Verstehen* premise asserts that human beings can and must be understood in a manner different from other objects of study because humans have purposes and emotions; they make plans, construct cultures, and hold values that affect behavior. Their feelings and behaviors are influenced by consciousness, deliberation, and the capacity to think about the future. Human beings live in a world that has special meaning to them, and because their behavior has meaning, "human actions are intelligible in ways that the behavior of nonhuman objects is not" (Strike 1972:28). Human and social sci-

> ### VERSTEHEN?
>
> *The following story is passed around among management consultants. It seems that very late at night the president of a multinational corporation was standing in front of a paper shredder, trying to figure out how to turn it on. The building was deserted except for the cleaning staff, one of whom happened by. The president asked for help, explaining that what he was working on was very important and couldn't wait until morning. The cleaning person was glad to be of help, turned on the machine, took the sheet of paper from the president, and fed it into the shredder just as the president said, "I only need you to make one copy."*

ences need methods different from those used in agricultural experimentation and physical sciences because human beings are different from plants and nuclear particles. The *Verstehen* tradition stresses understanding that focuses on the meaning of human behavior, the context of social interaction, an empathic understanding based on personal experience, and the connections between mental states and behavior. The tradition of *Verstehen* places emphasis on the human capacity to know and understand others through empathic introspection and reflection based on direct observation of and interaction with people. "*Verstehen* thus entails a kind of empathic identification with the actor. It is an act of psychological reenactment— getting inside the head of an actor to understand what he or she is up to in terms of motives, beliefs, desires, thoughts, and so on" (Schwandt 2000:192).

Max Weber brought the term *empathy* into social science to emphasize the importance of comprehending the motives and feelings of people in a social-cultural context.

Both *Verstehen* and empathy depend largely on qualitative data. Verstehen is an attempt to "crack the code" of the culture, that is, detect the categories into which a culture codes actions and thoughts.... Empathy in evaluation is the detection of emotions manifested in the program participants and staff, achieved by evaluators' becoming aware of similar or complementary emotions in themselves. (Meyers 1981:180)

A qualitative strategy of inquiry proposes an active, involved role for the social scientist. "Hence, insight may be regarded as the core of social knowledge. It is arrived at by being on the inside of the phenomena to be observed.... It is participation in an activity that generates interest, purpose, point of view, value, meaning, and intelligibility, as well as bias" (Wirth 1949:xxii). This is a quite different scientific process from that envisioned by the classical, experimental approach to science, but it is still an empirical, (i.e., data-based), scientific perspective. The qualitative perspective "in no way suggests that the researcher lacks the ability to be scientific while collecting the data. On the contrary, it merely specifies that it is crucial for validity—and, consequently, for reliability —to try to picture the empirical social world as it actually exists to those under investigation, rather than as the researcher imagines it to be" (Filstead 1970:4), thus the importance of such qualitative approaches as participant observation, depth interviewing, detailed description, and case studies.

These qualitative inquiry methods provide opportunities to achieve empathy and give the researcher an empirical basis for describing the perspectives of others. Chapter 1 cited the framework of humanistic psychologist Clark Moustakas, who has described this nonjudgmental empathic stance as "Being-In" another's world—immersing oneself in another's world by listening deeply and attentively so as to enter into the other person's experience and perception.

I do not select, interpret, advise, or direct.... Being-In the world of the other is a way of going wide open, entering in as if for the first time, hearing just what is, leaving out my own thoughts, feelings, theories, biases.... I enter with the intention of understanding and accepting perceptions and not presenting my own view or reactions.... I only want to encourage and support the other person's expression, what and how it is, how it came to be, and where it is going. (Moustakas 1995:82-83)

At first, the phrase "empathic neutrality" may appear to be an oxymoron, combining contradictory ideas. Empathy, however, describes a stance toward the people one encounters—it communicates understanding, interest, and caring. Neutrality suggests a stance toward their thoughts, emotions, and behaviors—it means being nonjudgmental. Neutrality can actually facilitate rapport and help build a relationship that supports empathy by disciplining the researcher to be open to the other person and nonjudgmental in that openness. Rapport and empathy, however, must not be taken for granted, as Radhika Parameswaran (2001) found in doing fieldwork among young middle-class women in urban India who read Western romance fiction.

Despite their eventual willingness to share their fears and complaints about gendered social pressures, I still wonder whether these young women would have been more open about their sexuality with a Westerner who might be seen as less likely to judge them based on cultural expectations of women's behavior in Indian society. The well-known word rapport, which is often used to signify acceptance and warm relationships between informants and researchers, was thus something I could not take for granted despite being an insider; all I could claim was an imperfect rapport. (Parameswaran 2001:69)

Evaluation presents special challenges for rapport and neutrality as well. After fieldwork, an evaluator may be called on to render judgments about a program as part of data interpretation and formulating recommendations, but during fieldwork, the focus should be on rigorously observing and interviewing to understand the people and situation being studied. This nuanced relationship between neutrality and empathy will be discussed further in both the data collection and analysis chapters.

A Dynamic, Developmental Perspective

*T*here is nothing permanent except change.

—Heraclitus (Ancient Greece)

A questionnaire is like a photograph. A qualitative study is like a documentary film. Both offer images. One, however— the photograph—captures and freezes a moment in time, like recording a respondent's answer to a survey question at a moment in time. The other—the film— offers a fluid sense of development, movement, and change.

Qualitative evaluation researchers, for example, conceive of programs as dynamic and developing, with "treatments" changing in subtle but important ways as staff learns what does and doesn't work, as clients move in and out, and as conditions of delivery are altered. A primary challenge, then, becomes describing and understanding these dynamic program processes and their holistic effects on participants so as to provide information for program improvement. In contrast, an experimental design for an evaluation typically conceives of the program as a fixed thing, like a measured amount of fertilizer applied to a crop—*a* treatment, *an* intervention—that has predetermined, measurable outcomes. Inconsistency in the treatment, instability in the intervention, changes in the program, variability in program processes, and diversity in participants' experiences undermine the logic of an experimental design because these developments—all natural, even inevitable, in real-world programs—call into question what the "treatment" or experiment actually is.

Naturalistic inquiry assumes the ever-changing world posited by the observation in the ancient Chinese proverb that one never steps into the same river twice. Change is a natural, expected, and inevitable part of human experience, and documenting change is a natural, expected, and intrinsic part of fieldwork. Rather than trying to control, limit, or direct change, naturalistic inquirers expect change, anticipate the likelihood of the unanticipated, and are prepared to go with the flow of change. One gets this sense of pursuing change in the comment by anthropologist Williams cited earlier: "I'm tracking something—killing —that's moving very rapidly in the culture." Part of her inquiry task is to track cultural changes the way an epidemiologist tracks a disease. As a result, reading a good qualitative case study gives the sense of reading a good story. It has a beginning, a middle, and an ending—though not necessarily an end.

🔲 Analysis Strategies for Qualitative Inquiry

Unique Case Orientation

"Six windows on respect" is how Harvard sociologist Sara Lawrence-Lightfoot (2000:13) describes the six detailed case studies, each a full chapter, she presents in her book *Respect*. The cases offer different angles on the meaning and experience of respect in modern society as illuminated by a nurse-midwife, a pediatrician, a teacher, an artist, a law school professor, and a pastoral therapist/AIDS activist. Before drawing themes and contrasts from this small, purposeful sample, and before naming the six angles they represent, Lawrence-Lightfoot had the task of constructing the unique cases to tell these distinct stories. Her first task, then, was to undertake the "art and science of portraiture" (Lawrence-Lightfoot and Davis 1997). From these separate portraits, she fashions a stained glass mosaic that depicts and illuminates *Respect*.

I undertook a study of a national fellowship award program that had had more than 600 recipients over a 20-year period. A survey had been done to get the fellows' opinions about select issues, but the staff wanted more depth, richness, and detail to really understand patterns of fellowship use and impact. With a team of researchers, we conducted 40 in-depth, face-to-face interviews and wrote case studies. Through inductive analysis, we subsequently identified distinct enabling processes and impacts, and we created a framework that depicted relationships between status at the time of the award, enabling processes, and impacts. The heart of the study remained the 40 case studies. To read only the framework analysis without reading the case studies would be to lose much of the richness, depth, meaning, and contribution of qualitative research and

evaluation. That is what is meant by the "unique case orientation" of qualitative inquiry.

Case studies are particularly valuable in program evaluation when the program is individualized, so the evaluation needs to be attentive to and capture individual differences among participants, diverse experiences of the program, or unique variations from one program setting to another. As noted earlier, a case can be a person, an event, a program, an organization, a time period, a critical incident, or a community. Regardless of the unit of analysis, a qualitative case study seeks to describe that unit in depth and detail, holistically, and in context.

Inductive Analysis and Creative Synthesis

Benjamin Whorf's development of the famous Whorf hypothesis—that language shapes our experience of the environment and that words shape perceptions and actions, a kind of linguistic relativity theory (Schultz 1991)—provides an instructive example of inductive analysis. Whorf was an insurance investigator assigned to look into explosions in warehouses. He discovered that truck drivers were entering "empty" warehouses smoking cigarettes and cigars. The warehouses, it turned out, often contained invisible, but highly flammable gases. He interviewed truckers and found that they associated the word *empty* with *harmless* and acted accordingly. From these specific observations and findings, he *inductively* formulated his general theory about language and perception that has informed a half-century of communications scholarship (Lee 1996).

Qualitative inquiry is particularly oriented toward exploration, discovery, and inductive logic. Inductive analysis begins with

QUALITATIVE COMPARATIVE ANALYSIS

Understanding unique cases can be deepened by comparative analysis. Indeed, constant comparative analysis is a central analytical approach in grounded theory, one of the major schools of qualitative inquiry (discussed in Chapters 3 and 8). Comparisons can also be important in illuminating differences between programs in evaluation. Indeed, evaluation theorist Michael Scriven (1993) has asserted in his monograph Hard-Won Lessons in Program Evaluation that "noncomparative evaluations are comparatively useless" (p. 58).

Leonardo da Vinci's (ca. 1519) insight into color contrasts offers a metaphor for qualitative comparative analysis: "In order to attain a color of the greatest possible perfection, one has to place it in the neighborhood of the directly contrary color: thus one places black with white, yellow with blue, green with red" (cited in Boring 1942).

specific observations and builds toward general patterns. Categories or dimensions of analysis emerge from open-ended observations as the inquirer comes to understand patterns that exist in the phenomenon being investigated.

Inductive analysis contrasts with the hypothetical-deductive approach of experimental designs that require the specification of main variables and the statement of specific research hypotheses *before* data collection begins. A specification of research hypotheses based on an explicit theoretical framework means that general constructs provide the framework for understanding specific observations or cases. The investigator must then decide in advance what vari-

ables are important and what relationships among those variables can be expected.

The strategy of inductive designs is to allow the important analysis dimensions to emerge from patterns found in the cases under study without presupposing in advance what the important dimensions will be. The qualitative analyst seeks to understand the multiple interrelationships among dimensions that emerge from the data without making prior assumptions or specifying hypotheses about the linear or correlative relationships among narrowly defined, operationalized variables. For example, an inductive approach to program evaluation means that understanding the nature of the "intervention" emerges from direct observations of program activities and interviews with participants. In general, theories about what is happening in a setting are grounded in and emerge from direct field experience rather than being imposed a priori as is the case in formal hypothesis and theory testing.

The straightforward contrast between closed-ended questionnaires and open-ended interviews in Chapter 1 illustrated the difference between deductive and inductive approaches at the simplest level. A structured, multiple-choice questionnaire requires a deductive approach because items must be predetermined based on some theory or preordinate criteria, for example, program goals about what is important to measure. An open-ended interview, by way of contrast, permits the respondent to describe what is meaningful and salient without being *pigeon holed* into standardized categories.

In practice, these approaches are often combined. Some evaluation or research questions may be determined deductively, while others are left sufficiently open to permit inductive analyses based on direct observations. While the quantitative/experimental approach is largely hypothetical-

Pigeon Holing

The problem with some pigeons is they refuse to stay in their pigeon holes.

deductive and the qualitative/naturalistic approach is largely inductive, a study can include elements of both strategies. Indeed, over a period of inquiry, an investigation may flow from inductive approaches, to find out what the important questions and variables are (exploratory work), to deductive hypothesis-testing or outcome measurement aimed at confirming and/or generalizing exploratory findings, then back again to inductive analysis to look for rival hypotheses and unanticipated or unmeasured factors.

The precise nature of inductive analysis depends, in part, on the purpose of the analysis and the number and types of cases in a study. Where there are several cases to be compared and contrasted, an inductive approach begins by constructing individual cases, without pigeon holing or categorizing those cases. That is, the first task is to do a careful job independently writing up the separate cases. Once that is done, cross-case analysis can begin in search of patterns and themes that cut across individual experiences. The initial focus is on full understanding of individual cases before those unique cases are combined or aggregated thematically. This helps ensure that emergent categories and discovered patterns are *grounded* in specific cases and their contexts (Glaser and Strauss 1967).

Just as writers report different creative processes, so too qualitative analysts have different ways of working. Although software programs now exist to facilitate working with large amounts of narrative data and substantial guidance can be offered about the steps and processes of content analysis, making sense of multiple interview transcripts and pages of field notes cannot be reduced to a formula or even a standard series of steps. There is no equivalent of a statistical significance test or factor score to tell the analyst when results are important or what quotations fit together under the same theme. Finding a way to *creatively synthesize* and present findings is one of the challenges of qualitative analysis, a challenge that will be explored at length in Part 3 of this book. For the moment, I can offer a flavor of that challenge with another excerpt from my interview with anthropologist Williams. Here she describes part of her own unique analytic process.

> My current project follows up work that I have always done, which is to study categories and classifications and their implications. Right now, as I said, the focus of my work is on killing and the desire to kill and the categories people create in relation to killing. Part of it right now focuses on the death penalty, but mainly on killing. My fascination is with the links between category distinctions, commitments, and the desire to kill for those commitments. That's what I study.
>
> I track categories, like "serial killers" or "death row inmates." The business of constantly transforming people into acts and acts into people is part of the way loyalties, commitments, and hatreds are generated. So I'm a classifier. I study classification—theories of classification. A lot of categories have to do with very abstract things; others have to do with very concrete things like skin color. But ultimately, the classification of a kill is what I'm focusing on now. I've been asking myself lately, for the chapter I've been working on, "Is there a fundamental difference, for example, in the way we classify to kill?" Consider the percentage of people classified as "death worthy"—the way we classify to justify the death penalty.
>
> As I write, moving back and forth between my tapes and my interviews, I don't feel that I have to follow some fixed outline or that I have to code things to come out a certain way. Sometimes I listen to a tape and I start to think

that I should rewrite this part of this chapter. I had completely forgotten about this tape. It was done in early '98 or late '97 and maybe I hadn't listened to it or looked at the transcript for a while, and I've just finished a chapter or section of a chapter. I pull that tape off the shelf. I listen to it. I go back to the transcript and I start writing again. I start revising in ways that it seems to me that tape *demands*.

As Williams describes her analysis and writing process, she offers insight into what it means when qualitative researchers say they are "working to be true to the data" or that their analytical process is "data driven." Williams says, "I start revising in ways that it seems to me that tape *demands*." It is common to hear qualitative analysts say that, as they write their conclusions, they keep going back to the cases; they reread field notes; and they listen again to interviews. Inductive analysis is built on a solid foundation of specific, concrete, and detailed observations, quotations, documents, and cases. As thematic structures and overarching constructs emerge during analysis, the qualitative analyst keeps returning to fieldwork observations and interview transcripts, working from the bottom up, staying grounded in the foundation of case write-ups, and thereby examining emergent themes and constructs in light of what they illuminate about the case descriptions on which they are based. That is inductive analysis.

Holistic Perspective

Holography is a method of photography in which the wave field of light scattered by an object is captured as an interference pattern. When the photographic record—the hologram—is illuminated by a laser, a three-dimensional image appears. Any piece of a hologram will reconstruct the entire image.

This has become a metaphor for thinking in new ways about the relationships between parts and wholes. The interdependence of flora, fauna, and the physical environment in ecological systems offers another metaphor for what it means to think and analyze holistically.

Researchers and evaluators analyzing qualitative data strive to understand a phenomenon or program as a whole. This means that a description and interpretation of a person's social environment, or an organization's external context, is essential for overall understanding of what has been observed during fieldwork or said in an interview. This holistic approach assumes that the whole is understood as a complex system that is greater than the sum of its parts. The analyst searches for the totality or unifying nature of particular settings—the *gestalt*. Psychotherapist Fritz Perls (1973) made the term *gestalt* equivalent with a holistic perspective in psychology. He used the example of three sticks that are just three sticks until one places them together to form a triangle. Then they are much more than the three separate sticks combined: They form a new whole.

> A gestalt may be a tangible thing, such as a triangle, or it may be a situation. A happening such as a meeting of two people, their conversation, and their leave-taking would constitute a completed situation. If there were an interruption in the middle of the conversation, it would be an incomplete gestalt. (Brown 1996:36)

The strategy of seeking gestalt units and holistic understandings in qualitative analysis contrasts with the logic and procedures of evaluation studies conducted in the analytical tradition of "let's take it apart and see how it works." The quantitative-experimental approach to evaluation, for example, re-

quires operationalization of independent and dependent variables with a focus on their statistical covariance. Outcomes must be identified and measured as specific variables. Treatments and programs must also be conceptualized as discrete, independent variables. The characteristics of program participants are also described by standardized, quantified dimensions. Sometimes the variables of interest are derived from program goals, for example, student achievement test scores, recidivism statistics for a group of juvenile delinquents, sobriety rates for participants in chemical dependency treatment programs. At other times, the variables measured are indicators of a larger construct. For example, community well-being may be measured by such rates for delinquency, infant mortality, divorce, unemployment, suicide, and poverty (Brock, Schwaller, and Smith 1985). These variables are statistically manipulated or added together in some linear fashion to test hypotheses and draw inferences about the relationships among separate indicators, or the statistical significance of differences between measured levels of the variables for different groups. The essential logic of this approach is as follows: (1) Key program outcomes and processes can be represented by separate independent variables, (2) these variables can be quantified, and (3) relationships among these variables are best portrayed statistically.

The primary critique of this logic by qualitative-naturalistic evaluators is that such an approach (1) oversimplifies the complexities of real-world programs and participants' experiences, (2) misses major factors of importance that are not easily quantified, and (3) fails to portray a sense of the program and its impacts as a whole. To support holistic analysis, the qualitative inquirer gathers data on multiple aspects of the setting under study to assemble a comprehensive and complete

HOLISTIC UNDERSTANDING IN GENETICS

The work of geneticist Barbara McClintock, winner of the Nobel prize, illustrates holistic inquiry. She sought to understand the organization and functions of genes in relation to the rest of the cell, within the organism as a whole:

> *She sought a feel for the whole. Rather than dismissing exceptional cases as irrelevant to general theory, she focused on anomalous pigmentation of individual plants. Instead of starting with an hypothesis prescribing what she expected and framing the questions for the material to answer, as in most controlled experiments, she felt the need to "let the experiment tell you what it wants to do" and to "listen to the material."*
>
> *She followed each unique seedling through its life in the field.... At times, she became so engrossed in examining individual cells in a grain of corn through her microscope that she felt as if she were down there within the cell, the same size as* the chromosomes, and could see how they were interacting. In such ways, she developed what she called a "feeling for the organism."

Her unique understanding let her to question the genetic theory of Watson and Crick: that DNA contained a cell's vital information, which was copied onto the RNA and acted as a blueprint for genetic traits. She thought that this "master molecule theory" claimed to explain too much and did not acknowledge the differences between small simple organisms and large complex multicellular ones. More important, it treated DNA as a central autonomous actor, sending out information one way, through a genetic organization structure hierarchically, like a classic bureaucracy. McClintock showed that genetic organization is more complex and interdependent. The DNA itself adapts to outside factors and can be reprogrammed by signals from the environment to meet the survival needs of the organism. In essence, information flows both ways. (Schmidt 1993: 528)

picture of the social dynamic of the particular situation or program. This means that at the time of data collection, each case, event, or setting under study, though treated as a unique entity with its own particular meaning and its own constellation of relationships emerging from and related to the context within which it occurs, is also thought of as a window into the whole. Thus capturing and documenting history, interconnections, and system relationships are part of fieldwork.

The advantages of using quantitative variables and indicators are parsimony, precision, and ease of analysis. Where key elements can be quantified with validity, reliability, and credibility, and where necessary statistical assumptions can be met (e.g., linearity, normality, and independence of mea-

surement), then statistical portrayals can be quite powerful and succinct. The advantages of qualitative portrayals of holistic settings and impacts are that greater attention can be given to nuance, setting, interdependencies, complexities, idiosyncrasies, and context. John Dewey (1956) articulated what a holistic approach means for both teaching and research if one wants to gain insight into and understand the world of the child:

> The child's life is an integral, a total one. He passes quickly and readily from one topic to another, as from one spot to another, but is not conscious of transition or break. There is no conscious isolation, hardly conscious distinction. The things that occupy him are held together by the unity of the personal and social interests which his life carries along. . . . [His]

universe is fluid and fluent; its contents dissolve and reform with amazing rapidity. But after all, it is the child's own world. It has the unity and completeness of his own life. (pp. 5-6)

Qualitative sociologist Irwin Deutscher (1970) commented that despite the totality of our personal experiences as living, working human beings, social scientists have tended to focus their research on parts to the virtual exclusion of wholes:

We knew that human behavior was rarely if ever directly influenced or explained by an isolated variable; we knew that it was impossible to assume that any set of such variables was additive (with or without weighting); we knew that the complex mathematics of the interaction among any set of variables was incomprehensible to us. In effect, although we knew they did not exist, we defined them into being. (p. 33)

While many would view this intense critique of variable analysis as too extreme, the reaction of many program staff to scientific research is like the reaction of Copernicus to the astronomers of his day: "With them," he observed, "it is as though an artist were to gather the hands, feet, head, and other members for his images from diverse models, each part excellently drawn, but not related to a single body, and since they in no way match each other, the result would be monster rather than man" (from Kuhn 1970:83).

How many program staffs have complained of the evaluation research monster?

It is no simple task to undertake holistic analysis. The challenge is "to seek the essence of the life of the observed, to sum up, to find a central unifying principle" (Bruyn 1966:316). Again, Shapiro's (1973) work in evaluating innovative Follow Through classrooms is instructive. She found that standardized test results could not be interpreted without understanding the larger cultural and institutional context in which the individual child is situated. Taking context seriously, the topic of the next section, is an important element of holistic analysis.

An illuminative example of holistic thinking came to me from a Portuguese colleague. He told of driving in a remote area of his country when he came upon a sizable herd of sheep being driven along the road by a shepherd. Seeing that he would be delayed until the sheep could be turned off the road, he got out of the car and struck up a conversation with the shepherd.

"How many sheep do you have?" he asked.

"I don't know," responded the young man.

Surprised at this answer, the traveler asked, "How do you keep track of the flock if you don't know how many sheep there are? How would you know if one was missing?"

The shepherd seemed puzzled by the question. Then he explained, "I don't need to count them. I know each one and I know the whole flock. I would know if the flock was not whole."

Context Sensitivity

*A*ny single act from any single person, put out of context, is damnable.

—Actor Kevin Spacey accepting the 2000 Academy Award
for Best Performance by an Actor in the film
American Beauty, explaining the film's message

A Holistic Perspective

Let's move, now, from sheep to elephants. One of the classic tales used to illustrate the relationship between parts and wholes is the story of the nine blind people and the elephant. Each person touches only one part of the elephant and therefore knows only that part. The person touching the ears thinks an elephant is like a large, thin fan. The person touching the tail thinks the elephant is like a rope. The person touching the truck thinks of a snake. The legs feel like tree trunks, the elephant's side like a tall wall. And so it goes. The holistic point is that one must put all of these perspectives together to get a full picture of what an elephant actually looks like.

But such a picture will still be limited, even distorted, if the only place one sees the elephant is in the zoo or at the circus. To understand the elephant—how it developed, how it uses its trunk, why it is so large—one must see it on the African savanna or in the Asian jungle. In short, one must see it *in context* and as part of an ecological *system* in relation to other flora and fauna, in its natural environment.

When we say to someone, "You've taken my comment out of context," we are saying, *You have distorted what I said*, changed its meaning by omitting critical context.

In Victor Hugo's great classic *Les Misérables*, we first encounter Jean Valjean as a hardened criminal and common thief; then we learn that he was originally sentenced to five years in prison for stealing a loaf of bread for his sister's starving family. That added context for his "crime" changes our understanding. The battle over standardized sentencing guidelines in the criminal justice system is partly a debate about how much to allow judges sway in taking into account context and individual circumstances in pronouncing sentences.

Naturalistic inquiry preserves natural context. Social psychology experiments under laboratory conditions strip observed actions from context. But that is the point of such laboratory experiments—to generate findings that are context free. The scientific ideal of generalizing across time and space is the ideal of identifying principles that do not depend on context. In contrast, qualitative inquiry elevates context as critical to understanding. Portraitist Sara Lawrence-Lightfoot (1997) explains why she finds context "crucial to the documentation of human experience and organizational culture":

> By context, I mean the setting—physical, geo-graphic, temporal, historical cultural, aesthetic —within which action takes place. Context becomes the framework, the reference point, the map, the ecological sphere; it is used to place people and action in time and space and as a resource for understanding what they say and do. The context is rich in clues for interpreting the experience of the actors in the setting. We have no idea how to decipher or decode an action, a gesture, a conversation, or an exclamation unless we see it embedded in context. (p. 41)

Voice and Perspective: Reflexivity

ABSTRACT OF A SCHOOL ACHIEVEMENT STUDY

This study will delineate the major factors that affect school achievement. Instruments were selected to measure achievement based on validity and reliability criteria. Decisions were made about administering the tests in conjunction with administrators taking into account time and resource constraints. A regression model was constructed to test relationships between various background variables and demonstrated achievement. School records were reviewed and coded to ascertain students' background characteristics. Data were obtained on 120 students from four classrooms. The extraction of significant predictor variables is the purpose of the final analysis. Interviews were conducted with teachers and principals to determine how test scores were used. The analysis concludes with the researcher's interpretations. The researcher wishes to thank those who cooperated in this study.

This journal article abstract represents academic writing as I was taught to do it in graduate school. This writing style still predominates in scholarly journals and books. No human being is visible in this writing. The passive voice reigns. Instruments were selected; decisions were made; a model was constructed; records were reviewed and coded; data were obtained; predictor variables were extracted; interviews were conducted. The warmth of thanks is extended by a role, the researcher: "The researcher wishes to thank those who cooperated." The third-person, passive voice communicates a message: This work is about procedures not people. This academic style is employed to project a sense of objectivity, control, and authority. The overall impression is mechanical, robotlike, distant, detached, systematic, and procedural. The research is the object of attention. Any real, live human being, subject to all the usual foibles of being human, is barely implied, generally disguised, hidden away, and kept in the background.

Contrast that academic voice with my explanation of how I analyzed a 10-day coming-of-age experience with my son in the Grand Canyon. (I presented part of the analysis of that experience as Exhibit 1.3 in the first chapter.) Here's an excerpt in which I describe the analytical process.

> I'm not sure when the notion first took hold of me that articulating alternative coming of age paradigms might help elucidate our Canyon

experience. Before formally conceptualizing contrasting paradigm dimensions, I experienced them as conflicting feelings that emanated from my struggle to sort out what I wanted my son's initiation to be, while also grappling with defining my role in the process. I suppose the idea of alternative paradigms first emerged the second night as I paced the narrow beach where White Creek intersects Shinumo and pondered the Great Unconformity [a geologic reference] as metaphor for the gap between tribal approaches to initiation and coming of age for contemporary youth. In the weeks and months after our Canyon experience, far from languishing in the throes of retox as I expected, the idea of contrasting paradigms stayed with me, as did the Canyon experience. I started listing themes and matching them with incidents and turning points along the way. The sequence of incidents became this book and the contrasting themes became the basis for this closing chapter, a way for me to figure out how what started out as an initiation become a humanist coming of age celebration. (Patton 1999a:332)

The contrast between the traditional academic voice and the personal voice of qualitative analysis recalls philosopher and theologian Martin Buber's (1923) influential distinction between "I-It" and "I-Thou" relationships. An I-It relationship regards other human beings from a distance, from a superior vantage point of authority, as objects or subjects, things in the environment to be examined and placed in abstract cause-effect chains. An I-Thou perspective, in contrast, acknowledges the humanity of both self and others and implies relationship, mutuality, and genuine dialogue.

The perspective that the researcher brings to a qualitative inquiry is part of the context for the findings. A human being is the instrument of qualitative methods. A real, live person makes observations, takes field notes, asks interview questions, and interprets responses. Self-awareness, then, can be an asset in both fieldwork and analysis. Developing appropriate self-awareness can be a form of "sharpening the instrument" (Brown 1996:42). The methods section of a qualitative study reports on the researcher's training, preparation, fieldwork procedures, and analytical processes. This is both the strength and weakness of qualitative methods, the strength in that a well-trained, experienced, and astute observer adds value and credibility to the inquiry, while an ill-prepared, inexperienced, and imperceptive observer casts doubt on what is reported. Judgments about the significance of findings are thus inevitably connected to the researcher's credibility, competence, thoroughness, and integrity. Those judgments, precisely because they are acknowledged as inevitably personal and perspective dependent, at least to some extent, invite response and dialogue, rather than just acceptance or rejection.

Reflexivity has entered the qualitative lexicon as a way of emphasizing the importance of self-awareness, political/cultural consciousness, and ownership of one's perspective.

> In the rush of interest in qualitative research in the past 15 years, few topics have developed as broad a consensus as the relevance of analytic "reflexivity." By most accounts, reflexivity is a deconstructive exercise for locating the intersections of author, other, text, and world, and for penetrating the representational exercise itself. (MacBeth 2001:35)

Being reflexive involves self-questioning and self-understanding, for "all understanding is self-understanding" (Schwandt 1997a:xvi). To be reflexive, then, is to undertake an ongoing examination of *what I know* and *how I know it*, "to have an ongoing conversation about experience while simultaneously living in the moment" (Hertz 1997: viii). Reflexivity reminds the qualitative inquirer to be attentive to and conscious of the cultural, political, social, linguistic, and ideological origins of one's own perspective and voice as well as the perspective and voices of those one interviews and those to whom one reports. Exhibit 2.2 depicts this reflexive triangulation.

Writing in the first-person, active voice communicates the inquirer's self-aware role in the inquiry: "I started listing themes and matching them with incidents and turning points along the way." The passive voice does not: "Themes were listed and matched to incidents and turning points along the way." Judith Brown (1996) captured the importance of the first-person voice in the title of her book *The I in Science: Training to Utilize Subjectivity in Research.* By subjectivity she means "the domain of experiential self-knowledge" (p. 1). Voice reveals and communicates this domain.

But voice is more than grammar. A credible, authoritative, authentic, and trustworthy voice engages the reader through rich description, thoughtful sequencing, appropriate use of quotes, and contextual clarity so that the reader joins the inquirer in the search for meaning. And there are choices of voice: the didactic voice of the teacher; the searching, logical voice of the sleuth; the narrator voice of the storyteller; the personal voice of the autoethnographer; the doubting voice of the skeptic; the intimacy of the insider's voice; the detachment of the outsider's voice; the searching voice of uncertainty; and the excited voice of discovery, to offer but a few examples. Just as point of view and voice have become focal points of writing good fiction and nonfiction, as in Nancy Mairs's (1997) *Voice Lessons: On Becoming a (Woman) Writer,* so too qualitative analysts are having to learn about, take into

account, and communicate perspective and voice. Balancing critical and creative analyses, description and interpretation, or direct quotation and synopsis also involves issues of perspective, audience, purpose, and voice. No rules or formula can tell a qualitative analyst precisely what balance is right or which voice to use, only that finding both balance and voice is part of the work and challenge of qualitative inquiry, what Lewis (2001) has acknowledged as "the difficulty of trying to situate the I in narrative research" (p. 109).

In addition to *finding voice,* the critical and creative writing involved in qualitative analysis and synthesis challenge the inquirer to *own one's voice and perspective.* Here, we owe much to feminist theory for highlighting and deepening our understanding of the intricate and implicate relationships between language, voice, and consciousness (e.g., Gilligan 1982; Minnich 1990). We are challenged by postmodern critiques of knowledge to be clear about and own our authorship of whatever we propound, to be self-reflective, to acknowledge biases and limitations, and to honor multiple perspectives (Greene 1998a, 1998b; Mabry 1997) while "accepting incredulity and doubt as modal postmodern responses to all attempts to explain ourselves to ourselves" (Schwandt 1997b:102). From struggles to locate and acknowledge the inevitably political and moral nature of evaluative judgments, we are challenged to connect voice and perspective to *praxis*—acting in the world with an appreciation for and recognition of how those actions inherently express social, political, and moral values (Schwandt 1989, 2000) and to personalize evaluation (Kushner 2000), both by owning our own perspective and by taking seriously the responsibility to communicate authentically the perspectives of those we encounter during our inquiry. These represent some

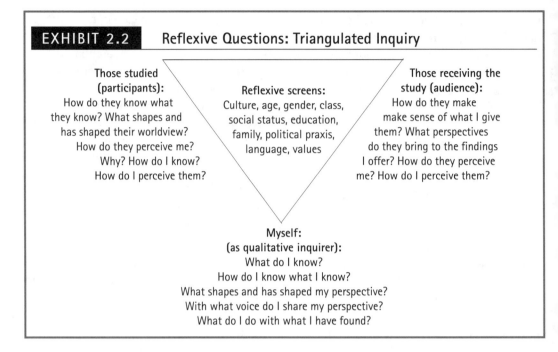

EXHIBIT 2.2   Reflexive Questions: Triangulated Inquiry

Those studied
(participants):
How do they know what
they know? What shapes and
has shaped their worldview?
How do they perceive me?
Why? How do I know?
How do I perceive them?

Reflexive screens:
Culture, age, gender, class,
social status, education,
family, political praxis,
language, values

Those receiving the
study (audience):
How do they make
make sense of what I give
them? What perspectives
do they bring to the findings
I offer? How do they perceive
me? How do I perceive them?

Myself:
(as qualitative inquirer):
What do I know?
How do I know what I know?
What shapes and has shaped my perspective?
With what voice do I share my perspective?
What do I do with what I have found?

of the more prominent contextual forces that have elevated the importance of owning voice and perspective in qualitative analysis.

It takes no great self-awareness or self-confidence to report a statistically significant *t* test with confidence intervals based on a formula and calculations easily replicated and confirmed. It can take considerable self-awareness and confidence to report: I coded these 40 interviews, these are the themes I found, here is what I think they mean, and here is the process I undertook to arrive at those meanings. The latter statement calls for, even demands, a sense of voice and perspective.

🔲 From Strategic Ideals to Practical Choices

The 12 themes of qualitative inquiry reviewed in this chapter are strategic ideals:

real-world observations through naturalistic inquiry; openness, responsiveness, and flexibility through emergent designs; focus through purposeful sampling; richness and depth through qualitative data; use of all of one's capacities through personal experience and engagement; balancing the critical and creative through a stance of empathic neutrality; sensitivity to dynamic processes and systems; appreciation of idiosyncrasies through a unique case orientation; insight and understanding through inductive analysis, contextual sensitivity, and a holistic perspective; and authenticity and trustworthiness through ownership of voice and perspective. These are not absolute and universal characteristics of qualitative inquiry, but rather strategic ideals that provide a direction and framework for developing specific designs and concrete data collection tactics.

Ideally, a pure qualitative inquiry strategy includes all the themes and dimensions identified in this chapter. For example, in an ideal naturalistic/inductive inquiry the re-searcher neither manipulates the setting under study nor predetermines what variables or categories are worth measuring. In practice, however, it is important to recognize that **actually conducting holistic-inductive analysis and implementing naturalistic inquiry are always a matter of degree.** In making this point, Guba (1978) has depicted the practice of naturalistic inquiry as a wave on which the investigator moves from varying degrees of a "discovery mode" to varying emphasis of a "verification mode" in attempting to understand the real world. As fieldwork begins, the inquirer is open to whatever emerges from the data, a discovery or inductive approach. Then, as the inquiry reveals patterns and major dimensions of interest, the investigator will begin to focus on verifying and elucidating what appears to be emerging—a more deductive approach to data collection and analysis. In essence, what is discovered may be verified by going back to the world under study and examining the extent to which the emergent analysis *fits* the phenomenon and *works to explain* what has been observed. Glaser and Strauss (1967), in their classic framing of grounded theory, described what it means for results to fit and work: "By 'fit' we mean that the categories must be readily (not forcibly) applicable to and indicated by the data under study; by 'work' we mean that they must be meaningfully relevant to and be able to explain the behavior under study" (p. 3). Discovery and verification mean moving back and forth between induction and deduction, between experience and reflection on experience, and between greater degrees and lesser degrees of naturalistic inquiry.

In program evaluation in particular, the evaluator may, through feedback of initial findings to program participants and staff, begin to affect the program quite directly and intentionally (given the job of helping improve the program), thus moving away from a purely naturalistic approach. As evaluative feedback is used to improve the program, the evaluator may then move back into a more naturalistic stance to observe how the feedback-induced changes in the program unfold.

In the same vein, the attempt to understand a program or treatment as a whole does not mean that the investigator never becomes involved in component analysis or in looking at particular variables, dimensions, and parts of the phenomenon under study. Rather, it means that the qualitative inquirer consciously works back and forth between parts and wholes, separate variables, and complex, interwoven constellations of variables in a sorting-out then putting-back-together process. While staying true to a strategy that emphasizes the importance of a holistic picture of the program, the qualitative evaluator recognizes that certain periods of fieldwork may focus on component, variable, and less-than-the-whole kinds of analysis.

The practice and practicalities of fieldwork also mean that the strategic mandate to "get close" to the people and setting under study is neither absolute nor fixed. Closeness to and involvement with the people under study are most usefully viewed as variable dimensions. The personal styles and capabilities of evaluators will permit and necessitate variance along these dimensions. Variations in types of programs and evaluation purposes will affect the extent to which an evaluator can or ought to get close to the program staff and participants. Moreover, closeness is likely to vary over the course of an evaluation. At times the evaluator may become totally immersed in the program experience. These periods of immersion may be followed by times of withdrawal and distance (for personal as well as methodological reasons), to be followed still later by new experiences of immersion in and direct experience with the program.

Nor is it necessary to be a qualitative methods purist. Qualitative data can be collected and used in conjunction with quantitative data. Today's evaluator must be sophisticated about matching research methods to the nuances of particular evaluation questions and the idiosyncrasies of specific stakeholder needs. Such an evaluator needs a large repertoire of research methods and techniques to use on a variety of problems. Thus, an evaluator may be called on to use any and all social science research methods, including analyses of quantitative data, questionnaires, secondary data analysis, cost-benefit and cost-effectiveness analyses, standardized tests, experimental designs, unobtrusive measures, participant observation, and in-depth interviewing. The evaluation researcher works with intended users of the findings to design an evaluation that includes any and all data that will help shed light on important evaluation questions, given constraints of resources and time. Such an evaluator is committed to research designs that are relevant, meaningful, understandable, and able to produce useful results that are valid, reliable, and believable. On many occasions a variety of data collection techniques and design approaches may be used together. Multiple methods and a variety of data types can contribute to methodological rigor. The ideal in evaluation designs is methodological appropriateness, design flexibility, and situational responsiveness in the service of utility (Patton 1997a)—not absolute allegiance to some ideal standard of paradigm purity and methodological orthodoxy.

Beyond Competing
Inquiry Paradigms

Having presented the strategic ideals of qualitative inquiry and noted variations in their practical implementation and attainment, before closing this chapter I want to acknowledge and comment on the controversy that sometimes engulfs qualitative methods. Students attempting to do qualitative dissertations can get caught up in and may have to defend, philosophically as well as methodologically, the use of qualitative inquiry to skeptical committee members who define doctoral-level work as rigorous hypothesis testing. Evaluators may encounter policymakers and funders who dismiss qualitative data as mere anecdote. The statistically addicted may poke fun at what they call the "softness" of qualitative data. (In Western society, where anything can be and often is sexualized, the distinction between "hard" data and "soft" data has additional nuances of meaning and innuendo.) Such encounters derive from a long-standing methodological paradigms war. Though many have pronounced the war and even the debate over (cf. Cook 1995; Greene 1998a:36; Patton 1997a: 290-95), not everyone has adopted a stance of methodological enlightenment and tolerance, namely, that methodological orthodoxy, superiority, and purity should yield to methodological appropriateness, pragmatism, and mutual respect. Therefore, a brief review of the paradigms debate is in order. (Elsewhere I have provided a more extensive review of the methodological paradigms debate; Patton 1997a: 265-99, 1988c.)

Philosophers of science and methodologists have been engaged in a long-standing epistemological debate about the nature of "reality" and knowledge. That philosophical debate finds its way into research and evaluation in arguments over the goals of empirical studies and differences of opinion about what constitutes "good" research. In its simplest and most strident formulation, this debate has centered on the relative value of two different and competing inquiry paradigms: (1) using quantitative and experimental methods to generate and test hypothetical-deductive generalizations versus (2) using qualitative and naturalistic approaches to inductively and holistically understand human experience and constructed meanings in context-specific settings. For example, Taylor and Bogdan (1984) contrast the *Verstehen* tradition, rooted in qualitative phenomenology, to measurement-oriented positivism as follows:

> Two major theoretical perspectives have dominated the social science scene. The first, *positivism*, traces its origins in the social sciences to the great theorists of the nineteenth and early twentieth centuries and especially to Auguste Comte and Emile Durkheim. The positivist seeks the *facts* or *causes* of social phenomena apart from the subjective states of individuals. Durkheim told the social scientist to consider social facts, or social phenomena, as "things" that exercise an external influence on people.
>
> The second theoretical perspective, which, following the lead of Deutscher, we will describe as *phenomenological*, has a long history in philosophy and sociology. The phenomenologist is committed to *understanding* social phenomena from the actor's own perspective. He or she examines how the world is experienced. The important reality is what people perceive it to be. (pp. 1-2)

Debate about these contrasting and competing perspectives has been an important part of the history of research and evaluation, but, as Chapters 3, 4, and 9 will show,

the variety of inquiry approaches has expanded well beyond the simplistic dichotomy between quantitative and qualitative paradigms. In contrast to these two classically opposed orthodoxies, this book offers a pragmatic strategy of matching concrete methods to specific questions, including the option of tactically mixing methods as needed and appropriate. My practical (and controversial) view is that one can learn to be a good interviewer or observer, and learn to make sense of the resulting data, without first engaging in deep epistemological reflection and philosophical study. Such reflection and study can be helpful to those so inclined, but it is not a prerequisite for fieldwork. Indeed, it can be a hindrance. Getting some field experience first, then studying philosophy of science, has much to recommend it as a learning strategy. Otherwise, it's all abstractions. Still, the paradigms debate is part of our methodological heritage and knowing a bit about it, and its distortions (Shadish 1995b, 1995c), may deepen appreciation for the importance of a strategic approach to methods decision making.

A paradigm is a worldview—a way of thinking about and making sense of the complexities of the real world. As such, paradigms are deeply embedded in the socialization of adherents and practitioners. Paradigms tell us what is important, legitimate, and reasonable. Paradigms are also normative, telling the practitioner what to do without the necessity of long existential or epistemological consideration. But it is this aspect of paradigms that constitutes both strength and weakness—a strength in that it makes action relatively easy, a weakness in that the very reason for action is hidden in the unquestioned assumptions of the paradigm.

Are there paradigms after death?

Scientists work from models acquired through education and through subsequent exposure to the literature often without quite knowing or needing to know what characteristics have given these models the status of community paradigms. . . . That scientists do not usually ask or debate what makes a particular problem or solution legitimate tempts us to suppose that, at least intuitively, they know the answer. But it may only indicate that neither the question nor the answer is felt to be relevant to their research. Paradigms may be prior to, more binding, and more complete than any set of rules for research that could be unequivocally abstracted from them. (Kuhn 1970:46)

But what does all this matter to the student interested in pursuing some research or evaluation question? It matters because paradigm-derived biases are the source of the distinctions mentioned earlier between "hard" data and "soft" data, empirical studies versus "mere anecdotes," and "objective" research versus "subjective" studies. These labels reveal value-laden prejudices about what constitute credible and valuable contributions to knowledge. Such prejudices and paradigmatic blinders limit methodological choices, flexibility, and creativity. Adherence to a methodological paradigm can lock researchers into unconscious patterns of perception and behavior that disguise the biased, predetermined nature of their methods "decisions." Methods decisions tend to stem from disciplinary prescriptions, concerns about scientific status, old methodological habits, and comfort with what the researcher knows best. Training and academic socialization tend to make researchers biased in favor of and against certain approaches.

While one may still encounter people who rigidly confess allegiance to only quantitative or qualitative methods, most practitioners appear to have become eclectic and pragmatic. Looking back, we can now see that the qualitative-quantitative debate oversimplified and often confused methodological and philosophical issues. For example, the notion that some combinations of methods and philosophy ever constituted consistent, coherent, and stable paradigms has proved problematic. Shadish (1995c), for example, in introducing an important set of articles aimed at "de-Kuhnifying" the debate, concluded that "there is little empirical evidence in support of such a Kuhnian paradigm portrayal. . . . [T]he relevant conceptual and philosophical issues are far more complex than the simple quantitative-qualitative dichotomy implies" (p. 48). Chapter 9 will revisit the quantitative-qualitative paradigms debate in more depth as part of our examination of issues that affect judgments about the quality and credibility of qualitative methods.

Pragmatism

*E*very thinker puts some portion of an apparently stable world in peril.

—John Dewey (1929)

While a paradigm offers a coherent worldview, an anchor of stability and certainty in the real world sea of chaos, operating narrowly within any singular paradigm can be quite limiting. As a pragmatist, I take issue as much with the purist, one-sided advocacy of Lincoln and Guba (1985), who believe that naturalistic inquiry is the only valid and meaningful way to study human beings, as I do with the narrow, intolerant stance of Boruch and Rindskopf (1984), who assert that randomized experiments are "the standard against which other designs for impact evaluation are judged" (p. 21). My pragmatic stance aims to supersede one-sided paradigm allegiance by increasing the concrete and practical methodological options available to researchers and evaluators. Such pragmatism means judging the quality of a study by its intended purposes, available resources, procedures followed, and results obtained, all within a particular context and for a specific audience. When a new drug is tested before being made available to the general population, a double-blind randomized experiment to determine efficacy is the design of choice, with careful attention to controlled and carefully measured dosage and outcome interactions, including side effects. But if the concern is whether people take the new drug appropriately, and one wants to know what people in a group think about the new drug (e.g., an antidepressant), how they make sense of taking or not taking it, what they believe about themselves as a result of experiencing the drug, and how those around them deal with it, then in-depth interviews and observations are the place to start. The importance of understanding alternative research paradigms is to sensitize researchers and evaluators to the ways in which their methodological prejudices, derived from their disciplinary socialization experiences, may reduce their methodological flexibility and adaptability.

I reiterate: Being pragmatic allows one to eschew methodological orthodoxy in favor of *methodological appropriateness* as the primary criterion for judging methodological quality, recognizing that different methods are appropriate for different situations. Situational responsiveness means designing a study that is appropriate for a specific inquiry situation or interest. A major purpose of this book, and the focus of Chapter 4, is to identify the kinds of research questions and program evaluation situations for which qualitative inquiry is the appropriate method of choice.

Paradigms are really about epistemology, ontology, and philosophy of science. As such, paradigms are important theoretical constructs for illuminating fundamental assumptions about the nature of reality. But at the pragmatic level of making concrete methods decisions, this chapter's emphasis

on strategic choices has conveyed, I hope, the idea that a wide range of possibilities exists when selecting methods. The point is to do what makes sense, report fully on what was done, why it was done, and what the implications are for findings. Chapter 5 is devoted to design issues, including design flexibility, using multiple methods, and making practical decisions.

A Sufi story about the wise fool Mulla Nasrudin illustrates the importance of understanding the connections between strategic ideals and practical tactics in real-world situations. Real-world situations seldom resemble the theoretical ideals taught in the classroom.

Ideal Conditions for Research: A Cautionary Tale

In his youth, Nasrudin received training in a small monastery noted for its excellence in the teaching of martial arts. Nasrudin became highly skilled in self-defense and after two years of training both his peers and his teachers recognized his superior abilities.

Each day, it was the responsibility of one of the students to go to the village market to beg for alms and food. It happened that a small band of three thieves moved into the area. They observed how the monastery obtained food daily and began hiding along the path the students had to take back to the monastery. As a returning student returned, laden with food and alms, the thieves would attack. After three days of such losses, the monastery's few supplies were exhausted. It was Nasrudin's turn to go to the village market. His elders and peers were confident that Nasrudin's martial arts skills were more than sufficient to overcome the small band of thieves.

At the end of the day, Nasrudin returned ragged, beaten, and empty-handed. Everyone was amazed. Nasrudin was taken immediately before the Master. "Nasrudin," he asked, "how is it that with all your skill in our ancient arts of defense, you were overcome?"

"But I did not use the ancient arts," replied Nasrudin.

All present were dumbfounded. An explanation was demanded.

"All of our competitions are preceded by great and courteous ceremony," Nasrudin explained. "We have learned that the opening prayers, the ceremonial cleansing, the bow to the East—these are essential to the ancient ways. The ruffians seemed not to understand the necessity for these things. I didn't find the situation ideal enough to use the methods you have taught us, Master."

On more than one occasion, researchers or evaluators have told me of their belief in the *potential* usefulness of qualitative methods, but they tell me, "I just haven't found the ideal situation in which to use them."

Ideal situations are rare, but we will consider throughout this book the questions and conditions in which qualitative strategies and methods offer advantages. In Chapter 4, I will present a range and variety of situations and inquiry problems that particularly lend themselves to qualitative inquiry. Chapter 5 will then discuss in more detail some of the methodological trade-offs involved in adapting the strategic ideals of qualitative methods to the practical realities of conducting research and evaluation in the field. Chapters devoted to observation, interviewing, analysis, and enhancing the quality and credibility of qualitative studies follow that design chapter. To lay the groundwork for in-depth review of applications and methods, the next chapter examines alternative theoretical frameworks that are closely associated with and used to guide qualitative inquiry.

🖬 Note

1. Excerpts in this chapter from the interview with Brackette F. Williams are used with her permission.

3

Variety in Qualitative Inquiry

Theoretical Orientations

Special Gifts _____

"Tell us again, Master, how it was in the beginning."

"In the beginning special gifts were given to different groups of people. The caregivers were endowed with compassion for the less fortunate. The engineers were given the ability to see what was not yet there. The carpenters were given patience to set straight lines and perfect angles. The technicians were provided with diligence so that they might conscientiously follow the blueprints and detailed directions of others. The experimental scientists were given the certain belief that the world could be manipulated according to their vision of it. The qualitative inquirers were gifted with a passion for depth, detail, and understanding meanings. And so it went until, finally, there remained one last group and one last gift. These were the explorers. To them was given the gift of curiosity that they might forever see new worlds and uncover the many wonders of the world."

"But what of the evaluators?" the children asked. "You have not mentioned their special gift."

Halcolm smiled. "The evaluators, dear children, were spread throughout all the other groups, each endowed with the special gift of his or her own group, and each using that gift in a special way."

"But does that not make for much arguing among evaluators about who has the most special gift of all?"

Halcolm grinned.

—From Halcolm's *Origins of Human Species*

From Core Strategies to Rich Diversity

The last chapter presented 12 primary threads that are woven through the tapestry of qualitative inquiry. A central point of that chapter was that different purposes, situations, questions, and resources will affect the degree to which such qualitative ideals as naturalistic inquiry, a holistic perspective, and inductive analysis can be realized in practice. Yet, despite variation along the several dimensions of qualitative inquiry, there are still core strategies and directions that differentiate a qualitative/naturalistic strategy from a quantitative/experimental one, as well as places where they can usefully be combined to complement each other (e.g., Tashakkori and Teddlie 1998). This chapter will present the rich menu of alternative possibilities *within* qualitative research by focusing on different theoretical perspectives that are associated with qualitative inquiry.

Qualitative inquiry is not a single, monolithic approach to research and evaluation. Discussions such as that in Chapter 2 that focus on differentiating primary strategies of qualitative/naturalistic methods from those of quantitative/experimental methods can leave the impression that there are only two methodological or paradigmatic alternatives. In fact, as we "turn inward in qualitative research," we find "an exhilarating and at times exhausting proliferation of types *within* the qualitative paradigm (Page 2000:3).

> When one looks more closely . . . the apparent unity of the qualitative approach vanishes, and one sees considerable diversity. What has been called "qualitative research" conveys different meanings to different people. Needless to say, this has caused considerable confusion. . . . A major source of the confusion lies in discussing qualitative research as if it were *one* approach. (Jacob 1988:16)

Major social sciences have drawn on and contributed to qualitative methods in different ways depending on the interests of theorists and methodologists in a particular discipline (cf. Brizuela et al. 2000; Kuhns and Martorana 1982). The language of discourse also varies. As Schwandt (1997a) has observed in his very useful dictionary of qualitative terminology:

> Qualitative inquiry . . . is a set of multiple practices in which words in methodological and philosophical vocabularies acquire different meanings in their use or in particular acts of speaking about the meaning of the practice. These different ways of speaking form something more like a constellation of contested practices than an integrated, readily surveyable order. There are multiple sources and kinds of disputes, but generally they involve different ways of conceiving of the aim of qualitative inquiry stemming from different traditions of thought. (p. xiv)

Those coming new to qualitative inquiry are understandably confused and even discombobulated by the diverse terminology and contested practices they encounter. Phenomenology. Hermeneutics. Ethnomethodology. Semiotics. Heuristics. Phenomenography. Such language! Exhibit 3.1 reproduces a letter of lamentation I received following publication of the first edition of this book, which did not include the current chapter.

This chapter sorts through some of the major perspectives and traditions that inform the rich variety that is qualitative inquiry. We shall look at how varying theoretical traditions emphasize different questions and how these particular emphases can

EXHIBIT 3.1	Which Approach Is Right?

Help!

Dear Dr. Patton:

I desperately need your help. I am a graduate student in education, planning to do my dissertation observing classrooms and teachers identified as innovative and effective. I want to see if they share any common approaches or wisdom that might be considered "best practices." I took this idea to one professor who asked me if I was proposing a phenomenological or grounded theory study. When I asked what the difference was, he said it was my job to find out. I've read about both but am still confused. Another professor told me I could do a qualitative study, but that asking about "best practices" meant that I was a positivist not a phenomenologist. Another grad student was told to "use a hermeneutic framing," but she's in a different department with a different topic. I'm a former schoolteacher and, I think, a pretty good observer and interviewer. I got very excited reading your book about the value of in-depth observations and interviewing, and that's where I got the idea for my dissertation, but now I'm being told I have to fit into one of these categories. Please tell me which one is right for my study. I don't care which one it is. I just want to get on with studying innovative classrooms. I feel lost and am on the verge of just doing a questionnaire where these philosophy questions don't seem to get asked. But if you can tell me which approach is right, I might still be able to do what I want to do. Help!!!

Dear _____:

Your dilemma is common. The distinctions you're being asked to make are, indeed, difficult—and not everyone agrees about what these terms and traditions mean. I didn't include them in my book in the hopes that the methods of in-depth interviewing and observation could stand on their own. As you've discovered, you don't need a class in philosophy to design good questionnaires, though an argument can be made that people using questionnaires and statistics would benefit from reflection on their epistemological (nature and justification of knowledge) and ontological (nature of reality) assumptions. Unfortunately, a lot of qualitative courses spend more time on epistemology than methods, which may make students better philosophers than interviewers. Some balance is needed. Your professors are doing you a service by having you struggle with understanding different qualitative schools of thought because what approach you take does make a difference—and students of qualitative inquiry should be expected to know at least the major competing and contrasting traditions, just as those doing statistical tests need to understand what different tests do. In the next edition of my book I'll include a chapter reviewing major philosophical and methodological traditions. But that won't help you now.

To answer your question directly, there is no "right" approach any more than there is a "right" fruit—apples, oranges, passion fruit. What you eat is a matter of personal taste, availability, price, history, and preference. Since you are also serving others (your doctoral committee), their preferences come into play, as you well know. Each tradition of qualitative inquiry offers a different emphasis, framework, or focus. I am reluctant to offer a recommendation about which tradition fits your work best, but

(continued)

EXHIBIT 3.1   Continued

until the next edition of my book is out with a new chapter that sorts through the various traditions, I feel obliged to offer you some guidance. So, here are three alternatives to consider.

First, because you portray yourself as a pragmatic, experienced practitioner, you could frame your study as qualitative, utilization-focused evaluation research [Patton 1997a]. You have to specify intended users for your study (for example, innovative teachers and curriculum designers) and intended uses (facilitating discussing about "effective practices"). This puts you in a tradition of generating practical and useful knowledge for action in the tradition of reflective practice [Schon 1983]. Your focus would be perceived patterns of effectiveness.

If that doesn't work and your committee insists on a more explicitly philosophical or theoretical framework for your inquiry, you might consider either "social constructionism" or "realism," which are two of the most general (and contradictory) of the traditions informing qualitative inquiry. I must warn you that there are competing versions of constructionism and realism (academics without arguments are like paraders without costumes or sports teams without uniforms—it's how the players differentiate themselves and figure out who to applaud). Either of these traditions will guide you in thinking about how people in particular contexts (in your case, schools) individually and collectively construct meaning and knowledge (in your case, effective or "best" practices).

The third alternative involves a change of topic, which may sound like bad news. The good news is that you've already collected a lot of the data. You could do a dissertation on the social constructions of qualitative paradigms using your professors as subjects. Obviously, you've already been doing participant observation on this topic. Or you might do a hermeneutic study of qualitative terminology. Or a phenomenological study on the experience of graduate students trying to frame a qualitative study. Or a heuristic inquiry into your own experience of qualitative design. Or. . . . but that's where you started out, isn't it.

Best wishes, whatever you decide.
Michael Quinn Patton

---

affect the analytical framework that guides fieldwork and interpretation. Understanding the divergent theoretical and philosophical traditions that have influenced qualitative inquiry is especially important in the design stage when the focus of fieldwork and interviewing is determined. Weaving together theory-based inquiry traditions and qualitative methods will reveal a rich tapestry with many threads of differing texture, color, length, and purpose.

This chapter will be of particular interest to social scientists conducting basic or applied research, and students doing dissertations, because their work is typically based on and aimed at contributing to theory. The next chapter, in contrast, will focus on practical and concrete evaluation and action research questions appropriate for qualitative inquiry, though theoretical understandings can be important for practitioners and policy analysts because "theoretical conceptions shape public arguments, giving people the concepts they use and shaping the alternatives they consider" (Nussbaum 2001:35). Taken together, this chapter and the next offer a broad range of goals for and approaches to qualitative research. Chapter 5 will then integrate theoretical and practical concerns by introducing a typology of research purposes to elucidate the design, methods, and analysis implications of varying purposes.

Alternative Ways of Distinguishing Qualitative Traditions

There is no definitive way to categorize the various philosophical and theoretical perspectives that have influenced and that distinguish types of qualitative inquiry. Lincoln and Guba (2000) identify five "alternative inquiry paradigms": positivism, postpositivism, critical theory, constructivism, and participatory. Schwandt (2000) discusses "three epistemological stances for qualitative inquiry: interpretivism, hermeneutics, and social constructionism." Crotty (1998) also offers three primary epistemological influences: objectivism, constructionism, and subjectivism; these, he posits, have influenced in varying degrees different theoretical perspectives: positivism (and postpositivism), interpretivism (symbolic interaction, phenomenology, hermeneutics), critical inquiry, feminism, and postmodernism. Creswell (1998) distinguishes "five qualitative traditions of inquiry": biography, phenomenology, grounded theory, ethnography, and case study.

While there is some overlap among these frameworks, there are also important differences reflecting varying experiences with and emphases within the history of qualitative research. Denzin and Lincoln (2000b) in their introduction to the *Handbook of Qualitative Research* trace six phases of qualitative research history that help explain the dramatically varying conceptions of what constitutes qualitative research.

1. During the "traditional period" of colonial research (up to World War II), ethnographers, influenced by positivism, strove for objectivity in their fieldwork and reports.

2. The "modernist phase" (to the 1970s) was a time in which qualitative researchers emphasized methodological rigor and procedural formalism as they sought acceptance within social science and reacted against postpositivism's emergent emphasis on interpretivism.

3. During the "blurred genres phase" (1970-1986), a large number of alternative approaches emerged, creating competition and confusion, the legacy of which remains in the daunting jargon and labels of qualitative perspectives: structuralism, symbolic interactionism, phenomenology, ethnomethodology, critical theory, semiotics, neopositivism, micro-macro descriptivism, neo-Marxism, poststructuralism, naturalism, constructionism, and deconstructionism.

4. Next came the "crisis of representation" that focused on issues of reflexivity, power, privilege, race, gender, and socioeconomic class—all of which undermined traditional notions of validity and neutrality.

5. The "fifth moment" describes recent history and is characterized as "a triple crisis of representation, legitimation, and praxis" (p. 17) in which the inevitably creative and interpretive nature of

qualitative writing is put under the microscope, including the perspective of the qualitative writer, and searching questions are raised about how to evaluate the quality of qualitative research and evaluation. During this period, more activist, explicitly political, and participatory approaches sought legitimacy as, for example, in "empowerment evaluation" (Fetterman, Kaftarian, and Wandersman 1996) and using qualitative/interpretive writing "to advance the promises of radical democratic racial justice embodied in the post-civil rights, Chicana/Chicano and Black Arts Aesthetic movements" (Denzin 2000a:256).

6. In the sixth phase, which Denzin and Lincoln call "postexperimental," the boundaries of qualitative inquiry are expanded to include creative nonfiction, autobiographical ethnography, poetic representations, and multimedia presentations.

They clearly expect qualitative inquiry to continue developing in new directions for they call the future the "seventh moment" —or perhaps this will be the moment of rest, when qualitative researchers cease debating their differences and celebrate the marvelous variety of their creations.

Foundational Questions

This chapter, in contrast with the work of qualitative theorists and historians cited above, distinguishes theoretical perspectives by their foundational questions. A foundational or burning question, like the mythical burning bush of Moses, blazes with heat (controversy) and light (wisdom) but is not consumed (is never fully answered). Disci-

plines given birth by the mother of all disciplines, philosophy, can be distinguished by their core burning questions. For sociology, the burning question is the Hobbesian question of order: What holds society or social groups together? What keeps them from falling apart? Psychology asks: Why do individuals think, feel, and act as they do? Political science asks: What is the nature of power, how it is distributed, and with what consequences? Economics studies how resources are produced and distributed.

Disciplines and subdisciplines reveal layers of questions. Biologists inquire into the nature and variety of life. Botanists ask how plants grow, while agriculturists investigate producing food, and agronomists narrow their focus still further to field crops.

To be sure, reducing any complex and multifaceted discipline to a singular burning question oversimplifies. But what is gained are clarity and focus about what distinguishes one lineage of inquiry from another. It is precisely that clarity and focus I shall strive for in identifying the burning questions that distinguish major lineages of qualitative inquiry. In doing so, I shall displease those who prefer to separate paradigms from philosophies from theoretical orientations from design strategies. For example, social constructivism may be viewed as a paradigm, ethnography may be considered a research strategy, and symbolic interactionism may be examined as a theoretical framework. However, distinctions between paradigmatic, strategic, and theoretical dimensions within any particular approach are both arguable and somewhat arbitrary. Therefore, I have circumvented those distinctions by focusing on and distinguishing foundational questions as the basis for understanding and contrasting long-standing and emergent qualitative inquiry approaches.

🔳 Theoretical Traditions and Orientations

Ethnography

Foundational question:
  What is the culture of this group
  of people?

Ethnography, the primary method of anthropology, is the earliest distinct tradition of qualitative inquiry. The notion of culture is central to ethnography. *Ethnos* is the Greek word for "a people" or cultural group. The study of *ethnos* then, or ethnography, is "devoted to describing ways of life of humankind . . . , a social scientific description of a people and the cultural basis of their peoplehood" (Vidich and Lyman 2000:38). Ethnographic inquiry takes as its central and guiding assumption that any human group of people interacting together for a period of time will evolve a culture. Culture is that collection of behavior patterns and beliefs that constitutes "standards for deciding what is, standards for deciding what can be, standards for deciding how one feels about it, standards for deciding what to do about it, and standards for deciding how to go about doing it" (Goodenough 1971:21-22). The primary method of ethnographers is participant observation in the tradition of anthropology. This means intensive fieldwork in which the investigator is immersed in the culture under study. While ethnographers share an interest in culture, there is debate about the nature of its essence (Douglass 2000) as well as several different styles of ethnography, including the classic holistic style of Benedict and Mead, the semiotic style of Boas and Geertz, and the behaviorist style of the Whitings (Sanday 1983).

Anthropologists have traditionally studied nonliterate cultures in remote settings, what were often thought of as "primitive" or "exotic" cultures. As a result, anthropology and ethnographers became intertwined with Western colonialism, sometimes resisting imperialism in efforts to sustain native cultures and sometimes as handmaidens to conquering empires as their findings were used to overcome resistance to change and manage subjugated peoples.

Modern anthropologists apply ethnographic methods to the study of contemporary society and social problems, for example, technological diffusion, globalization, environmental degradation, poverty, the gap between rich and poor, and societal breakdown (Scudder 1999); education (Spindler and Hammond 2000); addiction (Agar 1986; Agar and Reisinger 1999); child labor (Kenny 1999); intercultural understanding in schools (Jervis 1999); and international border conflicts (Hart 1999), to give but a few of many examples. The importance of understanding culture, especially in relation to change efforts of all kinds, is the cornerstone of "applied ethnography" as it has emerged in modern society (Chambers 2000). This can be seen in the ongoing reports of members of the Society for Applied Anthropology since its founding in 1941. Whyte (1984), for example, has collected a number of classic examples of ethnographic fieldwork applied to problems of industrial democracies.

Since the 1980s, understanding culture has become central in organizational studies (Morgan 1986, 1989; Pettigrew 1983) and in much organizational development work (Raia and Margulies 1985; Louis 1983), including major efforts to change an organization's culture (Schein 1985; Silverzweig and Allen 1976). Organizational ethnography has a distinguished history that can be

Cross-cultural perspective

traced back to the influential Hawthorne electric plant study that began in 1927 (Schwartzman 1993). Ethnography has also emerged as an approach to program evalua-tion (Fetterman 1984, 1989) and applied edu-cational research (Dobbert 1982). Programs develop cultures, just as organizations do. The program's culture can be thought of as

---

EXHIBIT 3.2	Culture, Culture Everywhere: Sample of Media Headlines

- "Stopping the Culture of Violence"
  (applied alternatively to gangs, families, neighborhoods, television shows, hockey games, even politics)
- "Inside the Culture of Sports"
  (Nike culture, Little League culture, "soccer mom" culture)
- "Learn the Culture of Day-Trading Stocks"
  (virtual trading culture, online business culture)
- "Girls and the Barbie Doll Culture"
  (or boys and the G.I. Joe action figure culture, kids and the *Star Wars* culture)
- "Eat Right: Fast Food Culture"
  ("Golden Arches Culture Around the World")
- "The Culture of Negative Political Campaigning: Why It Wins"
- Music, dance, or art culture
- Postmodern culture
- Virtual culture (aka Internet or Web culture)

---

part of the program's treatment. As such, the culture affects both program processes and outcomes. Improving a program, then, may include changing the program's culture. An ethnographic evaluation would both facilitate and assess such change.

Ironically, perhaps, awareness of the importance of culture has found its way into popular culture and mass media to such an extent that the term shows up nearly ubiquitously as an implied explanation for all kinds of social problems and phenomena, as shown in Exhibit 3.2.

Ethnographic methods continue to develop as new approaches emerge, for example, *Doing Team Ethnography* (Erickson and Stull 1998), and new issues surface, for example, *Ethnographic Decision Tree Modeling* (Gladwin 1989) or *Writing the New Ethnography* (Goodall 2000). Other ethnographic methodologists continue to delve deeply into classic issues such as paradigms for

thinking about ethnographic research (LeCompte and Schensul 1999), *Living the Ethnographic Life* (Rose 1990), *Selecting Ethnographic Informants* (Johnson 1990), and how to write ethnographies (Atkinson 1992) or write the methods section in ethnographic reports (Stewart 1998). The *Ethnographer's Toolkit* has been published (Schensul and LeCompte 1999).

While traditionally ethnographers have used the methods of participant observation and intensive fieldwork to study everything from small groups to nation-states, what it means to "participate" or be in the "field" or even be a "group" has changed with the World Wide Web and the emergence of the *virtual ethnographer*—studying people connected through distributed electronic environments (Ruhleder 2000). Nevertheless, whether doing ethnography in virtual space, a nonliterate community, a multinational corporation, or an inner-city school, what makes the approach distinct is the matter of interpreting and applying the findings from a *cultural perspective* (Wolcott 1980:59; Chambers 2000:852).

Autoethnography and Evocative Forms of Inquiry

Foundational question:
   How does my own experience of this culture connect with and offer insights about this culture, situation, event, and/or way of life?

We turn now from the earliest qualitative tradition, ethnography, to the latest and still emergent approach: autoethnography. Ethnography and autoethnography might be thought of as bookends, or opposite ends of a qualitative continuum, that frame a large number of distinct qualitative approaches to be reviewed in this chapter. By considering them one after the other throughout this chapter, it is hoped you'll get a sense of the range of issues that distinguish qualitative approaches.

Ethnography first emerged as a method for studying and understanding the *other*. It was fascination with "exotic otherness" that attracted Europeans to study the peoples of Africa, Asia, the South Sea Islands, and the Americas. "The life world of the 'primitive' was thought to be the window through which the prehistoric past could be seen, described, and understood" (Vidich and Lyman 2000:46). In the United States, for educated, White, university-based Americans the *others* were Blacks, American Indians, recent immigrants, working-class families, and the inner-city poor (and for that matter, anyone else not well educated, White, and university based). In recent times, when ethnography began to be used in program eval-

uations, the other became the program client, the student, the welfare recipient, the patient, the alcoholic, the homeless person, the victim, the perpetrator, or the recidivist. In organizational studies, the other was the worker, the manager, the leader, the follower, and/or the board of directors. The others were observed, interviewed, described, and their culture conceptualized, analyzed, and interpreted. Capturing and being true to the perspective of those studied, what came to be called the *emic* perspective, or the insider's perspective, was contrasted with the ethnographer's perspective, the *etic*, or outsider's, view. The etic viewpoint of the ethnographer implied some important degree of detachment or "higher" level of conceptual analysis and abstraction. To the extent that ethnographers reported on their own experiences as participant observers, it was primarily methodological reporting related to how they collected data and how, or the extent to which, they maintained detachment. To "go native" was to lose perspective.

In the new postcolonial and postmodern world at the beginning of the 21st century, the relationship between the observed and the observer has been called into question at every level. Postcolonial sensitivities raise questions about imbalances of power, wealth, and privilege between ethnographers and those they would study, including critical political questions about how findings will be used. Postmodern critiques and deconstruction of classic ethnographies have raised fundamental questions about how the values and cultural background of the observer affect what is observed while also raising doubts about the desirability, indeed, the possibility, of detachment. Then there is the basic question of how an ethnographer might study her or his own culture. What if there is no *other* as the focus of study, but I want to study the culture of my own

---

| EXHIBIT 3.3 | Varieties of Autoethnography: A Partial Lexicology |

David Hayano (1979) is credited with originating the term *autoethnography* to describe studies by anthropologists of their own cultures. In their extensive review, Ellis and Bochner (2000) focus on studying one's own culture and oneself as part of that culture to understand and illuminate a way of life. They cite a large number of phrases that have emerged both to support this emergent frontier of qualitative inquiry and to confuse exactly what it is. In the end, they conclude, "increasingly, autoethnography has become the term of choice in describing studies and procedures that connect the personal to the cultural" (p. 740).

Other terms include

Autobiographical ethnography	Lived experience
Auto-observation	Literary ethnography
Ethnographic poetics	Narrative ethnography
Creative analytic practice ethnography	Native ethnography
Critical autobiography	Narratives of the self
Ethnic autobiography	New ethnography
Ethnographic memoir	Personal ethnography
Ethnobiography	Personal experience narratives
Ethnographic autobiography	Personal narratives
Ethnographic stories	Postmodern ethnography
Evocative narratives	Reflexive ethnography
Experimental ethnography	Self-ethnography
First-person accounts	Self-stories
Indigenous ethnography	Socioautobiography
Interpretive biography	Sociopoetics

---

group, my own community, my own organization, and the way of life of people like me, or people I regularly encounter, or my own cultural experiences?

These developments have contributed to the emergence of *autoethnography*—studying one's own culture and oneself as part of that culture—and its many variations. Goodall (2000) calls this the "new ethnography": "creative narratives shaped out of a writer's personal experiences within a culture and addressed to academic and public audiences" (p. 9). Exhibit 3.3 offers a list of many, but not all, of the terms that have emerged to describe variations in this general approach. Carolyn Ellis (Ellis and Bochner 2000) describes it this way:

Autoethnography is an autobiographical genre of writing and research that displays multiple layers of consciousness, connecting the personal to the cultural. Back and forth autoethnographers gaze, first through an ethnographic wide-angle lens, focusing outward on social and the cultural aspects of their personal experience; then, they look inward, exposing a vulnerable self that is moved by and may move through, refract, and resist cultural interpretations. As they zoom backward and forward, inward and outward, distinctions between the personal and cultural become blurred, sometimes beyond distinct recognition. Usually written in first-person voice, autoethnographic texts appear in a variety of forms—short stories, poetry, fiction, novels, photographic essays, personal essays, journals, fragmented and layered writing, and social science prose. In these texts, concrete action, dialogue, emotion, embodiment, spirituality, and self-consciousness are featured, appearing as relational and institutional stories affected by history, social structure, and culture, which themselves are dialectically revealed through action, feeling, thought, and language. (p. 739)

In autoethnography, then, you use your own experiences to garner insights into the larger culture or subculture of which you are a part. Great variability exists in the extent to which autoethnographers make themselves the focus of the analysis, how much they keep their role as social scientist in the foreground, the extent to which they use the sensitizing notion of culture, at least explicitly, to guide their analysis, and how personal the writing is. At the center, however, what distinguishes autoethnography from ethnography is self-awareness about and reporting of one's own experiences and introspections as a primary data source. Ellis describes this process as follows:

I start with my personal life. I pay attention to my physical feelings, thoughts, and emotions. I use what I call systematic sociological introspection and emotional recall to try to understand an experience I've lived through. Then I write my experience as a story. By exploring a particular life, I hope to understand a way of life. (Ellis and Bochner 2000:737)

In writing about his experiences in a "New Age ashram located in Pennsylvania," Bruner (1996) confronted the intersection of the ethnographic and the personal:

What started out as part of my personal life was soon transformed into part of my professional life. The point is that, for an ethnographer, any experience—at home or abroad, of self or of other—offers the potential to become fieldwork. . . . For me, my personal and my ethnographic persona have become so intertwined that it would be impossible to separate them even if I wanted to do so. (p. 317)

Anthropologist Mary Catherine Bateson's (2000) autoethnographic description of teaching a seminar at Spelman College in Atlanta, Georgia, includes detailed attention to the personal challenge she experienced in trying to decide how to categorize students of different ages in contemporary American universities, for example, by calling older participants "elders." Aaron Turner (2000) of Brunel University in the United Kingdom has explored using one's own body as a source of data in ethnography, what he calls "embodied ethnography."

Such personal writing is controversial among qualitative theorists because of its "rampant subjectivism" (Crotty 1998:48). Many social science academics object to the way it blurs the lines between social science and literary writing. One sociologist told me angrily that those who want to write creative nonfiction or poetry should find their way to the English Department of the university and leave sociology to sociologists. Richardson (2000b), in contrast, sees the integration of art, literature, and social science as precisely the point, bringing together creative and critical aspects of inquiry. She suggests that what these various new approaches and emphases share is that "they are produced through *creative analytic practices*," which leads her to call "this class of ethnographies *creative analytic practice ethnography*" (Richardson 2000b:929). While the ethnographic aspect of this work is constructed on a foundation of careful research and fieldwork (p. 937), the creative element resides primarily in the writing, which she emphasizes is, itself, "a *method of inquiry*, a way of finding out about yourself and your topic" (p. 923).

But how is one to judge the quality of such nontraditional social scientific approaches that encourage personal and creative ethnographic writing? Richardson (2000b) has responded to this challenge by asserting that *creative analytic practice ethnography* should be held to "high and difficult standards; mere novelty does not suffice" (p. 937). She offers five criteria of quality drawn from both science and creative arts.

1. *Substantive contribution:* Does this piece contribute to our understanding of social life? Does the writer demonstrate a deeply grounded (if embedded) social scientific perspective? How has this perspective informed the construction of the text?

2. *Aesthetic merit:* Does this piece succeeded aesthetically? Does the use of creative analytic practices open up the text, invite interpretive responses? Is the text artistically shaped, satisfying, complex, and not boring?

3. *Reflexivity:* How has the author's subjectivity been both a producer and a product of this text? Is there adequate self-awareness and self-exposure for the reader to make judgments about the point of view?

4. *Impact:* Does this affect me? Emotionally? Intellectually? Does it generate new questions? Move me to write? Move me to try new research practices? Move me to action?

5. *Expression of a reality:* Does this text embody a fleshed out, embodied sense of lived experience? Does it seem a "true"

—a credible—account of a cultural, social, individual, or communal sense of the "real"? (Richardson 2000a:254, 2000b:937)

These criteria open up the possibility of new writing formats. Elliot Eisner (1996), a former president of the American Educational Research Association, has argued that a novel as a form of qualitative reporting could be a legitimate form for a doctoral dissertation in social science or education. In that vein, he has suggested that in "the new frontier in qualitative research methodology" an artistic qualitative social science contribution can be assessed by the "number and quality of the questions that the work raises" as much as by any conclusions offered (Eisner 1997:268). In this regard, eminent evaluator Ernie House (1991) reminds us that where evaluation reports are concerned, the possibility of fiction is always a subtext: "Our evaluation report proved to be so readable many people became enraptured by it. Some said it read like a novel. Others said it was a novel" (p. 113).

Poetry is another artistic genre that has emerged in ethnographic reporting. Glesne (1997) converted interview transcripts into poems because she found poetry better captured and communicated what her interview with an 86-year-old professor in Puerto Rico opened up and revealed. Richardson (1998) has published a number of fieldwork-based poems, reflecting his view that poetry offers a language especially well-suited "for those special, strange, even mysterious moments when bits and pieces suddenly coalesce . . . , when the ethnographer, away from home and in a strange culture, has a heightened sense of the frailty of being human. In such a sense, poetry appears to be a way of communicating instances when we feel truth has shown its face" (p. 451). Travisano (1998) included po-

HONORING ONE'S OWN EXPERIENCE

"One writes out of one thing only—one's own experience. Everything depends on how relentlessly one forces from this experience the last drop, sweet or bitter, it can possibly give. This is the only real concern of the artist, to recreate out of the disorder of life that order which is art" (Baldwin 1990: Introduction).

etry in his "autobiography of an ethnic identity" in which he explored his lived experience of becoming Italian American.

These new frontiers of qualitative inquiry and reporting, combining art and science, are also leading to the integration of multiple forms in a single work. Consider Denzin's (2000b) "Rock Creek History," which he describes as "an experimental, mixed-genre narrative, combining autoethnography with other evocative writing forms, including narratives of the self. Using the techniques of fiction, I tell a story about myself and my experiences with nature, the sacred, and a small Montana River named Rock Creek" (p. 71). He also calls his writing a "performance-based project" that draws on multiple writing forms and traditions including, in addition to those already noted, "the ethnographic story, nature writing, literary nonfiction, the personal memoir, and cultural criticism" (p. 79).

Ellis (Ellis and Bochner 2000) warns that autoethnographic writing is hard to do:

It's amazingly difficult. It's certainly not something that most people can do well. Most social scientists don't write well enough carry it off. Or they're not sufficiently introspective about their feelings or motives, or the contra-

dictions they experience. Ironically, many aren't observant enough of the world around them. The self-questioning autoethnography demands is extremely difficult. So is confronting things about yourself that are less than flattering. Believe me, honest autoethnography exploration generates a lot of fears and doubts—and emotional pain. Just when you think you can't stand the pain anymore, well, that's when the real work has only begun. Then there's the vulnerability of revealing yourself, not being able to take back what you've written or having any control over how readers interpret it. It's hard not to feel your life is being critiqued as well as your work. It can be humiliating. And the ethical issues. Just wait until you've written about family members and loved ones who are part of your story. (p. 738)

Part of the challenge in autoethnographic writing is finding and owning one's voice. In the last chapter, I contrasted the third-person passive voice of traditional academic writing with the first-person active voice of qualitative inquiry. Autoethnography increases the importance of voice and raises the stakes because an authentic voice enhances the authenticity of the work, while an inauthentic voice undermines it. Voice reveals the author's identity (Ivanic 1998). The tone of voice may be expressive, reflective, searching, academic, or critical, as in what Church (1995) has called the "forbidden narratives" of "critical autobiography" in social science. In voice resides Richardson's (2000b) fifth criterion for judging quality cited earlier, what she called *"expression of a reality:* Does this text embody a fleshed out, embodied sense of lived experience? Does it seem a 'true'—a credible—account of a cultural, social, individual, or communal sense of the 'real'?"* (p. 937).

These issues are being raised in a number of disciplinary genres. Historian Edmund

Morris won a Pulitzer Prize for his biography of America's 26th president, Theodore Roosevelt. Partly on this basis, he was chosen as the "official" biographer of former president Ronald Reagan. The resulting work (E. Morris 2000) proved highly controversial because to tell the story of Reagan's life as he felt it needed to be told, he created a fictional character based on himself and fabricated encounters with Reagan at various points that led him to first-person reflections as if he had actually witnessed and participated in these events and encounters. Thus, a traditional and highly respected historian introduced a form of quasi-autoethnographic literary fiction into a standard biography in order to have a point of view from which to recount his subject's life.

In my own major effort at autoethnographic inquiry (Patton 1999a), the struggle to find an authentic voice—authentic first to me, then to others who know me, and finally to those who do not know me— turned what I thought would be a one-year effort into seven years of often painful, discouraging writing. And I was only writing about a 10-day period, a Grand Canyon hike with my son in which we explored what it means to *come of age*, or be initiated into adulthood, in modern society. My son started and graduated from college while I was learning how to tell the story of what we experienced together. To make the story work as a story and make scattered interactions coherent, I had to rewrite conversations that took place over several days into a single evening's dialogue, I had to reorder the sequence of some conversations to enhance the plot line, and I had to learn to follow the novelist's mantra to "show don't tell," advice particularly difficult for those of us who make our living telling. More difficult still was revealing my emotions, foibles,

doubts, weaknesses, and uncertainties. But once the story was told, the final chapter of the book that contrasts alternative coming-of-age/initiation paradigms (Exhibit 1.1 in Chapter 1) emerged relatively painlessly. I've included as Appendix 3.1 at the end of this chapter an excerpt from the book as an example of autoethnographic writing.

Johnstone (2000) argues that "interest in the individual voice" within anthropology can be understood, at least in part, "within the context of a larger shift toward a more phenomenological approach to language" (p. 405). Autoethnography integrates ethnography with personal story, a specifically autobiographical manifestation of the more general "turn to biographical methods in social science" that strive to "link macro and micro levels of analysis . . . [and] provide a sophisticated stock of interpretive procedures for relating the personal and the social" (Chamberlayne, Bornat, and Wengraf 2000:2-3). Art Bochner (Ellis and Bochner 2000) has reflected on what this means:

> What is the point of a storied life? Narrative truth seeks to keep the past alive in the present. Stories show us that the meanings and significance of the past are incomplete, tentative, and revisable according to contingencies of our present life circumstances, the present from which we narrate. Doesn't this mean that the stories we tell always run the risk of distorting the past? Of course, it does. After all, stories rearrange, redescribe, invent, omit, and revise. They can be wrong in numerous ways—tone, detail, substance, etc. Does this attribute of storytelling threaten the project of personal narrative? Not at all, because a story is not a neutral attempt to mirror the facts of one's life. . . .
>
> Life and narrative are inextricably connected. Life both anticipates telling and draws

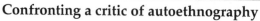

Confronting a critic of autoethnography

meaning from it. Narrative is both about living and part of it. (pp. 745-46)

By opening this chapter with the contrast between ethnography and autoethnography, we have moved from the beginnings of qualitative methods in anthropological fieldwork more than a century ago, where the ethnographer was an outsider among exotically distinct nonliterate peoples, to the most recent manifestation of qualitative inquiry in the postmodern age of mass communications, where autoethnographers struggle to find a distinct voice by documenting their own experiences in an increasingly all-encompassing and commercialized global culture. To further sharpen contrasts in qualitative approaches, the next two sections illuminate some of the philosophical underpinnings that have informed and shaped qualitative methods, including ethnography and autoethnography, by contrasting the foundational question of reality-oriented research and evaluation (postpositivist realism) with that of postmodern constructivism and social construction.

Truth and Reality-Oriented Correspondence Theory: Positivist, Realist, and Analytic Induction Approaches

Foundational questions:
What's really going on in the real world? What can we establish with some degree of certainty? What are plausible explanations for verifiable patterns? What's the truth insofar as we can get at it? How can we study a phenomenon so that our findings correspond, insofar as it's possible, to the real world?

What these questions have in common is the presumption that there is a real world with verifiable patterns that can be observed and predicted—that reality exists and truth is worth striving for. Reality can be elusive and truth can be difficult to determine, but describing reality and determining truth are the appropriate goals of scientific inquiry. Working from this perspective, researchers and evaluators seek methods that yield correspondence with the "real world," thus this is sometimes called a *correspondence* perspective.

Reality-oriented inquiry and the search for truth have fallen on hard times in this skeptical postmodern age when honoring multiple perspectives and diverse points of view has gained ascendancy in reaction to the oppressive authoritarianism and dogmatism that seemed so often to accompany claims of having found "Truth." Yet, many people, especially policymakers and those who commission evaluation research, find it difficult to accept the notion that all explanations and points of view hold equal merit. Some people in programs seem to be helped more than others. Some students seem to learn more than others. Some claims of effectiveness are more plausible and have more merit than others. To test a claim of effectiveness by bringing data to bear on it, including qualitative data, is to be engaged in a form of reality testing that uses evidence to examine assertions and corroborate claims. In this section, we shall examine how to recognize and engage in a reality-testing or reality-oriented approach to qualitative inquiry. In so doing, I shall minimize philosophical discourse and focus primarily on the practical implications of this orientation, but a brief foray into philosophical foundations is necessary to provide a context for practice.

Philosophical inquiry into truth and reality involves examining the nature of knowledge itself, how it comes into being and is transmitted through language. *Positivism,* following Auguste Comte, asserted that only verifiable claims based directly on experience could be considered genuine knowledge. Comte was especially interested in distinguishing the empirically based "positive knowledge" of experience from theology and metaphysics, which depended on fallible human reason and belief. *Logical positivism,* developed by the Vienna Circle in Austria and the Berlin School in Germany in the early part of the 20th century, added to the emphasis on direct experience from positivism a *logic-based* commitment "to theory development using a rigorous procedural language such as symbolic logic. Knowledge comes either from direct experience or indirectly from inferences from experience through the procedural language" (Shadish 1995b:64). Logical positivism subsequently came to be associated with philosophical efforts to specify basic requirements for what could be considered *scientific* knowledge, which included the search for universal laws through empirical verification of logically deduced hypotheses with key concepts and variables operationally defined and carefully formulated to permit replication and falsification. Thus, real knowledge (as opposed to mere beliefs) was limited to what could be logically deduced from theory, operationally measured, and empirically replicated. Such severe, narrow, and rigorous requirements turned out to severely limit what could pass for knowledge and to demand more certainty than the complex world of social phenomena could yield. Though influential in the first half of the 20th century, logical positivism has been "almost universally rejected" as a basis for social science inquiry (Campbell 1999a:132). The legacy of the fleeting influence of logical positivism is that the term lives on as an epithet hurled in

paradigm debates and routinely used incorrectly though persistently. Shadish (1995b) argues that one would be hard-pressed to find any contemporary social scientist, philosopher, or evaluator who really adheres to the tenets of logical positivism. Rather, "the term has become the linguistic equivalent of 'bad,' a rhetorical device aimed at depriving one's opponent of credibility by name-calling. This is particularly true in the quantitative-qualitative debate where some qualitative theorists are fond of labeling all quantitative opponents as logical positivists," a fundamental but common "error" (p. 64).

Logical empiricism and postpositivism, which take into account the criticisms against and weaknesses of rigid positivism, now inform much contemporary social science research, including reality-oriented qualitative inquiry. *Logical empiricism,* a more moderate version of logical positivism (Schwandt 2001), seeks unity in science, through both theory formulation and methodological inquiry, and asserts that there are no fundamental methodological differences between natural and social sciences. *Postpositivism,* as articulated by eminent methodologist Donald T. Campbell in his collected writings about and vision for an "experimenting society" (Campbell and Russo 1999), recognizes that discretionary judgment is unavoidable in science, that proving causality with certainty in explaining social phenomena is problematic, that knowledge is inherently embedded in historically specific paradigms and is therefore relative rather than absolute, and that all methods are imperfect, so multiple methods, both quantitative and qualitative, are needed to generate and test theory, improve understanding over time of how the world operates, and support informed policy making and social program decision making. While modest in asserting what can be known with any certainty, postpositivists do assert that it is possible, using empirical evidence, to distinguish between more and less plausible claims, to test and choose between rival hypotheses, and to distinguish between "belief and *valid* belief" (Campbell 1999b:151, emphasis added).

Given this brief philosophical and epistemological overview, what are the practical implications for qualitative inquiry of operating within a reality-oriented perspective? It means using the language and concepts of mainstream science to design naturalistic studies, inform data gathering in the field, analyze results, and judge the quality of qualitative findings. Thus, if you are a researcher or evaluator operating from a reality-oriented stance, you worry about validity, reliability, and objectivity (e.g., Peräkylä 1997). You realize that completely value-free inquiry is impossible, but you worry about how your values and preconceptions may affect what you see, hear, and record in the field, so you wrestle with your values, try to make any biases explicit, take steps to mitigate their influence through rigorous field procedures, and discuss their possible influence in reporting findings. You may establish an "audit trail" to verify the rigor of your fieldwork and confirmability of the data collected because you want to minimize bias, maximize accuracy, and report impartially believing that "inaccuracy and bias are unacceptable in any case study" (U.S. General Accounting Office [GAO] 1987:51). In reporting, you emphasize the empirical findings—good, solid description and analysis—not your own personal perspective or voice, though you acknowledge that some subjectivity and judgment may enter in. You include triangulation of data sources and analytical perspectives to increase the accuracy and credibility of findings (Patton 1999b). Your criteria for quality include the

CONSTRUCTED, EVER-CHANGING REALITY

"Each moment of our lives, each thing we say, is equally true and false. It is true, because at the very moment we are saying it that is the only reality, and it is false because the next moment another reality will replace it" (Simic 2000:11).

"truth value" and plausibility of findings; credibility, impartiality, and independence of judgment; confirmability, consistency, and dependability of data; and explainable inconsistencies or instabilities (GAO 1987:53). You may even *generalize* case study findings, depending on the cases selected and studied, to generate or test theory (Yin 1989:44, 1999b), establish causality (Ragin 1987, 2000), or inform program improvement and policy decisions from patterns established and lessons learned (GAO 1987:51). In short, you incorporate the language and principles of 21st-century science into naturalistic inquiry and qualitative analysis to convey a sense that you are dedicated to getting as close as possible to what is really going on in whatever setting you are studying. Realizing that absolute objectivity of the pure positivist variety is impossible to attain, you are prepared to admit and deal with imperfections in a phenomenologically messy and methodologically imperfect world, but you still believe that objectivity is worth striving for. As Kirk and Miller (1986) assert,

Objectivity, though the term has been taken by some to suggest a naive and inhumane version of vulgar positivism, is the essential basis of all good research. Without it, the only reason the reader of the research might have for accepting the conclusions of the investigator would be an authoritarian respect for the person of the author. Objectivity is a simultaneous realization of as much reliability and validity as possible. Reliability is the degree to which the finding is independent of accidental circumstances of the research, and validity is the degree to which the finding is interpreted in a correct way. (p. 20)

In the introduction to their widely used and influential sourcebook *Qualitative Data Analysis,* Miles and Huberman (1984) stated modestly: "We think of ourselves as logical positivists who recognize and try to atone for the limitations of that approach. Soft-nosed logical positivists, maybe" (p. 19). They went on to explain what this means and, in so doing, provide a succinct summary of the reality-oriented approach to qualitative research:

We believe that social phenomena exist not only in the mind but also in the objective world—and that there are some lawful and reasonably stable relationships to be found among them. . . . Given our belief in social regularities, there is a corollary: Our task is to express them as precisely as possible, attending to their range and generality and to the local and historical contingencies under which they occur.

So, unlike some schools within social phenomenology, we consider it important to evolve a set of valid and verifiable *methods* for capturing these social relationships and their causes. We want to interpret and explain these phenomena *and* have confidence that others, using the same tools, would arrive at analogous conclusions. (Miles and Huberman 1984:19-20)

Ten years later, in their revised and expanded qualitative sourcebook, Miles and Huberman called themselves "realists"

rather than logical positivists, further evidence that "the weight of criticisms" against logical positivism has "caused its internal collapse" (Schwandt 2001:150). Realism as a qualitative stance is clearly reality oriented, and much of the language quoted above remains in the revised edition. They acknowledge that knowledge is socially and historically constructed, and they "affirm the existence and importance of the subjective, the phenomenological, the meaning-making at the center of life." Then they return to their core reality-oriented stance:

Our aim is to register and "transcend" these processes by building theories to account for a real world that is both bounded and perceptually laden, and to test these theories in our various disciplines.

Our tests do not use "covering laws" or the deductive logic of classical positivism. Rather, our explanations flow from an account of how differing structures produced the events we observed. We aim to account for events, rather than simply to document their sequence. We look for an individual or a social process, a mechanism, a structure at the core of events that can be captured to provide a *causal description* of the forces at work.

Transcendental realism calls both for causal explanation and for the evidence to show that each entity or event is an instance of that explanation. So we need not only an explanatory structure but also a grasp of the particular configuration at hand. That is one reason why we have tilted toward more inductive methods of study. (Miles and Huberman 1994:4)

Analytic induction offers a specific form of inductive analysis that begins deductively, by formulating propositions or hypotheses, and then examines a particular case in depth to determine if the facts of the case support the hypothesis. If it fits, another case is studied, and so forth, in the search for generalizations. If a case does not support the hypothesis, that is, it is a *negative case,* the hypothesis is revised. The aim is to explain a phenomenon satisfactorily using qualitative, case-based inquiry (Schwandt 2001; Vidich and Lyman 2000:57-58; Ryan and Bernard 2000: 786-87; Gilgun 1995; Taylor and Bogdan 1984: 127-28). Chapter 8 on analysis discusses the analytical strategies of analytic induction in more detail and provides examples.

While analytic induction focuses on method, realism focuses first on philosophy. Realist philosophy (Baert 1998:189-97; Putnam 1987, 1990) has recently has been adapted by Mark, Henry, and Julnes (2000) and Pawson and Tilley (1997) as offering the foundation for a reality-oriented approach to evaluation research that includes qualitative inquiry.

> Realism presumes the existence of an external world in which events and experiences are triggered by underlying (and often unobservable) mechanisms and structures (Bhaskar, 1975). Commonsense realism also gives standing to everyday experiences. It is antiformalist in the sense of not expecting logical, formal solutions to vexing problems such as the nature of truth. And it places a priority on practice and the lessons drawn from practice. . . . As realists, we see no meaningful epistemological difference between qualitative and quantitative methods. Instead we see both as assisted sensemaking techniques that have specific benefits and limitations. And as commonsense realists, we believe that although there is a world out there to be made sense of, the specific constructions and construals that individuals make are critical and need to be considered. (Mark et al. 2000:15-16)

Throughout this section, I have used the term *reality-oriented* qualitative inquiry to describe this perspective because labels

such as logical positivism, postpositivism, logical empiricism, realism, transcendental realism, and objectivism are jargon-ish, have disputed definitions, and carry negative connotations for many, so they come with lots of baggage. I have attempted to be descriptive about the reality-oriented, correspondence theory perspective by focusing on its core, foundational questions as articulated at the beginning of this section. While, as the next section will show, many qualitative methodologists assert that qualitative inquiry is inherently constructionist or phenomenological in perspective, the reality-oriented perspective remains widespread, even dominant, in those arenas of research practice where scientific credibility carries a premium. These arenas include many dissertation committees in traditional disciplines where qualitative dissertations are just beginning to be allowed, in summative evaluation and policy studies where mere "anecdotal" evidence is demeaned, and in fields such as medical research where double-blind experimental studies remain the gold standard. To emphasize this latter point, I close this review of reality-oriented qualitative inquiry with an excerpt from a medical journal in which health researchers are defending qualitative research to an audience known to be skeptical. Their approach is to associate qualitative research closely with accepted and credible forms of experimental research. Such a perspective epitomizes the reality-testing orientation:

> What, then, does the qualitative researcher do once he or she accomplishes a careful and trustworthy understanding of the language and behavior of an individual human being? Here is where we rely on our positivist skills and methods. . . . [O]nce we carefully examine and articulate that which we understand one human being to be doing, we attempt to collate the language and behavior of many hu-

man beings, so many that we might be able to test the relationships, for example, between setting and behavior or between age and hope. Included within the domains of qualitative science or narrative research, then, are efforts to generalize, to predict, and to relate initial states to outcomes. These efforts require the same evidence-based activities that are used in testing any hypotheses. (Charon, Greene, and Adelman 1998:68)

Social Construction and Constructivism

Foundational questions:
How have the people in this setting constructed reality? What are their reported perceptions, "truths," explanations, beliefs, and world-view? What are the consequences of their constructions for their behaviors and for those with whom they interact?

Constructivism begins with the premise that the human world is different from the natural, physical world and therefore must be studied differently (Guba and Lincoln 1990). Because human beings have evolved the capacity to interpret and *construct* reality—indeed, they cannot do otherwise —the world of human perception is not real in an absolute sense, as the sun is real, but is "made up" and shaped by cultural and linguistic constructs. To say that the socially constructed world of humans is not physically real like the sun doesn't mean that it isn't perceived and experienced as real by real people. W. I. Thomas, a distinguished sociologist and a founding symbolic interactionist, formulated what has become known as Thomas's theorem: *What is defined or perceived by people as real is real in its consequences* (Thomas and Thomas 1928:572). So

---

TWO VIEWS OF OBJECTIVITY

"Whether you are managing an organization or trying to manage your own life, your ability to cope successfully, to succeed —even survive—depends on objectivity. The Japanese word sunao *translates roughly as 'the untrapped mind.' It describes the ability to see the world as it is, not as one wishes it to be"* (management consultants Arnold Brown and Edith Weiner, quoted in Safire and Safire 1991: 158).

* * *

"If I were objective or if you were objective or if anyone was, he would have to be put away somewhere in an institution because he'd be some sort of vegetable" (journalist David Brinkley, public television interview, December 2, 1968).

---

constructivists study the multiple realities constructed by people and the implications of those constructions for their lives and interactions with others. Shadish (1995b) reminds us that social constructionism "refers to constructing *knowledge about* reality, not constructing reality itself" (p. 67). Constructionists commonly assume that humans "do not have direct access to a singular, stable, and fully knowable external reality. All of our understandings are contextually embedded, interpersonally forged, and necessarily limited" (Neimeyer 1993:1-2). Any notion of "truth," then, becomes a matter of "consensus among informed and sophisticated constructors, not of correspondence with an objective reality." Likewise, the notion of an objective "fact" has no meaning "except within some value framework." It follows that "there cannot be an 'objective' assessment of any proposition" (Guba and Lincoln 1989:44). Social construction, or

---

EXHIBIT 3.4   Constructivism Versus Constructionism

Michael Crotty (1998) makes an important and useful distinction between constructivism and constructionism, a distinction that illustrates how the process of social construction unfolds among scholars. It remains to be seen whether this distinction will gain widespread use since the two terms are so difficult to distinguish and easy to confuse.

"It would appear useful, then, to reserve the term *constructivism* for the epistemological considerations focusing exclusively on 'the meaning-making activity of the individual mind' and to use *constructionism* where the focus includes 'the collective generation [and transmission] of meaning' " (p. 58). . . .

"Whatever the terminology, the distinction itself is an important one. Constructivism taken in this sense points out the unique experience of each of us. It suggests that each one's way of making sense of the world is as valid and worthy of respect as any other, thereby tending to scotch any hint of a critical spirit. On the other hand, social constructionism emphasizes the hold our culture has on us: it shapes the way in which we see things (even in the way in which we feel things!) and gives us a quite definite view of the world" (p. 58).

---

constructivist philosophy, is built on the thesis of *ontological relativity*, which holds that all tenable statements about existence depend on a worldview, and no worldview is uniquely determined by empirical or sense data about the world. Hence, two people can live in the same empirical world, even though one's world is haunted by demons, and the other's, by subatomic particles. Exhibit 3.4 distinguishes the worldviews of constructionism and constructivism, which are often used interchangeably.

How all-encompassing is the constructionist view? Michael Crotty (1998) asserts,

It is not just our thoughts that are constructed for us. We have to reckon with the social construction of emotions. Moreover, constructionism embraces the whole gamut of meaningful reality. All reality, as meaningful reality, is socially constructed. There is no exception. . . . The chair may exist as a phenomenal object regardless of whether any consciousness is aware of its existence. It exists *as a chair*, however, only if conscious beings construe it as a chair. As a chair, it too "is constructed, sus-

tained and reproduced through social life." (pp. 54-55)

Elsewhere Crotty uses the example of a tree:

What the "commonsense" view commends to us is that the tree standing before us is a tree. It has all the meaning we ascribe to a tree. It would be a tree, with that same meaning, whether anyone knew of its existence or not. We need to remind ourselves here that it is human beings who have constructed it as a tree, given it the name, and attributed to it the associations we make with trees. It may help if we recall the extent to which those associations differ even within the same overall culture. "Tree" is likely to bear quite different connotations in a logging town, an artists' settlement and a treeless slum. (p. 43)

How, then, does operating from a constructionist perspective actually affect qualitative inquiry? Let's consider its impact on program evaluation. A constructionist evaluator would expect that different stakeholders involved in a welfare program (e.g., staff, clients, families of clients, administrators, funders) would have different experiences and perceptions of the program, all of which deserve attention and all of which are experienced as real. The constructionist evaluator would attempt to capture these different perspectives through open-ended interviews and observations, and then would examine the implications of different perceptions (or multiple "realities") but would not pronounce which set of perceptions was "right" or more "true" or more "real," as would a reality-oriented (postpositivist) evaluator. Constructivist evaluators could compare clients' perceptions and social constructions with those of funders or program staff and could interpret the effects of differences on attainment of stated program goals, but they would not value staff perceptions as more real or meaningful. In constructivist evaluation, then, "the claims, concerns, and issues of stakeholders serve as organizational foci (the basis for determining what information is needed)" (Guba and Lincoln 1989:50).

Indeed, if constructivist evaluators were also operating from a social justice framework, they might give added weight to the perspectives of those with less power and privilege in order to "give voice" to the disenfranchised, the underprivileged, the poor, and others outside the mainstream (Weiss and Greene 1992:145). In the evaluation of a diversity project in a school district in Saint Paul, Minnesota, a major part of the design included capturing and reporting the experiences of people of color. Providing a way for African American, Native American, Chicano-Latino, and Hmong parents to tell their stories to mostly White, corporate funders was an intentional part of the design, one approved by those same White corporate funders. The final report was written as a "multivocal, multicultural" presentation that presented different experiences with and perceptions of the program's im-

pacts rather than reaching singular conclusions. The medium of the report carried the message that multiple voices needed to be heard and valued as a manifestation of diversity (Stockdill et al. 1992). The findings were used for both formative and summative purposes, but the parents and many of the staff were most interested in using the evaluation processes to make themselves heard by those in power. *Being heard* was an end in itself quite separate from use of findings.

Guba and Lincoln (1989) included among the primary assumptions of constructivism the following, whether for evaluation or research more generally:

- "Truth" is a matter of consensus among informed and sophisticated constructors, not of correspondence with objective reality.

- "Facts" have no meaning except within some value framework, hence there cannot be an "objective" assessment of any proposition.

- "Causes" and effects do not exist except by imputation. . . .

- Phenomena can only be understood within the context in which they are studied; findings from one context cannot be generalized to another; neither problems nor solutions can be generalized from one setting to another. . . .

- Data derived from constructivist inquiry have neither special status nor legitimation; they represent simply another construction to be taken into account in the move toward consensus. (pp. 44-45)

Guba and Lincoln (1990:148) summarize the constructivist perspective as being ontologically relativist, epistemologically subjectivist, and methodologically hermeneutic and dialectic. The thread throughout is the emphasis on the socially constructed nature of reality as distinguishing the study of human beings from the study of other natural phenomena.

The idea that social groups such as street gangs or religious adherents construct their own realities has a long history in sociology, especially the sociology of knowledge (e.g., Berger and Luckmann 1967). It wasn't until this idea of socially constructed knowledge was applied to scientists that constructionism became an influential methodological paradigm. No work has been more influential in that regard than Thomas Kuhn's classic *The Structure of Scientific Revolutions* (1970). Before Kuhn, most people thought that science progressed through heroic individual discoveries that contributed to an accumulating body of knowledge that got closer and closer to the way the world really worked. In contrast, Kuhn argued that tightly organized communities of specialists were the central forces in scientific development. Ideas that seemed to derive from brilliant individual scientific minds were actually shaped by and dependent on paradigms of knowledge that were socially constructed and enforced through group consensus. Rather than seeing scientific inquiry as progressing steadily toward truth about nature, he suggested that science is best seen as a series of power struggles between adherents of different scientific worldviews.

Kuhn emphasized the power of preconceived and socially constructed ideas to control the observations of scientists. He insisted that without the focusing effect of agreed-on constructs, investigators would not be able actually to engage in research. A fully "open" mind would not be able to focus on the details necessary to engage in "normal" science, that is, testing specific propositions derived from a theory or "scientific paradigm." What made this contribution so important was the widespread pre-

sumption that scientists, rather than being bound by preconceptions, were open-minded, value free, and unencumbered by inherited ideas. Kuhn applied to science the kind of language normally used to describe confrontations between opposing political and ideological communities, especially during revolutions. He argued (and showed with natural science examples) that communities of scientists, like ideological or religious communities, were organized by certain traditions that periodically came under strain when new problems arose that couldn't be explained by old beliefs. New explanations and ideas would then compete until the old ideas were discarded or revised, sometimes sweepingly. But the competition was not just intellectual. Power was involved. The leaders of scientific communities wielded power in support of their positions just as political leaders do. The assessment of Kuhn's contribution, three decades after his work first appeared, by Berkeley historian David Hollinger shows the importance of his analysis: "*The Structure of Scientific Revolutions* presented the strongest case ever made for the dependence of valid science on distinctly constituted, historically particular human communities" (Hollinger 2000:23).

Scientists constitute a critical case for social constructionism. If scientific knowledge is socially constructed and consensually validated, as opposed to consisting of empirical truths validated by nature, then surely all knowledge is socially constructed. "Accordingly, not only the social scientist but equally the natural scientist has to deal with realities that, as meaningful realities, are socially constructed. They are on equal footing in this respect" (Crotty 1998:55).

Kuhn's analysis, though remaining controversial and heavily critiqued (e.g., Fuller 2000), became a cornerstone of the postmodern skepticism about scientific truth.

Postmodernism, Radavich (2001) asserts, has become "the most prevalent mode of thinking in our time. . . . Postmodernist discourse is precisely the discourse that denies the possibility of ontological grounding" (p. 6). In other words, no truth or "true meaning" about any aspect of existence is possible, at least not in any absolute sense; it can only be constructed. To understand constructionism and its implications for qualitative inquiry, a brief review of postmodernism may be helpful in that it has shaped contemporary intellectual discourse in both science and art.

Belief in science as generating truth was one of the cornerstones of modernism inherited from the Enlightenment. Postmodernism attacked this faith in science by questioning its capacity to generate truth, in part because, like all human communications, it is dependent on language, which is socially constructed and, as such, distorts reality. Postmodernism asserts that no language, not even that of science, can provide a direct window through which one can view reality. Language inevitably and inherently is built on the assumptions and worldview of the social group that has constructed it and the culture of which it is a part. Thus, language does not and cannot fully capture or represent reality, a posture called the "crisis of representation" (Denzin and Lincoln 2000b; Turner 1998:598). Translated into Kuhn's framework, scientific language and constructs are paradigm based and dependent.

It follows from this that the continuity of knowledge over time and across cultures is called into question. Modernism's faith in science included the assumption that knowledge increased over time and that such accumulation constituted continuous progress toward deeper and deeper truths. "Postmodernists argue that because there is not a truth that exists apart from the ideological interests of humans, discontinuity of

FROM ENLIGHTENMENT TO POSTMODERNISM

"All movements tend to extremes, which is approximately where we are today. The exuberant self-realization that ran from romanticism to modernism has given rise now to philosophical postmodernism (often called poststructuralism, especially in its more political and sociological expressions). Postmodernism is the ultimate polar antithesis of the Enlightenment. The difference between the two extremes can be expressed roughly as follows: Enlightenment thinkers believe we can know everything, and radical postmodernists believe we can know nothing" (Harvard sociobiologist E. O. Wilson 1998:21).

knowledge is the norm, and a permanent pluralism of cultures is the only real truth that humans must continually face" (Turner 1998:599). Constructionism, then, consistent with postmodernism, is relativistic in stance, meaning knowledge is viewed as relative to time and place, never absolute across time and space, thus the reluctance to generalize and the suspicion of generalizations asserted by others.

Power comes into the picture here because, as views of reality are socially constructed and culturally embedded, those views dominant at any time and place will serve the interests and perspectives of those who exercise the most power in a particular culture. By exercising control over language, and therefore control over the very categories of reality that are opened to consciousness, those in power are served.

Scientific knowledge, then, is socially constructed like all other knowledge systems and, as such, is relative to and contingent on the methods and paradigms within which it was generated. "Science, like any knowledge system, is based on incorrigible assumptions, is an abstraction from physical reality, is in need of reification and stabilization through the processes of institutionalization and emotional investment, and is bent on systematically subjugating other knowledge systems to assert its own reality" (Turner 1998:614). Some postmodernists and constructivists question the possibility of ever finding and expressing true reality, even in the physical world, because language creates a screen between human beings and physical reality. "Vocabularies are useful or useless, good or bad, helpful or misleading, sensitive or coarse, and so on; but they are not 'more objective' or 'less objective' nor more or less 'scientific' " (Rorty 1994:57). This is because discovering the "true nature of reality" is not the real purpose of language; the purpose of language is to communicate the social construction of the dominant members of the group using the language.

The postmodern perspective, and its many variations—for postmodernism is not a unitary perspective (e.g., Pillow 2000; Constas 1998)—has given rise to an emphasis on *deconstruction*, which means to take apart the language of a text to expose its critical assumptions and the ideological interests being served. Perspective and power occur as hand in glove in postmodern critiques. Social constructions are presumed to serve someone's interests, usually those of the powerful. As Denzin (1991) has asserted with reference to deconstructing mass media messages, a critical analysis should "give a voice to the voiceless, as it deconstructs those popular culture texts which reproduce stereotypes about the powerless" (p. 153). Thus, deconstruction constitutes a core analytical tool of constructivists.

In deconstructing constructionism and constructivism, one finds a range of assump-

tions and positions, from the radical "absolutely no reality ever" to a milder "let's capture and honor different perspectives about reality." These positions share an interest in the subjective nature of human perceptions and skepticism about the possibility of objectivity. Reality-oriented researchers, in kind, are skeptical of the subjective knowledge of constructivism. How contentious is the debate? One gets some sense of the gulf that can separate these views from an assessment of postmodernism and constructivism by Rutgers mathematician Norman Levitt (1998) in an article titled "Why Professors Believe Weird Things": "Scientific evidence—which is to say the only meaningful evidence—cannot be neutralized by 'subjective knowledge,' which is to say bullshit" (p. 34). He goes on to comment on constructivism as a particular manifestation of postmodernism: "a particular technique for getting drunk on one's own words" (p. 35).

Thomas Schwandt (1997a) in his very useful dictionary of qualitative terms strikes a more conciliatory tone, recognizing that the rhetoric of constructivism can sound radical (and silly) if taken too literally:

> Although some versions of *constructivism* do appear to deny reality, many (if not most, I suspect) qualitative inquirers have a common-sense realist *ontology*, that is, they take seriously the existence of things, events, structures, people, meanings, and so forth in the environment as independent in some way from their experience with them. And they regard society, institutions, feelings, intelligence, poverty, disability, and so on as being just as "real" as the toes on their feet and the sun in the sky. (p. 134)

Further deconstructing the phrase "social construction," one may find "inescapable connotations of manufacturing," as if people sat around and made things up. But

DECONSTRUCTION EXEMPLAR: THE CONCEPT OF ENTREPRENEURSHIP

Ogbor (2000) has examined "mythicizing and reification in entrepreneurial discourse." He discusses "the effects of ideological control in conventional entrepreneurial discourses and praxis." Following postmodernist, deconstructionist, and critical theory traditions, the ideas expressed about the phenomenon of entrepreneurship are deconstructed to reveal "the dysfunctional effects of ideological control both in research and in praxis." Ogbor argues that the concept of entrepreneurship is "discriminatory, gender-biased, ethnocentrically determined and ideologically controlled, sustaining not only prevailing societal biases, but serving as a tapestry for unexamined and contradictory assumptions and knowledge about the reality of entrepreneurs" (p. 605).

to say that people produce the world is not the same as saying that they are solipsists, that they are able to fashion the world according to their whims. . . . [O]ne cannot ordinarily produce an imaginary or nonsensical phenomenon and expect to be taken seriously. The mistake is to think of the process of production as one that is free of constraints when in fact it is a structure of constraints. (Watson and Goulet 1998:97)

Attending to the social construction of reality, then, points us not only to what is constructed but to how it is constructed and the very question of what it means to say it is constructed. For an excellent review of these issues in both the social and natural sciences, see Hacking (2000).

DUALIST AND MONIST CONSTRUCTIONISM

Distinguishing dualist from monist approaches to social constructionism takes the deconstruction process through one final filter.

Dualist constructionism distinguishes between actual states of affairs and perceptions, interpretations, or reactions to those affairs. . . . When Berger and Luckmann (1967) say that the Sociology of Knowledge "must concern itself with whatever passes for 'knowledge' in a society" (p. 3), their putting knowledge in quotation marks demonstrates a commitment to a dualist position. There is knowledge then there is "knowledge." The latter will be treated as knowledge by some social group, but judgment can be made on the ultimate validity of this group's claims, determining whether "knowledge" really is knowledge. . . .

If the approach to the domain of inquiry is dualist this means that the analyst distinguishes between the objective features of the domain and members' representations of those features. The dualist is prepared to judge the adequacy of the members' representations (beliefs, interpretation). If the approach to the domain is monist, then there are only members' representations, the adequacy of which cannot be raised as an issue; there are no objective features in the domain upon which to base a judgment of the adequacy, for example, of a claim of racism. There are only representations of features, for example, the representation/claim of racism. (Heap 1995:54)

We can conclude by emphasizing the basic contributions of social construction and constructivist perspectives to qualitative inquiry, namely, the emphasis on capturing and honoring multiple perspectives; attending to the ways in which language as a social and cultural construction shapes, distorts, and structures understandings; how meth-

ods determine findings; and the importance of thinking about the relationship between the investigator and the investigated, espe- cially the effects of inequitable power dy- namics—and how that relationship affects what is found.

Phenomenology

Foundational question:
  What is the meaning, structure, and essence of the lived experience of this phenomenon for this person or group of people?

"Phenomenology asks for the very nature of a phenomenon, for that which makes a some-'thing' what it is—and without which it could not be what it is" (Van Manen 1990:10). The initial clarity of this definition can fade rapidly because the term *phenomenology* has become so popular and has been so widely embraced that its meaning has become confused and diluted. It can refer to a philosophy (Husserl 1967), an inquiry paradigm (Lincoln 1990), an interpretive theory (Denzin and Lincoln 2000b:14), a social science analytical perspective or orientation (Harper 2000:727; Schutz 1967, 1970), a major qualitative tradition (Creswell 1998), or a research methods framework (Moustakas 1994). Varying forms complicate the picture even more; transcendental, existential, and hermeneutic phenomenology offer different nuances of focus—the essential meanings of individual experience, the social construction of group reality, and the language and structure of communication, respectively (Schwandt 2001:191-94). Phenomenological traditions in sociology and psychology vary in unit of analysis, group or individual (Creswell 1998:53). Adding further confusion to the mix, the term *phenomenography* was coined by Ulrich Sonnemann (1954) to emphasize "a descriptive recording of immediate subjective experience as reported" (p. 344). (For an annotated bibliography of phenomenographic research, see Bruce and Gerber 1997.)

What these various phenomenological and phenomenographic approaches share in common is a focus on exploring how human beings make sense of experience and transform experience into consciousness, both individually and as shared meaning. This requires methodologically, carefully, and thoroughly capturing and describing how people experience some phenomenon—how they perceive it, describe it, feel about it, judge it, remember it, make sense of it, and talk about it with others. To gather such data, one must undertake in-depth interviews with people who have *directly* experienced the phenomenon of interest; that is, they have "lived experience" as opposed to secondhand experience.

> Phenomenology aims at gaining a deeper understanding of the nature or meaning of our everyday experiences. . . .
>
> Anything that presents itself to consciousness is potentially of interest to phenomenology, whether the object is real or imagined, empirically measurable or subjectively felt. Consciousness is the only access human beings have to the world. Or rather, it is by virtue of being conscious that we are already related to the world. Thus all we can ever know must present itself to consciousness. Whatever falls outside of consciousness therefore falls outside the bounds of our possible lived experience. . . . A person cannot reflect on lived experience while living through the experience. For example, if one tries to reflect on one's anger while being angry, one finds that the anger has already changed or dissipated. Thus, phenomenological reflection is not *introspective* but *retrospective*. Reflection on lived experience is always recollective; it is reflection on experience that is already passed or lived through. (Van Manen 1990:9-10).

The phenomenon that is the focus of inquiry may be an emotion—loneliness, jeal-

Hi, I'm a graduate student, and I'm learning about a new type of research that focuses on the "lived experience" of different life events. I just have a few questions..

Phenomenological abduction

ousy, anger. The phenomenon may be a relationship, a marriage, or a job. The phenomenon may be a program, an organization, or a culture.

Phenomenology as a philosophical tradition was first used in the development of a rigorous science by the German philosopher Edmund H. Husserl (1859-1938). The work of Alfred Schutz (1899-1959) was an important influence in applying and establishing phenomenology as a major social science perspective (Schutz 1977). Other important influences have been Merleau-Ponty (1962), Whitehead (1958), Giorgi (1971), and Zaner (1970). More recently, phenomenology has become an important influence in certain approaches to psychotherapy (Moustakas 1988, 1995).

By phenomenology Husserl (1913) meant the study of how people describe things and experience them through their senses. His most basic philosophical assumption was that *we can only know what we experience* by attending to perceptions and meanings that awaken our conscious awareness. Initially, all our understanding comes from sensory experience of phenomena, but that experience must be described, explicated, and interpreted. Yet, descriptions of experience and interpretations are so intertwined that they often become one. Interpretation is essential to an understanding of experience and the experience includes the interpretation. Thus, phenomenologists focus on how we put together the phenomena we experience in such a way as to make sense of the world and, in so doing, develop a worldview. There is no separate (or objective) reality for people. There is only what they know their experience is and means. The subjective experience incorporates the objective thing and becomes a person's reality, thus the focus on meaning making as the essence of human experience.

> From a phenomenological point of view, we are less interested in the factual status of particular instances: whether something happened, how often it tends to happen, or how the occurrence of an experience is related to the prevalence of other conditions or events. For example, phenomenology does not ask, "How do these children learn this particular material?" but it asks, "What is the nature or essence of the experience of learning (so that I can now better understand what this particular learning experience is like for these children)?" (Van Manen 1990:10)

There are two implications of this perspective that are often confused in discussing qualitative methods. The first implication is that what is important to know is what people experience and how they interpret the world. This is the subject matter, the focus, of phenomenological inquiry. The second implication is methodological. The only way for us to really know what another person experiences is to experience the phenomenon as directly as possible for ourselves. This leads to the importance of participant observation and in-depth interviewing. In either case, in reporting phenomenological findings, "the essence or nature of an experience has been adequately described in language if the description reawakens or shows us the lived quality and significance of the experience in a fuller and deeper manner" (Van Manen 1990:10).

There is one final dimension that differentiates a phenomenological approach: the assumption that *there is an essence or essences to shared experience.* These essences are the core meanings mutually understood through a phenomenon commonly experienced. The experiences of different people are bracketed, analyzed, and compared to identify the essences of the phenomenon, for example, the essence of loneliness, the essence of being a mother, or the essence of being a participant in a particular program. The assumption of essence, like the ethnographer's assumption that culture exists and is important, becomes the defining characteristic of a purely phenomenological study. *"Phenomenological research is the study of essences"* (Van Manen 1990:10). Phenomenologists are

rigorous in their analysis of the experience, so that basic elements of the experience that are common to members of a specific society, or all human beings, can be identified. This last point is essential to understanding the philosophical basis of phenomenology, yet it is often misunderstood. On the other hand, each person has a unique set of experiences which are treated as truth and which determine that individual's behavior. In this sense, truth (and associate behavior) is totally unique to each individual. Some researchers are misled to think that they are using a phenomenological perspective when they study four teachers and describe their four unique views. A phenomenologist assumes a commonality in those human experiences and must use rigorously the method of bracketing to search for those commonalities. Results obtained from a phenomenological study can then be related to and integrated with those of other phenomenologists studying the same experience, or phenomenon. (Eichelberger 1989:6)

In short, conducting a study with a phenomenological focus (i.e., getting at the essence of the experience of some phenomenon) is different from using phenomenology to philosophically justify the methods of qualitative inquiry as legitimate in social science research. Both contributions are important. But a phenomenological study (as opposed to a phenomenological perspective) is one that focuses on descriptions of what people experience and how it is that they experience what they experience. One can employ a general phenomenological perspective to elucidate the importance of using methods that capture people's experience of the world without conducting a phenomenological study that focuses on the essence of shared experience (at least that is my experience and interpretation of the phenomenon of phenomenology).

Heuristic Inquiry

Foundational question:
What is my experience of this phenomenon and the essential experience of others who also experience this phenomenon intensely?

Heuristics is a form of phenomenological inquiry that brings to the fore the personal experience and insights of the researcher.

"Heuristic" research came into my life when I was searching for a word that would meaningfully encompass the processes that I believed to be essential in investigations of human experience. The root meaning of heuristic comes from the Greek word *heuriskein*, meaning to discover or to find. It refers to a process of internal search through which one discovers the nature and meaning of experience and develops methods and procedures for further investigation and analysis. The self of the researcher is present throughout the process and, while understanding the phenomenon with increasing depth, the researcher also experiences growing self-awareness and self-knowledge. Heuristic processes incorporate creative self-processes and self discoveries. (Moustakas 1990b:9)

There are two focusing or narrowing elements of heuristic inquiry within the larger framework of phenomenology. First, the researcher must have personal experience with and intense interest in the phenomenon under study. Second, others (coresearchers) who are part of the study must share an intensity of experience with the phenomenon. Heuristics is not inquiry into casual experience. Heuristic inquiry focuses on intense human experiences, intense from the point of view of the investigator and coresearchers. It is the combination of personal experience and intensity that yields an understanding of the essence of the phenomenon. "Heuristics is concerned with meanings, not measurements; with essence, not appearance; with quality, not quantity; with experience, not behavior" (Douglass and Moustakas 1985:42).

The reports of heuristic researchers are filled with the discoveries, personal insights, and reflections of the researchers. Discovery comes from being wide open to the thing itself, a recognition that one must relinquish control and be tumbled about with the newness and drama of a searching focus, "asking questions about phenomena that disturb and challenge" (Douglass and Moustakas 1985:47).

The uniqueness of heuristic inquiry is the extent to which it legitimizes and places at the fore these personal experiences, reflections, and insights of the researcher. The researcher, then, comes to understand the essence of the phenomenon through shared reflection and inquiry with coresearchers as they also intensively experience and reflect on the phenomenon in question. A sense of connectedness develops between researcher and research participants in their mutual efforts to elucidate the nature, meaning, and essence of a significant human experience.

The fundamental methods text on heuristic inquiry is by the primary developer of this approach, Clark Moustakas (1990b). His classic works in this tradition include studies of loneliness (1961, 1972, 1975) and humanistic therapy (1995). Other examples are Bernthal (1990), Clark (1988), Hawka (1986), Weidman (1985), Katz (1987), Cheyne (1988), Marino (1985), and Craig (1978). Heuristic inquiry has strong roots in humanistic psychology (Maslow 1956, 1966; Rogers 1961, 1969, 1977) and Polanyi's (1962) emphasis on personal knowledge, indwelling, and the tacit dimension (1967). "Tacit knowing operates behind the scenes, giving birth to the hunches and vague, formless insights that characterize heuristic discovery" (Douglass and Moustakas 1985:49). Polanyi explained tacit knowing as the inner essence of human understanding, what we know but can't articulate.

> Tacit knowing now appears as an act of indwelling by which we gain access to a new meaning. When exercising a skill we literally dwell in the innumerable muscular acts which contribute to its purpose, a purpose which constitutes their joint meaning. Therefore, since all understanding is tacit knowledge, all understanding is achieved by indwelling. (Polanyi 1967:160)

The rigor of heuristic inquiry comes from systematic observation of and dialogues with self and others, as well as depth interviewing of coresearchers. This mode of inquiry "affirms the possibility that one can live deeply and passionately in the moment, be fully immersed in mysteries and miracles, and still be engaged in meaningful research experience" (Craig 1978:20).

> The power of heuristic inquiry lies in its potential for disclosing truth. Through exhaustive self-search, dialogues with others, and creative depictions of experience, a comprehensive knowledge is generated, beginning as a series of subjective and developing into a systematic and definitive exposition. (Douglass and Moustakas 1985:40)

Heuristic inquiry is derived from but different from phenomenology in four major ways (Douglass and Moustakas 1985):

1. Heuristics emphasizes connectedness and relationship, while phenomenology encourages more detachment in analyzing an experience.

2. Heuristics leads to "depictions of essential meanings and portrayal of the intrigue and personal significance that imbue the search to know," while phenomenology emphasizes definitive descriptions of the structures of experience.

3. Heuristics concludes with a "creative synthesis" that includes the researcher's intuition and tacit understandings, while phenomenology presents a distillation of the structures of experience.

4. "Whereas phenomenology loses the persons in the process of descriptive analysis, in heuristics the research participants remain visible in the examination of the data and continue to be portrayed as whole persons. Phenomenology ends with the essence of experience; heuristics retains the essence of the person in experience" (p. 43).

Systematic steps in the heuristic inquiry process lead to the "definitive exposition" of experiential essence: immersion, incubation, illumination, explication, and creative synthesis (Moustakas 1990a).

What is important about heuristics for my purpose here, that is, describing variety in qualitative inquiry, is that heuristic research epitomizes the phenomenological emphasis on meanings and knowing through personal experience; it exemplifies and places at the fore the way in which the researcher is the primary instrument in qualitative inquiry; and it challenges in the extreme traditional scientific concerns about researcher objectivity and detachment, as in autoethnography (described earlier in this chapter). In essence, it personalizes inquiry and puts the experience (and voice) of the inquirer front and center throughout.

If I am investigating the meaning of delight, then delight hovers nearby and follows me around. It takes me fully into its confidence and I take it into mine. Delight becomes a lingering presence; for awhile, there is only delight. It opens me to the world in a joyous way and takes me into a richness, playfulness and childlikeness that move freely and effortlessly. I'm ready to see, feel, touch or hear whatever opens me to a fuller knowledge and understanding of the experience of delight. (Moustakas 1990b:11)

Qualitative Heuristics: A German Alternative Tradition

Since no authority exists to monitor and sort out nomenclature, conflicts in usage occur, contributing to confusion and the importance of reaffirming the admonition to always define one's terms. Heuristic inquiry, à la Clark Moustakas and discussed in the previous section, has a nomenclature rival in "qualitative heuristics," an approach developed at the University of Hamburg, Germany, which aims to "bring back the qualities of systematic exploration and discovery into psychological and sociological research" (Kleining and Witt 2000:1). It is based on four rules.

Rule 1. The research person should be open to new concepts and change his or her preconceptions if the data are not in agreement with them.

Rule 2. The topic of research is preliminary and may change during the research process. It is only fully known after being successfully explored.

Rule 3. Data should be collected under the paradigm of maximum structural variation of perspectives. Variation of the sample and of research methods avoids one-sidedness of representation of the topic; variation of questions avoids just one answer. If researchers assume that a variable may influence the data they should implement variations. Structural variations mean sampling of positions in reference to the topic, i.e., when studying an emotion, the collection of data past and present, before and after its occurrence, in different situations, from different respondents, if possible from different times and cultures, by different methods, etc.

Rule 4.   The analysis is directed toward discovery of similarities. It locates similarities, accordance, analogies or homologies within these most diverse and varied data. It tries to overcome differences. The rule follows Simmel's famous chapter on method saying that "out of complex phenomena the homogenous will be extracted . . . and the dissimilar paralyzed." (Kleining and Witt 2000: online)

This approach emphasizes "introspection" as a critical part of the analytical process, an element also central to "heuristic inquiry" in the tradition of humanistic psychology. However, neither heuristic inquiry as articulated by Moustakas (1990b) nor this German alternative labeled "qualitative heuristics" can be derived directly from the common dictionary definition of *heuristics*, defined as techniques to assist learning or techniques for exploratory problem solving—though neither approach conflicts explicitly with the dictionary definition. Those who lament such variations in meanings, denotations, and connotations may find some comfort in Ambrose Bierce's ([1906] 1999) *Devil's Dictionary* definition of lexicographer:

A pestilent fellow who, under the pretense of recording some particular stage in the development of a language, does what he can to arrest its growth, stiffen its flexibility and mechanize its methods. For your lexicographer, having written his dictionary, comes to be considered "as one having authority," whereas his function is only to make a record, not to give a law. . . . Recognizing the truth that language must grow by innovation if it grow at all, makes new words and uses the old in an

unfamiliar sense, has no following and is tartly reminded that "it isn't in the dictionary" —although down to the time of the first lexicographer (Heaven forgive him!) no author ever had used a word that was in the dictionary. In the golden prime and high noon of English speech; when from the lips of the great Elizabethans fell words that made their own meaning and carried it in their very sound; when a Shakespeare and a Bacon were possible, and the language now rapidly perishing at one and slowly renewed at the other was in vigorous growth and hardy preservation— sweeter than honey and stronger than a lion —the lexicographer was a person unknown, the dictionary a creation which his Creator had not created him to create. (p. 110)

Ethnomethodology

Foundational question:

How do people make sense of their everyday activities so as to behave in socially acceptable ways?

Where heuristic inquiry focuses on issues of intense personal interest, ethnomethodology focuses on the ordinary, the routine, the details of everyday life. Harold Garfinkel (1967) invented the term. While working with the Yale cross-cultural files, Garfinkel came across such labels as "ethnobotany," "ethnophysiology," and "ethnophysics." At the time he was studying jurors. He decided that the deliberation methods of the jurors, or for that matter of any group, constituted an "ethnomethodology" wherein *ethno* refers to the "availability to a member of common-sense knowledge of his society as common-sense knowledge of the 'whatever' " (Turner 1974:16). For the jurors this was their ordinary, everyday understanding of what it meant to deliberate as a juror. Such an understanding made jury duty possible.

Ethnomethodology studies the social order "by combining a phenomenological sensibility with a paramount concern for everyday social practice" (Gubrium and Holstein 2000:490). Wallace and Wolf (1980) defined ethnomethodology as follows: "If we translated the 'ethno' part of the term as 'members' (of a group) or 'folk' or 'people,' then the term's meaning can be stated as: members' methods of making sense of their social world" (p. 263). Ethnomethodology gets at the norms, understandings, and assumptions that are taken for granted by people in a setting because they are so deeply understood that people don't even think about why they do what they do. It studies "the ordinary methods that ordinary people use to realize their ordinary actions" (Coulon 1995:2). Rooted in phenomenology, ethnomethodology has been particularly important in sociology.

> Ethnomethodology is, as the name suggests, a study of methods. It asks not why, but how. It asks how people get things done—how they transform situations or how they persevere, situation "unchanged," step by step, and moment to moment. As its name also suggests, it is interested in ordinary methods, the methods of the people rather than their theorists. (Watson and Goulet 1998:97)

Ethnomethodologists elucidate what a complete stranger would have to learn to become a routinely functioning member of a group, a program, or a culture. To do this, ethnomethodologists conduct depth interviews and undertake participant observation. They stray from the nonmanipulative and unobtrusive strategies of most qualitative inquiry in employing "ethnomethodological experiments." During these experiments, the researcher "violates the scene" and disrupts ordinary activity by do-

ing something out of the ordinary. A very simple and well-known such experiment is turning to face the other people on an elevator instead of facing the doors. When they conduct such qualitative experiments, "the researchers are interested in what the subjects do and what they look to in order to give the situation an appearance of order, or to 'make sense' of the situation" (Wallace and Wolf 1980:278). Garfinkel (1967) offered a number of such experiments (see especially pp. 38, 42, 47, 79, and 85).

Ethnomethodologists also have special interests in observing naturally occurring experiments where people are thrust into new or unexpected situations that require them to make sense of what is happening, "situations in which meaning is problematic" (Wallace and Wolf 1980:280). Such situations include intake into a program, immigration clearance centers, the first few weeks in a new school or job, and major transition points or critical incidents in the lives of people, programs, and organizations.

In some respects, ethnomethodologists attempt to make explicit what might be called the group's "tacit knowledge," to extend Polanyi's (1967) idea of tacit knowledge from the individual to the group. Heuristic inquiry reveals tacit knowledge through introspection and intersubjective inquiry with coresearchers. Ethnomethodologists get at a group's tacit knowledge by forcing it to the surface through disrupting violations of ordinary experience, since ordinary routines are what keep tacit knowledge at an unconscious, tacit level.

In short, ethnomethodologists "bracket or suspend their own belief in reality to study the reality of everyday life" (Taylor and Bogdan 1984:11). Elucidating the taken-for-granted realities of everyday life in a program or organization can become a force for understanding, change, and establishing a new reality based on the kind of everyday environment desired by people in the setting being studied. The findings of an ethnomethodological evaluation study would create a programmatic self-awareness that would, in principle at least, facilitate program change and improvement.

Symbolic Interaction

Foundational question:
  What common set of symbols
  and understandings has emerged
  to give meaning to people's
  interactions?

Symbolic interaction is a social-psychological approach most closely associated with George Herbert Mead (1934) and Herbert Blumer (1969). It is a perspective that places great emphasis on the importance of meaning and interpretation as essential human processes in reaction against behaviorism and mechanical stimulus-response psychology. People create shared meanings through their interactions, and those meanings become their reality. Blumer articulated three major premises as fundamental to symbolic interactionism:

1. Human beings act toward things on the basis of the meanings that the things have for them.

2. The meaning of things arises out of the social interaction one has with one's fellows.

3. The meanings of things are handled in and modified through an interpretative process used by the person in dealing with the things he or she encounters.

These premises led Blumer to qualitative inquiry as the only real way of understanding how people perceive, understand, and interpret the world. Only through close contact and direct interaction with people in open-minded, naturalistic inquiry and inductive analysis could the symbolic interactionist come to understand the symbolic world of the people being studied. Blumer was also one of the first to use *group* discussion and interview methods with key informants. He considered a carefully selected group of naturally acute observers and well-informed people to be a real "panel of experts" about a setting or situation, experts who would take the researcher inside the phenomenon of interest, for example, drug use. As we shall see in the chapter on interviewing, group interviews and focus groups have now become highly valued and widely used qualitative methods.

Labeling theory—the proposition that what people are called has major consequences for social interaction—has been a primary focus of inquiry in symbolic interaction. For example, using a sample of 46 participants in a 12-step group, Debtors Anonymous, Hayes (2000) studied how people who are unable to manage their finances responsibly come to feel shame. In program evaluation, labeling theory can be applied to such terms as *dropouts* and *at-risk* youth because language matters to staff and participants and can affect how they approach attaining desired outcomes (Hopson 2000; Patton 2000).

Though this theoretical perspective emerged in the 1930s, symbolic interactionists are showing that they can keep up with the times, for example, by applying their perspective to "cybersex" on the Internet. Waskul, Douglass, and Edgley (2000) have suggested that the new technologies of computer-mediated communication

allow us to examine the nature of human interaction in a uniquely disembodied environment that potentially transforms the nature of self, body, and situation. Sex—fundamentally a bodily activity—provides an ideal situation for examining these kinds of potential transformations. In the disembodied context of on-line interaction both bodies and selves are fluid symbolic constructs emergent in communication and are defined by sociocultural standards. Situations such as these are suggestive of issues related to contemporary transgressions of the empirical shell of the body, potentially reshaping body-to-self-to-social-world relationships. (p. 375)

For our purposes, the importance of symbolic interactionism to qualitative inquiry is its distinct emphasis on the importance of symbols and the interpretative processes that undergird interactions as fundamental to understanding human behavior. For program evaluation, organizational development, and other applied research, the study of the original meaning and influence of symbols and shared meanings can shed light on what is most important to people, what will be most resistant to change, and what will be most necessary to change if the program or organization is to move in new directions. The subject matter and methods of symbol interactionism also emphasize the importance of paying attention to how particular interactions give rise to symbolic understandings when one is engaged in changing symbols as part of a program improvement or organizational development process.

A related theoretical tradition informing some qualitative inquiry is *semiotics*, a blend of linguistics and social science, which focuses on the analysis of signs by studying the rules or forms of language as well as the relationship between language and human behavior (Manning 1987). "The importance of a study of language, as opposed to a scien-

tific study of a space-time event like a solar eclipse or rat behavior," Walker Percy (1990:150) has explained, "is that as soon as one scratches the surface of the familiar and comes face to face with the nature of language," one also finds oneself face to face with the nature and essence of being human. This is so because semiotics, in working to "unite logical analysis with the explanatory enterprise of science" (p. 243), has hit upon the fruitful insight that humans are distinctively sign-using and symbol-generating animals. Thus, semiotics offers a framework for "analyzing talk and text" (Silverman 2000:826) or studying "organizational symbolism" (Jones 1996). The foundational question of semiotics is: How do signs (words, symbols) carry and convey meaning in particular contexts?

Hermeneutics

Foundational question:
    What are the conditions under which a human act took place or a product was produced that make it possible to interpret its meanings?

In this brief (or not-so-brief, *depending on your perspective*) excursion through the variety of qualitative inquiry, we depart now from phenomenology and its derivative approaches: heuristic research, ethnomethodology, and symbolic interactionism. Hermeneutics is yet a different theoretical approach that can inform qualitative inquiry and also help put all the other theoretical orientations in this chapter in perspective in that it reminds us that what something means depends on the cultural context in which it was originally created as well as the cultural context within which it is subsequently interpreted. This is a reminder that each of the theoretical perspectives presented in this chapter emerged from a particular context to address specific concerns at that time. As we adopt and adapt those perspectives to current inquiries, we do so in a different historical, scholarly, and cultural context.

Hermeneutic philosophy, first developed by Frederich Schleiermacher (1768-1834) and applied to human science research by Wilhelm Dilthey (1833-1911) and other German philosophers, focuses on the problem of *interpretation*. Hermeneutics provides a theoretical framework for interpretive understanding, or meaning, with special attention to context and original purpose. The term *hermeneutics* derives from the Greek word *hermeneuein*, meaning to understand or interpret.

> There is an obvious link between *hermeneuein* and the god Hermes. Hermes is the fleet-footed divine messenger (he has wings on his feet!). As a messenger, he is the bearer of knowledge and understanding. His task is to explain to humans the decisions of the gods. Whether *hermeneuein* derives from Hermes or the other way round is not certain. (Crotty 1998:88)

In modern usage, hermeneutics offers a perspective for interpreting legends, stories, and other texts, especially biblical and legal texts. To make sense of and interpret a text, it is important to know what the author wanted to communicate, to understand intended meanings, and to place documents in a historical and cultural context (Palmer 1969). Following that principle, hermeneutics itself must be understood as part of a 19th- and 20th-century "broad movement away from an empiricist, logical atomistic, designative, representational account of meaning and knowledge.... Logical empiri-cism worked from a conception of knowledge as correct representation of an independent reality and was (is) almost exclusively interested in the issue of establishing the validity of scientific knowledge claims" (Schwandt 2000:196). In other words, hermeneutics challenged the assertion that an interpretation can ever be absolutely correct or true. It must remain only and always an *interpretation*. The meaning of a text, then, is negotiated among a community of interpreters, and to the extent that some agreement is reached about meaning at a particular time and place, that meaning can only be based on consensual community validation. Texts, then, must be "situated" within some literacy context (Barton, Hamilton, and Ivanic 1999).

Kvale (1987) has suggested,

> The attempts to develop a logic of validation within the hermeneutical tradition are relevant for clarifying the validity of interpretation in the qualitative research interview.
>
> The interpretation of meaning is characterized by a *hermeneutical circle,* or spiral. The understanding of a text takes place through a process where the meaning of the separate parts is determined by the global meaning of text. In principle, such a hermeneutical explication of the text is an infinite process while it ends in practice when a sensible meaning, a coherent understanding, free of inner contradictions has been reached. (p. 62)

Kneller (1984) has offered four principles for hermeneutic inquiry and analysis that can be applied beyond the interpretation of legends, literature, and historical documents:

1. Understanding a human act or product, and hence all learning, is like interpreting a text.

2. All interpretation occurs within a tradition.

3. Interpretation involves opening myself to a text (or its analogue) and questioning it.

4. I must interpret a text in the light of my situation (p. 68).

Hermeneutic researchers use qualitative methods to establish context and meaning for what people do. Hermeneutists "are much clearer about the fact that they are *constructing* the 'reality' on the basis of their interpretations of data with the help of the participants who provided the data in the study. . . . If other researchers had different backgrounds, used different methods, or had different purposes, they would likely develop different types of reactions, focus on different aspects of the setting, and develop somewhat different scenarios" (Eichelberger 1989:9). For concrete examples of hermeneutic investigations in psychology, see Packer and Addison (1989).

Thus, one must know about the researcher as well as the researched to place any qualitative study in a proper, hermeneutic context. Hermeneutic theory argues that one can only interpret the meaning of something from some perspective, a certain standpoint, a praxis, or a situational context, whether one is reporting on one's own findings or reporting the perspectives of people being studied (and thus reporting their standpoint or perspective). These ideas have become commonplace in much contemporary social science and are now fundamental, even basic, in qualitative inquiry, but such was not always the case. Two centuries of philosophical dialogue provide our current foundation for understanding the centrality of interpretivism in qualitative research. As Crotty (1998) concluded after his review of the historical development of hermeneutics and its influence on qualitative theory, "Our debt to the hermeneutic tradition is large" (p. 111).

Narratology or Narrative Analysis

Foundational questions:
What does this narrative or story reveal about the person and world from which it came? How can this narrative be interpreted so that it provides an understanding of and illuminates the life and culture that created it?

Hermeneutics originated in the study of written texts. Narratology, or narrative analysis, extends the idea of text to include in-depth interview transcripts, life history narratives, historical memoirs, and creative nonfiction. The hermeneutical perspective, with its emphasis on interpretation and context, informs narrative studies, as do interpretivist social science, literary nonfiction, and literary criticism. Narrative studies are also influenced by phenomenology's emphasis on understanding lived experience and perceptions of experience. "Todorov coined the term *narratology* in 1969 in an effort to elevate the form 'to the status of an object of knowledge for a new science' " (Riessman 1993:1).

Personal narratives, family stories, suicide notes, graffiti, literary nonfiction, and life histories reveal cultural and social patterns through the lens of individual experiences. Rhetoric of all kinds can be fodder for narrative analysis, for example, the rhetoric of politicians or teachers (Graham 1993). The "biographical turn in social science" (Chamberlayne et al. 2000) or the "narrative turn" in qualitative inquiry (Bochner 2001) honors people's stories as data that can stand on their own as pure description of experience, worthy as narrative documentary of *experience* (the core of phenomenology) or analyzed for connections between the psychological, sociological, cultural, political, and dramatic dimensions of human experience. Robert Coles, Harvard professor of psychiatry and medical humanities (his title offers interesting narratological fodder), has written *The Call of Stories* (1989) as a basis for teaching, learning, and moral reflection. Michael White and David Epston in *Narrative Means to Therapeutic Ends* (1990) look at the power of stories in the lives of individuals and families and the connection between storytelling and therapy. They suggest that people have adjustment difficulties because the story of their life, as created by themselves or others, does not match their *lived experience*. They propose that therapists can help their patients by guiding them in rewriting their life stories.

The idea of "story," of personal narrative, intersects with our earlier look at autoethnography in which the researcher's story becomes part of the inquiry into a cultural phenomenon of interest. The language of story carries a connotation different from that of case study. For example, in program evaluations, people may be invited to share their stories instead of being asked to participate in case studies. The central idea of narrative analysis is that stories and narratives offer especially translucent windows into cultural and social meanings.

Much of the methodological focus in narrative studies concerns the nature of interpretation, as in Norman Denzin's seminal qualitative works *Interpretive Biography* (1989a), *Interpretive Interactionism* (1989b), and *Interpretive Ethnography* (1997b). Interpretation of narrative poses the problem of how to analyze "talk and text" (Silverman 2000). Tom Barone (2000) has entered into literary nonfiction to hone his interpretive aesthetic:

All great literature, I think, lures those who experience it away from the shores of literal truth and out into uncharted waters where meaning is more ambiguous. . . .

Ultimately, I erased the boundary between the realm of text which purports to give only the facts and that of the metaphor-laden story which dares (as Sartre once put it) to lie in order to tell the truth. But I did so haltingly, and not in a single confident stroke of understanding. Indeed, my insight came only gradually, after confronting a form of writing that aims to straddle the boundary between actual and virtual worlds, one foot firmly planted in each. These works are hybrids of textual species, essays/stories written in a literary style but shelved (curiously) in the nonfiction section of the library. (pp. 61-62)

Here we have an example of personal narrative in the form of the narrative researcher's report of his journey into cross-genre exploration of the nature of textual interpretation. Later he uses narrative as a method for exploring what it means to be a professional educational researcher, exploring the narratives researchers construct about themselves and implications of those narratives for their relationships with non-researchers (Barone 2000:201-28).

Tierney (2000), in contrast, examines historical biographies and *testimonios* to explore interpretive challenges in using life histories in the postmodern age. His narrative analysis looks at the intersection of the interpreted purpose of a text, the constructed and interpreted "truth" of a text, and the *persona* of the author in text creation, all of which are called into interpretive question in the postmodern age.

Tedlock (2000) examines different genres of ethnography as constituting varying forms of narrative. She distinguishes life histories and memoirs from "narrative ethnography," a hybrid form that was created

Budding narratologist

in and attempts to portray accurately the biographies of people in the culture studied but also to include ethnographers' own experiences in their texts. She assesses this as a "sea change in ethnographic representa-

tion" because it unsettled "the boundaries that had been central to the notion of a self studying an other" and replaced it with an "ethnographic interchange" between self and other within a single text (pp. 460-61).

Narrative analysis has also now emerged as a specific approach to studying organizations. As such, it takes at least four forms:

1. organizational research that is written in storylike fashion (tales from the field);

2. organizational research that collects organizational stories (tales of the field);

3. organizational research that conceptualizes organizational life as story making and organizational theory as story reading (interpretative approaches); and

4. a disciplinary reflection that takes the form of literary critique (Czarniawska 1998:13-14).

Stories are at the center of narrative analysis, whether they be stories of teaching (Preskill and Jacobvitz 2000), stories of and by students (Barone 2000:119-31), stories of participants in programs (Kushner 2000), stories of fieldwork (Van Maanen 1988), stories of relationships (Bochner, Ellis, and Tillman-Healy 1997), or stories of illness (Frank 1995, 2000). How to interpret stories and, more specifically, the texts that tell the stories, is at the heart of narrative analysis.

Ecological Psychology

Foundational question:
What is the relationship between human behavior and the environment?

Several theoretical perspectives that inform qualitative inquiry are associated with particular disciplines. For example, hermeneutics is derived from linguistics and philosophy. Ethnography is the primary method of anthropology, while ethnomethodology and symbolic interaction developed out of sociology. Heuristic inquiry is grounded in humanistic psychology. A different psychology-based perspective is *ecological psychology*, which represents a different tradition and theoretical orientation because it makes different assumptions about what is important to understand about the human experience (Jacob 1987).

Robert Barker (1968) and Herbert Wright (1967) of the University of Kansas developed ecological psychology drawing heavily on natural history field studies. They see individuals and the environment as interdependent (Barker and Wright 1955; Barker et al. 1978; Schoggen 1978). They begin with pure, detailed descriptions of an individual in an environment. They observe (as spectators, *not* participant observers) "streams of behavior" that are subsequently analyzed in terms of presumed goal-directed actions. "Coders draw upon their ordinary knowledge and perceptions to infer the goals that actors intend to achieve, marking off segments of narrative descriptions into segments leading toward specific goals" (Jacob 1988:17). The ecological metaphor can also inform psychological clinical research by seeking "to understand the patient's concern within the context of his or her life world—the patient's personal, family, community, and ecological stories" (Miller and Crabtree 2000:617).

The unit of analysis in ecological psychology is primarily the individual, but Barker and Schoggen (1973) have also applied this approach in delineating *Qualities of Community Life*. What makes this approach of potential interest for program evaluation and organizational or community development is the focus on goal-directed behavior.

They assume that there are subjective aspects to behavior which they examine in terms of the goals of human behavior. They also assume that there is a subjective aspect to the environments which they usually discuss in terms of a person's emotional reactions to the environment. For example, they might be concerned whether a boy does an activity unwillingly or unhappily. (Jacob 1988:17)

Ecological psychologists also focus on delineating the central features of *behavior settings,* the particular constellations of places, things, and times that constitute a definitive environment. Such an approach can help make explicit what variety of environments program participants or organization members experience.

While ecological psychologists begin with detailed, qualitative descriptions based on observations in natural environments, their coding schemes and analysis procedures are quantitative. Segments of goal-directed behavior and characteristics of behavior settings are coded numerically and analyzed statistically. This illustrates a point to which we shall return later: One can go from the thick description of qualitative data to quantitative analysis, but not vice versa. One cannot generate thick description and qualitative narrative from original quantitative data.

The focus in ecological psychology on the relationship between human behavior and the environment provides a good transition to the next perspective, systems theory, which is much more comprehensive and interdisciplinary in examining the context for human actions in programs, organizations, and communities.

A Systems Perspective and Systems Theory

Foundational question:
How and why does this system as a whole function as it does?

LITERARY ECOLOGY

"Literary ecology is the study of biological themes and relationships which appear in literary works. It is simultaneously an attempt to discover what roles have been played by literature in the ecology of the human species. Many academic disciplines must contribute to the study of literary ecology. Literary form must be reconciled if possible with the forms and structures of nature as they are defined by ecological scientists, for both are related to human perceptions of beauty and balance. Characters in literature may also be analyzed as typical or atypical representatives of the human species, and their behavior compared to patterns of behavior among other animals as described by contemporary ethology. Philosophical ideas defining the relationship between humans and nature are often expressed or implied in literary works, revealing a history of human beliefs concerning the meaning of natural processes, and also revealing the cultural ideologies which have contributed to our contemporary ecological crisis. Most important, literary ecology makes it possible for us to study the function of literary art as it influences the survival of the human species" (Meeker 1980:29).

Parallel to the historical philosophical and methodological paradigms debate between positivists and constructivists, there has been another and corresponding paradigms debate about mechanistic/linear constructions of the world versus organic/systems constructions. This debate has been particularly intense among classic organizational theorists (Burns and Stalker 1972; Azumi and Hage 1972; Lincoln 1985; Gharajedaghi 1985; Morgan 1986, 1989). It includes concern about definitions of closed systems versus open systems, and the implications of such boundary definitions for research, theory, and practice in understanding programs, organizations, entire societies, and even the whole world (Wallerstein 1980).

It is important to note at the outset that the term *systems* has many and varied meanings. In the digital age, systems analysis often means looking at the interface between hardware and software, or the connectivity of various networks. The idea of "systems thinking" was popularized as the crucial "fifth discipline" of organizational learning in Peter Senge's (1990) best-selling book. A number of management consultants have made systems thinking and analysis the centerpiece of their organizational development work (e.g., Ackoff 1987, 1999a, 1999b; Kim 1993, 1994, 1999; Anderson and Johnson 1997). Indeed, over the past 30 years, since publication of Ludwig Von Bertalanffy's classic *General System Theory* (1976), a vast literature has developed about systems theory and applied systems research (e.g., Checkland 1999). Some of it is highly quantitative and involves complex computer applications and simulations. Given this broad and multifaceted context, my purpose is quite modest. I want to call to the reader's attention three points: (1) A systems perspective is becoming increasingly important in dealing with and understanding real-world complexities, viewing things as whole entities embedded in context and still larger wholes; (2) some approaches to systems research lead directly to and depend heavily on qualitative inquiry; and (3) a systems orientation can be very helpful in framing questions and, later, making sense out of qualitative data.

Holistic thinking is central to a systems perspective. A system is a whole that is both greater than and different from its parts. Indeed, a system cannot validly be divided into independent parts as discrete entities of inquiry because the effects of the behavior of the parts on the whole depend on what is happening to the other parts. The parts are so interconnected and interdependent that any simple cause-effect analysis distorts more than it illuminates. Changes in one part lead to changes among all parts and the system itself. Nor can one simply add the parts in some linear fashion and get a useful sense of the whole.

Gharajedaghi and Ackoff (1985:23) are quite insistent that a system as a whole cannot be understood by analysis of separate parts. They argue that "the essential properties of a system are lost when it is taken apart; for example, a disassembled automobile does not transport and a disassembled person does not live." Furthermore, the function and meaning of the parts are lost when separated from the whole. Instead of taking things apart, they insist that a systems approach requires "synthetic thinking":

Synthetic thinking is required to explain system behavior. It differs significantly from analysis. In the first step of analysis the thing to be explained is taken apart: in synthetic thinking it is taken to be a part of a larger whole. In the second step of analysis, the contained parts are explained: in synthetic thinking, the containing whole is explained. In the final step of analysis, knowledge of the parts is aggregated into knowledge of the whole: in synthetic thinking understanding of the containing whole is disaggregated to explain the parts. It does so by revealing their *role* or *function* in that whole. Synthetic thinking reveals function rather than structure: it reveals why a system works the way it does, but not how it does so. Analysis and synthesis are complementary: neither replaces the other. Systems thinking incorporates both.

Because the effects of the behavior of the parts of a system are interdependent, it can be shown that if each part taken separately is made to perform as efficiently as possible, the system as a whole will not function as effectively as possible. For example, if we select from all the automobiles available the best carburetor, the best distributor, and so on for each part required for an automobile, and then try to assemble them, we will not even obtain an automobile, let alone the best one, because *the parts will not fit together.* The performance of a system is not the sum of the independent effects of its parts; it is the product of their interactions. Therefore, effective management of a system requires managing the interactions of its parts, not the actions of its parts taken separately. (Gharajedaghi and Ackoff 1985:23-24)

This kind of systems thinking has profound implications for program evaluation and policy analysis where the parts are often evaluated in terms of strengths, weaknesses, and impacts with little regard for how the parts are embedded in and interdependent with the whole program or policy (Patton 1999c). For example, Benko and Sarvimaki (2000) applied systems theory as a framework for patient-focused evaluation in nursing and other health care areas. Such a framework, they found, allowed complex features of processes in health care to appear by conducting simultaneous analyses of relationships on different levels and with different methods. This contrasts with the mostly one-level, reductionist designs that have usually been employed in nursing and health care research. Their "systemic model" offered insights into system dynamics in both "downward" and "upward" directions—and the interconnections of these systems dynamics in affecting patient care and outcomes.

In addition to their influence in organizational development, systems approaches

have become very important in family research and therapy (Schultz 1984; Montgomery and Fewer 1988; Rosenblatt 1985; Miller and Winstead-Fry 1982; Hoffman 1981). A systems approach has also become one of the central orientations to international development efforts in recent years. Specifically, the farming systems approach to development (Farming Systems Support Project [FSSP] 1986) illustrates some unique ways of engaging in qualitative inquiry to support development, intervention, and evaluation from a systems perspective. The farming systems approach to evaluation and research is worth examining in detail because it has developed as a theory-based yet practical solution to agricultural development problems.

In the first three decades following World War II, much international development was conceived as direct technology transfer from more developed to less developed countries. Scientists and change agents made technology transfer recommendations within their disciplinary areas of specialization, for example, crops, livestock, water, and so on. This approach to development epitomized a mechanistic orientation.

In reaction to the dismal failures of the mechanistic, specialized technology transfer approach to development, a farming systems approach emerged (Shaner, Philipp, and Schmehl 1982b). Several elements are central to a farming systems perspective, elements that lead directly to qualitative methods of research.

1. Farming systems research and development (FSRD) is a *team effort* (Shaner, Philipp, and Schmehl 1982a).

2. FSRD is *interdisciplinary.* The team consists of representatives from a mix of both agricultural and social science disciplines (Cernea and Guggenheim 1985).

3. FSRD takes place *in the field,* on real farms, not at a university or government experiment station (Simmons 1985).

4. FSRD is *collaborative*—scientists and farmers work together on agricultural productivity within the goals, values, and situation of participating farmers (Galt and Mathema 1987).

5. FSRD is *comprehensive,* including attention to all farm family members; all farming operations, both crops and livestock; all labor sources; all income sources; and all other factors that affect small farm development (Harwood 1979).

6. FSRD is *inductive and exploratory,* beginning by open-ended inquiry into the nature of the farming system from the perspective of those in the system (Holtzman 1986).

7. FSRD begins with *qualitative description.* The first team task is fieldwork to qualitatively describe the system (Sands 1986).

8. FSRD is *sensitive to context,* placing the farming system in the larger agro-ecological, cultural, political, economic, and policy environments of which it is a part (Shaner et al. 1982a).

9. FSRD is *interactive, dynamic, and process oriented.* The interdisciplinary team begins with inductive exploration, then moves to trying out system changes, observing the effects, and adapting to emergent findings. The work is ongoing and developmental (FSSP 1986).

10. FSRD is *situationally responsive and adaptive.* There are many variations in FSRD projects depending on priority problems, available resources, team member preferences, and situation-specific possibilities (Sands 1986; FSSP 1987).

A farming systems approach includes both qualitative and quantitative forms of inquiry. It includes direct observations, informal interviews, naturalistic fieldwork, and inductive analysis, all within a systems framework. Well over 100 such projects in FSRD have been undertaken worldwide (FSSP 1987). There may be no larger-scale example of efforts to integrate naturalistic inquiry, quantitative methods, and a systems perspective through interdisciplinary evaluation and research teamwork for the purpose of promoting long-term social and economic developments.

FSRD is just one example of a systems approach to intervention, research, and evaluation. What this and other systems approaches illustrate is that the complex world of human beings cannot be fully captured and understood by simply adding up carefully measured and fully analyzed parts. At the *system* level (the whole program, the whole farm, the whole family, the whole organization, the whole community), there is a qualitative difference in the kind of thinking that is required to make sense of what is happening. Qualitative inquiry facilitates that qualitative difference in understanding human or "purposeful systems" (Ackoff and Emery 1982).

A final story will reinforce this point, the fable of the nine blind people and the elephant, which I used in the second chapter to illustrate the importance of context, and which I repeat here because it illustrates so well the real challenge of systems thinking. Besides, good stories have layers of meaning, and this one has phenomenological, hermeneutic, and even ethnographic implications, which the reader may want to reflect on, but I'll simply reintroduce it as a systems tale. Ironically, it is often offered as an example of systems thinking, but is, in its usual Western telling, actually quite linear and mechanical.

As the story goes, nine blind people encounter an elephant. One touches the ear and proclaims that an elephant is like a fan. Another touches the trunk and says the elephant most surely resembles a snake. The third feels the elephant's massive side and insists that it is like a wall. Yet, a fourth, feeling a solidly planted leg, counters that it more resembles a tree trunk. The fifth grabs hold of the tail and experiences the elephant as a rope. And so it goes, each blindly touching only a part and generalizing inappropriately to the whole. The usual moral of the story is that only by putting all the parts together in right relation to each can one get a complete and whole picture of the elephant.

Yet, from a systems perspective, such a picture yields little real understanding of the elephant. To understand the elephant, it must be seen and understood in its natural ecosystem, whether in Africa or Asia, as one element in a complex system of flora and fauna. Only in viewing the movement of a herd of elephants across a real terrain, over time and across seasons, in interaction with plants, trees, and other animals will one begin to understand the evolution and nature of elephants and the system of which elephants are a part. That understanding can never come at a zoo.

Thus, are we reminded of the challenge —and importance—of bringing a systems perspective into qualitative inquiry.

Chaos and Complexity Theory: Nonlinear Dynamics

Foundational question:
What is the underlying order, if any, of disorderly phenomena?

What are disorderly phenomena? The weather, waterfalls, fluids in motion, volcanoes, galaxies—and human beings, human

groups, programs. Chaos or complexity theorists and researchers are primarily theoretical physicists, meteorologists, biologists, and other natural scientists. Chaos research has developed as a highly quantitative specialty requiring supercomputer calculations (Cambel 1992). But the assumptions that undergird chaos theory pose challenges to social science research at the most fundamental levels of basic conceptualization.

Complexity theory is already being viewed as a new paradigm of natural science (Nadel and Stein 1995; Murali 1995; Hall 1993; Holte 1993; Waldrop 1992; Gleick 1987; Cronbach 1988). At least at the level of metaphor, chaos and complexity notions are being used to inform approaches to economics (Ormerod 2001), anthropology (Agar 1999), organizational development (Eoyang 1997; Allison 2000), and leadership (Wheatley 1992). The concepts of system and complexity are often closely related. For example, the self-organization of systems, as premised by complexity theory, implies the maintenance of a certain level of organization or the improvement of the systems (Rhee 2000). As social scientists begin to understand its assumptions, complexity theory about nonlinear dynamics may become a new paradigm for approaching human complexities. In the meantime, theory and research about nonlinear dynamics (complexity) raise questions about how we bring order to what we observe—a fundamental epistemological problem for all forms of inquiry, including qualitative inquiry. In Exhibit 3.5 (p. 126), I offer some teasers from Gleick's (1987) popularization of chaos theory to suggest implications for qualitative inquiry.

At this point, complexity theory offers, perhaps more than anything else, a new set of metaphors for thinking about what we observe, how we observe, and what we know as a result of our observations. Chaos theory challenges our need for order and prediction, even as it offers new ways to fulfill those needs. While much chaos research is highly mathematical, making sense of results seems to depend heavily on metaphors. Here is an intersection with qualitative inquiry that holds particular promise because much work in qualitative analysis, organizational development, and programs includes resort to metaphor (Patton 2000; Ronai 1999; Brady 1998). Indeed, Gleick (1987) offers a metaphor to explain the very nature of inquiry into chaos: "It's like walking through a maze whose walls rearrange themselves with every step you take" (p. 24).

This metaphor fits a great deal of fieldwork in real-world settings, but the implications can be so threatening to our need for order that we ignore the rearranging walls and describe the maze with a single, static diagram. If nothing else, the history and emergent ideas of chaos theory may give us the comfort and courage to describe nonlinear dynamics (chaos) when we find it, without imposing false order to fulfill the presumed traditional purpose of analysis. Chaos theory challenges us to deal with unpredictability and indeterminism in human behavior (Cziko 1989)—and therefore in the interventions (programs) we devise to alter human behavior as well as the unpredictability and indeterminism of the methods we use to study and evaluate those interventions.

Michael Agar, a distinguished anthropologist, used complexity theory, especially the work of John Holland (1995, 1998), to interpret fieldwork findings in his study of a heroin epidemic among suburban youth in Baltimore County, Maryland. He concluded:

> Complexity [theory] served, at least at the metaphorical level, to better define a research problem—explaining heroin trends—and it helps articulate why traditional social research has not answered this most basic question of drug research: How and why do trends occur? It also points at the kind of data we need to obtain and organize to do just that, however difficult that data might be to obtain. Furthermore, complexity handles some current anthropological research issues—like the inclusion of the researcher, broadening historical and political context, and the issue of prediction—as part of its central themes. With characteristics like holism, emergence, and feedback that map onto anthropological assumptions more so than any previous formal models, complexity is clearly worth a closer look. (Agar 1999:119)

The metaphors of chaos, complexity, and nonlinear dynamics open up new possibilities for doing fieldwork in and understanding those settings that feel like walking through a maze whose walls rearrange themselves with every step you take.

Grounded Theory

*T*he grounded theory approach is the most influential paradigm for qualitative research in the social sciences today.

—Norman K. Denzin (1997a:18)

Foundational question:
  What theory emerges from
  systematic comparative analysis
  and is grounded in fieldwork so
  as to explain what has been and
  is observed?

Now we turn from the fluidity of chaos to the solidity of the ground, specifically, *grounded theory.* Most of the theoretical perspectives examined thus far focus on a particular aspect of human experience: Ethnography focuses on culture, ethnomethodology on everyday life, symbolic interactionism on symbolic meanings in behavior, semiotics on signs, hermeneutics on interpretations, and phenomenology on lived experience. Their theoretical frameworks direct us to particular aspects of human experience as especially deserving of attention in our attempt to make sense of the social world. In contrast, **grounded theory focuses on the process of generating theory rather than a particular theoretical content.** It emphasizes steps and procedures for connecting induction and deduction through the constant comparative method, comparing research sites, doing theoretical sampling, and testing emergent concepts with additional fieldwork.

Concern for theory development is often quite marked in the literature on qualitative methods. The writings of Glaser (1978, 2000), Strauss and Corbin (1998), Denzin (1978b), Lofland and Lofland (1984), Blumer (1969), Whyte (1984), and Becker (1970), to name but a few well-known qualitative methodologists, take as a major focus the task of theory construction and verification. What distinguishes the discussion of theory in much of the literature on qualitative methods is the *emphasis on inductive strate-gies of theory development* in contrast to theory generated by logical deduction from a priori assumptions.

In contrasting grounded theory with logico-deductive theory and discussing and assessing their relative merits in ability to fit and work (predict, explain, and be relevant), we have taken the position that the adequacy of a theory for sociology today cannot be divorced from the process by which it is generated. Thus one canon for judging the usefulness of a theory is how it was generated —and we suggest that it is likely to be a better theory to the degree that it has been inductively developed from social research. . . . Generating a theory from data means that most hypotheses and concepts not only come from the data, but are systematically worked out in relation to the data during the course of the research. *Generating a theory involves a process of research.* (Glaser and Strauss 1967:5-6)

This theory-method linkage is of great concern in many of the orientations examined in this chapter. The idea of a theory-method linkage means that how you study the world determines what you learn about the world. Grounded theory depends on methods that take the researcher into and close to the real world so that the results and findings are grounded in the empirical world. Herbert Blumer (1978) has offered a metaphor for explaining what it means to generate grounded theory by being immersed in the empirical world:

The empirical social world consists of on-going group life and one has to get close to this life to know what is going on in it. The metaphor that I like is that of lifting the veils that obscure or hide what is going on. The task of scientific study is to lift the veils that cover the area of group life that one purposes to study.

EXHIBIT 3.5	Complexity (Chaos) Theory Precepts and Qualitative Inquiry Implications

Chaos Precepts and Assumptions (Gleick 1987)	Implications for Qualitative Inquiry on Human Systems
1. "Nonlinearity means that the act of playing the game has a way of changing the rules" (p. 24).	1. The entry of the researcher into a setting may do more than create problems of validity and reactivity. The researcher's entry may make it a different setting altogether—and forever.
2. A butterfly in Beijing flapping its wings may affect the weather in New York—next month or next year. "The butterfly effect" has a technical name: Sensitive dependence on initial conditions (p. 23).	2. Small, minute events can make critical differences. Qualitative importance is not dependent on quantitative magnitude. For want of a nail . . . , the war was lost.
3. A deterministic system can produce much more than just periodic behavior. There can be "wild disorder" among "islands of structure." "A complex system can give rise to turbulence and coherence at the same time," each of which is important (p. 56).	3. Much qualitative analysis attempts to bring order from chaos, identifying patterns in the noise of human complexity. Chaos theory suggests we need to learn to observe, describe, and value disorder and turbulence without forcing patterns onto genuine, meaningful chaos.
4. "Simple systems can do complicated things" (p. 167).	4. What presumptions do we bring to field-work and analysis about *simplicity* and *complexity*? These are not neutral terms.
5. "A healthy body is a chaotic one; when you reach an equilibrium in biology you are dead" (p. 298).	5. How do we observe and describe dynamic, constantly changing phenomena without imposing a static structure by the very boundaries we create in seeking to define and understand?
6. "On the collective scale and on the personal scale, the ideas of chaos advance in different ways and for different reasons" (p. 316).	6. Chaos theory's meanings and implications for qualitative inquiry in human settings remain to be developed.

The veils are not lifted by substituting, in whatever degree, preformed images for first-hand knowledge. The veils are lifted by getting close to the area and by digging deep in it through careful study. Schemes of meth-odology that do not encourage or allow this betray the cardinal principle of respecting the nature of one's empirical world. . . . [T]he merit of naturalistic study is that it respects and stays close to the empirical domain. (p. 38)

All of the approaches to theory and research in this chapter use qualitative methods to stay grounded in the empirical world. Yet, they vary considerably in their conceptualizations of what is important to ask and consider in elucidating and understanding the empirical world. While the phrase "grounded theory" is often used as a general reference to inductive, qualitative analysis, as an identifiable approach to qualitative inquiry it consists of quite specific methods and systematic procedures (Glaser 2000, 2001). In their book on techniques and procedures for developing grounded theory, Strauss and Corbin (1998:13) emphasized that analysis is the interplay between researchers and data, so what grounded theory offers as a framework is a set of "coding procedures" to "help provide some standardization and rigor" to the analytical process. Grounded theory is meant to "build theory rather than test theory." It strives to "provide researchers with analytical tools for handling masses of raw data." It seeks to help qualitative analysts "consider alternative meanings of phenomenon." It emphasizes being "systematic and creative simultaneously." Finally, it elucidates "the concepts that are the building blocks of theory." Glaser (1993) and Strauss and Corbin (1997) have collected together in edited volumes a range of grounded theory exemplars that include several studies of health (life after heart attacks, emphysema, chronic renal failure, chronically ill men, tuberculosis, Alzheimer's disease), organizational headhunting, abusive relationships, women alone in public places, selfhood in women, prison time, and characteristics of contemporary Japanese society.

While grounded theory has become widely thought of as an approach specific to qualitative inquiry, Glaser (2000) does not limit it in that way:

Let me be clear. Grounded theory is a general method. It can be used on any data or combination of data. It was developed partially by me with quantitative data. It is expensive and somewhat hard to obtain quantitative data, especially in comparison to qualitative data. Qualitative data are inexpensive to collect, very rich in meaning and observation, and very rewarding to collect and analyze. So, by default, due to ease and growing use, grounded theory is being linked to qualitative data and is seen as a qualitative method, using symbolic interaction, by many. Qualitative grounded theory accounts for the global spread of its use.

I can only caution the reader not to confuse this empirical use and the spread of its use with the fact that it is a general method. In some quarters of research, grounded theory is considered qualitative, symbolic interaction research. It is a kind of takeover that makes routine qualitative research sound good by positive stigma. Only highly trained grounded theory researchers can see the difference and the confusion. Much of it revolves around the notion of emergence versus forcing and the lack of use of all the grounded theory methodological steps. Any kind of data can be constantly compared. However, it is prudent for researchers to go with qualitative grounded theory when that is where the resources are to do it and when that is where researchers can reap career and personal rewards. (p. 7)

Grounded theory has opened the door to qualitative inquiry in many traditional academic social science and education departments, especially as a basis for doctoral dissertations, in part, I believe, because of its overt emphasis on the importance of and specific procedures for generating theory. In addition, I suspect its popularity may owe much to the fact that it unabashedly admonishes the researcher to strive for "objectivity." As discussed earlier in this chapter, the postmodern attack on objectivity has found its way into qualitative inquiry through constructivism, hermeneutic interpretivism, and the emphasis on subjective experience in phenomenology. Emergent autoethnographic and heuristic approaches to qualitative inquiry place even greater emphasis on the researcher's personal and subjective experience. Those social scientists and academics who find some value in the methods of qualitative inquiry, namely, in-depth interviewing and observation, but who eschew the philosophical underpinnings of constructivism and interpretivism can find comfort in the attention paid to objectivity in grounded theory.

> It is important to maintain a balance between the qualities of objectivity and sensitivity when doing analysis. Objectivity enables the researcher to have confidence that his or her findings are a reasonable, impartial representation of a problem under investigation, whereas sensitivity enables creativity and the discovery of new theory from data. (Strauss and Corbin 1998:53)

At the same time, the language of "grounded theory" has found its way into the constructivist literature. Charmaz (2000) compares "objectivist" (reality-oriented) and constructivist approaches to grounded theory and, though she finds examples of both, believes that the majority of grounded theorists are objectivist in orientation.

> Objectivist grounded theory accepts the positivistic assumption of an external world that can be described, analyzed, explained, and predicted: truth, but with a small *t*. . . . It assumes that different observers will discover this world and describe it in similar ways. (p. 524)

She believes that the guidelines for grounded theory offered by Strauss and Corbin (1990, 1998) "structure objectivist grounded theorists' work. These guidelines are didactic and prescriptive rather than emergent and interactive" (Charmaz 2000: 524). In contrast, she believes that in a constructivist grounded theory, "causality is suggestive, incomplete, and indeterminate. . . . It looks at how 'variables' are grounded —given meaning and played out in subjects' lives. . . . Their meanings and actions take priority over researchers' analytic interests and methodological technology" (p. 524). To illustrate a constructivist approach to grounded theory, she presents to the reader the kinds of questions she would ask to study a topic such as pain:

> I start by viewing the topic of pain subjectively as a feeling, an experience that may take a variety of forms. Then I ask these questions: What makes pain, pain? (That is, what is essential to the phenomenon as defined by those who experience it?) What defining properties or characteristics do ill people attribute to it? When do they do so?. . . . How does the person experience this pain, and what, if anything, does he or she do about it? My questions aim to get at meaning, not at truth. As a result, a constructivist grounded theory may remain at a more intuitive, impressionistic level than an objectivist approach. (Charmaz 2000:526)

Beyond drawing on the inductive and layered emphases in grounded theory à la Strauss and Corbin, it is hard to see how what Charmaz describes is different from basic phenomenological inquiry. As a matter of philosophical distinctness, then, grounded theory is best understood as fundamentally realist and objectivist in orientation, emphasizing disciplined and procedural ways of getting the researcher's biases out of the way but adding healthy doses of creativity to the analytic process. We shall consider the analytic procedures of grounded theory in more detail in the chapter on analyzing qualitative data. As a theoretical framework, I have included it in this chapter because of its emphasis on generating theory as the primary purpose of qualitative social science and its overt embrace of objectivity as a research stance.

Orientational Qualitative Inquiry: Feminist Inquiry, Critical Theory, and Queer Theory as Examples

One of the strengths of qualitative methods is the inductive, naturalistic inquiry strategy of approaching a setting without predetermined hypotheses. Rather, understanding and theory emerge from fieldwork experiences and are grounded in the data. The problem is how to approach the field with an open mind. Phenomenology includes recommended procedures for becoming clear about and taking into account biases and predispositions during both fieldwork and analysis so as to get at the true essence of the phenomenon under study. Hermeneutics takes the position that nothing can be interpreted free of some perspective, so the first priority is to capture the perspective and elucidate the context of the people being studied. The researcher's own perspective must also be made explicit, as must any other tradition or perspective brought to bear when interpreting meanings.

Orientational qualitative inquiry goes one step farther. Orientational qualitative inquiry eschews any pretense of open-mindedness in the search for grounded or emergent theory. Orientational qualitative inquiry begins with an explicit theoretical or ideological perspective that determines what conceptual framework will direct fieldwork and the interpretation of findings. For example, one can undertake a study from a feminist perspective, a Marxist perspective, a capitalist perspective, or a Freudian perspective, among others. In these instances, the ideological *orientation* or perspective of the researcher determines the focus of inquiry.

A feminist perspective presumes the importance of gender in human relationships and societal processes and *orients* the study in that direction (Guerrero 1999b; Ribbens and Edwards 1998; Maguire 1996; Reinharz 1992; Glennon 1983; Smith 1979). Principles of feminist inquiry (Guerrero 1999a:15-22; Thompson 1992) can include

- a sense of connectedness and equality between researcher and researched;

- explicitly acknowledging and valuing "women's ways of knowing" including integrating reason, emotion, intuition, experience, and analytic thought;

- participatory processes that support consciousness-raising and researcher reflexivity; and

- going beyond knowledge generation, beyond "knowledge for its own sake," to engage in using knowledge for change, especially "knowledge about women that will contribute to women's liberation and emancipation" (Guerrero 1999a: 16-17).

How does the lens of gender shape and affect our understandings and actions?

Philosopher Elizabeth Minnich has investigated the ways in which conceptual approaches to classifying human beings, embedded historically, culturally, and politically, continue to shape our thinking through the very language and categories available to us. Her book on the subject,

Transforming Knowledge (1990, forthcoming), speaks precisely and insightfully to the orientation of feminist inquiry.

> The *root problem* reappears in different guises in all fields and throughout the dominant tradition. It is, simply, that while the majority of humankind was excluded from education and the making of what has been called knowledge, *the dominant few not only defined themselves as the inclusive kind of human but also as the norm and the ideal.* A few privileged men defined themselves as constituting mankind/humankind and simultaneously saw themselves as akin to what mankind/humankind ought to be in fundamental ways that distinguished them from all others. Thus, at the same time they removed women and non-privileged men within their culture and other cultures from "mankind," they justified that exclusion on the grounds that the excluded were by nature and culture "lesser" people (if they even thought of the others as having "cultures"). Their notion of who was properly human was *both* exclusive *and* hierarchical with regard to those they took to be properly subject to them—women in all roles; men who worked with their hands; male servants and slaves; women and men from many other cultures.
>
> Thus, they created root definitions of what it means to be human that, with the concepts and theories that flowed from and reinforced those definitions, made it difficult to think well about, or in the mode of, anyone other than themselves, just as they made it difficult to think honestly about the defining few. (Minnich 1990:37-38)

The concepts and conceptual frameworks we use, whether unconsciously as a matter of tradition and training or intentionally as a matter of choice, carry embedded messages about what and who is important. Feminist inquiry challenges the phenomenological notion that one can cleanse oneself of such fundamental language-based conceptions when doing fieldwork and data analysis. Moreover, feminist inquiry provides not only conceptual and analytical direction but also methodological orientation in emphasizing participatory, collaborative, change-oriented, and empowering forms of inquiry.

A quite different theoretical framing for inquiry would be a Freudian orientation that assumes that individual behavior must be understood as a manifestation of the struggle between id, ego, and superego as influenced by very early childhood relationships and sexual experiences that have left their mark on the unconscious. Orientations can be combined, as in a feminist psychoanalytical framework (Eichenbaum and Orbach 1983).

Racism and ethnicity can be another defining lens—or orientation—for qualitative inquiry in research and evaluation (Ladson-Billings 2000; Stanfield 1999; Patton 1999d), as can inclusiveness (Mertens 1998, 1999). "Queer theory," an orientational approach focused on sexual orientation, "took social constructionist insights and added a post-structuralist critique of the unified, autonomous self," so a lesbian, gay, bisexual, and transgender orientation informs inquiry as "a deconstructive enterprise, taking apart the view of a self defined by something at its core, be it sexual desire, race, gender, nation, or class" (Gamson 2000:348).

One of the most influential orientational frameworks is "critical theory," which focuses on how injustice and subjugation shape people's experiences and understandings of the world.

> A critical social theory is concerned in particular with issues of power and justice and the ways that the economy, matters of race, class, and gender, ideologies, discourses, education,

religion and other social institutions and cultural dynamics interact to construct a social system. . . . Inquiry that aspires to the name *critical* must be connected to an attempt to confront the injustice of a particular society. . . . Research thus becomes a transformative endeavor unembarrassed by the label *political* and unafraid to consummate a relationship with emancipatory consciousness. (Kincheloe and McLaren 2000:281, 291)

Thus, what gives critical theory its name —what makes it *critical*—is that it seeks not just to study and understand society but rather to critique and change society. Influenced by Marxism, informed by the presumption of the centrality of class conflict in understanding community and societal structures (Crotty 1998; Heydebrand 1983; Carchedi 1983), and updated in the radical struggles of the 1960s, critical theory provides a framework—both philosophy and methods—for approaching research and evaluation as fundamentally and explicitly political, and as change-oriented forms of engagement. Fonte (2001) offers an example of critical theory applied to public policy. Fonte applies the perspective of Marxist intellectual Antonio Gramsci to contemporary American politics, considering how dominant and subordinate groups based on race and gender struggle over power in ways that make every aspect of life political.

Within any of these theoretical or ideological orientations one can undertake qualitative inquiry, but the focus of inquiry is determined by the framework within which one is operating and findings are interpreted and given meaning from the perspective of that preordinate theory. Such qualitative inquiry, therefore, aims to describe and explain *specific* manifestations of already-presumed general patterns. Such inquiry is aimed at confirmation and elucidation rather than discovery. I have chosen the

term *orientational* to describe such studies because they are oriented in a particular direction or framed from a specific perspective. *Orientational* is a more neutral term than ideologically based inquiry.

The extent to which any particular study is orientational is a matter of degree. Ethnographic studies can be viewed as orientational to the extent that they presume the centrality of culture in explaining human experience. "Critical ethnography" (Thomas 1993) combines the focus on culture with the commitment to use findings for change. Symbolic interactionism is orientational in focusing on the importance of the meanings that emerge as people define situations through interpersonal interactions. Orientational qualitative inquiry is a legitimate and important approach to theoretical or ideological elaboration, confirmation, and elucidation. **What is required is that the researcher be very clear about the theoretical framework being used and the implications of that perspective on study focus, data collection, fieldwork, and analysis.**

Variety in Qualitative Inquiry: Different Answers to Core Questions

Exhibit 3.6 summarizes the theoretical and philosophical perspectives presented in this chapter. This is not an exhaustive list of theoretical possibilities, but it does include the most common conceptual and philosophical frameworks—and it certainly documents the variety of perspectives that can inform qualitative inquiry.

No consensus exists about how to classify the varieties of qualitative research. As noted in the opening of this chapter, but worth repeating as a review of variety in qualitative inquiry, Crotty (1998:5) elabo-

---

EXHIBIT 3.6 | Variety in Qualitative Inquiry: Theoretical Traditions

Perspective	Disciplinary Roots	Central Questions
1. Ethnography	Anthropology	What is the culture of this group of people?
2. Autoethnography	Literary arts	How does my own experience of this culture connect with and offer insights about this culture, situation, event, and/or way of life?
3. Reality testing: Positivist and realist approaches	Philosophy, social sciences, and evaluation	What's really going on in the real world? What can we establish with some degree of certainty? What are plausible explanations for verifiable patterns? What's the truth insofar as we can get at it? How can we study a phenomenon so that our findings correspond, as much as possible, to the real world?
4. Constructionism/ constructivism	Sociology	How have the people in this setting constructed reality? What are their reported perceptions, "truths," explanations, beliefs, and worldview? What are the consequences of their constructions for their behaviors and for those with whom they interact?
5. Phenomenology	Philosophy	What is the meaning, structure, and essence of the lived experience of this phenomenon for this person or group of people?
6. Heuristic inquiry	Humanistic psychology	What is my experience of this phenomenon and the essential experience of others who also experience this phenomenon intensely?
7. Ethnomethodology	Sociology	How do people make sense of their everyday activities so as to behave in socially acceptable ways?
8. Symbolic interaction	Social psychology	What common set of symbols and understandings has emerged to give meaning to people's interactions?

---

rated five major theoretical perspectives as the foundations of social research: positivism (and postpositivism), interpretivism (which includes phenomenology, hermeneutics, and symbolic interactionism), critical inquiry, feminism, and postmodernism (to which he adds an "etc." to suggest the open-ended nature of such a classification). Creswell (1998) also settled on five tradi-

tions of qualitative inquiry, but a different five: biography, phenomenology, grounded theory, ethnography, and case study. Jacob (1987) chose yet a different five for a qualitative taxonomy: ecological psychology, holistic ethnography, ethnography of communication, cognitive anthropology, and symbolic interactionism. Schwandt (2000) highlighted "three epistemological stances

Perspective	Disciplinary Roots	Central Questions
9. Semiotics	Linguistics	How do signs (words, symbols) carry and convey meaning in particular contexts?
10. Hermeneutics	Linguistics, philosophy, literary criticism, theology	What are the conditions under which a human act took place or a product was produced that makes it possible to interpret its meanings?
11. Narratology/ narrative analysis	Social sciences (interpretive): Literary criticism, literary nonfiction	What does this narrative or story reveal about the person and world from which it came? How can this narrative be interpreted to understand and illuminate the life and culture that created it?
12. Ecological psychology	Ecology, psychology	How do individuals attempt to accomplish their goals through specific behaviors in specific environments?
13. Systems theory	Interdisciplinary	How and why does this system as a whole function as it does?
14. Chaos theory: Nonlinear dynamics	Theoretical physics, natural sciences	What is the underlying order, if any, of disorderly phenomenon?
15. Grounded theory	Social sciences, methodology	What theory emerges from systematic comparative analysis and is grounded in fieldwork so as to explain what has been and is observed?
16. Orientational: Feminist inquiry, critical theory, queer theory, among others	Ideologies: Political, cultural, and economic	How is X perspective manifest in this phenomenon?

for qualitative inquiry": interpretivism, hermeneutics, and social constructivism. Denzin and Lincoln (2000a) organized their review of qualitative variety around seven historical periods and seven "paradigms/theories": positivist/postpositivist, constructivist, feminist, ethnic, Marxist, cultural studies, and queer theory. Wolcott (1992) created a family tree of 20 distinct branches showing different "qualitative strategies." Tesch (1990) identified 27 varieties. Having examined some of the various attempts to classify qualitative approaches, Miles and Huberman (1994) concluded, "As comprehensive and clarifying as these catalogs and taxonomies may be, they turn out to be basically incommensurate, both in the way different qualitative strands are defined and in the criteria used to distinguish them. The mind boggles in trying to get from one to another" (p. 5).

Adding to this complexity is the practice of combining some perspectives. For example, one can do a heuristic feminist (orientational) study, that is, undertake a heuristic inquiry from a feminist perspective. Or do "critical ethnography" (Thomas 1993), combing elements of critical theory and ethnography. Bentz and Shapiro (1998) have offered what they call "mindful inquiry" as a synthesis of phenomenology, hermeneutics, critical theory, and Buddhism. From phenomenology they take the focus on experience and consciousness. From hermeneutics they take the focus on texts, on the process of understanding, and on letting new meanings emerge from the research process. From critical theory they direct attention to the social and historical context of both the researcher and the research topic, including attention to domination, injustice, and oppression. From Buddhism they take the focus on becoming aware of one's own "addictions" and attachments and on practicing compassion. In positing this synthesis, they aim to place the researcher, rather than research techniques, at the center of the research process. This adds something of a reflexive, autoethnographic orientation as another foundation of mindful inquiry because the mindful inquirer uses awareness of personal, social, and historical context, and personal ways of knowing, to shape the research.

The variety of qualitative frameworks is distinguished by answers to six core questions (one for each day of the week plus a day left over to integrate your answers):

- *What do we believe about the nature of reality?* (ontological debates concerning the possibility of a singular, verifiable reality and truth vs. the inevitability of socially constructed multiple realities)

- *How do we know what we know?* (epistemological debates about the possibility and desirability of objectivity, subjectivity, causality, validity, general- izability)

- *How should we study the world?* (methodological debates about what kinds of data and design to emphasize for what purposes and with what consequences)

- *What is worth knowing?* (philosophical debates about what matters and why)

- *What questions should we ask?* (disciplinary and interdisciplinary debates about the importance of various burning questions, inquiry traditions, and areas of inquiry)

- *How do we personally engage in inquiry?* (praxis debates about interjecting personal experiences and values into the inquiry, including issues of voice and political action)

The same program, organization, or community studied by researchers from different perspectives will lead to quite different studies even though they might all undertake observations, interviews, and document analysis. Nor would it necessarily be possible to synthesize the descriptions and findings of such different studies even though they took place in the same setting. When researchers operate from different frameworks, their results will not be readily interpretable by or meaningful to each other. While the frameworks provide guidance and a basis for interaction among researchers operating within the same framework, the different theoretical frameworks constitute barriers that impede interaction across and among different perspectives. In effect, each theoretical framework is a miniparadigm with its own internal logic and assumptions.

This means one cannot reasonably ask which theoretical framework is "right," best, or most useful. It depends on what one wants to do and which assumptions one shares. Gareth Morgan (1983) stated the problem quite succinctly after presenting a variety of research perspectives:

> There was the question as to how the reader could come to some conclusion regarding the contrary nature, significance, and claims of the different perspectives. . . . I realized that there was a major problem here. . . . There is a fallacy in the idea that the propositions of a system can be proved, disproved, or evaluated on the basis of axioms within that system. . . . This means that it is not possible to judge the validity or contribution of different research perspectives in terms of the ground assumptions of any one set of perspectives, since the process is self-justifying. Hence the attempts in much social science debate to judge the utility of different research strategies in terms of universal criteria based on the importance of generalizability, predictability and control, explanation of variance, meaningful understanding, or whatever are *inevitably flawed: These criteria inevitably favor research strategies consistent with the assumptions that generate such criteria as meaningful guidelines for the evaluation of research.* It is simply inadequate to attempt to justify a particular style of research in terms of assumptions that give rise to that style of research. . . . Different research perspectives make different kinds of knowledge claims, and the criteria as to what counts as significant knowledge vary from one to another. (pp. 14-15)

In other words, readers must make their own decisions about the relative value of any given perspective. Each has strengths. Each has limitations. There is no universal standard that can be applied to choose among these different frameworks. Quite the contrary, the diversity itself is a good indicator of the complexity of human phenomena and the challenges involved in conducting research.

Finally, a caution would seem in order about the danger of reifying the theoretical distinctions offered in this chapter. Take a look again at Exhibit 3.1, my reply to a letter from a graduate student desperate to figure out what category of inquiry she fit into. The boundaries between perspectives remain fuzzy. Adherents within each perspective can be found arguing about what is essential to that perspective. Tom Schwandt, who has studied these distinctions as much as anyone and is the lexicographer of the *Dictionary of Qualitative Inquiry* (2001), offers this reflection on theoretical distinctions:

> It seems to be a uniquely American tendency to categorize and label complicated theoretical perspectives as either this or that. Such labeling is dangerous, for it blinds us to enduring issues, shared concerns, and points of tension that cut across the landscape of the movement, issues that each inquirer must come to terms with in developing an identity as a social inquirer. In wrestling with the ways in which these philosophies forestructure our efforts to understand what it means to "do" qualitative inquiry, what we face is not a choice of which label—interpretivist, constructivist, hermeneuticist, or something else—best suits us. Rather, we are confronted with choices about how each of us wants to live the life of a social inquirer. (Schwandt 2000:205)

🔄 Pragmatism

Having documented the variety of theoretical perspectives that inform qualitative inquiry, we now leave the world of theory and enter the world of practice and pragmatism. Not all questions are theory based. Indeed, the quite concrete and practical questions of people working to make the world a better place (and wondering if what they're doing is working) can be addressed without plac-

---

EXHIBIT 3.7	Sample Internet E-mail Discussion Groups (listservs) and Sites Relevant to Qualitative Inquiry and Theory

1. Ethnography-in-education@mailbase.ac.uk: Use of ethnographic research methods in education; to subscribe, send this message to mailbase@mailbase.ac.uk: join ethnography-in-education firstname lastname

2. Ethno@cios.org: Ethnomethodology/conversation analysis; to subscribe, send this message to comserve@cios.org: join ethno ourname

3. http://www.tgsa.edu/online/cybrary/phenom.html: Phenomenology

4. http://www.ped.gu.se/biorn/phgraph/home.html: Phenomenography

5. www.groundedtheory.com/vidseries1.html: Grounded theory Web site

6. Q-METHOD@listserv.kent.edu: Q Methodology discussion list on this broad approach to the study of subjectivity; to subscribe, send this message to listserv@listserv.kent.edu: subscribe Q-METHOD ourname; for help contact Q-Method-request@listserv.kent.edu

7. BIOG-METHODS@mailbase.ac.uk: Biographical Methods for the Social Sciences; to subscribe, send this message to mailbase@mailbase.ac.uk: join BIOG-METHODS
LASTNAME

8. PSYCH-NARRATIVE@massey.ac.nz: A discussion of narrative in everyday life; to subscribe, send this message to majordomo@massey.ac.nz: subscribe psych-narrative

9. www.chass.utoronto.ca/epc/srb/cyber/cyber.html: Cyber Semiotic Institute

10. www.shop.affinia.com/ppsesystemstheory/Store1/: Systems theory site

11. H-ORALHIST@h-net.msu.edu: H-Net/Oral History Association Discussion List on Oral History; to subscribe, send this message to listserv@h-net.msu.edu subscribe H-ORALHIST
LASTNAME AFFILIATION

NOTE: Thanks to Judith Preissle, Aderhold Distinguished Professor, Social Foundations of Education, University of Georgia, for list subscription details. These sites and subscription details may change, and this list is not exhaustive. This list is meant to be suggestive of the qualitative analysis resources available through the Internet. See Chapter 1, Exhibit 1.5; Chapter 4, Exhibit 4.9; and Chapter 8, Exhibit 8.3, for additional qualitative resources through the Internet.

---

ing the study in one of the theoretical frameworks in this chapter. While these intellectual, philosophical, and theoretical traditions have greatly influenced the debate about the value and legitimacy of qualitative inquiry, it is not necessary, in my opinion, to swear vows of allegiance to any single epistemological perspective to use qualitative methods.

Indeed, I would go farther (at the risk of being heretical) and suggest that one need not even be concerned about theory. While students writing dissertations and academic scholars will necessarily be concerned with theoretical frameworks and theory generation, there is a very practical side to qualitative methods that simply involves asking open-ended questions of people and observing matters of interest in real-world settings in order to solve problems, improve programs, or develop policies. In short, **in real-world practice, methods can be separated from the epistemology out of which they have emerged.**

One can use statistics in straightforward ways without doing a philosophical literature review of logical empiricism or realism. One can make an interpretation without studying hermeneutics. And one can conduct open-ended interviews or make observations without reading treatises on phenomenology. **The methods of qualitative inquiry now stand on their own as reasonable ways to find out what is happening in programs and other human settings.**

The next chapter explores some of the ways in which qualitative inquiry can contribute to practical knowledge and pragmatic understandings. To help make that transition, this chapter ends with a practical, cautionary tale from Halcolm.

The Apple of Your Eye

After Halcolm had completed explaining to a scholarly assembly the many differing perspectives one could use in looking at the world, he was hungry. While he answered questions and continued the discussion, he sent a listener to inquire if the midday meal was ready. The messenger did not return, so Halcolm sent a second messenger. The second messenger did not return. So Halcolm went himself.

He found the two messengers, the chef, and three visiting scholars engaged in heated debate. Ignoring the debate, Halcolm asked, "Is the midday meal ready?"

The first and eldest visiting scholar responded, "I have been explaining to these young men that the state of the food is not the only issue in determining readiness. A meal is not just food. The meal must include those who would partake of the food, so the meal is not ready until everything is in order and those who would eat are assembled."

The second visiting scholar said, "I dared to taste the meal. From the perspective of a gourmet chef, this meal will never be ready. It is hopeless; let us return to the city."

The third visiting scholar said, "Readiness is a state of mind, not a physical state. Since the food has no mind, the food cannot be ready. Only people can be ready."

The chef added, "The midday meal is at midday every day. At midday the meal is ready. Why ask if the meal is ready? It is midday. This is the meal. Therefore the midday meal is ready."

With that, they all began talking at once making ever finer points, drawing ever narrower distinctions.

Halcolm, meanwhile, sat down and ate his midday meal.

A student asked why he had not joined the debate to clarify these important issues. Halcolm took another bite and replied, "The apple of your eye won't satisfy the emptiness in your stomach. There is a time to talk about the nature of eating—and there is a time to eat."

—From Halcolm's *Guide for Gourmands*

APPENDIX 3.1

🔄 🔄 🔄

Example of Autoethnographic Writing

Introduction. This excerpt is from the first chapter of *Grand Canyon Celebration: A Father-Son Journey of Discovery* (Patton 1999a). The excerpt combines inquiry into a cultural phenomenon of interest with personal reflection on and experience of that phenomenon, in this case, male coming of age in modern society.

My son Brandon and I were joined by Malcolm, a friend and our Grand Canyon guide.

Vishnu Metamorphism

To see the enormity of the Grand Canyon you have to be orbiting the Earth. To feel it, you have to descend within. To learn from it, you have only to stay awhile and be present. At least that's what Malcolm had claimed when he first urged me to hike with him from Apache Point to Elves Chasm years earlier. And learn I had, about bloody blisters, debilitating thirst, and the importance of moving quickly when a rock ledge gives way a thousand feet above the canyon floor, especially if you're standing on it at the time. Modest learnings. But they left an impression. As did the depth and beauty of the Canyon.

Malcolm had been bringing questions about his life to the Canyon for years. And getting answers. I had gotten no answers on that first trip. But that, Malcolm explained, was because I had brought no questions. Fair enough. I had come for the hike and a chance to walk among the oldest exposed rocks on the Earth's surface.

But I did get an idea. Standing atop Mount Huethawali and staring across the Colorado River at Holy Grail Temple, I imagined someday hiking with my son, then just entering toddlerhood, and initiating him into manhood there amidst buttes named King Arthur Castle, Guinevere Castle, and Excalibur, and gorges named Merlin Abyss and Modred Abyss. Malcolm called it a vision, which beguilingly transformed a passing notion into a quest, like framing a telephone doodle and calling it art. What better place for grandiosity than the Grand Canyon?

The gilt frame, however, didn't quite make it back with me to Minnesota. I realized that I lacked a few of the basic necessities for conducting an initiation. Tribal elders, for example. Hard to come by if you don't have a tribe. As are other essentials, like tradition, a sacred place, ritual, terrifying gods to appease, wisdom to pass on, and life-threatening tests for the initiate to pass (preferably ones that the initiator has successfully survived). From what I recalled of anthropology, strong gender identity would also be a prerequisite. That, however, might be conjured up. I had felt a vague sense of something while gazing toward Lancelot Point. Malcolm suggested that the Canyon was putting me in touch with my masculine collective unconscious. After ten days in the Canyon such things could be said without sounding absurd. Like eating freeze-dried food. It can taste gourmet scrumptious after a hard day hiking, but cooked at home, it's ghastly. So I found that my Canyon initiation vision didn't reconstitute well mixed with urban fluoridated water.

But it also didn't evaporate.

Malcolm now smiles and says he never doubted. I, on the other hand, still find myself amazed that we actually did return with Brandon for an initiation experience. And, being a social science researcher, I kept field notes. Not, I should add, because I had any premonition that they might reveal something important about a humanist approach to coming of age in contemporary society. I did it for family history and, I concede, out of habit. I had spent too many years in sociological observation to turn off that part of myself just because I had brought my eldest son into one of the most magnificent landscapes on earth after many years of anticipation. I considered leaving my scientific side behind. I even tried. Just be a father, I told myself. Just be in the Canyon. Be present with Brandon. Don't analyze it while it's happening. Stay with the experience.

Or were those Malcolm's admonitions? Certainly, some part of me was intrigued by Malcolm's belief that he got answers from the Canyon. And, unlike our first hike years earlier, this time I found I had come with a question, though I wasn't fully aware of it until our second night.

We were camped within the inner gorge, just short of the Colorado River, where White Creek flows out of Muav Canyon into Shinumo Creek. My aching body craved rest after two hard days hiking, but Brandon's after-dinner questions about how different cultures define manhood had left me tossing and turning. He slept near enough for me to hear his slow, even breathing. As I studied him, he rolled from his back onto his side, pulling his knees up fetus-like, almost, but not quite, transforming his gangling, 18-year-old frame into a picture of innocence. He looked like the question he had asked over dinner.

He had begun with a mocking tone: "So, this is my initiation. When do I find out about the manhood thing? I'm sure you two have come prepared with important insights. Might as well get on with it. I, your humble initiate, am all ears."

Our subsequent anthropological discussion about how different societies define manhood was rooted in cultural relativism as solidly as the large cottonwood that sheltered our campsite. The discussion had been serious, intense and surprisingly lacking in satisfaction. Not for Brandon. For me.

As I gazed at Brandon sleeping, voices argued with each other in my head. What does a modern father tell his son about being a man? Some voices, recorded in my memory long ago, rasped repeatedly like a worn needle stuck in scratched grooves from the waxen days of graduate school. Others, more recently entered, played intermittently through the scratches. The messages from different eras competed to be heard, rising to a discordant crescendo, like being caught in a small gym between opposing fans and their blaring pep bands at a championship basketball game—exhilarating only if you know which side to cheer for.

Such imagery being incongruent with my peaceful environs, though I enjoy both debate and athletic competition, I redirected my inner musings to the steady gurgle of nearby rapids and the chirping melodies of the canyon night. I quietly got up to stroll back and forth along the creek, pondering what I wanted to pass on to Brandon about the nature of manhood. I paused in the shadow of ancient rock and listened as Shinumo's rapids asserted the constant flow of the present. I tried out possibilities on a disinterested moon: metaphors of male incandescence and female florescence.

What was left to tell Brandon that he hadn't already heard from me *ad nauseam*? I could affirm that the moon is disinterested, that the Canyon is rock, and that life offers many pathways for being a man and developing as a person, none of them certain. I could offer perspective and Canyon-inspired metaphors. . . .

This trip, this "initiation," felt like a last chance. When, if ever again, would I have Brandon's undivided attention? Or at least some part of it? I was not quite so delusional as to believe I could attain the impossibly high standard of "undivided attention" with a member in good standing of the generation that grew up on channel-surfing. But I did have ten uninterrupted days and nights with Brandon. No outside influences. No competition from television, telephones, friends or work.

Ten whole days with my son in the Grand Canyon. Ten days before he left home for college and the rest of his adult life. Ten final days. A last chance.

I returned to where Brandon slept and, gazing at him, considered whether it much mattered what I had to say—words, after all, being only words. But words matter in my world, as do answers. Thought matters. And so I thought some more until, under the influence of that elixir unique to the small hours when the body is exhausted and the internal dialogue worn down, I experienced at last a euphoria of analogical clarity. It came as I turned and peered into the dark gorge through which we had descended. That very afternoon, we had traversed the Canyon's Great Unconformity, in one step passing through a gap of 250 million years across a space that had once been filled with massive mountains. Recalling that moment took me through what felt like a parallel unconformity, insignificant by standards of Canyon time, but huge when measured on the modest scale of human evolution. Canyon metaphor offered sociological insight. Malcolm would later say the Canyon had answered my question.

The Canyon's Great Unconformity had once been filled with towering Precambrian formations of Bass Limestone, Hakatai Shale, Shinumo Quartzite, Dox Sandstone, and Cardenas Basalts 800 million to one-and-a-quarter billion

AUTOETHNOGRAPHY

years old. They had been turned sideways and thrust up higher than the Rockies by monumental tectonic movements. During this churning, twisting and thrusting, even more ancient rocks were exposed in places: hardened magma of Zoroaster Granites and the oldest rock in the Grand Canyon, the metamorphosed lava-black Vishnu Schist, 1.7 billion years old. Over millions of years these mountains were eroded until the space they once occupied was filled with sandstone deposited by encroaching seas.

When we arrived at the Great Unconformity, we joked about what it meant to arrive some place that isn't there. As we hiked on within the depths of the inner canyon, we marveled at the dramatic transition from sand and gravel to sculptured stone, its significance gradually penetrating with the cold feel of the marble-like rock. Now, inspired by the memory of that geologic gap, I contemplated the chasm that exists between modern society and ancient times. Many experience the gap as a painful loss. Lately, contemporary male elders have been trying to fill in the gap, build a bridge back or at least make a connection. They hope a return to ancient initiation rites will help close the gap. I had been attracted by that possibility myself, but Brandon's reactions during our hike down said it wouldn't work, at least not for modern young people who have tasted choice, experienced the power of intellect, learned to value individuality and abhor control. The Great Unconformity impressed on me the gap between past and present when societal customs have been eroded to the point of vanishing. Our ancestral past will necessarily and inevitably remain a foundation, like the ancient Vishnu Schist, formed by 75,000 pounds per square inch of tectonic pressure and named for the Hindu god, the Preserver. The Tapeats formation now rises atop that preserved foundation, but is neither part of it nor continuous in time.

I imagined a contemporary coming of age journey that recognizes ancient foundations of human experience, but is separate and distinct in accordance with modern discontinuities and the great unconformity of human potential in our times—a coming of age process that does not require the societal equivalent of 75,000 pounds per square inch of pressure to assure conformity. Indeed, a coming of age process that does not even have conformity as its goal. That would be the greatest unconformity.

In elucidating the role of traditional initiation for Brandon, Malcolm, my longtime friend and Canyon guide, also an anthropologist and family therapist, had explained that initiation rites functioned to psychologically separate sons from parental domination in tribal societies with extended families where generations would live together in a confined village space. But in modern society, just the opposite is the case. Our children are separated from us by daycare, schools, music, television, peer groups and easy geographic mobility. The challenge of contemporary times is not to provide for the physical and psychological separation of children from parents. Society has evolved multiple mechanisms for detachment. Parents and children today are subjected to unprecedented centrifugal forces. The challenge now is to bond.

I thought I had come to the Grand Canyon for a ritual of initiation—recognizing and celebrating Brandon's manhood. But as we had descended into the inner Canyon, the focus shifted for me. There, in the moonlight, I admitted why. He was leaving home and going off to college. We needed no ceremony to recognize his independence. It was not in doubt. Nor was his manhood. What I craved, that ancient rituals could not provide and had not been designed to arrange, was connection.

Abruptly, propelled by the force of illusory insight, I turned again away from the rapids toward Brandon and sleep. A piercing pain in my leg stopped me. I had connected with a Prickly Pear cactus. Examining the offending thorn, I heard my voice say: "Reality-check." Suddenly self-conscious, I looked around, then laughed out loud at the ridiculous figure I presented: pacing the canyon floor dressed only in the ephemeral threads of an emerging sociological paradigm shift.

SOURCE: Patton (1999a:21-27). Copyright © 1999 by Michael Quinn Patton.

4

Particularly Appropriate
Qualitative Applications

Apprenticeship in Pragmatism _____

A young carpenter, at the beginning of his career, came to Halcolm in distress. He had studied diligently to master carpentry. At the completion of his apprenticeship, the master carpenters said that his technical competence and skill were unmatched for one so young.

Halcolm knew all this, for word of the young man's mastery had reached even the great one. Yet, Halcolm could also see that the young carpenter was in great distress. "What troubles you?" Halcolm asked gently.

"My parents, my townspeople, my master teachers have been most generous. Upon completion of my apprenticeship, they joined together to give me a fine set of tools. I have been trained by the best. I am told that my skills are—what can I say without being immodest?—my skills are adequate." The young man paused, his distress obvious and growing even as he spoke.

"Then what is the problem?" asked Halcolm. The young man looked down, embarrassed in the presence of the great one. It was a long time before he spoke, and then only in a whisper. "I have nothing to build."

"Ah, I see," said Halcolm.

"No one will give me any orders," continued the young man.

"Let me make some inquiries," offered Halcolm. "Return in a week and I'll tell you what I have learned."

The seven days were as an agonizing eternity for the young man. At last it was time to find out what Halcolm had learned through his discrete interviews with a few knowledgeable and well-connected people.

"I have confirmed all that you told me," Halcolm began. "Your skill is much respected. Your tools are the finest, given with much affection. Your competence is not in doubt. And yet, you have nothing to build."

The young man waited for Halcolm to continue.

"During your apprenticeship you did the latticework on the new cathedral. The craftsmanship you displayed is admired by all. You designed and constructed the intricate woodwork of the new town hall directrix—another work of great art admired even by your masters. You carved and installed the elaborate wine racks in the guardian's estate. In all these efforts you have distinguished yourself and pleased those for whom you built."

The young man was pleased but perplexed as he heard Halcolm affirm the quality of his work. Indeed, hearing the affirmations deepened his distress at finding himself now with nothing to build. Halcolm continued.

"You now have nothing to build because the townspeople believe your artistry and craftsmanship are far superior to their simple needs. They need simple chairs, tables, and doors. You work on cathedrals, town halls, and estates. You have designed objects of great beauty and complexity. You have not designed and built objects of great simplicity and practicality. To do the latter only looks easier, but takes no less skill.

"Build me a simple, functional, and practical bookcase at reasonable cost, and let us see what the townspeople think. Apply your skills to the everyday needs of the people and you shall not lack for work."

Halcolm expected the young man to be delighted at the prospect of a solution to his problem—and regular employment. Instead, he saw the distress deepen into despair.

"I do not know how to build simple, practical, and functional things," lamented the young man. "I have never applied my skills and my tools to such things."

"Then your apprenticeship is not over," said Halcolm.

And they went down to Halcolm's workshop where the young man began to learn anew.

—From Halcolm's *Applied Arts and Sciences*

🔄 Practical Purposes and Concrete Questions

Qualitative methods are first and foremost *research* methods. They are ways of finding out what people do, know, think, and feel by observing, interviewing, and analyzing documents. The last chapter reviewed how qualitative methods contribute to generating and confirming social science theory. This chapter reviews how qualitative methods can contribute to *useful* evaluation, *practical* problem solving, real-world decision making, action research, policy analysis, and organizational or community development. This chapter offers examples of how qualitative methods can help answer concrete questions, support development, and improve programs. All of these are ways of contributing to what is sometimes called "action science" (Argyris, Putnam, and Smith 1985).

Qualitative methods are not appropriate for every inquiry situation. The aim of this chapter is to illustrate when it may be particularly appropriate to use qualitative methods. Certain purposes, questions, problems, and situations are more consonant with qualitative methods than others. This chapter samples some of the research and evaluation questions for which qualitative inquiry strategies are especially appropriate and powerful. The actual and potential applications of qualitative methods are so diverse that this review, while including a great variety of applications, is far from exhaustive. My purpose is to expand the horizons of what is possible and appropriate for both practitioners and decision makers. Because the opportunities for qualitative inquiry are so vast, the examples offered here can be no more than teasers, merely hinting at the enormous array of qualitative applications that are possible.

Moreover, I have not examined in this chapter how the varying theoretical and paradigmatic approaches discussed in the previous chapter might affect inquiry into any of these practical issues. For example, one might examine program quality, the first topic below, phenomenologically, ethnographically, or heuristically—to cite but three possibilities. Or one might simply conduct interviews and gather observation data to answer concrete program and organizational questions without working explicitly with a particular theoretical, paradigmatic, or philosophical perspective. Well-trained and thoughtful interviewers can get meaningful answers to practical questions without making a paradigmatic or philosophical pledge of allegiance. Pragmatic and utilitarian frameworks can guide qualitative inquiry on their practical and applied underpinnings without having to be attached to or derived from a theoretical tradition. Pragmatism, then, is the foundational orientation of this chapter.

A Focus on Quality

*C*ome, give us a taste of your quality.

—William Shakespeare, *Hamlet*, Act II, scene ii

Quality care. Quality education. Quality parenting. Quality time. Total quality management. Continuous quality improvement. Quality control. Quality assurance. Malcolm

Baldridge National Quality Award. Quality is the watchword of our times. People in "knowledge-intensive societies . . . prefer 'better' to 'more' " (Cleveland 1989:157). *More* requires quantitative dimensions; *better* evokes qualitative criteria.

At the most fundamental level, the debates about abortion, on the one hand, and death with dignity and physician-assisted suicide, on the other, concern, in part, what is meant by "quality of life" (Humphrey 1991). Kenneth E. Boulding (1985), one of the most prominent intellectuals of the modern era, devoted a book to the grand and grandiose topic of human betterment. In that book, he defined development as "the learning of quality" (Chapter 8). He struggled, ultimately in vain, to define "quality of life." He found the idea beyond determinative explication and certainly beyond numerical measurement. It is a subject particularly well suited for in-depth, holistic qualitative inquiry.

Concern for quality surrounds us in the postmodern age. Quality has become the primary marketing theme of our time, for example, "Quality Is Job One" (Ford Motor advertising slogan). Customers demand quality. This may stem, at least in part, from the fact that in the busy lives we now lead, at least in postindustrial society, we simply don't have time for things to break down. We don't have time to wait for repairs. We can't afford the lost productivity of not having things work (either products or programs). We have taken to heart the admonition that, in the long run, it is cheaper do it right the first time—whatever "it" or "right" may refer to. It is within this larger societal context that we shall examine what qualitative inquiry brings to the challenge of studying and evaluating *quality.*

The current mania spotlighting quality can give the impression that this is a relatively recent concern, but the founders of the

quality movement—W. Edwards Deming and Joseph M. Juran—were preaching quality in manufacturing before World War II. In the 1930s, for example, Juran was applying concepts of empowered worker teams and continuous quality improvement to reduce defects at Western Electric's Hawthorne Works in Chicago (Deutsch 1998; Juran 1951). Deming and his disciples have long viewed quality from the customer's perspective, defining quality as meeting or exceeding customer expectations. More than 20 years ago, Philip B. Crosby (1979) wrote a best-selling book on "the art of making quality certain." Some of his assertions have become classic:

- The first struggle, and it is never over, is to overcome the "conventional wisdom" regarding quality (p. 7).

- The cost of quality is the expense of doing things wrong (p. 11).

- Quality is ballet, not hockey (p. 13).

- The problem of quality management is not what people don't know about. The problem is what they think they do know (p. 13).

- Quality management is a systematic way of guaranteeing that organized activities happen the way they are planned. . . . Quality management is needed because nothing is simple anymore, if indeed it ever was (p. 19).

Efforts to implement these and other principles swelled crescendo-like into a national movement as management consultants everywhere sang of total quality management and continuous quality improvement. The music began in the corporate sector, but by the early 1990s the "cult of total quality" had permeated deeply into the government and nonprofit sectors (Walters

1992). The Malcolm Baldridge National Quality Awards became, and remain, the pinnacle of recognition that the mountain-top of quality has been reached.

Nor was concern about quality limited to management books. Robert Pirsig's classic *Zen and the Art of Motorcycle Maintenance* (1984) was an investigation into quality and excellence, themes he revisited in *Lila* (1991) as he explored the "metaphysics of quality."

> What the Metaphysics of Quality adds to James' *pragmatism* and his *radical empiricism* is the idea that the primal reality from which subjects and objects spring is *value*. By doing so it seems to unite pragmatism and radical empiricism into a single fabric. Value, the pragmatic test of truth, is also the primary empirical experience. The metaphysics of quality says pure experience is value. Experience which is not valued is not experienced. The two are the same. This is where value fits. Value is not at the tail-end of a series of superficial scientific deductions that puts it somewhere in a mysterious undetermined location in the cortex of the brain. Value is at the very front of the empirical procession. (Pirsig 1991:365)

An important policy question of our time is whether educational quality can be achieved through state-imposed standards and mandates. One example of the difference between theory and practice in this regard is captured astutely in a case study by Goodson and Foote (2001) that describes what happened when a highly successful, innovative, and creative alternative to traditional education was confronted by the demands of contemporary standardized accountability. They chronicle the resistance of a particular school, the Durant School, to the imposition of state standards and mandated tests in an effort, ironically, to maintain the

school's documented history of high-quality education.

Understanding what people value and the meanings they attach to experiences, from their own personal and cultural perspectives, are major inquiry arenas for qualitative inquiry. This is especially true when making judgments about quality, or *valuing*, which brings us to evaluation and quality assurance.

Quality Assurance and Program Evaluation

Program evaluation and quality assurance have developed as separate functions with distinct purposes, largely separate literatures, different practitioners, and varying jargon. Each began quite narrowly, but each has broadened its scope, purposes, methods, and applications to the point where there is a great deal of overlap and, most important, both functions can now be built on a single, comprehensive program information system.

Program evaluation traces its modern beginnings to the educational testing work of Thorndike and colleagues in the early 1900s. Program evaluation was originally focused on measuring attainment of goals and objectives, that is, finding out if a program "works," that is, if it's effective. This came to be called *summative evaluation*, which originally relied heavily on experimental designs and quantitative measurement of outcomes. In recent years, program improvement (formative) evaluation has become at least as important and pervasive as summative evaluation (Patton 1997a).

Quality assurance (QA) in the United States had its official birth with the passage of the Community Mental Health Act Amendments of 1975 (Public Law 94-63). This law required federally funded commu-

QUALITY AS A PERVASIVE CONCERN

"The field of program evaluation is not monolithic, but rather is shaped by an ever-increasing range of approaches, each of which, to varying degrees, reflects evaluation's dual role as a theoretical endeavor and a form of socio-political inquiry. Indeed, today evaluators are confronted with a dizzying array of approaches, each emphasizing different purposes and endorsing different methodologies to guide practice. Yet, no matter which goals are pursued and which methods are employed, all evaluation involves an effort to conceptualize, comprehend, and convey the quality of the program" (Benson, Hinn, and Lloyd 2001: Introduction).

nity mental health centers to have QA efforts with utilization and peer review systems. Its purpose was to assure funders, including insurers and consumers, that established standards of care were being provided. QA systems involve data collection and evaluation procedures to document and support the promise made by health and mental health care providers to funding sources, including third-party insurance carriers and consumers, "that certain standards of excellence are being met. It usually involves measuring the quality of care given to individual clients in order to improve the appropriateness, adequacy, and effectiveness of care" (Lalonde 1982:352-53). As QA systems have developed, special emphasis has been placed on detecting problems, correcting deficiencies, reducing errors, and protecting individual patients. In addition, QA aims to control costs of health care by preventing overutilization of services and overbilling by providers.

Important methods of QA include clinical case investigations and peer reviews. All cases that fail to meet certain standards are reviewed in depth and detail. For example, patients who remain hospitalized beyond an accepted or expected period may trigger a review. An original difference between program evaluation and QA was that QA focused on individuals on a case-by-case basis, while program evaluation focused on the overall program. The traditional concerns with unique individual cases and quality in QA systems continue to be quite consonant with qualitative methods. Moreover, QA efforts have now moved beyond health care to the full spectrum of human service programs and government services (Human Services Research Institute 1984).

In-depth reviews of the quality of care for participants in programs can draw heavily on clinical case files only if the files contain appropriate and valid information. When files are to be used for research and evaluation purposes, clinicians need special training and support in how to gather and report highly descriptive qualitative data in clinical case files (Cox 1982). Because there can be great variation in the quality of clinical case records, particularly the descriptive quality, a program of QA must include evaluation of and attention to the quality of qualitative data available for QA purposes.

Moreover, it is useful to distinguish quality control from quality enhancement. Quality control efforts identify and measure minimum acceptable results, for example, minimum competency testing in schools or maximum acceptable waiting times before seeing a physician in an emergency room. Quality enhancement, in contrast, focuses on excellence, that is, levels of attainment well beyond minimums. Quality control requires clear, specific, standardized, and measurable levels of acceptable results. Excellence, however, often involves individu-

EXHIBIT 4.1	Comparing Program Evaluation and Quality Assurance
Program Evaluation	*Quality Assurance*
1. Focus on program processes and outcomes	1. Focus on individual processes and outcomes
2. Aggregate data	2. Individual clinical cases
3. Goals-based judgment	3. Professional-based judgment
4. Intended for decision makers	4. Intended for clinical staff

alization and professional judgment that cannot and should not be standardized. Excellence is manifest in quality responses to special cases or especially challenging circumstances. Thus, while quality control relies on standardized statistical measures, comparisons, and benchmarks, quality enhancement relies more on nuances of judgment that are often best captured qualitatively through case studies and cross-case comparisons.

Traditionally, given their different origins, program evaluation and QA have had different emphases. These differences are summarized in Exhibit 4.1.

The distinctions between QA and program evaluation have lost much of their importance as both functions have expanded. Program evaluation has come to pay much more attention to program processes, implementation issues, and qualitative data. QA has come to pay much more attention to outcomes, aggregate data, and cumulative information over time. What has driven the developments in both program evaluation and QA—and what now makes them more similar than different—is concern about program improvement and gathering really useful information. Both functions had their origins in demands for accountability. QA began with a heavy emphasis on quality

control, but attention has shifted to concern for quality enhancement. Program evaluation began with an emphasis on summative judgments about whether a program was effective or not but has shifted to improving program effectiveness. In their shared concern for gathering useful information to support program improvement, program evaluation and QA now overlap and find common ground. Accountability demands can be well served, in part, by evidence that programs are improving.

Both accountability and program improvement require comprehensive program information systems. We've learned that such systems should be designed with the direct involvement of intended users; that information systems should be focused on critical success factors (not data on every variable a software expert can dream up); that systems should be streamlined with utility in mind; and that program improvement systems benefit from both qualitative and quantitative information, both case data and aggregate data. Indeed, harking back to the opening discussion about total quality management and continuous quality improvement, the systems that support such efforts began with a heavy emphasis on statistical process control and "objective" indicators of performance, but have come increasingly to value *qualitative perspectives on quality.* It turns out that one of the particular strengths of qualitative inquiry, perhaps commonsensically, is illuminating the nature and meaning of *quality* in particular contexts. This takes on added significance since "quality of life has become a commonly used concept and is showing growing significance in economic and political terms . . . [and] has two aspects, psychological and environmental, [yet] some researchers have totally neglected the perception of the people" (Turksever and Atalik 2001:163).

There are many aspects of program operations, including implementation activities and client outcomes, that can be measured in terms of relative quantity. It makes sense to count the number of people who enter a program, the number who leave the program, and the number who receive or report some concrete benefit from the program. However, many attributes of programs do not lend themselves to counting. Even the quantitative scaling of quality attributes is an inadequate way of capturing either program quality or the effect of a program on the quality of life experienced by participants during and after the program.

For example, school outcomes can be looked at both in terms of quantity of change and quality of change. Quantity of change may involve the number of books read; a score on a standardized achievement test; the number of words spelled correctly; and the number of interactions with other students, the teacher, or people of a different race. Each of these outcomes has a corresponding quality dimension that requires description rather than scaling. Thus, to find out *what it means* to a student to have read a certain number of books is an issue of quality. How those books affected the student personally and intellectually is a question of quality. In contrast to counting the correct number of words spelled, the quality issue focuses on what spelling *means* to the student. How is spelling integrated into the student's approach to writing? How does the student think about spelling, approach spelling, feel about spelling? The answer to such questions requires description of individual students' perspectives and situations such that the meaning of the experience for the students is elucidated.

The same distinction holds with regard to programs that emphasize deinstitutionalization—for example, community mental health programs, community corrections, and community-based programs for the elderly. It is possible to count the number of people placed in the community. It is possible even to measure on standardized scales certain attributes of their lives and livelihoods. It is possible to have them subjectively rate various aspects and dimensions of quality of life. However, to fully grasp the meaning of a change in life for particular persons it is necessary to develop a description of life quality that integrates interdependent dimensions of quality into a whole that is placed in context: What is their daily life like? Who do they interact with? How do they perceive their lives? How do they make sense of what they experience? What do they say about the path they are on? How do they talk about their quality of life? What do they compare themselves to when deciding how well they're doing? These are areas of qualitative inquiry that support quality enhancement efforts and insights.

Quality has to do with nuance, with detail, and with the subtle and unique things that make a difference between the points on a standardized scale. In-depth quality descriptions can illuminate what the lives and perspectives of two different people are like, one of whom responded on a scale of 5 points that an experience was "highly satisfactory," while the other responded that it was an "extremely satisfying" experience.

This is not a question of interval versus ordinal scaling, but one of meanings. What do programs mean to participants? What is the quality of their experiences? Answers to such questions require detailed, in-depth, and holistic descriptions that represent people in their own terms and that get close enough to the situation being studied to understand firsthand the nuances of quality.

The failure to find statistically significant differences in comparing people on some outcome measure does not mean that there are no important differences among those people on those outcomes. The differences may simply be qualitative rather than quantitative. A carpenter is reported to have explained this point to William James. The carpenter, having worked for many different people, observed, "There is very little difference between one man and another; but what little there is, is very important." Those differences are differences of quality.

⑤ Evaluation Applications

Outcomes Evaluation

For programs engaged in healing, transformation, and prevention, the best source and form of information are client stories. It is through these stories that we discover how program staff interact with clients, with other service providers, and with family and friends of their clients to contribute to outcomes, and how the clients, themselves, grow and change in response to program inputs and other forces and factors in their lives. There is a richness here that numbers alone cannot capture. It is only for a story not worth telling, due to its inherent simplicity, that numbers will suffice. (Kibel 1999:13)

Outcomes evaluation has become a central focus, if not the central focus, of account-

ability-driven evaluation. The accountability movement is not so much about achieving quality (the previous section) as it is about demonstrating responsible use of public funds to achieve politically desired results. The U.S. Government Performance and Results Act (GPRA) of 1994 mandates outcomes reporting by government agencies. Philanthropic foundations are demanding outcomes evaluation (Porter and Kramer 1999) as are health care systems (Morse, Penrod, and Hupcey 2000). Indeed, in every arena of action—health, education, criminal justice, employment, international development—emphasis has shifted from providing services to attaining priority outcomes. A good example of this emphasis is the widely used United Way (1996) manual *Measuring Program Outcomes:*

In growing numbers, service providers, governments, other funders, and the public are calling for clearer evidence that the resources they expanded actually produce benefits for people. Consumers of services and volunteers who provide services want to know that programs to which they devote their time really make a difference. That is, they want better accountability for the use of resources. One clear and compelling answer to the question of "Why measure outcomes?" is: To see if programs really make a difference in the lives of people. (p. 4)

However, reading this manual one would think that the only way to document outcomes attainment is with numbers. The focus is entirely on numerical indicators of outcomes and statistics in accomplishments. Percentage increases in desired outcomes (e.g., higher achievement test scores) and percentage decreases in undesirable outcomes (e.g., reductions in rates of child abuse and neglect) are important to provide concrete evidence of overall patterns of effectiveness. What such statistics cannot do, however, is show the human faces behind the numbers. This is important to provide critical context when interpreting statistical outcomes as well as to make sure that the numbers can be understood as representing meaningful changes in the lives of real people.

In an adult literacy program, the test results showed an average increase of 2.7 grade levels over a three-month period. The people in this sample included

- a Puerto Rican man who was learning to read English so that he could help his young daughter with schoolwork;

- an 87-year-old African American grandmother who, having worked hard throughout her life to make sure that her children and grandchildren completed school, was now attending to her own education so that she could read the Bible herself; and

- a manager in a local corporation who years earlier had lied on her job application about having a high school diploma and was now studying at night to attain a general equivalency diploma (GED).

In judging the effectiveness of this program and making decisions about its future, it can be as important to understand the stories behind the numbers as to have the statistics themselves. One can justifiably criticize the past reporting practices of many human service agencies for having been limited to successful anecdotes with no accountability reporting on overall patterns of the effectiveness. However, swinging the pendulum to the other extreme of only reporting aggregate statistics presents its own problems and limitations. Numbers are subject to selection and distortion no less than anecdotes. Well-crafted case studies can tell the stories

behind the numbers, capture unintended impacts and ripple effects, and illuminate dimensions of desired outcomes that are difficult to quantify (e.g., what it *means* for someone to become "self-sufficient"). Such qualitative data can add significantly to statistical reporting to create a more comprehensive accountability system.

Detailed case studies can be even more important when evaluating outcomes attainment for program improvement (as opposed to external accountability reporting). To simply know that a targeted indicator has been met (or not met) provides little information for program improvement. Getting into case details better illuminates what worked and didn't work along the journey to outcomes—the kind of understanding a program needs to undertake improvement initiatives.

Exhibit 4.2 (p. 155) presents highlights of a case study from an employment training program. In addition to illuminating what the outcome of a "job placement" actually meant to a particular participant, the case documents attainment of hard-to-measure outcomes such as "understanding the American workplace culture" and "speaking up for oneself" that can be critical to long-term job success for an emigrant like the woman in the story.

We'll return to the theme of documenting outcomes through stories near the end of this chapter in the Capturing and Communicating Stories section. The next section, however, looks at the special capacity of qualitative inquiry to document individualized outcomes in programs that especially value individualization.

Evaluating Individualized Outcomes

Individualization means matching program services and treatments to the needs of

OUTCOME MAPPING AND THE OUTPUT/OUTCOME/DOWNSTREAM IMPACT BLUES

Terry Smutylo and his colleagues in the Evaluation Unit of the International Development Research Centre (IDRC), Ottawa, Canada, have long been working to overcome threats to learning in development programs. They have observed that longer-term outcomes and impacts often occur a long way downstream from program implementation and may not take the form anticipated. These longer-term outcomes depend on responsiveness to context-specific factors, creating diversity across initiatives. The outcomes examined include the depth and breadth of involvement by many stakeholders, processes that become results in and of themselves when done in ways that are sustainable. These characteristics make it difficult for external agencies (a) to identify and attribute specific outcomes to specific components of their programs and (b) to aggregate and compare results across initiatives. IDRC has developed an approach titled "outcome mapping," a methodology that can be used to create planning, monitoring, and evaluation mechanisms enabling organizations to document, learn from, and report on their achievements. It is designed to assist in understanding an organization's results while recognizing that contributions by other actors are essential to achieving the kinds of sustainable,

large-scale improvements in human and ecological well-being toward which the organization is working. The innovations introduced in outcome mapping offer ways of overcoming some of the barriers to learning faced by evaluators. Attribution and measuring downstream results are dealt with through a more direct focus on transformations in the actions of the main actors. The methodology has also shown promise for across-portfolio learning in that it facilitates standardization of indicators without losing the richness in each case's story, thus combining quantitative and qualitative approaches. (For more information, see their Web site: http://www.idrc.ca/evaluation.)

To help funders and grantees understand the complexities of measuring outcomes and impacts, Terry has written a song, The Output/Outcome/Downstream Impact Blues, that he performs with great gusto, playing guitar as he sings. I first heard Terry perform the song at the launching of the African Evaluation Association in Nairobi, Kenya, in 1999. He kindly gave me permission to reproduce it here. In the future, we'll undoubtedly be able to incorporate sound into books, but for the moment the lyrics alone must suffice.

The Output/Outcome/Downstream Impact Blues

by Terry Smutylo, director, Evaluation International Development Research Centre, Ottawa, Canada

There's a tricky little word
That's getting too much use
In development programs
It's prone to abuse
It's become an obsession
Now we're all in the act,
Because survival depends
On that elusive "impact."

(continued)

Chorus

'Cause it's impact any place
Impact anytime
You may find it 'round the corner
Or much farther down the line.
But if you look for attribution
You are never going to lose
Those Output Outcome Downstream
  Impact Blues.

When donors look for impact
They really want to see
A pretty little picture
Of their fantasy
And here is something
Evaluators should never do
Use a word like "impact"
Without thinking it through.

Donors often say,
And this is a fact
Get out there and show us
Your impact
You must change peoples' lives
And help us take the credit
Or next time you want funding
You just might not get it.

Recipients are always
Eager to please
When we send our evaluators
Overseas
To search for indicators
Of verifiable impact
Surprising the donors
What they bring back.

Impact, they find,
When it does occur
Comes from many factors
And we're not sure
What we can
Attribute to who
'Cause impact is the product
Of what many people do.

So donors wake up
From your impossible dream
You drop in your funding
A long way upstream
The waters they flow,
They mingle, they blend
So how can you take credit
For what comes out in the end?

SOURCE: Copyright © 2001 by Terry Smutylo. Used with permission.

individual clients. Successful social and educational programs adapt their interventions to the needs and circumstances of specific individuals and families (Schorr 1988:257). Flexibility, adaptability, and individualization can be important to the effectiveness of educational and human service programs. Highly individualized programs operate under the assumption that outcomes will be different for different clients. Not only will outcomes vary along specific common dimensions, but outcomes will be qualitatively different and will involve qualitatively different dimensions for different clients. Under such conditions, program

staff are justifiably reluctant to generate standardized criteria and scales against which all clients are compared. They argue that their evaluation needs are for documentation of the unique outcomes of individual clients rather than for measures of outcomes standardized across all clients.

There are numerous examples of individualized programs or treatments. Open education, for example, is partly a model of educational processes that assumes that the outcomes of education for each child are unique. Open and experiential approaches to education offer diverse activities to achieve diverse and individualized

EXHIBIT 4.2	Behind the Numbers of an Employment Program: The Story of Li

Outcome Statistics
- Completed WORK program, stayed in job placement one year.
- Highest wage before WORK program, $8.25 without benefits; wage following WORK
- program completion, $11.75 with benefits, more than a 42% increase.
- Graduated from technical school with a 3.66 GPA (out of 4.0)
- TABE test (math and language skills): reading, 7th grade equivalent; language, 4th grade; spelling, 10.6; math computation, 12.9—highest score possible, and applied math, 9.9. Average increase: 5.4 grade levels.
- Participation data: attended 89 classes at WORK, missed 6 and was late to 1.

Outcome Story

Li entered the employment program called "WORK" two years after she arrived in the United States from Vietnam. As a recent immigrant, Li faced language and cultural barriers at school, at work, and in her day-to-day living. She was originally from Saigon City, where she took the national test to study at the university but failed both times she took it. She gained entrance to the Vietnamese Technical College, where she completed a degree in payroll and human resources when she was 23. She soon went to work for a Vietnamese company as an accountant.

Li married a man from North Vietnam despite her family's opposition. Li and her husband were not accepted in either of their parents' homes, even though tradition calls for the married couple to live in the home of the husband's parents. As a result, the couple rented a small room where they struggled to improve their lives. Shortly after the birth of their daughter, the couple discovered that they might be eligible to go to the United States because the U.S. government was granting visas to former officers of the Vietnamese army. After successfully negotiating the difficult application and emigration process, they arrived in Minnesota where they knew no one. According to Li, her husband began treating her very badly. He immediately got a job but would not give her any financial support. Within a year he

deserted her. She found a cleaning job at a bakery and later at a hotel. Li had always believed that through education she would get ahead, so she again took up the study of accounting, begun in Vietnam, by enrolling in a local technical college four months after arriving in the United States. After two years in the United States, she found a data entry job for a retail business where she received $8.25 per hour without benefits. She lost that job when she had to stay home for a week to care for her very sick daughter. She then went on welfare.

Li first heard about the employment program, WORK, from some friends at the technical college. She entered and concentrated on improving her English, technical skills, and assertiveness with support from program staff. WORK provided tuition assistance, cost-of-living support, and bus passes. She also received tutoring in accounting (1.5 hours per week) from the program's accountant. The program secured for her a work experience placement at a local bank at a rate of $7.25 per hour. This work environment proved very stressful because her language skills were inadequate and she was teased and harassed by other workers.

The WORK program supported her leaving the bank job so that she could more intensively study business English, refine her workplace communications skills, and enhance her ac-

(continued)

EXHIBIT 4.2	Continued

counting software skills. The program case records show that at times she expressed feelings of hopelessness. Her staff worker counseled her to focus on all the barriers that she had overcome by moving to this country and her hopes for a positive future for her daughter. The program supported her return to the technical college where she graduated with dual diplomas in accounting and data entry. Shortly thereafter, she began interviewing for jobs. She went through more than seven interviews with different companies before she received a final job offer of an accounting position at a retail firm. She said that she had expected more help with placement from the program than she got. According to WORK staff, there was some confusion about their role in finding a placement for participants. At any rate, Li persevered and felt good about the result: "Even though I failed many interviews and I thought I might never get a job, all the staff encouraged me to keep trying. They talked to me about my good qualities. They were all positive, not negative. In the end, they really helped me get a good job even though I didn't understand the limits of their role at the time."

While her language and math tests showed great improvement (from elementary-level results to high school-level results over the two-year period in WORK), Li says that what was most important was what she learned at WORK about how to be professional in the workplace and how "to mesh with American culture." Li specifically mentioned that she found it important to learn interviewing skills, since the interview is not common in Vietnam. She emphasized that WORK played a critical role in helping her find a professional job in "American corporate culture," explaining, "I compare myself with my friends at the Tech College and even now they don't have a job. If I didn't have WORK, I probably wouldn't have a job either." The program staff emphasized the challenges Li faced in gaining confidence and learning how to speak up for herself, issues that the staff continued to work on with her after her job placement.

Li believes that WORK played a vital role in supporting her to overcome the challenges in her life. She said, "I can talk to staff about any problem—about my job, money, and my daughter. I talk to them to figure things out and solve problems. Even now that I have a job, I call and get help from staff." She recounted getting help dealing with a fellow worker who was making life difficult for her. Program staff talked her through the process of discussing the situation with her supervisor and getting help to resolve the situation. Li said, "Even though I wasn't successful at home with my husband, I feel like WORK is my family now. It makes people feel safe here. The staff encourages us to go forward. If there is a problem, they help us solve it. The important thing is that we treat each other like a family. I learned so many things here. Things I can't get in school. I learned interview skills, workplace skills, empowerment skills. I learned English that is more effective

outcomes. Moreover, the outcomes of having engaged in a single activity may be quite different for different students. For example, a group of primary school students may take a field trip, followed by dictating stories to the teachers and volunteers about that field trip, and then learning to read their stories. For some students such a process may in-on a professional level for communication. WORK helps us not be afraid. They gave me a computer and some cost-of-living support, and they paid for a pronunciation class. They helped me so much."

A friend of Li's interviewed for this case study reported that WORK was "especially helpful to Li in making the adjustment from her culture to this culture. It was a touchstone for her. It helped her in her adapting. It was vital." Li now works full time. She wakes at 5:30 a.m., catches the bus at 6:30, arrives at work at 7:30, and begins work at 8:00. She works until 4:30 p.m. and immediately takes the bus, arriving home at 5:30. Several times a week, Li swims after work at a local community pool. Each evening she prepares dinner for her daughter and helps her with her homework. After her daughter goes to bed, Li frequently works on her computer to improve her skills, or does other self-study.

Li says that she is still working on communicating better in the workplace. Her supervisor said in an interview: "We encouraged her to become more assertive. We wanted her to know that it's okay to stand up for herself. It's okay to be more assertive. It's the American way. She's learning." Her job supervisor continued: "WORK has been here a couple of times to sit and talk with myself and the personnel manager when we were having difficulty with Li and one coworker. We wanted their input on what to do. So we all kind of worked together to try and solve the problem. They worked really well with us and are continuing to do so."

Li feels that her primary challenge is the fact that she is a "foreigner." She says, "An American learns one thing and I have to learn double. I'm slower than another American worker, because it's all new for me."

According to Li, her "life has changed a lot because of WORK." She explained that before she received WORK support, it was hard to imagine herself in a professional position in an office environment in this country. Li noted, "I was so excited to get an office job. It is the luckiest thing in my life, and the biggest challenge." According to Li, one result of her effort with WORK is that she feels she can talk and interact with anyone at work or in the community. She's more secure in dealing with others and has more confidence in herself. In addition, Li is able to manage her own financial situation and make confident decisions about raising her daughter. Her interactions with her daughter have improved and she says that she is no longer ashamed of her divorce.

Li's future includes short-term and long-term goals. In the short term, she would like to save money to buy the software for Professional Payroll Accounting, complete the training, and move into payroll accounting. She doesn't see herself staying at her current company for more than several years. Eventually, she would like to go back to school to become a CPA and increase her income to support herself and her daughter. One day, Li hopes to travel to Vietnam to visit her mother.

volve learning about the mechanics of language: sentence structure, parts of speech, and verb conjugation, for example. For other students the major outcome of such a process may be learning how to spell certain words. For other students the important outcome may be having generated an idea from a particular experience. For yet other students the important outcome may have been something that was learned in the exercise or experience itself, such as knowledge about the firehouse or the farm that was visited. Other students may become more articulate as a result of the dictation exercise. Still other students may have learned to read better as a result of the reading part of the exercise. The critical point is that **a common activity for all students can result in drastically different outcomes for different students** depending on how they approach the experience, what their unique needs were, and which part of the activity they found most stimulating. Educators involved in individualized approaches, then, need evaluation methods that permit documentation of a variety of outcomes, and they resist measuring the success of complex, individualized learning experiences by any limited set of standardized outcome measures (e.g., improved reading scores, better spelling, or more knowledge about some specific subject). Qualitative case studies offer a method for capturing and reporting individualized outcomes.

A similar case can be made with regard to the individualization of leadership development, criminal justice, community mental health, job training, welfare, and health programs. Take, for example, the goal of increased independence among a group of clients receiving treatment in a community mental health center. It is possible to construct a test or checklist that can be administered to a large group of people measuring their relative degrees of independence. Indeed, such tests exist. They typically involve checking off what kind of activities a person takes responsibility for, such as personal hygiene, transportation, initiatives in social interaction, food preparation, and so on. In many programs, measuring such criteria in a standardized fashion provides the information that program staff would like to

have. However, in programs that emphasize individualization of treatment and outcomes, program staff may argue, quite justifiably, that **independence has a different meaning for different people under different life conditions.** Thus, for example, for one person independence may have to do with a changing family dynamic and changed relationships with parents. For another person independence may have to do with nonfamily relationships—that is, interactions with persons of the opposite sex, social activities, and friendships. For still other clients the dominant motif in independence may have to do with employment and economic factors. For still others it has to do with learning to live alone. While clients in each case may experience a similar psychotherapeutic intervention process, the meaning of the outcomes for their personal lives will be quite different. What program staff wants to document under such conditions is the unique meaning of the outcomes for each client. Staff members need descriptive information about what a client's life was like on entering treatment, the client's response to treatment, and what the client's life was like following treatment. They also want to report documented outcomes within the context of a client's life for "*successful programs see the child in the context of the family and the family in the context of its surroundings*" (Schorr 1988:257). Such descriptive information results in a set of individual case studies. By combining these case histories, it is possible to construct an overview of the patterns of outcomes for a particular treatment facility or modality.

The more a program moves beyond training in standard basic competencies to more individualized development, the more qualitative case studies will be needed to capture the range of outcomes attained. A leadership program that focuses on basic concepts of planning, budgeting, and communications skills may be able to measure outcomes with a standardized instrument. But a leadership program that engages in helping participants think in systems terms about how to find leverage points and intervention strategies to transform their own organizations will need case studies of the actual transformation efforts undertaken by participants, for their individual endeavors are likely to vary significantly. One may be the director of a small community-based nonprofit organization. Another may be a middle-level government manager. Still another may be part of a large national organization. "Transformation" will mean very different things in these different settings. Under such circumstances, qualitative case study methods and design strategies can be particularly useful for evaluation of individualized participant outcomes and organization-level impacts.

Process Studies

A focus on process involves looking at *how* something happens rather than or in addition to examining outputs and outcomes. Evaluations vary in their emphasis on process in part because programs vary in their attention to process. Some therapy approaches in psychology are highly process oriented in that they focus on the relationship between the client and therapist, how the client is approaching issues, how the client feels about the process, and the nature of the interactions that occur during therapy, rather than focusing only or primarily on behavioral outcomes. Groups, programs, even entire organizations may be characterized as highly "process oriented" if how members and participants feel about what is happening is given as much attention as the results achieved. There are styles of community and organizational development that operate on the premise "What we do is no more important than *how* we do it." This statement

means that actively involving people in the development process is an end in itself, not just a means to some more concrete end; the process *is* the point rather than simply the means of arriving at some other point. The journey, not the destination, is what matters. For example, a planning process for a community or organization may be carried out with a heavy emphasis on participation and involvement such that building relationships and mutual understandings along the way is at least as important as the focus of the actual plan produced. The process, in such a case, becomes the outcome. That is, producing a plan (the apparent intended outcome) actually becomes a means to building community (the real desired outcome).

In contrast, other interventions and programs play down process. The emphasis is on results and outcomes. Even in these cases, however, some process is undertaken to achieve results and understanding the process-outcomes relationship necessitates documenting and understanding processes.

Process evaluations study process. Qualitative inquiry is highly appropriate for studying process because (1) depicting process requires detailed descriptions of how people engage with each other, (2) the experience of process typically varies for different people so their experiences need to be captured in their own words, (3) process is fluid and dynamic so it can't be fairly summarized on a single rating scale at one point in time, and (4) participants' perceptions are a key process consideration.

Process evaluations aim at elucidating and understanding the internal dynamics of how a program, organization, or relationship operates. Process studies focus on the following kinds of questions: What are the things people experience that make this program what it is? How are clients brought into the program, and how do they move through the program once they are participants? How is what people do related to what they're trying to (or actually do) accomplish? What are the strengths and weaknesses of the program from the perspective of participants and staff? What is the nature of staff-client interactions?

A process evaluation requires sensitivity to both qualitative and quantitative changes in programs throughout their development, which typically means monitoring and describing the details of the program's implementation. Process evaluations not only look at formal activities and anticipated outcomes, but they also investigate informal patterns and unanticipated interactions. A variety of perspectives may be sought from people with dissimilar relationships to the program, that is, inside and outside sources.

Process data permit judgments about the extent to which the program or organization is operating the way it is supposed to be operating, revealing areas in which relationships can be improved as well as highlighting strengths of the program that should be preserved. Process descriptions are also useful in permitting people not intimately involved in a program—for example, external funders, public officials, and external agencies—to understand how a program operates. This permits such external persons to make more intelligent decisions about the program. Formative evaluations aimed at program improvement often rely heavily on process data. Finally, process evaluations are particularly useful for dissemination and replication of model interventions where a program has served as a demonstration project or is considered to be a model worthy of replication at other sites. By describing and understanding the details and dynamics of program processes, it is possible to isolate critical elements that have contributed to program successes and failures.

A process study is especially appropriate when the following kinds of statements are made about some intervention, relationship, organization, or program:

We take people through a developmental process made up of a series of steps or phases.

The nature of our process is what makes us unique.

We are a very process-oriented place.

We need to spend more time processing what's going on.

I'm having trouble getting a handle on the process.

What is the process? Is it the same for everyone? Is the process working for people?

A good example of what can emerge from a process study comes from an evaluation of the efforts of outreach workers at a prenatal clinic in a low-income neighborhood. The outreach workers were going door to door identifying women, especially teenagers, in need of prenatal care in order to get them into the community prenatal clinic. Instead of primarily doing recruiting, however, the process evaluation found that the outreach workers were spending a great deal of time responding to immediate problems they were encountering, for example, need for rat control, need for English as a second language classes, and protection from neglect, abuse, or violence (Philliber 1989). The actual interactions that resulted from the door-to-door contacts turned out to be significantly different from the way the door-to-door process was designed and conceptualized. These findings, which emerged from interviews and observations, had important implications for staff recruitment and training, and for how much time needed to be allocated to cover a neighborhood.

Implementation Evaluation

A prominent theme running through the preceding sections is that qualitative methods are particularly useful for capturing differences among people and programs. Evaluating individualized outcomes, developing unique case studies of people and programs, and documenting the local diversity within national or statewide programs— these are evaluation research issues for which qualitative strategies are particularly appropriate. This section looks more closely at the appropriateness of qualitative methods for evaluating program implementation.

It is important to know the extent to which a program is effective after it is fully implemented, but to answer that question it is important to learn the extent to which the program was actually implemented. In his seminal study *Social Program Implementation,* Walter Williams (1976) concluded, "The lack of concern for implementation is currently *the crucial impediment* to improving complex operating programs, policy analysis, and experimentation in social policy areas" (p. 267).

In *Utilization-Focused Evaluation* (Patton 1997a), I suggested that if one had to choose between implementation information and outcomes information because of limited evaluation resources, there are many instances in which implementation information would be of greater value. A decision maker can use implementation information to make sure that a policy is being put into operation according to design—or to test the very feasibility of the policy. Unless one knows that a program is operating according to design, there may be little reason to expect it to produce the desired outcomes. Furthermore, until the program is implemented and a "treatment" is believed to be in operation, there may be little reason even to bother

evaluating outcomes. Where outcomes are evaluated without knowledge of implementation, the results seldom provide a direction for action because the decision maker lacks information about what produced the observed outcomes (or lack of outcomes). Pure pre-post outcomes evaluation is the "empty box" approach to evaluation.

One important way of studying program implementation is to gather detailed, descriptive information about what the program is doing. Implementation evaluations answer the following kinds of questions: What do clients in the program experience? What services are provided to clients? What does staff do? What is it like to be in the program? How is the program organized? As these questions indicate, implementation evaluation includes attention to inputs, activities, processes, and structures.

Implementation evaluations tell decision makers what is going on in the program, how the program has developed, and how and why programs deviate from initial plans and expectations. **Such deviations are quite common and natural,** as demonstrated in the findings of RAND's classic "Change Agent Study" of 293 federal programs supporting educational change (McLaughlin 1976). That study found that national programs are implemented incrementally by adapting to local conditions, organizational dynamics, and programmatic uncertainties.

> Where implementation was successful, and where significant change in participant attitudes, skills, and behavior occurred, implementation was characterized by a process of mutual adaptation in which project goals and methods were modified to suit the needs and interests of the local staff and in which the staff changed to meet the requirements of the project. This finding was true even for highly technological and initially well-specified pro-

jects; unless adaptations were made in the original plans or technologies, implementation tended to be superficial or symbolic, and significant change in participants did not occur. (McLaughlin 1976:169)

If a process of ongoing adaptation to local conditions characterizes program implementation, then the methods used to study implementation should correspondingly be open-ended, discovery oriented, and capable of describing developmental processes and program changes. Qualitative methods are ideally suited to the task of describing such program implementation.

Failure to monitor and describe the nature of implementation, case by case, program by program, can render useless standardized, quantitative measures of program outcomes. The national evaluation of Follow Through was a prime example of this point. Follow Through was a planned variation "experiment" in compensatory education featuring 22 different models of education to be tested in 158 school districts on 70,00 children throughout the nation. The evaluation alone employed 3,000 people to collect data on program effectiveness. The multimillion-dollar evaluation focused almost entirely on standardized outcomes aimed at making possible comparisons of the effectiveness of the 22 models. It was assumed in the evaluation plan that models could be and would be implemented in some systematic, uniform fashion. Eugene Tucker (1977) of the U.S. Office of Education, however, has poignantly described the error of this assumption:

> It is safe to say that evaluators did not know what was implemented in the various sites. Without knowing what was implemented it is virtually impossible to select valid effectiveness measures. . . . Hindsight is a marvelous teacher and in large scale experimentations an expensive one. (pp. 11-12)

The Follow Through data analysis showed greater within-group variation than between-group variation; that is, the 22 models failed to show treatment effects as such. Most effects were null, some were negative, but "of all our findings, the most pervasive, consistent, and suggestive is probably this: *The effectiveness of each Follow Through model depended more on local circumstances than on the nature of the model*" (Anderson 1977:13). The evaluators, however, failed to study the local circumstances that affected variations in program implementation and outcomes. "Little remains in the existing Follow Through evaluation that specifically addresses the problem of how well, and by what process, program models are implemented" (Elmore 1976:119).

The study of these important program implementation questions requires case data rich with the details of program content and context. Because it is impossible to anticipate in advance how programs will adapt to local conditions, needs, and interests, it is impossible to anticipate what standardized quantities could be used to capture the essence of each program's implementation. Under these evaluation conditions, a strategy of naturalistic inquiry is particularly appropriate. For a more extensive discussion of evaluating program implementation, see King, Morris, and Fitz-Gibbon (1987) and Patton (1997a: Chapter 9).

Logic Models and Theories of Action

A logic model or theory of action depicts, usually in graphic form, the connections between program inputs, activities and processes (implementation), outputs, immediate outcomes, and long-term impacts. For example, the classic educational model of the popular DARE (Drug Abuse Resistance

Education) program in schools followed the following simple logic model: (1) Recruit and train select police officers (inputs) to teach children the dangers of drug use; (2) have the police, in uniform, teach children in special classes in school (implementation); and, as a result, the children will (3) find the teaching credible (process evaluation) and (4) learn facts about drugs (cognitive outcome), which will (5) convince them not to use drugs (attitude change outcome), which will (6) result in students not using drugs (behavior change outcome), which will ultimately show up in community indicators showing less drug use (impact). At least that was the model, or theory. In practice, evaluations of DARE consistently showed that the theory didn't work in practice.

Attention to program theory has become a major focus of evaluation research (see Rogers et al. 2000), and with that attention has come some confusion about terminology. I distinguish a logic model from a theory of change. The only criterion for a logic model is that it be, well, *logical*, that is, that it portrays a reasonable, defensible, and sequential order from inputs through activities to outputs, outcomes, and impacts. A theory of change or theory of action, in contrast, bears the burden of specifying and explaining assumed, hypothesized, or tested causal linkages. Logic models are *descriptive*. Theory of change and theory of action models are *explanatory* and *predictive*. The connotative difference between a "theory of change" and "theory of action," though the phrases are often used interchangeably, is that theory of change is more research based and scholarly in orientation, whereas a theory of action is practitioner derived and practice based.

The results of a logic modeling or theory-of-action exercise can make a dramatic difference in how people understand a program. A group of national and local pro-

THE LOGIC MODEL CHALLENGE

"The extent to which immediate and intermediate goals can be divorced from ultimate goals as valid in themselves poses a difficult question. Certainly there is a tremendous amount of activity, perhaps the largest portion of all public service work, devoted to the successful attainment of immediate and intermediate goals which appear to have only a very indirect bearing upon ultimate goals" (Suchman 1967:55).

gram staff, administrators, and evaluation researchers spent a day together working on a logic model for a program, Road to Recovery, that transported cancer patients to treatment. As a result of thorough contextual analysis and interviews with key informants, including patients and volunteer drivers, the program was reconceptualized as a *treatment compliance strategy* aimed at cancer control rather than just a transportation program. The reason for transporting patients was to ensure complete and consistent treatment. This reconceptualization had significant implications for how the program was implemented, the outcomes that were measured, and the importance of the program in relation to American Cancer Society priorities.

Organizational theorist Chris Argyris (1982) introduced what has become a classic distinction between "espoused theories" and "theories-in-use." The espoused theory is what people say they do; it's the official version of how the program or organization operates. The theory-in-use is what really happens. Interviewing supervisory or managerial staff and administrators, and analyzing official documents, reveals the espoused theory. Interviewing participants and frontline staff, and directly observing the program, reveals the theory-in-use. The resulting analysis can include comparing the stated ideals (espoused theory) with real priorities (theory-in-use) to help all concerned understand the reasons for and implications of discrepancies.

This ideal-actual comparison can support organizational development to improve effectiveness. It also helps move toward a reasonably realistic depiction of the program that can be put to a summative test, that is, one can study the extent to which the model or treatment actually accomplishes the hypothesized and desired outcomes and impacts. But such a study can take place only when the model has been described in realistic terms. Qualitative inquiry is especially appropriate for achieving that description.

Evaluability Assessments

Evaluability assessments (Wholey 1979, 1994; Smith 1989) are conducted through interviews, document analysis, and observations to determine whether a program is sufficiently well conceptualized and consistently implemented to undertake a formal and rigorous evaluation, especially a summative evaluation aimed at determining overall effectiveness. Clarifying the program logic model or theory of action (previous section) is also an important purpose of many evaluability assessments. In essence, an evaluability assessment involves making sure that the program treatment or model is clearly identifiable and logical; that outcomes are clear, specific, and evaluable; and that implementation strategies are reasonably and logically related to expected outcomes.

One reason evaluability assessment has become an important preevaluation tool is that by helping programs get ready for evaluation, the process acknowledges the common need for a period of time for evaluators to work with program staff, administrators, funders, and participants on clarifying goals and strategies—making them realistic, meaningful, agreed on, and evaluable. Evaluability assessments often include interviews and focus groups with diverse program constituencies to determine how much consensus there is among various stakeholders about a program's goals and intervention strategies and to identify where differences lie. Based on this kind of contextual analysis, an evaluator can work with primary intended users of the evaluation to plan a strategy for goals clarification and logic model development.

Studies of evaluability assessments (Rog 1985; Smith 1989) have found that the process of qualitative inquiry often becomes a formative evaluation as program staff members learn about the strengths and weaknesses of their program conceptualizations. The evaluability assessments become improvement-oriented experiences that lead to significant program changes rather than just a planning exercise preparing for summative evaluation.

Comparing Programs:
Focus on Diversity

We have frequently encountered the idea that a program is a fixed, unchanging object, observable at various times and places. A common administrative fiction, especially in Washington, is that because some money associated with an administrative label (e.g., Head Start) has been spent at several places and over a period of time, entities spending the money are comparable from time to time and from place to place. Such assumptions can easily lead to evaluation-research disasters. Programs differ from place to place because places differ. (Edwards, Guttentag, and Snapper 1975:142)

Individualizing services to clients has been one major theme of social action and educational programs in recent years. Another closely related theme has been the importance of adapting programs to local community needs and circumstances as discussed earlier in the Implementation Evaluation section of this chapter. While some basic framework of how programs should function may originate in Washington, D.C., Ottawa, Brussels, or Canberra or some state or provincial capital, it is clear that program implementation at the local level seldom follows exactly the proposed design. When an evaluation requires gathering data from several local sites, quantitative measures may be appropriate for comparing local programs along standardized dimensions, but qualitative descriptions are necessary to capture the unique diversities and contrasts that inevitably emerge as local programs adapt to local needs and circumstances. Local sites that are part of national or even international programs show considerable variation in implementation and outcomes. These variations are not such that they can be fully captured and measured along standardized scales; they are differences in *kind*— differences in content, process, goals, implementation, politics, context, outcomes, and program quality. To understand these differences, a holistic picture of each unique site is needed.

Using only standardized measures to compare programs can seriously distort what is actually occurring in diverse sites. Consider data from a national educational program that measured staff-student ratios across the country. A few programs had student-staff ratios as high as 75:1 according to the uniform measures used; other programs had student-staff ratios as small as 15:1.

What these data did not reveal was that some of the programs with large student-staff ratios made extensive use of volunteers. These regularly participating additional volunteer staff made the real student-adult ratios much smaller. The global and uniform reporting of the data, however, did not allow for that nuance to be recorded.

A good example of the diversity that can emerge from attention to the qualitative differences among programs is Sharon Feiman's (1977) classic study of national teacher center programs. Although funded as a single national program with common core goals and the shared label "teacher centers," Feiman found that three quite different *types* of center programs had emerged, what she called "behavioral" centers, "humanistic" centers, and "developmental" centers. Differences among the three types are summarized in Exhibit 4.3.

Feiman's analysis highlights the ways in which different teacher centers were trying to accomplish different outcomes through distinct approaches to teacher center programming. Uniform, quantitative measures applied across all programs might capture some of these critical differences, and such measures have the advantage of facilitating direct comparisons. However, qualitative descriptions permit documentation of deeper and unanticipated program differences, idiosyncrasies, and uniquenesses. If decision makers want to understand variations in program implementation and outcomes, qualitative case studies of local programs can provide such detailed information, as with the Carnegie Foundation's excellent *Portraits of High Schools* (Perrone 1985). Thus, qualitative data are necessary to give a complete evaluation picture of local variations within national programs, a picture that is necessarily incomplete so long as the only data available are aggregated and

EXHIBIT 4.3	Types of Teacher Centers	
Types of Centers	Primary Process for Working With Teachers	Primary Outcomes of the Process
Behavioral centers	Curriculum specialists directly and formally instruct teachers.	Teachers adopt comprehensive curriculum systems and methods.
Humanistic centers	Informal, undirected teacher exploration; "teachers select their own treatments."	Teachers feel supported and important; pick up concrete and practical ideas and materials for immediate use in classes.
Developmental centers	Advisers establish warm, interpersonal, and trusting relationships with teachers over time.	Teachers think in new ways about what they do and why they do it, developing new insights and fundamental skills and capabilities.

SOURCE: Feiman (1977).

standardized statistics about these diverse programs.

Prevention Evaluation

There may be nothing more difficult to evaluate than prevention—the nonoccurrence of some problem. Yet, there is no more important direction for the long-term solution of health and social problems than prevention efforts (Sociometrics 1989). The usual designs for evaluating prevention programs use experimental and control groups or time-series designs. In an experimental design, a sample targeted for prevention is compared with one that is not. There are often ethical problems with such designs (e.g., withholding needed services from the control group), and there can be problems in control, that is, the control group may be subject to some other intervention. A 10-year study of heart disease prevention found no differences between treatment and control groups because the whole society moved toward healthier lifestyle practices during the 1980s, essentially wiping out the control aspect of the intended control group. Time-series designs examine drops in indicators of interest, for example, teenage suicide or alcoholism, but, again, there are serious problems determining the causes of changes in indicators.

Qualitative data can add an important dimension to prevention evaluations by finding out the extent to which desired attitude and behavior changes linked to prevention actually occur. Interviews with teenagers about their decisions regarding sexual activity will reveal if teenagers are using prevention practices and ideas. This helps get at more than whether the desired outcome was achieved. It helps illuminate how those in the targeted group think about and understand what is being attempted.

An excellent example of prevention-oriented qualitative inquiry is Agar's (1999) study of heroin use among suburban youth in Baltimore County, Maryland. His fieldwork looked at how young people begin to experiment with heroin and the stories that are generated and disseminated based on initial experimentation. Those early stories tend to be positive: "Heroin puts one into a blissful, relaxed, dreamy state; the stresses, strains, and worries of everyday life fall away." Over time, positive stories are followed by negative stories as some youth become addicted and a few overdose. "The image of the addict, as opposed to the experimenter, was uniformly and strongly negative among the youth we interviewed, mostly based on their own observations or stories they had heard." As a result of his in-depth work on how heroin addiction spreads through the youth community, Agar (1999) learned how to be more effective in prevention education:

> I learned in the heroin lecture to emphasize the dangers of sliding into physical dependency —true addiction—and what post-addicted life was like. The theme contrasts with the normal approach, which conveys to youth that addiction and death may occur even with one experiment. Since youth rely on stories to evaluate drug effects and since so many stories contradict the normal premise, drug education loses its credibility. (pp. 115-16)

His fieldwork also included looking at supply and demand of heroin, and the larger system of which drug use was apart, all using qualitative methods to enhance efforts to prevent heroin use.

We evaluated a prevention program aimed at helping elderly people remain living in their homes, that is, preventing institutionalization. In some cases, the delay in institutionalization was only six months to a year. Through volunteer visits, home nursing care, and meals on wheels programs, however, elderly people could con-

tinue living in their homes, sometimes years beyond what would otherwise have been possible. While statistical data could document comparative death rates, hospitalization rates, and costs, only direct interviews and observations could reveal quality-of-life differences—what it meant to these elderly people to stay in their own homes. I remember in particular the story of one very frail woman in her 80s who took the interviewer to into her bathroom, opened her medicine cabinet, pointed to a bottle of capsules and said, "If they come to take me away, I'll excuse myself for a moment, come in here, and take these pills. I'm never leaving here. Never." This scenario was all clearly worked out in her mind and routinely practiced mentally. Understanding prevention includes understanding what people think and do as a result of prevention efforts.

Documenting Development Over Time and Investigating System Changes

The final practical application in this section focuses on the utility and appropriateness of using qualitative methods to follow and document development changes. This returns us to the value of qualitative inquiry for process studies, discussed earlier in this chapter, for development is best understood as a process. Organizational development, community development, human development, leadership development, professional development—these are process-oriented approaches to facilitating change. Pre- and posttests do not do justice to dynamic development processes. Pre- and postmeasures imply a kind of linear, ever upward, less-to-more image of growth and development. In reality, development usually occurs in fits and starts, some upward or forward progress, then backsliding or consolidation. Pre- and posttesting tell you where you started and where you ended up, but not what happened along the way. Quantitative measures can parsimoniously capture snapshots of pre- and poststates, even some interim steps, but qualitative methods are more appropriate for capturing evolutionary and transformational developmental dynamics. For example, I worked with a new and innovative employment training program that was constantly reorganizing staff and participant teams, realigning courses, trying new mixes of activities, and restructuring as growth occurred. We found that even quarterly reflective practice sessions were insufficient to capture all the changes occurring. To study this highly dynamic program required ongoing fieldwork framed against a chaos theory metaphor (see Chapter 3) because the program development really was like walking through a maze whose walls rearrange themselves with every step you take—and it was a major challenge to develop a data collection process that could capture those rearrangements.

Even routine monitoring using a standardized management information system can provide only an overview of up-and-down patterns. A break in a trend line or sudden blips in a time series can indicate that some qualitative difference may have occurred. Statistical data from monitoring and information systems can be used to trigger more in-depth qualitative studies that focus on finding out what the changes in the statistical indicators mean. Consider this analogy from the northern climes: The thermometer on a furnace thermostat shows the temperature throughout winter; if the temperature starts falling quickly in a house, someone had better have a look at the furnace. Just monitoring the temperature gauge won't solve the problem. So it is with management information systems. Blips or changes in indicators are a signal that fieldwork is needed to find out what's really going on where the action is.

From Evaluation Issues to Evaluation Models

Thus far in this chapter, we have reviewed the appropriateness of qualitative inquiry for dealing with fairly common evaluation challenges: quality assurance and enhancement, documenting outcomes through case studies, capturing individualized outcomes, process studies and implementation evaluation, clarifying a program's theory or logic model by linking processes and implementation to outcomes, evaluability assessments, comparing diverse programs, evaluating prevention programs, documenting development over time, and investigating sudden changes in management information system indicators. This is by no means an exhaustive list of evaluation applications, but each in some way illustrates a *practice-oriented application* of qualitative methods, the focus of this chapter, in the sense that qualitative findings are used to improve programs, deal with real problems, or support concrete decision making rather than contribute to social science theory or generate knowledge as an end in itself. The next section reviews some of the major models of evaluation research that are most closely associated with qualitative methods: goal-free evaluation, responsive evaluation, illuminative evaluation, the transaction model, the connoisseurship or art criticism approach, and utilization-focused evaluation.

🔄 Evaluation Models

┼┤ *olopis kuntal baris:* Indonesian phrase uttered to gain extra strength
when carrying heavy objects.

—Howard Rheingold (1988:49)

Conducting an evaluation can be a heavy load. Evaluation models help with the heavy lifting. Models provide frameworks like the metal frame on a backpack that gives support and shape to the load on a hiker's back. Models offer evaluators structure and support. They structure certain method-ological decisions, offer guidance about the appropriate steps to follow in design, pro-vide direction in ways of dealing with stake-holders (Alkin 1997), and identify the im-portant issues to consider in undertaking a study. Models provide frameworks rather than recipes, helping evaluators and evalua-tion users identify and distinguish among alternative approaches. For example, the classic model of evaluation is goals-based evaluation, that is, measuring the extent to which a program or intervention has at-tained clear and specific objectives. One al-ternative to goals-based evaluation, consid-ered below, is "goal-free" evaluation. The models briefly presented here have in com-mon that they have been closely associated with or heavily rely on qualitative methods.

Goal-Free Evaluation

In the classic model of evaluation, the fo-cus is on the *intended* services and outcomes of a program—its goals. However, an evalu-ator can turn up some very interesting re-sults by undertaking fieldwork in a program *without* knowing the goals of the program, or at least without designing the study with goal attainment as the primary focus. Philos-opher-evaluator Michael Scriven (1972b) first proposed the idea of goal-free evalua-tion. Essentially, goal-free evaluation means doing fieldwork and gathering data on a broad array of actual effects or outcomes, then comparing the observed outcomes with the actual needs of program partici-pants. The evaluator makes a deliberate at-tempt to avoid all rhetoric related to pro-gram goals; no discussion about goals is held with staff; no program brochures or proposals are read; only the program's ob-servable outcomes and documentable ef-fects are studied in relation to participant needs. There are four primary reasons for doing goal-free evaluation:

1. to avoid the risk of narrowly studying stated program objectives and thereby missing important unanticipated out-comes;

2. to remove the negative connotations at-tached to the discovery of unanticipated effects: "The whole language of 'side-effect' or 'secondary effect' or even 'un-anticipated effect' tended to be a put-down of what might well be the crucial achievement, especially in terms of new priorities" (Scriven 1972b:1-2);

3. to eliminate the perceptual biases intro-duced into an evaluation by knowledge of goals; and

4. to maintain evaluator independence by avoiding dependence on goals—a staff or administrative creation and, often,

fiction—that can limit the evaluator's range and freedom of inquiry.

In Scriven's (1972b) own words:

> It seemed to me, in short, that consideration and evaluation of goals was an unnecessary but also a possibly contaminating step.... The less the external evaluator hears about the goals of the project, the less tunnel-vision will develop, the more attention will be paid to looking for actual effects (rather than checking on alleged effects). (p. 2)

Goal-free evaluation, in its search for "actual effects," employs an inductive and holistic strategy aimed at countering the logical-deductive limitations inherent in the usual goals-based approach to evaluation. Goal-free evaluation was a radical departure from virtually all traditional evaluation thinking and practice. For example, prominent evaluation researcher Peter Rossi (Rossi and Williams 1972) asserted that "a social welfare program (or for that matter any program) which does not have clearly specified goals cannot be evaluated without specifying some measurable goals. This statement is obvious enough to be a truism" (p. 18). Carol Weiss (1972) emphasized the centrality of goals in evaluation when she stated, "The goals must be clear so that the evaluator knows what to look for. . . . Thus begins the long, often painful process of getting people to state goals in terms that are *clear, specific,* and *measurable*" (pp. 24-26).

In contrast to the predominant goals-based approach to evaluation, goal-free evaluation opens up the option of gathering data directly on program effects and effectiveness without being constrained by a narrow focus on stated goals. Qualitative in-quiry is especially compatible with goal-free evaluation because it requires capturing directly the actual experiences of program participants in their own terms. Moreover, and in particular, goal-free evaluation requires the evaluator to suspend judgment about what the program is trying to do and to focus instead on finding out what is actually occurring in and as a result of the program. The evaluator can thus be open to whatever data emerge from the phenomena of the program itself and participants' experiences of the program. But, as Ernie House (1991) has reported, somewhat tongue-in-cheek, actually conducting a goal-free evaluation can be challenging for all concerned because during on-site fieldwork staff keep dropping hints about program goals:

> Many are indignant that you do not want to know their objectives and incensed at the idea of your looking at what they are doing rather than what they are professing. As they chauffeur you around in their car, some will blurt out the goals as if accidentally, with sly apologies for their indiscretion. Others will write them on restroom walls—anonymously. (p. 112)

It is important to note that goal-free evaluations can employ both quantitative and qualitative methods. Moreover, Scriven (1972b) has proposed that goal-free evaluations might be conducted in parallel with goals-based evaluations, but with separate evaluators using each approach to maximize the strengths and minimize the weaknesses of each approach. (For a more detailed discussion of goal-free evaluation, and critiques of this idea, see Alkin 1972; Patton 1997a.)

Transaction Models: Responsive and Illuminative Evaluation

R esponsive evaluation enables an alert reporter to capture the deep-felt opinions of those most affected by the program, a product of grassroots populism.

—Ernest House (1991:113)

Robert Stake's (1975) "responsive approach to evaluation" places particular emphasis on the importance of personalizing and humanizing the evaluation process. Being responsive requires having face-to-face contact with people in the program and learning firsthand about diverse stakeholders' perspectives, experiences, and concerns.

Responsive evaluation is an alternative, an old alternative, based on what people do naturally to evaluate things, they observe and react. . . . To do a responsive evaluation, the evaluator conceives of a plan of observations and negotiations. He arranges for various persons to observe the program, and with their help prepares brief narrative portrayals, product displays, graphs, etc. He finds out what is of value to his audiences, and gathers expressions of worth from various individuals whose points of view differ. Of course, he checks the quality of his records: he gets program personnel to react to the accuracy of his portrayals; and audience members to react to the relevance of his findings. He does most of this informally—iterating and keeping a record of action and reaction. (Stake 1975:14)

Guba and Lincoln (1981) have integrated naturalistic inquiry and responsive evaluation into an overall framework for improving the usefulness of evaluation results. The openness of naturalistic inquiry permits the evaluator to be especially sensitive to the differing perspectives of various stakeholders.

This sensitivity allows the evaluator to collect data and report findings with those differing perspectives clearly in mind, but with special attention to those whose perspectives are less often heard. Subsequently, Guba and Lincoln (1989) added an explicitly constructivist perspective to responsive evaluation in proposing "responsive constructivist evaluation" as the "fourth generation" of evaluation. The first generation focused on measurement; the second on description; the third on judgment; and the fourth generation of evaluation focuses on issues-derived, values-based perspectives. (See Chapter 3 for a discussion of constructivism.)

Responsive evaluation includes the following primary emphases:

1. identification of issues and concerns based on direct, face-to-face contact with people in and around the program;

2. use of program documents to further identify important issues;

3. direct, personal observations of program activities before formally designing the evaluation to increase the evaluator's understanding of what is important in the program, and what can/should be evaluated;

4. designing the evaluation based on issues that emerged in the preceding three steps, with the design to include continuing direct qualitative observations in the naturalistic program setting;

5. reporting information in direct, personal contact through themes and portrayals that are easily understandable and rich with description; and

6. matching information reports and reporting formats to specific audiences with different reports and different formats for different audiences.

Responsive evaluation is a form of what evaluation theorist Ernie House (1978) has called the "transaction model" of evaluation in that it "concentrates on the educational (or program) processes themselves. . . . It uses various informal methods of investigation and has been drawn increasingly to the case study as the major methodology . . . , [derived from] a subjectivist epistemology [that] tends to be naturalistic" (p. 5). It treats each case as unique and places prime emphasis on perception and knowing as a *transactional* process between researcher and research participant, thus the label for this model.

> One can study perceptions only by studying particular transactions in which the perceptions can be observed. All parties of the situation enter into the transaction as "active participants," and do not appear as separate already-existing entities. . . . [The evaluator] affects and is affected by the situation, thus he is part of the transaction. (House 1978:9)

Another variation on the transaction model is "illuminative evaluation," originally developed as an educational evaluation approach that emphasized context and interpretation.

> The aims of illuminative evaluation are to study the innovative program: how it operates; how it is influenced by the various school situations in which it is applied; what those directly concerned regard as its advantages and disadvantages; and how students' intellectual tasks and academic experiences are most affected. It aims to discover and document what it is like to be participating in the scheme, whether as teacher or pupil, and, in addition, to discern and discuss the innovation's most significant features, recurring, concomitant, and critical processes. In short, it seeks to address and to illuminate a complex array of questions. (Parlett and Hamilton 1976:144)

Transaction evaluation approaches are based on the same assumptions that undergird qualitative research: the importance of understanding people and programs in context; a commitment to study naturally occurring phenomena without introducing external controls or manipulation; and the assumption that understanding emerges most meaningfully from an inductive analysis of open-ended, detailed, descriptive data gathered through direct interactions and transactions with the program and its participants.

Connoisseurship Studies

While responsive evaluation places the program's stakeholders at the center of the evaluation process, *connoisseurship* evaluation places the evaluator's perceptions and expertise at the center of the evaluation process. The researcher as connoisseur or expert uses qualitative methods to study a program or organization, but does so from a particular perspective drawing heavily on his or her own judgments about what constitutes excellence, thus the term *connoisseur*. This is a practical and personalistic version of what I called "orientational qualitative inquiry" in the last chapter and what Eisner (1985:184) has called "prefigured," that is, the terms and focus of the "educational criticism" are determined in advance by the evaluator and those seeking the evaluation. Prefiguring, however, does not mean that the observer cannot be open to a new, emergent focus during fieldwork.

> A critic might be invited to a school or classroom without a prefigured focus and after several days or weeks perceive an aspect of the school or classroom that is of considerable significance but which could not have been anticipated. For example, one of my students received permission from a secondary school English teacher to observe and to write an educational criticism about her class. What emerged during my student's observation was the extraordinary way in which the teacher used satire in her teaching. It was not the case that the teacher was herself teaching satire; it was that she was satirical in her teaching. Such a process or an approach could hardly have been prefigured. The point here is that the focus of criticism can be either prefigured as a part of the research bargain between the critic and the teacher, or it can be emergent or it can be both. (Eisner 1985:184-85)

The art criticism model as a "connoisseurship" approach has been most fully articulated by Elliot W. Eisner (1985). The imagery of evaluators as "connoisseurs" making critical appraisals of programs is analogous to the traditional way in which literary and artistic connoisseurs and critics work, Eisner having had considerable experience as an art educator.

The connoisseur approach has many elements that relate to naturalistic inquiry. Central among these are direct observation and immersion in the setting under study. Educational criticism or connoisseurship is, according to Eisner, first and foremost descriptive, both factually and artistically. The factual component reports direct observations and interviews. "The artistic aspect of description is literary and metaphorical; indeed, it can even be poetic in places. . . . In order to optimize communication, the potential of language is exploited so that the

literary and the factual complement each other" (Eisner 1985:182).

This means that evaluative criticism or connoisseurship is also highly interpretive and makes value judgments about the merits of what has been described and interpreted, using criteria that are appropriate to the situation based on the expertise of the evaluator (the connoisseur) and the agreements struck with those who are a party to the study. In that regard, design and data collection decisions are explicitly political and subjective. While there is a qualitative research foundation to this kind of evaluative connoisseurship, the method also "requires no small degree of artistry" (Eisner 1985:187). The factual aspects of this approach to evaluation communicate knowledge. The artistic aspects convey not only knowledge of facts "but also knowledge of feeling. Art can be said to be that activity concerned with the creation of images of feeling. The situations, people, and objects we encounter are never without affect" (Eisner 1988:17). The connoisseur, then, is explicitly and purposefully a qualitative researcher and an artistic critic of the phenomenon being studied.

Utilization-Focused Evaluation

Utilization-focused evaluation (Patton 1997a) offers an evaluative process, strategy, and framework for making decisions about the content, focus, and methods of an evaluation. Utilization-focused evaluation begins with identification and organization of specific, relevant decision makers and information users (not vague, passive audiences) who will use the information that the evaluation produces. A focus on *intended use by intended users* undergirds and informs every design decision in the evaluation. The evaluator works with these intended users (often an evaluation task force representing several constituencies, e.g., program staff, clients, funders, administrators, board members, and community representatives) to focus relevant evaluation questions. From these questions flow the appropriate research methods and data analysis techniques.

Utilization-focused evaluation plans for use before data are ever collected. The question that underlies the ongoing interactions between evaluators and intended users is, "What difference will this study make?" The evaluator asks, "What would you *do* if you had answers to the questions you're asking?" In answering the evaluation questions of specific intended evaluation users, utilization-focused evaluation does not preclude the use of any of the full variety of methodological options available. Qualitative inquiry strategies may emerge as appropriate in a particular utilization-focused evaluation as a result of defining the information needs of the specific intended evaluation needs.

Creative, practical evaluators need a full repertoire of methods to use in studying a variety of issues. This repertoire should include but not be limited to qualitative methods. By offering intended users methodological options, utilization-focused evaluators collaborate in making critical design and data collection decisions so as to increase the intended users' understanding and buy-in thereby facilitating increased commitment to use findings. The evaluator's responsibility is to interact with decision makers about the strengths, weaknesses, and relative merits of various methods so that mutually agreed-on, informed methods decisions can be made. The evaluator may well challenge entrenched methodological biases while remaining ultimately respectful of the importance of users getting something they will believe in and use.

Measurement and methods decisions are not simply a matter of expertly selecting the best techniques. Researchers *and* decision makers operate within quite narrow methodological paradigms about what constitutes valid and reliable data, rigorous and scientific design, and personal or impersonal research methods. As I noted in discussing methodological paradigms (Chapter 2), most social scientists routinely apply those methods in which they have been trained with little sensitivity to the biases introduced by a particular data collection scheme. Social and behavioral scientists— experts in the ultimate subjectivity and arbitrariness of all human perception—are often least aware of their own sociomethodological biases and how these biases affect their view of the social program world. Yet, to be sure, social scientists are not the only participants in the evaluation process operating on the basis of selective perception; decision makers and program staff also hold conditioned views about research and methods. One of the tasks to be accomplished during the interactions between evaluators and intended evaluation users is to mutually explore design and data biases so that the evaluation generates information that is useful and believable to all concerned.

Utilization-focused evaluation was developed from a study of the factors that seemed to explain variations in the actual use of evaluations. That study used qualitative methods to study the uses of 20 federal health evaluations. Our study team interviewed evaluators, funders, and program managers to find out how evaluation findings were used (Patton 1997a). Many others have since confirmed and elaborated the major elements of utilization-focused evaluation, again using qualitative methods (Alkin, Daillak, and White 1979; King and Pechman 1982; Campbell 1983; Holley and Arboleda-Florez 1988; Ferguson 1989). The utilization-focused approach was further refined through experience and practice and

EVALUATION OF FAITH-BASED PROGRAMS

First, some context for international readers: Shortly after being elected president of the United States, George W. Bush introduced legislation and created a White House office to support funding religious organizations engaged in social and educational programs. Such religious efforts are called "faith-based" in the current political lexicon.

In a Q & A session following a speech on enhancing evaluation use, I was asked to comment on the effectiveness of "faith-based" programs.

<u>*My response:*</u>

"From an evaluation perspective, any program is faith-based unless and until it has evaluation evidence of effectiveness. By that criterion, most programs have always been and remain essentially faith-based."

by studying how well-known and effective evaluators actually consult with clients and conduct themselves in doing evaluation research. Utilization-focused evaluation, then, is a process for creatively and flexibly interacting with intended evaluation users about their information needs and alternative methodological options, taking into account the decision context in which an evaluation is undertaken.

🖳 Interactive and Participatory Applications

Thus far, this chapter has been describing various evaluation issues that are especially appropriate for qualitative inquiry and some specific evaluation models that are closely associated with and rely heavily on qualitative methods. The next sections in this chapter review interactive applications of qualitative methods—practical and pragmatic forms of inquiry in which the researcher is especially sensitive to the perspectives of others and interacts closely with them in designing and/or implementing the study. Such interactive approaches that are especially congruent with qualitative methods include efforts to personalize and humanize research and evaluation, working with stakeholders to harmonize program and evaluation values, action learning and reflective practice, appreciative inquiry, facilitating collaboration with coresearchers through participatory research, supporting democratic dialogue and deliberation, and supporting democracy through process use.

Personalizing and Humanizing Evaluation

One reason for using qualitative methods in evaluation and organizational development processes is that such strategies may be perceived and experienced by program staff and participants as personal in nature, what Michael Cernea (1991) has called "putting people first." Programs that are based on humanistic concerns and principles often resist any kind of quantification because of the perception that numbers and standardized categorization are cold, hard, and impersonal. The issue here is not whether such objections are reasonable. The point is that such objectification feels real to those who hold such views. In programs where staff, funders, and/or participants feel this way, evaluations that rely on quantitative measurement may be rejected out of hand.

The personal nature of qualitative inquiry derives from its openness, the evaluator's close contact with the program, and the procedures of observation and in-depth interviewing, particularly the latter, that communicate respect to respondents by making *their* ideas and opinions (stated in their own terms) the important data source for the evaluation. Kushner's book *Personalizing Evaluation* (2000) epitomizes this emphasis especially in advocating that the perspective of participants be given primacy:

> I will be arguing for evaluators approaching programs through the experience of individuals rather than through the rhetoric of program sponsors and managers. I want to emphasize what we can learn about programs from Lucy and Ann. This does not mean ignoring the rights of program managers and sponsors with access to evaluation. There is no case for using evaluation against any stakeholder group; though there is a case for asserting a compensatory principle in favor of those who start out with relatively lower levels of access to evaluation. I don't think there is a serious risk of evaluators losing touch with their contractual obligations to report on programs and to support program management and improvement; I don't think there is a danger that evaluators will ever lose their preoccupation with program effects. There is always a risk, however, that evaluators lose contact with people; and a danger that in our concern to report on programs and their effects we lose sight of the pluralism of programs. So my arguments will robustly assert the need to address "the person" in the program. (pp. 9-10)

Qualitative methods may also be perceived as more personal because of their inductive nature. This means that, again, rather than imposing on people or a program some predetermined model or hypotheses, the results unfold in a way that takes into account idiosyncrasies, uniqueness, and complex dynamics. Finally, quali-

tative methods may be perceived as more humanistic and personal simply by avoiding numbers.

Personalizing and humanizing evaluation are particularly important for education, therapy, and development efforts that are based on humanistic values (Patton 1990). Humanistic values that undergird both qualitative inquiry and humanistic approaches to intervention and change include the core principles listed in Exhibit 4.4. Where people in a program, organization, or community hold these kinds of values, qualitative inquiry is likely to *feel* particularly appropriate.

Harmonizing Program and Evaluation Values

The suggestion that one reason for using qualitative methods is that such strategies may be perceived by program staff and program clients as more personal in nature opens up a whole range of potential philosophical, political, and value orientations that can influence methods decisions. The argument here is that it can be appropriate and desirable to include among the criteria for making methods decisions the value orientations of the intended users of the study. One example of a framework for supporting harmony between a program philosophy and evaluation approach is presented in Exhibit 4.5. This framework illustrates how the decision to use qualitative methods in evaluation can flow from the values of the people who will use the evaluation information.

Understanding, relevance, interest, and use are all increased when evaluators and users share values about methods. The final design of an evaluation depends on calculated trade-offs and weighing options, including political/philosophic/value considerations. The design also depends on

---

| EXHIBIT 4.4 | Common Principles Undergirding Qualitative Inquiry and Humanistic Values |

1. Each person or community is unique.

2. Each person or community deserves respect.

3. Equity, fairness, and mutual respect should be foundations of human interactions.

4. Change processes (and research) should be negotiated, agreed to, and mutually understood—not imposed, forced, or required.

5. One expresses respect for and concern about others by learning about them, their perspective, and their world—and by being personally involved.

6. Change processes should be person centered, attentive to the effects on real people as individuals with their own unique needs and interests.

7. Emotion, feeling, and affect are natural, healthy dimensions of human experience.

8. The change agent, therapist, or researcher is nonjudgmental, accepting, and supportive in respecting others' right to make their own decisions and live as they choose. The point is empowerment of others, not control or judgment.

9. People and communities should be understood in context and holistically.

10. The process (how things are done) is as important as the outcome (what is achieved).

11. Action and responsibility are shared; unilateral action is avoided.

12. Information should be openly shared and honestly communicated as a matter of mutual respect and in support of openness as a value.

---

opportunity, resources, time constraints, and commitment. What is to be avoided is the routine selection of a design without consideration of its strengths and weaknesses in relation to this complex constellation of both values and technical factors in an effort to make methods and values relatively harmonious.

Developmental Applications: Action Research, Action Learning, Reflective Practice, and Learning Organizations

> You learn something new every day. Actually, you learn something old every day. Just because you just learned it, doesn't mean it's new. Other people already knew it. Columbus is a good example.
>
> —George Carlin (1997:135)

A variety of organizational, program, and staff development approaches have emerged that involve inquiry within organizations aimed at learning, improvement,

EXHIBIT 4.5	Matching Program Philosophy and Evaluation Approach: An Illustration

What are the values of the school? And what are the values of the evaluation? Throughout the life of the school, three strong themes have emerged: (a) personalized curriculum, (b) the experiential nature of learning, and (c) the holistic nature of learning. The structures of the school organization, the formal goals of the school, emphases in classrooms, and investments of time and money in staff development activities have all placed strong value on these aspects of learning. These are not mutually exclusive, but are intricately intertwined. Their meaning for the school and for the evaluation of the school are described in the following excerpts from the Marcy Open School evaluation document.

Marcy Open School Philosophy	*Evaluation of Marcy Open School*
1. Personalized curriculum	1. Personalized evaluation
Curriculum will vary for each child as teaching extends from the interests, needs, and abilities of each child or group of children. The school personnel seek to be aware of each child as an individual, and of potential learning activities and materials. The individual child, the teacher, and the parents make decisions on the curriculum.	The determination of the success of the school will vary depending upon the values and perspectives of interested people. This evaluation will present a statement of what was made available by the school and of what was accomplished by children in the school. Decisions as to the success of the school and as to the validity of those activities must be left to the individual reading the evaluation report, according to his or her own perspective.
2. Experiential nature of learning	2. Experiential nature of evaluation
The school seeks to have the children experience language rather than only learning to read, to experience computation rather than only to learn math, to be in and to learn from the community rather than only to learn about social studies. Participants in the school believe that experience is the best transmitter of knowledge. Furthermore, the child is expected to interact with his [or her] environment—to have an effect upon it in the process of experiencing it—to change it or to recognize ways in which he [or she] seeks to move toward change.	This evaluation will attempt to provide an opportunity for the reader to experience the school and its children. It will provide not only charts and statistics, but photographs, drawings, and works of children and adults. Even so, it is acknowledged that, at best, any such report can only be an imperfect representation of the school and its processes. Furthermore, this report is not presented as a final document representing the accomplishments of the school. It is, instead, presented as a report-in-process, to be reacted to and sent back for new descriptions, new data, about which its readers may be concerned.

Marcy Open School Philosophy	*Evaluation of Marcy Open School*
3. Holistic nature of learning	3. Holistic evidence for evaluation
Much emphasis has been placed on the interrelatedness of learning. Organizational structures, activities, and materials are considered in terms of their multidimensionality of goals. Goal statements and staff development activities give conscious attention to children's feelings about themselves and their world, how those relate to the child's relationships with others and how those relate to the child's interest and ability in learning. The staff seeks activities that allow the child to experience the relationship between language, computation, and other knowledge rather than compartmentalizing them into separate content areas.	Three of the school's goals for children have been chosen for special attention in this evaluation. They include a range of process, content, and context typical of the goal statement as a whole. The evidence presented attempts to observe a natural order of events as they happen in the school with a minimum of distortion through departmentalization. Both objective figures and subjective judgments are included and are considered valid. The provisioning of the school and the activities and products of the children are viewed, insofar as it's possible, in terms of their multidimen- sionality of effect.

SOURCE: Olson 1974.

and development (e.g., Argyris and Schon 1978; Senge 1990; Watkins and Marsick 1993; Aubrey and Cohen 1995; Torres, Preskill, and Piontek 1996). These efforts are called various things: "action learning" (Pedler 1991; McNamara 1996), "team learning" (Jarvis 2000), "reflective practice" (Schon 1983, 1987; Tremmel 1993), "action research" (Whyte 1989; Gore and Zeichner 1995; Stringer 1996), internal evaluation (Sonnichsen 2000; Love 1991), or organizational development (Patton 1999c). These problem-solving and learning-oriented processes often use qualitative inquiry and case study approaches to help a group of people reflect on ways of improving what they are doing or understand it in new ways.

For example, the teaching staff of an evening basic skills adult education program undertook an action learning inquiry into the experiences of students who had recently immigrated to the United States. Each staff person interviewed three students and wrote short case studies based on the students' reports about their experiences enter-

ing the program. In an ongoing "reflective practice group," the teachers shared their cases and interpreted the results. Based on these reflections and thematic cross-case analysis, staff members revised their emphasis on goal setting as the priority first step in the program. The interviews showed that new immigrants lacked sufficient experience with and knowledge of American educational and employment opportunities to set meaningful and realistic goals. As a result, students typically acquiesced to counselor suggestions just to get the mandated goal-setting forms completed, but they came out of the orientation without any substantial commitment to or ownership of what were supposedly their own goals. Here we have an example of a short-term, rapid turn-around qualitative inquiry for reflective practice or action learning aimed at program improvement. By participating in the process, staff members also deepened their sensitivity to the perspectives and needs of new immigrant students, thereby developing professionally.

Inaction research

The learning that occurs as a result of these processes is twofold: (1) The inquiry can yield specific insights and findings that can change practice, and (2) those who participate in the inquiry learn to think more systematically about what they are doing and their own relationship to those with whom they work, what Bawden and Packham (1998) have called "systemic praxis." In many cases, the specific findings are secondary to the more general learnings that result from being involved in the process, what I have called "process use" as opposed to findings use (Patton 1997a). Process use is greatly enhanced in "developmental evaluation" (Patton 1994; 1997a) in which the purpose of the evaluation is ongoing learning, internal improvement, and program development rather than generating reports and summative judgments for external audiences or accountability.

A lot of attention in recent years has been paid to action learning as a way of helping people in organizations cope with change. Mwaluko and Ryan (2000) offer a case study showing how action learning programs can succeed if they are carefully designed and implemented systemically to deal with organic, cultural, and power complexities. In qualitative terms, this means action learning inquiry that is holistic, grounded, and sensitive to context.

Harvey and Denton (1999) examined the twin and interrelated themes of "organizational learning" and the "learning organization" in the business sector. The qualitative research underpinning their study was conducted over a three-year period (1994-1997) and involved detailed examination of organizational learning aspirations and practices within the British operations of five major manufacturing companies. Sixty-six interviewees were classified into three groups: strategy, human resources, and research and development (R&D). They identified a set of six antecedents that together explain the rise to prominence of emphasis on organizational learning: (1) the shift in the relative importance of factors of production away from capital toward labor, particularly intellectual labor; (2) the ever more rapid pace of change in the business environment; (3)

widespread acceptance of knowledge as a prime source of competitive advantage; (4) the greater demands being placed on all businesses by customers; (5) increasing dissatisfaction, among managers and employees, with the traditional, command-and-control management paradigm; and (6) the intensely competitive nature of global business. Their analysis of qualitative interviews featured the interplay of thoughts and feelings between management practitioners and organizational theorists in getting inside the idea of organizational learning. While they focused on business applications, the idea of being a learning organization has also become a prominent theme in the nonprofit, government, and philanthropic sectors (Sonnichsen 1993; Preskill and Torres 1999; Preskill and Preskill 1997). Qualitative inquiry as practiced through the lenses of action learning and reflective practice can be one of the foundations of a learning organization.

Appreciative Inquiry

Appreciative inquiry (AI) has emerged as a popular organizational development approach that emphasizes building on an organization's assets rather than focusing on problems, or even problem solving. Conceived and described in the work of David Cooperrider and his colleagues at Case Western Reserve's School of Organization Behavior (Watkins and Cooperrider 2000), AI is being offered by its advocates as "a worldview, a paradigm of thought and understanding that holds organizations to be affirmative systems created by humankind as solutions to problems. It is a theory, a mind-set, and an approach to analysis that leads to organizational learning and creativity" (Watkins and Cooperrider 2000:6). As such, "AI reflects the core values of OD [organizational development]," stated editors

Sorensen, Yaeger, and Nicoll (2000:4) in introducing a special issue of the journal *OD Practitioner* devoted to AI.

What interests us here is that AI is grounded in qualitative understandings and prescribes a particular process of qualitative inquiry within an organization that includes a dialogue process among participants based on their interviewing each other. They ask each other questions that "elicit the creative and life-giving events experienced in the workplace" (Watkins and Cooperrider 2000:9):

1. Looking at your entire experience with the organization, remember a time when you felt most alive, most fulfilled, or most excited about your involvement in the organization. . . .

2. Let's talk for a moment about some things you value deeply; specifically, the things you value about yourself, about the nature of your work, and about this organization. . . .

3. What do you experience as the core factors that give life to this organization? Give some examples of how you experience those factors.

4. What three wishes would you make to heighten the vitality and health of this organization? (p. 9)

These questions aim at generating specific examples, stories, and metaphors about positive aspects of organizational life. Participants in the process analyze the results in groups looking for the themes and topics that can become the foundation for positive organizational development going forward.

For example, if the original data suggest that COMMITMENT is an important factor in many of the stories about the best of times in the organization, then the workgroup might choose to ask more questions from others in the workplace about their experiences with commitment. This second round of interviews produces information about four to six topics that become the basis for building "possibility propositions" that describe how the organization will be in the future. Each topic or theme can be fashioned into a future statement. And these statements become an integral part of the vision for the organization. Often this process is completed with a future search conference that uses the appreciative inquiry data as a basis for imaging a positive and creative future for the organization. (Watkins and Cooperrider 2000:10)

AI has been criticized for being unbalanced and uncritical in its emphasis (critics say *over*emphasis) on accentuating the positive. It may even, ironically, discourage inquiry by discouraging constructive criticism (Golembiewski 2000). Whether it endures as a viable and popular approach to organizational development remains to be seen, but its questioning strategies could be incorporated into more balanced approaches. AI integrates inquiry and action within a particular developmental framework that guides analysis and processes of group interaction. The qualitative questioning and thematic analysis processes constitute a form of intervention by the very nature of the questions asked and the assets-oriented framework used to guide analysis. In this way, inquiry and action are completely integrated. Other forms of participatory inquiry also seek integration of inquiry and action.

Participatory Research and Evaluation: Valuing and Facilitating Collaboration

Let's start with three quite different examples of participatory qualitative inquiry.

In the film *Awakenings,* based on Dr. Oliver Sacks's real-life experiences in a New York institution for mentally ill people (Sacks 1973), Dr. Sacks (played by Robin Williams as the character Dr. Malcolm Sayer) engages the assistance of nurses, orderlies, janitorial staff, and even patients in joint efforts to discover what might reach certain patients suffering from a rare form of catatonia. The film powerfully displays a form of collaborative research in which trained researchers and nonresearchers undertake an inquiry together. One orderly tries music. A nurse tries reading to patients. A volunteer tries card games. Together they figure out what works.

In an African village, the women were skeptical of public health workers' admonitions to use well water rather than surface water for drinking during the rainy season. Going to the well was more work. Instead of simply trying to convince the women of the wisdom of this public health advice, the extension educators created an experiment in which half the village used well water and half used surface water. They kept track of illnesses with matchsticks. At the end of three months, the villagers could see for themselves that there were many more matchsticks in the surface water group. By participating in the study rather than just receiving results secondhand, the findings became more meaningful to them and more useful.

Early in my career, I was commissioned by a provincial deputy minister in Canada to undertake an evaluation in a school division he considered mediocre. I asked what he wanted the evaluation to focus on. "I don't care what the focus is," he replied. "I just want to get people engaged in some way. Education has no life there. Parents aren't involved. Teachers are just putting in time. Administrators aren't leading. Kids are bored. I'm hoping that having them participate in an evaluation will stir things up and get people involved again."

When conducting research in a collaborative mode, professionals and nonprofessionals become coresearchers. Humanistic research and heuristic inquiry (Douglass and Moustakas 1985) value collaboration, as does "cooperative inquiry" (Heron 1996). Participatory action research (Wadsworth 1993a, 1993b; King and Lonnquist 1994a, 1994b) encourages joint collaboration within a mutually acceptable ethical framework to understand and/or solve organizational or community problems. Feminist methods are participatory in that "the researcher invites members of the setting to join her in creating the study" (Reinharz 1992:184). "Empowerment evaluation" aims to foster "self-determination" among those who participate in the inquiry process (Fetterman 2000a; Fetterman, Kaftarian, and Wandersman 1996). This can involve forming "empowerment partnerships" between researchers and participants (Weiss and Greene 1992) and teaching participants to do research themselves (Wadsworth 1984). In-depth interviewing and description-oriented observations are especially useful methods for supporting collaborative inquiry because the methods are accessible to and understandable by people without much technical expertise.

Interest in participatory research has exploded in recent years, especially as an element of larger community change efforts (Stoecker 1999). The principal researcher trains the coresearchers to observe, interview, reflect, and/or keep careful records or diaries. Those involved come together periodically to share in the data analysis process. The purpose of such shared inquiry is typically to elucidate and improve the nature of practice in some arena of action.

Qualitative, collaborative research efforts in educational settings have a distinguished history. John Elliott (1976) worked with classroom teachers as coresearchers doing action research "developing hypotheses about classrooms from teachers' practical constructs." Bill Hull (1978) worked with teachers in a reflective, research-oriented process to study children's thinking. The Boston Women's Teachers' Group (1986) was organized as a research collaborative for studying the effects of teaching on teachers. Eleanor Duckworth's (1978) classic evaluation of an African primary science program was collaborative in approach.

Genuinely collaborative approaches to research and evaluation require power sharing. One of the negative connotations often associated with evaluation is that it is something done *to* people. Participatory evaluation, in contrast, involves working *with* people. Instead of being research subjects, the people in the research setting become "co-investigators." The process is facilitated by the researcher, but is controlled by the people in the program or community. They undertake a formal, reflective process for their own development and empowerment.

Participatory evaluation has been used with great success as part of international and community development efforts by a number of nongovernmental organizations (NGOs) and private voluntary organizations (PVOs) in the Third World (e.g., Aubel 1993). A collaborative group called Private Agencies Collaborating Together (PACT) published the excellent users guide *Participatory Evaluation* (1986) as well as the more general *Evaluation Sourcebook* (Pietro 1983). The guide includes techniques for actively involving nonliterate people as active participants in evaluating the development efforts they experience, often using qualitative methods.

The processes of participation and collaboration have an impact on participants and collaborators quite beyond whatever findings or report they may produce by working together. In the process of participating in research, participants are exposed to and have the opportunity to learn the logic of evidence-based inquiry and the discipline of evidentiary reasoning. Skills are acquired in problem identification, criteria specification, and data collection, analysis, and interpretation. Through acquisition of inquiry skills and ways of thinking, a collaborative inquiry process can have an impact beyond the findings generated from a particular study.

Moreover, people who participate in creating something tend to feel more ownership of what they have created and make more use of it. Active participants in research and evaluation, therefore, are more likely to feel ownership not only of *their* findings but also of the inquiry process itself. Properly, sensitively, and authentically done, it becomes *their* process. Participants and collaborators can be community members, villagers, organizational workers, program staff, and/or program participants (e.g., clients, students, farmers). Sometimes administrators, funders, and others also participate, but the usual connotation is that the primary participants are "lower down" in the hierarchy. **Participatory evaluation is bottom-up.** The trick is to make sure that participation is genuine and authentic, not just token or rhetorical, especially in participative evaluation, where differing political and stakeholder agendas often compete (Fricke and Gill 1989).

Norman Uphoff (1991) has published "A Field Guide for Participatory Self-Evaluation" aimed at grassroots community development projects. After reviewing a number of such efforts, he concluded:

If the process of self-evaluation is carried out regularly and openly, with all group members participating, the answers they arrive at are in

themselves not so important as what is learned from the discussion and from the process of reaching consensus on what questions should be used to evaluate group performance and capacity, and on what answers best describe their group's present status. (p. 272)

It was not a group's specific questions or answers that Uphoff found most affected the groups he observed. It was the process of reaching consensus about questions and engaging with each other in the meaning of the answers turned up. The process of participatory self-evaluation, in and of itself, provided useful learning experiences for participants.

Viewing participatory inquiry as a means of creating an organizational culture committed to ongoing learning, as discussed in the previous section, has become an important theme in recent literature linking program evaluation to "learning organizations" (e.g., King 1995; Leeuw, Rist, and Sonnichsen 1993). "The goal of a participatory evaluator is eventually to put him- or herself out of work when the research capacity of the organization is self-sustaining" (King 1995:89). Indeed, the "self-evaluating organization" (Wildavsky 1985) constitutes an important direction in the institutionalization of evaluation logic and processes.

I advise caution and care in using the label "participatory inquiry," "empowerment evaluation," or "collaborative research," for these terms mean different things to different people—and serve different purposes. Some use these terms interchangeably or as mutually reinforcing concepts. Wadsworth (1993a) distinguished "research *on* people, *for* people or *with* people" (p. 1). Levin (1993) distinguished three purposes for collaborative research: (1) the pragmatic purpose of increasing use of findings by those involved as emphasized by, for example, Cousins and Earl (1992); (2) the philosophical or method-

	Principles of Fully Participatory and Genuinely
EXHIBIT 4.6	**Collaborative Inquiry**

- The inquiry process involves participants in learning inquiry logic and skills, for example, the nature of evidence, establishing priorities, focusing questions, interpreting data, data-based decision making, and connecting processes to outcomes.

- Participants in the process *own* the inquiry. They are involved authentically in making major focus and design decisions. They draw and apply conclusions. Participation is real, not token.

- Participants work together as a group and the inquiry facilitator supports group cohesion and collective inquiry.

- All aspects of the inquiry, from research focus to data analysis, are undertaken in ways that are understandable and meaningful to participants.

- The researcher or evaluator acts as a facilitator, collaborator, and learning resource; participants are coequal.

- The inquiry facilitator recognizes and values participants' perspectives and expertise and works to help participants recognize and value their own and each other's expertise.

- Status and power differences between the inquiry facilitator and participants are minimized, as much as possible, practical, and authentic, without patronizing or game playing.

ological purpose of grounding data in participants' perspectives; and (3) the political purpose of mobilizing for social action, for example, empowerment evaluation or what is sometimes called "emancipatory" research (Cousins and Earl 1995:10). A fourth purpose, identified here, is teaching inquiry logic and skills. Since no definitive definitions exist for "participatory" and "collaborative evaluation," these phrases must be defined and given meaning in each setting where they're used. Exhibit 4.6 presents primary principles for fully participatory and genuinely collaborative inquiry. This list can be a starting point for working with participants in a research or evaluation setting to decide what principles they want to adopt for their own process.

Regardless of the terminology—participatory, collaborative, cooperative, or empowerment—these approaches share a commitment to involving the people in the setting being studied as co-inquirers, at least to some important extent, though the degree and nature of involvement vary widely. My purpose here has been to point out that these participatory approaches often employ qualitative methods because those methods are understandable, teachable, and usable by people without extensive research training.

Supporting Democratic Dialogue and Deliberation

Most of this chapter has examined relatively small-scale applications of qualitative methods in evaluating programs, developing organizations, supporting planning processes and needs assessments, and providing insights into communities. This section considers a much larger agenda, that of strengthening democracy. House and

Howe (2000) have articulated three requirements for evaluation done in a way that supports democracy: *inclusion, dialogue,* and *deliberation.* They worry about the power that
derives from access to evaluation and the
implications for society if only the powerful
have such access.

> We believe that the background conditions for
> evaluation should be explicitly democratic so
> that evaluation is tied to larger society by dem-
> ocratic principles argued, debated, and ac-
> cepted by the evaluation community. Evalua-
> tion is too important to society to be purchased
> by the highest bidder or appropriated by the
> most powerful interest. Evaluators should
> be self-conscious and deliberate about such
> matters. . . .
>
> If we look beyond the conduct of individ-
> ual studies by individual evaluators, we can
> see the outlines of evaluation as an influential
> societal institution, one that can be vital to the
> realization of democratic societies. Amid the
> claims and counterclaims of the mass media,
> amid public relations and advertising, amid
> the legions of those in our society who repre-
> sent particular interests for pay, evaluation
> can be an institution that stands apart, reliable
> in the accuracy and integrity of its claims. But
> it needs a set of explicit democratic principles
> to guide its practices and test its intuitions.
> (House and Howe 2000:4)

Qualitative inquiry figures into this democratic approach to evaluation because, as
discussed in the section on participatory research, qualitative methods are especially
accessible to and understandable by nonresearchers, and because case studies can be
an excellent resource for supporting inclusion and dialogue. In Europe, the democratic evaluation model of Barry MacDonald
(1987) illustrates these emphases. He argued
that "the democratic evaluator" recognizes
and supports value pluralism with the con-

sequence that the evaluator should seek to
represent the full range of interests in the
course of designing an evaluation. In that
way, an evaluator can support an informed
citizenry, the sine qua non of strong democracy, by acting as information broker between groups who want and need knowledge of each other. The democratic
evaluator must make the methods and techniques of evaluation accessible to nonspe-
cialists, that is, the general citizenry. Mac-
Donald's democratic evaluator seeks to
survey a range of interests by assuring confidentiality to sources, engaging in negotiation between interest groups, and making
evaluation findings widely accessible. The
guiding ethic is the public's right to know.

Saville Kushner (2000) has carried forward, deepened, and updated MacDonald's
democratic evaluation model. He sees evaluation as a form of personal expression and
political action with a special obligation to
be critics of those in power. He uses qualitative methods to place at the center of evaluation the experiences of people in programs.
The experiences and perceptions of the people in programs, the supposed beneficiaries,
are where, for Kushner, we will find the intersection of Politics (big *P*—Policy) and politics (small *p*—people). He uses qualitative
case studies to capture the perspectives of
real people—children and teachers and parents—and the realities of their lives in program settings as *they* experience those realities. He feels a special obligation to focus on,
capture, report, and therefore honor the
views of marginalized peoples. He calls this
"personalizing evaluation," but the larger
agenda is strengthening democracy. Consider these reflections on the need for evaluators and evaluations to address questions
of social justice and the democratic contract:

> Where each social and educational program
> can be seen as a reaffirmation of the broad so-

cial contract (that is, a re-confirmation of the bases of power, authority, social structure, etc.), each program evaluation is an opportunity to review its assumptions and consequences. This is commonly what we do at some level or another. *All programs expose democracy and its failings; each program evaluation is an assessment of the effectiveness of democracy in tackling issues in the distribution of wealth and power and social goods.* Within the terms of the evaluation agreement, taking this level of analysis into some account, that is, renewing part of the social contract, is to act more authentically; to set aside the opportunity is to act more inauthentically, that is, to accept the fictions. (Kushner 2000:32-33, emphasis added)

While MacDonald, Kushner, and House and Howe make explicit linkages between evaluation and democracy, a number of other evaluation approaches imply such linkages by emphasizing various degrees and types of stakeholder participation and involvement and, correspondingly, evaluator responsiveness. For reviews of the variety of such approaches and distinctions among them, see Cousins and Earl (1995) and Alkin (1997). The work of Mertens (1998, 1999) on "inclusive evaluation" and the "empowerment evaluation" model of Fetterman et al. (1996) offer additional examples of evaluation approaches that emphasize qualitative inquiry and support democratic principles, social justice, and explicitly political foundations of evaluation in support of those whose stakes tend to be underrepresented in policy discussions because they are marginalized economically, socially, and politically.

Taken together, these writings on evaluation's role in supporting democratic processes reflect a significant shift in the nature of evaluation's real and potential contribution to strengthening democracy. A decade ago, the emphasis was all on increasing use

of findings for enhanced decision making and program improvement and, therefore, making sure that findings reflected the diverse perspectives of multiple stakeholders, including the less powerful and participants in programs (instead of just staff, administrators, and funders). While this thrust remains important, a parallel and reinforcing use of evaluation focuses on *helping people learn to think and reason evaluatively,* and how rendering such help can contribute to strengthening democracy over the long term. I turn now to elaborate that contribution.

Supporting Democracy Through Process Use: Helping the Citizenry Weigh Evidence and Think Evaluatively

Let me begin by offering some context for reflecting on the role of knowledge creation in relation to democracy. In the autumn of 2000, I had the opportunity to participate in a seminar sponsored by the Italian Evaluation Society. While in Rome I visited the Forum, wandered among the ruins of ancient Rome, and spent some meditative time in the remains of the Senate seeking inspiration about what I might say regarding evaluation's potential contributions to democracy, the theme of the European Evaluation Society conference in Lausanne, Switzerland, where I was headed after Rome. Nothing came to me in the Forum, at least nothing about evaluation. I couldn't get past vivid images of Caesar's death in that place as portrayed by Shakespeare. After leaving the Forum, I walked across to the Coliseum, where gladiators did battle before emperors and citizens of Rome. There, standing in the platform area reserved for the senators, I got a distinct image. I imagined an evaluator presenting important policy findings to the citizens of Rome in the Coliseum. At the end of the report, the emperor would invite the crowd to render a thumbs-up or thumbs-down on the evaluation. Thumbs- up would mean a laurel wreath, coin of the realm, and an all-expenses-paid trip to present at the annual meeting of the Imperial Evaluation Society. Thumbs-down would mean the lions got fed. I left the Coliseum quickly thinking how fortunate I was to be engaged in evaluation at a time when the stakes, though high, are not quite so high as my Coliseum vision and when, instead, in the beautiful city of Lausanne, in the year 2000, an international community of professionals met together to spin visions of strengthening democracy by the ways in which we engage in evaluation and applied research.

So what is the connection between qualitative inquiry and democracy?

Start with the premise that a healthy and strong democracy depends on an informed citizenry. A central contribution of policy research and evaluation, then, is to help ensure an informed electorate by disseminating findings as well as to help the citizenry weigh evidence and think evaluatively. This involves thinking processes that must be learned. It is not enough to have trustworthy and accurate information (the informed part of the informed citizenry). People must also know how to use information, that is, to weigh evidence, consider inevitable contradictions and inconsistencies, articulate values, interpret findings, deal with complexity, and examine assumptions, to note but a few of the things meant by "thinking evaluatively." Moreover, in-depth democratic thinking includes political sophistication about the origins and implications of the categories, constructs, and concepts that shape what we experience as information and "knowledge" (Minnich forthcoming).

Philosopher Hannah Arendt was especially attuned to this foundation of democ-

racy. Having experienced totalitarianism, then having fled it, she devoted much of her life to studying it and its opposite, democracy. She believed that thinking thoughtfully in public deliberations and acting democratically were intertwined. Totalitarian- ism is built on and sustained by deceit and thought control. To resist efforts by the powerful to deceive and control thinking, Arendt believed that people needed to practice thinking. Toward that end she developed "eight exercises in political thought" (Arendt 1968). She wrote that "experience in thinking . . . can be won, like all experience in doing something, only through practice, through exercises" (p. 4). From this point of view, might we consider every evaluation an opportunity for those involved to practice thinking? This would mean that every evaluation is an opportunity to strengthen democracy by teaching people how to think evaluatively. In this regard, we might aspire to have policy research, action research, participatory research, and collaborative evaluation do what Arendt hoped her exercises in political thought would do, namely, give us "experience in *how* to think." Her exercises do not prescribe "what to think or which truths to hold"; rather, they focus on the act and process of thinking. For example, she thought it important to help people think conceptually, to "discover the real origins of original concepts in order to distill from them anew their original spirit which has so sadly evaporated from the very keywords of political language—such as freedom and justice, authority and reason, responsibility and virtue, power and glory—leaving behind empty shells" (Arendt 1968:14-15). Might we add to her conceptual agenda for examination and public dialogue such terms as *outcomes* and *performance indicators, interpretation* and *judgment,* and *beneficiary* and *stakeholder,* among many evaluative possibilities?

Helping people learn to think evaluatively by participating in real evaluation exercises is what I've come to call "process use" (Patton 1997a, 1998). I have defined process use as relating to and being indicated by individual changes in thinking and behaving that occur among those involved in evaluation as a result of the learning that occurs *during the evaluation process.* (Changes in program or organizational procedures and culture may also be manifestations of process impacts, but that is not our focus here.) This means an evaluation can have dual tracks of impact in strengthening democracy: (1) a more informed electorate through use of findings and (2) a more thoughtful and deliberative citizenry though helping people learn to think and engage each other evaluatively.

One way of thinking about process use is to recognize that evaluation constitutes a cultural perspective of sorts. When we engage other people in the evaluation process, we are providing them with a cross-cultural experience. This culture of evaluation, which we as evaluators take for granted in our own way of thinking, is quite alien to many of the people with whom we work at program levels. Examples of the values of evaluation include clarity, specificity, and focusing; being systematic and making assumptions explicit; operationalizing program concepts, ideas, and goals; distinguishing inputs and processes from outcomes; valuing empirical evidence; and separating statements of fact from interpretations and judgments. These values constitute ways of thinking that are not natural to people and, indeed, quite alien to many. When we take people through a process of participatory research or evaluation—at least in any kind of stakeholder involvement or collaborative process, they are in fact learning how to think in these ways. Inter-

viewing a variety of people and understanding in-depth case examples are especially effective ways of enhancing nonresearcher involvement in evaluation and research to help them increase their capacity to think about evidence and draw appropriate conclusions from data.

Helping people learn to think in these ways can have a more enduring impact from a study than use of specific findings generated in that same study. Findings have a very short half-life—to use a physical science metaphor. They deteriorate very quickly as the world changes rapidly. Specific findings typically have a small window of relevance. In contrast, learning to think and act evaluatively can have an ongoing impact. The experience of being involved in an evaluation, then, for those stakeholders actually involved can have a lasting impact on how they think, on their openness to reality testing, on how they view the things they do, and on their capacity to engage thoughtfully in democratic processes.

Democratic evaluations debunk the myth that methods and measurement decisions are purely technical. Nonresearchers then become savvier about both the technical and nontechnical dimensions of evaluation. Moreover, we know that use is enhanced when practitioners, decision makers, and other users fully understand the strengths and weaknesses of evaluation data and that such understanding is increased by being involved in making methods decisions. We know that use is enhanced when intended users participate in making sure that as trade-offs are considered, as they inevitably are because of limited resources and time, the path chosen is informed by relevance. We know that use is enhanced when users buy into the design and find it credible and valid within the scope of its intended purposes as determined by them. And we know that when evaluation findings are presented, the substance is less likely to be undercut by debates about methods if users have been involved in those decisions prior to data collection (Patton 1997a).

At its roots, participatory evaluations are informed by a fundamental confidence in the wisdom of an informed citizenry and a willingness to engage ordinary citizens respectfully in all aspects of evaluation, including methodological discussions and decisions. This point is worth emphasizing because some—not all, to be sure, but some—resistance to participatory evaluation derives from the status associated with research expertise and an elitist or patronizing attitude toward nonresearchers (they are, after all, "subjects"). Egon Guba (1978) has described in powerful language this archetype:

It is my experience that evaluators sometimes adopt a very supercilious attitude with respect to their clients; their presumptuousness and arrogance are sometimes overwhelming. We treat the client as a "child-like" person who needs to be taken in hand; as an ignoramus who cannot possibly understand the tactics and strategies that we will bring to bear; as someone who doesn't appreciate the questions he *ought* to ask until we tell him—and what we tell him often reflects our own biases and interests rather than the problems with which the client is actually beset. The phrase "Ugly American" has emerged in international settings to describe the person who enters into a new culture, immediately knows what is wrong with it, and proceeds to foist his own solutions onto the locals. In some ways I have come to think of evaluators as "Ugly Americans." And if what we are looking for are ways to manipulate clients so that they will fall in with *our* wishes and cease to resist our

blandishments, I for one will have none of it. (p. 1)

For others who will have none of it, one way to address the issue of methodological quality in democratic evaluations is to reframe the policy analyst's function from an emphasis on generating expert judgments to an emphasis on supporting informed dialogue, including methodological dialogue. The traditional expert-based status of researchers, scholars, and evaluators has fueled the notion that we provide scientifically based answers and judgments to policymakers while, by our independence, we ensure accountability to the general public. Playing such a role depends on a knowledge paradigm in which correct answers and independent judgments can be conceived of existing. However, postmodernism, deconstruction, critical theory, feminist theory, empowerment evaluation, and constructivism, among other perspectives, share skepticism about the traditional truth-oriented knowledge paradigm. They offer, in contrast, an emphasis on interest-acknowledged interpretations articulated and discussed within an explicit context (political, social, historical, economic, and cultural). Constructivist orientations to qualitative inquiry have played a critical role in the emergence of dialogical forms of inquiry and analysis. Participatory methods have increased the access of nonresearchers to both research findings and processes. In combination, constructivist, dialogical, and participatory approaches offer a vision of research and evaluation that can support deliberative democracy in the postmodern knowledge age. Such a grandiose, even bombastic, vision derives from recognition that in this emergent knowledge age, researchers have larger responsibilities than just publishing in academic journals.

🔁 Special Applications

$\mathcal{I}$f you come to a fork in the road, take it.

—Yogi Berra

These final sections examine some special applications and situations where qualitative strategies are especially appropriate: the need for unobtrusive measures; state-of-the-art considerations; adding depth, detail, and meaning to quantitative analyses; rapid reconnaissance; capturing and communicating stories; legislative auditing and monitoring; futuring applications; and breaking routines.

The Need for Unobtrusive Measures

Qualitative strategies can be particularly appropriate where the administration of standardized instruments, assigning people to comparison groups, and/or the collection of quantitative data would affect program operations by being overly intrusive. Examples of unobtrusive measures include observing and measuring wear and tear on carpets placed in front of different museum exhibits to evaluate visitor interest in different exhibits; observing people in a public place, as a participant in whatever is going on, without taking notes; and using documents or reports prepared for other purposes (e.g., clinical case notes) to generate research case data in situations where no additional human subject protection permission is required because the data are routinely collected and findings will be reported only in the aggregate.

Observations of program activities and informal interviews with participants can often be carried out in a less obtrusive fashion than having everyone complete a test or questionnaire. Indeed, administration of such instruments may produce artificial results because respondents are affected by the process, what measurement specialists call "reactivity," a source of invalidity in measurement. Educational researcher Edna Shapiro (1973), to her surprise, found this to be precisely the case in her study of innovative Follow Through classrooms. She found that standardized tests biased evaluation results by imposing an obtrusive and controlled stimulus in an environment where spontaneity, creativity, and freedom of expression were valued and encouraged. Shapiro found that the results of the test measured response to a stimulus (the test) that was essentially alien to the experience of the children. Because the classrooms she studied relied substantially less on paper-and-pencil skills than traditional schools, and because student progress was monitored daily on a personal basis without the use of written examinations, student outcomes in these classrooms could not be "objectively" measured by the sudden introduction of standardized tests.

I assumed that the internalized effects of different kinds of school experience could be observed and inferred only from responses in test situations, and that the observation of teaching and learning in the classroom should be considered auxiliary information, useful chiefly to document the differences in the children's group learning experiences. . . . The findings of this study, with the marked disparity between classroom responses and test responses, have led me to reevaluate this rationale. This requires reconsideration of the role of classroom data, individual test situation data, and the relation between them. . . . The individual's responses in the test situation have conventionally been considered the primary means to truth about psychological functioning. Test behavior, whether considered as a sign or sample of underlying function, is treated as a pure measure. Yet, the test situation is a unique interpersonal context in which what is permitted and encouraged, acceptable and unacceptable, is carefully defined, explicitly and implicitly. *Responses to tests are therefore made under very special circumstances. The variables that influence the outcome are different from those which operate in the classroom.* (Shapiro 1973:532-34, emphasis added)

In their imaginative classic, *Unobtrusive Measures,* Webb et al. (1966) discussed at length the problems of "reactive measurement effects." A basic theme of their work was that research participants' awareness that they are part of a study (as they complete questionnaires or take tests) might distort and confound the study's findings. Their documentation of the sources and nature of reactivity problems in scholarly social science research makes it highly likely that such problems are magnified in evaluation research (see Holley and Arboleda-Florez 1988). While qualitative methods are also subject to certain reactivity problems (to be discussed in later chapters), the less formal and less obtrusive nature of some qualitative strategies can reduce or even eliminate distorting reactivity.

State-of-the-Art Considerations: Lack of Proven Quantitative Instrumentation

Another reason for using qualitative methods is that for particular phenomena or

outcomes, no acceptable, valid, and reliable measures exist. The extent to which one believes that particular instruments, such as personality tests, are useful, valid, and reliable can be a matter of debate and judgment. Moreover, for desired program outcomes where measures have not been developed and tested, it can be more appropriate to gather descriptive information about what happens as a result of program activities than to use some scale that has the merit of being quantitative but whose validity and reliability are suspect.

Creativity is a prime example. While there are some instruments that purport to measure creativity, the applicability of those instruments in diverse situations is at least open to question. Thus, a program that aims to support students or participants in being more creative might do better to document in detail the activities, products, behaviors, feelings, and actual creations of participants instead of administering some standardized instrument of marginal or dubious relevance. Qualitative documentation can be inspected and judged by interested evaluation users to make their own interpretations of the extent to which creativity was exhibited by the products produced.

Even such hallowed concepts as self-esteem are open to considerable controversy when it comes to specifying measurement criteria. In addition, for people whose self-esteem is already quite high, instruments that measure self-esteem will not be very sensitive to incremental changes that may be important to the people involved. For staff development or leadership training programs that include enhanced self-esteem as an outcome goal, it may be more useful to do case studies to document changes experienced by participants rather than rely on a standardized measurement scale of problematic relevance and sensitivity.

The same point can be made with regard to controversy surrounding even long-standing measurement instruments. The use of standardized achievement tests to measure student learning is a prime example. Strong arguments have been made attacking the relevance of universal, standardized achievement tests for the evaluation of particular local programs (Perrone 1977). The way in which norm-referenced, standardized achievement tests are constructed reduces their relevance and validity for particular local programs, especially those that serve populations where scores are likely to cluster at the lower or higher extremes of the normal curve. For such programs, more accurate evaluation results can be produced through documentation of actual student portfolios, that is, developing case histories of what students can do and have done over time rather than relying on their responses to a standardized instrument administered under artificial conditions at a moment in time (Carini 1975, 1979; Buxton 1982).

A related state-of-the-art consideration is exploratory research. In new fields of study where little work has been done, few definitive hypotheses exist and little is known about the nature of the phenomenon, qualitative inquiry is a reasonable beginning point for research. Excellent examples of such exploratory research are Angela Browne's (1987) study *When Battered Women Kill*; a qualitative study of female child sexual offenders in a Minnesota treatment program (Mathews, Matthews, and Speltz 1989); follow-up interviews documenting the effects of reunification on sexually abusive families (Matthews, Raymaker, and Speltz 1991); Jane Gilgun's (1991) work on the resilience of and intergenerational transmission of child sexual abuse; and related frontline, small- scale studies of family sexual abuse (Patton 1991). These studies oc-

curred at a time when family violence and child sexual abuse were just emerging into societal consciousness and as a focus of scholarly inquiry. Exploratory work of this kind is the way that new fields of inquiry are developed, especially in the policy arena.

Confirmatory and Elucidating Research: Adding Depth, Detail, and Meaning to Quantitative Analyses

At the opposite end of the continuum from exploratory research is the use of qualitative methods to add depth and detail to completed studies that used quantitative data where the statistical results indicate global patterns generalizable across settings or populations. For example, when a large-scale survey has revealed certain marked and significant patterns of responses, it is often helpful to fill out the meaning of those patterns through in-depth study using qualitative methods. The quantitative data identify areas of focus; the qualitative data give substance to those areas of focus. Consider: What did people really mean when they marked that answer on the questionnaire? What elaborations can respondents provide to clarify responses? How do the various dimensions of analysis fit together as a whole from the perspective of respondents? Follow-up interviews with a subsample of respondents can provide meaningful additional detail to help make sense out of and interpret survey results. Qualitative data can put flesh on the bones of quantitative results, bringing the results to life through in-depth case elaboration.

Moreover, while the role of qualitative research in exploratory inquiry is relatively well understood, the confirmatory and elucidating roles of qualitative data are less well appreciated. Adding depth and detail to statistical findings is one aspect of confirmation and elucidation. Within major traditions of theory-oriented qualitative inquiry (Chapter 3), qualitative methods are also the methods of choice in extending and deepening the theoretical propositions and understandings that have emerged from previous field studies. In short, qualitative inquiry is not just for exploratory purposes.

Rapid Reconnaissance

Sometimes information is needed quickly. Indeed, this is increasingly the case in our rapidly changing world. There may be no time to search the literature, develop hypotheses, select probabilistic samples based on definitive population enumerations, and develop, pilot test, and administer new instruments. One major advantage of qualitative methods is that you can get into the field quickly.

Experimental, deductive, hypothesis-testing strategies can require a lot of front-end work. You've got to be quite certain about design and instrumentation *before* data collection because once the study is under way, changes in design and measurement undermine both internal and external validity. Naturalistic inquiry, in contrast, permits the researcher to enter the field with relatively little advance conceptualization, allowing the inquirer to be open to whatever becomes salient to pursue. The design is emergent and flexible. The questions unfold as the researcher pursues what makes sense.

Rapid reconnaissance or "rapid assessment" (Beebe 2001) connotes doing fieldwork quickly, as does "quick ethnography" (Handwerker 2001). In our highly dynamic world, it's important to stay close to the action. Best-selling author Tom Peters (1987) called his field-based, close-to-the-action management approach "thriving on chaos." He included the admonition to managers to

spend less time planning and more time out in the trenches talking to people and watching what's going on.

In crisis epidemiological work, as in the outbreak of highly contagious diseases (e.g., the Ebola virus in Africa) or the emergence of AIDS, rapid reconnaissance teams made up of medical personnel, public health researchers, and social scientists are deployed to investigate the crisis and determine immediate interventions and longer-term actions needed. The film *And the Band Played On*, about the early incidences of the HIV virus before it had been identified and named, shows the intensity of this kind of interview-based, snowball-sampling (getting new contacts from each person interviewed), and field-based crisis reconnaissance inquiry.

In the late 1980s, cooperative extension services in the United States adopted a new approach to programming based on rapid response to emergent issues (Patton 1987b, 1988a; Dalgaard et al. 1988). This meant doing ongoing "environmental scanning," which included content analysis of newspapers and periodicals, conducting focus groups with emerging new client groups, interviewing key informants well placed to identify cutting-edge issues, and making systematic observations of what is happening in counties and regions throughout the United States. Issues teams worked together using both quantitative and qualitative information to identify trends, scan the environment, and formulate new programs based on emergent issues. These teams sometimes undertake rapid reconnaissance fieldwork to get detailed, descriptive information about a developing situation, for example, an influx or out-migration of new people in an area; the impact of sudden economic changes in a county; the sudden appearance of a crop disease or pest; or a rapid increase in some problem such as teenage pregnancies, crack cocaine-addicted new-borns, homelessness, or elderly persons in need of long-term care. Action research teams can do rapid reconnaissance on these issues quickly, going where the action is, talking to people and observing what is happening.

The farming systems approach to international development was developed using rapid reconnaissance teams (Shaner, Philipp, and Schmehl 1982a, 1982b). Interdisciplinary teams conduct fieldwork and informal interviews to construct an initial, exploratory, and qualitative portrayal of the farming system in a particular agroecological area. Through the fieldwork, which may last from one to three weeks, the teams are able to identify system characteristics, farmers' needs, extension possibilities, and new applied agricultural research priorities. The Caribbean Agricultural Extension Project, for example, used 10-day rapid reconnaissance studies in each of 10 different islands to assess needs and develop interventions for the extension services in those countries (Alkin and Patton 1987; Alkin et al. 1989; Patton 1988b).

In the farming systems literature, these rapid reconnaissance surveys are often called *sondeos* after the Spanish word meaning "sounding." A *sondeo* is a qualitative "sounding out" of what is happening. Informal interviews and observations are done on farms and in homes to document and understand variations within some defined geographical area. Once interventions begin, either research or extension interventions, the *sondeos* may be periodically repeated to monitor system changes and development, as well as to evaluate the interventions.

The point here is that the very nature of qualitative inquiry makes it possible to get into the field quickly to study emerging phe-nomena and assess quickly developing situations in a world of rapid change.

Capturing and Communicating Stories

> To keep my head straight I reserve certain words for specialized meanings—case study and ethnography are two such labels. I write stories, not case studies, although readers of my stories may mistakenly call them ethnographic research or case studies. Were I doing ethnography or ethnology, which I never do, I would have a much heavier burden. I would have to address questions of validity, of theory contribution, of com- pleteness, of generality, of replicability. . . . A story documents a given milieu in an attempt to communicate the general spirit of things. The story need not test theory; need not be complete; and need not be robust in either time or depth. (Denny 1978:1)

In *The Springboard*, Stephen Denning (2001) explains "how storytelling ignites action in knowledge-era organizations." He teaches storytelling as a powerful and formal discipline for organizational change and knowledge management. What he calls "springboard" stories are those that communicate new or envisioned strategies, structures, identities, goals, and values to employees, partners, and even customers. He argues that storytelling has the power to transform individuals and organizations. He offers as an example his frustrated efforts, as director of knowledge management of the World Bank, to convince colleagues to share information throughout the organization. His reports and graphs were not proving effective in making his case, so he told the staff a story. In 1995, a health care worker in Zambia was searching for a treatment for malaria. He found what he needed at the Web site of the Centers for Disease Control.

The story communicated what his memos had not: the potential life-and-death importance of having critical knowledge available and easily accessible to any World Bank worker in any remote place in the world.

In another management book, *Managing By Storying Around,* David Armstrong (1992) turns the noun *story* into a verb, *storying,* to emphasize the direct and active impact of constructing stories to influence organizational values and culture. Shaw, Brown, and Bromiley (1998) reported how capturing and using "strategic stories" helped the multinational 3M company improve their business planning both internally, for those involved, and externally, for those to whom strategic results were reported: "A good story (and a good strategic plan) defines relationships, a sequence of events, cause and effect, and a priority among items—*and those elements are likely to be remembered as a complex whole*" (p. 42).

Qualitative inquiry can be used to discover, capture, present, and preserve the stories of organizations, programs, communities, and families. Barry Kibel (1999) developed a process for capturing the "success stories" of clients in programs and aggregating them in a method he called "results mapping." His approach involves an arduous and rigorous coding process that can be challenging to manage, but the fundamental idea is that "for programs engaged in healing, transformation, and prevention, the best source and form of information are client stories" (Kibel 1999:13).

Story collecting can be integrated into ongoing program evaluation, monitoring, and development (organizational learning) processes. For example, the Institute of Land and Food Resources at the University of Melbourne in Australia developed a story-based change-monitoring approach called "most significant changes" (Dart et al. 2000; Davies 1996) that involves several steps. First, key program stakeholders and participants (e.g., farmers in an extension program) come to an agreement on which "domains of change" to monitor with stories. Second, monthly stories of change written by farmers and field staff are collected. Third, volunteer reviewers and evaluators using agreed-on criteria select the "most significant stories" during regional and statewide committee meetings. Last, at the end of the year a document is produced containing all the "winning" stories. This document forms the basis for a round-table discussion with "key influentials" and funders of the project, who then also select the most significant stories according to their views. "This approach goes beyond merely capturing and documenting client stories; each story is accompanied by the storyteller's interpretation, and after review the stories are also accompanied by the reviewer's interpretation. One of the ideas behind the process is that it promotes a slow but extensive dialog up and down the project hierarchy each month" (Dart 2000). See Exhibit 4.7 for an example of a "most significant change" story. This story also illustrates a qualitative approach to outcomes documentation discussed earlier in this chapter.

Cognitive scientists have found that stories are more memorable and better support learning and understanding than nonstory narratives (Shaw et al. 1998:42). Language scholar Richard Mitchell (1979) has observed, "Our knowledge is made up of the stories we can tell, stories that must be told in the language that we know. . . . Where we can tell no story, we have no knowledge" (p. 34).

As I noted in the last chapter in discussing narrative analysis, which focuses on stories as a particular form of qualitative inquiry, the language of "storytelling" is less

---

EXHIBIT 4.7	**Example of a "Most Significant Change" Story**

Title: "I'll Not Be Milking Cows When I'm 55"

Name of person recording story: Mark Saddington, dairy farmer

Region: Gippsland

Date of narration: Round 2—August 21, 1998

Who was involved: Farmer and family

When did it happen: 1998

What happened? We did the pilot Dairy Business Focus Program in March, and for the first time, my wife came along. We were able to look at our farm as a business, not just as a farm. As a consequence of doing the program, we did a few sums and made a few decisions. We worked out that we can afford to have her on the farm, and she has left her job at the bank. We will generate enough income on the farm to make it more profitable for her to be here. The kids will benefit from seeing her a lot more, and they won't be in day care. So far this year, this has made the calving so much easier, we have a joint input, and it has been such a turn around in my lifestyle. It has been so good.

    We actually went to the accountant yesterday to get some financial advice on how we should be investing off-farm. He was amazed that what we are doing is treating the farm as a business. I said: "Now everything that we earn on this farm is going to be put away so that I am not milking cows when I am 55 years old!"

    We have got a debt-reduction program running for the next 12 months, but after that the money will be channeled to off-farm investment. I want to retire young enough to enjoy what we have been working towards for the last 20 or 30 years. My boss is 77 and is still working on the farm. If I am that fit when I am his age, I want to be touring around the world.

    It has opened up our lives. We are now looking at off-farm investment, as capital investment on-farm is not that great. We are not going to invest in new machinery but are going to invest in contractors to do any work we can't do. There is no point buying new machinery, as it depreciates. Instead, we will buy shares and invest off the farm. This proves that you can farm on 120 cows, you don't have to get big, and you don't have to milk a lot of cows. It just depends what you do with your money. If only we could educate the younger farmers to think ahead instead buying the largest SS Commodore or the latest dual cab. I followed the same track for a few years until we sat down and worked out where we were going and where we could be. We made a few mistakes in the past, but the past is the past.

Feedback from the statewide committee:
- This story generated lots of discussion. But is it really about profitability or quality of life or changes in farm practice?
- The general consensus was that there needed to be more detail in the story for it to be clearly about profitability.
- It is a really powerful story that shows considerable change.

(continued)

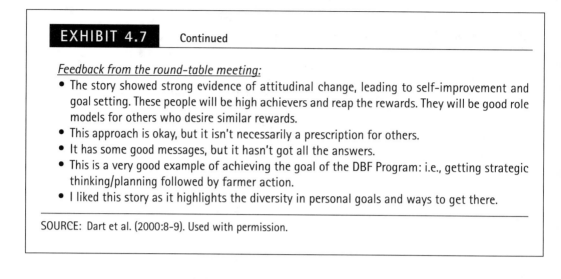

intimidating to nonresearchers than the language of "case studies" or "ethnography," words that sound heavy and academic. It makes quite a difference when talking to people in a community to say, "We'd like to hear and record your stories" versus "We'd like to do a case study of you."

One of my favorite stories was told by anthropologist Gregory Bateson (1978), the story of attempts to create a computer that could think like human beings. Two scientists became particularly enthralled with this idea and devoted their lives to the quest. Each time they thought they had succeeded, their efforts failed critical tests and they had to go back to the drawing board to search still deeper for the breakthrough that would lead to a computer that could truly think. They made revisions and adaptations based on all their prior failures until finally they felt more hopeful than ever that they had succeeded. The computer program passed all the preliminary tests. They became increasingly excited. The moment arrived for the penultimate test. They asked the computer: "Can you think like a human being?"

The computer processed the question and on the screen appeared the answer: "That question reminds me of a story." They knew then they had succeeded.

Legislative Auditing and Monitoring

W e've funded nine of these so-called regional transportation coordinating boards around the state and we have no real idea who's involved, how well they're working, or even what they're really doing. We need an independent perspective on what the hell's going on. Think you can find out?

—Phone inquiry from a state legislator

On occasion some legislative body or board that has mandated and appropriated funds to a new program wants information about the extent to which the program is operating in accordance with legislative intent. Legislative intent may involve achieving certain outcomes or may focus on whether some mandated delivery specifications are being followed. Sometimes the precise nature of the legislated delivery system is only vaguely articulated. For example, such mandates as "deinstitutionalization," "decentralization," "services integration," and "community-based programming" involve varied conceptualizations of legislative intent that do not lend themselves easily to quantitative specification. Indeed, for the evaluator to unilaterally establish some quantitative measure of deinstitutionalization that provides a global, numerical summary of the nature of program operations may hide more than it reveals.

To monitor the complexities of program implementation in the delivery of government services, it can be particularly helpful to decision makers to have detailed case descriptions of how programs are operating and what they're accomplishing. Such legislative monitoring would include descriptions of program facilities, decision making, outreach efforts, staff selection procedures, the nature of services offered, and descriptions from clients about the nature and results of their experiences. An exemplar of such an effort is an in-depth study of "transportation partnerships" throughout Minnesota that included case studies in each region and an extensive cross-case analysis of patterns and variations (DeCramer 1997).

Busy legislators cannot be expected to read in detail a large number of such histories. Rather, legislators or funders are likely to be particularly interested in the case histories of those programs that are within their own jurisdiction or legislative district. More generally, legislative staff members who are particularly interested in the program can be expected to read such case histories with some care. From a political point of view, programs are more likely to be in trouble or cause trouble for legislators because they failed to follow legislative intent in implementation rather than because they failed to achieve desired outcomes. In this case, **the purpose of legislative monitoring or auditing is to become the eyes and ears of the legislature or board.** This means providing program descriptions that are sufficiently detailed and evocative that the legislator or legislative staff can read such descriptions and have a good idea of what that program is really like. Having such descriptions enables legislators to decide whether their own interpretations of legislative intent are being met. The observation of a parent education program reported in the first chapter is an example of fieldwork done for the purpose of monitoring legislative intent. There are excellent program evaluation units within a number of state legislative audit commissions that use fieldwork to do policy research and evaluation for legislators. When done well, such fieldwork goes beyond simple compliance audits by using qualitative methods to get at program processes, implementation details, and variations in impacts.

Detailed case histories may also be of considerable service to the programs being monitored because a case history permits them to tell their own story in some detail. Thus, where they have deviated from legislative intent, such case histories would be expected to include information from program administrators and staff about constraints under which the program operates and the decisions staff has made that give the program its character. At the same time, the collection of such case histories through site visits and program monitoring need not neglect the possibility for including more global statements about statewide patterns in programs, or even nationwide patterns. It is quite possible through content analysis to identify major patterns of program operations and outcomes for a number of separate cases. Thus, qualitative methods used for legislative monitoring allow one to document common patterns across programs as well as unique developments within specific programs.

Futuring Applications: Anticipatory Research and Prospective Policy Analysis

J am often surprised, but I am never taken by surprise.

—Robert E. Lee, U.S. Civil War general

Lee's statement captures, in essence, what it means to anticipate the future. Our rapidly changing world has increased interest in and need for futures studies. Such work has moved beyond the supermarket tabloids to become a focus of scholarly inquiry (e.g., Helmer 1983). Much futures work involves statistical forecasting and computer simulations. There are, however, also qualitative inquiry futuring research strategies.

One important futuring tool is scenario construction (Edmunds 1978; Godet 1987; Fitzsimmons 1989). Scenarios are narrative portrayals of future systems. A scenario can be constructed for an organization, a community, a farming system, a society, or any other unit of interest. Useful scenarios are highly descriptive. One technique for writing scenarios is to base the scenario on imagined future fieldwork. The scenario is written as if it were a qualitative study of that future system. As such, it would include interview results, observational findings, and detailed descriptions of the phenomenon of interest.

Qualitative methods can also be used to gather the data for scenario development. The Minnesota Extension Service undertook a community development effort in rural ar-

eas called Project Future. Part of the development effort involved teams of community members interviewing people in their own communities about their visions, expectations, hopes, and fears for the future. The community teams then analyzed the results and used them to construct alternative future scenarios for their community. The community next reviewed these scenarios, changed them through discussion, and selected a future to begin creating. (This is also a form of participatory research discussed earlier in this chapter.) Ethnographic futures research can be part of a community development process (Domaingue 1989; Textor 1980).

The Evaluation Unit of the U.S. General Accounting Office (GAO) developed methods for "prospective studies" to help policymakers anticipate the implications and consequences of proposed laws. Prospective studies can include interviewing key knowledgeables in a field to solicit the latest and best thinking about a proposal, sometimes feeding back the findings for a second round of interviews (a qualitative Delphi technique). Prospective methods can also include doing a synthesis of existing knowledge to pull together a research base that will help inform policy making. The GAO

Futures Research

Somebody sent some researchers here thinking they could get some interviews from people interested in the long-term future. But I get off work in just 15 minutes. Are you interested?

© 2002 Michael Quinn Patton and Michael Cochran

handbook *Prospective Methods* (1989) includes attention to qualitative and quantitative synthesis techniques, with particular attention to the problem of drawing together diverse data sources, including case studies. Indeed, the *Prospective Methods* guidebook presents much of the material in a case study format.

Rapid reconnaissance fieldwork can also be used for anticipatory or futuring research. Being able to get into the field quickly to get a sense of emerging developments can be critical to futures-oriented needs assessment techniques and forward-looking planning processes. The content analysis techniques of qualitative inquiry, especially media analysis (Naisbitt and Aburdene 1990; Merriam and Makower 1988; Naisbitt 1982), are central to many

futuring research efforts. Constructing futures scenarios can also be an effective way to contextualize evaluation findings and recommendations, to help decision makers think about the varying future conditions that could affect implementation of alternative recommendations (Patton 1988d, 1997a: 328-29).

In summary, while most evaluation work involves looking at the effectiveness of past efforts in order to improve the future effectiveness of interventions, a futuring perspective involves anticipatory research and forward thinking in order to affect current actions toward creating desirable futures. Qualitative inquiry can play a role in both studies of the past and anticipatory research on the future.

Breaking the Routine:
Generating New Insights

Being futures oriented includes being open and flexible. Both individuals and organizations can easily become trapped in routine ways of doing things, including routine ways of thinking about and conducting evaluations or engaging in research. Thus, I end this chapter with one final rationale for using qualitative methods: breaking the routine or "making the familiar strange" (Erickson 1973:10). Programs and organizations that have established ongoing evaluation systems or management information approaches may have become lulled into a routine of producing statistical tables that are no longer studied with any care. Inertia and boredom can seriously reduce the usefulness of program evaluation results. After program staff or other decision makers have seen the same statistical results used in the same kinds of statistical tables year after year, those results can begin to have a numbing effect. Even though the implications of those results may vary somewhat from year to year, the very format used to report the data can reduce the impact of the reports.

Mao Tse-tung commented on the tendency of human beings to settle into numbing routines when he said that a revolution is needed in any system every 20 years. Revolutions in the collection of evaluation data may be needed much more often. One such revolution may be to introduce a totally new approach to evaluation simply for the purpose of attracting renewed attention to the evaluation process. At the time, changing the method may produce new insights or at least force people to deal with the old insights in a new way.

Of course, collection of qualitative data can also become routine. Programs based on a humanistic philosophy and/or programs with an emphasis on individualization may find that the collection of qualitative data has become a routine and that new insights can be gained through even the temporary use of some quantitative measures. This suggestion for periodically changing methods derives from a concern with enhancing the use of evaluation research. Given the ease with which human beings and social systems settle into inertia and routine, evaluators who want their results to make a difference need to find creative ways to get people to deal with the empirical world. Exploring methodological variations may be one such approach.

It is also worth noting that evaluators can settle into routines and inertia. Evaluators who have been using the same methods over and over may have lost the cutting edge of their own creativity. Utilization-focused evaluators need to have at their disposal a large repertoire of possible data collection techniques and approaches. Evaluators can be more helpful to programs if they themselves are staying alert to the many possibilities available for looking at the world. Indeed, a change in methods may do as much or more to reenergize the evaluator as it does to renew the program evaluation process.

🔄 Summary: A Vision of the Utility of Qualitative Methods

As I was completing this book, my local coffee shop went out of business. It had been open only two years, having been part of a surge of new coffee shops that sprang up throughout the United States as Americans fell in love with cappuccino. This particular coffee shop was unique because it was also a biker hangout. That is, it catered to aficionados of large Harley-Davidson motorcycles affectionately called "Hawgs." The owners, Scott and Connie, a young husband-and-wife team, were also bikers. Because the coffee shop was only a block from my office, I had become a regular, despite my lacking the appropriate leather attire and loud steel machine. One morning, Connie mentioned that she had decided to have laser surgery to correct her nearsighted vision. I left for a trip wishing her a positive outcome from the surgery. When I returned two weeks later the coffee shop was closed and I found a barely legible, handwritten note on the door:

> *Closed indefinitely—vision problem*

I made inquiries at a nearby gasoline station, but all I learned was that the shop had closed very suddenly without notice. Some three weeks later, I happened to see Scott riding his motorcycle on the street and waved him over to ask how Connie was doing. He said she was fine. What about the sign on the coffee shop door? That had nothing to do with Connie's surgery, he explained. "I just couldn't vision myself serving coffee the rest of my life."

This chapter has been aimed at helping you decide if you can envision yourself interviewing people, doing fieldwork, constructing case studies, and otherwise using qualitative methods in practical applications. Exhibit 4.8 lists the applications offered in this chapter, situations and questions for which qualitative methods are particularly appropriate. These are by no means exhaustive of the possibilities for applying qualitative approaches, but they suggest the wide range of arenas in which qualitative methods can be and are being used.

New applications of qualitative methods continue to emerge as people in a variety of endeavors discover the value of in-depth, open-ended inquiry into people's perspectives and experiences. For example, Wasson (2000) has reported that members of the design profession have begun using qualitative methods, especially ethnography, "because it provides a window onto the ways consumers interact with products in their everyday lives" (p. 377). Designers, in developing innovative products and services, must be concerned with satisfying the needs of users of their products. Qualitative methods, including extensive use of videotape to capture people using products and services, offer designers insights into the cultural and environmental contexts within which real consumers use real products. Exhibit 4.9 offers examples of Internet-based resources that can help you monitor new developments in qualitative applications.

The emphasis in this chapter on practical and useful applications stands in contrast to the philosophical and theoretical focus of the previous chapter. Taken together, these two chapters demonstrate the importance of qualitative inquiry to both social science theory and practice-oriented inquiry, especially in evaluation and organizational development.

Practical applications of qualitative methods emerge from the power of observation, openness to what the world has to teach, and inductive analysis to make sense out of the world's lessons. While there are elegant philosophical rationales and theoretical underpinnings to qualitative inquiry, the practical applications come down to a few very basic and simple ideas: Pay attention, listen and watch, be open, think about what you hear and see, document systematically (memory is selective and unreliable), and apply what you learn.

The story of the invention of modern running shoes illustrates these principles and provides a helpful metaphor to close this chapter. The design of sneakers varied little until the 1960s when competitive runners began to turn to lighter-weight shoes. Reducing the weight of shoes clearly improved performance, but problems of traction re-

EXHIBIT 4.8	Qualitative Inquiry Applications: Summary Checklist of Particularly Appropriate Uses of Qualitative Methods

Studies Focusing on Quality
　Understanding and illuminating quality
　Quality assurance

Evaluation Applications
　Outcomes evaluation
　Evaluating individualized outcomes
　Process studies
　Implementation evaluation
　Logic models and theories of action
　Evaluability assessments
　Comparing programs: Focus on diversity
　Prevention evaluation
　Documenting development over time and investigating system changes

Evaluation Models
　Goal-free evaluation
　Transaction models: Responsive and illuminative evaluation
　Connoisseurship studies
　Utilization-focused evaluation

Interactive and Participatory Applications
　Personalizing and humanizing evaluation
　Harmonizing program and evaluation values
　Developmental applications: Action research, action learning, reflective practice, and
　　learning organizations
　Appreciative inquiry
　Participatory research and evaluation: Valuing and facilitating collaboration
　Supporting democratic dialogue and deliberation
　Supporting democracy through process use: Helping the citizenry weigh evidence and think
　　evaluatively

Special Applications
　Unobtrusive measures
　State-of-the-art considerations: Lack of proven quantitative instrumentation
　Confirmatory and elucidating research: Adding depth, detail, and meaning to quantitative
　　analyses
　Rapid reconnaissance
　Capturing and communicating stories
　Legislative monitoring and auditing
　Futuring applications: Anticipatory research and prospective policy analysis
　Breaking the routine: Generating new insights

mained. A running coach, Bill Bowerman, went into the sneaker business in 1962. He paid close attention to the interest in lighter-weight shoes and the problems of traction.

One morning while he was making waffles, he had an idea. He heated a piece of rubber in the waffle iron to produce the first waffle-shaped sole pattern that became the world standard for running shoes (Panati

EXHIBIT 4.9	Sample Internet E-mail Discussion Groups (listservs) and Sites Relevant to Qualitative Applications and Practice

1. EVALTALK@bama.ua.edu: American Evaluation Association (AEA) Discussion List; to subscribe, send this message to listserv@bama.ua.edu: subscribe evaltalk ourname
   AEA home page with links to evaluation organizations, training programs, and Internet resources: www.eval.org

2. ARLIST-L@scu.edu.au: Action Research Mailing List; to subscribe, send this message to listproc@scu.edu.au: subscribe ARLIST-L
   LASTNAME

3. ARMNET-L@scu.edu.au: Action research methodology network; to subscribe, send this message to listproc@scu.edu.au: subscribe ARMNET-L firstname lastname

4. Organizational development Web site: www.mnodn.org

5. Organizational Development Network: www.ODNetwork.org

6. Evaluation Center at Western Michigan University: www.wmich.edu/evalctr/

7. World Bank Evaluation Unit Web site: www.wbln0018.worldbank.org/wbies/wbievalu.nsf

8. Empowerment Evaluation:
   www.stanord.edu/~davidf/EmpowermentWorkshopCSAP/sld001.htm

9. IVSA@pdomain.uwindsor.ca: International Visual Sociology Association; to subscribe, send this message to listserv@pdomain.uwindsor.ca: subscribe ivsa ourname

NOTE: These sites and subscription details may change, nor is this list exhaustive. This list is meant to be suggestive of the qualitative analysis resources available through the Internet. For other Internet resources, see Chapter 1, Exhibit 1.5; Chapter 3, Exhibit 3.7; and Chapter 8, Exhibit 8.3.

1987:298-99). Subsequently, engineers and computers would be used to design and test the best waffle patterns for different athletic purposes. But the initial discovery came from Bowerman's paying attention, being open, making connections, drawing on personal experience, getting a feel for what was possible, exploration, documenting his initial results, and applying what he learned.

While later chapters will present in detail techniques for increasing the validity and reliability of qualitative data through rigorous fieldwork and highly skilled interviewing, the essence of qualitative inquiry is paying attention, being open to what the world has to show us, and thinking about what it means. C. Wright Mills (1961) quoted Nobel Prize winning physicist Percy Bridgman in this regard:

> There is no scientific method as such, but the vital feature of the scientist's procedures has been merely to do his utmost with his mind, *no holds barred.* (p. 58)

PART 2

Qualitative Designs and Data Collection

- Always be suspicious of data collection that goes according to plan.

- Research subjects have also been known to be people.

- The evaluator's scientific observation is some person's real-life experience. Respect for the latter must precede respect for the former.

- Total trust and complete skepticism are twin losers in the field. All things in moderation, especially trust and skepticism.

- Evaluators are presumed guilty until proven innocent.

- Make sure when you yield to temptation in the field that it appears to have something to do with what you are studying.

- A fieldworker should be able to sweep the floor, carry out the garbage, carry in the laundry, cook for large groups, go without food and sleep, read and write by candlelight, see in the dark, see in the light, cooperate without offending, suppress sarcastic remarks, smile to express both pain and hurt, experience both pain and hurt, spend time alone, respond to orders, take sides, stay neutral, take risks, avoid harm, be confused, seem confused, care terribly, become attached to nothing. . . . The nine-to-five set need not apply.

- Always carry extra batteries and getaway money.

—From Halcolm's *Fieldwork Laws*

5

Designing Qualitative Studies

The First Evaluation _____

The young people gathered around Halcolm. "Tell us again, Teacher of Many Things, about the first evaluation."

"The first evaluation," he began, "was conducted a long, long time ago, in ancient Babylon when Nebuchadnezzar was king. Nebuchadnezzar had just conquered Jerusalem in the third year of the reign of Jehoiakim, King of Judah. Now Nebuchadnezzar was a shrewd ruler. He decided to bring carefully selected children of Israel into the palace for special training so that they might be more easily integrated into Chaldean culture. This special program was the forerunner of the compensatory education programs that would become so popular in the 20th century. The three-year program was royally funded with special allocations and scholarships provided by Nebuchadnezzar. The ancient text from the Great Book records that

> the king spake unto Ashpenaz the master of his eunuchs that he should bring certain of the children of Israel, and of the king's seed, and of the princes; children in whom was no blemish, but well-favored and skillful in all wisdom, and cunning in knowledge, and understanding science, and such as had ability in them to stand in the king's palace, and whom they might teach the learning and the tongue of the Chaldeans.
>
> And the king appointed them a daily provision of the king's meat, and of the wine which he drank; so nourishing them three years, that at the end thereof they might stand before the king. (Daniel 1:3-5)

"Now this program had scarcely been established when the program director, Ashpenaz, who happened also to be prince of the eunuchs, found himself faced with a student rebellion led by a radical named Daniel, who decided for religious reasons that he would not consume the king's meat and wine. This created a serious problem for the director. If Daniel and his coconspirators did not eat their dormitory food, they might fare poorly in the program and endanger not only future program funding but also the program director's head! The Great Book says:

> But Daniel purposed in his heart that he would not defile himself with the portion of the king's meat, nor with the wine which he drank; therefore he requested of the prince of the eunuchs that he might not defile himself.
>
> And the prince of the eunuchs said unto Daniel, I fear my lord the king, who hath appointed your meat and your drink; for why should he see your faces worse liking than the children which are of your sort? Then shall ye make me endanger my head to the king. (Daniel 1:8, 10)

"At this point, Daniel proposed history's first educational experiment and program evaluation. He and three friends (Hananiah, Mishael, and Azariah) would be placed on a strict vegetarian diet for ten days, while other students continued on the king's rich diet of meat and wine. At the end of ten days the program director would inspect the treatment group for any signs of physical deterioration and judge the productivity of Daniel's alternative diet plan. Daniel proposed the experiment thusly:

> Prove thy servants, I beseech thee, ten days; and let them give us pulse to eat, and water to drink. Then let our countenances be looked upon before thee, and the countenance of the children that eat of the portion of the king's meat: and as thou seest, deal with thy servants.
>
> So he consented to them in this matter, and proved them ten days. (Daniel 1:12-14)

"During the ten days of waiting Ashpenaz had a terrible time. He couldn't sleep, he had no appetite, and he had trouble working because he was preoccupied worrying about how the evaluation would turn out. He had a lot at stake. Besides, in those days they hadn't quite worked out the proper division of labor so he had to play the roles of both program director and evaluator. You see. . . ."

The young listeners interrupted Halcolm. They sensed that he was about to launch into a sermon on the origins of the division of labor when they still wanted to hear the end of the story about the origins of evaluation. "How did it turn out?" they asked. "Did Daniel end up looking better or worse from the new diet? Did Ashpenaz lose his head?"

"Patience, patience," Halcolm pleaded. "Ashpenaz had no reason to worry. The results were quite amazing. The Great Book says that

> at the end of ten days their countenances appeared fairer and fatter in flesh than all the children which did eat the portion of the king's meat.

Thus, Melzar took away the portion of their meat, and the wine that they should drink; and gave them pulse.

As for these four children, God gave them knowledge and skill in all learning and wisdom; and Daniel had understanding in all visions and dreams. Now at the end of the days that the king had said he should bring them in, then the prince of the eunuchs brought them in before Nebuchadnezzar. And in all matters of wisdom and understanding, that the king inquired of them, he found them ten times better than all the magicians and astrologers that were in all his realm. (Daniel 1:15-18, 20)

"And that, my children, is the story of the first evaluation. Those were the good old days when evaluations really got used. Made quite a difference to Ashpenaz and Daniel. Now off with you—and see if you can do as well."

—From Halcolm's *Evaluation Histories*

A Meta-Evaluation

A meta-evaluation is an evaluation of an evaluation. A great deal can be learned about evaluation designs by conducting a meta-evaluation of history's first program evaluation. Let us imagine a panel of experts conducting a rigorous critique of this evaluation of Babylon's compensatory education program for Israeli students:

1. Small sample size (*N* = 4).

2. Selectivity bias because recruitment into the program was done by "creaming," that is, only the best prospects among the children of Israel were brought into the program.

3. Sampling bias because students were self-selected into the treatment group (diet of pulse and water).

4. Failure to clearly specify and control the nature of the treatment, thus allowing for the possibility of treatment contamination because we don't know what

other things, aside from a change in diet, either group was involved in that might have explained the outcomes observed.

5. Possibility of interaction effects between the diet and the students' belief system (i.e., potential Hawthorne and halo effects).

6. Outcome criteria vague: Just what is "countenance"?

7. Outcome measurement poorly operationalized and nonstandardized.

8. Single observer with deep personal involvement in the program introduces possibility of selective perception and bias in the observations.

9. Validity and reliability data are not reported for the instruments used to measure the final, summative outcome ("he found them ten times better than all the magicians and astrologers").

10. Possible reactive effects from the students' knowledge that they were being evaluated.

Despite all of these threats to internal validity, not to mention external validity, the information generated by the evaluations appears to have been used. The 10-day formative evaluation was used to make a major decision about the program, namely, to change the diet for Daniel and his friends. The end-of-program summative evaluation conducted by the king was used to judge the program a success. (Daniel did place first in his class.) Indeed, it would be difficult to find a more exemplary model for the uses of evaluation in making educational policy decisions than this "first evaluation" conducted under the auspices of Nebuchadnezzar so many years ago. This case study is an exemplar of evaluation research having an immediate, decisive, and lasting impact on an educational program. Modern evaluation researchers, flailing away in seemingly futile efforts to affect contemporary governmental decisions, can be forgiven a certain nostalgia for the "good old days" in Babylon when evaluation really made a difference.

But should the results have been used? Given the apparent weakness of the evaluation design, was it appropriate to make a major program decision on the basis of data generated by such a seemingly weak research design?

I would argue that not only was use impressive in this case, it was also appropriate because the research design was exemplary. Yes, exemplary, because the study was set up in such a way as to provide precisely the information needed by the program director to make the decision he needed to make. Certainly, it is a poor research design to study the relationship between nutrition and educational achievement. It is even a poor design to decide if *all* students should be placed on a vegetarian diet. But those were not the issues. The question the director faced was whether to place four specific students on a special diet at their request.

The information he needed concerned the consequences of that specific change and *only* that specific change. He showed no interest in generalizing the results beyond those four students, and he showed no interest in convincing others that the measures he made were valid and reliable. Only he and Daniel had to trust the measures used, and so data collection (observation of countenance) was done in such a way as to be meaningful and credible to the primary intended evaluation users, namely, Ashpenaz and Daniel. If any bias existed in his observations, given what he had at stake, the bias would have operated against a demonstration of positive outcomes rather than in favor of such outcomes.

While there are hints of whimsy in the suggestion that this first evaluation was exemplary, I do not mean to be completely facetious. I am serious in suggesting that the Babylonian example is an exemplar of utilization-focused evaluation. It contains and illustrates all the factors modern evaluation researchers have verified as critical from studies of utilization (Patton 1997a). The decision makers who were to use findings generated by the evaluation were clearly identified and deeply involved in every stage of the evaluation process. The evaluation question was carefully focused on needed information that could be used in the making of a specific decision. The evaluation methods and design were appropriately matched to the evaluation question. The results were understandable, credible, and relevant. Feedback was immediate and utilization was decisive. Few modern evaluations can meet the high standards for evaluation set by Ashpenaz and Daniel more than 3,000 years ago.

This chapter discusses some ways in which research designs can be appropriately matched to evaluation questions in an attempt to emulate the exemplary match be-

Observing countenance

tween evaluation problem and research design achieved in the Babylonian evaluation. As with previous chapters, I shall emphasize the importance of being both strategic and practical in creating evaluation designs. Being strategic begins with being clear about the purpose of the intended research or evaluation.

🖐 Clarity About Purpose: A Typology

Purpose is the controlling force in research. Decisions about design, measurement, analysis, and reporting all flow from purpose. Therefore, the first step in a research process is getting clear about purpose. The centrality of purpose in making methods decisions becomes evident from examining

alternative purposes along a continuum from theory to action:

1. *Basic research:* To contribute to fundamental knowledge and theory

2. *Applied research:* To illuminate a societal concern

3. *Summative evaluation:* To determine program effectiveness

4. *Formative evaluation:* To improve a program

5. *Action research:* To solve a specific problem

Basic and applied researchers publish in scholarly journals, where their audience is other researchers who will judge their contributions using disciplinary standards of rigor, validity, and theoretical import. In contrast, evaluators and action researchers publish reports for specific stakeholders who will use the results to make decisions, improve programs, and solve problems.

Standards for judging quality vary among these five different types of research. Expectations and audiences are different. Reporting and dissemination approaches are different. Because of these differences, the researcher must be clear at the beginning about which purpose has priority. No single study can serve all of these different purposes and audiences equally well. With clarity about purpose and primary audience, the researcher can go on to make specific design, data-gathering, and analysis decisions to meet the priority purpose and address the intended audience.

In the Babylonian example, the purpose was simply to find out if a vegetarian diet would negatively affect the healthy appearances (countenances) of four participants —not *why* their countenances appeared healthy or not (a causal question), but *whether* the dietary change would affect countenance (a descriptive question). The design, therefore, was appropriately simple to yield descriptive data for the purpose of making a minor program adjustment. No contribution to general knowledge. No testing or development of theory. No generalizations. No scholarly publication. No elaborate report on methods. Just find out what would happen to inform a single decision about a possible program change. The participants in the program were involved in the study; indeed, the idea of putting the diet to an empirical test originated with Daniel. In short, we have a very nice example of simple *formative evaluation.*

The king's examination of program participants at the end of three years was quite different. We might infer that the king was judging the overall value of the program.

Did it accomplish his objectives? Should it be continued? Could the outcomes he observed be attributed to the program? This is the kind of research we have come to call *summative evaluation*—summing up judgments about a program to make a major decision about its value, whether it should be continued, and whether the demonstrated model can or should be generalized to and replicated for other participants or in other places.

Now imagine that researchers from the University of Babylon wanted to study the diet as a manifestation of culture in order to develop a theory about the role of diet in transmitting culture. Their sample, their data collection, their questions, the duration of fieldwork, and their presentation of results would all be quite different from the formative evaluation undertaken by Ashpenaz and Daniel. The university study would have taken much longer than 10 days and might have yielded empirical generalizations and contributions to theory, yet would not have helped Ashpenaz make his simple decision. On the other hand, we might surmise that University of Babylon scholars would have scoffed at an evaluation done in 10 days, even a formative one. Different purposes. Different criteria for judging the research contribution. Different methods. Different audiences. Different kinds of research.

These are examples of how purpose can vary. In the next section, I shall present a more formal framework for distinguishing these five different research purposes and examine in more depth the implications of varying purposes for making design decisions. Previous chapters have presented the nature and strategies of qualitative inquiry, philosophical and theoretical foundations, and practical applications. In effect, the reader has been presented with a large array of options, alternatives, and variations.

How does one sort it all out to decide what to do in a specific study? The answer is to get clear about purpose. The framework that follows is meant to facilitate achieving this necessary clarity about purpose while also illustrating how one can organize a mass of observations into some coherent typology —a major analytical tool of qualitative inquiry. The sections that follow examine each type of research: basic research, applied research, summative evaluation research, formative evaluation, and action research.

Basic Research

The purpose of basic research is knowledge for the sake of knowledge. Researchers engaged in basic research want to understand how the world operates. They are interested in investigating a phenomenon to get at the nature of reality with regard to that phenomenon. The basic researcher's purpose is to understand and explain.

Basic researchers typically work within specific disciplines, such as physics, biology, psychology, economics, geography, and sociology. The questions and problems they study emerge from traditions within those disciplines. Each discipline is organized around attention to basic questions, and the research within that discipline derives from concern about those basic questions. Exhibit 5.1 presents examples of fundamental questions in several disciplines.

The fundamental questions undergirding each discipline flow from the basic concerns and traditions of that discipline. Researchers working within any specific disciplinary tradition strive to make a contribution to knowledge in that discipline and thereby contribute to answering the fundamental questions of the discipline. The most prestigious contribution to knowledge takes the form of a *theory* that explains the phenomenon under investigation. Basic researchers

work to generate new theories or test existing theories. Doctoral students are typically expected to make theoretical contributions in their dissertations. Theories encapsulate the knowledge of a discipline.

Basic researchers are interested in formulating and testing theoretical constructs and propositions that ideally generalize across time and space. The most powerful kinds of findings in basic science are those findings that are universal, such as Boyle's law in physics that the volume of a gas at constant temperature varies inversely with the pressure exerted on it. Basic researchers, then, are searching for fundamental patterns of the universe, the earth, nature, society, and human beings. For example, biologists have discovered that "changes in DNA are inherited, but changes in proteins (specifically, in their amino acid sequence) are not . . . , perhaps the only universal truth biologists have" (Smith 2000:43). Social science, to date, is markedly short of "universal truths." Nevertheless, generalizations across time and space remain the Holy Grail of basic research and theory.

The findings of basic research are published in scholarly books, journals, and dissertations. Each discipline has its own traditions, norms, and rules for deciding what constitutes valid research in that discipline. To be published in the major journals of any particular discipline, scientists must engage in the kind of research that is valued by the researchers in that disciplinary tradition.

Chapter 3 reviewed theoretical traditions closely associated with qualitative inquiry, for example, ethnography and phenomenology. Qualitative inquiry also contributes to basic research through inductive theory development, a prominent example being the "grounded theory" approach of Glaser and Strauss (1967), essentially an inductive strategy for generating and confirming theory that emerges from close involvement and di-

EXHIBIT 5.1	Fundamental Disciplinary Questions
Anthropology	What is the nature of culture? How does culture emerge? How is it transmitted? What are the functions of culture?
Psychology	Why do individuals behave as they do? How do human beings behave, think, feel, and know? What is normal and abnormal in human development and behavior?
Sociology	What holds groups and societies together? How do various forms of social organization emerge and what are their functions? What are the structures and processes of human social organizations?
Political science	What is the nature of power? How is power organized, created, distributed, and used?
Economics	How do societies and groups generate and distribute scarce resources? How are goods and services produced and distributed? What is the nature of wealth?
Geography	What is the nature of and variations in the earth's surface and atmosphere? How do various forms of life emerge in and relate to variations in the earth? What is the relationship between the physical characteristics of an area and the activities that take place in that area?
Biology	What is the nature of life? What are variations in the forms of life? How have life forms emerged and how do they change?

rect contact with the empirical world. Basic qualitative research typically requires a relatively lengthy and intensive period of fieldwork. The rigor of field techniques will be subject to peer review. Particular attention must be given to the accuracy, validity, and integrity of the results.

An example of interdisciplinary theory development comes from work in basic economic anthropology studying craft commercialization and the product differentiation that ordinarily accompanies increased craft sales. Artisans in emerging markets, such as those in rural Mexico, typically innovate and develop specialties in an attempt to establish a niche for themselves in a complex economic environment. Chibnik's (2000) basic research on commercial woodcarving in Oaxaca has led to the theory that such market segmentation resembles the later stages of product life cycles described in the business literature and is somewhat analogous to the proliferation of equilibrium species in mature or climax stages of ecological successions. Chibnik examined both market demands and the initiative of artisans and found that local artisans do not have total freedom in their attempts to create market niches since they are restricted by their abilities and the labor and capital they can mobilize. This is a classic example of interdisciplinary theory generation and testing bridging economics, ethnology, and ecology.

Applied Research

Applied researchers work on human and societal problems. In the example just cited, had Chibnik examined the problem of creating new markets for rural artisans and offered possible solutions for increased marketing, the work would have constituted applied rather than basic research. The purpose of applied research is to contribute knowledge that will help people understand the nature of a problem in order to intervene, thereby allowing human beings to more effectively control their environment. While in basic research the source of questions is the traditions within a scholarly discipline, in applied research the source of questions is in the problems and concerns experienced by people and articulated by policymakers.

Applied researchers are often guided by the findings, understandings, and explanations of basic research. They conduct studies that test *applications* of basic theory and disciplinary knowledge to real-world problems and experiences. The results of applied research are published in journals that specialize in applied research within the traditions of a problem area or a discipline.

Societal concerns have given rise to a variety of new fields that are interdisciplinary in nature. These emerging fields reflect the long-standing criticism by policymakers that universities have departments but society has problems. Applied interdisciplinary fields are especially problem oriented rather than discipline oriented. For example, work on environmental studies often involves researchers from a number of disciplines. In agricultural research, the field of integrated pest management (IPM) includes researchers from entomology, agronomy, agricultural economics, and horticulture. Fields of interdisciplinary research in the social sciences include gerontology, criminal justice studies, women's studies, and family research. Exhibit 5.2 offers examples of applied *interdisciplinary* research questions for economic anthropology, social psychology, political geography, and educational and organizational development. Notice the difference between these questions and the kinds of questions asked by basic researchers in Exhibit 5.1. Applied researchers are trying to understand how to deal with a significant societal problem, while basic researchers are trying to understand and explain the basic nature of some phenomenon.

Applied qualitative researchers are able to bring their personal insights and experiences into any recommendations that may emerge because they get especially close to the problems under study during fieldwork. Audiences for applied research are typically policymakers, directors and managers of intervention-oriented organizations, and professionals working on problems. Timelines for applied research depend a great deal on the timeliness and urgency of the problem being researched. A good example of applied research is *Emerging Drug Problems*, a work sponsored by the U.S. General Accounting Office (1998) that examined new street drugs, recent research on addiction, and alternatives for public policy.

In contrast to basic researchers, who ultimately seek to generalize across time and space, applied research findings typically are limited to a specific time, place, and condition. For example, a researcher studying the nature of family problems in the 1980s

EXHIBIT 5.2	Sample Interdisciplinary Applied Research Questions
Applied economic anthropology	How can the prosperous economy of an isolated, small minority group be preserved when that group encounters new competition from the encroaching global economy?
Applied social psychology	How can a group within a large organization develop cohesion and identity within the mission and values of its parent structure and culture?
Applied political geography	How can people of previously isolated towns, each with its own history of local governance, come together to share power and engage in joint decision making at a regional level?
Applied educational and organizational development	How can students from different neighborhoods with varied ethnic and racial backgrounds be integrated in a new magnet school?

would not expect those problems to be the same as those experienced by families in the 1880s. While the research might include making such comparisons, applied researchers understand that problems emerge within particular time and space boundaries.

Evaluation Research: Summative and Formative

Once solutions to problems are identified, policies and programs are designed to intervene in society and bring about change. It is hoped that the intervention and changes will be effective in helping to solve problems. However, the effectiveness of any given human intervention is a matter subject to study. Thus, the next point on the theory-to-action research continuum is the conduct of evaluation and policy research to test the effectiveness of specific solutions and human interventions.

While applied research seeks to understand societal problems and identify poten-

tial solutions, evaluations examine and judge the processes and outcomes aimed at attempted solutions. Evaluators study programs, policies, personnel, organizations, and products. Evaluation research can be conducted on virtually any explicit attempt to solve problems or bring about planned change. As illustrated in the Daniel story of history's "first evaluation" that opened this chapter, evaluators distinguish two quite different purposes for evaluation: (1) summative evaluations that judge overall effectiveness to inform major decisions about whether a program should continue and (2) formative evaluations that aim to improve programs.

Summative evaluations serve the purpose of rendering an overall judgment about the effectiveness of a program, policy, or product for the purpose of saying that the *evaluand* (thing being evaluated) is or is not effective and, therefore, should or should not be continued, and has or does not have the potential of being generalizable to other situations. A summative decision implies a

Are they doing research or evaluation?

summing-up judgment or a summit (from the mountaintop) decision, for example, to expand a pilot program to new sites or move it from temporary (pilot test or demonstra- tion) funding to more permanent funding, or it may lead to program or policy termina- tion. Summative evaluations seldom rely entirely, or even primarily, on qualitative data and naturalistic inquiry because of decision makers' interest in measuring standardized outcomes, having controlled comparisons, and making judgments about effectiveness from relatively larger samples with statistical pre-post and follow-up results. Qualitative data in summative evaluations typically add depth, detail, and nuance to quantitative findings, rendering insights through illuminative case studies and examining individualized outcomes and issues of quality or excellence—applications discussed in Chapter 4. Harkreader and Henry (2000) have provided an excellent discussion of the challenges of rendering summative judgments about merit and worth; they use as their example comparative quantitative performance data from Georgia schools to assess a democratic reform initiative. Fetterman (2000b) shows how qualitative data can be the primary basis for a summative evaluation. His evaluation of STEP, a 12-month teacher education program in the Stanford University School of Education, included fieldwork immersion in the program, open-ended interviews with all students, focus groups, observations of classrooms, interviews with faculty, digital photography of classroom activities, and qualitative analysis of curricular materials, as well as a variety of surveys and outcome measures. The summative evaluations of a democratic reform initiative in Georgia and of Stanford's STEP program both followed and built on extensive formative evaluation work, the purpose of which we now examine.

Formative evaluations, in contrast to summative ones, serve the purpose of improving a specific program, policy, group of staff (in a personnel evaluation), or product. Formative evaluations aim at *forming* (shaping) the thing being studied. No attempt is made in a formative evaluation to generalize findings beyond the setting in which the

evaluation takes place. Formative evaluations rely heavily on process studies, implementation evaluations, case studies, and evaluability assessments (see Chapter 4). Formative evaluations often rely heavily, even primarily, on qualitative methods. Findings are context specific.

Although formative and summative remain the most basic and classic distinctions in evaluation, other evaluation purposes have emerged in recent years in "a world larger than formative and summative" (Patton 1996b). New purposes include ongoing "developmental evaluation" for program and organizational development and learning (Patton 1994; Preskill and Torres 1999); empowering local groups through evaluation participation (Fetterman 2000a; Patton 1997b); and using the processes of evaluation (*process use*) to build staff capacity for data-based decision making and continuous improvement (Patton 1997a: 87-113, 1998). For our analysis here, however, these and related approaches to evaluation share the general purpose of improvement and can be included within the broad category of formative research along our theory-to-action continuum. In addition, some evaluation studies are now designed to generate generalizable knowledge about effective practices across different projects or programs based on cluster evaluations, lessons learned, "better" practices, and meta-analyses (Patton 1997a:70-75). This knowledge-generating approach to evaluation research, to the extent that it aims to discover general principles of effective practice rather than render judgment about the merit or worth of a specific intervention, falls roughly within the category "applied research" in this theory-to-action continuum. However, the emergence and increased importance of knowledge-generating evaluations illustrate why these five categories (basic, applied, summative, formative, and action research) cannot be thought of as fixed or exhaustive; rather, this typology provides general guidance to major formations in the research landscape without charting every hill and valley in that varied and complex territory that research has become.

Action-Oriented, Problem-Solving Research

The final category along the theory-to-action continuum is action research. Action research aims at solving specific problems within a program, organization, or community. Action research explicitly and purposefully becomes part of the change process by engaging the people in the program or organization in studying their own problems in order to solve those problems (Whyte 1989). As a result, the distinction between research and action becomes quite blurred and the research methods tend to be less systematic, more informal, and quite specific to the problem, people, and organization for which the research is undertaken.

Both formative evaluation and action research focus on specific programs at specific points in time. There is no intention, typically, to generalize beyond those specific settings. The difference between formative evaluation and action research centers on the extent to which the research is systematic, the different kinds of problems studied, and the extent to which there is a special role for the researcher as distinct from the people being researched.

In formative evaluation, there is a formal design and the data are collected and/or analyzed, at least in part, by an evaluator. Formative evaluation focuses on ways of improving the effectiveness of a program, a policy, an organization, a product, or a staff unit. In action research, by way of contrast, design and data collection tend to be more

informal, the people in the situation are often directly involved in gathering the information and then studying themselves, and the results are used internally to attack specific problems within a program, organization, or community. While action research may be used as part of an overall organizational or community development process, it most typically focuses on specific problems and issues within the organization or community rather than on the overall effectiveness of an entire program or organization. Thus, along this theory-to-action-research continuum, action research has the narrowest focus.

The findings of formative evaluation and action research are seldom disseminated beyond the immediate program or organization within which the study takes place. In many instances, there may not even be a full written research report. Publication and dissemination of findings are more likely to be through briefings, staff discussions, and oral communications. Summaries of findings and recommendations will be distributed for discussion, but the formality of the reporting and the nature of the research publications are quite different from those in basic, applied, or even summative evaluation research.

An example of action research comes from a small rural community in the Midwest in which the town board needed to decide what to do with a dilapidated building on a public park. They got a high school class to put together a simple telephone survey to solicit ideas about what to do with the building. They also conducted a few focus groups in local churches. The results showed that the townspeople preferred to fix up the building and restore it as a community center rather than tear it down. The action research process took about a month. Based on the findings, a local committee was formed to seek volunteers and funds for the restora-

INACTION RESEARCH

Educational researcher J. Ronald Gentile (1994) noticed the increasing popularity and importance of action research and wondered about the value of all the work involved: "While there are some advantages of action research, the disadvantages are that the researcher must collect a lot of data, carefully observing both the behaviors of interest and the conditions under which they occur. Following that, one has to score the data, a process that sometimes requires inventing ways to categorize them, analyze them, and draw inferences that are appropriate for the sample, design, and so forth. The problem with action research, in other words, is that it requires too much action. Fortunately, I discovered an alternative to action research that is probably best labeled 'inaction' research" (p. 30).

Three examples of Inaction Research:

Statistics in service of the Id—"The invention or use of statistics to support some preconceived belief or entrepreneurial motive" (p. 30).

Scholarship as inaction research—Making up quotations where the researcher knows what the interviewee really meant to say but didn't say quite right, so the inaction researcher helps out by making up the needed quotation; also, "inventing new terminology that, by definition, has no historical usage" so no literature review is needed because there is no literature (p. 31).

Happiness quotients—"Exposing people to a program or product and then following up with a one-page questionnaire asking how well they liked the program or product" thereby giving the appearance of having done an evaluation without all the cost, inconvenience and difficulties of conducting real fieldwork (p. 31).

tion, thereby solving the town board's problem of what to do with the building—an example of action-oriented, problem-solving research.

The Purpose of Purpose Distinctions

It is important to understand variations in purpose along this theory-to-action continuum because different purposes typically lead to different ways of conceptualizing problems, different designs, different types of data gathering, and different ways of publicizing and disseminating findings. These are only partly issues of scholarship. Politics, paradigms, and values are also part of the landscape.

Researchers engaged in inquiry at various points along the continuum can have very strong opinions and feelings about researchers at other points along the continuum, sometimes generating opposing opinions and strong emotions. Basic and applied researchers, for example, would often dispute even calling formative and action research by the name *research*. The standards that basic researchers apply to what they would consider good research excludes even some applied research because it may not manifest the conceptual clarity and theoretical rigor in real-world situations that basic researchers value. Formative and action researchers, on the other hand, may attack basic research for being esoteric and irrelevant.

Debates about the meaningfulness, rigor, significance, and relevance of various approaches to research are regular features of university life. On the whole, within universities and among scholars, the status hierarchy in science attributes the highest status to basic research, secondary status to applied research, little status to summative evaluation research, and virtually no status to formative and action research. The status hierarchy is reversed in real-world settings, where people with problems attribute the greatest significance to action and formative research that can help them solve their problems in a timely way and attach the least importance to basic research, which they consider remote and largely irrelevant to what they are doing on a day-to-day basis.

The distinctions along the continuum are not only distinctions about purpose and how one conducts research, but they also involve the issue of what one calls what one does. In other words, a person conducting basic research for the purpose of contributing to theory within a discipline may find it helpful to call that work *applied research* to get certain kinds of funding. Summative evaluation researchers may describe what they are doing as *formative evaluation* to make their work more acceptable to program staff resistant to being studied. On the other hand, applied researchers may call what they are doing *basic research* to increase its acceptability among scholars.

In short, there are no clear lines dividing the points along the continuum. Part of what determines where a particular kind of research falls along the continuum is how the researcher describes what is being done and its purpose. Different reviewers of the same piece of research might well use a different label to describe it. What is important for our purposes is that researchers understand the implications of these distinctions, the choices involved, and the implications of

those choices for both the kind of research undertaken and the researcher's status as a professional within various social groups.

Exhibit 5.3 summarizes some of the major differences among the different kinds of research.

Examples of Types of Research Questions: A Family Research Example

To further clarify these distinctions, it may be helpful to take a particular issue and look at how it would be approached for each type of research. For illustrative purposes, let's examine the different kinds of questions that can be asked about families for different research purposes. All of the research questions in Exhibit 5.4 focus on families, but the purpose and focus of each type of research are quite different. With clarity about purpose, it is possible to turn to consideration of specific design alternatives and strategies. Clarity about purpose helps in making decisions about critical trade-offs in research and designs, our next topic.

⑤ Critical Trade-Offs in Design

Purposes, strategies, and trade-offs— these themes go together. A discussion of design strategies and trade-offs is necessitated by the fact that **there are no perfect research designs.** There are always trade-offs. Limited resources, limited time, and limits on the human ability to grasp the complex nature of social reality necessitate trade-offs.

The very first trade-offs come in framing the research or evaluation questions to be studied. The problem here is to determine the extent to which it is desirable to study one or a few questions in great depth or to

EXHIBIT 5.3 A Typology of Research Purposes

Types of Research	Purpose	Focus of Research	Desired Results	Desired Level of Generalization	Key Assumptions	Publication Mode	Standard for Judging
Basic research	Knowledge as an end in itself; discover truth	Questions deemed important by one's discipline or personal intellectual interest	Contribution to theory	Across time and space (ideal)	The world is patterned; those patterns are knowable and explainable.	Major refereed scholarly journals in one's discipline, scholarly books	Rigor of research, universality and verifiability of theory
Applied research	Understand the nature and sources of human and societal problems	Questions deemed important by society	Contributions to theories that can be used to formulate problem-solving programs and interventions	Within as general a time and space as possible, but clearly limited application context	Human and societal problems can be understood and solved with knowledge.	Specialized academic journals, applied research journals within disciplines, interdisciplinary problem-focused journals	Rigor and theoretical insight into the problem
Summative evaluation	Determine effectiveness of human interventions and actions (programs, policies, personnel, products)	Goals of the intervention	Judgments and generalizations about effective types of interventions and the conditions under which those efforts are effective	All interventions with similar goals	What works one place under specified conditions should work elsewhere.	Evaluation reports for program funders and policymakers, specialized journals	Generalizability to future efforts and to other programs and policy issues
Formative evaluation	Improve an intervention: A program, policy, organization, or product	Strengths and weaknesses of the specific program, policy, product, or personnel being studied	Recommendations for improvements	Limited to specific setting studied	People can and will use information to improve what they're doing.	Oral briefings; conferences; internal report; limited circulation to similar programs, other evaluators	Usefulness to and actual use by intended users in the setting studied
Action research	Solve problems in a program, organization, or community	Organization and community problems	Immediate action; solving problems as quickly as possible	Here and now	People in a setting can solve problems by studying themselves.	Interpersonal interactions among research participants; informal unpublished	Feelings about the process among research participants, feasibility of the solution generated

EXHIBIT 5.4	Family Research Example: Research Questions Matched to Research Category
Basic research	What are variations in types of families and what functions do those variations serve?
Applied research	What is the divorce rate among different kinds of families in the United States and what explains different rates of divorce among different groups?
Summative evaluation	What is the overall effectiveness of a publicly funded educational program that teaches family members communication skills where the desired program outcomes are enhanced communications among family members, a greater sense of satisfaction with family life, effective parenting practices, and reduced risk of divorce?
Formative evaluation	How can a program teaching family communications skills be improved? What are the program's strengths and weaknesses? What do participants like and dislike?
Action research	A self-study in a particular organization (e.g., church, neighborhood center) to figure out what activities would be attractive to families with children of different ages to solve the problem of low participation in family activities.

study many questions but in less depth—the "boundary problem" in naturalistic inquiry (Guba 1978). Once a potential set of inquiry questions has been generated, it is necessary to begin the process of prioritizing those questions to decide which of them ought to be pursued. For example, for an evaluation, should all parts of the program be studied or only certain parts? Should all clients be interviewed or only some subset of clients? Should the evaluator aim at describing all program processes or only certain selected processes in depth? Should all outcomes be examined or only certain outcomes of particular interest to inform a pending decision? These are questions that are discussed and negotiated with intended users of the evaluation. In basic research, these kinds of questions are resolved by the nature of the theoretical contribution to be made. In dissertation research, the doctoral committee provides guidance on focusing.

And always there are fundamental constraints of time and resources.

Converging on focused priorities typically proves more difficult than the challenge of generating potential questions at the beginning of a study or evaluation. Doctoral students can be especially adept at avoiding focus, conceiving instead of sweeping, comprehensive studies that make the whole world their fieldwork oyster. In evaluations, once involved users begin to take seriously the notion that they can learn from finding how whether what they think is being accomplished by a program is what is really being accomplished, they soon generate a long list of things they'd like to find out. The evaluation facilitator's role is to help them move from a rather extensive list of potential questions to a much shorter list of realistically possible questions and finally to a focused list of essential and necessary questions.

Review of relevant literature can also bring focus to a study. What is already known? Unknown? What are the cutting-edge theoretical issues? Yet, reviewing the literature can present a quandary in qualitative inquiry because it may bias the researcher's thinking and reduce openness to whatever emerges in the field. Thus, sometimes a literature review may not take place until after data collection. Alternatively, the literature review may go on simultaneously with fieldwork, permitting a creative interplay among the processes of data collection, literature review, and researcher introspection (Marshall and Rossman 1989:38-40). As with other qualitative design issues, trade-offs appear at every turn, for there are decided advantages and disadvantages to reviewing the literature before, during, or after fieldwork—or on a continual basis throughout the study.

A specific example of possible variations in focus will illustrate the kinds of trade-offs involved in designing a study. Suppose some educators are interested in studying how a school program affects the social development of school-age children. They want to know how the interactions of children with others in the school setting contribute to the development of social skills. They believe that those social skills will be different for different children, and they are not sure of the range of social interactions that may occur, so they are interested in a qualitative inquiry that will capture variations in program experience and relate those experiences to individualized outcomes. What, then, are trade-offs in determining the final focus?

We begin with the fact that any given child has social interactions with a great many people. The first problem in focusing, then, is to determine how much of the social reality experienced by children we should attempt to study. In a narrowly focused study, we might select one particular set of interactions and limit our study to those— for example, the social interactions between teachers and children. Broadening the scope somewhat, we might decide to look only at those interactions that occur in the classroom, thereby increasing the scope of the study to include interactions not only between teacher and child but also among peers in the classroom and between any volunteers and visitors to the classroom and the children. Broadening the scope of the study still more, we might decide to look at all of the social relationships that children experience in schools; in this case we would move beyond the classroom to look at interactions with other personnel in the school—for example, the librarian, school counselors, special subject teachers, the custodian, and/or school administrative staff. Broadening the scope of the study still further, the educators might decide that it is important to look at the social relationships children experience at home as well as at school so as to understand better how children experience and are affected by both settings, so we would include in our design interactions with parents, siblings, and others in the home. Finally, one might look at the social relationships experienced throughout the full range of societal contacts that children have, including church, clubs, and even mass media contacts.

A case could be made for the importance and value of any of these approaches, from the narrowest focus, looking only at student-teacher interactions, to the broadest focus, looking at students' full, complex social world. Now let's add the real-world constraint of limited resources—say, $50,000 and three months—to conduct the study. At some level, any of these research endeavors could be undertaken for $50,000. But it becomes clear, immediately, that there are trade-offs between breadth and depth. A highly focused study of the student-teacher relationship could consume our entire budget but allow us to investigate the issue in great depth. On the other hand, we might attempt to look at all social relationships that children experience but to look at each of them in a relatively cursory way in order, perhaps, to explore which of those relationships is primary. (If school relationships have very little impact on social development in comparison with relationships outside the school, policymakers could use that information to decide whether the school program ought to be redesigned to have greater impact on social development or, alternatively, if the school should forget about trying to directly affect social development at all.) **The trade-offs involved are the classic trade-offs between breadth and depth,** which we now turn to in more depth.

Breadth Versus Depth

In some ways, the differences between quantitative and qualitative methods involve trade-offs between breadth and depth. Qualitative methods permit inquiry into selected issues in great depth with careful attention to detail, context, and nuance; that data collection need not be constrained by predetermined analytical categories contributes to the potential breadth of qualitative inquiry. Quantitative instruments, on the other hand, ask standardized questions that limit responses to predetermined categories (less breadth and depth). This has the advantage of making it possible to measure the reactions of many respondents to a limited set of questions, thus facilitating comparison and statistical aggregation of the data. By contrast, qualitative methods typi-

cally produce a wealth of detailed data about a much smaller number of people and cases.

However, the breadth versus depth trade-off also applies within qualitative design options. Human relations specialists tell us that we can never *fully* understand the experience of another person. The design issue is how much time and effort we are willing to invest in trying to increase our understanding about any single person's experiences. So, for example, we could look at a narrow range of experiences for a larger number of people or a broader range of experiences for a smaller number of people. Take the case of interviews. Interviewing with an instrument that provides respondents with largely open-ended stimuli typically takes a great deal of time. In an education study, I developed an open-ended interview for elementary students consisting of 20 questions that included items such as "What do you like most about school?" and "What don't you like about school?" These interviews took between half an hour and two hours depending on students' ages and how articulate they were. It would certainly have been possible to have longer interviews. Indeed, I have conducted in-depth interviews with people that ran 6 to 16 hours over a period of a couple of days. On the other hand, it would have been possible to ask fewer questions, make the interviews shorter, and probe in less depth.

Or consider another example with a fuller range of possibilities. It is possible to study a single individual over an extended period of time—for example, the study, in depth, of one week in the life of one child. This involves gathering detailed information about every occurrence in that child's life and every interaction involving that child during the week of the study. With more focus, we might study several children during that week but capture fewer events. With a still more limited approach, say, a daily half-hour interview, we could interview yet a larger number of children on a smaller number of issues. The extreme case would be to spend all of our resources and time asking a single question of as many children as we could interview given time and resource constraints.

No rule of thumb exists to tell a researcher precisely how to focus a study. The extent to which a research or evaluation study is broad or narrow depends on purpose, the resources available, the time available, and the interests of those involved. In brief, these are not choices between good and bad but choices among alternatives, all of which have merit.

Units of Analysis

A design specifies the unit or units of analysis to be studied. Decisions about samples, both sample size and sampling strategies, depend on prior decisions about the appropriate unit of analysis to study. Often individual people, clients, or students are the unit of analysis. This means that the primary focus of data collection will be on what is happening to individuals in a setting and how individuals are affected by the setting. Individual case studies and variation across individuals would focus the analysis.

Comparing groups of people in a program or across programs involves a different unit of analysis. One may be interested in comparing demographic groups (males compared with females, Whites compared with African Americans) or programmatic groups (dropouts vs. people who complete the program, people who do well vs. people who do poorly, people who experience group therapy vs. people who experience individual therapy). One or more groups are

selected as the unit of analysis when there is some important characteristic that separates people into groups and when that characteristic has important implications for the program.

A different unit of analysis involves focusing on different parts of a program. Different classrooms within a school might be studied, making the classroom the unit of analysis. Outpatient and inpatient programs in a medical facility could be studied. The intake part of a program might be studied separately from the service delivery part of a program as separate units of analysis. Entire programs can become the unit of analysis. In state and national programs where there are a number of local sites, the appropriate unit of analysis may be local projects. The analytical focus in such multisite studies is on variations among project sites more than on variations among individuals within projects.

Different units of analysis are not mutually exclusive. However, each unit of analysis implies a different kind of data collection, a different focus for the analysis of data, and a different level at which statements about findings and conclusions would be made. Neighborhoods can be units of analysis or communities, cities, states, cultures, and even nations in the case of international programs.

One of the strengths of qualitative analysis is looking at program units holistically. This means doing more than aggregating data from individuals to get overall program results. When a program, group, organization, or community is the unit of analysis, qualitative methods involve observations and description focused directly on that unit: The program, organization, or community, not just the individual people, becomes the case study focus in those settings.

Particular events, occurrences, or incidents may also be the focus of study (unit of analysis). For example, a quality assurance effort in a health or mental health program might focus only on those critical incidents in which a patient fails to receive expected or desirable treatment. A criminal justice evaluation could focus on violent events or instances in which juveniles run away from treatment. A cultural study may focus on celebrations.

Sampling can also involve time period strategies, for example, continuous and ongoing observation versus fixed-interval sampling in which one treats units of time (e.g., 15-minute segments) as the unit of observation. "The advantage of fixed-interval sampling over continuous monitoring are that fieldworkers experience less fatigue and can collect more information at each sampling interval than they could on a continuous observation routine" (Johnson and Sackett 1998:315). *Time sampling* (sampling periods or units of time) can be an especially important approach because programs, organizations, and communities may function in different ways at different times during the year. Of course, in some programs there never seems to be a good time to collect data. In doing school evaluations in the United States, I've been told by educators to avoid collecting data before Halloween because the school year is just getting started and the kids and teachers need time to get settled in. But the period between Halloween and Thanksgiving is really too short to do very much, and, then, of course, after Thanksgiving everybody's getting ready for the holidays, so that's not a typical or convenient period. It then takes students a few weeks after the winter break to get their attention focused back on school and then the winter malaise sets in and both teachers and students become deeply depressed with the endlessness of winter (at least in northern climes). Then, of course, once spring hits, attention is focused on the close of school and

the kids want to be outside, so that's not an effective time to gather data. In African villages, I was given similar scenarios about the difficulties of data collection for every month in the annual cycle of the agricultural season. A particular period of time, then, is both an important context for a study and a sampling issue.

There are limits to how much one can apply logic in trying to calculate all of the possible consequences of sampling options, whether the decision is about which time periods to sample or which activities to observe. The trick is to keep coming back to the criterion of usefulness. What data collected during what time period describing what activities will most likely illuminate the inquiry? For evaluation, what focus of inquiry will be most useful? There are no perfect evaluation designs, only more and less useful ones.

The key issue in selecting and making decisions about the appropriate unit of analysis is to decide what it is you want to be able to say something about at the end of the study. Do you want to have findings about individuals, families, groups, or some other unit of analysis? For scholarly inquiries, disciplinary traditions provide guidance about relevant units of analysis. For evaluations, one has to determine what decision makers and primary intended users really need information about. Do they want findings about the different experiences of individuals in programs, or do they want to know about variations in program processes at different sites? Or both? Such differences in focus will be critical to the design but may not be easy to determine. A decision maker is unlikely to say to the evaluator, "The unit of analysis we want to study is ____." The evaluator must be able to hear the real issues involved in the decision maker's questions and translate those issues into the appropriate unit of analysis, then check out that translation with the intended evaluation users.

Exhibit 5.5 presents some alternative units of analysis. Clarity about the unit of analysis is needed to select a study sample. In Chapter 2, I identified purposeful sampling as one of the core distinguishing strategic themes of qualitative inquiry. The next section presents variations in, rationales for, and the details of how to design a study based on a purposeful sample.

🖻 Purposeful Sampling

T is the motive exalts the action.

—Margaret Preston, 1875

Perhaps nothing better captures the difference between quantitative and qualitative methods than the different logics that undergird sampling approaches.

Qualitative inquiry typically focuses in depth on relatively small samples, even single cases ($N = 1$), selected *purposefully*. Quantitative methods typically depend on larger samples selected randomly. Not only are the techniques for sampling different, but the very logic of each approach is unique because the purpose of each strategy is different.

The logic and power of random sampling derive from statistical probability theory. A random and statistically representative sample permits confident generalization from a sample to a larger population. Random sampling also controls for selection bias. The purpose of probability-based random sampling is generalization from the sample to a population and control of selectivity errors.

What would be "bias" in statistical sampling, and therefore a weakness, becomes intended focus in qualitative sampling, and therefore a strength. The logic and power of purposeful sampling lie in selecting *information-rich cases* for study in depth. Information-rich cases are those from which one can learn a great deal about issues of central importance to the purpose of the inquiry, thus the term *purposeful* sampling. Studying information-rich cases yields insights and in-depth understanding rather than empirical generalizations. For example, if the purpose of an evaluation is to increase the effectiveness of a program in reaching lower-socioeconomic groups, one may learn a great deal more by studying in depth a small number of carefully selected poor families than by gathering standardized information from a large, statistically representative sample of the whole program. Purposeful sampling focuses on selecting information-rich cases whose study will illuminate the questions under study. Purposeful sampling is sometimes called *purposive* or *judgment* sampling: "In judgment sampling, you decide the purpose you want informants (or communities) to serve, and you go out to find some" (Bernard 2000:176). There are several different strategies for purposefully selecting information-rich cases. The logic of each strategy serves a particular purpose.

1. *Extreme or deviant case sampling.* This strategy involves selecting cases that are

EXHIBIT 5.5	Examples of Units of Analysis for Case Studies and Comparisons

People Focused	*Structure Focused*
Individuals	Projects
Small, informal groups (friends, gangs)	Programs
Families	Organizations
	Units in organizations

Perspective/Worldview Based

People who share a culture

People who share a common experience or perspective, for example, dropouts, graduates, leaders, parents, Internet listserv participants, survivors

Geography Focused

Neighborhoods	Villages
Cities	Farms
States	Regions
Countries	Markets

Activity Focused

Critical incidents	Time periods
Celebrations	Crises
Quality assurance violations	Events

Time Based

Particular days, weeks, or months	Vacations
Winter break	Rainy season
Ramadan	Dry season
Full moons	School term
A political term of office	An election period

NOTE: These are not mutually exclusive categories.

information rich because they are unusual or special in some way, such as outstanding successes or notable failures. The influential study of America's best-run companies, published as *In Search of Excellence,* exemplifies the logic of purposeful, extreme group sampling. This study was based on a sample of 62 companies "never intended to be per- fectly representative of U.S. industry as a whole . . . [but] a list of companies considered to be innovative and excellent by an informed group of observers of the business scene" (Peters and Waterman 1982:19). Lisbeth Schorr (1988) used a similar strategy in studying especially effective programs for families in poverty, published as the influential book *Within Our Reach*. Stephen Covey's (1990) best-selling book *The 7 Habits of Highly Effective People* is based on a purposeful, extreme group sampling strategy. Studies of leadership have long focused on identifying the characteristics of highly successful leaders, as in Collins's (2001) case studies of 11 corporate executives in whom "extreme personal humility blends paradoxically with intense professional will" (p. 67), what he calls "Level 5 leaders," the highest level in his model. In the early days of AIDS research when HIV infections almost always resulted in death, a small number of cases of people infected with HIV who did not develop AIDS became crucial outlier cases that provided important insights into directions researchers should take in combating AIDS.

Sometimes cases of dramatic failure offer powerful lessons. The legendary UCLA basketball coach John Wooden won 10 national championships from 1964 through 1975, an unparalleled sports achievement. But the game he remembered the most and said he learned the most from was UCLA's 1974 overtime loss to North Carolina State in the semifinals (quoted in the *Los Angeles Times*, December 21, 2000). Wooden's focus on that game—that extreme case—illustrates the learning psychology of extreme group purposeful sampling.

This is also the sampling psychology behind Jim Paul's (1994) book *What I Learned Losing a Million Dollars*. A former governor of the Chicago Mercantile Exchange, he made thousands of trades in many commodities over a long and distinguished career, but what he reports learning the most from was a highly unusual combination of mistakes in which he lost more than $1 million in a few weeks of trading soy beans —an extreme but illuminative case. He reports that he ultimately learned to be a winner by carefully studying and learning from losing.

An excellent applied research example is Angela Browne's (1987) study *When Battered Women Kill*. She conducted in-depth studies of the most extreme cases of domestic violence to elucidate the phenomenon of battering and abuse. The extreme nature of the cases is what renders them so powerful. Browne's book is an exemplar of qualitative inquiry using purposeful sampling for applied research.

In evaluation, the logic of extreme case sampling is that lessons may be learned about unusual conditions or extreme outcomes that are relevant to improving more typical programs. Let's suppose that we are interested in studying a national program with hundreds of local sites. We know that many programs are operating reasonably well, even quite well, and that other programs verge on being disasters. We also know that most programs are doing "OK." This information comes from knowledgeable sources who have made site visits to enough programs to have a basic idea about what the variation is. The question is this: How should programs be sampled for the study? If one wanted to precisely document the natural variation among programs, a random sample would be appropriate, preferably a random sample of sufficient size to be truly representative and permit generalizations to the total population of programs. However, some information is already available on what program variation is like. The question of more immediate interest may concern *illuminative cases*. With limited resources and limited time, an evaluator might learn more by intensively studying one or more examples of really poor programs and one or more examples of really excellent programs. The evaluation focus, then, becomes a question of understanding under what conditions programs get into trouble and under what conditions

SAMPLING THE BEST

Evaluating the Caribbean Agricultural Extension Project posed a challenge: how to provide funders with decision-relevant information about the long-term potential of agricultural extension in eight English-speaking Caribbean countries. The first phase of the project involved needs assessment, planning, and capacity building. These processes laid the foundation for training agricultural extension agents who would, it was hoped, help improve the productivity and profitability of small farms. However, a critical funding decision about the potential of the project had to be made at the end of the first phase before actual training of extension agents had begun and prior to any impact on farmers. No data existed on the effectiveness of extension that could be used to calculate potential effectiveness. Funders were asking for concrete estimates of future impact, not just some hoped-for productivity increase pulled out of the air. The solution was to study a purposeful sample of "the best."

Each agricultural extension service established a process for identifying and recognizing its own "outstanding agricultural extension agent." Those agents were each asked to identify five farm families whose farm productivity the agent believed he or she had in-

creased. Independent case studies were done on these 40 farm families (5 families in each of the 8 countries).

This sample was purposefully "biased" to establish case-based goals for increased extension effectiveness while also showing the diversity of small farm situations and the variety of extension agent practices. It could be expected that the typical extension agent would have somewhat less impact on farmers than these outstanding agents. However, by gathering data about the impacts of the "best," it was possible to provide project funders with concrete examples of what might be accomplished over time if more extension agents were trained in the practices of the "best." These data allowed potential second-phase funders to engage the question: Given the impacts of those extension agents identified as the best, is it worth funding a training program aimed at creating more extension agents following those "best" practices? Without these concrete cases to examine, the funding decision would have been based on abstract discussion and speculative guesses about extension agent activities and impacts. Having real cases to examine made the resulting discussions concrete, focused, and data based. The second phase was funded.

programs exemplify excellence. It is not even necessary to randomly sample poor programs or excellent programs. The researchers and intended users involved in the study think through **what cases they could learn the most from** and those are the cases that are selected for study.

In a single program the same strategy may apply. Instead of studying some representative sample of people in the setting, the evaluator may focus on studying and understanding selected cases of special interest, for example, unexpected dropouts or outstanding successes. In an evaluation of the Caribbean Agricultural Extension Project, we did case studies of the "outstanding extension agent" selected by peers in each of eight Caribbean countries to help the program develop curriculum and standards for improving extension practice. The sample was purposefully "biased," not to make the program look good, but rather to learn from those who were exemplars of good practice. In many instances, more can be learned from intensively studying exemplary (information-rich) cases than can be learned from statistical depictions of what the average case is like. In other evaluations, detailed information about special cases can be used to supplement statistical data about the normal distribution of participants. In statistical terms, extreme case sampling focuses on *outliers* (the endpoints of the bell-shaped curve normal distribution) that are often ignored in aggregate data reporting.

Ethnomethodologists use a form of extreme case sampling when they do their field experiments. Ethnomethodologists are interested in everyday experiences of routine living that depend on deeply understood, shared understandings among people in a setting (see Chapter 3). One way of exposing these implicit assumptions and norms on which everyday life is based is to create disturbances that deviate greatly from the norm. Observing the reactions to someone eating like a pig in a restaurant and then interviewing people about what they saw and how they felt would be an example of studying a deviant sample to illuminate the ordinary.

In essence, the logic of extreme group sampling is that extreme cases may be information-rich cases precisely because, by being unusual, they can illuminate both the unusual and the typical. In proposing an extreme group sample, as in all purposeful sampling designs, the researcher has an obligation to present the rationale and expected benefits of this strategy as well as to note its weakness (lack of generalizability).

2. *Intensity sampling.* Intensity sampling involves the same logic as extreme case sampling but with less emphasis on the extremes. An intensity sample consists of information-rich cases that manifest the phe-

nomenon of interest intensely (but not extremely). Extreme or deviant cases may be so unusual as to distort the manifestation of the phenomenon of interest. Using the logic of intensity sampling, one seeks excellent or rich examples of the phenomenon of interest, but not highly unusual cases.

Heuristic research (Chapter 3) uses intensity sampling. Heuristic research draws explicitly on the intense personal experiences of the researcher, for example, experiences with loneliness or jealousy. Coresearchers who have experienced these phenomena intensely also participate in the study. The heuristic researcher is not typically seeking pathological or extreme manifestations of loneliness, jealousy, or whatever phenomenon is of interest. Such extreme cases might not lend themselves to the reflective process of heuristic inquiry. On the other hand, if the experience of the heuristic researcher and his or her coresearchers is quite mild, there won't be much to study. Thus, the researcher seeks a sample of sufficient intensity to elucidate the phenomenon of interest.

The same strategy can be applied in a program evaluation. Extreme successes or unusual failures may be discredited as being too extreme or unusual to yield useful information. Therefore, the evaluator may select cases that manifest sufficient intensity to illuminate the nature of success or failure, but not at the extreme.

Intensity sampling involves some prior information and considerable judgment. The researcher or evaluator must do some exploratory work to determine the nature of the variation in the situation under study, then sample intense examples of the phenomenon of interest.

3. *Maximum variation (heterogeneity) sampling.* This strategy for purposeful sampling aims at capturing and describing the

central themes that cut across a great deal of variation. For small samples, a great deal of heterogeneity can be a problem because individual cases are so different from each other. The maximum variation sampling strategy turns that apparent weakness into a strength by applying the following logic: Any common patterns that emerge from great variation are of particular interest and value in capturing the core experiences and central, shared dimensions of a setting or phenomenon.

How does one maximize variation in a small sample? One begins by identifying diverse characteristics or criteria for constructing the sample. Suppose a statewide program has project sites spread around the state, some in rural areas, some in urban areas, and some in suburban areas. The evaluation lacks sufficient resources to randomly select enough project sites to generalize across the state. The evaluator can study a few sites from each area and at least be sure that the geographical variation among sites is represented in the study. While the evaluation would describe the uniqueness of each site, it would also look for common themes across sites. Any such themes take on added importance precisely because they emerge out of great variation. For example, in studying community-based energy conservation efforts statewide using a maximum heterogeneity sampling strategy, I constructed a matrix sample of 10 communities in which each community was as different as possible from every other community on such characteristics as size, form of local government (e.g., strong mayor/weak mayor), ethnic diversity, strength of the economy, demographics, and region. In the analysis, what stood out across these diverse cases was the importance of a local, committed cadre of people who made things happen.

In a study of the MacArthur Foundation Fellowship Program, the design focused on case studies of individual fellowship recipients. Over 20 years of awards, more than 600 people had received fellowships. We had sufficient resources to do only 40 case studies. We maximized sample variation by creating a matrix in which each person in the sample was as different as possible from others using dimensions such as nature of work, stage in career, public visibility, institutional affiliation, age, gender, ethnicity, geographic location, mobility, health status, nationality, and field of endeavor. The thematic patterns of achievement that emerged from this diversity allowed us to construct a model to illuminate the primary dimensions of and factors in the award's impact. A theme song emerged from all the scattered noise. That's the power of maximum variation (heterogeneity) sampling.

Thus, when selecting a small sample of great diversity, the data collection and analysis will yield two kinds of findings: (1) high-quality, detailed descriptions of each case, which are useful for documenting uniquenesses, and (2) important shared patterns that cut across cases and derive their significance from having emerged out of heterogeneity. Both are important findings in qualitative inquiry.

4. *Homogeneous samples.* In direct contrast to maximum variation sampling is the strategy of picking a small, homogeneous sample, the purpose of which is to describe some particular subgroup in depth. A program that has many different kinds of participants may need in-depth information about a particular subgroup. For example, a parent education program that involves many different kinds of parents may focus a qualitative evaluation on the experiences of single-parent female heads of household because that is a particularly difficult group to reach and hold in the program.

Focus group interviews are based typically on homogeneous groups. Focus groups involve open-ended interviews with groups of five to eight people on specially targeted or focused issues. The use of focus groups in evaluation will be discussed at greater length in the chapter on interviewing. The point here is that sampling for focus groups typically involves bringing together people of similar backgrounds and experiences to participate in a group interview about major issues that affect them.

5. *Typical case sampling.* In describing a culture or program to people not familiar with the setting studied, it can be helpful to provide a qualitative profile of one or more typical cases. These cases are selected with the cooperation of key informants, such as program staff or knowledgeable participants, who can help identify who and what are typical. Typical cases can also be selected using survey data, a demographic analysis of averages, or other statistical data that provide a normal distribution of characteristics from which to identify "average-like" cases. Keep in mind that the purpose of a qualitative profile of one or more typical cases is to describe and illustrate what is typical to those unfamiliar with the setting—not to make generalized statements about the experiences of all participants. The sample is illustrative not definitive.

When entire programs or communities are the unit of analysis, the processes and effects described for the typical program may be used to provide a frame of reference for case studies of "poor" or "excellent" sites. When the typical site sampling strategy is used, the site is specifically selected because it is not in any major way atypical, extreme, deviant, or intensely unusual. This strategy is often appropriate in sampling villages for community development studies in Third World countries. A study of a typical village

illuminates key issues that must be considered in any development project aimed at that kind of village.

In evaluation and policy research, the interests of decision makers will shape the sampling strategy. I remember an evaluation in which the key decision makers had made their peace with the fact that there will always be some poor programs and some excellent programs, but the programs they really wanted more information about were what they called "those run-of-the-mill programs that are so hard to get a handle on precisely because they are so ordinary and don't stand out in any definitive way." Given that framing, we employed typical case sampling. It is important, when using this strategy, to attempt to get broad consensus about which cases are typical—and what criteria are being used to define typicality.

6. *Critical case sampling.* Critical cases are those that can make a point quite dramatically or are, for some reason, particularly important in the scheme of things. A clue to the existence of a critical case is a statement to the effect that "if it happens there, it will happen anywhere," or, vice versa, "if it doesn't happen there, it won't happen anywhere." Another clue to the existence of a critical case is a key informant observation to the effect that "if that group is having problems, then we can be sure all the groups are having problems."

Looking for the critical case is particularly important where resources may limit the evaluation to the study of only a single site. Under such conditions, it makes strategic sense to **pick the site that would yield the most information and have the greatest impact on the development of knowledge.** While studying one or a few critical cases does not technically permit broad generalizations to all possible cases, *logical generalizations* can often be made from the weight of evidence produced in studying a single, critical case.

Physics provides a good example of such a critical case. In Galileo's study of gravity, he wanted to find out if the weight of an object affected the rate of speed at which it would fall. Rather than randomly sampling objects of different weights in order to generalize to all objects in the world, he selected a critical case—the feather. If in a vacuum, as he demonstrated, a feather fell at the same rate as some heavier object (a coin), then he could logically generalize from this one critical comparison to all objects. His finding was both useful and credible because the feather was a convincing critical case.

Critical cases can be found in social science and evaluation research if one is creative in looking for them. For example, suppose national policymakers want to get local communities involved in making decisions about how their local program will be run, but they aren't sure that the communities will understand the complex regulations governing their involvement. The first critical case is to evaluate the regulations in a community of well-educated citizens; if they can't understand the regulations, then less educated folks are sure to find the regulations incomprehensible. Or conversely, one might consider the critical case to be a community consisting of people with quite low levels of education: "If they can understand the regulations, anyone can."

Identification of critical cases depends on recognition of the key dimensions that make for a critical case. For example, a critical case might come from a particularly difficult program location. If the funders of a new program are worried about recruiting clients or participants into a program, it may make sense to study the site where resistance to the program is expected to be greatest to provide the most rigorous test of program recruitment. If the program works in that site,

it could work anywhere. That makes the critical case an especially information-rich exemplar, therefore worthy of study as the centerpiece in a small or "N of 1" sample.

World-renowned medical hypnotist Milton H. Erickson became a critical case in the field of hypnosis. Erickson was so skillful that he became widely known for "his ability to succeed with 'impossibles'—people who have exhausted the traditional medical, dental, psychotherapeutic, hypnotic and religious avenues for assisting them in their need, and have not been able to make the changes they desire" (Grinder, DeLozier, and Bandler 1977:109). If Milton Erickson couldn't hypnotize a person, no one could. He was able to demonstrate that, under his definition of hypnosis, anyone could be hypnotized.

7. Snowball or chain sampling. This is an approach for locating information-rich key informants or critical cases. The process begins by asking well-situated people: "Who knows a lot about _____? Whom should I talk to?" By asking a number of people who else to talk with, the snowball gets bigger and bigger as you accumulate new information-rich cases. In most programs or systems, a few key names or incidents are mentioned repeatedly. Those people or events, recommended as valuable by a number of different informants, take on special importance. The chain of recommended informants would typically diverge initially as many possible sources are recommended, then converge as a few key names get mentioned over and over.

The Peters and Waterman (1982) study *In Search of Excellence* began with snowball sampling, asking a broad group of knowledgeable people to identify well-run companies. Rosabeth Moss Kanter's (1983) study of innovation reported in *The Change Masters* focused on 10 core case studies of the "most innovative" companies. She began by asking corporate experts for candidate companies to study. Nominations snowballed as she broadened her inquiry and then converged into a small number of core cases nominated by a number of different expert informants.

8. *Criterion sampling.* The logic of criterion sampling is to review and study all cases that meet some predetermined criterion of importance, a strategy common in quality assurance efforts. For example, the expected range of participation in a mental health outpatient program might be 4 to 26 weeks. All cases that exceed 28 weeks are reviewed to find out why the expected range was exceeded and to make sure the case was being appropriately handled. Or a quality assurance standard may be that all patients entering a hospital emergency room, who are not in a life-threatening situation, receive care within 2 hours. Cases that exceed this standard are reviewed.

Critical incidents can be a source of criterion sampling. For example, all incidents of client abuse in a program may be objects of in-depth evaluation in a quality assurance effort. All former mental health clients who commit suicide within three months of release may constitute a sample for in-depth, qualitative study. In a school setting, all students who are absent 25% or more of the time may merit the in-depth attention of a case study. The point of criterion sampling is to be sure to understand cases that are likely to be information rich because they may reveal major system weaknesses that become targets of opportunity for program or system improvement.

Criterion sampling can add an important qualitative component to a management information system or an ongoing program monitoring system. All cases in the data system that exhibit certain predetermined criterion characteristics are routinely identified for in-depth, qualitative analysis. Criterion sampling also can be used to identify cases from standardized questionnaires for in-depth follow-up, for example, all respondents who report having experienced ongoing workplace discrimination. (This strategy can only be used where respondents have willingly supplied contact information.)

9. *Theory-based sampling, operational construct sampling, and theoretical sampling.* A more conceptually oriented version of criterion sampling is theory-based sampling. The researcher samples incidents, slices of life, time periods, or people on the basis of their potential manifestation or representation of important theoretical constructs. Buckholt (2001) studied people who met theory-derived criteria for being "resilient" in a study of resilience among adult abuse survivors. The sample becomes, by definition and selection, representative of the phenomenon of interest.

When one is studying people, programs, organizations, or communities, the population of interest can be fairly readily determined. Constructs, however, do not have as clear a frame of reference:

For sampling operational instances of constructs, there is no concrete target population. . . . Mostly, therefore, we are forced to select on a purposive basis those particular instances of a construct that past validity studies, conventional practice, individual intuition, or consultation with critically minded persons suggest offer the closest correspondence to the construct of interest. Alternatively, we can use the same procedures to select multiple operational representations of each construct, chosen because they overlap in representing the critical theoretical components of the construct and because they differ from each other on irrelevant dimensions. This second form of sampling is called multiple operationalism, and it depends more heavily on individual judgment than does the random sampling of persons from a well-designated, target population. Yet, such judgments, while inevitable, are less well understood than formal sampling methods and are largely ignored by sampling experts. (Cook, Leviton, and Shadish 1985: 163-64)

Operational construct sampling simply means that one samples for study real-world examples (i.e., *operational* examples) of the constructs in which one is interested. Studying a number of such examples is called "multiple operationalism" (Webb et al. 1966). For example, classic diffusion of innovations theory (Rogers 1962) predicts that early adopters of some innovation will be different in significant ways from later adopters. Doing cases studies on early and late adopters, then, would be an example of theory-based sampling. Such samples are often necessarily purposefully selected because the population of all early and late adopters may not be known, so random sampling is not an option.

Theoretical sampling is what grounded theorists define as "sampling on the basis of the emerging concepts, with the aim being to explore the dimensional range or varied conditions along which the properties of concepts vary" (Strauss and Corbin 1998: 73). In grounded theory, theoretical sampling supports the constant comparative method of analysis. That is, one does theoretical sampling in grounded theory in order to use the constant comparative method of analysis. The two go hand in glove, connecting design and analysis. Theoretical sampling permits elucidation and refinement of the variations in, manifestations of, and meanings of a concept as it is found in the data gathered during fieldwork. The constant comparative method involves systematically examining and refining variations in emergent and grounded concepts. Variations in the concept must be sampled to rigorously compare and contrast those variations. (See Chapters 3 and 8 for more detailed discussions of grounded theory.)

10. *Confirming and disconfirming cases.* In the early part of qualitative fieldwork, the evaluator is exploring—gathering data and watching for patterns to emerge. Over time, the exploratory process gives way to confirmatory fieldwork. This involves testing ideas, confirming the importance and meaning of possible patterns, and checking out the viability of emergent findings with new data and additional cases. This stage of fieldwork requires considerable rigor and integrity on the part of the evaluator in looking for and sampling confirming *as well as disconfirming* cases.

Confirmatory cases are additional examples that fit already emergent patterns; these cases confirm and elaborate the findings, adding richness, depth, and credibility. Disconfirming cases are no less important at this point. These are the examples that don't fit. They are a source of rival interpretations as well as a way of placing boundaries around confirmed findings. They may be "exceptions that prove the rule" or exceptions that disconfirm and alter what appeared to be primary patterns.

The source of questions or ideas to be confirmed or disconfirmed may be from stakeholders or previous scholarly literature rather than the evaluator's fieldwork. An evaluation may in part serve the purpose of confirming or disconfirming stakeholders' or scholars' hypotheses, these having been identified during early, conceptual evaluator-stakeholder design discussions or literature reviews.

Thinking about the challenge of finding confirming and disconfirming cases emphasizes the relationship between sampling and research conclusions. **The sample determines what the evaluator will have something to say about—thus the importance of sampling carefully and thoughtfully.**

11. *Stratified purposeful sampling.* Stratified samples are samples within samples. A stratified random sample, for example, might stratify by socioeconomic status within a larger population so as to make generalizations and statistically valid comparisons by social class as well as to generalize to the total population.

Purposeful samples can also be stratified and nested by combining types of purposeful sampling. So, for example, one might combine typical case sampling with maximum heterogeneity sampling by taking a stratified purposeful sample of above average, average, and below average cases. This represents less than a full maximum variation sample, but more than simple typical case sampling. The purpose of a stratified purposeful sample is to capture major variations rather than to identify a common core, although the latter may also emerge in the analysis. Each of the strata would constitute a fairly homogeneous sample. This strategy differs from stratified random sampling in that the sample sizes are likely to be too small for generalization or statistical representativeness.

12. *Opportunistic or emergent sampling.* Fieldwork often involves on-the-spot decisions about sampling to take advantage of new opportunities during actual data collection. Unlike experimental designs, emergent qualitative designs can include the option of adding to a sample to take advantage of unforeseen opportunities *after* fieldwork has begun. Being open to following wher-

ever the data lead is a primary strength of qualitative fieldwork strategies. This permits the sample to emerge during fieldwork.

During fieldwork, it is impossible to observe everything. Decisions must be made about what activities to observe, which people to observe and interview, and when to collect data. These decisions cannot all be made in advance. The purposeful sampling strategies discussed above provide direction for sampling but often depend on some knowledge of the setting being studied. Opportunistic, emergent sampling takes advantage of whatever unfolds as it unfolds.

In Chapter 2, I identified emergent flexible designs as one of the core strategic themes of qualitative inquiry and cited as an exemplar the anthropologist Brackette F. Williams and her fieldwork on how Americans view violence in America:

> I do impromptu interviews. I don't have some target number of interviews in mind or predetermined questions. It depends on the person and the situation. Airports, for example, are a good place for impromptu interviews with people. So sometimes, instead of using airport time to write, I interview people about the death penalty or about killing or about death in their life. It's called *opportunity sampling.* . . . I'm following where the data take me, where my questions take me. (personal interview)

Few qualitative studies are as fully emergent and open-ended as the fieldwork of Williams. Her approach exemplifies emergent opportunity sampling.

13. *Purposeful random sampling.* A purposeful sampling strategy does not automatically eliminate any possibility for random selection of cases. For many audiences, random sampling, even of small samples, will substantially increase the credibility of the

results. I recently worked with a program that annually appears before the state legislature and tells "war stories" about client successes and struggles, sometimes even including a few stories about failures to provide balance. To enhance the credibility of their reports, the director and staff decided to begin collecting evaluation information more systematically. Because they were striving for individualized outcomes, they rejected the notion of basing the evaluation entirely on a standardized pre-post instrument. They wanted to collect case histories and do in-depth case studies of clients, but they had very limited resources and time to devote to such data collection. In effect, staff at each program site, many of whom serve 200 to 300 families a year, felt that they could only do 10 or 15 detailed, in-depth clinical case histories each year. We systematized the kind of information that would be going into the case histories at each program site and then set up a random procedure for selecting those clients whose case histories would be recorded in depth, thereby systematizing and randomizing their collection of war stories. While they cannot generalize to the entire client population on the basis of 10 cases from each program site, they will be able to tell legislators that the stories they are reporting were randomly selected **in advance of knowledge of how the outcomes would appear** and that the information collected was comprehensive. The credibility of systematic and randomly selected case examples is considerably greater than the personal, ad hoc selection of cases selected and reported *after* the fact—that is, after outcomes are known.

It is critical to understand, however, that this is a *purposeful random sample,* not a representative random sample. **The purpose of a small random sample is credibility, not representativeness.** A small, purposeful random sample aims to reduce suspicion about why certain cases were selected for study, but such a sample still does not permit statistical generalizations.

14. *Sampling politically important cases.* Evaluation is inherently and inevitably political (see Turpin 1989; Palumbo 1987; Patton 1987b). A variation on the critical case strategy involves selecting (or sometimes avoiding) a politically sensitive site or unit of analysis. For example, a statewide program may have a local site in the district of a state legislator who is particularly influential. By studying carefully the program in that district, evaluation data may be more likely to attract attention and get used. This does not mean that the evaluator then undertakes to make that site look either good or bad, depending on the politics of the moment. That would clearly be unethical. Rather, sampling politically important cases is simply a strategy for trying to increase the usefulness and relevance of information where resources permit the study of only a limited number of cases.

The same political perspective (broadly speaking) may inform case sampling in applied or even basic research studies. A political scientist or historian might select the election year 2000 Florida vote-counting case, the Clinton impeachment effort, Nixon's Watergate crisis, or Reagan's Iran-Contra scandal for study not only because of the insights they provide about the American system of government but because of the likely attention such a study would attract. A sociologist's study of a riot or a psychologist's study of a famous suicide would likely involve some attention during sampling to the public and political importance of the case.

15. *Convenience sampling.* Finally, there is the strategy of sampling by convenience: doing what's fast and convenient. This is

probably the most common sampling strategy—and the least desirable. Too often evaluators using qualitative methods think that because the sample size they can study will be too small to permit generalizations, it doesn't matter how cases are picked, so they might as well pick ones that are easy to access and inexpensive to study. **While convenience and cost are real considerations, they should be the last factors to be taken into account** after strategically deliberating on how to get the most information of greatest utility from the limited number of cases to be sampled. Purposeful, strategic sampling can yield crucial information about critical cases. **Convenience sampling is neither purposeful nor strategic.**

Information-Rich Cases

Exhibit 5.6 summarizes the 15 purposeful sampling strategies discussed above, plus a 16th approach—combination or mixed purposeful sampling. For example, an extreme group or maximum heterogeneity approach may yield an initial potential sample size that is still larger than the study can handle. The final selection, then, may be made randomly—a combination approach. Thus, these approaches are not mutually exclusive. Each approach serves a somewhat different purpose. Because research and evaluations often serve multiple purposes, more than one qualitative sampling strategy may be necessary. In long-term fieldwork, all of these strategies may be used at some point.

The underlying principle that is common to all these strategies is selecting information-rich cases—cases from which one can learn a great deal about matters of importance and therefore worthy of in-depth study.

In the process of developing the research design, the evaluator or researcher is trying to consider and anticipate the kinds of arguments that will lend credibility to the study as well as the kinds of arguments that might be used to attack the findings. Reasons for site selections or individual case sampling need to be carefully articulated and made explicit. Moreover, it is important to be open and clear about a study's limitations, that is, to anticipate and address criticisms that may be made of a particular sampling strategy, especially from people who think that the only high-quality samples are random ones.

Having weighed the evidence and considered the alternatives, evaluators and primary stakeholders make their sampling decisions, sometimes painfully, but always with the recognition that there are no perfect designs. The sampling strategy must be selected to fit the purpose of the study, the resources available, the questions being asked, and the constraints being faced. This holds true for sampling strategy as well as sample size.

🔄 Sample Size

Qualitative inquiry is rife with ambiguities. There are purposeful strategies instead of methodological rules. There are inquiry approaches instead of statistical formulas. Qualitative inquiry seems to work best for people with a high tolerance for ambiguity. (And we're still only discussing design. It gets worse when we get to analysis.)

Nowhere is this ambiguity clearer than in the matter of sample size.

I get letters. I get calls. I get e-mails.

Is 10 a large enough sample to achieve maximum variation?

I started out to interview 20 people for two hours each, but I've lost 2 people. Is 18 large enough, or do I have to find 2 more?

EXHIBIT 5.6   Sampling Strategies

Type	*Purpose*
Random probability sampling	Representativeness: Sample size a function of population size and desired confidence level.
1. Simple random sample	Permit generalization from sample to the population it represents.
2. Stratified random and cluster samples	Increase confidence in making generalizations to particular subgroups.
Purposeful sampling	Select information-rich cases strategically and purposefully; specific type and number of cases selected depends on study purpose and resources.
1. Extreme or deviant case (outlier) sampling	Learning from unusual manifestations of the phenomenon of interest, for example, outstanding successes/notable failures; top of the class/dropouts; exotic events; crises.
2. Intensity sampling	Information-rich cases that manifest the phenomenon intensely, but not extremely, for example, good students/poor students; above average/below average.
3. Maximum variation sampling—purposefully picking a wide range of cases to get variation on dimensions of interest	Document unique or diverse variations that have emerged in adapting to different conditions. Identify important common patterns that cut across variations (cut through the noise of variation).
4. Homogeneous sampling	Focus; reduce variation; simplify analysis; facilitate group interviewing.
5. Typical case sampling	Illustrate or highlight what is typical, normal, average.
6. Critical case sampling	Permits logical generalization and maximum application of information to other cases because if it's true of this one case, it's likely to be true of all other cases.
7. Snowball or chain sampling	Identify cases of interest from sampling people who know people who know people who know what cases are information rich, that is, good examples for study, good interview participants.
8. Criterion sampling	Picking all cases that meet some criterion, for example, all children abused in a treatment facility. Quality assurance.
9. Theory-based sampling, operational construct sampling, or theoretical sampling	Finding manifestations of a theoretical construct of interest so as to elaborate and examine the construct and its variations.

(continued)

EXHIBIT 5.6　　Continued

Type	Purpose
10. Confirming and disconfirming cases	Elaborating and deepening initial analysis; seeking exceptions; testing variation.
11. Stratified purposeful sampling	Illustrate characteristics of particular subgroups of interest; facilitate comparisons.
12. Opportunistic or emergent sampling	Following new leads during fieldwork; taking advantage of the unexpected; flexibility.
13. Purposeful random sampling (still small sample size)	Add credibility when potential purposeful sample is larger than one can handle. Reduces bias within a purposeful category. (Not for generalizations or representativeness.)
14. Sampling politically important cases	Attract attention to the study (or avoid attracting undesired attention by purposefully eliminating from the sample politically sensitive cases).
15. Convenience sampling	Do what's easy to save time, money, and effort. Poorest rationale; lowest credibility. Yields information-poor cases.
16. Combination or mixed purposeful sampling	Triangulation; flexibility; meet multiple interests and needs.

I want to study just one organization, but interview 20 people in the organization. Is my sample size 1 or 20 or both?

My universal, certain, and confident reply to these questions is this: "It depends."

There are no rules for sample size in qualitative inquiry. Sample size depends on what you want to know, the purpose of the inquiry, what's at stake, what will be useful, what will have credibility, and what can be done with available time and resources.

Earlier in this chapter, I discussed the trade-offs between breadth and depth. With the same fixed resources and limited time, a researcher could study a specific set of experiences for a larger number of people (seeking breadth) or a more open range of experiences for a smaller number of people (seeking depth). In-depth information from a small number of people can be very valuable, especially if the cases are information rich. Less depth from a larger number of people can be especially helpful in exploring a phenomenon and trying to document diversity or understand variation. I repeat, the size of the sample depends on what you want to find out, why you want to find it out, how the findings will be used, and what resources (including time) you have for the study.

To understand the problem of small samples in qualitative inquiry, it's necessary to place these small samples in the context of probability sampling. A qualitative inquiry sample *only seems small* in comparison with the sample size needed for representativeness when the purpose is generalizing from a sample to the population of which it is a part. Suppose there are 100 people in a program to be evaluated. It would be necessary to randomly sample 80 of those people (80%) to make a generalization at the 95% confidence level. If there are 500 people in the program, 217 people must be sampled (43%) for the same level of confidence. If there are 1,000 people, 278 people must be sampled (28%), and if there are 5,000 people in the population of interest, 357 must be sampled (7%) to achieve a 95% confidence level in the generalization of findings. At the other extreme, if there are only 50 people in the program, 44 must be randomly sampled (88%) to achieve a 95% level of confidence. (See Fitz-Gibbon and Morris [1987:163] for a table on determining sample size from a given population.)

The logic of purposeful sampling is quite different. The problem is, however, that the utility and credibility of small purposeful samples are often judged on the basis of the logic, purpose, and recommended sample sizes of probability sampling. Instead, purposeful samples should be judged according to the purpose and rationale of the study: Does the sampling strategy support the study's purpose? The sample, like all other aspects of qualitative inquiry, must be judged in context—the same principle that undergirds analysis and presentation of qualitative data. Random probability samples cannot accomplish what in-depth, purposeful samples accomplish, and vice versa.

Piaget contributed a major breakthrough to our understanding of how children think by observing his own two children at length and in great depth. Freud established the field of psychoanalysis based originally on fewer than 10 client cases. Bandler and Grinder (1975a, 1975b) founded neurolinguistic programming (NLP) by studying three renowned and highly effective therapists: Milton Erickson, Fritz Perls, and Virginia Satir. Peters and Waterman (1982) for-

mulated their widely followed eight principles for organizational excellence by studying 62 companies, a very small sample of the thousands of companies one might study. Sands (2000) did a fine dissertation studying a single school principal, describing the leadership of a female leader who entered a challenging school situation and brought about constructive change.

Clair Claiborne Park's (2001) single case study of her daughter's autism reports 40 years of data on every stage of her development, language use, emotions, capacities, barriers, obsessions, communication patterns, emergent artistry, and challenges overcome and challenges not overcome. Park and her husband made systematic observations throughout the years. Eminent medical anthropologist Oliver Saks reviewed the data and determined in his preface to the book that more data are available on the woman in this extraordinary case study than on any other autistic human being who has ever lived. Here, then, is the epitome of $N = 1$, in-depth inquiry.

The validity, meaningfulness, and insights generated from qualitative inquiry have more to do with the information richness of the cases selected and the observational/analytical capabilities of the researcher than with sample size.

This issue of sample size is a lot like the problem students have when they are assigned an essay to write.

Student: "How long does the paper have to be?"

Instructor: "Long enough to cover the assignment."

Student: "But how many pages?"

Instructor: "Enough pages to do justice to the subject—no more, no less."

Lincoln and Guba (1985) recommend sample selection "to the point of redundancy.... In purposeful sampling the size of the sample is determined by informational considerations. If the purpose is to maximize information, the sampling is terminated when no new information is forthcoming from new sampled units; thus *redundancy* is the primary criterion" (p. 202).

This strategy leaves the question of sample size open, another example of the emergent nature of qualitative inquiry. There remains, however, the practical problem of how to negotiate an evaluation budget or get a dissertation committee to approve a design if you don't have some idea of sample size. Sampling to the point of redundancy is an ideal, one that works best for basic research, unlimited timelines, and unconstrained resources.

The solution is judgment and negotiation. I recommend that qualitative sampling designs specify *minimum samples* based on expected reasonable coverage of the phenomenon given the purpose of the study and stakeholder interests. One may add to the sample as fieldwork unfolds. One may change the sample if information emerges that indicates the value of a change. The design should be understood to be flexible and emergent. Yet, at the beginning, for planning and budgetary purposes, one specifies a minimum expected sample size and builds a rationale for that minimum, as well as criteria that would alert the researcher to inadequacies in the original sampling approach and/or size.

In the end, sample size adequacy, like all aspects of research, is subject to peer review, consensual validation, and judgment. What is crucial is that the sampling procedures and decisions be fully described, explained, and justified so that information users and peer reviewers have the appropriate context for judging the sample. The researcher or evaluator is obligated to discuss how the sample affected the findings, the strengths and weaknesses of the sampling procedures, and any other design decisions that are relevant for interpreting and understanding the reported results. Exercising care not to overgeneralize from purposeful samples, while maximizing to the full the advantages of in-depth, purposeful sampling, will do much to alleviate concerns about small sample size.

🔄 Emergent Designs and Protection of Human Subjects

Emergent designs pose special problems for institutional review boards (IRBs) charged with approving research designs to ensure protection of human subjects. Such boards typically want to know, in advance of fieldwork, who will be interviewed and the precise questions that will be asked. If the topic is fairly innocuous and the general line of questioning relatively unobtrusive, an IRB may be willing to approve the framework of an emergent design with sample questions included, but without full sample specification and a formal interview instrument.

Another approach is to ask for approval in stages. This means initially asking for approval for the general framework of the inquiry and specifically for the first exploratory stage of fieldwork, including procedures for assuring confidentiality and informed consent, then returning periodically (e.g., quarterly or annually) to update the design and its approval. This is cumbersome for both the researcher and the IRB, but it is a way of meeting IRB mandates and still implementing an emergent design. This staged-approval approach can also be used when the evaluator is developing the design jointly with program staff and/or participants and therefore cannot specify the full design at the beginning of the participatory process.

🖺 Methodological Mixes

A study may employ more than one sampling strategy. It may also include multiple types of data. The chapters on interviewing, observation, and analysis will include information that will help in making design decisions. Before turning to those chapters, however, I want to briefly discuss the value of using multiple methods in research and evaluation.

Triangulation

*T*he method must follow the question. Campbell, many decades ago, promoted the concept of triangulation—that every method has its limitations, and multiple methods are usually needed.

—Gene V. Glass eulogizing pioneering methodologist Donald T. Campbell, quoted in Tashakkori and Teddlie (1998:22)

Triangulation strengthens a study by combining methods. This can mean using several kinds of methods or data, including using both quantitative and qualitative approaches. Denzin (1978b) has identified four basic types of triangulation: (1) *data triangulation,* the use of a variety of data sources in a study; (2) *investigator triangulation,* the use of several different researchers or evaluators; (3) *theory triangulation,* the use of multiple perspectives to interpret a single set of data, and (4) *methodological triangulation,* the use of multiple methods to study a single problem or program.

The term *triangulation* is taken from land surveying. Knowing a single landmark only locates you somewhere along a line in a direction from the landmark, whereas with two landmarks (and your own position being the third point of the triangle) you can take bearings in two directions and locate yourself at their intersection (Fielding and Fielding 1986:23). The term *triangulation* also works metaphorically to call to mind the world's strongest geometric shape—the triangle (e.g., the form used to construct geode-

sic domes à la Buckminster Fuller). The logic of triangulation is based on the premise that

no single method ever adequately solves the problem of rival causal factors. Because each method reveals different aspects of empirical reality, multiple methods of observations must be employed. This is termed triangulation. I now offer as a final methodological rule the principle that multiple methods should be used in every investigation. (Denzin 1978b:28)

Triangulation is ideal. It can also be expensive. A study's limited budget and time frame will affect the amount of triangulation that is practical, as will political constraints (stakeholder values) in an evaluation. Certainly, one important strategy for inquiry is to employ multiple methods, measures, researchers, and perspectives— but to do so reasonably and practically.

Most good researchers prefer addressing their research questions with any methodological tool available, using the pragmatist credo of "what works." For most researchers committed to the thorough study of a research problem, method is secondary to the research question itself, and the underlying worldview hardy enters the picture, except in the most abstract sense. (Tashakkori and Teddlie 1998:22)

A rich variety of methodological combinations can be employed to illuminate an inquiry question. Some studies intermix interviewing, observation, and document analysis. Others rely more on interviews than observations, and vice versa. Studies that use only one method are more vulnerable to errors linked to that particular method (e.g., loaded interview questions, biased or untrue responses) than studies that use multiple methods in which different types of data provide cross-data validity checks. Using multiple methods allows inquiry into a research question with "an arsenal of methods that have nonoverlapping weaknesses in addition to their complementary strengths" (Brewer and Hunter 1989:17).

However, a common misunderstanding about triangulation is that the point is to demonstrate that different data sources or inquiry approaches yield essentially the same result. But the point is really to *test for* such consistency. Different kinds of data may yield somewhat different results because different types of inquiry are sensitive to different real-world nuances. Thus, understanding inconsistencies in findings across different kinds of data can be illuminative. Finding such inconsistencies ought not be viewed as weakening the credibility of results, but rather as offering opportunities for deeper insight into the relationship between inquiry approach and the phenomenon under study.

Triangulation within a qualitative inquiry strategy can be attained by combining both interviewing and observations, mixing different types of purposeful samples (e.g., both intensity and opportunity sampling),

or examining how competing theoretical perspectives inform a particular analysis (e.g., the transcendental phenomenology of Husserl vs. the hermeneutic phenomenology of Heidegger). A study can also be designed to cut across inquiry approaches and achieve triangulation by combining qualitative and quantitative methods, a strategy discussed and illustrated in the next section.

Mixing Data, Design, and Analysis Approaches

Borrowing and combining distinct elements from pure or coherent methodological strategies can generate creative mixed inquiry strategies that illustrate variations on the theme of triangulation. We begin by distinguishing measurement, design, and analysis components of the hypothetico-deductive (quantitative/experimental) and holistic-inductive (qualitative/naturalistic) paradigms. The ideal-typical qualitative methods strategy is made up of three parts: (1) qualitative data, (2) a holistic-inductive design of naturalistic inquiry, and (3) content or case analysis. In the traditional hypothetico-deductive approach to research, the ideal study would include (a) quantitative data from (b) experimental (or quasi-experimental) designs and (c) statistical analysis.

Measurement, design, and analysis alternatives can be mixed to create eclectic designs, like customizing an architectural plan to tastefully integrate modern, postmodern, and traditional elements, or preparing an elegant dinner with a French appetizer, a Chinese entrée, and an American dessert—not to everyone's taste, to be sure, but the possibilities are endless. At least that's the concept. To make the idea of mixed elements more concrete and to illustrate the creative possibilities that can emerge out of a flexible

Triangulation

approach to research, it will help to examine alternative design possibilities for a single program evaluation. The examples that follow have been constructed under the artificial constraint that only one kind of measurement, design, and analysis could be used in each case. In practice, of course, the possible mixes are much more varied, because any given study could include several measurement approaches, varying design approaches, and varying different analytical approaches to achieve triangulation.

The Case of Operation Reach-Out: Variations in Program Evaluation Design

Let's consider design alternatives for a comprehensive program aimed at high school students at high risk educationally (poor grades, poor attendance, poor attitudes toward school), with highly vulnerable health (poor nutrition, sedentary life-style, high drug use), and who are likely candidates for delinquency (alienated from dominant societal values, running with a "bad" crowd, and angry). The program consists of experiential education internships through which these high-risk students get individual tutoring in basic skills, part-time job placements that permit them to earn income while gaining work exposure, and participation in peer group discussions aimed at changing health values, establishing a positive peer culture, and increasing social integration. Several evaluation approaches are possible.

PURE HYPOTHETICAL-DEDUCTIVE APPROACH TO EVALUATION: EXPERIMENTAL DESIGN, QUANTITATIVE DATA, AND STATISTICAL ANALYSIS

The program does not have sufficient resources to serve all targeted youth in the population. A pool of eligible youth is established with admission into the program on a random basis and the remaining group receives no immediate treatment intervention. Before the program begins and one year later, all youth, both those in the program and those in the control group, are administered standardized instruments measuring school achievement, self-esteem, anomie, alienation, and locus of control. Rates of school attendance, illness, drug use, and delinquency are obtained for each group. When all data have been collected at the end of the year, comparisons between the control and experimental groups are made using inferential statistics.

PURE QUALITATIVE STRATEGY: NATURALISTIC INQUIRY, QUALITATIVE DATA, AND CONTENT ANALYSIS

Procedures for recruiting and selecting participants for the program are determined entirely by the staff. The evaluator finds a convenient time to conduct an in-depth interview with new participants as soon as they are admitted into the program, asking students to describe what school is like for them, what they do in school, how they typically spend their time, what their family life is like, how they approach academic tasks, their views about health, and their behaviors/attitudes with regard to delinquent and criminal activity. In brief, participants are asked to describe themselves and their social world. The evaluator observes program activities, collecting detailed descriptive data about staff-participant interactions and conversations, staff intervention efforts, and youth reactions. The evaluator finds opportunities for additional in-depth interviews with participants to find out how they view the program, what kinds of experiences they are having, and what they're do-

ing. Near the end of the program, in-depth interviews are conducted with the participants to learn what behaviors have changed, how they view things, and what their expectations are for the future. Interviews are also conducted with program staff and some parents. These data are content analyzed to identify the patterns of experiences participants bring to the program, what patterns characterize their participation in the program, and what patterns of change are reported by and observed in the participants.

MIXED FORM: EXPERIMENTAL DESIGN, QUALITATIVE DATA, AND CONTENT ANALYSIS

As in the pure experimental form, potential participants are randomly assigned to treatment and control groups. In-depth interviews are conducted with all youth, both those in the treatment group and those in the control group, and both before the program begins and at the end of the program. Content and thematic analyses are performed so that the control and experimental group patterns can be compared and contrasted. (For a detailed example combining experimental controls and ethnography, see Maxwell, Bashook, and Sandlow 1987.)

MIXED FORM: EXPERIMENTAL DESIGN, QUALITATIVE DATA, AND STATISTICAL ANALYSIS

Participants are randomly assigned to treatment and control groups, and in-depth interviews are conducted both before the program and at its end. These interview data, in raw form, are then given to a panel of judges, who rate each interview along several outcome dimensions operationalized as a 10-point scale. For both the "pre" interview and the "post" interview, the judges assign ratings on such dimensions as likelihood of success in school (*low* = 1, *high* = 10), likelihood of committing criminal offenses (*low* = 1, *high* = 10), commitment to education, commitment to engaging in productive work, self-esteem, and manifestation of desired nutritional and health habits. Inferential statistics are then used to compare these two groups. Judges make the ratings without knowledge of which participants were in which group. Outcomes on the rated scales are also statistically related to background characteristics of participants.

MIXED FORM: NATURALISTIC INQUIRY, QUALITATIVE DATA, AND STATISTICAL ANALYSIS

As in the pure qualitative form, students are selected for the program on the basis of whatever criteria staff members choose to apply. In-depth interviews are conducted with all students before and at the end of the program. These data are then submitted to a panel of judges, who rate them on a series of dimensions similar to those listed in the previous example. Change scores are computed for each individual, and changes are statistically related to background characteristics of the students to determine in a regression format which characteristics of students are likely to predict success in the program. In addition, observations of program activities are rated on a set of scales developed to quantify the climate attributes of activities: for example, the extent to which the activity involved active or passive participation, the extent to which student-teacher interaction was high or low, the extent to which interactions were formal or informal, and the extent to which participants had input into program activities. Quantitative ratings of activities based on qualitative descriptions are then aggregated to provide an overview of the treatment environment of the program.

MIXED FORM: NATURALISTIC INQUIRY, QUANTITATIVE DATA, AND STATISTICAL ANALYSIS

Students are selected for the program according to staff criteria. The evaluator enters the program setting without any predetermined categories of analysis or presuppositions about important variables or variable relationships. The evaluator observes important activities and events in the program, looking for the types of behaviors and interactions that will emerge. For each significant type of behavior or interaction observed, the evaluator creates a category and then uses a time and space sampling design to count the frequency with which those categories of behavior and interaction are exhibited. The frequency of the manifestation of observed behaviors and interactions are then statistically related to such characteristics as group size, duration of the activity, staff-student ratios, and social/physical density.

Alternative Pure and Mixed Strategies

Exhibit 5.7 summarizes the six alternative design scenarios we created and just reviewed for evaluation of "Operation Reach-Out." As these alternative designs illustrate, purity of approach is only one option. Inquiry strategies, measurement approaches, and analysis procedures can be mixed and matched in the search for relevant and useful information. That said, it is worth considering the case for maintaining the integrity and purity of qualitative and quantitative paradigms. The 12 themes of qualitative inquiry described in the second chapter (Exhibit 2.1) do fit together as a coherent strategy. The openness and personal involvement of naturalistic inquiry mesh well with the openness and depth of qualitative data.

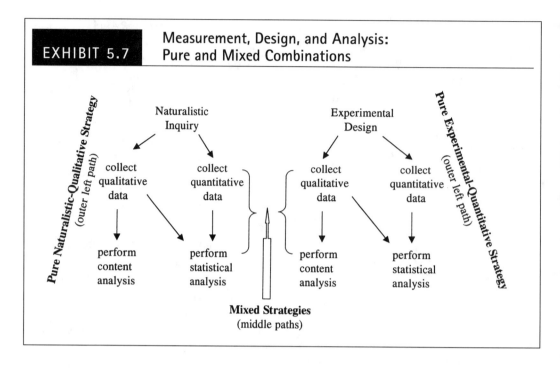

EXHIBIT 5.7

Measurement, Design, and Analysis:
Pure and Mixed Combinations

Genuine openness flows naturally from an inductive approach to analysis, particularly an analysis grounded in the immediacy of direct fieldwork and sensitized to the desirability of holistic understanding of unique human settings.

Likewise, there is an internal consistency and logic to experimental designs that test deductive hypotheses derived from theoretical premises. These premises identify the key variables to consider in testing theory or measuring, controlling, and analyzing hypothesized relationships between program treatments and outcomes. The rules and procedures of the quantitative-experimental paradigm are aimed at producing internally valid, reliable, replicable, and generalizable findings.

Guba and Lincoln (1988) have argued that the internal consistency and logic of each approach, or paradigm, mitigates against methodological mixing of different inquiry modes and data collection strate-

gies. Their cautions are not to be dismissed lightly. Mixing parts of different approaches is a matter of philosophical and methodological controversy. Yet, the practical mandate in evaluation (Patton 1981) to gather the most relevant possible information for evaluation users outweighs concerns about methodological purity based on epistemological and philosophical arguments. The intellectual mandate to be open to what the world has to offer surely includes methodological openness. In practice, it is altogether possible, as we have seen, to combine approaches, and to do so creatively (Patton 1987a). Just as machines that were originally created for separate functions such as printing, faxing, scanning, and copying have now been combined into a single integrated technological unit, so too methods that were originally created as distinct, stand-alone approaches can now be combined into more sophisticated and multifunctional designs.

Advocates of methodological purity argue that a single evaluator cannot be both deductive and inductive at the same time, or cannot be testing predetermined hypotheses and still remain open to whatever emerges from open-ended, phenomenological observation. Yet, in practice, human reasoning is sufficiently complex and flexible that it is possible to research predetermined questions and test hypotheses about certain aspects of a program while being quite open and naturalistic in pursuing other aspects of a program. In principle, this is not greatly different from a questionnaire that includes both fixed-choice and open-ended questions. The extent to which a qualitative approach is inductive or deductive varies along a continuum. As evaluation fieldwork begins, the evaluator may be open to whatever emerges from the data, a discovery or inductive approach. Then, as the inquiry reveals patterns and major dimensions of interest, the evaluator will begin to focus on verifying and elucidating what appears to be emerging—a more deductively oriented approach to data collection and analysis.

The extent to which a study is naturalistic in design is also a matter of degree. This applies particularly with regard to the extent to which the investigator places conceptual constraints on or makes presuppositions about the program or phenomenon under study. In practice, the naturalistic approach may often involve moving back and forth between inductive, open-ended encounters and more hypothetical-deductive attempts to verify hypotheses or solidify ideas that emerged from those more open-ended experiences, sometimes even manipulating something to see what happens.

These examples of variations in qualitative approaches are somewhat like the differences between experimental and quasi-experimental designs. Pure experiments are the ideal; quasi-experimental designs often represent what is possible and practical. Likewise, full participant observation over an extended period of time is the qualitative ideal. In practice, many acceptable and meaningful variations to qualitative inquiry can be designed.

This spirit of adaptability and creativity in designing studies is aimed at being pragmatic, responsive to real-world conditions and, when doing evaluations, to meeting stakeholder information needs. Mixed methods and strategies allow creative research adaptations to particular settings and questions, though certain designs pose constraints that exclude other possibilities. It is not possible, for example, for a program to operate as an experiment by assigning participants to treatment and control groups while at the same time operating the program under naturalistic inquiry conditions in which all eligible participants enter the program (and thus there is no control group and no random assignment). Another incompatibility: Qualitative descriptions can be converted into quantitative scales for purposes of statistical analysis, but it is not possible to work the other way around and convert purely quantitative measures into detailed, qualitative descriptions.

Design and Methods Decisions

Which research design is best? Which strategy will provide the most useful information to decision makers? No simple and universal answer to that question is possible. The answer in each case will depend on the purpose of the study, the scholarly or evaluation audience for the study (what intended users want to know), the funds available, the political context, and the interests/abilities/biases of the researchers. Exhibit 5.8

EXHIBIT 5.8   Design Issues and Options

Issues	*Design Options and Concerns*
1. What is the primary purpose of the study?	Basic research, applied research, summative evaluation, formative evaluation, action research. (See Exhibits 5.1-5.4)
2. What is the focus of study?	Breadth versus depth trade-offs.
3. What are the units of analysis?	Individuals, groups, program components, whole program, organizations, communities, critical incidents, time periods, etc. (See Exhibit 5.5)
4. What will be the sampling strategy or strategies?	Purposeful sampling, probability sampling. Variations in sample size from a single case study to a generalizable sample. (See Exhibit 5.6)
5. What types of data will be collected?	Qualitative, quantitative, or both. (See Exhibit 5.7)
6. What type and degree of control will be exercised?	Naturalistic inquiry (no control), experimental design, quasi-experimental.
7. What analytical approach or approaches will be used?	Inductive, deductive. Content or thematic analysis, statistical analysis, combinations. (See Exhibit 5.7)
8. How will the validity of and confidence in the findings be addressed?	Triangulation options, multiple data sources, multiple methods, multiple perspectives, multiple investigators.
9. Time issues: When will the study occur? How will the study be sequenced or phased?	Long-term fieldwork, rapid reconnaissance, exploratory phase to confirmatory phase, fixed times versus open timelines.
10. How will logistics and practicalities be handled?	Gaining entry to the setting, access to people and records, contracts, training, endurance, etc.
11. How will ethical issues and matters of confidentiality be handled?	Informed consent, protection of human subjects, reactivity, presentation of self, etc.
12. What resources will be available? What will the study cost?	Personnel, supplies, data collection, materials, analysis time and costs, reporting/publishing costs.

---

summarizes the issues discussed in this chapter that must be addressed in designing a study.

In qualitative inquiry, the problem of design poses a paradox. The term *design* sug-

gests a very specific blueprint, but "design in the naturalistic sense . . . means planning for certain broad contingencies without, however, indicating exactly what will be done in relation to each" (Lincoln and Guba

TWO DESIGN PERSPECTIVES

An Old Joke Told in Methods Classes

A renowned heart surgeon described his new methods to a rapt audience at a medical convention. From the back of the room someone asked: "Did you randomly assign half your patients to the old treatment and half to the new, in order to test it?"

From the rostrum, in an arrogant huff, the surgeon replied: "Of course not. Why would I sentence half my patients to premature death by depriving them of the better treatment?"

From the back of the room: "But how did you know which half?"

The Qualitative Version

A renowned heart surgeon described his new methods to a rapt audience at a medical convention. He presented detailed results of 20 in-depth cases, all of them long-term successes. From the back of the room someone asked: "Did you randomly assign half your patients to the old treatment and half to the new, in order to test it?"

From the rostrum, with a caring, compassionate tone, the surgeon replied: "I tried to. I sent out invitations worldwide to statisticians asking for volunteers willing to be part of a control group and forgo my new treatment if they got heart disease. None volunteered."

1985:226). A qualitative design needs to remain sufficiently open and flexible to permit exploration of whatever the phenomenon under study offers for inquiry. Qualitative designs continue to be *emergent* even after data collection begins. The degree of flexibility and openness is, however, also a matter of great variation among designs.

What is certain is that different methods can produce quite different findings. The challenge is to figure out which design and methods are most appropriate, productive, and useful in a given situation. Martin Trow (1970) points out (quite nicely, I think) the difference between arguments about which methods are most appropriate for studying a particular problem and arguments about the intrinsic and universal superiority of one method over another:

Every cobbler thinks leather is the only thing. Most social scientists, including the present

writer, have their favorite research methods with which they are familiar and have some skill in using. And I suspect we mostly choose to investigate problems that seem vulnerable to attack through these methods. But we should at least try to be less parochial than cobblers. Let us be done with the arguments of participant observation *versus* interviewing —as we have largely dispensed with the arguments for psychology *versus* sociology—and get on with the business of attacking our problems with the widest array of conceptual and methodological tools that we possess and they demand. This does not preclude discussion and debate regarding the relative usefulness of different methods for the study of specific problems or types of problems. But that is very different from the assertion of the general and inherent superiority of one method over another on the basis of some intrinsic qualities it presumably possesses. (p. 149)

Sophisticated emergent design strategy

Choices

*E*very path we take leads to fantasies about the path not taken.

—Halcolm

This chapter has suggested that research and evaluation should be built on the foundation of a "paradigm of choices" rather than become the handmaiden of any single and inevitably narrow disciplinary or methodological paradigm. But be careful, the Sufis would warn us, for the exercise of real choice can be elusive. Trow admonishes us to "at least try to be less parochial than cobblers." The evaluation sage, Halcolm, might suggest that all too often the methods decisions made become like the bear's "decision" to like honey.

One day, in a sudden impulse of generosity, a bear decided to enlighten the other animals in the forest about the marvelous properties of honey. The bear assembled all the other animals together for his momentous announcement.

"I have studied the matter at great length," began the bear, "and I have decided that honey is the best of all foods. Therefore, I have chosen to like honey. I am going to describe to you the perfect qualities of honey, which, due to your past prejudices and lack of experience, you have ignored. Then you will be able to make the same rational decision that I have made.

"Honey comes conveniently packaged in beautifully shaped prisms of the most delicate texture. It's ready to eat, slides down the throat ever so easily, is a highly nutritious source of energy, digests smoothly, and leaves a lingering taste of sweetness on the palate that provides pleasure for hours. Honey is readily available and requires no special labor to produce since bees do all the work. Its pleasing aroma, light weight, resistance to spoilage, and uniformly high quality make it a food beyond compare. It comes ready to consume—no peeling, no killing, no tearing open—and there's no waste. What's more, it has so many uses; it can be eaten alone or added to enhance any other food.

"I could go on and on, but suffice it to say that I have studied the situation quite objectively and at great length. A fair and rational analysis leads to only one conclusion. Honey is the supreme food and any reasonable animal will undoubtedly make the same conscious decision I have made. I have chosen to like honey."

6

Fieldwork Strategies and Observation Methods

Folk Wisdom About Human Observation

*J*n the fields of observation, chance favors the prepared mind.

—Louis Pasteur (1822-1895)

*P*eople only see what they are prepared to see.

—Ralph Waldo Emerson (1803-1882)

Every student who takes an introductory psychology or sociology course learns that human perception is highly selective. When looking at the same scene or object, different people will see different things. What people "see" is highly dependent on their interests, biases, and backgrounds. Our culture shapes what we see, our early childhood socialization forms how we look at the world, and our value systems tell us how to interpret what passes before our eyes. How, then, can one trust observational data?

In their classic guide for users of social science research, Katzer, Cook, and Crouch (1978) titled their chapter on observation "Seeing Is Not Believing." They open with an oft-repeated story meant to demonstrate the problem with observational data.

Once at a scientific meeting, a man suddenly rushed into the midst of one of the sessions. Another man with a revolver was chasing him. They scuffled in plain view of the assembled researchers, a shot was fired, and they rushed out. About twenty seconds had elapsed. The chairperson of the session immediately asked all present to write down an account of what they had seen. The observers did not know that the ruckus had been planned, rehearsed, and photographed. Of the forty reports turned in, only one was less than 20 percent mistaken about the principal facts, and most were more than 40 percent mistaken. The event surely drew the undivided attention of the observers, was in full view at close

range, and lasted only twenty seconds. But the observers could not observe all that happened. Some readers chuckled because the observers were researchers, but similar experiments have been reported numerous times. They are alike for all kinds of people. (Katzer et al. 1978:21-22)

Using this story to cast doubt on all varieties of observational research manifests two fundamental fallacies: (1) These researchers were not trained as social science observers, and (2) they were not prepared to make observations at that particular moment. **Scientific inquiry using observational methods requires disciplined training and rigorous preparation.**

The fact that a person is equipped with functioning senses does not make that person a skilled observer. The fact that ordinary persons experiencing any particular incident will highlight and report different things does not mean that *trained and prepared observers* cannot report with accuracy, authenticity, and reliability that same incident.

Training to become a skilled observer includes

- learning to pay attention, see what there is to see, and hear what there is hear;

- practice in writing descriptively;

- acquiring discipline in recording field notes;

- knowing how to separate detail from trivia to achieve the former without being overwhelmed by the latter;

- using rigorous methods to validate and triangulate observations; and

- reporting the strengths and limitations of one's own perspective, which requires both self-knowledge and self-disclosure.

Training observers can be particularly challenging because so many people think that they are "natural" observers and therefore have little to learn. Training to become a skilled observer is a no less rigorous process than the training necessary to become a skilled survey researcher or statistician. People don't "naturally" know how to write good survey items or analyze statistics—and people don't "naturally" know how to do systematic research observations. All forms of scientific inquiry require training and practice.

Careful preparation for entering into fieldwork is as important as disciplined training. Though I have considerable experience doing observational fieldwork, had I been present at the scientific meeting where the shooting scene occurred my recorded observations might not have been significantly more accurate than those of my less trained colleagues because *I would not have been prepared to observe what occurred* and, lacking that preparation, would have been seeing things through my ordinary eyes rather than my scientific observer's eyes.

Preparation has mental, physical, intellectual, and psychological dimensions. Pasteur said, "In the fields of observation, chance favors the prepared mind." Part of preparing the mind is learning how to concentrate during the observation. Observation, for me, involves enormous energy and concentration. I have to "turn on" that concentration—"turn on" my scientific eyes

and ears, my observational senses. A scientific observer cannot be expected to engage in systematic observation on the spur of the moment any more than a world-class boxer can be expected to defend his title spontaneously on a street corner or an Olympic runner can be asked to dash off at record speed because someone suddenly thinks it would be nice to test the runner's time. Athletes, artists, musicians, dancers, engineers, *and* scientists require training and mental preparation to do their best. Experiments and simulations that document the inaccuracy of spontaneous observations made by untrained and unprepared observers are no more indicative of the potential quality of observational methods than an amateur community talent show is indicative of what professional performers can do.

Two points are critical, then, in this introductory section. First, the folk wisdom about observation being nothing more than selective perception is true in the ordinary course of participating in day-to-day events. Second, the skilled observer is able to improve the accuracy, authenticity, and reliability of observations through intensive training and rigorous preparation. The remainder of this chapter is devoted to helping evaluators and researchers move their observations from the level of ordinary looking to the rigor of systematic seeing.

The Value of Direct Observations

I'm often asked by students: "Isn't interviewing just as good as observation? Do you really have to go see a program directly to evaluate it? Can't you find out all you need to know by talking to people in the program without going there and seeing it firsthand?"

I reply by relating my experience evaluating a leadership development program with two colleagues. As part of a formative evaluation aimed at helping staff and funders clarify and improve the program's design before undertaking a comprehensive follow-up study for a summative evaluation, we went through the program as participant observers. After completing the six-day leadership retreat, we met to compare experiences. Our very first conclusion was that we would never have understood the program without personally experiencing it. It bore little resemblance to our expectations, what people had told us, or the official program description. Had we designed the follow-up study without having participated in the program, we would have completely missed the mark and asked inappropriate questions. To absorb the program's language, understand nuances of meaning, appreciate variations in participants' experiences, capture the importance of what happened outside formal activities (during breaks, over meals, in late-night gatherings and parties), and feel the intensity of the retreat environment—nothing could have substituted for direct experience with the program. Indeed, what we observed and experienced was that participants were changed as much or more by what happened outside the formal program structure and activities as by anything that happened through the planned curriculum and exercises.

The first-order purposes of observational data are to *describe* the setting that was observed, the activities that took place in that setting, the people who participated in those activities, and the meanings of what was observed from the perspectives of those observed. The descriptions should be factual, accurate, and thorough without being cluttered by irrelevant minutiae and trivia. The quality of observational reports is judged by the extent to which that observation permits the reader to enter into and understand the situation described. In this way, evaluation users, for example, can come to understand program activities and impacts through detailed descriptive information about what has occurred in a program and how the people in the program have reacted to what has occurred.

Naturalistic observations take place *in the field*. For ethnographers, the field is a cultural setting. For qualitative organizational development researchers, the field will be an organization. For evaluators, the field is the program being studied. Many terms are used for talking field-based observations including *participant observation, fieldwork, qualitative observation, direct observation,* and *field research.* "All these terms refer to the circumstance of being in or around an on-going social setting for the purpose of making a qualitative analysis of that setting" (Lofland 1971:93).

Direct, personal contact with and observations of a setting have several advantages. First, through direct observations the inquirer is better able to understand and capture the context within which people interact. Understanding context is essential to a holistic perspective.

Second, firsthand experience with a setting and the people in the setting allows an inquirer to be open, discovery oriented, and inductive because, by being on-site, the observer has less need to rely on prior conceptualizations of the setting, whether those prior conceptualizations are from written documents or verbal reports.

A third strength of observational fieldwork is that the inquirer has the opportunity to see things that may routinely escape awareness among the people in the setting. For someone to provide information in an interview, he or she must be aware enough to report the desired information. Because

Fieldwork Variations

all social systems involve routines, participants in those routines may take them so much for granted that they cease to be aware of important nuances that are apparent only to an observer who has not become fully immersed in those routines.

The participant observer can also discover things no one else has ever really paid attention to. One of the highlights of the leadership training program we experienced was the final evening banquet at which staff was roasted. For three nights, after training ended, participants worked to put together a program of jokes, songs, and skits for the banquet. Staff were never around for these preparations, which lasted late into the night, but they had come to count on this culminating event. Month after month for two years each completely new training group had organized a final banquet event to both honor and make fun of staff. Staff assumed that either prior participants passed on this tradition or it was a nat-

ural result of the bonding among participants. We learned that neither explanation was true. What actually occurred was that, unbeknownst to program staff, the dining hostess for the hotel where participants stayed initiated the roast. After the second evening's meal, when staff routinely departed for a meeting, the hostess would tell participants what was expected. She even brought out a photo album of past banquets and offered to supply joke books, costumes, music, or whatever. This 60-year-old woman had begun playing what amounted to a major staff role for one of the most important processes in the program—and the staff didn't know about it. We learned about it by being there.

A fourth value of direct observation is the chance to learn things that people would be unwilling to talk about in an interview. Interviewees may be unwilling to provide information on sensitive topics, especially to strangers. A fifth advantage of fieldwork is the opportunity to move beyond the selective perceptions of others. Interviews present the understandings of the people being interviewed. Those understandings constitute important, indeed critical, information. However, it is necessary for the inquirer to keep in mind that interviewees are always reporting perceptions—selective perceptions. Field observers will also have selective perceptions. By making their own perceptions part of the data—a matter of training, discipline, and self-awareness—observers can arrive at a more comprehensive view of the setting being studied than if forced to rely entirely on secondhand reports through interviews.

Finally, getting close to the people in a setting through firsthand experience permits the inquirer to draw on personal knowledge during the formal interpretation stage of analysis. Reflection and introspection are important parts of field research. The impressions and feelings of the observer become part of the data to be used in attempting to understand a setting and the people who inhabit it. The observer takes in information and forms impressions that go beyond what can be fully recorded in even the most detailed field notes.

> Because [the observer] sees and hears the people he studies in many situations of the kind that normally occur for them, rather than just in an isolated and formal interview, he builds an ever-growing fund of impressions, many of them at the subliminal level, which give him an extensive base for the interpretation and analytic use of any particular datum. This wealth of information and impression sensitizes him to subtleties which might pass unnoticed in an interview and forces him to raise continually new and different questions, which he brings to and tries to answer in

succeeding observations. (Becker and Geer 1970:32)

Observation-Based Evaluation and Applied Research in a Political World

The preceding review of the advantages of fieldwork strikes me as fairly straightforward but a bit abstract. In a moment, we'll consider the details of how to do fieldwork, but to inform that transition and reinforce the importance of direct observation in the real world, let me offer a perspective from the world of children's stories. Some of the most delightful, entertaining, and suspenseful fairy tales and fables concern tales of kings who discard their royal robes to take on the apparel of peasants so that they can move freely among their people to really understand what is happening in their kingdoms. Our modern-day kings and political figures are more likely to take television crews with them when they make excursions among the people. They are unlikely to go out secretly disguised, moving through the streets anonymously, unless they're up to mischief. It is left, then, to applied researchers and evaluators to play out the fable, to take on the appropriate appearance and mannerisms that will permit easy movement among the people, sometimes secretly, sometimes openly, but always with the purpose of better understanding what the world is really like. They are then able to report those understandings to our modern-day version of kings so that policy wisdom can be enhanced and programmatic decisions enlightened. At least that's the fantasy. Turning that fantasy into reality involves a number of important decisions about what kind of fieldwork to do. We turn now to those decisions.

🔄 Variations in Observational Methods

W e shall not cease from exploration
And the end of all our exploring
Will be to arrive where we started
And know the place for the first time.[1]

—T. S. Eliot (1888-1965)

Observational research explores the world in many ways. Deciding which observational approaches are appropriate for evaluation or action research involves different criteria than those same decisions made to undertake basic social scientific research. These differences emerge from the nature of applied research, the politics of evaluation, the nature of contract funding in most evaluations, and the accountability of evaluators to information users. Thus, while field methods have their origins in basic anthropological and sociological field methods, using these methods for evaluation often requires adaptation. The sections that follow will discuss both the similarities and differences between evaluation field methods and basic research field methods.

Variations in Observer Involvement: Participant or Onlooker or Both?

The first and most fundamental distinction that differentiates observational strategies concerns the extent to which the observer will be a *participant* in the setting being studied. This involves more than a simple choice between participation and nonparticipation. The extent of participation is a continuum that varies from complete immersion in the setting as full participant to complete separation from the setting as spectator, with a great deal of variation along the continuum between these two end points.

Nor is it simply a matter of deciding at the beginning how much the observer will participate. The extent of participation can change over time. In some cases, the researcher may begin the study as an onlooker and gradually become a participant as fieldwork progresses. The opposite can also occur. An evaluator might begin as a complete participant to experience what it is like to be initially immersed in the program and then gradually withdraw participation over the period of the study until finally taking the role of occasional observer from an onlooker stance.

Full participant observation constitutes an omnibus field strategy in that it "simultaneously combines document analysis, interviewing of respondents and informants, direct participation and observation, and introspection" (Denzin 1978b: 183). If, on the other hand, an evaluator observes a program as an onlooker, the processes of observation can be separated from interviewing. In participant observation, however, no such separation exists. Typically, anthropological fieldworkers combine in their field notes data from personal, eyewitness observation with information gained from informal, natural interviews and informants' descriptions (Pelto and Pelto 1978:5). Thus, the participant observer employs multiple and overlapping data collection strategies: being fully engaged in experiencing the setting (participation) while at the same time observing and talking with other participants about whatever is happening.

In the leadership program I evaluated through participant observation, I was a full participant in all exercises and program activities using the field of evaluation as my leadership arena (since all participants had to have an arena of leadership as their focus). As did other participants, I developed close relationships with some people as the week progressed, sharing meals and conversing late into the night. I sometimes took detailed notes during activities if the activity permitted (e.g., group discussion), while at other times I waited until later to record notes (e.g., after meals). If a situation suddenly became emotional, for example during a small group encounter, I would cease to take notes so as to be fully present as well as to keep my note taking from becoming a distraction. Unlike other participants, I sat in on staff meetings and knew how staff viewed what was going on. Much of the time I was fully immersed in the program experience as a participant, but I was also always aware of my additional role as evaluation observer.

The extent to which it is possible for an evaluator to become a participant in a program will depend partly on the nature of the program. In human service and education programs that serve children, the evaluator cannot participate as a child but may be able to participate as a volunteer, parent, or staff member in such a way as to develop the perspective of an insider in one of those adult roles. Gender can create barriers to participant observation. Males can't be participants in female-only programs (e.g., battered women's shelters). Females doing fieldwork in nonliterate cultures may not be permitted access to male-only councils and ceremonies. Programs that serve special populations may also involve natural limitations on the extent to which the evaluator

can become a full participant. For example, a researcher who is not chemically dependent will not be able to become a full participant, physically and psychologically, in a chemical dependency program, even though it may be possible to participate in the program as a client. Such participation in a treatment program can lead to important insights and understanding about what it is like to be in the program; however, the evaluator must avoid the delusion that participation has been complete. This point is illustrated by an exchange between an inmate and a student who was doing participant observation in a prison.

Inmate: "What are you in here for, man?"

Student: "I'm here for a while to find out what it's like to be in prison."

Inmate: "What do you mean— 'find out what it's like' ?"

Evaluator: "I'm here so that I can experience prison from the inside instead of just studying what it's like from out there."

Inmate: "You got to be jerkin' me off, man. 'Experience from the inside . . . ' ? Shit, man, you can go home when you decide you've had enough can't you?"

Evaluator: "Yeah."

Inmate: "Then you ain't never gonna know what it's like from the inside."

Social, cultural, political, and interpersonal factors can limit the nature and degree of *participation* in participant observation. For example, if the participants in a program all know each other intimately they may object to an outsider trying to become part of their close circle. Where marked social class differences exist between a sociologist and people in a neighborhood, access will be more difficult; likewise, when, as is often the case, an evaluator is well educated and middle class while welfare program clients are economically disadvantaged and poorly educated, the participants in the program may object to any ruse of "full" participant observation. Program staff will sometimes object to the additional burden of including an evaluator in a program where resources are limited and an additional participant would unbalance staff-client ratios. Thus, in evaluation, the extent to which full participation is possible and desirable will depend on the precise nature of the program, the political context, and the nature of the evaluation questions being asked. Adult training programs, for example, may permit fairly easy access for full participation by evaluators. Offender treatment programs are much less likely to be open to participant observation as an evaluation method. Evaluators must therefore be flexible, sensitive, and adaptive in negotiating the precise degree of participation that is appropriate in any particular observational study, especially where reporting timelines are constrained so entry into the setting must be accomplished relatively quickly. Social scientists who can take a long time to become integrated into the setting under study have more options for fuller participant observation.

As these examples illustrate, full and complete participation in a setting, what is sometimes called "going native," is fairly rare, especially for a program evaluation. Degree of participation and nature of observation vary along a wide continuum of possibilities. **The ideal in evaluation is to design and negotiate that degree of participation that will yield the most meaningful data about the program given the characteristics of the participants, the nature of staff-participant interactions, the sociopolitical context of the program, and the information needs of intended evaluation users.** Likewise, in applied and basic re-

search, the purpose, scope, length, and setting for the study will dictate the range and types of participant observation that are possible.

One final caution: The researcher's plans and intentions regarding the degree of program involvement to be experienced may not be the way things actually turn out. Lang and Lang (1960) report that two scientific participant observers who were studying audience behavior at a Billy Graham evangelical crusade made their "decision for Christ" and left their observer posts to walk down the aisle and join Reverend Graham's campaign. Such are the occupational hazards (or benefits, depending on your perspective) of real-world fieldwork.

Insider and Outsider Perspectives: Emic Versus Etic Approaches

> People who are insiders to a setting being studied often have a view of the setting and any findings about it quite different from that of the outside researchers who are conducting the study. (Bartunek and Louis 1996)

Ethnosemanticist Kenneth Pike (1954) coined the terms *emic* and *etic* to distinguish classification systems reported by anthropologists based on (1) the language and categories used by the people in the culture studied, an emic approach, in contrast to (2) categories created by anthropologists based on their analysis of important cultural distinctions, an etic approach. Leading anthropologists such as Franz Boas and Edward Sapir argued that the only meaningful distinctions were those made by people within a culture, that is, from the emic perspective. However, as anthropologists turned to more comparative studies, engaging in cross-cultural analyses, distinctions that cut across cultures had to be made based on the anthropologist's analytical perspective, that is, an etic perspective. The etic approach involved "standing far enough away from or outside of a particular culture to see its separate events, primarily in relation to their similarities and their differences, as compared to events in other cultures" (Pike 1954:10). For some years a debate raged in anthropology about the relative merits of emic versus etic perspectives (Pelto and Pelto 1978:55-60; Headland, Pike, and Harris 1990), but, as often happens over time, both approaches came to be understood as valuable, though each contributes something different. Nevertheless, tension between these perspectives remains:

> Today, despite or perhaps because of the new recognition of cultural diversity, the tension between universalistic and relativistic values remains an unresolved conundrum for the Western ethnographer. In practice, it becomes this question: By which values are observations to be guided? The choices seem to be either the values of the ethnographer or the values of the observed—that is, in modern parlance, either the *etic* or the *emic*. . . . Herein lies a deeper and more fundamental problem: How is it possible to understand the other when the other's values are not one's own? This problem arises to plague ethnography at a time when Western Christian values are no longer a surety of truth and, hence, no longer the benchmark from which self-confidently valid observations can be made. (Vidich and Lyman 2000:41)

Methodologically, the challenge is to do justice to both perspectives during and after fieldwork and to be clear with one's self and one's audience how this tension is managed.

A participant observer shares as intimately as possible in the life and activities of the setting under study in order to develop *an insider's view* of what is happening, the emic perspective. This means that the participant observer not only sees what is happening but feels what it is like to be a part of the setting or program. Anthropologist Hortense Powdermaker (1966) has described the basic assumption undergirding participant observation as follows: "To understand a society, the anthropologist has traditionally immersed himself in it, learning, as far as possible, to think, see, feel and sometimes act as a member of its culture and at the same time as a trained anthropologist from another culture" (p. 9).

Experiencing the setting or program as an insider accentuates the participant part of participant observation. At the same time, the inquirer remains aware of being an outsider. The challenge is to combine participation and observation so as to become capable of understanding the setting as an insider while describing it to and for outsiders.

> Obtaining something of the understanding of an insider is, for most researchers, only a first step. They expect, in time, to become capable of thinking and acting within the perspective of two quite different groups, the one in which they were reared and—to some degree—the one they are studying. They will also, at times, be able to assume a mental position peripheral to both, a position from which they will be able to perceive and, hopefully, describe those relationships, systems and patterns of which an inextricably involved insider is not likely to be consciously aware. For what the social scientist realizes is that while the outsider simply does not know the meanings or the patterns, the insider is so immersed that he may be oblivious to the fact that patterns exist. . . . What fieldworkers eventually produce out of the tension developed by this ability to shift their point of view depends upon their sophistication, ability, and training. Their task, in any case, is to realize what they have experienced

and learned and to communicate this in terms that will illumine. (Wax 1971:3)

Who Conducts the Inquiry? Solo and Team Versus Participatory and Collaborative Approaches

The ultimate in insider perspective comes from involving the insiders as coresearchers through collaborative or participatory research. Collaborative forms of fieldwork, participatory action research, and empowerment approaches to evaluation have become sufficiently important and widespread to make *degree of collaboration* a dimension of design choice in qualitative inquiry. Participatory action research has a long and distinguished history (Kemmis and McTaggart 2000; Whyte 1989). Collaborative principles of feminist inquiry include connectedness and equality between researchers and researched, participatory processes that support consciousness-raising and researcher reflexivity, and knowledge generation that contributes to women's liberation and emancipation (Olesen 2000; Guerrero 1999a:15-22; Thompson 1992). In evaluation, Cousins and Earl (1995) have advocated participatory and collaborative approaches to evaluation primarily to increase use of findings. Empowerment evaluation, often using qualitative methods (Fetterman 2000a; Fetterman, Kaftarian, and Wandersman 1996), involves the use of evaluation concepts and techniques to foster self-determination and help people help themselves by learning to study and report on their own issues and concerns.

What these approaches have in common is a style of inquiry in which the researcher or evaluator becomes a facilitator, collaborator, and teacher in support of those engaging in their own inquiry. While the findings from such a participatory process may be useful, a supplementary agenda is often to increase participants' sense of being in control of, deliberative about, and reflective on their own lives and situations. Chapter 4 discussed these approaches as examples of how qualitative inquiry can be applied in support of organizational or program development and community change.

Degrees of collaboration vary along a continuum. At one end is the solo fieldworker or a team of professionals; what characterizes this end of the continuum is that researchers completely control the inquiry. At the other end are collaborations with people in the setting being studied, sometimes called "coresearchers"; they help design the inquiry, collect data, and are involved in analysis. Along the middle of the continuum are various degrees of partial and periodic (as opposed to continuous) collaboration.

Overt Versus Covert Observations

A traditional concern about the validity and reliability of observational data has been the effects of the observer on what is observed. People may behave quite differently when they know they are being observed versus how they behave naturally when they don't think they're being observed. Thus, the argument goes, covert observations are more likely to capture what is really happening than are overt observations where the people in the setting are aware they are being studied.

Researchers have expressed a range of opinions concerning the ethics and morality of conducting covert research, what Mitchell (1993:23-35) calls "the debate over secrecy." One end of the continuum is represented by Edward Shils (1959), who absolutely opposed all forms of covert research including "any observations of private behavior, however technically feasible, without the explicit and fully informed permission of the person to be observed." He argued that there should be full disclosure of the purpose of any research project and that even participant observation is "morally obnoxious . . . manipulation" unless the observer makes explicit his or her research questions at the very beginning of the observation (Shils 1959, quoted in Webb et al. 1966:vi).

At the other end of the continuum is the "investigative social research" of Jack Douglas (1976). Douglas argued that conventional anthropological field methods have been based on a consensus view of society that views people as basically cooperative, helpful, and willing to have their points of view understood and shared with the rest of the world. In contrast, Douglas adopted a conflict paradigm of society that led him to believe that any and all covert methods of research should be considered acceptable options in a search for truth.

> The investigative paradigm is based on the assumption that profound conflicts of interest, values, feelings and actions pervade social life. It is taken for granted that many of the people one deals with, perhaps all people to some extent, have good reason to hide from others what they are doing and even to lie to them. Instead of trusting people and expecting trust in return, one suspects others and expects others to suspect him. Conflict is the reality of life; suspicion is the guiding principle. . . . It's a war of all and no one gives anyone anything for nothing, especially truth. . . .
>
> All competent adults are assumed to know that there are at least four major problems lying in the way of getting at social reality by asking people what is going on and that these problems must be dealt with if one is to avoid being taken in, duped, deceived, used, put on, fooled, suckered, made the patsy, left holding the bag, fronted out and so on. These four

problems are (1) misinformation, (2) evasions, (3) lies, and (4) fronts. (Douglas 1976:55, 57)

Just as degree of participation in fieldwork turned out to be a continuum of variations rather than an all-or-none proposition, so too is the question of how explicit to be about the purpose of fieldwork. The extent to which participants in a program under study are informed that they are being observed and are told the purpose of the research has varied historically from full disclosure to no disclosure, with a great deal of variation along the middle of this continuum (Junker 1960). Discipline-based ethics statements (e.g., American Psychological Association, American Sociological Association) now generally condemn deceitful and covert research. Likewise, institutional review board (IRB) procedures for the protection of human subjects have severely constrained such methods. They now refuse to approve protocols in which research participants are deceived about the purpose of a study, as was commonly done in early psychological research. One of the more infamous examples was Stanley Milgram's New Haven experiments aimed at studying whether ordinary people would follow the orders of someone in authority by having these ordinary citizens administer what they were told were behavior modification electric shocks to help students learn, shocks that appeared to the unsuspecting citizens to go as high as 450 volts despite the screams and protests heard from supposed students on the other side of a wall. The real purpose of the study, participants later learned, was to replicate Nazi prison guard behavior among ordinary American citizens (Milgram 1974).

IRBs also refuse to approve research in which people are observed and studied without their knowledge or consent, as in the infamous Tuskegee Experiment. For

40 years, physicians and medical researchers, under the auspices of the U.S. Public Health Service, studied untreated syphilis among Black men in and around the county seat of Tuskegee, Alabama, without the informed consent of the men studied, men whose syphilis went untreated so that the progress of the disease could be documented (Jones 1993). Other stories of abuse and neglect by researchers doing covert studies abound. In the late 1940s and early 1950s, schoolboys at the Walter E. Fernald State School in Massachusetts were routinely served breakfast cereal doused with radioactive isotopes, without permission of the boys or their guardians, for the dissertation of a doctoral student in nutritional biochemistry. In the 1960s, the U.S. Army secretly sprayed a potentially hazardous chemical from downtown Minneapolis rooftops onto unsuspecting citizens to find out how toxic materials might disperse during biological warfare. Native American children on the Standing Rock Sioux Reservation in the Dakotas were used to test an unapproved and experimental hepatitis A vaccine without the knowledge or approval of their parents. In the 1960s and 1970s, scientists tested skin treatments and drugs on prisoners in a Philadelphia county jail without informing them of potential dangers.

Doctoral students frustrated by having their fieldwork delayed while they await IRB approval need to remember that they are paying for the sins of their research forebears for whom deception and covert observations were standard ways of doing their work. Those most subject to abuse were often the most vulnerable in society—children, the poor, people of color, the sick, people with little education, women and men incarcerated in prisons and asylums, and children in orphanages or state correctional schools. Anthropological research was com-

missioned and used by colonial administrators to maintain control over indigenous peoples. Protection of human subjects procedures are now an affirmation of our commitment to treat all people with respect. And that is as it should be. But the necessity for such procedures comes out of a past littered with scientific horrors for which those of us engaging in research today may still owe penance. At any rate, we need to lean over backward to be sure that such history is truly behind us—and that means being ever vigilant in fully informing and protecting the people who honor us by agreeing to participate in our research, whether they be homeless mothers (Connolly 2000) or corporate executives (Collins 2001).

However, not all research and evaluation falls under IRB review, so the issue of what type and how much disclosure to make remains a matter of debate, especially where the inquiry seeks to expose the inner workings of cults and extremist groups, or those whose power affects the public welfare, for example, corporations, labor union boards, political parties, and other groups with wealth and/or power. For example, Maurice Punch (1985, 1989, 1997), formerly of the Nijenrode Business School in the Netherlands, has written about the challenges of doing ethnographic studies of corruption in both private and public sector organizations, notably the police.

One classic form of deception in fieldwork involves pretending to share values and beliefs in order to become part of the group being studied. Sociologist Richard Leo carefully disguised his liberal political and social views, instead feigning conservative beliefs, to build trust with police and thereby gain admission to interrogation rooms (Allen 1997:32). Sociologist Leon Festinger (1956) infiltrated a doomsday cult by lying about his profession and pretending to believe in the cult's prophecies. Sociologist Laud Humphreys (1970) pretended to be gay to gather data for his dissertation on homosexual encounters in public parks. Anthropologist Carolyn Ellis (1986) pretended to be just visiting friends when she studied a Chesapeake Bay fishing culture. Her negative portrayals made their way back to the local people, many of whom were infuriated. She later expressed remorse about her deceptions (Allen 1997).

In traditional scholarly fieldwork, the decision about the extent to which observations would be covert was made by researchers balancing the search for truth against their sense of professional ethics. In evaluation research, the information users for whom the evaluation is done have a stake in what kind of methods are used, so the evaluator alone cannot decide the extent to which observations and evaluation purposes will be fully disclosed. Rather, the complexities of program evaluation mean that there are several levels at which decisions about the covert-overt nature of evaluation observations must be made. Sometimes only the funders of the program or of the evaluation know the full extent and purpose of observations. On occasion, program staff may be informed that evaluators will be participating in the program, but clients will not be so informed. In other cases, a researcher may reveal the purpose and nature of program participation to fellow program participants and ask for their cooperation in keeping the evaluation secret from program staff. On still other occasions, a variety of people intimately associated with the program may be informed of the evaluation, but public officials who are less closely associated with the program may be kept "in the dark" about the fact that observations are under way. Sometimes the situation becomes so complex that the evaluator may lose track of who knows and who doesn't

know, and, of course, there are the classic situations where everyone involved knows that a study is being done and who the evaluator is—but the evaluator doesn't know that everyone else knows.

In undertaking participant observation of the community leadership program mentioned earlier, my two evaluation colleagues and I agreed with the staff to downplay our evaluation roles and describe ourselves as "educational researchers" interested in studying the program. We didn't want participants to think that *they* were being evaluated and therefore worry about our judgments. Our focus was on evaluating the program, not participants, but to avoid increasing participant stress we simply attempted to finesse our evaluation role by calling ourselves educational researchers.

Our careful agreement on and rehearsal of this point with the staff fell apart during introductions (at the start of the six-day retreat) when the program director proceeded to tell participants—for 10 minutes—that we were *just* participants and they didn't have to worry about our evaluating them. The longer he went on reassuring the group that they didn't have to worry about us, the more worried they got. Sensing that they were worried, he increased the intensity of his reassurances. While we continued to refer to ourselves as educational researchers, the participants thereafter referred to us as evaluators. It took a day and a half to recover our full participating roles as the participants got to know us on a personal level as individuals.

Trying to protect the participants (and the evaluation) had backfired and made our entry into the group even more difficult than it otherwise would have been. However, this experience sensitized us to what we subsequently observed to be a pattern in many program situations and activities throughout the week, and became a major finding of the evaluation: staff overprotection of and condescending attitudes toward participants.

Based on this and other evaluation experiences, I recommend full and complete disclosure. People are seldom really deceived or reassured by false or partial explanations—at least not for long. Trying to run a ruse or scam is simply too risky and adds to evaluator stress while holding the possibility of undermining the evaluation if (and usually when) the ruse becomes known. Program participants, over time, will tend to judge evaluators first and foremost as people not as evaluators.

The nature of the questions being studied in any particular evaluation will have a primary effect on the decision about who will be told that an evaluation is under way. In formative evaluations where staff members and/or program participants are anxious to have information that will help them improve their program, the quality of the data gathered may be enhanced by overtly soliciting the cooperation of everyone associated with the program. Indeed, the ultimate acceptance and usefulness of formative information may depend on such prior disclosure and agreement that a formative evaluation is appropriate. On the one hand, where program funders have reason to believe that a program is corrupt, abusive, incompetently administered, and/or highly negative in impact on clients, it may be decided that an external, covert evaluation is necessary to find out what is really happening in the program. Under such conditions, my preference for full disclosure may be neither prudent nor practical. On the other hand, Whyte (1984) has argued that "in a community setting, maintaining a covert role is generally out of the question" (p. 31).

Finally, there is the related issue of confidentiality. Those who advocate covert research usually do so with the condition that reports conceal names, locations, and other identifying information so that the people who have been observed will be protected from harm or punitive action. Because the basic researcher is interested in truth rather than action, it is easier to protect the identity of informants or study settings when doing scholarly research. In evaluation research, however, while the identity of who said what may be possible to keep secret, it is seldom possible to conceal the identity of a program, and doing so may undermine the utility of the findings.

Evaluators and decision makers will have to resolve these issues in each case in accordance with their own consciences, evaluation purposes, political realities, and ethical sensitivities.

Variations in Duration of Observations

Another important dimension along which observational studies vary is the length of time devoted to data gathering. In the anthropological tradition of field research, a participant observer would expect to spend six months at a minimum, and often years, living in the culture being observed. The fieldwork of Napoleon Chagnon (1992) among the Yanomami Indians in the rain forest at the borders of Venezuela and Brazil spanned a quarter century. To develop a holistic view of an entire culture or subculture takes a great deal of time, especially when, as in the case of Chagnon, he was documenting changes in tribal life and threats to the continued existence of these once-isolated people. The effects of his long-term involvement on the people he studied became controversial (Geertz 2001; Tierney 2000a, 2000b), a matter we shall take up later. The point here is that fieldwork in basic and applied social science aims to unveil the interwoven complexities and fundamental patterns of social life—actual, perceived, constructed, and analyzed. Such studies take a long time.

Educational researcher Alan Peshkin offers a stellar example of a committed fieldworker who lived for periods of time in varied settings in order to study the intersections between schools and communities. He did fieldwork in a Native American community; in a high school in a stable, multiethnic midsized city in California; in rural, east-central Illinois; in a fundamentalist Christian school; and in a private, residential school for elites (Peshkin 1986, 1997, 2000b). To collect data, he and his wife Maryann lived for at least a year in and with the community that he was studying. They shopped locally, attended religious services, and developed close relationships with civic leaders as well as teachers and students.

In contrast, evaluation and action research typically involve much shorter durations in keeping with their more modest aims: generating useful information for action. To be useful, evaluation findings must be timely. Decision makers cannot wait for years while fieldworkers sift through mountains of field notes. Many evaluations are conducted under enormous pressures of time and limited resources. Thus, the duration of observations will depend to a considerable extent on the time and resources available in relation to the information needs and decision deadlines of primary evaluation users. Later in this chapter we'll include reflections from an evaluator about what it was like being a part-time, in-and-out observer of a program for eight months, but only present 6 hours a week out of the program's 40-hour week.

On the other hand, sustained and ongoing evaluation research may provide annual findings while, over years of study, accumulating an archive of data that serves as a source of more basic research into human

and organizational development. Such has been the case with the extraordinary work of Patricia Carini (1975, 1979) at the Prospect School in North Bennington, Vermont. Working with the staff of the school to collect detailed case records on students of the school, she established an archive with as much as 12 years of detailed documentation about the learning histories of individual students and the nature of the school programs they experienced. Her data included copies of the students' work (completed assignments, drawings, papers, projects), classroom observations, teacher and parent observations, and photographs. Any organization with an internal evaluation information system can look beyond quarterly and annual reporting to building a knowledge archive of data to document development and change over years instead of just months. Participant observations by those who manage such systems can and should be an integral part of this kind of knowledge-building organizational data system that spans years, even decades.

On the other end of the time continuum are short-term studies that involve observations of a single segment of a program, sometimes for only an hour or two. Evaluations that include brief site visits to a number of program locations may serve the purpose of simply establishing the existence of certain levels of program operations at different sites. Chapter 1 presented just such an observation of a single two-hour session of an early childhood parent education program in which mothers discussed their child-rearing practices and fears. The site visit observations of some 20 such program sessions throughout Minnesota were part of an implementation evaluation that reported to the state legislature how these innovative (at the time) programs were operating in practice. Each site visit lasted no more than a day, often only a half day.

Sometimes an entire segment of a program may be of sufficiently short duration that the evaluator can participate in the complete program. The leadership retreat we observed lasted 6 days, plus three 1-day follow-up sessions during the subsequent year.

The critical point is that the length of time during which observations take place depends on the purpose of the study and the questions being asked, not some ideal about what a typical participant observation must necessarily involve. Field studies may be massive efforts with a team of people participating in multiple settings in order to do comparisons over several years. At times, then, and for certain studies, long-term fieldwork is essential. At other times and for other purposes, as in the case of short-term formative evaluations, it can be helpful for program staff to have an evaluator provide feedback based on just one hour of onlooker observation at a staff meeting, as I have also done.

My response to students who ask me how long they have to observe a program to do a good evaluation follows the line of thought developed by Abraham Lincoln during one of the Douglas-Lincoln debates. In an obvious reference to the difference in stature between Douglas and Lincoln, a heckler asked, "Tell us, Mr. Lincoln, how long do you think a man's legs ought to be?"

Lincoln replied, "Long enough to reach the ground."

Fieldwork should last long enough to get the job done—to answer the research questions being asked and fulfill the purpose of the study.

Variations in Observational Focus

The preceding sections have discussed how observations vary in the extent to which the observer participates in the setting being studied, the tension between insider versus outsider perspectives, the extent to which the purpose of the study is made explicit, and the duration of the observations. A major factor affecting each of these other dimensions is the scope or focus of the study or evaluation. The scope can be broad, encompassing virtually all aspects of the setting, or it can be narrow, involving a look at only some small part of what is happening.

Parameswaran (2001) wanted to interview young women in India who read Western romance novels. Thus, her fieldwork had a very narrow focus. But to contextualize what she learned from interviews, she sought "active involvement in my informants' lives beyond their romance reading." How did she do this?

I ate snacks and lunch at cafes with groups of women, went to the movies, dined with them at their homes, and accompanied them on shopping trips. I joined women's routine conversations during break times and interviewed informants at a range of everyday sites, such as college grounds, homes, and restaurants. I visited used-book vendors, bookstores, and lending libraries with several readers and observed social interactions between library owners and young women. To gain insight into the multidimensional relationship between women's romance reading and their experiences with everyday social discourse about romance readers, I interviewed young women's parents, siblings, teachers, bookstore managers, and owners of the lending libraries they frequented. (p. 75)

The tradition of ethnographic fieldwork has emphasized the importance of understanding whole cultural systems. The various subsystems of a society are seen as interdependent parts so that the economic system, the cultural system, the political system, the kinship system, and other specialized subsystems could only be understood in relation to each other. In reality, fieldwork and observations have tended to focus on a particular part of the society or culture because of specific investigator interests and the need to allocate the most time to those things that the researcher considered most important. Thus, a particular study might present an overview of a particular culture but then go on to report in greatest detail about the religious system of that culture.

In evaluating programs, a broad range of possible foci makes choosing a specific focus challenging. One way of thinking about focus options involves distinguishing various program processes sequentially: (1) processes by which participants enter a program (the outreach, recruitment, and intake components); (2) processes of orientation to and socialization into the program (the initiation period); (3) the basic activities that comprise program implementation over the course of the program (the service delivery system); and (4) the activities that go on around program termination, including follow-up activities and client impacts over time. It would be possible to observe only one of these program components, some combination of components, or all of the components together. Which parts of the program and how many are studied will clearly affect such issues as the extent to which the observer is a participant, who will know about the evaluation's purpose, and the duration of observations.

Chapter 5 discussed how decisions about the focus and scope of a study involve trade-offs between breadth and depth. The very first trade-off comes in framing the research questions to be studied. The problem is to determine the extent to which it is desirable and useful to study one or a few questions in great depth or to study more questions but each in less depth. Moreover, in emergent designs, the focus can change over time.

Dimensions Along Which Fieldwork Varies: An Overview

We've examined five dimensions that can be used to describe some of the primary variations in fieldwork. Those dimensions, discussed in the previous sections, are graphically summarized in Exhibit 6.1. These dimensions can be used to help design observational studies and make decisions about the parameters of fieldwork. They can also be used to organize the methods section of a report or dissertation in order to document how research or evaluation fieldwork actually unfolded.

⑤ What to Observe: A Sensitizing Framework

J keep six honest serving men.
They taught me all I knew:
Their names are What and Why and When
And How and Where and Who.[2]

—Rudyard Kipling

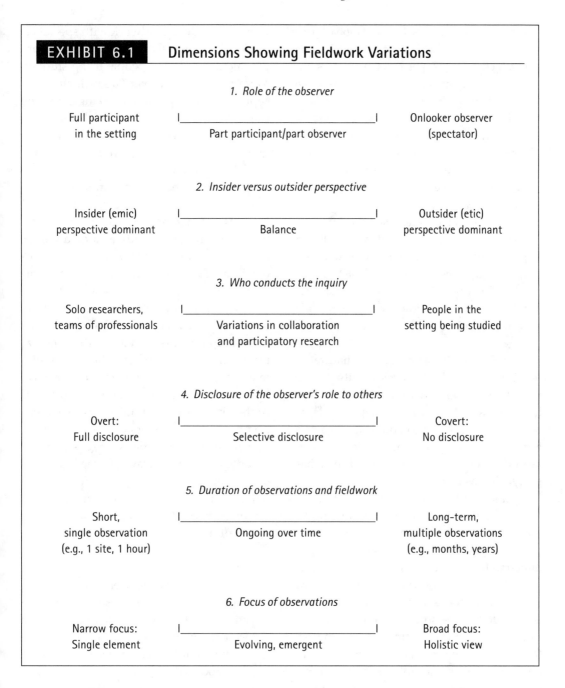

EXHIBIT 6.1   Dimensions Showing Fieldwork Variations

1. Role of the observer

Full participant | Part participant/part observer | Onlooker observer
in the setting | | (spectator)

2. Insider versus outsider perspective

Insider (emic) | Balance | Outsider (etic)
perspective dominant | | perspective dominant

3. Who conducts the inquiry

Solo researchers, | Variations in collaboration | People in the
teams of professionals | and participatory research | setting being studied

4. Disclosure of the observer's role to others

Overt: | Selective disclosure | Covert:
Full disclosure | | No disclosure

5. Duration of observations and fieldwork

Short, | Ongoing over time | Long-term,
single observation | | multiple observations
(e.g., 1 site, 1 hour) | | (e.g., months, years)

6. Focus of observations

Narrow focus: | Evolving, emergent | Broad focus:
Single element | | Holistic view

NASA space scientist David Morrison (1999) has noted that in astronomy, geology, and planetary science, observation precedes theory generation "and the journals in these fields never require the authors to state a 'hypothesis' in order to publish their results" (p. 8).

A recent example is the famous Hubble Space Telescope Deep Field in which the telescope obtained a single exposure of many days duration of one small field in an unremarkable part of the sky. The objective was to see fainter and farther than ever before, and thus to find out what the universe was like early in its history. No hypothesis was required—just the unique opportunity to look where no one had ever looked before and see what nature herself had to tell us.

In many other sciences the culture demands that funding proposals and published papers be written in terms of formulating and testing a hypothesis. But I wonder if this is really the way the scientific process works, or is this just an artificial structure imposed for the sake of tradition. (Morrison 1999:8)

Part of the value of open-ended naturalistic observations is the opportunity to see what there is to see without the blinders of hypotheses and other preconceptions. Pure observation. As Morrison put it so elegantly, just the unique opportunity to look where no one has ever looked before and see what the world has to show us.

That's the ideal. However, it's not possible to observe everything. The human observer is not a movie camera, and even a movie camera has to be pointed in the right direction to capture what is happening. For both the human observer and the camera there must be focus. In fieldwork, this focus is provided by the study design and the nature of the questions being asked. Once in the field, however, the observer must somehow organize the complex stimuli experienced so that observing that becomes and remains manageable.

Experienced observers often use "sensitizing concepts" to orient fieldwork. Qualitative sociologist and symbolic interactionist Herbert Blumer (1954) is credited with originating the idea of the sensitizing concept as a guide to fieldwork with special attention to the words and meanings that are prevalent among the people being studied. More generally, however, "a sensitizing concept is a starting point in thinking about the class of data of which the social researcher has no definite idea and provides an initial guide to her research" (van den Hoonaard 1997:2). Sensitizing concepts in the social sciences include loosely operationalized notions such as victim, stress, stigma, and learning organization that can provide some initial direction to a study as a fieldworker inquires into how the concept is given meaning in a particular place or set of circumstances being studied (Schwandt 2001).

Rudyard Kipling's poem about his "six honest serving men," quoted above, constitutes a fundamental and insightful sensitizing framework identifying the central elements of good description. In social science, "group process" is a general sensitizing concept as is the focus on outcomes in evaluation. Kinship, leadership, socialization, power, and similar notions are sensitizing in that they alert us to ways of organizing observations and making decisions about what to record. Qualitative methodologist Norman Denzin (1978a) has captured the essence of how sensitizing concepts guide fieldwork:

The observer moves from sensitizing concepts to the immediate world of social experience and permits that world to shape and modify his conceptual framework. In this way he moves continually between the realm of more general social theory and the worlds of native people. Such an approach recognizes that social phenomena, while displaying regularities, vary by time, space, and circumstance. The observer, then, looks for repeatable regularities. He uses ritual patterns of dress and body-spacing as indicators of self-image. He takes special languages, codes, and dialects as indicators of group boundaries. He studies his subject's prized social objects as indicators of prestige, dignity, and esteem hierarchies. He studies moments of interrogation and derogation as indicators of socialization strategies. He attempts to enter his subject's closed world of interaction so as to examine the character of private versus public acts and attitudes. (p. 9)

The notion of "sensitizing concepts" reminds us that observers do not enter the field with a completely blank slate. While the inductive nature of qualitative inquiry emphasizes the importance of being open to whatever one can learn, some way of organizing the complexity of experience is virtually a prerequisite for perception itself. Exhibit 6.2 presents examples of common sensitizing concepts for program evaluation and organizational studies. These common program concepts and organizational dimensions constitute ways of breaking the complexities of planned human interventions into distinguishable, manageable, and observable elements. The examples in Exhibit 6.2 are by no means exhaustive of evaluation and organizational sensitizing concepts, but they illustrate oft-used ways of organizing an agenda for inquiry. These concepts serve to guide initial observations as the evaluator or organizational analyst watches for incidents, interactions, and conversations that illuminate these sensitizing concepts in a particular program setting or organization. Highly experienced evaluators and organizational consultants have internalized some kind of sensitizing framework like this to the point where they would not need to list these concepts in a formal written design. Less experienced researchers and dissertation students will usually benefit from preparing a formal list of major sensitizing concepts in the formal design and then using those concepts to help organize and guide fieldwork, at least initially.

A note of caution about sensitizing concepts: When they become part of popular culture, they can lose much of their original meaning. Philip Tuwaletstiwa, a Hopi geographer, relates the story of a tourist cruising through Native American areas of the Southwest. He overheard the tourist, "all agog at half-heard tales about Hopi land," ask his wife, "Where are the *power places*?"

"Tell her that's where we plug-in TV," he said (quoted in Milius 1998:92).

Overused sensitizing concepts can become desensitizing.

🖻 Sources of Data

Poet David Wagoner (1999) tells those observing the modern world and afraid of being lost to follow the advice Native American elders gave the young when they were afraid of being lost in the forest:

Lost

Stand still. The trees ahead and bushes
    beside you
Are not lost. Where you are is called
    Here,
And you must trust it as a powerful
    stranger,
Must ask permission to know it and
    be known.
The forest breathes. Listen. It answers,
I have made this place around you.
If you leave it, you may come back
    again, saying Here.
No two trees are the same to Raven.
No two branches are the same to Wren.
If what a tree or a bush does is lost on
    you,
You are surely lost. Stand still. The
    forest knows
Where you are. You must let it find
    you.[3]

EXHIBIT 6.2   Examples of Sensitizing Concepts

Program Evaluation	Organizational Dimensions
Context	Mission/vision language
Goals	Centralization/decentralization of participation and decision making
Inputs	External boundary relationships: Open/closed
Recruitment	Routinness/nonroutinness of work, products, decisions
Intake	Leadership
Implementation	Communication patterns
Processes	Organizational culture
Output	Hierarchy: Layered/flat
Outcomes	Authority patterns
Products	Formal/informal networks
Impacts	Rewards/punishments, incentives/disincentives
Program theory	Success and failure messages/stories
Logic model	Degree of integration
Perceived	Competition/cooperation
Assets	
Barriers	
Strengths	
Weaknesses	
Incentives	
Disincentives	

The *what* and *how* of qualitative inquiry are closely linked. Sources of data are derived from inquiry questions. Knowing what we want to illuminate helps us determine sources of data for that illumination. The examples and illustrations that follow derive from and build on the sensitizing framework for program evaluation. Interspersed with this presentation of sources of evaluation data are examples of how to collect observational data. These strategies apply to other inquiry settings, but to provide coherent and in-depth illustrations, the examples that follow focus on program evaluation.

The Setting

Describing a setting, like a program setting, begins with the physical environment within which the program takes place. The description of the program setting should be sufficiently detailed to permit the reader to visualize that setting. In writing a program description, the observer, unlike the novelist, should avoid interpretive adjectives except as they appear in quotes from participants about their reactions to and perceptions of that environment. Such adjectives as *comfortable, beautiful, drab,* and *stimulating* interpret rather than describe —and interpret vaguely at that. More purely descriptive adjectives include

> colors ("a room painted blue with a blackboard at one end"),
>
> space ("a 40-foot-by-20-foot classroom with windows on one side"), and
>
> purpose ("a library, the walls lined with books and tables in the center").

Beginners can practice learning to write descriptively by sharing a description of a setting observed with a couple of people and asking them if they can visualize the setting described. Another helpful exercise involves two people observing the same environment and exchanging their descriptions, watching in particular for the use of interpretive adjectives instead of descriptive ones. Vivid description provides sufficient information that the reader does not have to speculate at what is meant. For example, simply reporting "a crowded room" requires interpretation. Contrast with this:

> The meeting room had a three-person couch across one side, six chairs along the adjoining walls next to the couch, and three chairs along the wall facing the couch, which included the door. With 20 people in the room, all standing, there was very little space between people. Several participants were overheard to say, "This room is really crowded."

Such descriptive writing requires attention to detail and discipline to avoid vague, interpretive phrases. But such writing can also be dull. Metaphors and analogies can enliven and enrich descriptions, helping readers connect through shared understandings and giving them a better *feel* for the environment being described. I once evaluated a wilderness education program that included time at the Grand Canyon. Exhibit 6.3 presents my feeble attempt to capture in words our first view of the Grand Canyon. Notice the metaphors that run through the description. Of course, this is one of those instances where a picture would be worth a mountain of words, which is why qualitative fieldwork increasingly includes photography and videography. This excerpt aims at offering *a sense of the physical environment* more than it offers a literal description because unless one has been there or seen pictures, the landscape is outside ordinary experience.

The physical environment of a setting can be important to what happens in that environment. The way the walls look in rooms, the amount of space available, how the space is used, the nature of the lighting, how people are organized in the space, and the interpretive reactions of program participants to the physical setting can be important information about both program implementation and the effects of the program on participants.

A common mistake among observers is to take the physical environment for granted. Thus, an evaluator may report that the program took place in "a school." The evaluator may have a mental image of "school" that matches what was observed, but schools vary considerably in size, appearance, and neighborhood setting. Even more so, the interiors of schools vary considerably. The same can be said for criminal justice settings, health settings, community mental health programs, and any other human service activity.

EXHIBIT 6.3	Example of Combining Description and Metaphor to Provide a Sense of Place

Context for a Wilderness Program: First View From Bright Angel Point at the Grand Canyon

We followed an asphalt path from the lodge a quarter mile to Bright Angel Point, perhaps the most popular tourist site at the Grand Canyon because of its relatively easy accessibility. With cameras aimed in all directions at the spectacular panorama, in a sea of domestic accents and foreign tongues, we waited our turn at the edge to behold the magnificent rock temples of Ottoman Amphitheater: Deva, Brahma, Zoroaster and, in the distance, Thor. Each rises a half mile above the undulating grayness of the stark Tonto Platform defining the eight-mile descent of Bright Angel Canyon, a narrow slit hiding the inner gorge that looks like it had been drawn in black ink to outline the base of the temples. Each begins as sheer Redwall that forms a massive foundation supporting a series of sloping sedimentary rock terraces, the Supai. These sweeping terraces, spotted green with sparse desert vegetation, point upward like arrow feathers to a white sandstone pedestal, the Coconino. A dark red pinnacle of Hermit shale uniquely crowns each temple. Eons of erosion have sculpted dramatic variations in every aspect save one: their common geologic history. I studied each separately, wanting to fix in my mind the differences between them, but the shared symmetry of strata melded them into a single, massive formation, a half mile high and many miles around. Behind me I heard a participant say softly to no one in particular, almost under her breath, "It's too awesome. I feel overwhelmed."

SOURCE: Adapted from Patton (1999a).

During site visits to early childhood education programs, we found a close association between the attractiveness of the facility (child-made decorations and colorful posters on the walls, well-organized learning materials, orderly teacher area) and other program attributes (parent involvement, staff morale, clarity of the program's goals and theory of action). An attractive, well-ordered environment corresponded to an engaging, well-ordered program. In observing as well as conducting workshops, I have noted how the arrangement of chairs affects participation. It is typically much easier to generate discussion when chairs are in a circle rather than in lecture style. The dim lighting of many hotel conference rooms seems to literally drain energy from people sitting in those rooms for long periods of time. Physical environments clearly affect people and programs.

Variations in the settings for a wilderness training program for which I served as participant observer provide an interesting example of how physical environments affect a program. The explicit purpose of holding the "field conferences" in the wilderness was to remove people from their everyday settings in largely urban environments surrounded by human-made buildings and the paraphernalia of modern industrial society. Yet, wilderness environments are no more uniform than the environments of human service programs. During the yearlong program, participants were exposed to four different wilderness environments: the autumn forest in the Gila wilderness of New Mexico; the rough terrain of Arizona's Kofa

Mountains in winter; the muddy, flooding San Juan River in the canyon lands of Utah during the spring; and among the magnificent rock formations of the Grand Canyon in summer, a desert environment. One focus of the evaluation, then, was to observe how participants responded to the opportunities and constraints presented by these different environments: forest, mountains, canyon-lined river, and Grand Canyon desert.

In addition, weather and seasonal differences accentuated variations among these environments. Program activities were clearly affected by the extent to which there was rain, cold, wind, and shelter. In the program's theory, weather uncertainties were expected to be a natural part of the program, offering natural challenges for the group to deal with. But the program theory also called for participants to engage deeply with each other during evening group discussions. During one 10-day winter field conference that was unusually cold and wet, participants were miserable, and it became increasingly difficult to carry on group discussions, thus reducing considerably the amount of group process time available and rushing the interactions that did occur because of participants' discomfort. Program staff learned that they needed to anticipate more clearly the possible variations in physical environments, plan for those variations, and include the participants in that planning so as to increase their commitment to continuing the process under difficult physical conditions.

The Human, Social Environment

Just as physical environments vary, so too do social environments. The ways in which human beings interact create social-ecological constellations that affect how partici-

pants behave toward each other in those environments. Rudolf Moos (1975) described the social-ecological view of programs as follows:

> The social climate perspective assumes that environments have unique "personalities," just like people. Personality tests assess personality traits or needs and provide information about the characteristic ways in which people behave. Social environments can be similarly portrayed with a great deal of accuracy and detail. Some people are more supportive than others. Likewise, some social environments are more supportive than others. Some people feel a strong need to control others. Similarly, some social environments are extremely rigid, autocratic, and controlling. Order, clarity, and structure are important to many people. Correspondingly, many social environments strongly emphasize order, clarity, and control. (p. 4)

In describing the social environment, the observer looks for the ways in which people organize themselves into groups and subgroups. Patterns and frequency of interactions, the direction of communication patterns (from staff to participants and participants to staff), and changes in these patterns tell us things about the social environment. How people group together can be illuminative and important. All-male versus all-female groupings, male-female interactions, and interactions among people with different background characteristics, racial identities, and/or ages alert the observer to patterns in the social ecology of the program.

Decision-making patterns can be a particularly important part of a program's social environment. Who makes decisions about the activities that take place? To what extent are decisions made openly, so that participants are aware of the decision-making process? How are decisions by staff communicated to participants? Answers to these questions are an important part of the description of a program's decision environment.

An observer's descriptions of a social environment will not necessarily be the same as the perceptions of that environment expressed by participants. Nor is it likely that all participants will perceive the setting's human climate in the same way. At all times it is critical that the observer record participants' comments in quotation marks, indicating the source—who said what?—so as to keep perceptions of participants separate from the observer's or evaluator's own descriptions and interpretations.

Historical Perspectives

Historical information can shed important light on the social environment. The history of a program, community, or organization is an important part of the context for research. Distinguished qualitative sociologist William Foote Whyte, sometimes called the father of sociological field research, has reflected on how he came to value historical research as a critical part of his fieldwork.

When we began our Peruvian research program, I viewed history as having little value for understanding the current scene. I thought I was only being sympathetic to the interests of our Peruvian researchers in suggesting that they gather historical data on each village for the last 50 years.

Fortunately, the Peruvians refused to accept the 50-year limit and in some cases probed up to 500 years in the history of villages or areas. Much of these data on rural communities would be of interest only to historians. However, understanding the paradox of the Mantaro Valley required us to go back to the conquest of Peru, and, in the Chancay Val-

OBSERVING NATURE

Observing animals and nature poses special challenges in overcoming the tendency to attribute human characteristics to flora and fauna. Harvard sociobiologist E. O. Wilson pulled no punches in assessing the consequences: "No intellectual vice is more crippling then defiantly self-indulgent anthropocentrism" (quoted by Leo Marx 1999:60).

ley, we traced the beginnings of the differentiation of Huayopampa from Pacaros back more than a century. (Whyte 1984:153)

Documenting and understanding the context of a program will require delving into its history. How was the program created and initially funded? Who were the original people targeted for program services, and how have target populations changed over time? To what extent and in what ways have goals and intended outcomes changed over time? What have staffing patterns been over time? How has the program's governance (board) been involved at various stages in the program's history? What crises has the program endured? If the program is embedded within a larger organizational context, what is the history of that organization in relation to the program? How has the larger political and economic environment changed over time, and how have those changes affected program development? What are the stories people tell about the program's history? These kinds of questions frame inquiry into the program's history to illuminate context.

In the 1990s, I evaluated a "free high school" that had been created during the struggles and turmoil of the 1960s. Little about the program's current programming could be understood outside the context of its historical emergence. The school's image of itself, its curriculum, and its policies had been handed down and adapted from that intense period of early development. Doing fieldwork in the 1990s could only be done by traversing the memories and legends of the school's historical emergence in the 1960s.

Planned Program Implementation Activities and Formal Interactions

Most evaluations focus at least some observations on planned program activities. What goes on in the program? What do participants and staff do? What is it like to be a participant? These are the kinds of questions evaluators bring to the program setting to document program implementation.

Build observations around activities that have a kind of unity about them: a beginning, some middle point, and a closure point—such things as a class session, a counseling session, meal time in the residential facility, a meeting of some kind, a home visit in an outreach program, a consultation, or a registration procedure. Attending to sequence illustrates how the inquiry progresses over the course of an observation. Initially, the observer will focus on how the activity is introduced or begun. Who is present at the beginning? What exactly was said? How did participants respond or react to what was said?

These kinds of basic descriptive questions guide the evaluator throughout the full sequence of observation. *Who* is involved? *What* is being done and said by staff and participants? *How* do they go about what they do? *Where* do activities occur? *When* do things happen? What are the variations in how participants engage in planned activities? How does it feel to be engaged in this activity? (The observer records his or her

own feelings as part of the observation.) How do behaviors and feelings change over the course of the activity?

Finally, the observer looks for closure points. What are the signals that a particular activity is being ended? Who is present at that time? What is said? How do participants react to the ending of the activity? How is the completion of this unit of activity related to other program activities and future plans?

Each unit of activity is observed and treated as a self-contained event for the purpose of managing field notes. The observation of a single session of the early childhood parent education program presented in Chapter 1 is an example. Each observed event or activity can be thought of as a mini-case write-up of a discrete incident, activity, interaction, or event. During analysis, one looks across these discrete units-of-activity cases for patterns and themes, but during the initial stages of fieldwork the observer will be kept busy just trying to capture self-contained units of activity without worrying yet about looking for patterns across activities.

Observing and documenting formal program activities will constitute a central element in evaluating planned program implementation, but to fully understand a program and its effects on participants, observations should not be restricted to formal, planned activities. The next section discusses observation of the things that go on between and around formal, planned program activities.

Informal Interactions and Unplanned Activities

If observers put away their seeing and observing selves as soon as a planned, formal activity ends, they will miss a great deal of data. Some programs build in "free" or un-structured time between activities, with the clear recognition that such periods provide opportunities for participants to assimilate what has occurred during formal program-matic activities as well as to provide partici-pants with necessary breathing space. Rarely, if ever, can a program or institution plan every moment of participants' time.

During periods of informal interaction and unplanned activity, it can be particu-larly difficult to organize observations be-cause people are likely to be milling around, coming and going, moving in and out of small groups, with some sitting alone, some writing, some seeking refreshments, and otherwise engaging in a full range of what may appear to be random behaviors. How, then, can the evaluator observer collect data during such a time?

This scenario illustrates beautifully the importance of staying open to the data and doing opportunity sampling. One can't an-ticipate all the things that might emerge dur-ing unplanned program time, so the ob-server watches, listens, and looks for opportunities to deepen observations, re-cording what people do, the nature of infor-mal interactions (e.g., what subgroups are in evidence), and, in particular, what people are saying to each other. This last point is particularly important. During periods of unplanned activity, participants have the greatest opportunity to exchange views and to talk with each other about what they are experiencing in the program. In some cases, the evaluator will simply listen in on conver-sations or there may be opportunities to con-duct informal interviews, either with a sin-gle participant in natural conversation or with some small group of people, asking normal, conversational questions:

So what did you think of what went on this morning?

Was it clear to you what they were trying to get at?

What did you think of the session today?

How do you think what went on today fits into this whole thing that we're involved in?

Such questioning should be done in an easy, conversational manner so as not to be intru-sive or so predictable that every time some-one sees you coming they know what ques-tions you're going to ask. "Get ready, here comes the evaluator with another endless set of questions." Also, when doing infor-mal, conversational interviewing, be sure that you are acting in accordance with ethi-cal guidelines regarding informed consent and confidentiality. (See the earlier discus-sion in this chapter about overt versus co-vert fieldwork.)

How something is said should be re-corded along with what is said. At a morn-ing break in the second day of a two-day workshop, I joined the other men in the restroom. As the men lined up to use the fa-cilities, the first man to urinate said loudly, "Here's what I think of this program." As each man finished he turned to the man be-hind him and said, "Your turn to piss on the program." This spontaneous group reaction spoke volumes more than answers to formal interview questions and provided much greater depth of expression than checking "very dissatisfied" on an evaluation ques-tionnaire.

Everything that goes on in or around the program is data. The fact that none of the participants talk about a session when it is over is data. The fact that people immedi-ately split in different directions when a ses-sion is over is data. The fact that people talk about personal interests and share gossip that has nothing to do with the program is data. In many programs, the most sig-nificant participant learnings occur during unstructured time as a result of interactions with other participants. To capture a holistic view of the program, the evaluator observer must stay alert to what happens during these informal periods. While others are on break, the observer is still working. No breaks for the dedicated field-worker! Well, not really. You've got to pace yourself and take care of yourself or your observations will deteriorate into mush. But you get the idea. You may be better off taking a break during part of a formal session time so you can work (collect data) while others are on break.

As happens in many programs, the participants in the wilderness education program I was observing/evaluating began asking for more free, unstructured time. When we weren't hiking or doing camp chores, a lot of time was spent in formal discussions and group activities. Participants wanted more free time to journal. Some simply wanted more time to reflect. Most of all, they wanted more time for informal interactions with other participants. I respected the privacy of one-to-one interactions when I observed them and would never attempt to eavesdrop. I would, however, watch for such interactions and, judging body language and facial expressions, I would speculate when serious interpersonal exchanges were taking place. I would then look for natural opportunities to engage each of those participants in conversational interviews, telling them I had noticed the intensity of their interaction and inquiring whether they were willing to share what had happened and what significance they attached to the interaction. Most appreciated my role in documenting the program's unfolding and its effects on participants and were open to sharing. It was on the basis of those informal interviews and observations that I provided formative feedback to staff about the importance of free time and helped alleviate the

feeling among some staff members that they had a responsibility to plan and account for every moment during the program.

Participant observation necessarily combines observing and informal interviewing. Observers need to be disciplined about not assuming they know the meaning to participants of what they observe without checking with those participants. During one period of unstructured time in the wilderness program, following a fairly intensive group activity in which a great deal of interpersonal sharing had taken place, I decided to pay particular attention to one of the older men in the group who had resisted involvement. Throughout the week he had taken every available opportunity to make it known that he was unimpressed with the program and its potential for impact on him. When the session ended, he immediately walked over to his backpack, pulled out his writing materials, and went off to a quiet spot where he could write. He continued writing, completely absorbed, until dinnertime an hour later. No one interrupted him. With his legs folded, his notebook in his lap, and his head and shoulders bent over the notebook, he gave off clear signals that he was involved, concentrating and working on something to which he was giving a great deal of effort.

I suspected as I watched that he was venting his rage and dissatisfaction with the program. I tried to figure out how I might read what he had written. I was so intrigued that I momentarily even considered covert means of getting my hands on his notebook, but quickly dismissed such unethical invasion of his privacy. Instead, I looked for a natural opportunity to initiate a conversation about his writing. During the evening meal around the campfire, I moved over next to him, made some small talk about the weather, and then began the following conversation:

"You know, in documenting experiences people are having, I'm trying to track some of the different things folks are doing. The staff have encouraged people to keep journals and do writing, and I noticed that you were writing fairly intensely before dinner. If you're willing to share, it would be helpful for me to know how you see the writing fitting into your whole experience with the program."

He hesitated, moved his food about in his bowl a little bit, and then said, "I'm not sure about the program or how it fits in or any of that, but I will tell you what I was writing. I was writing . . . ," and he hesitated because his voice cracked, "a letter to my teenage son trying to tell him how I feel about him and make contact with him about some things. I don't know if I'll give the letter to him. The letter may have been more for me than for him. But the most important thing that's been happening for me during this week is the time to think about my family and how important it is to me and I haven't been having a very good relationship with my son. In fact, it's been pretty shitty and so I wrote him a letter. That's all."

This short conversation revealed a very different side of this man and an important impact of the program on his personal and family life. We had several more conversations along these lines, and he agreed to be a case example of the family impacts of the program. Until that time, impacts on family had not even been among the expected or intended outcomes of the program. It turned out to be a major area of impact for a number of participants.

The Native Language of the Program

The lunatic, the lover, and the poet
Are of imagination all compact.
One sees more devils than vast hell can hold;
That is, the madman. The lover, all as frantic,
Sees Helen's beauty in a brow of Egypt.
The poet's eye, in a fine frenzy rolling,
Doth glance from heaven to earth, from earth to heaven;
And as imagination bodies forth the forms of things unknown,
The poet's pen turns them to shapes
And gives to airy nothing
A local habitation and a name.

—William Shakespeare,
A Midsummer Night's Dream, Act V, scene 1

As noted in Chapter 2, the Whorf hypothesis (Schultz 1991) alerts us to the power of language to shape our perceptions and experiences. As an insurance investigator, Benjamin Whorf was assigned to look into explosions in warehouses. He discovered that truck drivers were entering "empty" warehouses smoking cigarettes and cigars. The warehouses often contained invisible, but highly flammable gases. He interviewed truckers and found that they associated the word *empty* with *harmless* and acted accordingly. Whorf's job, in Shakespeare's terms, was to turn the truckers' perception of "airy nothing" into the shape of possible danger.

An anthropological axiom insists that one cannot understand another culture without understanding the language of the people in that culture. Language organizes our world for us by shaping what we see, perceive, and pay attention to. The things for which people have special words tell others what is important to that culture. Thus, as students learn in introductory anthropology, Eskimos have many words for snow and Arabs have many words for camel. Likewise, the artist has many words for red and different kinds of brushes.

Roderick Nash (1986), in his classic study *Wilderness and the American Mind*, traces how changing European American perceptions of "wilderness" has affected at the deepest levels our cultural, economic, and political perspectives on deserts, forests, canyons, and rivers. He traced the very idea of wilderness to the eighth-century heroic epic character Beowulf, whose bravery was defined by his courage in entering the *wildeor*—a place of wild and dangerous beasts, dark and foreboding forests, and untamed, primordial spirits. In the Judeo-Christian tradition, wilderness came to connote a place of uncontrolled evil that needed to be tamed and civilized, while Eastern cultures and religions fostered love of wilderness rather than fear. Nash credits the Enlightenment with offering new ways of thinking about wilderness—and new language to shape that changed thinking.

Moving from the wilderness to the interior territory of organizations, agencies, and programs, language still shapes experience and is therefore an important focus during fieldwork. Programs develop their own language to describe the problems they deal with in their work. Educators who work with learning disabled students have a com-

plex system of language to distinguish different degrees and types of retardation, a language that changes as cultural and political sensitivities change. People in criminal justice generate language for distinguishing types of offenders or "perps" (perpetrators). Fieldwork involves learning the "native language" of the setting or program being studied and attending to variations in connotations and situational use. The field notes and reports of the observer should include the exact language used by participants to communicate the flavor and meaning of "native" program language.

Language was especially important in the wilderness education program I evaluated. These were highly verbal people, well educated, reflective and articulate, who spent a lot of program time in group discussions. Program staff understood how words can shape experiences. They wanted participants to view the time in the wilderness as a professional development learning experience not a vacation, so staff called each week in the wilderness a "field conference." They hoped participants would see the program as a "conference" held in the "field." Despite the determined efforts of staff, however, the participants never adopted this language. Almost universally they referred to the weeks in the wilderness as "trips." During the second "field conference" the staff capitulated. Interestingly enough, that capitulation coincided with negative reactions by participants to some logistical inadequacies, unsuccessful program activities, and bad weather, all of which undercut the "conference" emphasis. Staff language reflected that change.

Other language emerged that illuminated participants' experiences. One of the participants expressed the hope of "detoxifying" in the wilderness. He viewed his return to his everyday world as "poisonous retoxification." The group immediately adopted this language of detoxification and retoxification to refer to "wilderness time" versus ordinary "urban civilization time," ultimately shortening the words to *detox* and *retox*. This language came to permeate the program's culture.

The discussions in the wilderness often reflected the physical environment in which program activities took place. Participants became skilled at creating analogies and metaphors to contrast their urban work lives with their wilderness experiences. After backpacking all day, participants could be heard talking about learning how to "pace myself in my work," or "shifting the burdens of responsibilities that I carry so that the load is more evenly balanced" (a reference to the experience of adjusting the weight of the backpack). In the mountains, after rock climbing, participants referred to "the danger in taking risks at work without support" (a reference to the *balay* system of climbing where someone supports the climber with a safety rope below). One discussion focused on how to "find toeholds and handholds" to bring about change back home, "to get on top of the steep wall of resistance in my institution." They even assigned numbers to degrees of back-home institutional resistance corresponding to the numbers used to describe the degree of difficulty of various rock climbs. On the river, participant language was filled with phrases like "going with the flow," "learning to monitor professional development like you read and monitor the current," and "trying to find my way out of the eddies of life."

Because of the power of language to shape our perceptions and experiences, most participants wanted to know the names of the rock formations, winding canyons, and river rapids we encountered, while others, following *Desert Solitaire* author Edward Abbey (1968), set for themselves the goal of suppressing the human tendency to personify natural forms. Thus began a sustained personal interest in how names in the wilderness shaped our experiences there (Patton and Patton 2001).

When I took my son into the Grand Canyon for a "coming of age" initiation experience (Patton 1999a), he reacted to the problem of finding words for that awesome environment by making up words. For example, upon seeing the Canyon for the very first time he whispered, "*Bue düden,*" which became our way of describing things too beautiful and awesome for ordinary words.

Capturing the precise language of participants honors the emic tradition in anthropology: recording participants' own understandings of their experiences. Observers must learn the language of participants in the setting or program they are observing in order to faithfully represent participants in their own terms and be true to their worldview.

Nonverbal Communication

Social and behavioral scientists have reported at length the importance of both verbal and nonverbal communication in human groups. While recording the language of participants, the observer should also attend to nonverbal forms of communication. For example, in educational settings nonverbal communication would include how students get the attention of or otherwise approach instructors, such as waving their hands in the air. In group settings a great deal of fidgeting and moving about may reveal things about attention and involvement. How participants dress, express affection, and sit together or apart are examples of nonverbal cues about social norms and patterns.

Again, the wilderness program provides informative examples. Hugging emerged as a nonverbal way of providing support at times of emotional distress or celebration, for example, a way to recognize when someone had overcome some particularly difficult challenge, like making it up across a ledge along a cliff face. But subgroups differed in amount of and comfort with hugging, and different field conferences manifested different amounts of hugging. When the group felt disparate, separated, with people on their own "trips," isolated from each other, little hugging occurred either in pairs or around the group campfire. When the depth of connection was deeper, shoulder-to-shoulder contact around the campfire was common and group singing was more likely. Over time, it became possible to read the tenor of the group by observing the amount and nature of physical contact participants were having with each other—and participants in groups with a lot of hugging and connectedness reported noticeably greater personal change.

In evaluating an international development project, I observed that the three host country nationals ("locals") had developed a subtle set of hand signals and gestures that the American staff never noticed. In meetings, the host country nationals regularly communicated with each other and operated as a team using these nonverbal signals. Later, having gained their confidence, I asked the local staff members about the gestures. They told me that the Americans had insisted that each person participate as an individual on an equal footing in staff meetings and, to support an atmosphere of openness, the Americans asked them not to use their own language during staff meetings. But the locals wanted to operate as a unit to counter the power of the Americans, so they developed subtle gestures to communicate with each other since they were denied use of their own language.

Parameswaran (2001) has described how she relied on reading nonverbal cues to tell how potential interviewees reacted to her subject matter, the study of young middle-class women in India who read Western romance novels. She had to depend on reading body language to pick up hostility, disapproval, support, or openness because the verbal formalities of some interactions offered fewer cues than nonverbal reactions. Among the young women, giggles, winks, animated interactions, lowered eyes, and direct gaze became cues about how the fieldwork was progressing.

A caution is in order here. Nonverbal behaviors are easily misinterpreted, especially cross-culturally. Therefore, whenever possible and appropriate, having observed what appear to be significant nonverbal behaviors, some effort should be made to follow up with those involved to find out directly from them what the nonverbal behaviors really meant. I confirmed with other participants in the wilderness program the importance of hugging as a mechanism that they themselves used to sense the tenor of the group.

Unobtrusive Observations

Being observed can make people self-conscious and generate anxiety, especially when the observations are part of an evaluation. Regardless of how sensitively observations are made, the possibility always exists that people will behave differently under conditions where an observation or evaluation is taking place than they would if the observer were not present.

> Even when well-intentioned and cooperative, the research subject's knowledge that he is participating in a scholarly search may confound the investigator's data. . . . It is important to note early that the awareness of testing need not, by itself, contaminate responses. It is a question of probabilities, but the probability

of bias is high in any study in which a respondent is aware of his subject status. (Webb et al. 1966:13)

Concern about reactions to being observed has led some social scientists to recommend covert observations as discussed earlier in this chapter. An alternative strategy involves searching for opportunities to collect "unobtrusive measures" (Webb et al. 1966). Unobtrusive measures are those made without the knowledge of the people being observed and without affecting what is observed.

Robert L. Wolf and Barbara L. Tymitz (1978) included unobtrusive measures in their naturalistic inquiry evaluation of the National Museum of Natural History at the Smithsonian Institution. They looked for "wear spots" as indicators of use of particular exhibit areas. They decided that worn rugs would indicate the popularity of particular areas in the museum. The creative evaluator can learn a number of things about a program by looking for physical clues. Dusty equipment or files may indicate things that are not used. Areas that are used a great deal by children in a school will look different—that is, more worn—than areas that are little used.

In a week-long staff training program for 300 people, I asked the kitchen to systematically record how much coffee was consumed in the morning, afternoon, and evening each day. Those sessions that I judged to be particularly boring had a correspondingly higher level of coffee consumption. Active and involving sessions showed less coffee consumption, regardless of time of day. (Participants could get up and get coffee whenever they wanted.)

In the wilderness program, the thickness of notebooks called "learning logs" became an unobtrusive indicator of how engaged participants were in self-reflective journal-

ing. All participants were provided with learning logs at the beginning of the first field conference and were encouraged to use them for private reflections and journaling. These three-ring binders contained almost no paper when first given to participants. Participants brought the learning logs back each time they returned to the wilderness. (The program involved four different trips over the course of a year.) The extent to which paper had been added to the notebooks was one indicator of the extent to which the logs were being used.

The personnel of the National Forest Service and the Bureau of Land Management have a kind of unobtrusive measure they use in "evaluating" the wilderness habits of groups that go through an area such as the San Juan River in Utah. The canyons along the San Juan River are a very fragile environment. The regulations for use of that land are essentially "take only photographs, leave only footprints." This means that all garbage, including human waste and feces, are to be carried out. It takes several days to go down the river. By observing the amount and types of garbage groups carry out, one can learn a great deal about the wilderness habits of various groups and their compliance with river regulations.

The creative observer, aware of the variety of things to be learned from studying physical and social settings, will look for opportunities to incorporate unobtrusive measures into fieldwork, thereby manifesting a "sympathy toward multi-method inquiry, triangulation, playfulness in data collection, outcroppings as measures, and alternatives to self report" (Webb and Weick 1983:210).

A particularly powerful example of unobtrusive fieldwork is Laura Palmer's (1988) study of letters and remembrances left at the Vietnam Veterans Memorial in Washington, D.C., a work she called *Shrapnel in the Heart*. For the unobtrusive part of her fieldwork,

Palmer sampled items left at the memorial, all of which are saved and warehoused by the U.S. government. She categorized and analyzed types of items and the content of messages. In some cases, because of identifying information contained in letters or included with objects (photographs, baby shoes, artwork), she was able, through intensive investigative work, to locate the people who left the materials and interview them. Their stories, the intrusive part of her study, combined with vivid descriptions of the objects that led her to them, offer dramatic and powerful insights into the effects of the Vietnam War on the lives of survivors. In one sense, her analysis of letters, journals, photos, and messages can be thought of as a nontraditional and creative form of document analysis, another important fieldwork strategy.

Documents

Records, documents, artifacts, and archives—what has traditionally been called "material culture" in anthropology—constitute a particularly rich source of information about many organizations and programs. Thus, archival strategies and techniques constitute part of the repertoire of field research and evaluation (Hill 1993). In contemporary society, all kinds of entities leave a trail of paper and artifacts, a kind of spoor that can be mined as part of fieldwork. Families keep photographs, children's schoolwork, letters, old Bibles with detailed genealogies, bronzed baby shoes, and other sentimental objects that can inform and enrich family case studies. People who commit suicide leave behind suicide notes that can reveal patterns of despair in a society (Wilkinson 1999). Gangs and others inscribe public places with graffiti. Organizations of all kinds produce mountains of records, both public and private. Indeed, an oft-

intriguing form of analysis involves comparing official statements found in public documents (brochures, board minutes, annual reports) with private memos and what the evaluation observer actually hears or sees occurring the program. Client files are another rich source of case data to supplement field observations and interviews. For example, Vesneski and Kemp (2000) coded and analyzed intake sheets and copies of family plans produced during more than 100 "family conferences" involving the extended families of abused or neglected children in child welfare decision making in the state of Washington.

At the very beginning of an evaluation or organizational fieldwork, access to potentially important documents and records should be negotiated. The ideal situation would include access to all routine records on clients, all correspondence from and to program staff, financial and budget records, organizational rules, regulations, memoranda, charts, and any other official or unofficial documents generated by or for the program. These kinds of documents provide the evaluator with information about many things that cannot be observed. They may reveal things that have taken place before the evaluation began. They may include private interchanges to which the evaluator would not otherwise be privy. They can reveal goals or decisions that might be otherwise unknown to the evaluator.

In evaluating the mission fulfillment of a major philanthropic foundation, I examined 10 years of annual reports. Each report was professionally designed, elegantly printed, and widely disseminated—and each report stated a slightly different mission for the foundation. It turned out that the president of the foundation wrote an annual introduction and simply stated the mission from memory. The publication designer routinely lifted this "mission statement" from the president's letter and highlighted it in bold font at the beginning of the report, often on the cover page. From year to year the focus changed until, over the course of 10 years, the stated mission had changed dramatically without official board action, approval, or even awareness. Further investigation through years of board minutes revealed that, in fact, the board had never adopted a mission statement at all, a matter of considerable surprise to all involved.

As this example shows, documents prove valuable not only because of what can be learned directly from them but also as stimulus for paths of inquiry that can be pursued only through direct observation and interviewing. As with all information to which an evaluator has access during observations, the confidentiality of program records, particularly client records, must be respected. The extent to which actual references to and quotations from program records and documents are included in a final report depends on whether the documents are considered part of the public record and therefore able to be publicized without breach of confidentiality. In some cases, with permission and proper safeguards to protect confidentiality, some information from private documents can be quoted directly and cited.

Program records can provide a behind-the-scenes look at program processes and how they came into being. In the wilderness program evaluation, program staff made their files available to me. I discovered a great deal of information not available to other program participants: letters detailing both conceptual and financial debates between the technical staff (who led the wilderness trips) and the project directors (who had responsibility for the overall management of the program). Without knowledge of those arguments it would have been impossible to fully understand the nature of the interactions between field staff and exec-

utive staff in the project. Disagreements about program finances constituted but one arena of communication difficulties during the program, including time in the wilderness. Interviews with those involved revealed quite different perceptions of the nature of the conflicts, their intensity, and their potential for resolution. While participants became aware of some arguments among staff, for the most part they were unaware of the origins of those conflicts and the extent to which program implementation was hampered by them.

My review of files also revealed the enormous complexity of the logistics for the wilderness education program. Participants (college deans, program directors, administrators) were picked up at the airport in vans and driven to the wilderness location where the field conference would take place. Participants were supplied with all the gear necessary for surviving in the wilderness. Prior to each field trip, staff had many telephone and written exchanges with individual participants about particular needs and fears. Letters from participants, especially those new to the wilderness, showed how little they understood about what they were getting into. One seasoned administrator and hard-core smoker inquired, with reference to the first 10-day hike in the heart of the Gila wilderness, "Will there be a place to buy cigarettes along the way?" Talk about being clueless! But by the end of the year of field trips, he had given up smoking. His letter of inquiry alerted me to the importance of this pre-post observation.

Without having looked over this correspondence, I would have missed the extent to which preparation for the one-week experiences in the wilderness consumed the time and energy of program staff. The intensity of work involved before the field conferences helped explain the behavior of staff once the field trips got under way. So much had gone into the preparations, virtually none of which was appreciated by or known to program participants, that program staff would sometimes experience a psychological letdown effect and have difficulty energizing themselves for the actual wilderness experience.

Learning to use, study, and understand documents and files is part of the repertoire of skills needed for qualitative inquiry. For an extended discussion of the interpretation of documents and material culture, see Hodder (2000).

Observing What Does Not Happen

The preceding sections have described the things one can observe in a setting or program. Observing activities, interactions, what people say, what they do, and the nature of the physical setting is important in a comprehensive approach to fieldwork. But what about observing what does *not* happen?

The potential absurdity of speculating about what does not occur is illustrated by a Sufi story. During a plague of locusts, the wise-fool Mulla Nasrudin, always looking on the bright side, went from village to village encouraging people by observing how fortunate they were that elephants had no wings. "You people don't realize how lucky you are. Imagine what life would be like with elephants flying overhead. These locusts are nothing."

To observe that elephants have no wings is indeed data. Moreover, elephants have no fins, claws, feathers, or branches. Clearly, once one ventures into the area of observing what does not happen, there are a near-infinite number of things one could point out. The "absence of occurrence" list could become huge. It is therefore with some cau-

tion that I include among the tasks of the observer that of noting what does not occur.

If social science theory, program goals, implementation designs, and/or proposals suggest that certain things ought to happen or are expected to happen, then it is appropriate for the observer or evaluator to note that those things did not happen. If a community where water is scarce shows no evidence of conflict over water rights, an anthropologist could be expected to report and explain this absence of community conflict. If a school program is supposed to, according to its funding mandate and goals, provide children with opportunities to explore the community and no such explorations occur, it is altogether appropriate for the evaluator to note said implementation failure. If the evaluator reported only what occurred, a question might be left in the mind of the reader about whether the other activities had occurred but had simply not been observed. Likewise, if a criminal justice program is supposed to provide one-to-one counseling to juveniles and no such counseling takes place, it is entirely appropriate for the evaluator to note the absence of counseling.

In observing early childhood programs, the absence of children's art on the walls in one center stood out. Indeed, the absence of any colorful posters or art of any kind stood out because all other centers' walls were covered with colorful displays. When I pointed this out, embarrassed staff members explained that they had set in motion a planning process for decorating the walls that had become bogged down and they had just neglected to get back to the issue because, they realized, they got gotten used to the way things were.

Thus, it can be appropriate to note that something did not occur when the observer's basic knowledge of and experience with the phenomenon suggests that the absence of some particular activity or factor is noteworthy. This clearly calls for judgment, common sense, and experience. As eminent qualitative methodologist Bob Stake (1995) has asserted:

> One of the principal qualifications of qualitative researchers is experience. Added to the experience of ordinary looking and thinking, the experience of the qualitative researcher is one of knowing what leads to significant understanding, recognizing good sources of data, and consciously and unconsciously testing out the veracity of their eyes and robustness of their interpretations. It requires sensitivity and skepticism. Much of this methodological knowledge and personality come from hard work under the critical examination of colleagues and mentors. (pp. 49-50)

Making informed judgments about the significance of nonoccurrences can be among the most important contributions an evaluator can make because such feedback can provide program staff members or other evaluation users with information that they may not have thought to request. Moreover, they may lack the requisite experience or awareness to have noticed the absence of that which the evaluator observes. For example, the absence of staff conflict is typically noteworthy because staff conflict is common. Similarly, absence of conflict between administrative levels (local, state, and federal) would be noteworthy because such conflict is, in my experience, virtually universal.

In many such cases, the observation about what did not occur is simply a restatement, in the opposite, of what did occur. That restatement, however, will attract attention in a way that the initial observation might not. For example, if one were observing a program being conducted in a multiracial community, it is possible that program goals would include statements about the necessity of staff being sensitive to the particular needs, interests, and cultural patterns of minorities, but there may not be specific mention of the desired racial composition of program staff. If, then, the evaluator observes that the staff of the program consists entirely of Caucasians, it is appropriate to report that the staff is all White, that is, no people of color are among the program staff, the importance of which derives from the location and nature of the program.

Observations of staff interaction and decision-making processes also provide opportunities for evaluators to note things that do not happen. If, over time, the observer notes that program planning processes never include participants' input in any systematic or direct way, it may well be appropriate for the evaluator to point out the absence of such input based on experiences indicating the significance of participant input in the planning processes of other programs.

My evaluation of the wilderness education program included observations about a number of things that did not occur. No serious injuries occurred at any of the six field conferences in the wilderness—important information for someone thinking about the possible risks involved in such a program. No participant refused to shoulder his or her share of the work that had to be done in order for the group to live and work together in the wilderness. This observation emerged from discussions with technical field staff who often worked with juveniles in wilderness settings where uneven sharing of cooking, cleaning, and related responsibilities often led to major group conflicts. The fact that the groups I observed never had to deal with one or two people not helping out was worth noting.

Perhaps the most important observation about what did not happen came from observing staff meetings. Over time, I noticed a pattern in which staff held meetings to make decisions about important issues, but no such decisions were made. Staff sometimes thought that a decision had been made, but closure was not brought to the decision-making process and no responsibility for follow-up was assigned. Many subsequent implementation failures and staff conflicts could be traced to ambiguities and differences of opinion that were left unresolved at staff meetings. By hearing me describe both what was and was not occurring, staff became more explicit and effective in making decisions. Reporting what did happen in staff meetings was important, but it was also extremely important to observe what did not happen.

Nested and Layered Case Studies During Fieldwork

> A case study is expected to catch the complexity of a single case. The single leaf, even a single toothpick, has unique complexities—but rarely will we care enough to submit it to case study. We study a case when it itself is of very special interest. We look for the detail of interaction with its context. Case study is the study of the particularity and complexity of a single case, coming to understand its activity within important circumstances. (Stake 1995:xi)

Months of fieldwork may result in a single case study that describes a village, community, neighborhood, organization, or program. However, that single case study is likely to be made up of many smaller cases—the stories of specific individuals, families, organizational units, and other groups. Critical incidents and case studies of specific bounded activities, like a celebra-

tion, may also be presented within the larger case. The qualitative analysis process typically centers on presentation of specific cases and thematic analysis across cases. Knowing this, fieldwork can be organized around nested and layered case studies, which means that some form of nested case sampling must occur.

Let me briefly review the centrality of case studies as a qualitative inquiry strategy. Chapter 1 opened by citing a number of well-known and influential books based on case studies, for example, *In Search of Excellence: Lessons From America's Best-Run Companies* by Peters and Waterman (1982), Angela Browne's important book *When Battered Women Kill* (1987), and Sara Lawrence-Lightfoot's six detailed case studies in *Respect* (2000:13). Chapter 2 presented the construction of *unique case studies* as a major strategic theme of qualitative inquiry. Chapter 3 reviewed theoretical perspectives that are inductively case based. Chapter 4 reviewed at some length the importance in qualitative evaluation of *capturing and reporting individualized outcomes* based on case studies of how participants in programs change during a program and whether they maintain those changes afterward. To illustrate this point, in the wilderness education program our evaluation team constructed case studies of participants using multiple sources of data from fieldwork: (1) background data gathered through interviews about participants' situations and perspectives upon entering the year of field conferences; (2) observations of their experiences during field conferences; (3) informal and conversational interviews with them during the wilderness trips; (4) quotations from formal group interviews (focus groups) held at various times during the trips; (5) excerpts from their journals and other personal writings when they were willing to share those with us, as they often were; and (6) follow-up telephone interviews with participants after each field trip and after the entire program was completed to track the impact of the program on individuals over time.

Let me pause at this point and note some confusion in the qualitative literature about terminology. For example, sociologists Hamel, Dufour, and Fortin (1993) ask:

> But is the case study a method? Or is it an approach? ... Case studies employ various methods. These can include interviews, participant observation, and field studies. Their goals are to reconstruct and analyze a case from a sociological perspective. It would thus be more appropriate to define the case study as an approach, although the term *case method* suggests that it is indeed a method. (p. 1)

Whatever term or phrase is used, case studies depend on clearly defining the object of study, that is, the case. But this too is complex.

When more than one object of study or unit of analysis is included in fieldwork, case studies may be layered and nested within the overall, primary case approach. William Foote Whyte's (1943) classic study *Street Corner Society* has long been recognized as an exemplar of the single-community ($N = 1$) case study (e.g., Yin 1989) even though his study of "Cornerville" includes the stories (case studies) of several individual lower-income youth, some of whom were striving to escape the neighborhood.

The wilderness program illustrates how case studies often are layered and nested. The three-year wilderness program constituted the overall, one might say *macro*, case study. The final evaluation report presented conclusions about the processes and outcomes of the overall program, a case example of a three-year wilderness education initiative. As Exhibit 6.4 (p. 300) shows, however, within that overall evaluation case study were nested individual case studies documenting individual experiences and outcomes; case studies of each yearlong group cohort; and case studies of each separate field conference, for example, the 10 days in the Gila wilderness or the 10 days in the Kofa Mountains. Slicing through the fieldwork and analysis in other ways were case studies of particular incidents, for example, the emotional catharsis experienced by one participant when she finally managed to overcome her terror and rappel down a cliff face, the whole group watching and urging her on, a process that took some 45 tense minutes. Other mini-cases consisted of different units of analysis. A full day's hike could be a case, as could running a specific dangerous rapid on the San Juan River. Each evening discussion constituted a case such that that over the three years, we had notes on over 80 discussions of various kinds. Staff meetings made for a different unit of analysis and therefore a different series of case studies. Thus, extended fieldwork can and typically does involve many mini- or micro-case studies of various units of analysis (individuals, groups, specific activities, specific periods of time, critical incidents), all of which together make up the overall case study, in this example, the final evaluation of the wilderness education program. Chapter 5 discusses at length various units of analysis and sampling strategies for case studies (see especially Exhibit 5.5 [p. 231] on units of analysis and Exhibit 5.6 [pp. 243-244] on purposeful sampling strategies).

Fieldwork, then, can be thought of as engaging in a series of multilayered and nested case studies, often with intersecting and overlapping units of analysis. One final case study deserves consideration—the observer's experiences and reactions. We turn to that now.

Observing Oneself

P hysician, heal thyself.
    Observer, observe thyself.

—Halcolm

In the second chapter, I identified voice and perspective, or reflexivity, as one of the central strategic themes of contemporary, postmodern qualitative inquiry. The term *reflexivity* has entered the qualitative lexicon as a way of emphasizing the importance of self-awareness, political/cultural conscious-ness, and ownership of one's perspective. Reflexivity reminds the qualitative inquirer to observe herself or himself so as to be at-tentive to and conscious of the cultural, po-litical, social, linguistic, and ideological ori-gins of her or his own perspective and voice as well as—and often in contrast to—the perspectives and voices of those she or he observes and talks to during fieldwork. Re-flexivity calls for self-reflection, indeed, crit-ical self-reflection and self-knowledge, and a willingness to consider how who one is af-fects what one is able to observe, hear, and understand in the field and as an observer and analyst. The observer, therefore, during fieldwork, must observe self as well as oth-ers, and interactions of self with others.

Once again, for continuity, I cite Para-meswaran (2001), who has written a won-derfully self-reflective account of her ex-perience returning to her native India to do fieldwork as a feminist scholar after being educated in United States.

> Because my parents were fairly liberal com-pared to many of my friends' parents, I grew up with a little more awareness than many middle- and upper-class Indians of the differ-ences between my life and that of the vast ma-jority of Indians. Although I questioned some restrictions that were specific to women of my class, I did not have the language to engage in a systematic feminist critique of patriarchy or nationalism. Feminism for me had been unfor-tunately constructed as an illness that struck highly Westernized intellectual Indian wom-en who were out of touch with reality. . . . [I]t was my dislocation from India to the relatively radicalized context of the United States that prompted my political development as a femi-nist and a woman of color. (p. 76)

Given this background and the contro-versial focus of her fieldwork (reading of Western romance novels by young Indian women), she identified reflexive questions to guide her reflexive inquiry during and af-ter fieldwork:

> How do kinship roles assigned to native schol-ars shape social interactions in the field? How can commitments to sisterhood make it diffi-cult for feminist ethnographers to achieve crit-ical distance and discuss female informants' prejudiced views? (p. 76)

Her personal inquiry into these questions, reflecting on her own fieldwork experiences (Parameswaran 2001), is a model of reflex-ivity.

Many year ago, Indian philosopher J. Krishnamurti (1964) commented on the challenges of self-knowledge. Although his reflections were directed to the importance of lifelong learning rather than to being re-flexive in fieldwork, his ruminations offer a larger context for thinking about how to ob-serve oneself, a context beyond concern

EXHIBIT 6.4	Nested, Layered, and Overlapping Mini–Case Studies During Fieldwork: Example From the Wilderness Education Program Evaluation

The wilderness education program evaluation illustrates how case studies often are layered and nested. Evaluation of the three-year wilderness program constituted the overall macro case study. Nested and layered within that overall evaluation were various mini-cases of overlapping and intersecting units of analysis that helped organize and frame fieldwork.

Macro Case Study: Final Evaluation Study of the Three-Year Program
Possible nested, layered, and overlapping mini-case studies

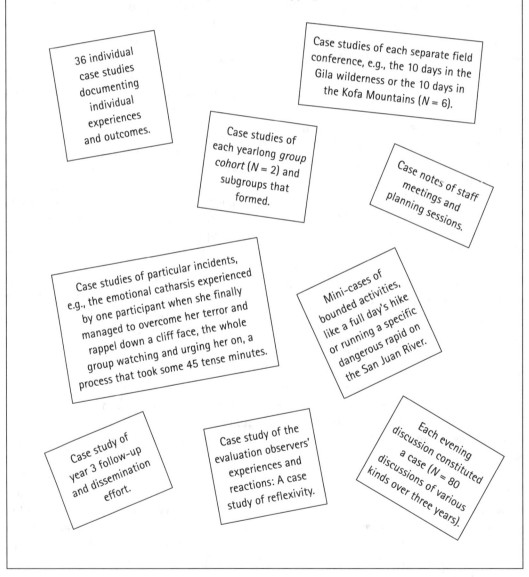

36 individual case studies documenting individual experiences and outcomes.

Case studies of each separate field conference, e.g., the 10 days in the Gila wilderness or the 10 days in the Kofa Mountains ($N = 6$).

Case studies of each yearlong group cohort ($N = 2$) and subgroups that formed.

Case notes of staff meetings and planning sessions.

Case studies of particular incidents, e.g., the emotional catharsis experienced by one participant when she finally managed to overcome her terror and rappel down a cliff face, the whole group watching and urging her on, a process that took some 45 tense minutes.

Mini-cases of bounded activities, like a full day's hike or running a specific dangerous rapid on the San Juan River.

Case study of year 3 follow-up and dissemination effort.

Case study of the evaluation observers' experiences and reactions: A case study of reflexivity.

Each evening discussion constituted a case ($N = 80$ discussions of various kinds over three years).

about methodological authenticity, though his advice applies to that as well.

> Self-knowledge comes when you observe yourself in your relationship with your fellow-students and your teachers, with all the people around you; it comes when you observe the manner of another, his gestures, the way he wears his clothes, the way he talks, his contempt or flattery *and your response*; it comes when you watch everything in you and about you and see yourself as you see your face in the mirror. . . . Now, if you can look into the mirror of relationship exactly as you look into the ordinary mirror, then there is no end to self-knowledge. It is like entering a fathomless ocean which has no shore. . . . ; if you can just observe what you are and move with it, then you will find that it is possible to go infinitely far. Then there is no end to the journey, and that is the mystery, the beauty of it. (Krishnamurti 1964:50-51, emphasis added)

I realize that Krishnamurti's phrase "There is no end to the journey" may strike terror in the hearts of graduate students reading this in preparation for dissertation fieldwork or evaluators facing a report deadline. But, remember, he's taking about lifelong learning, of which the dissertation or a specific evaluation report is but one phase. Just as most dissertations and evaluations are reasonably expected to contribute incremental knowledge rather than make major breakthroughs, so too the self-knowledge of reflexive fieldwork is but one phase in a lifelong journey toward self-knowledge—but it's an important phase and a commitment of growing significance as reflexivity has emerged as a central theme in qualitative inquiry.

The point here, which we shall take up in greater depth in the chapters on analysis and credibility, is that the observer must ulti-

mately deal with issues of authenticity, reactivity, and how the observational process may have affected what was observed as well as **how the background and predispositions of the observer may have constrained what was observed and understood.** Each of these areas of methodological inquiry depends on some degree of critical reflexivity.

Sources of Data Reviewed

This lengthy review of options in what to observe and sources of data for evaluation fieldwork began with the suggestion that a *sensitizing framework* can be useful as a tool to guide fieldwork. The list of data sources we've reviewed can be used to stimulate thinking about evaluation fieldwork possibilities. Other phenomena and other observational arenas would have different sensitizing frameworks or concepts. The following summarizes the observation and inquiry topics we've reviewed for evaluation:

- Description of the program setting/physical environment
- Description of the social environment
- Capturing historical perspectives
- Describing planned program implementation activities and structured interactions
- Observing informal interactions and unplanned activities
- Recording participants' special program language
- Observing nonverbal communication
- Watching for unobtrusive indicators
- Analyzing documents, files, records, and artifacts

- Commenting on notable nonoccurrences (what does not happen)

- Constructing nested and layered case studies during fieldwork for intersecting and overlapping units of analysis

- Observing oneself: Reflexivity

- Documenting individualized and common outcomes (Chapter 4)

Creativity in Fieldwork

No checklist can be relied on to guide all aspects of fieldwork. A participant observer must constantly make judgments about what is worth noting. Because it is impossible to observe everything, some process of selection is necessary. Plans made during design should be revised as appropriate when important new opportunities and sources of data become available. That's where flexibility and creativity help. Creativity can be learned and practiced (Patton 1987a). Creative fieldwork means using every part of oneself to experience and understand what is happening. Creative insights come from being directly involved in the setting being studied.

I shall return to the issue of creativity in considering the interpretation of field notes later in this chapter and again in the analysis chapter. For the moment, it is sufficient to acknowledge the centrality of creativity in naturalistic inquiry and to concur with Virginia Woolf:

Odd how the creative power at once brings the whole universe to order. . . . I mark Henry James' sentence: observe perpetually. Observe the oncome of age. Observe greed. Observe my own despondency. By that means it becomes serviceable. (quoted in Partnow 1978: 185)

⬚ Doing Fieldwork: The Data-Gathering Process

The purpose of the research has been clarified. The primary research questions have been focused. Qualitative methods using observations have been selected as one of the appropriate methods of data gathering. It is time to enter the field. Now begins the arduous task of taking field notes.

Field Notes

Many options exist for taking field notes. Variations include the writing materials used, the time and place for recording field notes, the symbols developed by observers as their own method of shorthand, and how field notes are stored. No universal prescriptions about the mechanics of and procedures for taking field notes are possible because different settings lend themselves to different ways of proceeding and the precise organization of fieldwork is very much a matter of personal style and individual work habits. **What is not optional is the taking of field notes.**

Aside from getting along in the setting, the fundamental work of the observer is the taking of field notes. Field notes are "the most important determinant of later bringing off a qualitative analysis. Field notes provide the observer's *raison d'être*. If . . . not doing them, [the observer] might as well not be in the setting" (Lofland 1971:102).

Field notes contain the description of what has been observed. They should contain everything that the observer believes to be worth noting. Don't trust anything to future recall. At the moment one is writing it is very tempting, because the situation is still fresh, to believe that the details or particular elements of the situation can be recalled later. If it's important as part of your con-

BOXED IN

Those who aspire to be creative are admonished to "think outside the box." This presumes that one has exhausted the possibilities of learning within the box. Before moving outside the box, make sure you know the box. Observe it. Look deep within. Find out the history of the box, how it came to be the box. What has it held? What has been taken from it? Examine the corners. Look underneath, on top, on all sides. Know the box. Understand the box. Learn what the box has to teach. Think inside the box. Only then will you truly be ready to "think outside the box."

—From Halcolm's *Boxing Guide*

sciousness as an observer, if it's information that has helped you understand the context, the setting, and what went on, then as soon as possible that information should be captured in the field notes.

First and foremost, field notes are descriptive. They should be dated and should record such basic information as where the observation took place, who was present, what the physical setting was like, what social interactions occurred, and what activities took place. Field notes contain the descriptive information that will permit you to return to an observation later during analysis and, eventually, permit the reader of the study's findings to experience the activity observed through your report.

The passages in Exhibit 6.5 on the next page illustrate different kinds of descriptive field notes. On the left side are vague and overgeneralized field notes. On the right side are more detailed and concrete field notes from the same observation.

These examples illustrate the problem of using general terms to describe specific ac-

tions and conditions. Words such as *poor, anger,* and *uneasy* are insufficiently descriptive. Such interpretive words conceal what actually went on rather than reveal the details of the situation. Such terms have little meaning for a person present for the observation. Moreover, the use of such terms in field notes, without the accompanying detailed description, means that the fieldworker has fallen into the bad habit of primarily recording interpretations rather than description. Particularly revealing are terms that can make sense only in comparison to something else. The phrase "poorly dressed" requires some frame of reference about what constitutes "good dress." No skill is more critical in fieldwork than learning to be descriptive, concrete, and detailed.

Field notes also contain what people say. Direct quotations, or as near as possible recall of direct quotations, should be captured during fieldwork, recording what was said during observed activities as well as responses garnered during interviews, both formal and conversational. Quotations provide the "emic perspective" discussed earlier—the insider's perspective—which "is at the heart of most ethnographic research" (Fetterman 1989:30).

Field notes also contain the observer's own feelings, reactions to the experience, and reflections about the personal meaning and significance of what has been observed. Don't deceive yourself into thinking that such feelings can be conjured up again simply by reading the descriptions of what took place. Feelings and reactions should be recorded at the time they are experienced, while you are in the field. Both the nature and intensity of feelings should be recorded. In qualitative inquiry, the observer's own experiences are part of the data. Part of the purpose of being in a setting and getting close to the people in the setting is to permit you to experience what it is like to be in that

---

EXHIBIT 6.5   Fieldnotes Comparisons

Vague and Overgeneralized Notes	Detailed and Concrete Notes
1. The new client was uneasy waiting for her intake interview.	1. At first the new client sat very stiffly on the chair next to the receptionist's desk. She picked up a magazine and let the pages flutter through her fingers very quickly without really looking at any of the pages. She set the magazine down, looked at her watch, pulled her skirt down, picked up the magazine again, set it back down, took out a cigarette and lit it. She watched the receptionist out of the corner of her eye and glanced at the two or three other people waiting in the room. Her eyes moved from people to the magazine to the cigarette to the people to the magazine in rapid succession, but avoided eye contact. When her name was finally called, she jumped like she was startled.
2. The client was quite hostile toward the staff person.	2. When Judy, the senior staff member, told the client that she could not just do whatever she wanted to do, the client began to yell, screaming that Judy couldn't couldn't control her life, accused Judy of being on a "power trip," and said that she'd "like to beat the shit out of her," then told her to "go to hell." The client shook her fist in Judy's face and stomped out of the room, leaving Judy standing there with her mouth open, looking amazed.
3. The next student who came in to take the test was very poorly dressed.	3. The next student who came into the room wore clothes quite different from the three previous students. The other students had hair carefully combed, clothes clean, pressed, and in good condition with colors coordinated. This new student wore soiled pants with a tear in one knee and a threadbare seat. His flannel shirt was wrinkled with one tail tucked into the pants and the other tail hanging out. His hair was disheveled and his hands looked liked he'd been playing in the engine of a car.

---

setting. If what it is like for you, the observer or participant observer, is not recorded in your field notes, then much of the purpose for being there is lost.

Finally, field notes include your insights, interpretations, beginning analyses, and working hypotheses about what is happening in the setting and what it means. While you should approach fieldwork with a disciplined intention not to impose preconceptions and early judgments on the phenomenon being experienced and observed, nevertheless, as an observer you don't be-

come a mechanical recording machine on entering the field. Insights, ideas, inspirations—and yes, judgments, too—will occur while making observations and recording field notes. It's not that you sit down early on and begin the analysis and, if you're an evaluator, make judgments. Rather, it's in the nature of our intellects that ideas about the meaning, causes, and significance of what we experience find their way into our minds. These insights and inspirations become part of the data of fieldwork and should be recorded in context in field notes.

I like to set off field interpretations with brackets. Others use parentheses, asterisks, or some other symbol to distinguish interpretations from description. The point is that interpretations should be understood to be just that, interpretations, and labeled as such. Field-based insights are sufficiently precious that you need not ignore them in the hopes that, if really important, they will return later.

Field notes, then, contain the ongoing data that are being collected. They consist of descriptions of what is being experienced and observed, quotations from the people observed, the observer's feelings and reactions to what is observed, and field-generated insights and interpretations. Field notes are the fundamental database for constructing case studies and carrying out thematic cross-case analysis in qualitative research.

Procedurally Speaking

When field notes are written will depend on the kind of observations being done and the nature of your participation in the setting being studied. In an evaluation of a parent education program, I was introduced to the parents by the staff facilitator and explained the purpose of the evaluation and assured the parents that no one would be identified. I then openly took extensive notes without participating in the discussions. Immediately following those sessions, I would go back over my notes to fill in details and be sure what I had recorded made sense. By way of contrast, in the wilderness education program I was a full participant engaged in full days of hiking, rock climbing, and rafting/kayaking. I was sufficiently exhausted by the end of each day that I seldom stayed awake making field notes by flashlight while others slept . Rather, each night I jotted down basic notes that I could expand during the time that others were writing in

their journals, but some of the expansion had to be completed after the weeklong field conference. In evaluating a leadership training program as a participant observer, the staff facilitator privately asked me not to take notes during group discussions because it made him nervous, even though most other participants were taking notes.

The extent to which notes are openly recorded during the activities being observed is a function of the observer's role and purpose, as well as the stage of participant observation. If the observer or evaluator is openly identified as a short-term, external, nonparticipant observer, participants may expect him or her to write down what is going on. If, on the other hand, one is engaged in longer-term participant observation, the early part of the process may be devoted to establishing the participant observer role with emphasis on participation so that open taking of notes is deferred until the fieldworker's role has been firmly established within the group. At that point, it is often possible to openly take field notes since, it is hoped, the observer is better known to the group and has established some degree of trust and rapport.

The wilderness program evaluation involved three 10-day trips ("field conferences") with participants at different times during the year. During the first field conference, I never took notes openly. The only time I wrote was when others were also writing. During the second field conference, I began to openly record observations when discussions were going on if taking notes did not interfere with my participation. By the third week, I felt I could take notes whenever I wanted to and I had no indication from anyone that they even paid attention to the fact that I was taking notes. By that time I had established myself as a participant, and my participant role was more primary than my evaluator role.

The point here is that evaluator observers must be strategic about taking field notes, timing their writing and recording in such a way that they are able to get their work done without unduly affecting either their participation or their observations. Given those constraints, **the basic rule of thumb is to write promptly,** to complete field notes as soon and as often as physically and programmatically possible.

Writing field notes is rigorous and demanding work. Lofland (1971) has described this rigor quite forcefully:

> Let me not deceive the reader. The writing of field notes takes personal discipline and time. It is all too easy to put off actually writing notes for a given day and to skip one or more days. For the actual writing of the notes may take as long or longer than did the observation! Indeed, a reasonable rule of thumb here is to expect and plan to spend as much time writing notes as one spent in observing. This is, of course, not invariant . . . but one point is inescapable. All the fun of actually being out and about monkeying around in some setting must also be met by cloistered rigor in committing to paper—and therefore to future usefulness—what has taken place. (p. 104)

⑤ Observations, Interviews, and Documentation: Bringing Together Multiple Perspectives

Fieldwork is more than a single method or technique. For example, evaluation fieldwork means that the evaluator is on-site (where the program is happening) observing, talking with people, and going through program records. Multiple sources of information are sought and used because no single source of information can be trusted to provide a comprehensive perspective on the program. By using a combination of observations, interviewing, and document analysis, the fieldworker is able to use different data sources to validate and cross-check findings. Each type and source of data has strengths and weaknesses. Using a combination of data types—triangulation, a recurring theme in this book— increases validity as the strengths of one approach can compensate for the weaknesses of another approach (Marshall and Rossman 1989: 79-111).

Limitations of observations include the possibility that the observer may affect the situation being observed in unknown ways, program staff and participants may behave in some atypical fashion when they know they are being observed, and the selective perception of the observer may distort the data. Observations are also limited in focusing only on external behaviors—the observer cannot see what is happening inside people. Moreover, observational data are often constrained by the limited sample of activities actually observed. Researchers and evaluators need other data sources to find out the extent to which observed activities are typical or atypical.

Interview data limitations include possibly distorted responses due to personal bias, anger, anxiety, politics, and simple lack of awareness since interviews can be greatly affected by the emotional state of the interviewee at the time of the interview. Interview data are also subject to recall error, reactivity of the interviewee to the interviewer, and self-serving responses.

Observations provide a check on what is reported in interviews; interviews, on the other hand, permit the observer to go beyond external behavior to explore feelings and thoughts.

Documents and records also have limitations. They may be incomplete or inaccurate. Client files maintained by programs are notoriously variable in quality and completeness, with great detail in some cases and virtually nothing in others. Document analysis, however, provides a behind-the-scenes look at the program that may not be directly observable and about which the interviewer might not ask appropriate questions without the leads provided through documents.

By using a variety of sources and resources, the evaluator observer can build on the strengths of each type of data collection while minimizing the weaknesses of any single approach. This mixed methods, triangulated approach to fieldwork is based on pragmatism (Tashakkori and Teddlie 1998) and is illustrated in my attempt to understand some of the problems involved in staff communication during the wilderness education evaluation. I mentioned this example earlier, but I'd like to expand it here.

As noted, two kinds of staff worked in the program: (1) those who had overall management and administrative responsibility and (2) the technical staff, who had responsibility for wilderness skills training, field logistics, and safety. The technical staff had extensive experience leading wilderness trips, but they also were skilled at facilitating group processes. During the trips, the lines of responsibility between technical staff and administrative staff were often blurred and, on occasion, these ambiguities gave rise to conflicts. I observed the emergence of conflict early on the first trip but lacked context for knowing what was behind these differences. Through interviews and casual conversations during fieldwork, I learned that all of the staff, both administrative and technical, had known each other prior to the program. Indeed, the program administrative directors had been the college professors of the technical staff while the latter were still undergraduate students. However, the technical staff had introduced the directors to the

wilderness as an environment for experiential education. Each of the staff members described in interviews his or her perceptions of how these former relationships affected the field operations of the program, including difficulties in communication that had emerged during planning sessions prior to the actual field conferences. Some of those conflicts were documented in letters and memos. Reading their files and correspondence gave me a deeper understanding of the different assumptions and values of various staff members. **But the documentation would not have made sense without the interviews, and the focus of the interviews came from the field observations. Taken together, these diverse sources of information and data gave me a complete picture of staff relationships.** Working back and forth among individual staff members and group staff meetings, I was able to use this information to assist staff members in their efforts to improve their communication during the final field conference. All three sources of information proved critical to my understanding of the situation, and that understanding enhanced my effectiveness in providing feedback as a formative evaluator.

The Technology of Fieldwork and Observation

The classic image of the anthropological fieldworker is of someone huddled in an African hut writing voluminously by lantern. Contemporary researchers, however, have available to them a number of technological innovations that, when used judiciously, can make fieldwork more efficient and comprehensive. First and foremost is the battery-operated tape recorder or dictaphone. For some people, myself included, dictating field notes saves a great deal of time while increasing the comprehensiveness of the report. Learning to dictate takes practice, effort, and critical review of early attempts. Tape recorders must be used judiciously so as not to become obtrusive and inhibit program processes or participant responses. A tape recorder is much more useful for recording field notes in private than it is as an instrument to be carried about at all times, available to put a quick end to any conversation into which the observer enters.

Portable computers have emerged as a fieldwork tool that can facilitate writing field notes. Cameras have become standard accessories in fieldwork. Photographs can help in recalling things that have happened as well as vividly capturing the setting for others. Digital photography and advances in printing and photocopying now make it possible to economically reproduce photographs in research and evaluation reports.

In the wilderness education evaluation, I officially became the group photographer, making photographs available to all of the participants. This helped legitimize taking photographs and reduced the extent to which other people felt it necessary to carry their own cameras at all times, particularly at times when it was possible that the equipment might be damaged. Looking at photographs during analysis helped me recall the details of certain activities that I had not fully recorded in my written notes. I relied heavily on photographs to add details to descriptions of places where critical events occurred in the Grand Canyon initiation story I wrote about coming of age in modern society (Patton 1999a).

Video photography is another technological innovation that has become readily accessible and common enough that it can sometimes be used unobtrusively. For example, in a formative evaluation of a staff training program I used videotapes to provide visual feedback to staff. Videotaping classrooms, training sessions, therapeutic interactions, and a host of other observational targets can sometimes be less intrusive than a note-taking evaluator. We had great success taking videos of mothers and children playing together in early childhood education centers. Of course, use of such equipment must be negotiated with program staff and participants, but the creative and judicious use of technology can greatly increase the quality of field observations and the utility of the observational record to others. Moreover, comfort with tape recorders and video cameras has made it increasingly possible to use such technology without undue intrusion when observing programs where professionals are the participants. In addition, sometimes videotapes originally done for research or evaluation can subsequently be used for future training, program development, and public relations, making the costs more manageable because of added uses and benefits. Evaluators learn to balance costs against benefits and look for multiple uses of more expensive techniques where there is a need to make judicious decisions about reducing expenses.

Visual technology can add an important dimension to fieldwork if the observer knows how to use such technology and uses it well—for there is much to learn beyond how to click the camera or turn on the video recorder, especially about integrating and analyzing visual data within a larger fieldwork context (Ball and Smith 1992). Moreover, a downside to visual technology has emerged, since it is now possible to not only capture images on film and video but also change and edit those images in ways that distort. In his extensive review of "visual methods" in qualitative inquiry, Douglas Harper (2000) concludes that "now that images can be created and/or changed digitally, the connection between image and 'truth' has been forever severed" (p. 721). This means that issues of credibility apply to using and reporting visual data as they do to other kinds of data.

Perhaps the ultimate in observer technology for fieldwork is the Stenomask, a sound-shielded microphone attached to a portable tape recorder that is worn on a shoulder strap. The handle of the Stenomask contains the microphone switch. The Stenomask allows the observer to talk into the recorder while an activity is occurring without people in the area being able to hear the dictation. Its use is limited to external, onlooker observations, as the following passage makes clear.

Two procedures precede any data taking. The first is orientation of the subject and as many other persons in the environment as are likely to be present during observations. . . . During this phase, the observer goes into the habitat and behaves exactly as he or she will during the actual recording. They wear the Stenomask, follow the subject about and run the machine, taking mock records. The purpose of these activities is exactly what is implied in the title, to adapt the subject and others in the environment to the presence of the observer and to reduce the effects of that presence to as near zero as possible. The cardinal rule of the observer during this time is to be completely nonresponding. It has been demonstrated over and over again that if the observer continues to resist all social stimuli from the subject and others (and some will occur despite the most careful orientation) by simply keeping the mask in place, looking busily at work and remaining nonrespond- ing, both subjects and others soon cease emitting stimuli to the observer and come to truly accept him or her as a present and sometimes mobile but completely nonresponding part of the environment, per-

haps somewhat like a rolling chair. (Scott and Eklund 1979:9-11).

The imagery of a fieldworker following a subject around through a day wearing a Stenomask offers a stark contrast to that of the traditional anthropologist doing participant observation and trying covertly to write notes during informal field interviews. Taking field notes can be nearly as intrusive as wearing a Stenomask, as illustrated in the fieldwork of anthropologist Carlos Castaneda. In the passage below, Castaneda (1973) reports on his negotiations with Don Juan to become his Native Indian key informant on sorcery and indigenous drugs. The young anthropologist records that Don Juan "looked at me piercingly."

"What are you doing in your pocket?" he asked, frowning. "Are you playing with your whanger?"

He was referring to my taking notes on a minute pad inside the enormous pockets of my windbreaker.

When I told him what I was doing he laughed heartily.

I said that I did not want to disturb him by writing in front of him.

"If you want to write, write," he said. "You don't disturb me." (pp. 21-22)

Whether one uses modern technology to support fieldwork or simply writes down what is occurring, some method of keeping track of what is observed must be established. In addition, the nature of the recording system must be worked out in accordance with the participant observer's role, the purpose of the study, and consideration of how the data-gathering process will affect the activities and persons being observed. Many of these issues and procedures must be worked out during the initial phase (entry period) of fieldwork.

☐ Stages of Fieldwork

Thus far, fieldwork has been described as if it were a single, integrated experience. Certainly, when fieldwork goes well it flows with a certain continuity, but it is useful to look at the evolution of fieldwork through identifiable stages. Three stages are most often discussed in the participant observation literature: the entry stage, the routinization of data-gathering period, and the closing stage. The following sections explore each of these stages, again using evaluative research as the primary example.

Entry Into the Field

The writings of anthropologists sometimes present a picture of the early period of fieldwork that reminds me of the character in Franz Kafka's haunting novel *The Castle*. Kafka's character is a wandering stranger, K., with no more identity than that initial. He doesn't belong anywhere, but when he arrives at the castle he wants to become part of that world. His efforts to make contact with the faceless authorities who run the castle lead to frustration and anxiety. He can't quite figure out what is going on, can't break through their vagueness and impersonal nature. He doubts himself; then he gets angry at the way he is treated; then he feels guilty, blaming himself for his inability to break through the ambiguous procedures for entry. Yet, he remains determined to make sense out of the incomprehensible regulations of the castle. He is convinced that, after all, where there are rules—and he does find that there are rules—they must fit together somehow, have some meaning, and manifest some underlying logic. There must be some way to make contact, to satisfy the needs of the authorities, to find some pattern of behavior that will permit him to be ac-

cepted. If only he could figure out what to do, if only he could understand the rules, then he would happily do what he was supposed to do. Such are the trials of entry into the field.

Entry into the field for evaluation research involves two separate parts: (1) negotiation with gatekeepers, whoever they may be, about the nature of the fieldwork to be done and (2) actual physical entry into the field setting to begin collecting data. These two parts are closely related, for the negotiations with gatekeepers will establish the rules and conditions for how one goes about playing the role of observer and how that role is defined for the people being observed. In traditional scholarly fieldwork for the purpose of basic or applied research, the investigator unilaterally decides how best to conduct the fieldwork. In evaluation studies, the evaluator will need to take into account the perspectives and interests of the primary intended users of the evaluation. In either case, interactions with those who control entry into the field are primarily strategic, figuring out how to gain entry while preserving the integrity of the study and the investigator's interests. The degree of difficulty involved varies depending on the purpose of the fieldwork and the expected or real degree of resistance to the study. Where the field researcher expects cooperation, gaining entry may be largely a matter of establishing trust and rapport. At the other end of the continuum are those research settings where considerable resistance, even hostility, is expected, in which case gaining entry becomes a matter of "infiltrating the setting" (Douglas 1976:167). And sometimes entry is simply denied. A doctoral student had negotiations for entry end abruptly in a school district where she had developed good relationships with school personnel and negotiations appeared to be going well. She later learned that she was denied entry far into the negotiation process because of community opposition. The local community had had a very bad experience with a university researcher more than 20 years earlier and still viewed all research with great suspicion.

A major difference between the entry process in anthropological or sociological research and the entry process for evaluation research is the extent to which fieldworkers are free to make up whatever story they want to about the purpose of the study. In scholarly research, the investigators represent only themselves and so they are relatively free to say whatever they want to say about why they are doing the research guided by the ethics of their discipline with regard to informed consent. The usual cross-cultural explanation is some variation of "I'm here because I would like to understand you better and learn about your way of life because the people from my culture would like to know more about you." While anthropologists admit that such an explanation almost never makes sense to indigenous peoples in other cultures, it remains a mainstay initial explanation until mutual reciprocities can be established with enough local people for the observation process to become established and accepted in its own right.

Evaluators and action researchers, however, are not just doing fieldwork out of personal or professional interest. They are doing the fieldwork for some decision makers and information users who may be either known or unknown to the people being studied. It becomes critical, then, that evaluators, their funders, and evaluation users give careful thought to how the fieldwork is going to be presented.

Because the word *evaluation* has such negative connotations for many people, having had negative experiences being evaluated, for example, at school or work, it may be ap-propriate to consider some other term to describe the fieldwork. In our onlooker, nonparticipatory observations for an implementation study of early childhood programs in Minnesota, we described our role to local program participants and staff as follows:

> We're here to be the eyes and ears for state legislators. They can't get around and visit all the programs throughout the state, so they've asked us to come out and describe for them what you're doing. That way they can better understand the programs they have funded. We're not here to make any judgments about whether your particular programs is good or bad. We are just here to be the eyes and ears for the legislature so that they can see how the legislation they've passed has turned into real programs. This is your chance to inform them and give them your point of view.

Other settings lend themselves to other terms that are less threatening than *evaluator*. Sometimes a fieldwork project can be described as *documentation*. Another term I've heard used by community-based evaluators is *process historian*. In the wilderness education program I was a full participant observer, and staff described my role to participants as "keeper of the community record," making it clear that I was not there to evaluate individual participants. The staff of the project explained that they had asked me to join the project because they wanted someone who did not have direct ego involvement in the success or outcomes of the program to observe and describe what went on, both because they were too busy running the program to keep detailed notes about what occurred and because they were too involved with what happened to be able to look at things dispassionately. We had agreed from the beginning that the community record I produced would be accessible to participants as well as staff.

In none of these cases did changing the language automatically make the entry process smooth and easy. Earlier in this chapter, I described our attempt to be viewed as "educational researchers" in evaluating a community leadership program. Everyone figured out almost immediately that we were really evaluators— and that's what participants called us. Regardless of the story told or the terms used, the entry period of fieldwork is likely to remain "the first and most uncomfortable stage of field work" (Wax 1971:15). It is a time when the observer is getting used to the new setting, and the people in that setting are getting used to the observer. Johnson (1975) suggests that there are two reasons why the entry stage is both so important and so difficult:

> First, the achievement of successful entree is a precondition for doing the research. Put simply, no entree, no research. . . . [P]ublished reports of researchers' entree experiences describe seemingly unlimited contingencies which may be encountered, ranging from being gleefully accepted to being thrown out on one's ear. But there is a more subtle reason why the matter of one's entrance to a research setting is seen as so important. This concerns the relationship between the initial entree to the setting and the validity of the data that is subsequently collected. The conditions under which an initial entree is negotiated may have important consequences for how the research is socially defined by the members of the setting. These social definitions will have a bearing on the extent to which the members trust a social researcher, and the existence of relations of trust between an observer and the members of a setting is essential to the production of an objective report, one which retains the integrity of the actor's perspective and its social context. (pp 50-51)

While the observer must learn how to behave in the new setting, the people in that setting are deciding how to behave toward the observer. Mutual trust, respect, and cooperation are dependent on the emergence of an exchange relationship, or reciprocity (Jorgensen 1989:71; Gallucci and Perugini 2000), in which the observer obtains data and the people being observed find something that makes their cooperation worthwhile, whether that something is a feeling of importance from being observed, useful feedback, pleasure from interactions with the observer, or assistance in some task. This *reciprocity model* of gaining entry assumes that some reason can be found for participants to cooperate in the research and that some kind of mutual exchange can occur.

Infiltration lies at the opposite end of the continuum from a negotiated, reciprocity model of entry. Many field settings are not open to observation based on cooperation. Douglas (1976:167-71) has described a number of infiltration strategies, including "worming one's way in," "using the crowbar to pry them open for our observations," showing enough "saintly submissiveness" to make members guilty enough to provide help, or playing the role of a "spineless boob" who could never possibly hurt the people being observed. He has also suggested using various ploys of misdirection where the researcher diverts people's attention away from the real purpose of the study. There is also the "phased-entrée tactic" by which the researcher who is refused entrée to one group begins by studying another group until it becomes possible to get into the group that is the real focus of the researcher's attention, for example, begin by observing children in a school when what you really want to observe are teachers or administrators.

Often the best approach for gaining entrée is the "known sponsor approach."

When employing this tactic, observers use the legitimacy and credibility of another person to establish their own legitimacy and credibility, for example, the director of an organization for an organizational study, a local leader, elected official, or village chieftain for a community study. Of course, it's important to make sure that the known sponsor is indeed a source of legitimacy and credibility. Some prior assessment must be made of the extent to which that person can provide halo feelings that will be positive and helpful. For example, in an evaluation, using a program administrator or funders as a known sponsor may increase suspicion and distrust among program participants and staff.

The initial period of fieldwork can be frustrating and give rise to self-doubt. The fieldworker may lie awake at night worrying about some mistake, some faux pas, made during the day. There may be times of embarrassment, feeling foolish, of questioning the whole purpose of the project, and even feelings of paranoia. The fact that one is trained in social science does not mean that one is immune to all the normal pains of learning in new situations. On the other hand, the initial period of fieldwork can also be an exhilarating time, a period of rapid new learning, when the senses are heightened by exposure to new stimuli, and a time of testing one's social, intellectual, emotional, and physical capabilities. The entry stage of fieldwork magnifies both the joys and the pains of doing fieldwork.

Evaluators can reduce the "stick-out-like-a-sore-thumb syndrome" by beginning their observations and participation in a program at the same time that participants are beginning the program. In traditional fieldwork, anthropologists cannot become children again and experience the same socialization into the culture that children experience. Evaluators, however, can often ex-perience the same socialization process that regular participants experience by becoming part of the initiation process and timing their observations to coincide with the beginning of a program. Such timing makes the evaluator one among a number of novices and substantially reduces the disparity between the evaluator's knowledge and the knowledge of other participants.

Beginning the program with other participants, however, does not assure the evaluator of equal status. Some participants may be suspicious that real difficulties experienced by the evaluator as a novice participant are phony—that the evaluator is play-acting, only pretending to have difficulty. On the first day of my participation in the wilderness education program, we had our first backpacking experience. The staff leader began by explaining that "your backpack is your friend." I managed to both pack and adjust my "friend" incorrectly. As a result, as soon as we hit the trail, I found that the belt around my waist holding the backpack on my hips was so tight that my friend was making my legs fall asleep. I had to stop several times to adjust the pack. Because of these delays and other difficulties I was having with the weight and carriage of the pack, I ended up as the last participant along the trail. The next morning when the group was deciding who should carry the map and walk at the front of the group to learn map reading, one of the participants immediately volunteered my name. "Let Patton do it. That way he can't hang back at the end of the group to observe the rest of us." No amount of protest from me seemed to convince the participants that I had ended up behind them all because I was having trouble hiking (working out my "friendship" with my backpack). They were convinced I had taken that position as a strategic place from which to evaluate what was happening. It is well to remember, then, that regardless of the nature of the fieldwork, during the entry stage more than at any other time, the observer is also the observed.

What You Say and What You Do

Fieldworkers' actions speak louder than their words. Researchers necessarily plan strategies to present themselves and their function, but participant reactions to statements about the researcher's role are quickly superseded by judgments based on how the person actually behaves.

The relative importance of words versus deeds in establishing credibility is partly a function of the length of time the observer expects to be in a setting. For some direct onlooker observations, the fieldworker may be present in a particular program for only a few hours or a day. The entry problem in such cases is quite different from the situation where the observer expects to be participating in the program over some longer period of time, as anthropologist Rosalie Wax has noted:

> All field workers are concerned about explaining their presence and their work to a host of people. "How shall I introduce myself?" they wonder, or, "what shall I say I am doing?" If the field worker plans to do a very rapid and efficient survey, questions like these are extremely important. The manner in which an interviewer introduces himself, the precise words he uses, may mean the difference between a first-rate job and a failure.... But if the field worker expects to engage in some variety of participant observation, to develop and maintain long-term relationships, to do a study that involves the enlargement of his own understanding, the best thing he can do is relax and remember that most sensible people do not believe what a stranger tells them. In the long run, his host will judge and trust him, not because of what he says about himself or

> about his research, but by the style in which he lives and acts, by the way in which he treats them. In a somewhat shorter run, they will accept or tolerate him because some relative, friend, or person they respect has recommended him to them. (Wax 1971:365)

William Foote Whyte (1984:37-63) has extracted and summarized entry strategies used in a number of groundbreaking sociological studies, including the Lynds' study of Middletown, W. Lloyd Warner's study of Yankee City, Burleigh Gardner's fieldwork in the deep South, Elliot Liebow's hanging around Tally's Corner, Elijah Anderson's fieldwork in a Black neighborhood, Ruth Horowitz's study of a Chicano neighborhood, Robert Cole's work in Japan, and Whyte's own experiences in Cornerville. They each had to adapt their entry strategy to the local setting and they all ended up changing what they had planned to do as they learned from the initial responses to their efforts to gain acceptance. These examples from those who paved for way for modern fieldworkers demonstrate the importance of careful attention to entry and the variety of approaches that are possible. The next section presents a concrete example from an evaluation by Joyce Keller.

AN ENTRY CASE EXAMPLE: THE PART-TIME OBSERVER

Introduction. The previous section contrasted the entry challenges for the one-shot onlooker observer with those of the long-term participant observer, but a great deal of middle ground exists between these extremes. In this section, Joyce Keller, a senior staff member of the Minnesota Center for Social Research at the time, describes her entry into fieldwork as a part-time observer.[4] Because limitations of time and resources are common in evaluation, many situations call for a part-time observer. Joyce's reflections capture some of the special entry problems associated with this "now you're here, now you're gone" role.

One word can describe my role, at least initially, in a recent evaluation assignment: ambiguous. I was to be neither a participant observer nor an outsider coming in for a brief but intensive stint. I was to allocate approximately six hours a week for seven months to observing the team development of a group of 23 professionals in an educational setting. At first, the ambiguity was solely on my side: What, really, was I to do? The team, too busy in the beginning with defining their own roles, had little time to consider mine. Later on, as I became accustomed to my task, the team's curiosity about my function began to grow.

In their eyes, I served no useful purpose that they could see. I was in the way a great deal of the time inhibiting their private conversations. On the other hand, they appeared to be concerned about what I was thinking. Some of them—most of them—began to be friendly, to greet me as I came in, to comment when I missed a team meeting. They came to see me as I saw myself: neither really part of the group nor a separate, removed force.

Observing their interaction perhaps six hours a week out of their 40-hour work week obviously meant that I missed a great deal. I needed to develop a sense of when to be present, to choose among group meetings, subgroup meetings, and activities when all the members were to come together. At the same time, I was working on other contracts which limited the amount of adjustable time available. "Flexible" was the way I came to define my weekly schedule; others, not as charitable, would probably have defined it as "shifty."

A hazard that I encountered as I filled my ambiguous, flexible role was that I soon discovered I was not high on the priority list to be notified in the event of schedule changes. I would have firmly in mind that a subgroup was to meet on Tuesday at 10:00 a.m. in a certain place. I would arrive to find no one there. Later, I would discover that on Monday the meeting had been changed to Wednesday afternoon and no one had been delegated to tell me. At no time did I seriously feel that the changes were planned to exclude me; on the contrary, the members' contrition about their oversight seemed quite genuine. They had simply forgotten me.

Another area of sudden change that caused me difficulty was in policy and procedure. What had seemed to be firm commitments on ways to proceed or tasks to be tackled were being ignored. I came to realize that while a certain amount of this instability was inherent in the program itself, other shifts in direction were outgrowths of planning sessions I had not attended or had not heard the results from after they had occurred. Therefore, keeping current became for me a high-priority activity. Not to do so would have added to my feeling of ambiguity. Also, if I had not operated with a certain degree of self-confidence, I would have felt somehow at fault for coming to a meeting at the wrong time or place or assuming that a certain decision, which the team had previously made, was still valid.

I began my observation of this team in its formative stage. Had I begun after the team was well established, my difficulties would have been greater. Nevertheless, many of the team members were already well acquainted with each other; all had been employees of the same school district over a period of time. They were much better versed in what they had come together to accomplish than I, whose only orientation was reading the proposal which, upon acceptance, had brought them together. I found also that the proposal and the way they planned to proceed were, in actuality, far from identical.

With my observer role to continue over many months, I realized that I must maintain the difficult position of being impartial. I could not be thought of by the team members as being closely aligned with their leaders, nor could I expect the leaders to talk candidly and openly with me if they believed that I would repeat their confidences to the group members. Reluctantly, for I discovered several team members with whom friendships could easily have developed, I declined invitations to social activities outside of working hours.

When I met with the group for the first time, I directed most of my energies to matching names and faces. I would be taking notes at most of the sessions and it was essential that I could record not only what was said but who said it. At the first session everyone, including me, wore a name tag. But within a few days, they were all well acquainted and had discarded their name tags; I was the only one still fumbling for names. While being able to greet each member by name was important, so was knowing something about each one's background. Coffee breaks allowed me to circulate among the group and carry on short conversations with as many as possible to try to fix in my mind who they were and where they came from, which provided insights into why they behaved in the group as they did.

Team members at first expressed a certain amount of enthusiasm for minutes to be taken of their meetings. This enthusiasm was short-lived, for willing volunteers to serve as secretary did not emerge. I was disappointed, for, had minutes been kept of the meetings and had I been able to rely on receiving copies, I would have concentrated solely on observing the interactions and would not have had to keep track of what

they were interacting about. I noted (and ignored) a few passing suggestions that since I was obviously taking notes maybe I could. . . .

I took copious notes before I began to develop a sense of what was or was not important to record. When I relaxed more and aimed for the tone of the meeting my understanding of the group increased. I had to realize that, as a part-time observer, it was impossible for me to understand all of what was said. My decision frequently was to let this portion of the meeting pass or to jot down a reminder to myself to ask clarifying questions later.

Side-stepping sensitive questions from both leaders and team members had to be developed into a fine art. As I became more finely tuned to the interactions, and most became aware that I was, I was frequently queried as to my perceptions of a particular individual or situation. On one occasion, I found a team member jumping into an elevator to ride two floors with me in a direction he didn't want to go so that he could ask me privately what I thought of another team member. My response was, "I think she's a very interesting person," or something equally innocuous, and received from him a highly raised eyebrow, since the woman in question had just behaved in a very peculiar manner at the meeting we had both just attended.

In-depth interviews with each team member began in the fourth month of my observation and was the mechanism which filled in many of the gaps in my understanding. The timing was perfect: I had gained enough familiarity with both personnel and project by that time so that I was knowledgeable, they had come to trust me, and they still cared deeply about the project. (This caring diminished for some as the project year drew to a close without any real hopes of refunding for a second year.) My interview design was intentionally simple and open-ended. What I wanted most was for them to talk about their experiences in terms of strengths and weaknesses.

The amount of new information diminished throughout the six weeks or so that was required to interview all team members. My own performance unquestionably diminished too as the weeks went on. It was difficult to be animated and interesting as I asked the same questions over and over, devised strategies with which to probe, and recorded perceptions and incidents which I had heard many times before.

Nevertheless, the interviews appear in retrospect to have been a necessary tool of the part-time observer. Bit by bit team members filled in holes in my information and their repeated references to particular situations and conditions reinforced for me what were sometimes at best only vague perceptions. Team members who appeared to be passive and quiet when I saw them at group meetings were often referred to by their team members as hard-working and creative when they were out in the field. The interviews also helped me become aware of misconceptions on my part caused by seeing only part of the picture, due to time constraints.

The experience was a new one for me, that of part-time observer. Quite frankly, this mode of evaluation probably will never be a favorite one. On the other hand, it provided a picture that no "snap-shot" evaluation method could have accomplished as interactions changed over time and in a situation where the full participant observer role was clearly not appropriate.

Routinization of Fieldwork: The Dynamics of the Second Stage

What did you learn in your readings today?" asked Master Halcolm. "We learned that a journey of a thousand miles begins with the first step," replied the learners.

"Ah, yes, the importance of beginnings," smiled Halcolm.

"Yet, I am puzzled," said a learner. "Yesterday I read that there are a thousand beginnings for every ending."

"Ah, yes, the importance of seeing a thing through to the end," affirmed Halcolm.

"But which is more important, to begin or end?"

"Two great self-deceptions are asserted by the world's self-congratulators: that the hardest and most important step is the first and that the greatest and most resplendent step is the last.

"While every journey must have a first and last step, my experience is that what ultimately determines the nature and enduring value of the journey are the steps in between. Each step has its own value and importance. Be present for the whole journey, learners that you are. Be present for the whole journey."

—Halcolm

During the second stage, after the fieldworker has established a role and purpose, the focus moves to high-quality data gathering and opportunistic investigation following emergent possibilities and building on what is observed and learned each step along the way. The observer, no longer caught up in adjustments to the newness of the field setting, begins to really *see* what is going on instead of just looking around. As Florence Nightingale said, "Merely looking at the sick is not observing."

Describing the second stage as "routinization of fieldwork" probably overstates the case. In emergent designs and ever-deepening inquiry, the human tendency toward routines yields to the ups and downs of new discoveries, fresh insights, sudden doubts, and ever-present questioning of others—and often of self. Discipline is needed to maintain high-quality, up-to-date field notes. Openness and perseverance are needed to keep exploring, looking deeper, diverging broader, and focusing narrower, always going where the inquiry and data take you. Fieldwork is intellectually challenging at times, mind-numbingly dull at times, and for many, an emotional roller coaster. Appendix 9.1 at the end of Chapter 9, "A Documenter's Perspective," offers the reflections of a participant observer conducting a school evaluation and grappling with changes in fieldwork over time.

One of the things that can happen in the course of fieldwork is the emergence of a strong feeling of connection with the people being studied. As you come to understand the behaviors, ideals, anxieties, and feelings of other people, you may find yourself identifying with their lives, their hopes, and their pain. This sense of identification and connection can be a natural and logical consequence of having established relationships of rapport, trust, and mutuality. For me, that awakening identification involves some realization of how much I have in common with these people whose world I have been permitted to enter. At times during fieldwork I feel a great separation from the people I'm observing, then at other times I feel a strong sense of our common humanity. For a fieldworker to identify, however briefly, with the people in a setting or for an evaluator to identify with the clients in a program can be a startling experience because social science observers are often quite separated from those they study by education, experience, confidence, and income. Such differences sometimes make the world of programs as exotic to evaluators as nonliterate cultures are exotic to anthropologists.

There come times, then, when a fieldworker must deal with his or her own feelings about and perspectives on the people being observed. Part of the sorting-out process of fieldwork is establishing an understanding of the relationship between the observed and the observer. When that happens, and as it happens, the person involved in fieldwork may be no less startled than Joseph Conrad's infamous character Marlowe in *Heart of Darkness*. Marlowe had followed Kurtz, the European ivory trader, up the deep river into the Congo where Kurtz had established himself as a mangod to the tribal people there. He used his position to acquire ivory, but to maintain his position he had to perform the indigenous rituals of human sacrifice and cannibalism. Marlowe, deeply enmeshed in the racism of his culture and time, was initially horrified by the darkness of the jungle and its peoples, but as he watched the rituals of those seeming savages, he found an emergent identification with them and even entertained the suspicion that they were *not* inhuman. He became aware of a linkage between himself and them:

They howled and leaped and spun, and made horrid faces; but what thrilled you was the thought of their humanity—like ours—the thought of your remote kinship with this wild and passionate uproar. Ugly. Yes, it was ugly enough; but if you were man enough you would admit to yourself that there was in you just the faintest trace of a response to the terrible frankness of that noise, a dim suspicion of there being a meaning in it which you—you so remote from the night of the first ages—comprehend. And why not? (Conrad 1960:70)

In this passage, Conrad chronicles the possibility of awakening to unexpected realizations and intense emotions in the course of encounters with the unknown and those who are different from us. In many ways, it is our common humanity, whether we are fully aware of it at any given moment or not, that makes fieldwork possible. As human beings, we have the amazing capability to become part of other people's experiences, and through watching and reflecting, we can come to understand something about those experiences.

As fieldwork progresses, the intricate web of human relationships can entangle the participant observer in ways that will create tension between the desire to become more enmeshed in the setting so as to learn more and the need to preserve some distance and perspective. Participant observers carry no immunity to the political dynamics of the settings being observed. Virtually any setting is likely to include subgroups of people who may be in conflict with other subgroups. These factions or cliques may either woo or reject the participant observer, but they are seldom neutral. During her fieldwork interviewing young women in India, Parameswaran (2001) reports efforts by parents and teachers to get her to inform on the women she interviewed or to influence them in a desired direction. She found herself in the middle of deep generational divisions between mothers and their daughters, teachers and students, bookstore owners and their clients. She could not risk deeply alienating or completely acquiescing to any of these important and competing groups, for they all affected her access and the ultimate success of her fieldwork.

In evaluations, the evaluator can be caught in the middle of tensions between competing groups and conflicting perspectives. For example, where divisions exist among the staff and/or the participants in a program, and such divisions are common, the evaluator will be invited, often subtly, to align with one subgroup or the other. Indeed, the evaluator may want to become part of a particular subgroup to gain further insight into and understanding of that subgroup. How such an alliance occurs, and how it is interpreted by others, can greatly affect the course of the evaluation.

My experience suggests that it is impractical to expect to have the same kind of relationship—close or distant—with every group or faction. Fieldworkers, human beings with their own personalities and interests, will be naturally attracted to some people more than others. Indeed, to resist those attractions may hinder the observer from acting naturally and becoming more thoroughly integrated into the setting or program. Recognizing this, the observer will be faced with ongoing decisions about personal relationships, group involvement, and how to manage differential associations without losing perspective on what the experience is like for those with whom the fieldworker is less directly involved.

Perhaps the most basic division that will always be experienced in program evaluation is the separation of staff and participants. While the rhetoric of many programs attempts to reduce the distinction between staff and participants, there is almost always a distinction between those who are paid for their responsibilities in the program (staff) and those who are primarily recipients of what the program has to offer (participants). Sociologically, it makes sense that staff and participants would be differentiated, creating a distance that can evolve into conflict or distrust. Participants will often view the evaluator as no different from the staff or administration, or even the funding sources —virtually any group except the participants. If the evaluator observer is attempting to experience the program as a participant, special effort will be required make participation real and meaningful and to become accepted, even trusted, by other participants. On the other hand, staff and administrators may be suspicious of the evaluator's relationships with funders or board members.

The point is not to be naive about the tangled web of relationships the participant observer will experience and to be thoughtful about how fieldwork, data quality, and the overall inquiry are affected by these connections and interrelationships, all of which have to be negotiated.

Lofland (1971) has suggested that participant observers can reduce suspicion and fear about a study by becoming openly aligned with a single broad grouping within a setting while remaining aloof from that grouping's own internal disputes.

Thus, known observers of medical schools have aligned themselves only with the medical students, rather than attempting to participate extensively with both faculty and students. In mental hospitals, known observers have confined themselves largely to mental patients and restricted their participation with staff. To attempt to participate with both, extensively and simultaneously, would probably have generated suspicion about the ob-

servers among people on both sides of those fences. (pp. 96-97)

In contrast to Lofland's advice, in evaluating the wilderness education program I found myself moving back and forth between a full participant role, where I was identified primarily as a participant, and a full staff role, where I was identified primarily with those who carried responsibility for directing the program. During the first field conference, I took on the role of full participant and made as visible as possible my allegiance to fellow participants while maintaining distance from the staff. Over time, however, as my personal relationships with the staff increased, I became more and more aligned with the staff. This coincided with a change of emphasis in the evaluation itself, with the earlier part of the fieldwork being directed at describing the participant experience and the latter part of the fieldwork being aimed at describing the workings of the staff and providing formative feedback.

However, I was always aware of a tension, both within myself and within the group at large, about the extent to which I was a participant or a staff member. I found that as my observational skills became increasingly valued by the program staff I had to more consciously and actively resist their desire to have me take on a more active and explicit staff role. They also made occasional attempts to use me as an informer, trying to seduce me into conversations about particular participants. The ambiguities of my role were never fully resolved. I suspect that such ambiguities were inherent in the situation and are to be expected in many evaluation fieldwork experiences.

Managing field relationships involves a different set of dynamics when the inquiry is collaborative or participatory. Under such designs, where the researcher involves others in the setting in fieldwork, a great deal of the work consists of facilitating the interactions with co-inquirers, supporting their data collection efforts, ongoing training in observation and interviewing, managing integration of field notes among different participant researchers, and monitoring data quality and consistency. These collaborative management responsibilities will reduce the primary researcher's own time for fieldwork and will affect how others in the settings, those who aren't participatory or collaborative researchers, view the inquiry and the fieldwork director, if that is the role taken on. In some cases, management of the collaborative inquiry effort is done by one of the participants and the trained fieldworker serves primarily as a skills and process trainer and consultant to the group. Clarity about these roles and divisions of labor can make or break collaborative, participatory forms of inquiry. Having shared values about collaboration does not guarantee actually pulling it off. Collaborative inquiry is challenging work, often frustrating, but when it works, the findings will carry the additional credibility of collaborative triangulation, and the results tend to be rewarding for all involved, with enduring insights and new inquiry skills for those involved.

Key Informants

One of the mainstays of much fieldwork is the use of key informants as sources of information about what the observer has not or cannot experience, as well as sources of explanation for events the observer has actually witnessed. *Key informants* are people who are particularly knowledgeable about the inquiry setting and articulate about their knowledge—people whose insights can prove particularly useful in helping an observer understand what is happening and why. Selecting key informants must be done carefully to avoid arousing hostility or an-

tagonisms among those who may resent or distrust the special relationships between the fieldworker and the key informant. Indeed, how—and how much—to make visible this relationship involves strategic thinking about how others will react and how their reactions will affect the inquiry. There's no formal announcement that the "position" of key informant is open, or that it's been filled; the key informant is simply that person or those persons with whom the researcher or evaluator is likely to spend considerable time.

Key informants must be trained or developed in their role, not in a formal sense, but because they will be more valuable if they understand the purpose and focus of the inquiry, the issues and questions under investigation, and the kinds of information that are needed and most valuable. Anthropologists Pelto and Pelto (1978) made this point in reflecting on their own fieldwork:

> We noticed that humans differ in their willingness as well as their capabilities for verbally expressing cultural information. Consequently, the anthropologist usually finds that only a small number of individuals in any community are good key informants. Some of the capabilities of key informants are systematically developed by the field workers, as they train the informants to conceptualize cultural data in the frame of reference employed by anthropologists. . . . The key informant gradually learns the rules of behavior in a role vis-à-vis the interviewer-anthropologist. (p. 72)

The danger in cultivating and using key informants is that the researcher comes to rely on them too much and loses sight of the fact that their perspectives are necessarily limited, selective, and biased. Data from informants represent perceptions, not truths. Information obtained from key informants should be clearly specified as such in the field notes so that the researcher's observations and those of the informants do not become confounded. This may seem like an obvious point, and it is, but over weeks and months of fieldwork it can become difficult to decipher what information came from what sources unless the fieldworker has a routine system for documenting sources and uses that system with great discipline, thoroughness, and care.

Key informants can be particularly helpful in learning about subgroups to which the observer does not or cannot have direct access. During the second year of the wilderness education program, one informal group, mostly women, dubbed themselves the "turtles" to set themselves apart from participants, mostly men, who had more experience in the wilderness and wanted to hike at a fast pace, climb the highest peaks, or otherwise demonstrate their prowess—a group they called somewhat disparagingly the "truckers" (trucks being unwelcome in the wilderness). Having had a full year of wilderness experiences the first year of the program, I didn't qualify to become an intimate part of the turtles. I therefore established an informant relationship with one of

the turtles, who willingly kept me informed about the details of what went on in that group. Without that key informant relationship, I would have missed some very important information about the kinds of experiences the turtle participants were having and the significance of the project to them.

While being part of any setting necessarily involves personal choices about social relationships and political choices about group alliances, the emphasis on making strategic decisions in the field should not be interpreted as suggesting that the conduct of qualitative research in naturalistic settings is an ever-exciting game of chess in which players and pieces are manipulated to accomplish some ultimate goal. Fieldwork certainly involves times of both exhilaration and frustration, but the dominant motifs in fieldwork are hard work, long hours to both do observations and keep up-to-date with field notes, enormous discipline, attention to details, and concentration on the mundane and day-to-day. The routinization of fieldwork is a time of concentrated effort and immersion in gathering data. Alas, let the truth be told: **The gathering of field data involves very little glory and an abundance of nose-to-the-grindstone drudgery.**

Bringing Fieldwork to a Close

Well, I've gotten to the end of the subject—of the page—of your patience and my time.

—Alice B. Toklas in a letter to Elizabeth Hansen, 1949

In traditional scholarly fieldwork within anthropology and sociology, it can be difficult to predict how long fieldwork will last. The major determinant of the length of the fieldwork is the investigator's own resources, interests, and needs. Evaluation and action research typically have quite spe-

cific reporting deadlines, stated in a contract, that affect the length of and resources available for fieldwork, and the intended uses of evaluative findings.

In the previous section, we looked at the many complex relationships that get formed during fieldwork, relationships with key informants, hosts, and sponsors in the setting who helped with entrée and may have supported ongoing fieldwork, helping solve problems and smooth over difficulties. In collaborative research, relationships with coresearchers will have deepened. In any extended involvement within a setting, friendships and alliances are formed. As fieldwork comes to an end, an exit or disengagement strategy is needed. While a great deal of attention has traditionally been paid to entering the field, much less attention has been given to the disengagement process, what Snow (1980) has called the "neglected problem in participant observation research."

One side of the coin is disengagement. The other side is reentry back to one's life after extended fieldwork or an all-consuming project. When I went to do graduate research in Tanzania, our team received a lot of support and preparation for entry, much of it aimed at avoiding culture shock. But when we returned home, we were given no preparation for what it would be like to return to America's highly commercial, materialistic, and fast-moving culture after months in an agrarian, community-oriented, slower-moving environment. The culture shock hit coming home, not going to Africa.

Interpersonal, cross-cultural, disengagement, and reentry issues all deserve attention as fieldwork comes to a close. Relationships with people change and evolve from entry, through the middle days, and into the end of fieldwork. So does the fieldworker's relationship with the data and engagement in the inquiry process. That changed engagement in the inquiry process is what I want to focus on here.

As you near completion of data gathering, having become fairly knowledgeable about the setting being observed, more and more attention can be shifted to fine-tuning and confirming observed patterns. Possible interpretations of and explanations for what

was observed show up more in the field notes. Some of these explanations have been offered by others; some occur directly to the observer. In short, analysis and interpretation will have begun even before the observer has left the field.

Chapter 9 discusses analysis strategies at length. At this point, I simply want to recognize the fact that data gathering and analysis flow together in fieldwork, for there is usually no definite, fully anticipated point at which data collection stops and analysis begins. One process flows into the other. As the observer gains confidence in the quality and meaningfulness of the data, sophisticated about the setting under study, and aware that the end draws near, additional data collection becomes increasingly selective and strategic.

As fieldwork draws to a close, the researcher is increasingly concerned with *verification* of already-collected data and less concerned with generating new inquiry leads. While in naturalistic inquiry one avoids imposing preconceived analytical categories on the data, as fieldwork comes to an end, experience with the setting will usually have led to thinking about prominent themes and dimensions that organize what has been experienced and observed. These emergent ideas, themes, concepts, and dimensions—generated inductively through fieldwork—can also now be deepened, further examined, and verified during the closure period in the field.

Guba (1978) has described fieldwork as moving back and forth between the discovery mode and the verification mode like a wave. The ebb and flow of research involves moving in and out of periods when the investigator is open to new inputs, generative data, and opportunistic sampling to periods when the investigator is testing out hunches, fine-tuning conceptualization, sifting ideas, and verifying explanations.

When fieldwork has gone well the observer grows increasingly confident that things make sense and begins to believe in the data. Glaser and Strauss (1967), commenting on grounded theory as an outcome of fieldwork, have described the feelings that the traditional field observer has as fieldwork moves to a close, data-based patterns have emerged, and the whole takes shape:

> The continual intermeshing of data collection and analysis has direct bearing on how the research is brought to a close. When the researcher is convinced that his conceptual framework forms a systematic theory, that it is a reasonably accurate statement of the matter studied, that it is couched in a form possible for others to use in studying a similar area, and that he can publish his results with confidence, then he has neared the end of his research. . . .
>
> Why does the researcher trust what he knows? . . . They are his perceptions, his personal experiences, and his own hard-won analyses. A field worker knows that he knows, not only because he has been in the field and because he has carefully discovered and generated hypotheses, but also because "in his bones" he feels the worth of his final analysis. He has been living with partial analyses for many months, testing them each step of the way, until he has built this theory. What is more, if he has participated in the social life of is subject, then he has been living by his anal - yses, testing them not only by observation and interview but also by daily living. (pp. 224-25)

This representation of bringing a grounded theory inquiry to a close represents the scholarly inquiry ideal. In the "contracted deliverables" world of program evaluation, with limited time and resources, and reporting schedules that may not permit as much fieldwork as is desirable, the evalu-

ator may have to bring the fieldwork to a close before that state of real confidence has fully emerged. Nevertheless, I find that there is a kind of Parkinson's law in fieldwork: As time runs out, the investigator feels more and more the pressure of making sense out of things, and some form of order does indeed begin to emerge from the observations. This is a time to celebrate emergent understandings even while retaining the critical eye of the skeptic, especially useful in questioning one's own confident conclusions.

Evaluation Feedback

In doing fieldwork for program evaluation, in contrast to theory-oriented scholarly field research, the evaluator observer must be concerned about providing feedback, making judgments, and generating recommendations. Thus, as the fieldwork draws to a close, the evaluator observer must begin to consider what feedback is to be given to whom and how.

Giving feedback can be part of the verification process in fieldwork. My own preference is to provide the participants and staff with descriptions and analysis, verbally and informally, and to include their reactions as part of the data. Part of the reciprocity of fieldwork can be an agreement to provide participants with descriptive information about what has been observed. I find that participants and staff are hungry for such information and fascinated by it. I also find that I learn a great deal from their reactions to my descriptions and analyses. Of course, it's neither possible nor wise to report everything one has observed. Moreover, the informal feedback that occurs at or near the end of fieldwork will be different from the findings that are reported formally based on the more systematic and rigorous analysis that must go on once the evaluator leaves the field. But that formal, systematic analysis will take more time, so while one is still in the field it is possible to share at least some findings and to learn from the reactions of those who hear those findings.

Timing feedback in formative evaluations can be challenging. When the purpose is to offer recommendations to improve the program, the program staff will usually be anxious to get that information "ASAP" (as soon as possible). The evaluator observer may even feel pressured to report findings prematurely, before having confidence in the patterns that seem to be emerging. I experienced this problem throughout the evaluation of the wilderness education program. During the first year, we met with the staff at the end of each field conference program (the three 10-day field conferences were spread out over a year) to discuss what we had observed and to share interpretations about those observations. At the very first feedback session, the staff reaction was, "I wish you'd told us that in the middle of the week, when we could have done something about it. Why'd you hold back? We could have used what you've learned to change the program right then and there."

I tried to explain that the implications of what I observed had only become clear to me an hour or two before our meeting when my coevaluator and I had sat down with our field notes, looked them over, and discussed their significance together. Despite this explanation, which struck me as altogether reasonable and persuasive and struck the staff as altogether disingenuous, from that moment forth a lingering distrust hung over the evaluation as staff periodically joked about when we'd get around to telling them what we'd learned next time. Throughout the three years of the project, the issue of timing feedback surfaced several times a year. As they came increasingly to value our feedback, they wanted it to come earlier and ear-

lier during each field conference. During the second field conference in the second year, when a number of factors had combined to make the program quite different from what the staff had hoped for, the end-of-the-conference evaluation feedback session generated an unusual amount of frustration from the staff because my analyses of what had happened had not been shared earlier. Again, I found some distrust of my insistence that those interpretations had emerged later rather than sooner as the patterns became clear to me.

Evaluators who provide formative feedback on an ongoing basis need to be conscientious in resisting pressures to share findings and interpretations before they have confidence about what they have observed and sorted out important patterns—not certainty, but at least some degree of confidence. The evaluator is caught in a dilemma: Reporting patterns before they are clearly established may lead program staff to intervene inappropriately; withholding feedback too long may mean that dysfunctional patterns become so entrenched that they are difficult, if not impossible, to change.

No ideal balance has ever emerged for me between continuing observations and providing feedback. Timing feedback is a matter of judgment and strategy, and it depends on the nature of the evaluator's relationship with program staff and the nature of the feedback, especially the balance between what staff will perceive as negative and positive feedback. When in doubt, and where the relationship between the evaluator and program staff has not stabilized into one of long-term trust, I counsel evaluator observers to err on the side of less feedback rather than more. As often happens in social relationships, negative feedback that was wrong is long remembered and often recounted. On the other hand, it may be a measure of the success of the feedback that program staff so fully adopt it that they make it their own and cease to credit the insights of the evaluator.

Once feedback is given, the role of the evaluator changes. Those to whom the feedback was presented are likely to become much more conscious of how their behavior and language are being observed. Thus, added to the usual effect of the fieldworker on the setting being observed, this feedback dimension of fieldwork increases the impact of the evaluator observer on the setting in which he or she is involved.

Though this problem of reactivity is accentuated in evaluation, it exists in any observational inquiry. As the researcher prepares to leave the field, and people react to that imminent departure, the impact of the researcher's presence on the setting may become visible in new ways. Because those effects have been of such major concern to people who engage in naturalistic inquiry, the final section in this chapter considers this question of how the observer affects what is observed.

🔄 The Observer and What Is Observed: Unity and Separation

The question of how the observer affects what is observed has natural as well as social science dimensions. The Heisenberg uncertainty principle states that the instruments used to measure velocity and position of an electron alter the accuracy of measurement. When the scientist measures the position of an electron, its velocity is changed, and when velocity is measured, it becomes difficult to capture precisely the electron's position. The process of observing affects what is observed. These are real effects, not just errors of perception or mea-

surement. The physical world can be altered by the intrusion of the observer. How much more, then, are social worlds changed by the intrusion of fieldworkers?

The effects of observation vary depending on the nature of the observation, the type of setting being studied, the personality and procedures of the observer, and a host of unanticipated conditions. Nor is it simply in fieldwork involving naturalistic inquiry that scientific observers affect what is observed. Experimentalists, survey researchers, cost-benefit analysts, and psychologists who administer standardized tests all affect the situations into which they introduce data collection procedures. The issue is not whether or not such effects occur; rather, the issue is how to monitor those effects and take them into consideration when interpreting data.

A strength of naturalistic inquiry is that the observer is sufficiently a part of the situation to be able to understand personally what is happening. Fieldworkers are called on to inquire into and be reflective about how their inquiry intrudes and how those intrusions affect findings. But that's not always easy. Consider the case of anthropologist Napoleon Chagnon, who did fieldwork for a quarter century among the isolated and primitive Yanomami Indians who lived deep in the rain forest at the borders of Venezuela and Brazil. He studied mortality rates by dispensing steel goods, including axes, as a way of persuading people to give him the names of their dead relatives in violation of tribal taboos. Brian Ferguson, another anthropologist knowledgeable about the Yanomami, believes that Chagnon's fieldwork destabilized relationships among villages, promoted warfare, and introduced disease. Chagon denies these charges but acknowledges extracting tribal secrets by giving informants gifts like beads and fishhooks, capitalizing on animosities between individuals, and bribing children for information when their elders were not around. He gave away machetes in exchange for blood samples for his genealogical studies. The long-term effects of his fieldwork have become a matter of spirited debate and controversy within anthropology (Geertz 2001; Tierney 2000a, 2000b).

At the other end of the intrusion continuum we find those qualitative designs where "intrusions" are intentionally designed because the qualitative inquiry is framed as an intended form of desired intervention. This is the case, for example, with collaborative and participatory forms of inquiry in which those people in the setting who become coresearchers are expected to be affected by participation in the inquiry. The processes of participation and collaboration can be designed and facilitated to have an impact on participants and collaborators quite beyond whatever findings they may generate by working together. In the process of participating in an evaluation, participants are exposed to and have the opportunity to learn the logic of research and the discipline of data-based reasoning. Skills are acquired in problem identification, criteria specification, and data collection, analysis, and interpretation. Acquisition of research skills and ways of thinking can have a longer-term impact than the use of findings from a particular evaluation study. This "learning from the process" as an outcome of participatory and collaborative inquiry experiences is called *process use* in contrast to findings use (Patton 1997a: Chapter 5, 1998, 1999c).

While it is not possible to know precisely how collaboration will affect coresearchers or to fully anticipate how an observer will affect the setting observer, both cases illustrate the need to be thoughtful about the interconnections between observers and observed. It is possible, however, when designing the study and making decisions about the observer's degree of participation in the setting, the visibility and openness of fieldwork, and the duration of fieldwork (see Exhibit 6.1 earlier in this chapter) to anticipate certain of the situations that may arise and to establish strategies for how those situations will be handled. For example, I have been involved as a participant observer- evaluator in a number of professional development programs where participants were expected to exercise increasing control over the curriculum as the program evolved. Had I fully participated in such participatory decision making, I could have influenced the direction of the program. Anticipating that problem and reviewing the implications with program staff, in each case I decided not to participate actively in participant-led decision making to the full extent I might have had I not been involved in the role of evaluator observer. The participatory and empowering philosophy of these programs called for each participant to articulate interests and help make happen those things that he or she wanted to have happen. In my role as evaluator observer, I had to reduce the extent to which I acted out that philosophy so as to limit my impact on the direction of the group. I aimed my involvement at a level where I would not appear withdrawn from the process, yet at the same time attempted to minimize my influence, especially where the group was divided on priorities.

Another example comes from evaluation of a community leadership program mentioned previously in this chapter. As a three-person team of participant observers, we participated fully in small-group leadership exercises. When the groups in which we participated were using concepts inappropriately or doing the exercise wrong, we went along with what participants said and did without making corrections. Had we really been *only* participants—and not participant evaluators—we would have offered corrections and solutions. Thus, our roles made us more passive than we tended naturally to be in order not to dominate the small groups. We had anticipated this possibility in the design stage prior to fieldwork and had agreed on this strategy at that time.

The role and impact of the evaluator observer can change over the course of fieldwork. Early in the wilderness program, I kept a low profile during participant-led planning discussions. Later in the program, particularly during the final field conference of the second year, I became more engaged in discussions about the future direction of the project.

Reporting on the relationship between the observer and the observed, then, and the ways in which the observer may have affected the phenomenon observed becomes part of the methodological discussion in published fieldwork reports and evaluation studies. In that methodological discussion (or the methods chapter of a dissertation), the observer presents data about the effects of fieldwork on the setting and people therein and also the observer's perspective on what has occurred. As Patricia Carini (1975) has explained, such a discussion acknowledges that findings inevitably are influenced by the observer's point of view during naturalistic inquiry:

> The observer has a point of view that is central to the datum and it is in the articulation—in the revelation of his point of view—that the datum of inquiry is assumed to emerge. In effect the observer is here construed as one moment of the datum and as such the fabric of his thought is inextricably woven into the datum as he is assumed to be constituent of its meaning. From this assumption it is possible to consider the relationship of the observer to the phenomenon under inquiry. Relatedness can be stated in many ways: opposition, identity, proximity, interpenetration, isolation, to name

only a few. All imply that the way in which a person construes his relationship to the phenomenal world is a function of his *point of view* about it. That is, relationship is not a given nor an absolute, but depends upon a personal perspective. It is also true that perspective can shift, the only necessity of a person's humanity being that he takes some stance in relationship to the events about him. (pp. 8-9)

Carini is here articulating the interdependence between the observer and what is observed. Prior to data collection, the fieldworker plans and strategizes about the hoped-for and expected nature of that interdependence. But things don't always unfold as planned, so observers must make some effort to observe themselves observing—and record the effects of their observations on the people observed and, no less important, reflect on changes they've experienced from having been in the setting. This means being able to balance observation with reflection and manage the tension between engagement and detachment.

Bruyn (1966), in his classic work on participant observation, articulated a basic premise of participant observation: the "role of the participant observer requires both detachment and personal involvement" (p. 14). To be sure, there is both tension and ambiguity in this premise. How it plays out in any given situation will depend on both the observer and the phenomenon being observed.

> Thus, we may observe at the outset that while the traditional role of the scientist is that of a neutral observer who remains unmoved, unchanged, and untouched in his examination of phenomena, the role of the participant observer requires sharing the sentiments of people in social situations; as a consequence he himself is changed as well as changing to some degree the situation in which he is a partici-

pant.... The effects are reciprocal for observer and observed. The participant observer seeks, on the one hand, to take advantage of the changes due to his presence in the group by recording these changes as part of his study, and on the other hand, to reduce the changes to a minimum by the manner in which he enters into the life of the group. (Bruyn 1966:14)

Whether one is engaged in participant observation or onlooker observation, what happens in the setting being observed will, to some extent, be dependent on the role assumed by the observer. Likewise, the nature of the data collected will, to some extent, be dependent on the role and perspective of the observer. And just as the presence of the observer can affect people observed, so too the observer can be affected.

The Personal Experience of Fieldwork

The intersection of social science procedures with individual capabilities and situational variation is what makes fieldwork a highly personal experience. At the end of her book *Doing Fieldwork*, Rosalie Wax (1971) reflected on how fieldwork changed her:

A colleague has suggested that I reflect on the extent to which I was changed as a person by doing field work. I reflected and the result astonished me. For what I realized was that I had not been greatly changed by the things I suffered, enjoyed or endured; nor was I greatly changed by the things I did (though they strengthened my confidence in myself). What changed me irrevocably and beyond repair were the things *learned*. More specifically, these irrevocable changes involved replacing mythical or ideological assumptions with the correct (though often painful) facts of the situation. (p. 363)

Fieldwork is not for everyone. Some, like Henry James, will find that "innocent and infinite are the pleasures of observation." Others will find observational research anything but pleasurable. Some students have described their experiences to me as tedious, frightening, boring, and "a waste of time," while others have experienced challenge, exhilaration, personal learning, and intellectual insight. More than once the same student has experienced both the tedium and the exhilaration, the fright and the growth, the boredom and the insight. Whatever the adjectives used to describe any particular individual's fieldwork, of this much we are assured: The experience of observing provides the observer with both experience and observations, the interconnection being cemented by reflection. No less an authority than William Shakespeare gives us this assurance.

Armado: "How hast thou purchased this experience?"

Moth: "By my penny of observation."

—*Love's Labour's Lost*

A Part of and Apart From the World Observed

The personal, perspective-dependent nature of observations can be understood as both a strength and a weakness, a strength in that personal involvement permits firsthand experience and understanding, and a weakness in that personal involvement introduces selective perception. In the deep engagement of naturalistic inquiry lies both its risks and its benefits. Reflection on that engagement, from inside and outside the phenomenon of interest, crowns fieldwork with reflexivity and makes the observer the

CHANCE DISCOVERY OR THE RESULT OF CAREFUL, DISCIPLINED OBSERVATION?

In 1949, an obscure Australian psychiatrist, John F. J. Cade, noticed that the urine of his manic patients was highly toxic to guinea pigs, and he began looking for the toxic chemical, which he suspected was uric acid.

> *He began experimenting with lithium urate, not because of any psychiatric properties of lithium, but because lithium urate was the most soluble salt of uric acid. To Cade's surprise, far from being toxic, the salt protected guinea pigs against the urine of manics, and it also sedated the animals, effects Cade found were due to the lithium. He immediately tried other lithium salts on himself and, when they proved safe, on ten hospitalized manic patients, all of whom recovered, some almost miraculously.*
>
> > *Cade's discovery is often characterized as serendipitous.... [However], the discovery of lithium as an antimanic agent resulted from one man's curiosity and powers of observation and deduction. (Kramer 1993:44)*

observed—even if only by oneself. So we repeat Halcolm's refrain that opened this chapter:

> Go out into the world. Live among the peoples of the world as they live. Learn their language. Participate in their rituals and routines. Taste of the world. Smell it. Watch and listen. Touch and be touched. Write down what you see and hear, how they think and how you feel.
>
> Enter into the world. Observe and wonder. Experience and reflect. To understand a world you must become part of that world while at the same time remaining separate, a part of and apart from.
>
> Go then, and return to tell what you see and hear, what you learn, and what you come to understand.

⑤ Summary Guidelines for Fieldwork

A reader who came to this chapter looking for specific fieldwork rules and clear procedures would surely be disappointed. Looking back over this chapter, the major theme seems to be, **What you do depends on the situation, the nature of the inquiry,** **the characteristics of the setting, and the skills, interests, needs, and point of view that you, as observer, bring to your engagement.** Yet, the conduct of observational research is not without direction. Exhibit 6.6 offers a modest list of 10 guidelines for fieldwork (not, please notice, commandments, just guidelines) by way of reviewing some of the major issues discussed in this chapter. Beyond these seemingly simple but deceptively complex prescriptions, the point remains that what you do depends on a great number of situational variables, your own capabilities, and careful judgment informed by the strategic themes for qualitative inquiry presented in the first chapter (Exhibit 2.1).

Having considered the guidelines and strategic themes for naturalistic field-based research, and after the situational constraints on and variations in the conduct of fieldwork have been properly recognized and taken into account in the design, there remains only the core commitment of qualitative inquiry to reaffirm. That core commitment was articulated by Nobel laureate Nicholas Tinbergen in his 1975 acceptance speech for the Nobel Prize in physiology

---

EXHIBIT 6.6   Summary Guidelines for Fieldwork

---

1. Design the fieldwork to be clear about the role of the observer (degree of participation); the tension between insider (emic) and outsider (etic) perspectives; degree and nature of collaboration with coresearchers; disclosure and explanation of the observer's role to others; duration of observations (short vs. long); and focus of observation (narrow vs. broad). (See Exhibit 6.1.)

2. Be descriptive in taking field notes. Strive for thick, deep, and rich description.

3. Stay open. Gather a variety of information from different perspectives. Be opportunistic in following leads and sampling purposefully to deepen understanding. Allow the design to emerge flexibly as new understandings open up new paths of inquiry.

4. Cross-validate and triangulate by gathering different kinds of data: observations, interviews, documents, artifacts, recordings, and photographs. Use multiple and mixed methods.

5. Use quotations; represent people in their own terms. Capture participants' views of their experiences in their own words.

6. Select key informants wisely and use them carefully. Draw on the wisdom of their informed perspectives, but keep in mind that their perspectives are selective.

7. Be aware of and strategic about the different stages of fieldwork.
   a. Build trust and rapport at the entry stage. Remember that the observer is also being observed and evaluated.
   b. Attend to relationships throughout fieldwork and the ways in which relationships change over the course of fieldwork, including relationships with hosts, sponsors within the setting, and coresearchers in collaborative and participatory research.
   c. Stay alert and disciplined during the more routine, middle phase of fieldwork.
   d. Focus on pulling together a useful synthesis as fieldwork draws to a close. Move from generating possibilities to verifying emergent patterns and confirming themes.
   e. Be disciplined and conscientious in taking detailed field notes at all stages of fieldwork.
   f. In evaluations and action research, provide formative feedback as part of the verification process of fieldwork. Time that feedback carefully. Observe its impact.

8. Be as involved as possible in experiencing the setting as fully as is appropriate and manageable while maintaining an analytical perspective grounded in the purpose of the fieldwork.

9. Separate description from interpretation and judgment.

10. Be reflective and reflexive. Include in your field notes and reports your own experiences, thoughts, and feelings. Consider and report how your observations may have affected the observed as well as how you may have been affected by what and how you've participated and observed. Ponder and report the origins and implications of your own perspective.

Constructivist _Rashomon_ heaven: Multiple and diverse perspectives

and medicine: _"watching_ and _wondering."_ Tinbergen explained that it was by watching and wondering that he had, despite being neither a physiologist nor a medical doctor, discovered what turned out to be a major breakthrough in our understanding of autism. His observations revealed that the major clinical research on autism did not hold up outside clinical settings. His "watching and wondering" allowed him to see that normal individuals, those not clinically labeled as autistic, exhibited under a variety of circumstances all of the behaviors described as autistic in clinical research. He also noted that children diagnosed as autistic responded in nonautistic ways outside the clinical setting. By observing people in a variety of settings and watching a full range of behaviors, he was able to make a major medical and scientific contribution. His research methodology: "watching and wondering."

🔲 Notes

1. Excerpt from "Little Gidding" in the _Four Quartets_ by T. S. Eliot. Copyright 1942 by T. S. Eliot; renewed 1970 by Esme Valerie Eliot. Reprinted by permission of Harcourt, Inc.

2. Excerpt from "The Elephant's Child," from _Just So Stories,_ by Rudyard Kipling. Used by permission of A. P. Watt Ltd. on behalf of The National Trust for Places of Historical Interest or Natural Beauty. Original publication 1902.

3. From _Traveling Light: Collected and New Poems._ Copyright © 1999 by David Wagoner. Used with permission of the University of Illinois Press.

4. Used with permission of Joyce Keller.

Between-Chapters Interlude

Outside to Inside, Inside to Outside

Shifting Perspectives

Preface

The preceding chapter on fieldwork included discussion of insider (emic) versus outsider (etic) perspectives. Understanding different perspectives from inside and outside a phenomenon goes to the core of qualitative inquiry. Experience affects perspective. Perspective shapes experience. In the next chapter, on interviewing, we shall continue to explore ways of capturing the experiences and getting deeply into the perspectives of those who have encountered whatever phenomenon interests us.

The reflections that follow look at the experience of mental illness from the inside and outside, and how being on the inside can dramatically change the view from the outside. Barbara Lee moved from the outside (Ph.D. researcher and mental health professional) to the inside as an involuntary participant observer (a patient in a locked mental health facility) and back again to the outside (as a professional pro-

gram evaluator). She recounts those transitions from outside to inside, and inside to outside, and how they have shaped her perspective on research and evaluation. Her reflections provide a poignant and insightful transition from our discussion of participant observation in the last chapter to interviewing strategies in the next chapter, both methods aimed at bridging insider-outsider perspectives. Barbara Lee generously wrote these reflections especially for this book. I thank Barbara for her openness, courage, commitment, and insights.

🖵 "Nothing About Us, Without Us"

I was a high school and junior high school science teacher, a school psychologist and guidance counselor, and finally an educational researcher, before I completed my Ph.D. (on the second try!). I had specifically sought that degree in my mid-40s to get evaluation and research skills, which I accomplished nicely at St. Louis University, in one of the few programs in the 1980s designed to train graduate students in evaluation theory and methodology.

Since I had been a scientist of some sort for all of my career life, I was a "natural" for the field of evaluation. I thought like a scientist. I was familiar with the practice of research in biology, bacteriology, and field botany and had a special interest in medicine. But through some quirks of fate and personality, I found myself working as a clinician, providing therapy and case management to people with severe mental disorders. Then, after having been gainfully employed my entire adult life, and successfully raising two children who had now produced one grandchild each, I was forced into the locked, psychiatric ward of a hospital for the third time in my life.

Back at work, after nearly two months in the hospital, I found myself, for the first time, looking at my professional work and reading professional literature with the eyes of one from the other side of the locked doors and medical charts.

The irony of my situation was obvious: I treated people like me! Thus began a shift of viewpoint that has radically altered my practice of evaluation in the field of mental health.

First, I had to throw out some grand assumptions. As a scientist, I trusted scientific method and worshipped at the same shrine of true experimental design and random assignment as everyone else. But now I was much more conscious that the "lab rats," the subjects of our research, literally have minds of their own. Some of the most treasured assumptions of mental health research were looking awfully different from inside the maze. Probably the most serious is that what I had assumed to be "treatment" from the viewpoint of the researcher now looked like mostly futile efforts that were most often experienced as punishment and threat from the viewpoint of "patient." I was not asked if I would go into the hospital. I was told I had to. If I got angry at something, someone gave me powerful medications that made me feel like a zombie.

While some of what happened in my hospitalization helped, much of what I experienced made me feel much worse. I was incarcerated and my jailers looked at me kindly, certain that I was being locked up, strapped to a bed, and injected with medications for my own good. Even though I actually entered the hospital "voluntarily," the threat of involuntary treatment and permanent damage to my ability to earn a living was the driving force that got me there, and kept me there, and taught me to "make nice" for the staff, lest they refuse to certify me sane and let me be free again.

As a human services program evaluator, I learned to do needs assessments, to use proven treatment methods in a package deal called a program, to gather data of various kinds—sometimes even from the people who were getting the program. I learned how to interpret the data gathered in the environmental context in which the program operated and how to get and report reliable and credible information to those who make decisions about programs. Sometimes, I admit, I even offered my own "expert" judgment about the value of the program. Now a whole new set of questions confronted me as a professional.

What can distort the perceptions of those I ask about "needs" and how much is the distortion? The providers believe they have the well-being of the clients at heart, but the clients may experience the treatments as more disabling than the symptoms of the disease. Clients are taught to mistrust their own symptom-distorted thoughts and are flatly ignored when psychotic, yet virtually all of them can make reasoned decisions if they have adequate information and are asked. It seems to be assumed that a psychiatric label defines the "needs" of people with severe mental illness. But other needs may be a consequence of a stingy health care system that won't provide necessary and expensive medications unless you are completely disabled, and social stigma makes it nearly impossible to get a good job with benefits after psychiatric hospitalizations. A clinician who admits to having a psychiatric label of severe mental illness will never be hired, so it can be survival as well as denial to deny even to oneself that one is one of "those crazies."

Providers are taught, in all sincerity and good intentions, to act in a kind of parental role toward clients, a benign dictatorship. But their "subjects" are people who have already had their dignity as adults medically removed, their privacy invaded, and the job and relationship underpinnings of American self-esteem destroyed; been told they will be sick for life; and been medicated so they cannot perform sexually or sometimes even read a good book. Is it any wonder that many of them (us) will accept survival as an adequate "quality of life"?

What are the limits of (a) theory about what the "problem" is; (b) the kinds, relevance, and quality of data collected in the past; and (c) the stakeholders' (mentally ill people) freedom to express themselves? Evaluation designs that test the effects of treatment programs on the individual don't address the problem of living in a neighborhood where life is stressful and taxis won't take you home after dark, and where the threatening voices might just as likely be real as hallucinated. The provider who is confined to the office and distance of a professional relationship will not know when there is abuse in the home the client never speaks of, because the abuser is someone they love or who controls their money as payee. Mental health workers are put in the role of defenders of the public purse, and then we wonder why clients feel their safety net of services threatened with every dollar they are given or earn and fail to trust their "providers."

In short, I may apply many of the same ideas, theories, methods, and interpretations as I always did as a program evaluator. But now I always question, not just the validity, reliability, and generalizability of the evaluation work itself but also the hidden assumptions that surround it. I will always be seeking to empower those disenfranchised by custom, poverty, and stigma. Furthermore, I will always be conscious of the fact that my work is always limited—and empowered—by the selection of data and methods to be used. But if I want to be part of the solution rather than part of the problem, I better be sure I know what the experience of different stakeholders really is, not constrained by the limited questions I may think to ask, or guided too narrowly by work done in the past.

As an evaluator, I now try to approach my task with equal measures of chutzpah and humility so that I will not fail to challenge all the assumptions, especially my own, nor ever assume that I have all of the questions, much less the answers, right. I have adopted the motto of the people who do not claim the title of "consumer," because they were not given true choice about treatment when they found themselves pinned with psychiatric labels: *"Nothing about us, without us."*

When was the last time you saw the clients who are the intended target of the program, sitting at the table with the evaluators and program providers, freely exchanging perspectives and ideas? For those who can answer truthfully, "Just last week, or last month": Thank you!

—Barbara Lee, Ph.D., prosumer and mental health program evaluator

7

Qualitative Interviewing

After much cloistered study, three youths came before Halcolm to ask how they might further increase their knowledge and wisdom. Halcolm sensed that they lacked experience in the real world, but he wanted to have them make the transition from seclusion in stages.

During the first stage he sent them forth under a six-month vow of silence. They wore the identifying garments of the muted truth-seekers so that people would know they were forbidden to speak. Each day, according to their instructions, they sat at the market in whatever village they entered, watching but never speaking. After six months in this fashion they returned to Halcolm.

"So," Halcolm began, "you have returned. Your period of silence is over. Your transition to the world beyond our walls of study has begun. What have you learned so far?"

The first youth answered, "In every village the patterns are the same. People come to the market. They buy the goods they need, talk with friends, and leave. I have learned that all markets are alike and the people in markets always the same."

Then the second youth reported, "I too watched the people come and go in the markets. I have learned that all life is coming and going, people forever moving to and fro in search of food and basic material things. I understand now the simplicity of human life."

Halcolm looked at the third youth: "And what have you learned?"

"I saw the same markets and the same people as my fellow travelers, yet I know not what they know. My mind is filled with questions. Where did the people come from? What were they thinking and feeling as they came and went? How did they happen to be at this market on this day? Who did they leave behind? How was today the same or different for them? I have failed, Master, for I am filled with questions rather than answers, questions for the people I saw. I do not know what I have learned."

Halcolm smiled. "You have learned most of all. You have learned the importance of finding out what people have to say about their experiences. You are ready now to return to the world, this time without the vow of silence.

"Go forth now and question. Ask and listen. The world is just beginning to open up to you. Each person you question can take you into a new part of the world. The skilled questioner and attentive listener know how to enter into another's experience. If you ask and listen, the world will always be new."

—From Halcolm's *Epistemological Parables*

Rigorous and Skillful Interviewing

The very popularity of interviewing may be its undoing as an inquiry method. In the contemporary "interview society" (Fontana and Frey 2000:646), so much interviewing is being done so badly that its credibility may be undermined. Television, radio, magazines, newsletters, and Web sites feature interviews. In their ubiquity, interviews done by social scientists become indistinguishable in the popular mind from interviews done by talk show hosts. The motivations of social scientists have become suspect, as have our methods. The popular business magazine *Forbes* (self-proclaimed "The Capitalist Tool") has opined, "People become sociologists because they hate society, and they become psychologists because they hate themselves" (quoted in Geertz 2001:19). Such glib sarcasm, anti-intellectual at the core, can serve to remind us that we bear the burden of demonstrating that our methods involve rigor and skill. Interviewing, seemingly straightforward, easy, and universal, can be done well or poorly. This chapter is about doing it well.

Inner Perspectives

Interviewing is rather like a marriage: everybody knows what it is, an awful lot of people do it, and yet behind each closed door there is a world of secrets.

—A. Oakley (1981:41)

We interview people to find out from them those things we cannot directly observe. The issue is not whether observational data are more desirable, valid, or meaningful than self-report data. The fact is that we cannot observe everything. We cannot observe feelings, thoughts, and intentions. We cannot observe behaviors that took place at some previous point in time. We cannot observe situations that preclude the presence of an observer. We cannot observe how people have organized the world and the meanings they attach to what goes on in the world. We have to ask people questions about those things.

The purpose of interviewing, then, is to allow us to enter into the other person's perspective. Qualitative interviewing begins with the assumption that the perspective of others is meaningful, knowable, and able to be made explicit. We interview to find out what is in and on someone else's mind, to gather their stories.

Program evaluation interviews, for example, aim to capture the perspectives of program participants, staff, and others associated with the program. What does the program look and feel like to the people involved? What are their experiences in the program? What thoughts do people knowledgeable about the program have concerning program operations, processes, and outcomes? What are their expectations? What changes do participants perceive in themselves as a result of their involvement in the program? It is the responsibility of the evaluator to provide a framework within which people can respond comfortably, accurately, and honestly to these kinds of questions.

Evaluators can enhance the use of qualitative data by generating relevant and high-quality findings. As Hermann Sudermann said in *Es Lebe das Leben I*, "I know how to listen when clever men are talking. That is the secret of what you call my influence." Evaluators must learn how to listen when knowledgeable people are talking. That may be the secret of their influence.

An evaluator, or any interviewer, faces the challenge of making it possible for the person being interviewed to bring the interviewer into his or her world. **The quality of the information obtained during an interview is largely dependent on the interviewer.** This chapter discusses ways of obtaining high-quality information by talking with people who have that information. We'll be delving into "the art of hearing" (Rubin and Rubin 1995).

This chapter begins by discussing three different types of interviews. Later sections consider the content of interviews: what questions to ask and how to phrase questions. The chapter ends with a discussion of how to record the responses obtained during interviews. This chapter emphasizes skill and technique as ways of enhancing the quality of interview data, but no less important is a genuine interest in and caring about the perspectives of other people. If what people have to say about their world is generally boring to you, then you will never be a great interviewer. Unless you are fascinated by the rich variation in human experience, qualitative interviewing will become drudgery. On the other hand, a deep and genuine interest in learning about people is insufficient without disciplined and rigorous inquiry based on skill and technique.

🖫 Variations in Qualitative Interviewing

*O*n her deathbed Gertrude Stein asked her beloved companion, Alice B. Toklas, "What is the answer?" When Alice, unable to speak, remained silent, Gertrude asked: "In that case, what is the question?"

The question in this section is how to format questions. There are three basic approaches to collecting qualitative data through open-ended interviews. They involve different types of preparation, conceptualization, and instrumentation. Each approach has strengths and weaknesses, and each serves a somewhat different purpose. The three alternatives are

- the informal conversational interview,
- the general interview guide approach, and
- the standardized open-ended interview.

These three approaches to the design of the interview differ in the extent to which interview questions are determined and standardized *before* the interview occurs.

The *informal conversational interview* relies entirely on the spontaneous generation of questions in the natural flow of an interaction, often as part of ongoing participant observation fieldwork. The persons being talked with may not even realize they are being interviewed. The *general interview guide approach* involves outlining a set of issues that are to be explored with each respondent before interviewing begins. The guide serves as a basic checklist during the interview to make sure that all relevant topics are covered. In contrast, the *standardized open-ended interview* consists of a set of questions carefully worded and arranged with the intention of taking each respondent through the same sequence and asking each respondent the same questions with essentially the same words. Flexibility in probing is more or less limited, depending on the nature of the interview and the skills of interviewers. The standardized open-ended interview is used when it is important to minimize variation in the questions posed to interviewees. Let's look at each approach in greater depth for each serves a different purpose and poses quite varying interviewer challenges.

The Informal Conversational Interview

The informal conversational interview is the most open-ended approach to interviewing. It is also called "unstructured interviewing" (Fontana and Frey 2000:652). The conversational interview offers maximum flexibility to pursue information in whatever direction appears to be appropriate, depending on what emerges from observing a particular setting or from talking with one or more individuals in that setting. Most of the questions will flow from the immediate context. Thus, the conversational interview constitutes a major tool of fieldwork and is sometimes referred to as "ethnographic interviewing." No predetermined set of questions would be appropriate under many emergent field circumstances where the fieldworker doesn't know beforehand what is going to happen, who will be present, or what will be important to ask during an event, incident, or experience.

Data gathered from informal conversational interviews will be different for each person interviewed. The same person may be interviewed on different occasions with questions specific to the interaction or event at hand. Previous responses can be revisited and deepened. This approach works particularly well where the researcher can stay in the setting for some period of time so as not to be dependent on a single interview opportunity. Interview questions will change over time, and each new interview builds on those already done, expanding information that was picked up previously, moving in new directions, and seeking elucidations and elaborations from various participants.

Being unstructured doesn't mean that conversational interviews are unfocused. Sensitizing concepts and the overall purpose of the inquiry inform the interviewing. But within that overall guiding purpose, the interviewer is free to go where the data and respondents lead.

The conversational interviewer must "go with the flow." Depending on how the interviewer's role has been defined, the people being interviewed may not know during any particular conversation that data are being collected. In many cases, participant observers do not take notes during such conversational interviews, instead writing down what they learned later. In other cases, it can be both appropriate and comfortable to take notes or even use a tape recorder.

The strength of the informal conversational method resides in the opportunities it offers for flexibility, spontaneity, and responsiveness to individual differences and situational changes. Questions can be personalized to deepen communication with the person being interviewed and to make use of the immediate surroundings and situation to increase the concreteness and immediacy of the interview questions.

A weakness of the informal conversational interview is that it may require a greater amount of time to collect systematic information because it may take several conversations with different people before a similar set of questions has been posed to each participant in the setting. Because this approach depends on the conversational skills of the interviewer to a greater extent than do more formal, standardized formats, this go-with-the-flow style of interviewing may be susceptible to interviewer effects, leading questions, and biases, especially with novices. The conversational interviewer must be able to interact easily with people in a variety of settings, generate rapid insights, formulate questions quickly and smoothly, and guard against asking questions that impose interpretations on the situation by the structure of the questions.

Data obtained from informal conversational interviews can be difficult to pull together and analyze. Because different questions will generate different responses, the researcher has to spend a great deal of time sifting through responses to find patterns that have emerged at different points in different interviews with different people. By contrast, interviews that are more systematized and standardized facilitate analysis but provide less flexibility and are less sensitive to individual and situational differences.

The Interview Guide

An interview guide lists the questions or issues that are to be explored in the course of an interview. An interview guide is prepared to ensure that the same basic lines of inquiry are pursued with each person interviewed. The interview guide provides topics or subject areas within which the interviewer is free to explore, probe, and ask questions that will elucidate and illuminate that particular subject. Thus, the interviewer remains free to build a conversation within a particular subject area, to word questions spontaneously, and to establish a conversational style but with the focus on a particular subject that has been predetermined.

The advantage of an interview guide is that it makes sure that the interviewer/evaluator has carefully decided how best to use the limited time available in an interview situation. The guide helps make interviewing a number of different people more systematic and comprehensive by delimiting in advance the issues to be explored. A guide is essential in conducting focus group interviews for it keeps the interactions *focused* while allowing individual perspectives and experiences to emerge.

Interview guides can be developed in more or less detail, depending on the extent to which the interviewer is able to specify important issues in advance and the extent to which it is important to ask questions in the same order to all respondents. Exhibit 7.1 provides an example of an interview guide used with participants in an employment training program. This guide provides a framework within which the interviewer would develop questions, sequence those questions, and make decisions about which information to pursue in greater depth. Usually, the interviewer would not be expected to go into totally new subjects that are not covered within the framework of the guide. The interviewer does not ask questions, for example, about previous employment or education, how the person got into the program, how this program compares with other programs the trainee has experienced, or the trainee's health. Other topics might still emerge during the interview, topics of importance to the respondent that are not listed explicitly on the guide and therefore would not normally be explored with each person interviewed. For example, trainees might comment on family support (or lack thereof) or personal crises. Comments on such concerns might emerge when, in accordance with the interview guide, the trainee is asked for reactions to program strengths, weaknesses, and so on, but if family is not mentioned by the respondent, the interviewer would not raise the issue.

An additional, more detailed example of an interview guide is included as Appendix 7.1 at the end of this chapter. The example in the chapter appendix, a "descriptive interview" developed by the Educational Testing Service Collaborative Research Pro-ject on Reading, illustrates how it is possible to use a detailed outline to conduct a series of interviews with the same respondents over the course of a year. The flexibility permitted by the interview guide approach will become clearer after reviewing the third strategy of qualitative interviewing: the standardized open-ended interview.

The Standardized Open-Ended Interview

This approach requires carefully and fully wording each question before the interview. For example, the interview guide for the employment training program in Exhibit 7.1 simply lists "work experiences" as a topic for inquiry. In a fully structured interview instrument, the question would be completely specified:

> You've told me about the courses you've taken in the program. Now I'd like to ask you about any work experiences you've had. Let's go back to when you first entered the program and go through each work experience up to the present. Okay? So, what was your first work experience?
>
> *Probes:* Who did you work for?
>
> What did you do?
>
> What do you feel you learned doing that?
>
> What did you especially like about the experience, if anything?
>
> What did you dislike, if anything?
>
> *Transition:* Okay, tell me about your next work experience.

Why so much detail? To be sure that each interviewee gets asked the same questions —the same stimuli—in the same way and the same order, including standard probes. A doctoral committee may want to see the

EXHIBIT 7.1	Evaluation Interview Guide for Participants in an Employment Training Program

What has the trainee done in the program?
- ✔ activities
- ✔ courses
- ✔ groups
- ✔ work experiences

Achievements?
- ✔ skills attained
- ✔ products produced
- ✔ outcomes achieved
- ✔ knowledge gained
- ✔ things completed
- ✔ what can the trainee do that is *marketable*?

How has the trainee been affected in areas other than job skills?
- ✔ feelings about self
- ✔ attitudes toward work
- ✔ aspirations
- ✔ interpersonal skills

What aspects of the program have had the greatest impacts?
- ✔ formal courses
- ✔ relationships with staff
- ✔ peer relationships
- ✔ the way treated in the program
- ✔ contacts
- ✔ work experiences

What problems has the trainee experienced?
- ✔ work related
- ✔ program related
- ✔ personal
- ✔ family, friends, world outside program

What are the trainee's plans for the future?
- ✔ work plans
- ✔ income expectations
- ✔ lifestyle expectations/plans

What does the trainee think of the program?
- ✔ strengths, weaknesses
- ✔ things liked, things disliked
- ✔ best components, poorest components
- ✔ things that should be changed

full interview protocol before approving a dissertation proposal. The institutional review board for protection of human subjects may insist on approving a structured interview, especially if the topic is controversial or intrusive. In evaluations, key stakeholders may want to be sure that they know what program participants will be asked. In team research, standardized interviews ensure consistency across interviewers. In multisite studies, structured interviews provide comparability across sites.

In participatory or collaborative studies, inexperienced and nonresearcher interviewers may be involved in the process, so standardized questions can compensate for variability in skills. Some evaluations rely on volunteers to do interviewing; at other times program staff may be involved in doing some interviewing; and in still other instances interviewers may be novices, students, or others who are not social scientists or professional evaluators. When a number of different interviewers are used, variations in data created by differences among interviewers will become particularly apparent if an informal conversational approach to data gathering is used or even if each interviewer uses a basic guide. The best way to guard against variations among interviewers is to carefully word questions in advance and train the interviewers not to deviate from the prescribed forms. The data collected are still open-ended, in the sense that the respondent supplies his or her own words, thoughts, and insights in answering the questions, but the precise wording of the questions is determined ahead of time.

When doing action research or conducting a program evaluation, it may only be possible to interview participants once for a short, fixed time, such as a half hour, so highly focused questions serve to establish priorities for the interview. At other times, it is possible and desirable to interview partic-

ipants before they enter the program, when they leave the program, and again some period of time (e.g., six months) after they have left the program. For example, a chemical dependency program would ask participants about sobriety issues before, during, at the end of, and after the program. To compare answers across these time periods, the same questions need to be asked in the same way each time. Such interview questions are written out in advance *exactly* the way they are to be asked during the interview. Careful consideration is given to the wording of each question before the interview. Any clarifications or elaborations that are to be used are written into the interview itself. Probes are placed in the interview at appropriate places to minimize interviewer effects by asking the same question of each respondent, thereby reducing the need for interviewer judgment during the interview. The standardized open-ended interview also makes data analysis easier because it is possible to locate each respondent's answer to the same question rather quickly and to organize questions and answers that are similar.

In summary, there are four major reasons for using standardized open-ended interviews:

1. The exact instrument used in the evaluation is available for inspection by those who will use the findings of the study.

2. Variation among interviewers can be minimized where a number of different interviewers must be used.

3. The interview is highly focused so that interviewee time is used efficiently.

4. Analysis is facilitated by making responses easy to find and compare.

In program evaluations, potential problems of legitimacy and credibility for qualitative data can make it politically wise to produce an exact interview form that the evaluator can show to primary decision makers and evaluation users. Moreover, when generating a standardized form, evaluation users can participate more completely in writing the interview instrument. They not only will know precisely what is going to be asked but, no less important, will understand what is *not* going to be asked. This reduces the likelihood of the data being attacked later because certain questions were missed or asked in the wrong way. By making it clear, in advance of data collection, exactly what questions will be asked, the limitations of the data can be known and discussed before evaluation data are gathered.

While the conversational and interview guide approaches permit greater flexibility and individualization, these approaches also open up the possibility, indeed, the likelihood, that more information will be collected from some program participants than from others. Those using the findings may worry about how conclusions have been influenced by qualitative differences in the depth and breadth of information received from different people.

In contrast, in fieldwork done for basic and applied research, the researcher will be attempting to understand the holistic worldview of a group of people. Collecting the same information from each person poses no credibility problem when each person is understood as a unique informant with a unique perspective. The political credibility of consistent interview findings across respondents is less of an issue under basic research conditions.

The weakness of the standardized approach is that it does not permit the interviewer to pursue topics or issues that were not anticipated when the interview was written. Moreover, a structured interview reduces the extent to which individual differences and circumstances can be queried.

To illustrate the standardized open-ended interview, three interviews have been reproduced in Appendix 7.2 at the end of this chapter. These interviews were used to gather information from participants in an Outward Bound wilderness program for disabled persons. The first interview was conducted at the beginning of the program, the second interview was used at the end of the 10-day experience, and the third interview took place six months after the program.

Combining Approaches

These contrasting interview strategies are by no means mutually exclusive.

A conversational strategy can be used within an interview guide approach, or you can combine a guide approach with a standardized format by specifying certain key questions exactly as they must be asked while leaving other items as topics to be explored at the interviewer's discretion. This combined strategy offers the interviewer flexibility in probing and in determining when it is appropriate to explore certain subjects in greater depth, or even to pose questions about new areas of inquiry that were not originally anticipated in the interview instrument's development. A common combination strategy involves using a standardized interview format in the early part of an interview and then leaving the interviewer free to pursue any subjects of interest during the latter parts of the interview. Another combination would include using the informal conversational interview early in an evaluation project, followed midway through by an interview guide, and then closing the program evaluation with a standardized open-ended interview to get systematic information from a sample of participants at the end of the program or when conducting follow-up studies of participants.

A *sensitizing concept* can provide the bridge across types of interviews. In doing follow-up interviews with recipients of Mac-Arthur Foundation Fellowships, the sensitizing concept "enabling," a concept central to the fellowship's purpose, allowed us to focus interviews on any ways in which receiving the fellowship had *enabled* recipients. "Enabling," or "being enabled," broadly defined and open-ended, gave interviewees room to share a variety of experiences and outcomes while also letting me identify some carefully worded, standardized questions for all interviewees, some interview guide topics that might or might not be pursued, and a theme for staying centered during completely open-ended conversations at the end of the interviews.

Summary of Interviewing Strategies

All three qualitative approaches to interviewing share the commitment to ask genuinely open-ended questions that offer the persons being interviewed the opportunity to respond in their own words and to express their own personal perspectives.

While the three strategies vary in the extent to which the wording and sequencing of questions are predetermined, no variation exists in the principle that the response format should be open-ended. The interviewer never supplies and predetermines the phrases or categories that must be used by respondents to express themselves as is the case in fixed-response questionnaires. The purpose of qualitative interviewing is to capture how those being interviewed view their world, to learn *their* terminology and judgments, and to capture the complexities of *their* individual perceptions and experiences. This openness distinguishes qualitative interviewing from the closed questionnaire or test used in quantitative studies. Such closed instruments force respondents to fit their knowledge, experiences, and feelings into the researcher's categories. The fundamental principle of qualitative interviewing is to provide a framework within which respondents can express *their own* understandings in their own terms.

Exhibit 7.2 summarizes variations in interview instrumentation. In reviewing this summary table, keep in mind that these are presented as pure types. In practice, any particular study may employ all or several of these strategies together.

🖫 Question Options

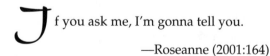

*I*f you ask me, I'm gonna tell you.

—Roseanne (2001:164)

Six kinds of questions can be asked of people. On any given topic, it is possible to ask any of these questions. Distinguishing types of questions forces the interviewer to be clear about what is being asked and helps the interviewee respond appropriately.

Experience and Behavior Questions

Questions about what a person does or has done aim to elicit behaviors, experiences, actions, and activities that would

EXHIBIT 7.2   Variations in Interview Instrumentation

Type of Interview	Characteristics	Strengths	Weaknesses
Informal conversational interview	Questions emerge from the immediate context and are asked in the natural course of things; there is no predetermination of question topics or wording.	Increases the salience and relevance of questions; interviews are built on and emerge from observations; the interview can be matched to individuals and circumstances.	Different information collected from different people with different questions. Less systematic and comprehensive if certain questions do not arise naturally. Data organization and analysis can be quite difficult.
Interview guide approach	Topics and issues to be covered are specified in advance, in outline form; interviewer decides sequence and wording of questions in the course of the interview.	The outline increases the comprehensiveness of the data and makes data collection somewhat systematic for each respondent. Logical gaps in data can be anticipated and closed. Interviews remain fairly conversational and situational.	Important and salient topics may be inadvertently omitted. Interviewer flexibility in sequencing and wording questions can result in substantially different responses from different perspectives, thus reducing the comparability of responses.
Standardized open-ended interview	The exact wording and sequence of questions are determined in advance. All interviewees are asked the same basic questions in the same order. Questions are worded in a completely open-ended format.	Respondents answer the same questions, thus increasing comparability of responses; data are complete for each person on the topics addressed in the interview. Reduces interviewer effects and bias when several interviewers are used. Permits evaluation users to see and review the instrumentation used in the evaluation. Facilitates organization and analysis of the data.	Little flexibility in relating the interview to particular individuals and circumstances; standardized wording of questions may constrain and limit naturalness and relevance of questions and answers.
Closed, fixed-response interview	Questions and response categories are determined in advance. Responses are fixed; respondent chooses from among these fixed responses.	Data analysis is simple; responses can be directly compared and easily aggregated; many questions can be asked in a short time.	Respondents must fit their experiences and feelings into the researcher's categories; may be perceived as impersonal, irrelevant, and mechanistic. Can distort what respondents really mean or experienced by so completely limiting their response choices.

have been observable had the observer been present. "If I followed you through a typical day, what would I see you doing? What experiences would I observe you having?" "If I had been in the program with you, what would I have seen you doing?"

Opinion and Values Questions

Questions aimed at understanding the cognitive and interpretive processes of people ask about opinions, judgments, and values—"head stuff" as opposed to actions and behaviors. Answers to these questions tell us what people *think* about some experience or issue. They tell us about people's goals, intentions, desires, and expectations. "What do you believe?" "What do you think about _____?" "What would you like to see happen?" "What is your opinion of _____?"

Feeling Questions

Emotional centers in the brain can be distinguished from cognitive areas. Feeling questions aim at eliciting emotions—*feeling* responses of people to their experiences and thoughts. Feelings tap the affective dimension of human life. In asking feeling questions—"How do you feel about that?"—the interviewer is looking for adjective responses: anxious, happy, afraid, intimidated, confident, and so on.

Opinions and feelings are often confused. It is critical that interviewers understand the distinction between the two in order to know when they have the kind of answer they want to the question they are asking. Suppose an interviewer asks, "How do you feel about that? The response is, "I think it's probably the best that we can do under the circumstances." The question about feelings

has not really been answered. Analytical, interpretive, and opinion statements are not answers to questions about feelings.

This confusion sometimes occurs because interviewers give the wrong cues when asking questions—for example, by asking opinion questions using the format "How do you feel about that?" instead of "What is your opinion about that?" or "What do you think about it?" When you want to understand the respondents' emotional reactions, you have to ask about *and listen for* feeling-level responses. When you want to understand what someone thinks about something, the question should explicitly tell the interviewee that you're searching for opinions, beliefs, and considered judgments—not feelings.

Knowledge Questions

Knowledge questions inquire about the respondent's factual information—what the respondent knows. Certain things are facts, such as whether it is against the law to drive while drunk and how the law defines drunkenness. These things are not opinions or feelings. Knowledge about a program may include knowing what services are available, who is eligible, what the rules and regulations of the program are, how one enrolls in the program, and so on. Cooke (1994), for example, reviews and assesses a variety of knowledge elicitation methods and techniques.

Sensory Questions

Sensory questions ask about what is seen, heard, touched, tasted, and smelled. Responses to these questions allow the interviewer to enter into the sensory apparatus of the respondent. "When you walk through the doors of the program, what do you see? Tell me what I would see if I walked through the doors with you." Or again: "What does the counselor ask you when you meet with him? What does he actually say?" Sensory questions attempt to have interviewees describe the stimuli that they experience. Technically, sensory data are a type of behavioral or experiential data—they capture the experience of the senses. However, the types of questions asked to gather sensory data are sufficiently distinct to merit a separate category.

Background/ Demographic Questions

Age, education, occupation, and the like are standard background questions that identify characteristics of the person being interviewed. Answers to these questions help the interviewer locate the respondent in relation to other people. Asking these questions in an open-ended rather than closed manner elicits the respondent's own categorical worldview. Asked about age, a person aged 55 might respond, "I'm 55" or "I'm middle-aged" or "I'm at the cusp of old age" or "I'm still young at heart" or "I'm in my mid-50s" or "I'm 10 years from retirement" or "I'm between 40 and 60" (smiling broadly) and so forth. Responses to open-ended, qualitative background inquiries tell us about how people categorize themselves in today's endlessly categorizing world. Perhaps nowhere is such openness more important and illuminative than in asking about race and ethnicity. For example, professional golfer Tiger Woods has African, Thai, Chinese, American Indian, and European ancestry—and resists being "assigned" to any single ethnic category. He came up with the name "Cablinasian" to describe his mixed heritage. In an increasingly diverse world with people of mixed ethnicity and ever-evolving labels (e.g., Negro,

Colored, Black, African American, Person of African descent), qualitative inquiry is a particularly appropriate way of finding out how people perceive and talk about their backgrounds.

Distinguishing Question Types

Behaviors, opinions, feelings, knowledge, sensory data, and demographics are common background questions possible to ask in an interview. Any kind of question one might want to ask can be subsumed in one of these categories. Keeping these distinctions in mind can be particularly helpful in planning an interview, designing the inquiry strategy, focusing on priorities for inquiry, and ordering the questions in some sequence. Before considering the sequence of questions, however, let's look at how the *dimension of time* intersects with the different kinds of questions.

The Time Frame of Questions

Questions can be asked in the present, past, or future tense. For example, you can ask someone what they're doing now, what they have done in the past, and what they plan to do in the future. Likewise, you can inquire about present attitudes, past attitudes, or future attitudes. By combining the time frame of questions with the different types of questions, we can construct a matrix that generates 18 different types of questions. Exhibit 7.3 shows that matrix.

Asking all 18 questions about any particular situation, event, or programmatic activity may become somewhat tedious, especially if the sequence is repeated over and over throughout the interview for different program elements. The matrix constitutes a set of options to help you think about what

EXHIBIT 7.3	A Matrix of Question Options		
Question Focus	*Past*	*Present*	*Future*
Behaviors/experiences			
Opinions/values			
Feelings/emotions			
Knowledge			
Sensory			
Background			

information is most important to obtain. To understand how these options are applied in an actual study, it may be helpful to review a real interview. The Outward Bound standardized interview in Appendix 7.2 at the end of this chapter can be used for this purpose. Try identifying which cell in the matrix (Exhibit 7.3) is represented by each question in the Outward Bound interviews.

Sequencing Questions

No recipe for sequencing questions can or should exist, but the matrix of questions suggests some possibilities. The challenges of sequencing vary, of course, for different strategies of interviewing. Informal conversational interviewing is flexible and responsive so that a predetermined sequence is seldom possible or desirable. In contrast, standardized open-ended interviews must establish a fixed sequence of questions to fit their structured format. I offer, then, some suggestions about sequencing.

I prefer to begin an interview with questions about noncontroversial present behaviors, activities, and experiences like "What

are you currently working on in school?" Such questions ask for relatively straightforward descriptions; they require minimal recall and interpretation. Such questions are, it is hoped, fairly easy to answer. They encourage the respondent to talk *descriptively.* Probes should focus on eliciting greater detail—filling out the descriptive picture.

Once some experience or activity has been described, then opinions and feelings can be solicited, building on and probing for interpretations of the experience. Opinions and feelings are likely to be more grounded and meaningful once the respondent has verbally "relived" the experience. Knowledge and skill questions also need a context. Such questions can be quite threatening if asked too abruptly. The interviewer doesn't want to come across as a TV game show host quizzing a contestant. So, for example, in evaluation interviewing, it can be helpful to ask knowledge questions ("What are the eligibility requirements for this program?") as follow-up questions about program activities and experiences that have a bearing on knowledge and skills ("How did you become part of the program?"). Finding out from people what they know works best once some rapport and trust have been established in the interview.

Questions about the present tend to be easier for respondents than questions about the past. Future-oriented questions involve considerable speculation, and responses to questions about future actions or attitudes are typically less reliable than questions about the present or past. I generally prefer to begin by asking questions about the present, then, using the present as a baseline, ask questions about the same activity or attitude in the past. Only then will I broach questions about the future.

Background and demographic questions are basically boring; they epitomize what people hate about interviews. They can also be somewhat uncomfortable for the respondent, depending on how personal they are. I keep such questions to a minimum and prefer to space them strategically and unobtrusively throughout the interview. I advise never beginning an interview with a long list of routine demographic questions. In qualitative interviewing, the interviewee needs to become actively involved in providing descriptive information as soon as possible instead of becoming conditioned to providing short-answer, routine responses to uninteresting categorical questions. Some background information may be necessary at the beginning to make sense out of the rest of the interview, but such questions should be tied to descriptive information about present life experience as much as possible. Otherwise, save the sociodemographic inquiries (age, socioeconomic status, birth order, and the like) for the end.

🔄 Wording Questions

An interview question is a stimulus aimed at eliciting a response from the person being interviewed. How a question is worded and asked affects how the interviewee responds. As Payne (1951) observed in his classic book on questioning, **asking questions is an art.** In qualitative inquiry, "good" questions should, at a minimum, be open-ended, neutral, singular, and clear. Let's look at each of these criteria.

Asking Truly Open-Ended Questions

Qualitative inquiry—strategically, philosophically, and therefore, methodologically —aims to minimize the imposition of predetermined responses when gathering data. It follows that questions should be asked in a truly open-ended fashion so people can respond in their own words.

The standard fixed-response item in a questionnaire provides a limited and predetermined list of possibilities: "How satisfied are you with the program? (a) very satisfied, (b) somewhat satisfied, (c) not too satisfied, (d) not at all satisfied." The closed and limiting nature of such a question is obvious to both questioner and respondent. Many researchers seem to think that the way to make a question open-ended is simply to leave out the structured response categories. But doing so does not make a question truly open-ended. It merely disguises what still amounts to a predetermined and implicit constraint on likely responses.

Consider the question "How satisfied are you with this program?" Asked without fixed response choices, this can appear to be an open-ended question. On closer inspection, however, we see that the dimension along which the respondent can answer has already been identified—*degree of satisfaction.* The interviewee can use a variety of modifiers for the word *satisfaction*—"pretty satisfied," "kind of satisfied," "mostly satisfied," and so on. But, in effect, the possible response set has been narrowly limited by the wording of the question. The typical range of answers will vary only slightly more than what would have been obtained had the categories been made explicit from the start while making the analysis more complicated.

A truly open-ended question does not presuppose which dimension of feeling or thought will be salient for the interviewee. The truly open-ended question allows the person being interviewed to select from among that person's full repertoire of possible responses those that are most salient. Indeed, in qualitative inquiry one of the things the inquiry is trying to determine is what dimensions, themes, and images/ words people use among themselves to describe their feelings, thoughts, and experiences. Examples, then, of truly open-ended questions would take the following format:

How do you feel about _____?
What is your opinion of _____?
What do you think of _____?

The truly open-ended question permits those being interviewed to take whatever direction and use whatever words they want to express what they have to say. Moreover, to be truly open-ended a question cannot be phrased as a dichotomy.

The Horns of a Dichotomy

Dichotomous response questions provide the interviewee with a grammatical structure suggesting a "yes" or "no" answer. Are you satisfied with the program? Have you changed as a result of your participation in this program? Was this an important experience for you? Do you know the proce-

dures for enrolling in the program? Have you interacted much with the staff in the program? By their grammatical form, all of these questions invite a yes/no reply.

In contrast, in-depth interviewing strives to get the person being interviewed to talk —to talk about experiences, feelings, opinions, and knowledge. Far from encouraging the respondent to talk, dichotomous response questions limit expression. They can even create a dilemma for respondents who may not be sure whether they are being asked a simple yes/no question or if, indeed, the interviewer expects a more elaborate response. Often, in teaching interviewers and reviewing their fieldwork, I've found that those who report having difficulty getting respondents to talk are posing a string of dichotomous questions that program the respondent to be largely reactive and binary.

Consider this classic exchange between a parent and teenager. Teenager returns home from a date:

Do you know that you're late?
Yeah.
Did you have a good time?
Yeah.
Did you go to a movie?
Yeah.
Was it a good movie?
Yeah, it was okay.
So, it was worth seeing?
Yeah, it was worth seeing.
I've heard a lot about it. Do you think I would like it?
I don't know. Maybe.
Anything else happen?
No. That's about it.

Teenager then goes off to bed. One parent turns to the other and says, "Sure is hard to get him to talk to us. I guess he's at the age where kids just don't want to tell their parents anything."

Dichotomous questions can turn an interview into an interrogation or quiz rather than an in-depth conversation. In everyday conversation, our interactions with each other are filled with dichotomous questions that we unconsciously ignore and treat as if they were open-ended questions. If a friend asks, "Did you have a good time?" you're likely to offer more than a yes/no answer. In a more formal interview setting, however, the interviewee will be more conscious of the grammatical structure of questions and is less likely to elaborate beyond "yes" or "no" when hit with dichotomous queries. Indeed, the more intense the interview situation, the more likely the respondent reacts to the "deep structure" stimulus of questions —which includes their grammatical framing—and to take questions literally (Bandler and Grinder 1975a, 1975b).

In training interviewers, I like to play a game where I will only respond literally to the questions asked without volunteering any information that is not clearly demanded in the question. I do this before explaining the difficulties involved in asking dichotomous questions. I have played this game hundreds of times and the interaction seldom varies. When getting dichotomous responses to general questions, the interviewer will begin to rely on more and more specific dichotomous response questions, thereby digging a deeper and deeper hole, which makes it difficult to pull the interview out of the dichotomous response pattern. Transcribed on page 356 is an actual interview from a training workshop. In the left column, I have recorded the interview that took place; the right column records truly open-ended alternatives to the dichotomous questions that were asked.

INTERVIEW DEMONSTRATION

Instruction: Okay, now we're going to play an interviewing game. I want you to ask me questions about an evaluation I just completed. The program being evaluated was a staff development demonstration project that involved taking professionals into a wilderness setting for a week. That's all I'm going to tell you at this point. I'll answer your questions as precisely as I can, but I'll only answer what you ask. I won't volunteer any information that isn't directly asked for by your questions.

The questions on the left (next page) illustrate a fairly extreme example of posing dichotomous questions in an interview. Notice that the open-ended questions on the right side generate richer answers and quite different information than was elicited from the dichotomous questions. In addition, dichotomous questions can easily become leading questions. Once the interviewer begins to cope with what appears to be a reluctant or timid interviewee by asking ever more detailed dichotomous questions, guessing at possible responses, the interviewer may actually impose those responses on the interviewee. One sure sign that this is happening is when the interviewer is doing more talking than the person being interviewed. Consider the excerpt on page 357 from an actual interview. The interviewee was a teenager who was participating in a chemical dependency program. The interview took place during the time the teenager was resident in the program.

The person conducting this interview said she wanted to find out two things in this portion of the interview: What experiences were most salient for John and how personally involved John was becoming in the experience. She has learned that the hot seat

Actual Questions Asked	Genuinely Open-Ended Alternatives With Richer Responses
Question: Were you doing a formative evaluation?	Q: What were the purposes of the evaluation?
Answer: Mostly.	A: First, to document what happened; then to provide feedback to staff and help them identify their "model"; and finally to report to funders.
Q: Were you trying to find out if the people changed from being in the wilderness?	Q: What were you trying to find out through the evaluation?
A: That was part of it.	A: Several things. How participants experienced the wilderness, how they talked about the experience, what meanings they attached to what they experienced, what they did with the experience when they returned home, and any ways in which it affected them.
Q: Did they change?	Q: What did you find out? How did participation in the program affect participants?
A: Some of them did.	A: Many participants reported "transformative" experiences—their term—by which they meant something life-changing. Others became more engaged in experiential education themselves. A few reported just having a good time. You'd need to read the full case studies to see the depth of variation and impacts.
Q: Did you interview people both before and after the program?	Q: What kinds of information did you collect for the evaluation?
A: Yes.	A: We interviewed participants before, during, and after the program; we did focus groups; we engaged in participant observation with conversational interviews; and we read their journals when they were willing. They also completed open-ended evaluation forms that asked about aspects of the program.
Q: Did you find that being in the program affected what happened?	Q: How do you think your participation in the program affected what happened?
A: Yes.	A: We've reflected a lot on that and we talked with staff and participants about it. Most agreed that the evaluation process made everyone more intentional and reflective—and that increased the impact in many cases.
Q: Did you have a good time?	Q: What was the wilderness experience like for you?
A: Yes.	A: First, I learned a great deal about participant observation and evaluation. Second, came to love the wilderness and have become an avid hiker. Third, I began what I expect will be a deep and lifelong friendship with one staff member.

was highly salient for John, but she really knows very little about the reasons for that salience. With regard to the question of his personal involvement, the only data she has come from his acquiescence to leading questions. In fact, if one lists the actual *data* from the interview—his verbatim responses—there is very little there:

Okay.

Yeah, . . . the hot seat.

Right.

One person does it every day.

Yeah, it depends.

Okay, let's see, hmmm . . . there was this guy yesterday who really got nailed. I mean he really caught a lot of crap from the group. It was really heavy.

No, it was them others.

Yeah, right, and it really got to him.

He started crying and got mad and one guy really came down on him and afterwards

Interview	Comments
Question: Hello, John. It's nice to see you again. I'm anxious to find out what's been happening with you. Can I ask you some questions about your experience?	The opening is dominated by the interviewer. No informal give-and-take. The interviewee is set up to take a passive/reactive role.
Answer: Okay.	
Q: I'd like you to think about some of the really important experiences you've had here. Can you think of something that stands out in your mind?	Introductory cue sentence is immediately followed by a dichotomous response question.
A: Yeah, . . . the hot seat.	John goes beyond the dichotomous response.
Q: The hot seat is when one person is the focus of attention for the whole group, right?	The interviewer has provided the definition rather than getting John's own definition of the hot seat.
A: Right.	
Q: So, what was it like . . . ? Was this the first time you've seen the hot seat used?	Began open-ended, then changed the question and posed a dichotomous question. The question is no longer singular or open.
A: One person does it every day.	Not really an answer to the question.
Q: Is it different with different people?	Question follows previous answer but still a dichotomous format.
A: Yeah, it depends.	
Q: Can you tell me about one that really stands out in your mind?	"Can you?" Is this an inquiry about willingness or memory or capacity or trust?
A: Okay, let's see, hmm . . . there was this guy yesterday who really got nailed. I mean, he really caught a lot of crap from the group. It was really heavy.	Before responding to the open request, John reacts to the dichotomous format.
Q: Did you say anything?	Dichotomous question.
A: No, it was them others.	
Q: So what was it like for you? Did you get caught up in it? You said it was really heavy. Was it heavy for you or just the group?	Multiple questions. Unclear connections. Ambiguous, multiple-choice format at the end.
A: Yeah, right, and it really got to him.	John's positive answer ("Yeah, right") is actually uninterpretable, given the questions asked.
Q: Did you think it was good for him? Did it help him?	Dichotomous questions.
A: He started crying and got mad and one guy really came down on him and afterwards they were talking and it seemed to be okay for him.	The question asks for a judgment. John wants to describe what happened. The narrowness of the interview questions are limiting his responses.
Q: So it was really intense?	Leading question, setting up an easy acquiescence response.
A: Yeah, it really was.	Acquiesces to leading question. Accepts interviewer's term, "intense," so we don't learn what word he would have chosen.
Q: And you got really involved.	Another leading question.
A: It was pretty heavy.	John doesn't actually respond to the question. Ambiguous response.
Q: Okay, I want to ask you some about the lecture part of the program. Anything else you want to say about the hot seat? (John doesn't answer verbally. Sits and waits for the next questions.)	Transition. John is cued that the hot seat questions are over. No response really expected.

they were talking, and it seemed to be okay for him.

Yeah, it really was.

It was pretty heavy.

The lack of a coherent story line in these responses reveals how little we've actually learned about John's perspective and experiences. Study the transcript and you'll find that the interviewer was talking more than the interviewee. The questions put the interviewee in a passive stance, able to confirm or deny the substance provided by the interviewer but not really given the opportunity to provide in-depth, descriptive detail in his own words.

Asking Singular Questions

One of the basic rules of questionnaire writing is that each item must be singular; that is, no more than one idea should be contained in any given question. Consider this example:

> How well do you know and like the staff in
> this program?
>
> (a) a lot
> (b) pretty much
> (c) not too much
> (d) not at all

This item is impossible to interpret in analysis because it asks two questions:

> (1) How well do you know the staff?
> (2) How much do you like the staff?

When one turns to open-ended interviewing, however, many people seem to think that singular questions are no longer called for. Precision gives way to vagueness and confused multiplicity, as in the illustration in this section. I've seen transcripts of interviews conducted by experienced and well-known field researchers in which several questions have been thrown together, which they might think are related, but which are likely to confuse the person being interviewed about what is really being asked.

> To help the staff improve the program, we'd
> like to ask you to talk about your opinion of

the program—what you think are the strengths and weaknesses of the program. What you like. What you don't like. What you think could be improved or should stay the same. Those kinds of things—and any other comments you have.

The evaluator who used this question regularly in interviewing argued that by asking a series of questions, he could find out which was most salient to the person being interviewed because the interviewee was forced to choose what he or she most cared about in order to respond to the question. The evaluator would then probe more specifically in those areas that were not answered in the initial question.

It's necessary to distinguish, then, between giving an overview of a series of questions at the beginning of a sequence, then asking each one singularly, and laying out a whole series of questions at once and seeing which one strikes a respondent's fancy. In my experience, multiple questions create tension and confusion because the person being interviewed doesn't really know what is being asked. An analysis of the strengths and weaknesses of a program is not the same as reporting what one likes and dislikes about a program. Likewise, recommendations for change may be unrelated to strengths, weaknesses, likes, and dislikes. The following is an excerpt from an interview with a parent participating in a family education program aimed at helping parents become more effective as parents.

> Question: Based on your experience, what
> would you say are the strengths of this
> program?
>
> Answer: The other parents. Different parents can get together and talk about what being a parent is like for them. The program is really parents with parents. Par-

Asking Clear, Singular Questions

Now, the <u>first</u> question I'd like to ask, just to get us started is how you happened to find out about the program; what it was like when you first came--you know, how you feel about it now, and what impact it's had on you...?

© 2002 Michael Quinn Patton and Michael Cochran

ents really need to talk to other parents about what they do, and what works and doesn't work. It's the parents, it really is.

Q: What about weaknesses?

A: I don't know . . . I guess I'm not always sure that the program is really getting to the parents who need it the most. I don't know how you do that, but I just think there are probably a lot of parents out there who need the program and . . . especially maybe single-parent families. And fathers. It's really hard to get fathers into something like this. It should just get to everybody and that's real hard.

Q: Let me turn now to your personal likes and dislikes about the program. What are some of the things that you have really liked about the program?

A: I'd put the staff right at the top of that. I really like the program director. She's really well educated and knows a lot, but she never makes us feel dumb. We can say anything or ask anything. She treats us like people, like equals even. I like the other parents. And I like being able to bring my daughter along. They take her into the child's part of the program, but we also have some activities together. But it's also good for her to have her activities with other kids and I get some time with other parents.

Q: What about dislikes? What are some things you don't like so much about the program?

A: I don't like the schedule much. We meet in the afternoons after lunch and it kind of breaks into the day at a bad time for me, but there isn't any really good time for all the parents and I know they've tried different times. Time is always going to be a hassle for people. Maybe they could just offer different things at different times. The room we meet in isn't too great, but that's no big deal.

Q: Okay, you've given us a lot of information about your experiences in the program, strengths and weaknesses you've observed, and some of the things you've liked and haven't liked so much. Now I'd like to ask you about your recommendations for the program. If you had the power to change things about the program, what would you make different?

A: Well, I guess the first thing is money. It's always money. I just think they should put, you know, the legislature should put more money into programs like this. I don't know how much the director gets paid, but I hear that she's not even getting paid as much as schoolteachers. She should get paid like a professional. I think there should be more of these programs and more money in them.

Oh, I know what I'd recommend. We talked about it one time in our group. It would be neat to have some parents who have already been through the program come back and talk with new groups about what they've done with their kids since they've been in the program, you know, like problems that they didn't expect or things that didn't work out, or just getting the benefit of the experiences of parents who've already been through the program to help new parents. We talked about that one day and thought that would be a neat thing to do. I don't know if it would work, but it would be a neat thing. I wouldn't mind doing it, I guess.

* * *

Notice that each of these questions solicited a different response. Strengths, weaknesses, likes, dislikes, and recommendations —each question meant something different and deserved to be asked separately. Qualitative interviewing can be deepened through thoughtful, focused, and distinct questions.

A consistent theme runs through this discussion of question formulation: **The wording used in asking questions can make a significant difference in the quality of responses elicited.** The interviewer who throws out a bunch of questions all at once to see which one takes hold puts an unnecessary burden on the interviewee to decipher what is being asked. Moreover, multiple questions asked at the same time suggest that the interviewer hasn't figured out what question should be asked at that juncture in the interview. Taking the easy way out by asking several questions at once transfers the burden of clarity from the interviewer to the interviewee.

Asking several questions at once can also waste precious interview time. Given multiple stimuli and not being sure of the focus of the question, the interviewee is free to go off in any direction at all, including tangents that are irrelevant to the issues under study. In evaluation interviews, for example, both interviewers and respondents typically have only so much time to give to an interview. To make the best use of that time, it is helpful to think through priority questions that will elicit relevant responses. This means that the interviewer must know what issues are important enough to ask questions about, and to ask those questions in a way that the person being interviewed can clearly identify what he or she is being asked—that is, to ask clear questions.

Clarity of Questions

*I*f names are not correct, language will not be in accordance with the truth of things.

—Confucius

The interviewer bears the responsibility to pose questions that make it clear to the interviewee what is being asked. Asking understandable questions facilitates establishing rapport. Unclear questions can make the person being interviewed feel uncomfortable, ignorant, confused, or hostile. Asking singular questions helps a great deal to make things clear. Other factors also contribute to clarity.

First, in preparing for an interview, find out what special terms are commonly used by people in the setting. For example, state and national programs often have different titles and language at the local level. CETA (Comprehensive Employment and Training Act) was designed as a national program in which local contractors were funded to establish and implement services in their area. We found that participants only knew these programs by the name of the local contractor, such as "Youth Employment Services," "Work for Youth," and "Working Opportunities for Women." Many participants in these programs did not even know they were in CETA programs. Conducting an interview with these participants where they were asked about their "CETA experience" would have been confusing and disruptive to the interview.

When I was doing fieldwork in Burkina Faso, the national government was run by the military after a coup d'état. Local officials carried the title "commandant" (commander). However, no one referred to the government as a military government. To do so was not only politically incorrect but risky. The appropriate official phrase man-dated by the rulers in Ouagadougou was "the people's government."

Second, clarity can be sharpened by understanding what language participants use among themselves in talking about a setting, activities, or other aspects of life. When we interviewed juveniles who had been placed in foster group homes by juvenile courts, we had to spend a good deal of preparatory time trying to find out how the juveniles typically referred to the group home parents, to their natural parents, to probation officers, and to each other in order to ask questions clearly about each of those sets of people. For example, when asking about relationships with peers, should we use the word *juveniles, adolescents, youth, teenagers,* or what? In preparation for the interviews, we checked with a number of juveniles, group home parents, and court authorities about the proper language to use. We were advised to refer to "the other kids in the group home." However, we found no consensus about how the kids in the group home referred to group home parents. Thus, one of the questions we had to ask in each interview was, "What do you usually call Mr. and Mrs. _____?" We then used the language given to us by that youth throughout the rest of the interview to refer to group home parents.

Third, providing clarity in interview questions may mean avoiding using labels altogether. This means that when asking about a particular phenomenon or program component, it may be better to first find out what the interviewee believes that phenomenon to be and then ask questions about the descriptions provided by the person being interviewed. In studying officially designated "open classrooms" in North Dakota, I interviewed parents who had children in those classrooms. However, many of the teachers and local school officials did not use the term "open" to refer to these classrooms because they wanted to avoid political conflicts and stereotypes that were sometimes associated with the notion of "open education." Thus, when interviewing parents we could not ask their opinions about open education. Rather, we had to pursue a sequence of questions like the following:

> What kinds of differences, if any, have you noticed between your child's classroom last year and the classroom this year? (Parent responds.)
>
> OK, you've mentioned several differences. Let me ask you your opinion about each of the things you've mentioned. What do you think about _____?

This strategy avoids the problem of collecting data that later turn out to be uninterpretable because you can't be sure what respondents meant by their responses. Their opinions and judgments are grounded in descriptions, in their own words, of what they've experienced and what they're assessing.

A related problem emerged in interviewing children about their classrooms. We wanted to find out how basic skills were taught in open classrooms. In preparing for the interviews, we learned that many teachers avoided such terms as "math time" or "reading time" because they wanted to integrate math and reading into other activities. In some cases, we learned during parent interviews, children reported to parents that they didn't do any math in school. These

same children would be working on projects, such as the construction of a model of their town using milk cartons that required geometry, fractions, and reductions to scale, but they did not perceive of these activities as math because they associated math with worksheets and workbooks. Thus, to find out that kind of math activities children were doing, it was necessary to talk with them in detail about specific projects and work they were engaged in without asking them the simple question "What kind of math do you do in the classroom?"

Another example of problems in clarity comes from follow-up interviews with mothers whose children were victims of sexual abuse. A major part of the interview focused on experiences with and reactions to the child protection agency, the police, the welfare workers, the court system, the school counselor, probation officers, and other parts of the enormously complex system constructed to deal with child sexual abuse. We learned quickly that mothers could seldom differentiate the parts of the system. They didn't know when they were dealing with the courts, the child protection people, the welfare system, or some treatment program. It was all "the system." They had strong feelings and opinions about the system, so our questions had to remain general, about the system, rather than specifically asking about the separate parts of the system (Patton 1991).

The theme running through these suggestions for increasing the clarity of questions centers on the importance of using language that is understandable and part of the frame of reference of the person being interviewed. It means taking special care to find out what language the interviewee uses. Questions that use the respondent's own language are most likely to be clear. This means being sensitive to "languaculture" by attending to "meanings that lead the researcher beyond the words into the nature of the speaker's world" (Agar 2000:93-94). This sensitivity to local language, the emic perspective in anthropology, is usually discussed in relation to data analysis in which a major focus is illuminating a setting or culture through its language. Here, however, we're discussing languaculture, not as an analytical framework but as a way of enhancing data collection during interviewing by increasing clarity, communicating respect, and facilitating rapport.

Using words that make sense to the interviewee, words that reflect the respondent's worldview, will improve the quality of data obtained during the interview. Without sensitivity to the impact of particular words on the person being interviewed, an answer may make no sense at all—or there may be no answer. A Sufi story makes this point quite nicely.

> A man had fallen between the rails in a subway station. People were all crowding around trying to get him out before the train ran him over. They were all shouting. "Give me your hand!" but the man would not reach up.
>
> Mulla Nasrudin elbowed his way through the crowd and leaned over the man. "Friend," he asked, "what is your profession?"
>
> "I am an income tax inspector," gasped the man.
>
> "In that case," said Nasrudin, "take my hand!"
>
> The man immediately grasped the Mulla's hand and was hauled to safety. Nasrudin turned to the amazed by-standers. "Never ask a tax man to give you anything, you fools," he said. (Shah 1973:68)

Before leaving the issue of clarity, let me offer one other suggestion: Be especially careful asking "why" questions.

Why to Take Care Asking "Why?"

> Three Zen Masters were discussing a flapping flag on a pole. The first observed dryly: "The flag moves."
>
> "No," said the second, "wind is moving."
>
> "No," said the third. "It is not flag. It is not wind. It is mind moving."

"Why" questions presuppose that things happen for a reason and that those reasons are knowable. "Why" questions presume cause-effect relationships, an ordered world, and rationality. "Why" questions move beyond what has happened, what one has experienced, how one feels, what one opines, and what one knows to the making of analytical and deductive inferences.

The problems in deducing causal inferences have been thoroughly explored by philosophers of science (Bunge 1959; Nagel 1961). On a more practical level and more illuminative of interviewing challenges, reports from parents about "why" conversations with their children document the difficulty of providing causal explanations about the world. The infinite regression quality of "why" questions is part of the difficulty engendered by using them as part of an interview. Consider this parent-child exchange:

Dad, why does it get dark at night?

Because our side of the earth turns away from the sun.

Dad, why does our side of the earth turn away from the sun?

Because that's the way the world was made.

Dad, why was the world made that way?

So that there would be light and dark.

Dad, why should there be dark? Why can't it just be light all the time?

Because then we would get too hot.

Why would we get too hot?

Because the sun would be shining on us all the time.

Why can't the sun be cooler sometimes?

It is, that's why we have night.

But why can't we just have a cooler sun?

Because that's the way the world is.

Why is the world like that?

It just is. Because.

Because why?

Just because.

Oh.

Daddy?

Yes.

Why don't you know why it gets dark?

In a program evaluation interview, it might seem that the context for asking a "why" question would be clearer. However, if a precise reason for a particular activity is what is wanted, it is usually possible to ask that question in a way that does not involve using the word *why*. Let's look first at the difficulty posed for the respondent by the "why" question, and then look at some alternative phrases.

"Why did you join this program?" The actual reasons for joining the program probably consist of some constellation of factors, including the influences of other people, the nature of the program, the nature of the person being interviewed, the interviewee's expectations, and practical considerations. It is unlikely that an interviewee can sort through all of these levels of possibility at once, so the person to whom the question is posed must pick out some level at which to respond.

- "Because it takes place at a convenient time." (*programmatic* reason)

- "Because I'm a joiner." (*personality* reason)

- "Because a friend told me about the program." (*information* reason)

- "Because my priest told me about the program and said he thought it would be good for me." (*social influence* reason)

- "Because it was inexpensive." (*economic* reason)

- "Because I wanted to learn about the things they're teaching in the program." (*outcomes* reason)

- "Because God directed me to join the program." (*personal motivation* reason)

- "Because it was there." (*philosophical* reason)

Anyone being interviewed could respond at any or all of these levels. The interviewer must decide before conducting the interview which of these levels carries sufficient importance to make it worth asking a question. If the primary evaluation question concerns characteristics of the program that attracted participants, then instead of asking, "Why did you join?" the interviewer should ask something like the following: "What was it about the program that attracted you to it?" If the evaluator is interested in learning about social influences that led to participation in a program, either voluntary or involuntary participation, a question like the following could be used:

Other people sometimes influence what we do. What other people, if any, played a role in your joining this program?

In some cases, the evaluator may be particularly interested in the characteristics of participants, so the question might be phrased in the following fashion:

> I'm interested in learning more about you as a person and your personal involvement in this program. What is it about you—your situation, your personality, your desires, whatever—what is it about you that you think led you to become part of this program?

When used as a probe, "why" questions can imply that a person's response was somehow inappropriate. "Why did you do that?" may sound like doubt that an action (or feeling) was justified. A simple "Tell me more, if you will, about your thinking on that" may be more inviting.

The point is that by thinking carefully about what you want to know, there is a greater likelihood that respondents will supply answers that make sense—and are relevant, usable, and interpretable. My cautions about the difficulties raised with "why" questions come from trying to analyze such questions when responses covered such a multitude of dimensions that it was clear different people were responding to different things. This makes analysis unwieldy.

Perhaps my reservations about the use of "why" questions come from having appeared the fool when asking such questions during interviews with children. In our open classroom interviews, several teachers had mentioned that children often became so involved in what they were doing that they chose not to go outside for recess. We decided to check this out with the children.

"What's your favorite time in school?" I asked a first grader.

"Recess," she answered quickly.

"Why do you like recess?"

"Because we go outside and play on the swings."

"Why do you go outside?" I asked.

"Because that's where the swings are!"

She replied with a look of incredulity that adults could ask such stupid questions, then explained helpfully: "If you want to swing on the swings, you have to go outside where the swings are."

Children take interview questions quite literally and so it becomes clear quickly when a question is not well thought out. It was during those days of interviewing children in North Dakota that I learned about the problems with "why" questions.

🔲 Rapport and Neutrality

Neutral Questions

As an interviewer, I want to establish rapport with the person I am questioning, but that rapport must be established in such a way that it does not undermine my neutrality concerning what the person tells me. Neutrality means that the person being interviewed can tell me anything without engendering either my favor or disfavor with regard to the content of her or his response. I cannot be shocked; I cannot be angered; I cannot be embarrassed; I cannot be saddened. Nothing the person tells me will make me think more or less of the person.

At the same time that I am neutral with regard to the content of what is being said to me, I care very much that that person is willing to share with me what she or he is saying. **Rapport is a stance vis-à-vis the person being interviewed. Neutrality is a stance vis-à-vis the content of what that person says.** Rapport means that I respect the people being interviewed, so what they say is important because of who is saying it. I want

to convey to them that their knowledge, experiences, attitudes, and feelings are important. Yet, I will not judge them for the content of what they say to me.

Rapport is built on the ability to convey empathy and understanding without judgment. Throughout this chapter, we have been considering ways of phrasing questions that facilitate the establishment of rapport through mutual understanding. In this section, I want to focus on ways of wording questions that are particularly aimed at conveying that important sense of neutrality.

Using Illustrative Examples in Questions

One kind of question wording that can help establish neutrality is the *illustrative ex-amples format*. When phrasing questions in this way I want to let the person I'm interviewing know that I've pretty much heard it all—the bad things and the good—and so I'm not interested in something that is particularly sensational, particularly negative, or especially positive. I'm really only interested in what that person's genuine experience has been like. I want to elicit open and honest judgments from people without making them worry about my judging what they say.

An example of the illustrative examples format is provided by a question taken from interviews we conducted with juvenile delinquents who had been placed in foster group homes. One section of the interview was aimed at finding out how the juveniles were treated by group home parents.

Okay, now I'd like to ask you to tell me how you were treated in the group home by the parents. Some kids have told us they were treated like one of the family; some kids have told us that they got knocked around and beat up by the group home parents; some kids have told us about sexual things that were done to them; some of the kids have told us about fun things and trips they did with the parents; some kids have felt they were treated really well and some have said they were treated pretty bad. What about you—how have you been treated in the group home?

A closely related approach is the *illustrative extremes format*—giving examples only of extreme responses. This question is from a follow-up study of award recipients who received a substantial fellowship with no strings attached.

How much of the award, if any, did you spend on entirely personal things to treat yourself well? Some fellows have told us they spent a sizable portion of the award on things like a new car, a hot tub, fixing up their house, personal trips, and family. Others spent almost nothing on themselves and put it all into their work. How about you?

In both the illustrative examples format and the illustrative extremes format, it is critical to avoid asking leading questions. Leading questions are the opposite of neutral questions; they give the interviewee hints about what would be a desirable or appropriate kind of answer. Leading questions "lead" the respondent in a certain direction. Below are questions I found on transcripts during review of an evaluation project carried out by a reputable university center.

We've been hearing a lot of really positive comments about this program. So what's your assessment?

and

We've already heard that this place has lots of troubles, so feel free to tell us about the troubles you've seen.

and

I imagine it must be horrible to have a child abused and have to deal with the system, so you can be honest with me. How bad was it?

Each of these questions builds in a response bias that communicates the interviewer's belief about the situation prior to hearing the respondent's assessment. The questions are leading in the sense that the interviewee can be led into acquiescence with the interviewer's point of view.

In contrast, the questions offered above to demonstrate the illustrative examples format included several dimensions to provide balance between what might be construed as positive and negative kinds of responses. I prefer to use the illustrative examples format primarily as a clarifying strategy after having begun with a simple, straightforward, and truly open-ended question: "What do you think about this program?" or "What has been your experience with the system?" Only if this initial question fails to elicit a thoughtful response, or if the interviewee seems to be struggling, will I offer illustrative examples to facilitate a deeper response.

Role-Playing and Simulation Questions

Providing context for a series of questions can help the interviewee hone in on relevant responses. A helpful context provides cues about the level at which a response is expected. One way of providing such a context is to role-play with persons being interviewed, asking them to respond to the interviewer as if he or she were someone else.

> Suppose I was a new person who just came into this program, and I asked you what I should do to succeed here. What would you tell me?

or

> Suppose I was a new kid in this group home, and I didn't know anything about what goes on around here. What would you tell me about the rules that I have to be sure to follow?

These questions provide a context for what would otherwise be quite difficult questions, for example, "How does one get the most out of this program?" or "What are the rules of this group home?" The role-playing format emphasizes the interviewees' expertise; that is, it puts them in the role of expert because they know something of value to someone else. The interviewee is *the insider with inside information.* The interviewer, in contrast, as an outsider, takes on the role of novice or apprentice. The "expert" is being asked to share his or her expertise with the novice. I've often observed interviewees become more animated and engaged when asked role-playing questions. They get into the role.

A variation on the role-playing format involves the interviewer dissociating somewhat from the question to make it feel less personal and probing. Consider these two difficult questions for a study of a tough subject: teenage suicide.

> What advice would you give someone your age who was contemplating suicide?

versus

> Think of someone you know and like who is moody. Suppose that person told you they were contemplating suicide. What would you tell them?

The first question comes across as abrupt and demanding, almost like an examination to see if they know the right answer. The second question, with the interviewee allowed to create a personal context, is softened and, it is hoped, more inviting. While this technique can be overused and can sound phony if asked insensitively, with the right intonation communicating genuine interest and used sparingly, with subtlety, the role-playing format can ease the asking of difficult questions to deepen answers and enhance the quality of responses.

Simulation questions provide context in a different way, by asking the person being interviewed to imagine himself or herself in the situation about which the interviewer is interested.

> Suppose I was present with you during a staff meeting; what would I see going on? Take me there.

or

> Suppose I was in your classroom at the beginning of the day when the students first come in. What would I see happening as the students came in? Take me to your classroom and let me see what happens during the first 10 to 15 minutes as the students arrive, what you'd be doing, what they'd be doing, what those first 15 minutes are like.

In effect, these questions ask the interviewee to become an observer. In most cases, a response to this question will require the interviewee to visualize the situation to be described. I frequently find that the richest and most detailed descriptions come from a series of questions that ask a respondent to reexperience and/or simulate some aspect of an experience.

Presupposition Questions

Presupposition questions involve a twist on the theme of empathic neutrality. Presuppositions have been identified by linguists as a grammatical structure that creates rapport by assuming shared knowledge and assumptions (Kartunnen 1973; Bandler and Grinder 1975a). Natural language is filled with presuppositions. In the course of our day-to-day communications, we often employ presuppositions without knowing we're doing so. By becoming aware of the effects of presupposition questions, we can use them strategically in interviewing. The skillful interviewer uses presuppositions to increase the richness and depth of responses.

What then, are presuppositions? Linguists Grinder and Bandler define presuppositions as follows:

> When each of us uses a natural language system to communicate, we assume that the listener can decode complex sound structures into meanings, i.e., the listener has the ability to derive the Deep-Structure meaning from the Surface-Structure we present to him auditorily. . . . [W]e also assume the complex skill of listeners to derive extra meaning from some Surface-Structures by the nature of their form. Even though neither the speaker nor the listener may be aware of this process, it goes on all the time. For example, if someone says: I want to watch *Kung Fu* tonight on TV we must understand that *Kung Fu* is on TV tonight in order to process the sentence "I want to watch . . ." to make any sense. These processes are called presuppositions of natural language. (Bandler and Grinder 1975a:241)

Used in interviewing, presuppositions communicate that the respondent has something to say, thereby increasing the likelihood that the person being interviewed will, indeed, have something to say. Consider the following question: "What is the most important experience you have had in the program?" This question presupposes that the respondent has had an important experience. The person of whom the question is asked, of course, has the option of responding, "I haven't had any important experiences." However, it is more likely that the interviewee will go directly to the issue of which experience to report as important, rather than dealing first with the question of whether or not an important experience has occurred.

Contrast the presupposition format— "What is the most important experience you have had in the program?"—to the following dichotomous question: "Have you had any experiences in the program that you would call really important?" This dichotomous framing of the question requires the person to make a decision about what an important experience is and whether one has occurred. The presupposition format bypasses this initial step by asking directly for description rather than asking for an affirmation of the existence of the phenomenon in question. Listed on page 70, on the left, are typical dichotomous response questions that are used to introduce a longer series of questions. On the right are presupposition questions that bypass the dichotomous lead-in query and, in some cases, show how adding "if any" creates a more neutral framing.

A naturalness of inquiry flows from presuppositions making more comfortable what might otherwise be embarrassing or intrusive questions. The presupposition includes the implication that what is presupposed is the natural way things occur. It is

🠗 Alternative Question Formats

Dichotomous Lead-In Question	Presupposition Lead-In Question
Do you feel you know enough about the program to assess its effectiveness?	How effective do you think the program is? (presupposes that a judgment can be made)
Have you learned anything from this program?	What, if anything, have you learned from this program? (presupposes that some learning is likely)
Do you do anything now in your work that you didn't do before the program began?	What, if anything, do you do now that you didn't do before the program began? (presupposes change)
Are there any conflicts among the staff?	What kinds of staff conflicts have occurred here? (presupposes conflicts)

natural for there to be conflict in programs. The presupposition provides a stimulus that asks the respondent to mentally access the answer to the question directly without making a decision about whether or not something has actually occurred.

I first learned about interview presuppositions from a friend who worked with the agency in New York City that had responsibility for interviewing carriers of venereal disease. His job was to find out about the carrier's previous sexual contracts so that those persons could be informed that they might have venereal disease. He had learned to avoid asking men, "Have you had any sexual relationships with other men?" Instead, he asked, "How many sexual contacts with other men have you had?" The dichotomous question carried the burden for the respondent of making a decision about some admission of homosexuality and/or promiscuity. The presupposition form of the open-ended question implied that some sexual contacts with other men might be quite natural and focused on the frequency of occurrence rather than whether or not such sexual contacts have occurred at all. The venereal disease interviewers found that they

were much more likely to generate open responses with the presupposition format than with the dichotomous response format.

The purpose of in-depth interviews is to find out what someone has to say. By presupposing that the person being interviewed does, indeed, have something to say, the quality of the descriptions received may be enhanced. However, a note of warning: Presuppositions, like any single form of questioning, can be overused. Presuppositions are *one* option. There are many times when it is more comfortable and appropriate to check out the relevance of a question with a dichotomous inquiry ("Did you go to the lecture?") before asking further questions ("What did you think of the lecture?").

Prefatory Statements and Announcements

Another technique for facilitating responses involves alerting the interviewee to what is about to be asked before it is actually asked. Think of it as warming up the respondent, or ringing the interviewee's mental doorbell. This is done with prefatory statements that introduce a question. These can serve two functions. First, a preface alerts interviewees to the nature of the question that is coming, directs their awareness, and focuses their attention. Second, an introduction to a question gives respondents a few seconds to organize their thoughts before responding. Prefaces, transition announcements, and introductory statements help smooth the flow of the interview. Any of several formats can be used.

The *transition* format announces that one section or topic of the interview has been completed and a new section or topic is about to begin.

We've been talking about the goals and objectives of the program. Now I'd like to ask you some questions about actual program activities. What are the major activities offered to clients in this program?

or

We've been talking about your personal experiences with this program. Now I'd like to ask your opinions about the program more generally, specifically, about the program's strengths and weaknesses. Let's begin with strengths. What would you say are the basic strengths of this program, from your point of view?

The transition format essentially says to the interviewee: "This is where we've been ... and this is where we're going. . . ." Questions prefaced by transition statements help maintain the smooth flow of an interview.

An alternative format is the *summarizing transition*. This involves bringing closure to a section of the interview by summarizing what has been said and asking if they have anything to add or clarify before moving on to a new subject.

Before we move on to the next set of questions, let me make sure I've got everything you said about the program goals and objectives. You said the program had five goals. First, . . . Second, . . .

Before I ask you some questions about program activities related to these goals, are there any additional goals or objectives that you want to add?

The *summarizing transition* lets the person being interviewed know that the interviewer is actively listening and recording what is being said. The summary invites the interviewee to make clarifications, corrections, or additions before moving on to a new topic.

The *direct announcement* format simply states what will be asked next. A preface to a question that announces its content can soften the harshness or abruptness of the question itself. Direct prefatory statements help make an interview more conversational and easy-flowing. The transcriptions below show two interview sequences, one without prefatory statements and the other with prefatory statements.

Question Without Preface	Interview With Direct Preface
How have you changed as a result of the program?	Now, let me ask you to think about any changes you see in yourself as a result of participating in this program. (pause) How, if at all, have you been changed by your experiences in this program?

The *attention-getting preface* goes beyond just announcing the next question to make a comment about the question. The comment may concern the importance of the question, the difficulty of the question, the openness of the question, or any other characteristic of the question that would help set the stage. Consider these examples:

> This next question is particularly important to the program staff. How do you think the program could be improved?

or

> This next question is purposefully vague so that you can respond in any way that makes sense to you. What difference has this program made to the larger community?

or

> This next question may be particularly difficult to answer with certainty, but I'd like to get your thoughts on it. In thinking about how you've changed during the last year, how much has this program caused those changes compared to other influences on your life at this time?

or

> This next question is aimed directly at getting your perspective. What's it like to be a client in this program?

or

> As you may know, this next issue has been both controversial and worrisome. What kind of staff is needed to run a program like this?

The common element in each of these examples is that some prefatory comment is made about the question to alert the interviewee to the nature of the question. The attention-getting format communicates that the question about to be asked has some unique quality that makes it particularly worthy of being answered.

Making statements about the questions being asked is a way for the interviewer to engage in some conversation during the interview without commenting judgmentally on the answers being provided by the interviewee. What is said concerns the questions and not the respondent's answers. In this fashion, the interview can be made more interesting and interactive. However, all of these formats must be used selectively and strategically. Constant repetition of the same format or mechanical use of a particular approach will make the interview more, rather than less, awkward.

Probes and Follow-Up Questions

Probes are used to deepen the response to a question, increase the richness and depth of responses, and give cues to the interviewee about the level of response that is desired. The word *probe* is usually best avoided in interviews—a little too proctological. The expression "Let me probe that further" can sound as if you're conducting an investigation of something illicit or illegal. Quite simply, a probe is a follow-up question used to go deeper into the interviewee's responses. As such, probes should be conversational, offered in a natural style and voice, and used to follow up initial responses.

One natural set of conversational probes consists of *detail-oriented questions*. These are the basic questions that fill in the blank spaces of a response.

> *When* did that happen?
> *Who* else was involved?
> *Where* were you during that time?
> *What* was your involvement in that situation?

How did that come about?

Where did that happen?

These *detail-oriented probes* are the basic "who," "where," "what," "when," and "how" questions that are used to obtain a complete and detailed picture of some activity or experience.

At other times, an interviewer may want to keep a respondent talking about a subject by using *elaboration probes*. The best cue to encourage continued talking is nonverbal—gently nodding your head as positive reinforcement. However, overenthusiastic head nodding may be perceived as endorsement of the content of a response or as wanting the person to stop talking because the interviewer has already understood what the respondent has to say. Gentle and strategic head nodding is aimed at communicating that you are listening and want to go on listening.

The verbal corollary of head nodding is the quiet "uh-huh." A combination may be necessary; when the respondent seems about to stop talking and the interviewer would like to encourage more comment, an "uh-huh" combined with a gentle rocking of the whole upper body can communicate interest in having the interviewee elaborate.

Elaboration probes also have direct verbal forms:

Would you elaborate on that?

Could you say some more about that?

That's helpful. I'd appreciate a bit more detail.

I'm beginning to get the picture. (The implication is that I don't have the full picture yet, so please keep talking.)

If something has been said that is ambiguous or an apparent non sequitur, a *clarification probe* may be useful. Clarification probes tell the interviewee that you need more information, a restatement of the answer, or more context.

You said the program is a "success." What do you mean by success?

I'm not sure I understand what you meant by that. Would you elaborate, please?

I want to make sure I understand what you're saying. I think it would help me if you could say some more about that.

A *clarification probe* should be used naturally and gently. It is best for the interviewer to convey the notion that the failure to understand is the fault of the interviewer and not a failure by the person being interviewed. The interviewer does not want to make the respondent feel inarticulate, stupid, or muddled. After one or two attempts at achieving clarification, it is usually best to leave the topic that is causing confusion and move on to other questions, perhaps returning to that topic at a later point.

Another kind of clarifying follow-up question is the *contrast probe* (McCracken 1988:35). The purpose of a contrast probe is to "give respondents something to push off against" by asking, "How does *x* compare to *y*?" This is used to help define the boundaries of a response. How does this experience/feeling/action/term compare to some other experience/feeling/action/term?

A major characteristic that separates probes from general interview questions is that probes are seldom written out in an interview. **Probing is a skill that comes from knowing what to look for in the interview, listening carefully to what is said and what is not said, and being sensitive to the feedback needs of the person being interviewed.** Probes are always a combination of verbal and nonverbal cues. Silence at the end of a response can indicate as effectively as anything else that the interviewer would like the person to continue. Probes are used to communicate what the interviewer wants. More detail? Elaboration? Clarity?

Probes, then, provide guidance to the person interviewed. They also provide the interviewer with a way to maintain control of the flow of the interview, a subject we now turn to.

◻ Process Feedback During the Interview

Previous sections have emphasized the importance of careful wording so that interview questions are clear. Clear wording concerns the content of the interview. This section emphasizes feedback about how the *process* is going.

A good interview feels like a connection has been established in which communication is flowing two ways. Qualitative research interviews differ from interrogations or detective-style investigations. The interviewer has a responsibility to communicate clearly what information is desired and why that information is important and to let the interviewee know how the interview is progressing.

An interview is an interaction. Kvale (1996) has emphasized this point by calling qualitative research interviews "Inter-Views" to highlight that an interchange occurs and a temporary interdependence is created. The interviewer provides stimuli to generate a reaction. That reaction from the interviewee, however, is also a stimulus to which the interviewer responds. **You, as the interviewer, must maintain awareness of how the interview is flowing, how the interviewee is reacting to questions, and what kinds of feedback are appropriate and helpful to maintain the flow of communication.**

Support and Recognition Responses

A common mistake among novices is failing to provide *reinforcement* and *feedback*. This means letting the interviewee know from time to time that the purpose of the interview is being fulfilled. Words of thanks, support, and even praise will help make the interviewee feel that the interview process is worthwhile and support ongoing rapport.

Your comments about program weaknesses are particularly helpful, I think, because identification of the kind of weaknesses you describe can really help in making changes in the program.

or

It's really helpful to get such a clear statement of what the program is like. That's just the kind of thing we're trying to get at.

or

We're about halfway through the interview now and from my point of view, it's going very well. You've been telling me some really important things. How's it going for you?

or

I really appreciate your willingness to express your feelings about that. You're helping me understand—and that's exactly why I wanted to interview you.

You can get clues about what kind of reinforcement is appropriate by watching the interviewee. When verbal and nonverbal behaviors indicate someone is really struggling with a question, going mentally deep within, working hard trying to form an answer, after the response it can be helpful for the interviewer to say, "I know that was a difficult question and I really appreciate your working with it because what you said was very meaningful and came out very clearly."

At other times, you may perceive that only a surface or shallow answer has been provided. It may then be appropriate to say something like the following: "I don't want to let that question go by without asking you to think about it just a little bit more, because I feel you've really given some important detail and insights on the other questions and I'd like to get more of your reflections about this question."

In essence, the interviewer, through feedback, is "training" the interviewee to provide high-quality and relevant responses.

Maintaining Control and Enhancing the Quality of Responses

Time is precious in an interview. Long-winded responses, irrelevant remarks, and digressions reduce the amount of time available to focus on critical questions. These problems exacerbate when the interviewer fails to maintain a reasonable degree of control over the process. Control is facilitated by (1) knowing what you want to find out, (2) asking focused questions to get relevant answers, (3) listening attentively to assess the quality and relevance of responses, and

(4) giving appropriate verbal and nonverbal feedback to the person being interviewed.

Knowing what you want to find out means being able to recognize and distinguish appropriate from inappropriate responses. It is not enough just to ask the right questions. The interviewer must listen carefully to make sure that the responses received provide answers to the questions that are asked. Consider the following exchange:

Question: What happens in a typical interviewer training session that you lead?

Answer: I try to be sensitive to where each person is at with interviewing. I try to make sure that I am able to touch base with each person so that I can find out how they're responding to their training, to get some notion of how each person is doing.

Question: How do you begin a session, a training session?

Answer: I believe it's important to begin with enthusiasm, to generate some excitement about interviewing.

In this interaction, the interviewer is asking descriptive, behavioral questions. The responses, however, are about beliefs and hopes. The answers do not actually describe what happened. Rather, they describe what the interviewee thinks *ought* to happen. Since the interviewer wants behavioral data, it is necessary to first recognize that the responses are not providing the kind of data desired, and then to ask appropriate questions that will lead to behavioral responses, something like this:

Interviewer: Okay, you try to establish contact with each person and generate enthusiasm at the beginning. What would help me now is to have you actually take me into a training ses-

sion. Describe for me what the room looks like, where the trainees are, where you are, and tell me what I would see and hear if I were right there in that session. What would I see you doing? What would I hear you saying? What would I see the trainees doing? What would I hear the trainees saying? *Take me into a session so that I can actually experience it.*

It is the interviewer's responsibility to work with the person being interviewed to facilitate the desired kind of responses. At times, it may be necessary to give very direct feedback about the kind of information that has been received and the kind that is desired.

Interviewer: I understand what you try to do during a training session—what you hope to accomplish and stimulate. Now I'd like you to describe to me what you actually do, not what you expect, but what I would actually see happening if I was present at the session.

It's not enough to simply ask a well-formed and carefully focused initial question. Neither is it enough to have a well-planned interview with appropriate basic questions. The interviewer must listen actively and carefully to responses to make sure that the interview is working. I've seen many well-written interviews that have resulted in largely useless data because the interviewer did not listen carefully and thus did not recognize that the responses were not providing the information needed. The first responsibility, then, in maintaining control of the interview is knowing what kind of data you are looking for and managing the interview so as to get quality responses.

Giving appropriate feedback to the interviewee is essential in pacing an interview and maintaining control of the interview process. Head nodding, taking notes, "uh-huhs," and silent probes (remaining quiet when a person stops talking to let them know you're waiting for more) are all signals to the person being interviewed that responses are on the right track. These techniques encourage greater depth in responses, but you also need skill and techniques to stop a highly verbal respondent who gets off the track. The first step in stopping the long-winded respondent is to cease giving the usual cues that encourage talking: stop nodding the head, interject a new question as soon as the respondent pauses for breath, stop taking notes, or call attention to the fact that you've stopped taking notes by flipping the page of the writing pad and sitting back, waiting. When these nonverbal cues don't work, you simply have to interrupt the long-winded respondent.

> Let me stop you here for a moment. I want to make sure I fully understand something you said earlier. (Then ask a question aimed at getting the response more targeted.)

or

> Let me ask you to stop for a moment because some of what you're talking about now I want to get later in the interview. First I need to find out from you. . . .

Interviewers are sometimes concerned that it is impolite to interrupt an interviewee. It certainly can be awkward, but when done with respect and sensitivity, the interruption can actually help the interview. It is both patronizing and disrespectful to let the respondent run on when no attention is being paid to what is said. It is respectful of both the person being interviewed and the interviewer to make good use of the short time available to talk. It is the responsibility of the interviewer to help the interviewee understand what kind of information is being requested and to establish a framework and context that makes it possible to collect the right kind of information.

Information that helps the interviewee understand the purpose of the overall interview and the relationship of particular questions to that overall purpose is important information that goes beyond simply asking questions. While the reason for asking a particular question may be absolutely clear to the interviewer, don't assume it's clear to the respondent. You communicate respect for persons being interviewed by giving them the courtesy of explaining why questions are being asked. Understanding the purpose of a question will increase the motivation of the interviewee to respond openly and in detail.

The overall purpose of the interview is conveyed in an opening statement. Specific questions within the interview should have a connection to that overall purpose. (We'll deal later with issues of informed consent and protection of human subjects in relation to opening statements of purpose. The focus here is on communicating purpose to improve responses. Later we'll review the ethical issues related to informing interviewees about the study's purpose.) While the opening statement at the beginning of an interview provides an overview about the purpose of the interview, it will still be appropriate and important to explain the purpose of particular questions at strategic points throughout the interview. Here are some examples from evaluation interviews.

> This next set of questions is about the program staff. The staff has told us that they don't really get a chance to find out how people in the program feel about what they do, so this part of the interview is aimed at giving them some direct feedback. But as we agreed at the beginning, the staff won't know who said what. Your responses will remain confidential.

or

> This next set of questions asks your background and experiences. The purpose of these questions is to help us find out how people with varying backgrounds have reacted to the program.

The One-Shot Question

Informal, conversational interviewing typically takes place as a natural part of fieldwork. It is opportunistic and often unscheduled. An opportunity arises to talk with someone and the interview is under way. More structured and scheduled interviewing takes place by way of formal appointments and evaluation site visits. Yet, the best-laid plans for scheduled interviews can go awry. You arrive at the appointed time and place only to find that the person to be interviewed is unwilling to cooperate or needs to run off to take care of some unexpected problem. When faced with such a situation, it is helpful to have a single, one-shot question in mind to salvage at least something. This *one-shot question* is the one you ask if you are only going to get a few minutes with the interviewee.

For an agricultural extension needs assessment, I was interviewing farmers in rural Minnesota. The farmers in the area were economically distressed and many felt alienated from politicians and professionals. I arrived at a farm for a scheduled interview, but the farmer refused to cooperate. At first, he refused to even come out of the barn to call off the dogs surrounding my truck. Finally, he appeared and said,

> I don't want to talk to you tonight. I know I said I would, but the wife and I had a tiff and I'm tired. I've always helped with your government surveys. I fill out all the forms the government sends. But I'm tired of it. No more. I don't want to talk.

I had driven a long way to get this interview. The fieldwork was tightly scheduled and I knew that I would not get another shot at this farmer, even if he later had a change of heart. And I didn't figure it would help much to explain that I wasn't from the government. Instead, to try to salvage the situation, I took my one-shot question, a question stimulated by his demeanor and overt hostility.

> I'm sorry I caught you at a bad time. But as long as I'm here, let me ask you just one quick question, then I'll be on my way. Is there anything you want to tell the bastards in St. Paul?

He hesitated for just a moment, grinned, and then launched into a tirade that turned into a full, two-hour interview. I never got out of the truck, but I was able to cover the entire interview (though without ever referring to or taking out the written interview schedule). At the end of this conversational interview, which had fully satisfied my data collection needs, he said, "Well, I've enjoyed talkin' with you, and I'm sorry about refusin' to fill out your form. I just don't want to do a survey tonight."

I told him I understood and asked him if I could use what he had told me as long as he wasn't identified. He readily agreed, having already signed the consent form when we set up the appointment. I thanked him for the conversation. My scheduled, structured interview had become an informal, conversational interview developed from a last-ditch, one-shot question.

Here's a different example. The story is told of a young ethnographer studying a village that had previously been categorized in anthropological studies as aggressive and war oriented. He sat outside the school at the end of the day and asked each boy who came out a one-shot question that must have seemed either very stupid or very European, or both. His question: "What do men do?" The responses he obtained overwhelmingly referred to farming and fishing, and almost none to warfare. In one hour, he had a totally different view of the society than that portrayed by previous researchers.

The Final or Closing Question

In the spirit of emergent interviewing, open-ended interviewing, it's important in formal interviews to provide an opportunity for the interviewee to have the final say: "That covers the things I wanted to ask. Anything you care to add?" I've gotten some my richest data from this question with interviewees taking me in directions it had never occurred to me to pursue. Or try this: "What should I have asked you that I didn't think to ask?"

Beyond Technique

We've been looking with some care at different kinds of questions in an effort to polish interviewing technique and increase question precision. Below I'll offer suggestions about the mechanics of managing data collection, things like recording the data and taking notes. Before moving on, though, it may be helpful to stand back and remember the larger purpose of qualitative inquiry so that we don't become overly technique oriented. You're trying to understand a person's world and worldview. That's why you ask focused questions in a sensitive manner. You're hoping to elicit relevant answers that are useful in understanding the interviewee's perspective. That's basically what interviewing is all about.

This chapter offers ideas about how to do quality interviews, but, ultimately, no recipe can prescribe the single right way of interviewing. No single correct format exists that

HOW MUCH TECHNIQUE?

Sociologist Peter Berger is said to have told his students, "In science as in love, a preoccupation with technique may lead to impotence."

To which Halcolm adds, "In love as in science, ignoring technique reduces the likelihood of attaining the desired results. The path of wisdom joins that of effectiveness somewhere between the outer boundaries of ignoring technique and being preoccupied with it."

is appropriate for all situations, and no particular way of wording questions will always work. The specific interview situation, the needs of the interviewee, and the personal style of the interviewer all come together to create a unique situation for each interview. Therein lies the challenge of qualitative interviewing.

Maintaining focus on gathering information that is useful, relevant, and appropriate requires concentration, practice, and **the ability to separate that which is foolish from that which is important.** In his great novel *Don Quixote*, Cervantes describes a scene in which Sancho is rebuked by Don Quixote for trying to impress his cousin by repeating deeply philosophical questions and answers that he has heard from other people, all the while trying to make the cousin think that these philosophical discourses were Sancho's own insights.

"That question and answer," said Don Quixote, "are not yours, Sancho. You have heard them from someone else."

"Whist, sir," answered Sancho, "if I start questioning and answering, I shan't be done till tomorrow morning. Yes, for if it's just a matter of asking idiotic questions and giving silly replies, I needn't go begging help from the neighbors."

"You have said more than you know, Sancho," said Don Quixote, "for there are some people who tire themselves out learning and proving things that, once learned and proved, don't matter a straw as far as the mind or memory is concerned." (Cervantes 1964: 682)

Regardless of which interview strategy is used—the informal conversational interview, the interview guide approach, or a standardized open-ended interview—the wording of questions will affect the nature and quality of responses received. So will careful management of the interview process. Constant attention to *both content and process,* with both informed by the purpose of the interview, will reduce the extent to which, in Cervantes's words, researchers and evaluators "tire themselves out learning and proving things that, once learned and proved, don't matter a straw as far as the mind or memory is concerned."

⑤ Mechanics of Gathering Interview Data

Recording the Data

No matter what style of interviewing you use and no matter how carefully you word questions, it all comes to naught if you fail to capture the actual words of the person being interviewed. The raw data of interviews are the actual quotations spoken by interviewees. Nothing can substitute for these data: the actual things said by real people. That's the prize sought by the qualitative inquirer.

Data interpretation and analysis involve making sense out of what people have said, looking for patterns, putting together what

Award-winning documentary filmmaker Errol Morris (The Thin Blue Line) invented the "Interrotron" to increase rapport and deepen eye contact when videotaping interviews. Morris believes that Americans are so comfortable with television sets that doing his interviews through a television enhances rapport. Morris asks his questions through a specially designed video camera in the same room with the interview subject. The interviewee sees and hears him on a television and responds by talking into the television. Morris, in turn, watches the interview live on TV. The whole interaction takes place face-to-face through televisions placed at right angles to each other in the same room.

is said in one place with what is said in another place, and integrating what different people have said. These processes occur primarily during the analysis phase after the data are collected. During the interviewing process itself—that is, during the data collection phase—the purpose of each interview is to record as fully and fairly as possible that particular interviewee's perspective. Some method for recording the verbatim responses of people being interviewed is therefore essential.

As a good hammer is essential to fine carpentry, a good tape recorder is indispensable to fine fieldwork. Tape recorders do not "tune out" conversations, change what has been said because of interpretation (either conscious or unconscious), or record words more slowly than they are spoken. (Tape recorders, do, however, break down and malfunction.) Obviously, a researcher doing conversational interviews as part of covert fieldwork does not walk around with a tape recorder. However, most interviews are arranged in such a way that tape recorders are appropriate if properly explained to the interviewee:

> I'd like to tape record what you say so I don't miss any of it. I don't want to take the chance of relying on my notes and maybe missing something that you say or inadvertently changing your words somehow. So, if you don't mind, I'd very much like to use the recorder. If at any time during the interview you would like to turn the tape recorder off, all you have to do is press this button on the microphone, and the recorder will stop.

Exhibit 7.4 lists a set of tips for getting high-quality recordings and transcriptions. These tips were prepared by transcribers who had worked on hundreds of hours of interviews and estimated that 20% of the tapes given to them, usually by graduate students, were so badly recorded as to be impossible to transcribe accurately—or at all. These tips will also help if, as is often recommended, you do either all or some of your own transcriptions as a way of more deeply immersing yourself in the data as a first step during analysis.

When it is not possible to use a tape recorder because of some sensitive situation, interviewee request, or tape recorder malfunction, notes must become much more thorough and comprehensive. It becomes critical to gather actual quotations. When the interviewee has said something that seems particularly important or insightful, it may be necessary to say, "I'm afraid I need to stop you at this point so that I can get down exactly what you said because I don't want to lose that particular quote. Let me read back to you what I have and make sure it is exactly what you said." This point emphasizes again the importance of capturing what people say in their own words.

But such verbatim note taking has become the exception now that most people are familiar and comfortable with tape recorders. More than just increasing the accuracy of data collection, using a tape recorder permits the interviewer to be more attentive to the interviewee. If you tried to write down every word said, you'd have a difficult time responding appropriately to interviewee needs and cues. Ironically, *verbatim* note taking can interfere with listening attentively. The interviewer can get so focused on note taking that the person speaking gets only secondary attention. Every interview is also an observation, and having one's eyes fixed on a notepad is hardly conducive to careful observation. In short, the interactive nature of in-depth interviewing can be seriously affected by an attempt to take verbatim notes. Lofland (1971) has made this point forcefully:

> One's full attention must be focused upon the interviewee. One must be thinking about probing for further explication or clarification of what he is now saying; formulating probes linking up current talk with what he has already said; thinking ahead to putting in a new question that has now arisen and was not taken account of in the standing guide (plus making a note at that moment so one will not forget the question); and attending to the interviewee in a manner that communicates to him that you are indeed listening. All of this is hard enough simply in itself. Add to that the problem of writing it down—even if one takes shorthand in an expert fashion—and one can see that the process of note-taking in the interview decreases one's interviewing capacity. Therefore, if conceivably possible, *tape record*; then one can interview. (p. 89)

So if verbatim note taking is neither desirable nor really possible, what kind of notes are taken during a tape-recorded interview?

EXHIBIT 7.4	Tips for Tape-Recording Interviews: How to Keep Transcribers Sane

1. Equipment
   a. Use an electrical outlet and external microphone whenever possible; they're more reliable.
   b. If you use batteries check them regularly and carry spares.
   c. The recorder should be clean and in good condition—check it before going to an interview.
   d. Use good-quality tapes of 60 minutes or less; longer tapes are more likely to stretch or break when transcribed.
   e. Take along extra cassette tapes.

2. Before the interview
   a. Choose a place for the interview that's quiet and free from interruptions.
   b. Place the microphone close to the respondent, then speak loud enough so that questions can be heard; most important, though, is hearing the responses.
   c. Set the recorder on a stable surface.
   d. Test the recording system.

3. During the interview
   a. Speak clearly and not too fast—the respondent will then be more likely to do the same.
   b. Ask the respondent to speak up if his or her voice starts to soften.
   c. Run a test with the respondent: Then rewind and listen so the respondent can hear whether he or she is speaking distinctly. Whether a problem is mechanical or personal, correct it before continuing.
   d. Don't rustle papers, cups, bottles, etc., near the microphone.
   e. Turn off the recorder during extended side conversations, breaks, or interruptions.
   f. Watch for tape breakage and tangling.
   g. Repeat the test if a tape change is necessary.
   i. At end of interview, say, "This is the end of interview with _____."

4. After the interview
   a. Listen to the start, middle, and end of the tape; list proper names and unfamiliar or unusual terminology to help the transcriber.
   b. Label tapes and return them to appropriate containers.
   c. Keep tapes and recorder in good condition; do not touch tapes or expose them to extreme temperatures.
   d. Give transcribers reasonable time to do a good job.

SOURCE: Prepared by transcribers at the Minnesota Center for Social Research, University of Minnesota.

Taking Notes During Interviews

The use of the tape recorder does not eliminate the need for taking notes, but does allow you to concentrate on taking strategic and focused notes, rather than attempting verbatim notes. Notes can serve at least four purposes:

1. Notes taken during the interview can help the interviewer formulate new questions as the interview moves along, particularly where it may be appropriate to check out something said earlier.

2. Looking over field notes before transcripts are done helps make sure the inquiry is unfolding in the hoped-for direction and can stimulate early insights that may be relevant to pursue in subsequent interviews while still in the field—the emergent nature of qualitative inquiry.

3. Taking notes about what is said will facilitate later analysis, including locating important quotations from the tape itself.

4. Notes are a backup in the event the recorder has malfunctioned or, as I've had happen, a tape is erased inadvertently during transcription.

When a tape recorder is being used during the interview, notes will consist primarily of key phrases, lists of major points made by the respondent, and key terms or words shown in quotation marks that capture the interviewee's own language. It is enormously useful to develop some system of abbreviations and informal shorthand to facilitate taking notes, for example, in an interview on leadership, write "L" instead of the full word. Some important conventions along this line include (1) using quotation marks *only* to indicate full and actual quotations; (2) developing some mechanism for indicating interpretations, thoughts, or ideas that may come to mind during the interview, for example, the use of brackets to set off one's own ideas from those of the interviewee; and (3) keeping track of questions asked as well as answers received. Questions provide the context for interpreting answers.

Note taking serves functions beyond the obvious one of taking notes. Note taking helps pace the interview by providing nonverbal cues about what's important, providing feedback to the interviewee about what kinds of things are especially "noteworthy"—literally. Conversely, the failure to take notes may indicate to the respondent that nothing of particular importance is being said. And don't start making out your shopping list while someone is droning on endlessly. They'll think you're taking notes, enchanted, and will keep on talking. The point is that taking notes affects the interview process.

After the Interview

The period after an interview or observation is critical to the rigor and validity of qualitative inquiry. This is a time for guaranteeing the quality of the data.

Immediately after a recorded interview, check the tape to make sure it was functioning properly. If, for some reason, a malfunction occurred, you should immediately make extensive notes of everything that can be remembered. Even if the tape functioned properly, the interviewer should go over the interview notes to make certain that they make sense, to uncover areas of ambiguity or uncertainty. If you find things that don't quite make sense, as soon possible, you should check back with the interviewee for clarification. This can often be done over the telephone. In my experience, people who are interviewed appreciate such a follow-up because it indicates the seriousness with which the interviewer is taking their responses. Guessing the meaning of a response is unacceptable; if there is no way of following up the comments with the respondent, then those areas of vagueness and uncertainty simply become missing data.

The immediate postinterview review is a time to record details about the setting and your observations about the interview. Where did the interview occur? Under what conditions? How did the interviewee react to questions? How well do you think you did asking questions? How was the rapport?

Answers to these questions establish a context for interpreting and making sense of the interview later. Reflect on the quality of information received. Did you find out what you really wanted to find out in the interview? If not, what was the problem? Poorly worded questions? Wrong topics? Poor rapport? Reflect on these issues and make notes on the interview process while the experience is still fresh in your minds. These process notes will inform the methodological section of your research report, evaluation, or dissertation.

This period after an interview or observation is a critical time of reflection and elaboration. It is a time of quality control to guarantee that the data obtained will be useful, reliable, and authentic. This kind of postinterview ritual requires discipline. Interviewing and observing can be exhausting, so much so that it is easy to forgo this time of reflection and elaboration, put it off, or neglect it altogether. To do so is to seriously undermine the rigor of qualitative inquiry. Interviews and observations should be scheduled so that sufficient time is available afterward for data clarification, elaboration, and evaluation. Where a team is working together, the whole team needs to meet regularly to share observations and debrief together. This is the beginning of analysis, because, while the situation and data are fresh, insights can emerge that might otherwise have been lost. Ideas and interpretations that emerge following an interview or observation should be written down and clearly marked as emergent, field-based insights to be further reviewed later.

I sometimes think about the time after an interview as a period for postpartum reflection, a time to consider what has been revealed or what has been birthed. In 18th-century Europe, the quaint phrase "in an interesting condition" became the gentile way of referring to an expectant mother in "polite company." The coming together of an interviewer and an interviewee makes for "an interesting condition." The interviewer is certainly expectant, as may be the interviewee. What emerged? What was created? Did it go OK? Is some form of triage necessary? As soon as a child is born, a few basic observations are made and tests are performed to make sure that everything is all right. That's what you're doing right after an interview—making sure everything came out OK.

Such an analogy may be a stretch for thinking about a postinterview debrief, but interviews are precious to those who hope to turn them into dissertations, contributions to knowledge, and evaluation findings. It's worth managing the interview process to allow time to make observations about, reflect on, and learn from each interview.

Up to this point we've been focusing on techniques to enhance the quality of the standard one-on-one interview. We turn now to some important variations in interviewing, such as think-aloud protocols, focus group interviews, and cross-cultural interviewing.

🖳 Special Applications and Issues

Think-Aloud Protocol Interviewing

Protocol analysis or, more literally, the *think-aloud protocol* approach, aims to elicit the inner thoughts or cognitive processes that illuminate what's going on in a person's head during the performance of a task, for example, painting or solving a problem. The point is to undertake interviewing as close to the action as possible. While someone engages in an activity, the interviewer asks questions and probes to get the person to talk about what the person is thinking as he or she does the task. In teaching rounds at hospitals, senior physicians do a version of this when they talk aloud about how they're engaging in a diagnosis while medical students listen, presumably learning the experts' thinking processes by hearing them in action. For details of the think-aloud protocol method, see Pressley and Afflerbach (1995) and Ericsson and Simon (1993).

Wilson (2000) used a protocol research design in a doctoral dissertation that investigated student understanding and problem solving in college physics. Twenty students in individual 45-minute sessions were videotaped and asked to talk aloud as they tried to solve three introductory physics problems of moderate difficulty involving Newton's second law. This involved a *concurrent* rather than *retrospective* approach, because students were engaged in thinking aloud and problem solving concurrently, as opposed to explaining their thinking and reasoning retrospectively after solving the problems. Wilson notes that concurrent designs are generally considered more reliable because the verbal data and protocols that are generated do not depend on subjects' short-term memory recall of the cognitive

processes and strategies they think were engaged while solving problems. Wilson was able to pinpoint the cognitive challenges that confronted students as they tried to derive the acceleration of a particle moving in various directions and angles with respect to a particular reference frame.

The basic strategy of think-aloud protocols involves getting people who are doing something to verbalize their thoughts and feelings as they do whatever they're doing. This can take some "training" of participants to get them used to verbalizing what are usually only internal dialogues with themselves.

Focus Group Interviews

A *focus group* interview is an interview with a small group of people on a specific topic. Groups are typically 6 to 10 people with similar backgrounds who participate in the interview for one to two hours. In a given study, a series of different focus groups will be conducted to get a variety of perspectives and increase confidence in whatever patterns emerge. Focus group interviewing was developed in recognition that many consumer decisions are made in a social context, often growing out of discussions with other people. Thus, market researchers began using focus groups in the 1950s as a way of stimulating the consumer group process of decision making to gather more accurate information about consumer product preferences (Higginbotham and Cox 1979). On the academic side, sociologist Robert K. Merton and associates wrote the seminal work on research-oriented focus group interviews in 1956: *The Focused Interview* (Merton, Riske, and Kendall 1956).

The focus group interview is, first and foremost, an interview. It is not a problem-solving session. It is not a decision-making group. It is not primarily a discussion,

though direct interactions among participants often occur. It is an *interview*. The twist
is that, unlike a series of one-on-one interviews, in a focus group participants get to
hear each other's responses and to make additional comments beyond their own original responses as they hear what other people
have to say. However, participants need not
agree with each other or reach any kind of
consensus. Nor is it necessary for people to
disagree. The object is to get high-quality
data in a social context where people can
consider their own views in the context of
the views of others.

Focus group expert Richard Krueger
(1994) explains that a focus group should be
"carefully planned" to obtain perceptions
"on a defined area of interest in a permissive,
nonthreatening environment. It is conducted . . . by a skilled interviewer. The discussion is comfortable and often enjoyable
for participants as they share their ideas and
perceptions. Group members influence each
other by responding to ideas and comments
in the discussion" (p. 6). Krueger prefers the
term *moderator* to *interviewer* because

> this term [*moderator*] highlights a specific func-
> tion of the interviewer—that of moderating or
> guiding the discussion. The term *interviewer*
> tends to convey a more limited impression of
> two-way communication between an inter-
> viewer and an interviewee. By contrast, the fo-
> cus group affords the opportunity for multiple
> interactions not only between the interviewer
> and respondent but among all participants in
> the group. The focus group is not a collection
> of simultaneous individual interviews, but
> rather a group discussion where the conversa-
> tion flows because of the nurturing of the
> moderator. (p. 100)

The combination of moderating and interviewing is sufficiently complex that

Krueger recommends that teams of two conduct the groups so that one person can focus
on facilitating the group while the other
takes detailed notes and deals with mechanics like as tape recorders, cameras, and any
special needs that arise, for example, someone needing to leave early or becoming
overwrought. Even when the interview is
recorded, good notes help in sorting out
who said what when the tape recording is
transcribed.

Focus group interviews have several advantages for qualitative inquiry.

- Data collection is cost-effective. In one
  hour, you can gather information from
  eight people instead of only one, significantly increasing sample size. "Focus
  group interviews are widely accepted
  within marketing research because they
  produce believable results at a reasonable cost" (Krueger 1994:8).

- Interactions among participants enhance data quality. Participants tend to
  provide checks and balances on each
  other, which weeds out false or extreme
  views (Krueger and Casey 2000).

- The extent to which there is a relatively
  consistent, shared view or great diversity of views can be quickly assessed.

- Focus groups tend to be enjoyable to participants, drawing on human tendencies
  as social animals.

Focus groups, like all forms of data collection, also have limitations.

- The number of questions that can be
  asked is greatly restricted in the group
  setting.

- The available response time for any particular individual is restrained in order
  to hear from everyone. A rule of thumb:

Postmodern *unfocused* group interview

With eight people and an hour for the group, plan to ask no more than 10 major questions.

■ Facilitating and conducting a focus group interview require considerable group process skill beyond simply asking questions. The moderator must manage the interview so that it's not dominated by one or two people and so that those participants who tend not to be highly verbal are able to share their views.

■ Those who realize that their viewpoint is a minority perspective may not be inclined to speak up and risk negative reactions.

■ Focus groups appear to work best when people in the group, though sharing similar backgrounds, are strangers to each other. The dynamics are quite different and more complex when participants have prior established relationships.

■ Controversial and highly personal issues are poor topics for focus groups (Kaplowitz 2000).

■ Confidentiality cannot be assured in focus groups. Indeed, in market research, focus groups are often videotaped so that marketers can view them and see for themselves the emotional intensity of people's responses.

■ "The focus group is beneficial for identification of major themes but not so much for the micro-analysis of subtle differences" (Krueger 1994:x).

■ Compared with most qualitative fieldwork approaches, focus groups typically have the disadvantage of taking place outside of the natural settings where social interactions normally occur (Madriz 2000:836).

As these strengths and limitations suggest, **the power of focus groups resides in their being focused.** The topics are narrowly focused, usually seeking reactions to something (a product, program, or shared experience) rather than exploring complex life issues with depth and detail. The groups are focused by being formed homogeneously. The facilitation is focused, keeping responses on target. Interactions among participants are focused, staying on topic. Use of time must be focused, because the time passes quickly. Despite some of the limitations introduced by the necessity of sharp focus, applications of focus groups are widespread and growing (Krueger and Casey 2000; Madriz 2000; Fontana and Frey 2000; Academy for Educational Development 1989; Morgan 1988). Focus groups remain a staple of market research where reactions to new or existing products can be explored. Focus groups have come to play an important role in quality management efforts where consumer feedback about services and programs is desired. The feedback from focus groups is typically more specific, meaningful, and animated than what can be obtained from individually filled out consumer questionnaires and surveys. Focus groups are conducted as part of a needs assessment process with both potential client groups and professionals who know the needs of client groups. Focus groups are being used with client and staff groups in program evaluation to identify a program's strengths, weaknesses, and needed improvements. Focus groups can be used at the end of a program, or even months after program completion, to gather perceptions about outcomes and impacts. Key community people can be interviewed in groups

when their views of a policy may be of interest to planners, organizers, and developers. Focus groups are used with special targeted populations in action research, for example, with program dropouts or community leaders. Organizational development consultants make widespread use of focus groups to identify major motifs of an organization's culture.

Private sector market research firms have developed substantial technology to support focus groups. Krueger (1994), who works mainly with public sector, education, and nonprofit groups, thinks that

> fancy facilities and technological devices are generally overrated. The private sector market research environment often cites these electronic and physical features as benchmarks of quality. The true benchmark is the quality of the discussion, which can easily erode when participants are overly fascinated, annoyed, or distracted by such devices as one-way mirrors, television cameras, and knobs and buttons. (p. x)

At the other end of the societal continuum from focus groups used for corporate marketing are community groups using focus groups as a form of community-wide documentation and, sometimes, organizing. Focus groups have entered into the repertoire of techniques for qualitative researchers and evaluators involved in participatory studies with coresearchers. For community research, collaborative action research, and participatory evaluations, local people who are not professional researchers are being successfully trained and supported to do focus groups (Krueger and King 1997).

Because the focus group "is a collectivistic rather than an individualistic research method," focus groups have also emerged as a collaborative and empowering approach in feminist research (Madriz 2000:

836). Sociologist and feminist researcher Esther Madriz (2000) explains:

> Focus groups allow access to research participants who may find one-on-one, face-to-face interaction "scary" or "intimidating." By creating multiple lines of communication, the group interview offers participants . . . a safe environment where they can share ideas, beliefs, and attitudes in the company of people from the same socioeconomic, ethnic, and gender backgrounds. . . .
>
> For years, the voices of women of color have been silenced in most research projects. Focus groups may facilitate women of color "writing culture together" by exposing not only the layers of oppression that have suppressed these women's expressions, but the forms of resistance that they use every day to deal with such oppressions. In this regard, I argue that focus groups can be an important element in the advancement of an agenda of social justice for women, because they can serve to expose and validate women's everyday experiences of subjugation and their individual and collective survival and resistance strategies. (pp. 835-36)

I experienced firsthand the potential of focus groups to provide safety in numbers for people in vulnerable situations. I conducted focus groups among low-income recipients of legal aid as one technique in an evaluation of services provided to people in a large public housing project. As the interview opened, participants, who came from different sections of the project and did not know each other, were reserved and cautious about commenting on problems they were experiencing. As one woman shared in vague terms a history of problems she had had in getting needed repairs, another woman jumped in and supported her, saying, "I know exactly what you're talking about and *who* you're talking about. It's re-

ally bad. Bad. Bad. Bad." She then shared her story. Soon others were telling similar stories, often commenting that they had no idea so many other people were having the same kind of problems. Several also commented at the end of the interview that they would have been unlikely to share their stories with me in a one-on-one interview because they would have felt individually vulnerable, but they drew confidence and a sense of safety and camaraderie from being part of the interview group.

On the other hand, Kaplowitz (2000) studied whether sensitive topics were more or less likely to be discussed in focus groups versus individual interviews. Ninety-seven year-round residents from the Chelem Lagoon region in Yucatan, Mexico, participated in one of 12 focus groups or 19 individual in-depth interviews. A professional moderator used the same interview guide to get reactions to a shared mangrove ecosystem. The 31 sessions generated more than 500 pages of transcripts, which were coded for the incidence of discussions of sensitive topics. The findings showed that the individual interviews were 18 times more likely to address socially sensitive discussion topics than the focus groups. In addition, the study found the two qualitative methods, focus groups and individual interviews, to be complementary to each other, each yielding somewhat different information.

Computer-based Internet interactions have created new forms of focus groups. Walston and Lissitz (2000) evaluated the feasibility and effectiveness of computer-mediated focus groups. They compared the reactions of computer-mediated and face-to-face participants in focus groups discussing academic dishonesty and found that the computer-mediated environment appeared to reduce members' anxiety about what the moderator thought of them, making it easier for them to share embarrassing information.

As focus groups have become more widely used in needs assessments, organizational development, and evaluation research, new approaches have emerged that adapt techniques to those purposes. Rossman and Rallis (1998:135), for example, have done focus groups with young children. The *Focus Group Kit* (Morgan 1997a, 1997b; Krueger 1997a, 1997b, 1997c; Krueger and King 1997) and *The Handbook for Focus Group Research* (Greenbaum 1997) are helpful resources for variations on focus groups.

The next section looks at group interviews more broadly.

Group Interviews

Not all group interviews are of the focus group variety. During fieldwork, unstructured conversational interviews may occur in groups that are not at all focused. In evaluating a community leadership program, much of the most important information came from talking informally with groups of people during breaks from the formal training. During the fieldwork for the wilderness education program described extensively in the last chapter, informal group interviews became a mainstay of data collection, sometimes with just 2 or 3 people, and sometimes in dinner groups as large as 10.

Parameswaran (2001) found important differences in the data she could gather in group versus individual interviews during her fieldwork in India. Moreover, she found that she had to do group interviews with the young women *before* she could interview them one-on-one. She was studying the reading of Western romance novels among female college students in India. She reports:

To my surprise, several young women did not seem happy or willing to spend time with me alone right away. When I requested the first group of women to meet me on an individual basis and asked if they could meet me during their breaks from classes, I was surprised and uncomfortable with the loud silence that ensued. . . .

When I faced similar questions from another group of women who also appeared to resist my appeals to meet with them alone, I realized that I had arrogantly encroached into their intimate, everyday rituals of friendship. . . . Knowing well that without collecting data from these possibly recalcitrant subjects, I had no project, I reluctantly changed my plans and agreed to accept their demands. I began talking to them in groups first, and gradually, more than 30 women agreed to meet me in individual sessions. Later, I discovered that they preferred to respond to me as a group first because they were wary about the kinds of questions I planned to ask about their sexuality and romance reading. The more public nature of group discussions meant that it was a safe space where I might hesitate to ask intrusive and personal questions. . . .

Group interviews in which women spoke about love, courtship, and heterosexual relations in Western romance fiction became opportunities to debate, contradict, and affirm their opinions about a range of gendered social issues in India such as sexual harassment of women in public places, stigmas associated with single women, expectations of women to be domestic, pressures on married women to obey elders in husbands' families, and the merits of arranged versus choice/love marriages. . . . In contrast to these collective sessions where young women's discussions primarily revolved around gender discrimination toward women as a group, in individual interviews, many women were much more talkative about restrictions on their sexuality, and several women shared their frustrations with immediate, everyday problems pertaining to family members' control over their movements. (Parameswaran 2001: 84-86)[1]

Parameswaran's work illustrates well the different kinds of data that can be collected from groups versus individuals, with both kinds of data being important in long-term or intensive fieldwork. I had similar experiences in Burkina Faso and Tanzania where villagers much preferred group interviews for formal and structured interactions, and the only way to get individual interviews was informally when walking somewhere or doing something with an individual. On several occasions, I tried scheduling and conducting individual interviews only to have many other people present when I arrived. Such cross-cultural differences in valuing individual versus group interactions provide a nice segue to the next section on cross-cultural interviewing.

🔲 Cross-Cultural Interviewing

*C*ulture and place demand our attention not because our concepts of them are definitive or authoritative, but because they are fragile and fraught with dispute.

—Jody Berland (1997:9)

Cross-cultural inquiries add layers of complexity to the already-complex interactions of an interview. The possibility for misunderstandings are increased significantly as documented in materials and training schemes aimed at cross-cultural sensitization (e.g., Brislin et al. 1986; Stewart 1985; Casse and Deol 1985; Harris and Moran 1979). Ironically, economic and cultural globalization, far from reducing the likelihood of misunderstandings, may simply make miscommunications more nuanced and harder to detect because of false assumptions about shared meanings. Whiting (1990) tellingly explores cross-cultural differences in his book *You Gotta Have Wa*, on how Americans and Japanese play seemingly the same game, baseball, quite differently—and then uses those differences as entrées into the two cultures. Frow and Morris (2000) have captured the challenges of "cross-cultural" engagement in the new millennium, when the very notion of "culture" is in flux:

The smooth professional consensus about the limits and potentials of culture does not easily emerge when new struggles, conversations, and alliances are forming across once-formidable geopolitical and even linguistic boundaries while old colonial hierarchies, spacings, and "structures of feeling" continue to shape the social meanings of events in landscapes newly produced or remade by economic globalization. For many scholars now, questions of identity and community are framed not only by issues of race, class, and gender but by a deeply political concern with place, cultural memory, and the variable terms of the scholars' access to an "international" space of debate dominated not only by Western preoccupations but by the English language. (p. 319)

Ethnographic interviewing has always been inherently cross-cultural but has the advantage of being grounded in long-term relationships and in-depth participant observation (Tedlock 2000). In this section, we focus on the problematic short-term studies for theses or student exchange projects and brief evaluation site visits sponsored by international development agencies and philanthropic foundations. In the latter case, teams of a few Westerners are flown into a developing country for a week to a month to assess a project, often with counterparts from the local culture. These rapid appraisals revolve around cross-cultural interviewing and are more vulnerable to misinterpretations and miscommunications than traditional, long-term anthropological fieldwork. Examples of the potential problems, presented in the sections that follow, will, I hope, help sensitize students, short-term site visitors, and evaluators to the precariousness of cross-cultural interviewing. As Rubin and Rubin (1995) have noted:

> You don't have to be a woman to interview women, or a sumo wrestler to interview sumo wrestlers. But if you are going to cross social gaps and go where you are ignorant, you have to recognize and deal with cultural barriers to communication. And you have to accept that how you are seen by the person being interviewed will affect what is said. (p. 39)

Language Differences

The data from interviews are words. It is tricky enough to be sure what a person means when using a common language, but words can take on a very different meaning in other cultures. In Sweden, I participated in an international conference discussing policy evaluations. The conference was conducted in English, but I was there two days, much of the time confused, before I came to understand that their use of the term *policy* corresponded to my American use of the term *program*. I interpreted policies from an American context, to be fairly general direc-

tives, often very difficult to evaluate because of their vagueness. In Sweden, however, policies were articulated and even legislated at such a level of specificity that they resembled programmatic prescriptions more than the vague policies that typically emanate from the legislative process in the United States.

The situation becomes more precarious when a translator or interpreter must be used. Special and very precise training of translators is critical. Translators need to understand what, precisely, you want them to ask and that you will need full and complete translation of responses as verbatim as possible. Interpreters often want to be helpful by summarizing and explaining responses. This contaminates the interviewee's actual response with the interpreter's explanation to such an extent that you can no longer be sure whose perceptions you have—the interpreter's or the interviewee's.

Some words and ideas simply can't be translated directly. People who regularly use the language come to know the unique cultural meaning of special terms. One of my favorites from the Caribbean is *liming*, meaning something like hanging out, just being, doing nothing—guilt free. In interviews for a Caribbean program evaluation, a number of participants said they were just "liming" in the program. That was not, however, meant as criticism, for liming is a highly desirable state of being, at least to participants. Funders viewed the situation somewhat differently.

Rheingold (2000) has published a whole book on "untranslatable words and phrases" with special meanings in other cultures. Below are four examples that are especially relevant to evaluators.

> *Schlimmbesserung* (German)—a so-called improvement that makes things worse

biga peula (Kiriwina, New Guinea)—potentially disruptive, unredeemable true statements

animater (French)—a word of respect for a person who can communicate difficult concepts to general audiences

ta (Chinese)—to understand things and thus take them lightly

In addition to the possibility of misunderstandings, there may be the danger of contracting culturally specific disease, including for some what the Chinese call *koro* —"the hysterical belief that one's penis is shrinking" (Rheingold 1988:59).

Attention to language differences cross-nationally can, it is hoped, make us more sensitive to barriers to understanding that can arise even among those who speak the same language. Joyce Walker undertook a collaborative study with 18 women who had written to each other annually for 25 years, 1968 to 1993. She involved them actively in the study, including having them confirm the authenticity of her findings. In reacting to the study, one participant reacted to the research language used: "Why call us a cohort? There must be something better—a group, maybe?" (Walker 1996:10).

Differing Norms and Values

The high esteem in which science is held has made it culturally acceptable in Western countries to conduct interviews on virtually any subject in the name of scholarly inquiry and the common good. Such is not the case worldwide. Researchers cannot simply presume that they have the right to ask intrusive questions. Many topics discussed freely in Western societies are taboo in other parts of the world. I have experienced cultures where it was simply inappropriate to ask questions of a subordinate about a super-

ordinate. Any number of topics may be insensitive to ask or indelicate if brought up by strangers, for example, family matters, political views, who owns what, how people came to be in certain positions, and sources of income.

Interviewing farmers for an agricultural extension project in Central America became nearly impossible to do because, for many, their primary source of income came from growing illegal crops. In an African dictatorship our needs assessment team found that we could not ask about "local" leadership because the country could have *only* one leader. Anyone taking on or being given the designation "local leader" would have been endangered. Interviewees can be endangered by insensitive and inappropriate questions, so can naive interviewers. I know of a case where an American female student was raped following an evening interview in a foreign country because the young man interpreted her questions about local sexual customs and his own dating experiences as an invitation to have sex.

As noted in the previous section on group interviews, different norms govern cross-cultural interactions. I remember going to an African village to interview the chief and finding the whole village assembled. Following a brief welcoming ceremony, I asked if we could begin the interview. I expected a private, one-on-one interview. He expected to perform in front of and involve the whole village. It took me a while to understand this, during which time I kept asking to go somewhere else so we could begin the interview. He did not share my concern about and preference for privacy. What I expected to be an individual interview soon became a whole-village group dialogue.

In many cultures, it is a breach of etiquette for an unknown man to ask to meet alone with a woman. Even a female interviewer may need the permission of a husband, brother, or parent to interview a village woman. A female colleague created a great commotion, and placed a woman in jeopardy, by pursuing a personal interview without permission from the male headman.

As difficult as cross-cultural interviewing may be, it is still far superior to standardized questionnaires for collecting data from nonliterate villagers. Salmen (1987) described a major water project undertaken by the World Bank based on a needs assessment survey. The project was a failure because the local people ended up opposing the approach used. His reflection on the project's failure included a comparison of survey and qualitative methods.

> Although it is difficult to reconstruct the events and motivation that led to the rejection there is little question that a failure of adequate communication between project officials and potential beneficiaries was at least partly responsible. The municipality's project preparation team had conducted a house-to-house survey in Guasmo Norte before the outset of the project, primarily to gather basic socioeconomic data such as family size, employment and income. The project itself, however, was not mentioned at this early stage. On the basis of this survey, World Bank and local officials had decided that standpipes would be more affordable to the people than household connections. It now appears, from hindsight, that the questionnaire survey method failed to elicit the people's negative attitude toward standpipes, their own criterion of affordability, or the opposition of their leaders who may have played on the negative feelings of the people to undermine acceptance of the project. Qualitative interviews and open discussions would very likely have revealed people's preferences and the political climate far better than did the preconstructed questionnaire. (Salmen 1987:37)

Appropriately, Salmen's book, published by the World Bank, is called *Listen to the People* and advocates qualitative methods for international project evaluation of development efforts.

Interviewers are not in the field to judge or change values and norms. Researchers are there to understand the perspectives of others. Getting valid, reliable, meaningful, and usable information in cross-cultural environments requires special sensitivity to and respect for differences. For additional discussion of cross-cultural research and evaluation, see Patton (1985) and Lonner and Berry (1986). For examples of doctoral dissertations based entirely on cross-cultural qualitative interviewing, see McClure (1989) and Sandmann (1989).

One final observation on international and cross-cultural evaluations may help emphasize the value of such experiences. Connor (1985) found that doing international evaluations made him more sensitive and effective in his domestic evaluation work. The heightened sensitivity we expect to need in exotic, cross-cultural settings can serve us well in our own cultures. Sensitivity to and respect for other people's values, norms, and worldviews is as needed at home as abroad.

⑤ Beyond Standard Interviewing: Creative Qualitative Modes of Inquiry

Thus far, this discussion of interviewing has focused on asking. However, insights into the lives and worlds of others can be elicited in many other ways.

Projection techniques are widely used in psychological assessment to gather information from people. The best-known projective test is probably the Rorschach. The general principle involved is to have people react to something other than a question—an ink-blot, picture, drawing, photo, abstract painting, film, story, cartoon, or whatever is relevant. This approach is especially effective in interviewing children, but it can be helpful with people of any age. I found, for example, when doing follow-up interviews two years after completion of a program that some photographs of the program site and a few group activities greatly enhanced recall.

Students can be interviewed about work they have produced. In the wilderness program evaluation, we interviewed participants about entries they shared from their journals. Walker (1996) used letters exchanged between friends as the basis for her study of a generation of American women. Holbrook (1996) contrasted official welfare case records with a welfare recipient's journals to display two completely different constructions of reality. Hamon (1996) used proverbs, stories, and tales as a starting point for her inquiry into Bahamian family life. Rettig, Tam, and Magistad (1996) extracted quotes from transcripts of public hearings on child support guidelines as a basis for their fieldwork. Laura Palmer (1988) used objects left in memory of loved ones and friends at the Vietnam Veterans Memorial in Washington, D.C., as the basis for her inquiry and later interviews. An ethnomusicologist will interview people as they listen and react to recorded music. The possibilities for creative interviewing stretch out before us like an ocean teeming with myriad possibilities, some already known, many more waiting to be discovered or created.

Robert Kegan and colleagues have had success basing interviews on reactions to 10 words in what they call the "subject-object interview . . . In order to understand how the interviewee organizes interpersonal and intrapersonal experiencing, real-life situations are elicited from a series of ten uniform probes" (Lahey et al. n.d.). The interviewee responds to 10 index cards, each listing an idea, concept, or emotion:

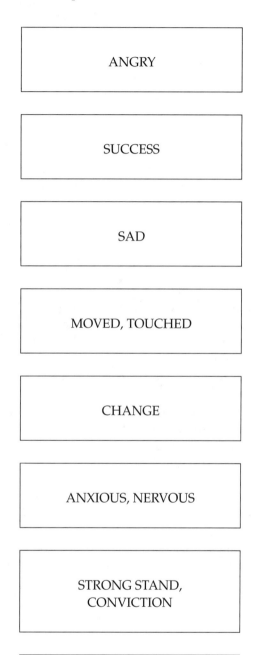

ANGRY

SUCCESS

SAD

MOVED, TOUCHED

CHANGE

ANXIOUS, NERVOUS

STRONG STAND, CONVICTION

TORN

```
┌─────────────────────────────────────┐
│                                       │
│          LOST SOMETHING               │
│                                       │
└─────────────────────────────────────┘

┌─────────────────────────────────────┐
│                                       │
│          IMPORTANT TO ME              │
│                                       │
└─────────────────────────────────────┘
```

Reactions to these words provide data for the interviewer to explore the interviewee's underlying epistemology or "principle of meaning-coherence" based on Kegan's work *The Evolving Self* (1982). The subject-object interview is a complex and sophisticated methodology that requires extensive training for proper application and theoretical interpretation. For my purposes, the point is that a lengthy and comprehensive interview interaction can be based on reaction to 10 deceptively simple ideas presented on index cards rather than fully framed questions.

The subject-object interview methodology illustrates another basis for interviewing: **including writing as part of the interview.** Prior to interviewing the research participants about the 10 ideas, they are given 15 to 20 minutes to jot down things on the index cards. They subsequently choose which cards to talk about and can use their jottings to facilitate their verbal responses. Such an approach gives interviewees a chance to think through some things before responding verbally.

Another substitute for straight questions in interviewing is to ask for explanations of or reactions to critical incidents. These can be selected by the interviewer based on previous fieldwork or previous interviews. The interviewer describes the critical incident to get the interviewee's perspective on what it means and how it relates to other experiences (McClure 1989). Interviewees can be invited to identify incidents they consider "critical" after which a dialogue ensues to determine what made the incident critical.

As these many examples illustrate, qualitative inquiry need not be confined to interview protocols and taking field notes. Researchers and evaluators have considerable freedom to creatively adapt qualitative methods to specific situations and purposes using anything that comes to mind—and works—as a way to enter into the world and worldview of others. Not only are there many variations in what stimuli to use and how to elicit responses, creative variations also exist for who conducts interviews.

Participant Interview Chain

As a participant observer in the wilderness training program for adult educators, I was involved in (1) documenting the kinds of experiences program participants were having and (2) collecting information about the effects of those experiences on the participants and their work situations. In short, the purpose of the evaluation was to provide formative insights that could be used to help understand the personal, professional, and institutional outcomes of intense wilderness experiences for these adult educators. But the two of us doing the evaluation didn't have sufficient time and resources to track everyone, 40 people, in depth. Therefore, we began discussing with the program staff ways in which the participants might become involved in the data collection effort to meet *both* program and evaluation needs. The staff liked the idea of involving participants thereby introducing them to observation and interviewing as ways of expanding their own horizons and deepening their perceptions.

The participants' backpacking field experience was organized in two groups. We used this fact to design a data collection approach that would fit with the programmatic needs for sharing information between the two groups. Participants were paired to interview each other. At the very beginning of the first trip, before people knew each other, all of the participants were given a short, open-ended interview of 10 questions. They were told that each of them, as part of their project participation, was to have responsibility for documenting the experiences of their pair-mate throughout the year. They were given a little bit of interview training, given a lot of encouragement about probing, and told to record responses fully, thereby taking responsibility for helping to build this community record of individual experiences. They were then sent off in pairs and given two hours to complete the interviews with each other, recording the responses by hand.

At the end of the 10-day experience, when the separate groups came back together, the same pairs of participants, consisting of one person from each group, were again given an interview outline and sent off to interview each other about their respective experiences. This served the program need for sharing of information *and* an evaluation need for the collection of information. The trade-off, of course, was that with the minimal interview training given the participants and the impossibility of carefully supervising, controlling, and standardizing the data collection, the results were of variable quality. This mode of data collection also meant that confidentiality was minimal and certain kinds of information might not be shared. But we gathered a great deal more data than we could have obtained if we had had to do all the interviews ourselves.

Limitations certainly exist as to how far one can push client involvement in data collection and analysis without interfering in

the program or burdening participants. But before those limits are reached, a considerable amount of useful information can be collected by involving program participants in the actual data collection process. I have since used similar participant interview pairs in a number of program evaluations with good results. The trick is to integrate the data collection into the program.

Data Collection by Program Staff

Program staff constitutes another resource for data collection that is often overlooked. Involving program staff in data collection raises objections about staff subjectivity, data contamination, loss of confidentiality, the vested interests of staff in particular kinds of outcomes, and the threat that staff members can pose to clients or students from whom they are collecting the data. Balancing these objections are the things that can be gained from staff involvement in data collection: greater staff commitment to the evaluation, increased staff reflectivity, enhanced understanding of the data collection process that comes from training staff in data collection procedures, increased understanding by staff of program participants' perceptions, increased data validity because of staff rapport with participants, and cost savings in data collection.

One of my first evaluation experiences involved studying a program to train teachers in open education at the University of North Dakota. Faculty were interested in evaluating that program, but there were almost no resources available for a formal evaluation. Certainly not enough funds existed to bring in an external evaluation team to design the study, collect data, and analyze the results. The main means of data collection consisted of in-depth interviews with student teachers in 24 different schools and classrooms throughout North Dakota and structured interviews with 300 parents who had children in those classrooms. The only evaluation monies available would barely pay for the transportation and the actual mechanical costs of data collection. Staff and students at the university agreed to do the interviews as an educational experience. I developed structured interview forms for both the teacher and parent interviews and trained all of the interviewers in a full-day session. Interviewers were assigned to geographical areas making sure that no one collected data from their own student teachers. The interviews were tape recorded and transcribed. I did follow-up interviews with a 5% sample as a check on the validity and reliability of the student and staff data.

After data collection, seminars were organized for staff and students to share their personal perceptions based on their interview experiences. Their stories related considerable impact on both staff and students. One outcome was the increased respect both staff and students had for the parents. They found the parents to be perceptive, knowledgeable, caring, and deeply interested in the education of their children. Prior to the interviewing, many of the interviewers had held fairly negative and derogatory images of North Dakota parents. The systematic interviewing had put them in a situation where they were forced to listen to what parents had to say, rather than telling parents what they (as educators) thought about things, and in learning to listen they had learned a great deal. The formal analysis of the data yielded some interesting findings that were used to make some changes in the program and the data provided a source of case materials that were adapted for us in training future program participants, but it is likely that the major and most lasting impact of the evaluation came from the

learnings of students and staff who participated in the data collection. That experiential impact was more powerful than the formal findings of the study, an example of "evaluation process use" (Patton 1997a)—using an evaluation process for participant and organizational learning.

By the way, had the interviewers been paid at the going commercial rate, the data collection could have cost at least $30,000 in personnel expenses. As it was, there were no personnel costs and a considerable human contribution was made to the university program by both students and staff.

Such participatory action research remains controversial. As Kemmis and McTaggart (2000) noted in their extensive review of participatory approaches:

> In most action research, including participatory action research, the researchers make sacrifices in methodological and technical rigor in exchange for more immediate gains in face validity: whether the evidence they collect makes sense to them in their context. For this reason, we sometimes characterize participatory action research as "low-tech" research: It sacrifices in methodological sophistication in order to generate timely evidence that can be used and further developed in a real-time process of transformation (of practices, practitioners, and practice settings). (p. 591)

Whether some loss of methodological sophistication is merited depends on the primary purpose of the inquiry and the primary intended users of the results. For an example of this trade-off, see Exhibit 7.5, which describes a project where former prostitutes were trained to facilitate focus groups with women leaving prostitution. Participatory research will have lower credibility among external audiences, especially among scholars who make rigor their pri-

---

<table>
<tr><td>**EXHIBIT 7.5**</td><td>**Training Nonresearchers as Focus Group Interviewers: Women Leaving Prostitution**</td></tr>
</table>

Rainbow Research studied the feasibility of developing a transitional housing program for prostituted women. To assist us we recruited 5 women who had been prostituted, trained them in focus group facilitation and had them do our interviews with women leaving prostitution. For them the experience was empowering and transformational. They were excited about learning a new skill, pleased to be paid for this work and thought it rewarding that it might benefit prostituted women. Especially thrilling for them during the interviews was the validation and encouragement they received from their peers for the work they were doing. Our work together also had its light moments. During a group simulation, our interviewers loudly and provocatively bantered with one another as they might have on the street.

Our interviewers were proud of their contribution. At project's end they requested certificates acknowledging the training they had received and the interviews successfully performed. And, because they had performed well, we were pleased to oblige. In the simulations they critiqued our interview guide, leading us to edit the language, content, order and length, introduce new questions and drop others. Clearly they had rapport with their peers based on shared discourse and experience, allowing them to gather information others without the experience of prostitution would have been hard-pressed to secure. This was apparent in the reliability of our data. Comparing across the interviews responses to the same items were highly consistent. For all concerned it was a positive experience, with findings that most definitely shaped our final recommendations.

SOURCE: By Barry B. Cohen, executive director of Rainbow Research, Inc., Minneapolis, Minnesota. Personal communication, 2000. Used by permission.

---

mary criterion for judging quality. Participants involved in improving their work or lives, however, lean toward pragmatism where *what is useful determines what is true.* As Kemmis and McTaggart (2000) conclude,

The inevitability—for participants—of having to live with the consequences of transformation provides a very concrete "reality check" on the quality of their transformative work, in terms of whether their practices are more efficaciousness, their understandings are clearer, and the settings in which they practice are more rational, just, and productive of the kinds of consequences they are intended to achieve. For participants, the point of collecting compelling evidence is to achieve these goals, or, more precisely, to avoid subverting them intentionally or unintentionally by their action. Evidence sufficient for this kind of "reality checking" can often be low-tech (in terms of research methods and techniques) or impressionistic (from the perspective of an outsider who lacks the contextual knowledge that the insider draws on in interpreting this evidence). But it may still be "high-fidelity" evidence from the perspective of understanding the nature and consequences of particular interventions in transformations made by participants, in their context—where they are privileged observers. (p. 592)

Interactive Group Interviewing and Dialogues

The involvement of program staff or clients as colleagues or coresearchers in action research and program evaluation changes the relationship between evaluators and staff, making it interactive and cooperative rather than one-sided and antagonistic. William Tikunoff (1980) used an "interactive research" approach in educational research and development projects. He found that putting teachers, researchers, and trainer/developers together as a team increased both the meaningfulness and the validity of the findings because teacher cooperation with and understanding of the research made the research less intrusive, thus reducing rather than increasing reactivity. Their discussions were a form of group interviews in which *they all asked each other questions.*

The problem of how research subjects or program clients will react to staff involvement in an evaluation, particularly involvement in data collection, needs careful scrutiny and consideration in each situation in which it is attempted. Reactivity is a potential problem in both conventional and nonconventional designs. Breaches of confidence and/or reactivity-biased data cannot be justified in the name of creativity. On the other hand, as Tikunoff's experiences indicate, interactive designs may increase the validity of data and reduce reactivity by making evaluation more visible and open, thereby making participants or clients less resistant or suspicious.

These approaches can reframe inquiry from a duality (interviewer-interviewee) to a dialogue in which all are co-inquirers. Miller and Crabtree (2000) advocate such a collaborative approach even in the usually closed and hierarchical world of medical and clinical research:

We propose that clinical researchers investigate questions emerging from the clinical experience with the clinical participants, pay attention to and reveal any underlying values and assumptions, and direct results toward clinical participants and policy makers. This refocuses the gaze of clinical research onto the clinical experience and redefines its boundaries so as to answer three questions: Whose question is it? Are hidden assumptions of the clinical world revealed? For whom are the research results intended? . . . Patients and clinicians are invited to explore their own and/or each other's questions and concerns with whatever methods are necessary. Clinical researchers share ownership of the research with clinical participants, thus undermining the patriarchal bias of the dominant paradigm and opening its assumptions to investigation. This is the situated knowledge . . . where space is created to find a larger, more inclusive vision of clinical research. (p. 616)

Creativity and Data Quality: Qualitative Bricolage

No definitive list of creative interviewing or inquiry approaches can or should be constructed. Such a list would be a contradiction in terms. Creative approaches are those that are situationally responsive and appropriate, credible to primary intended users, and effective in opening up new understandings. The approaches just reviewed are deviations from traditional research practice. Each idea is subject to misuse and abuse if applied without regard for ways in which the quality of data collected can be affected. I have not discussed such threats and possible errors in depth because I believe it is impossible to identify in the abstract and in advance all the trade-offs involved in balancing concerns for accuracy, utility, feasibility, and propriety. For example, having program staff do client interviews in an outcomes evaluation could (a) seriously reduce the validity and reliability of the data, (b) substantially increase the validity and reliability of the data, or (c) have no measurable effect on data quality. The nature and degree of effect would depend on staff relationships with clients, how staff were assigned to clients for interviewing, the kinds of questions asked, the training of the interviewers, attitudes of clients toward the program, the purposes to be served by the evaluation, the environmental turbulence of the program, and so on. Program staff might make better or worse interviewers than external evaluation researchers depending on these and other factors. An evaluator must grapple with these kinds of data quality questions for all designs, particularly nontraditional approaches.

Practical, but creative, data collection consists of using whatever resources are available to do the best job possible. Constraints always exist and do what constraints do—constrain. Our ability to think of alternatives is limited. Resources are always limited. This means data collection will be imperfect, so dissenters from research and evaluation findings who want to attack a study's methods can always find some grounds for doing so. A major reason for actively involving intended evaluation users in methods decisions is to deal with weaknesses and consider trade-off threats to data quality *before* data are collected. By strategically calculating threats to utility, as well as threats to validity and authenticity, it is possible to make practical decisions about the strengths of creative and nonconventional data collection procedures (Patton 1987a, 1997a).

The creative, adaptive inquirer using diverse techniques may be thought of as a "bricoleur." The term comes from Levi-Strauss (1966), who defined a bricoleur as a "jack of all trades or a kind of professional do-in-yourself person" (p. 17).

> The qualitative researcher as bricoleur or maker of quilts uses the aesthetic and material tools of his or her craft, deploying whatever strategies, methods, or empirical materials are at hand. If new tools or techniques have to be invented, or pieced together, then the researcher will do this. (Denzin and Lincoln 2000b:4)

Interdisciplinary scholar and artist Jose Cedillos has adopted the identity of Bricoleur and explained in personal terms how he came to the "bricolage arts" as his creative method of inquiry.

> I learned naïve Bricolage in the garbage dumps, our backs hemmed in by *la playa*, the nutrient edge of the Pacific Ocean. How could it be otherwise to a bunch of field-working native *Mestizos* at the disposable edge of industrial culture? I learned economic Bricolage from my *landsleit* on *La Frontera*, the border between Mexico in the U.S. The bilingual, bi-economic estuaries of Tijuana, Mexicali and the other border towns produced the entrepreneurial dynamism of the immigrant who works off the land and joins odd forms together to make a workable whole, usually by dent of sheer effort. . . .
>
> Bricolage means to combine odds and ends, fragments, in making something. The word comes from the French bricoleur, who traveled the countryside using odds and ends, materials at hand, to perform fix-it work. The power to employ the Bricolage creatively rested in perception, being able to spot materials nested in the environment and available. The Bricolage begins by disentangling perception from information and cognition. The trick is to see what is there, not just our brains speckled onto the environment. Seeing what is there releases information, rather like how, af-

ter a moment of stillness, an ecology begins to chirp and quiver again. (Cedillos forthcoming)

Bricolage, by taking broken things as its primary resource, is a trash methodology for deploying unbridled optimism in a perceptual world; a search technology for the aesthetic potential, the creativity edge everywhere. Bricolage operates in the pixeling surface of the dumps glistening like diamond fields streaked through with veins of gold and silver, and this brings one to see for oneself that the world is indeed layered like this. (Cedillos 1998:18-19)[2]

Creativity begins with being open to new possibilities, the bricolage of combining old things in new ways, including alternative and emergent forms of data collection, transformed observer-observed relations, and reframed interviewer-interviewee interconnections. Naturalistic inquiry calls for ongoing openness to whatever emerges in the field and during interviews. This openness means avoiding forcing new possibilities into old molds. The admonition to remain open and creative applies throughout naturalistic inquiry, from design through data collection and into analysis. Failure to remain open and creative can lead to the error made by a traveler who came across a peacock for the first time, a story told by Halcolm.

A traveler to a new land came across a peacock. Having never seen this kind of bird before, he took it for a genetic freak. Taking pity on the poor bird, which he was sure could not survive for long in such deviant form, he set about to correct nature's error. He trimmed the long, colorful feathers, cut back the beak, and dyed the bird black. "There now," he said, with pride in a job well-done, "you now look more like a standard guinea hen."

⑤ Specialized and Targeted Interview Approaches

This chapter has reviewed general principles of and approaches to in-depth qualitative interviewing. However, most researchers, evaluators, and practitioners specialize in working with and studying specific target populations using finely honed interviewing techniques. Interviewing "elites" or "experts" often requires an interactive style.

> Elites respond well to inquiries about broad topics and to intelligent, provocative, open-ended questions that allow them the freedom to use their knowledge and imagination. In working with elites, great demands are placed on the ability of the interviewer, who must establish competence by displaying a thorough knowledge of the topic or, lacking such knowledge, by projecting an accurate conceptualization of the problem through shrewd questioning. (Rossman and Rallis 1998:134)

Robert Coles (1990) became adept at interviewing children, as have Guerrero-Manalo (1999), Graue and Walsh (1998), Holmes (1998), and Greig and Taylor (1998). Rita Arditti (1999) developed special culturally and politically sensitive approaches for gaining access to and interviewing grandmothers whose children were among "the disappeared" during Argentina's military regime. Guerrero (1999a, 1999b) and colleagues have developed special participatory approaches for interviewing women in developing countries. Judith Arcana (1981, 1983) drew on her own experiences as a mother to become expert at interviewing 180 mothers for two books about the experiences of mothering (one about mothers and daughters, one about mothers and sons). At the other end of the continuum from Cole's delightful stories of childhood innocence are Jane Gilgun's haunting interviews with male sexual offenders and Angela Browne's intensive interviews with women incarcerated in a maximum security prison. Gilgun (1991, 1994, 1995, 1996, 1999) has conducted hundreds of hours of interviews with men who have perpetrated violent sex offenses against women and children, most of them having multiple victims. She learned to establish relationships with these men through repeated life history interviews, but did so without pretending to condone their actions and sometimes challenging their portrayals. Two examples offer a sense of the challenges for someone undertaking such work through long hours and horrific details. One man, engaged to be married at the time of his arrest, confessed to seven rapes; Gilgun interviewed him for a total of 14 hours over 12 different interviews, including detailed descriptions of his sexual violence. Another man molested more than 20 boys; at the time of his arrest he was married, sexually active with his wife, and a stepfather of two boys; she obtained 20 hours of tape over 11 interviews. These cases were particularly intriguing as purposeful samples because both men were White, college graduates in their early 30s who were employed as managers with major supervisory responsibilities and who came from upper-middle-class, two-parent, never-divorced families whose fathers held executive positions and whose mothers were professionals. Gilgun worked with an associate in transcribing and interpreting the interviews.

> The data were so emotionally evocative that we spent a great deal of time working through our personal responses. Almost two years went by before we found we had any facility in articulating the meanings of the discourses we identified in the informants' accounts. Their way of thinking was for the most part outside our frames of reference. As we struggled through these interpretive processes, we made notes of our responses. . . . Most compelling to us [was the men believing they were] entitled to take what they wanted and of defining persons and situations as they wished . . . , to suit themselves. Overall, the discourses they invoked served oppressive hegemonic ends. We also found that the men experienced chills, thrills, and intense emotional gratification as they imposed their wills on smaller, physically weaker persons. (Gilgun and McLeod 1999:175)

The life work of Angela Browne illustrates a similar commitment to in-depth, life history interviewing with people who are isolated from the mainstream and whose experiences are little understood by the general culture. After her groundbreaking 1987 study of women who kill violent partners in self-defense (*When Battered Women Kill*), Browne began gathering life history narratives from women incarcerated in a maximum security prison. These interviews, conducted in a small room off a tunnel in the middle of the facility and six hours in length, included women with lifetime histories of trauma, much of it at the hands of family members in early childhood. Some had witnessed brutal homicides; others were serving time for crimes of violence they had committed. Their stories were painful to tell and to hear. Interviews often were so emotionally draining that Browne came away exhausted, sometimes needing to debrief on both the impact of what she had heard and dynamics of the interviewing process. On several occasions, we had lengthy phone conversations immediately following interviews while she was still within the prison walls. This kind of extreme interviewing takes unusual skill, dedication, and self-knowledge, coupled with a keen interest in the dynamics of human interaction. Although Browne returned home drained after each full week of conducting these daylong interviews, her enthusiasm for the task and her appreciation of respondents' strength and lucidity never dimmed. As this is being written, Browne is writing a book about early exposure to violence as a part of women's pathway to prison, based on the life stories of the women she interviewed.

The works of Gilgun and Browne illustrate the intensity, commitment, long hours, and hard work involved with certain in-depth and life history approaches to interviewing. Robert Atkinson (1998) established the Center for the Study of Lives at the University of Southern Maine in 1988 to capture life stories and further develop methods for the "life story interview." Other methodological contributions along these lines include Cole and Knowles's (2000) *Doing Reflexive Life History Research,* Denzin's (1989a) *Interpretive Biography,* and *The Art and Science of Portraiture* by Sara Lawrence-Lightfoot and Jessica Hoffman Davis (1997):

> Portraiture is a method of qualitative research that blurs the boundaries of aesthetics and empiricism in an effort to capture the complexity, dynamics, and subtlety of human experience and organizational life. Portraitists seek to record and interpret the perspectives and experience of the people they are studying, documenting their voices and their visions—their authority, knowledge, and wisdom. The drawing of the portrait is placed in social and cultural context and shaped through dialogue between the portraitist and the subject, each one negotiating the discourse and shaping the evolving image. The relationship between the two is rich with meaning and resonance and

becomes the arena for navigating the empirical, aesthetic, and ethical dimensions of authentic and compelling narrative. (Lawrence-Lightfoot and Davis 1997:xv)

By explicitly combining "art and science," and making portraiture a negotiated cocreation between the social scientist and the person being depicted, portraiture as a method of qualitative inquiry has been subject to attack for being too much art and too little science (English 2000).

Holstein and Gubrium (1995) have conceptualized what they call "the active interview." Taking a constructionist perspective, they emphasize that an interview is a social interaction with interviewers and interviewees sharing in constructing a story and its meanings; that is, both are participants in the meaning-making process. Their work reminds us that one's theoretical orientation (Chapter 3) can have concrete methodological implications in how one thinks about and engages in data collection.

A different kind of challenge concerns how to manage the tremendous amount of data that can be, and usually are, collected during in-depth interviewing. Grant McCracken (1988) has contributed ways of bringing focus to "the long interview":

> [The long interview] is a sharply focused, rapid, highly intensive interview process that seeks to diminish the indeterminacy and redundancy that attends more unstructured research processes. The long interview calls for special kinds of preparation and structure, including the use of an open-ended questionnaire, so that the investigator can maximize the value of the time spent with the respondent. . . . In other words, the long interview is designed to give the investigator a highly efficient, productive, "stream-line" instrument of inquiry. (p. 7)

Qualitative inquiry includes methods adapted for particular disciplines such as psychology (Kopala and Suzuki 1999), as well as subspecializations such as health psychology (Murray and Chamberlain 1999), humanistic psychology (Moustakas 1990b, 1994, 1995, 1997), and methods of "transpersonal inquiry" that emphasize using intuition, empathy, and self-awareness (Braud and Anderson 1998). Specialized approaches to qualitative inquiry have been developed in organizational research (Van Maanen 1998; Lee 1998; Symon and Cassell 1998), social work (Padgett 1998), family studies (Sussman and Gilgun 1996), health research (Grbich 1998; Morse and Field 1995), nursing (Morse 1991), aging research (Gubrium and Sankar 1993), and cultural studies (McGuigan 1998; Alasuutari 1995), just to cite the range of examples.

Applications and methods of qualitative inquiry, especially interviewing techniques for specially targeted populations and specialized disciplinary approaches, continue to evolve as interest in qualitative methods grows exponentially (a metaphoric rather than statistical estimation). As applications and techniques have proliferated, so have concerns about the ethical challenges of qualitative inquiry, our next topic.

⑤ Ethical Challenges in Qualitative Interviewing

Interviews are interventions. They affect people. A good interview lays open thoughts, feelings, knowledge, and experience, not only to the interviewer but also to the interviewee. The process of being taken through a directed, reflective process affects the persons being interviewed and leaves them knowing things about themselves that they didn't know—or least were not fully aware of—before the interview. Two hours

or more of thoughtfully reflecting on an experience, a program, or one's life can be change inducing; 10, 15, or 20 hours of life history interviewing can be transformative —or not. Therein lies the rub. Neither you nor the interviewee can know, in advance, and sometimes even after the fact, what impact an interviewing experience will have or has had.

The purpose of a research interview is first and foremost to gather data, not change people. Earlier, in the section on neutrality, I asserted that an interviewer is not a judge. Neither is a research interviewer a therapist. Staying focused on the purpose of the interview is critical to gathering high-quality data. Still, there will be many temptations to stray from that purpose. It is common for interviewees to ask for advice, approval, or confirmation. Yielding to these temptations, the interviewer may become the interviewee—answering more questions than are asked.

On the other hand, the interviewer, in establishing rapport, is not a cold slab of granite—unresponsive to the human issues, including great suffering and pain, that may unfold during an interview. In a major farming systems needs assessment project to develop agricultural extension programs for distressed farm families during the farm crisis of the mid-1980s, I was part of a team of 10 interviewers (working in pairs) who interviewed 50 farm families. Many of these families were in great pain. They were losing their farms. Their children had left for the city. Their marriages were under stress. The two-hour interviews traced their family history, their farm situation, their community relationships, and their hopes for the future. Sometimes questions would lead to husband-wife conflict. The interviews would open old wounds, lead to second-guessing decisions made long ago, or bring forth painful memories of dreams never fulfilled.

People often asked for advice—what to do about their finances, their children, government subsidy programs, even their marriages. But we were not there to give advice. Our task was to get information about needs that might, or might not, lead to new programs of assistance. Could we do more than just ask our questions and leave? Yet, as researchers, could we justify in any way intervening? Yet again, our interviews were already an intervention. Such are the ethical dilemmas that derive from the power of interviews.

What we decided to do in the farm family interviews was leave each family a packet of information about resources and programs of assistance, everything from agricultural referrals to financial and family counseling. To avoid having to decide which families really needed such assistance, we left the information with all families—separate and identical packages for both husband and wife. When interviewees asked for advice during the interview, we could tell them that we would leave them referral information at the end of the interview.

While interviews may be intrusive in reopening old wounds, they can also be healing. In doing follow-up interviews with families who had experienced child sexual abuse, our team found that most mothers appreciated the opportunity to tell their stories, vent their rage against the system, and share their feelings with a neutral but interested listener. Our interviews with elderly residents participating in a program to help them stay in their homes and avoid nursing home institutionalization typically lasted much longer than planned because the elderly interviewees longed to have company and talk. When interviewees are open and willing to talk, the power of interviewing poses new risks. People will tell you things they never intended to tell you. This can be true even with reluctant or hostile interviewees, a fact depended on by journalists. Indeed, it seems at times that the very thing someone is determined *not* to say is the first thing they tell, just to release the psychological pressure of secrecy or deceit.

I repeat, people in interviews will tell you things they never intended to tell. Interviews can become confessions, particularly under the promise of confidentiality. But beware that promise. Social scientists can be summoned to testify in court. We do not have the legal protection that clergy and lawyers have. In addition, some information must be reported to the police, for example, evidence of child abuse. Thus, the power of interviewing can put the interviewees at risk. **The interviewer needs to have an ethical framework for dealing with such issues.**

There are also direct impacts on interviewers. The previous section described the wrenching interviews conducted by Jane Gilgun, with male sex offenders, and Angela Browne, with incarcerated women, and the physical and emotional toll of those interviews on them as interviewers exposed for hours on end to horrendous details of violence and abuse. In a family sexual abuse project (Patton 1991), the fieldwork director found that interviewers needed to be extensively debriefed, sometimes in support groups together, to help them process and deal with the things they heard. They could take in only so much without having some release, some safety valve for their own building anger and grief. Middle-class interviewers going into poor areas may be shocked and depressed by what they hear and see. It is not enough to do preparatory training before such interviewing. Interviewers may need debriefing— **and their observations and feelings can become part of the data on team projects.**

These examples are meant to illustrate the power of interviewing and why it is important to anticipate and deal with the ethical dimensions of qualitative inquiry. **Because qualitative methods are highly personal and interpersonal, because naturalistic inquiry takes the researcher into the real world where people live and work, and because in-depth interviewing opens up what is inside people—qualitative inquiry may be more intrusive and involve greater reactivity than surveys, tests, and other quantitative approaches.**

Exhibit 7.6 presents a checklist of ethical issues as a starting point in thinking through ethical issues in design, data collection, and analysis. The next section elaborates some issues of special concern. (For more comprehensive discussions of ethics in qualitative inquiry, see Christians 2000; Kvale 1996: 109-23; Rubin and Rubin 1995:93-105; Punch 1986, 1997; for ethics in evaluation and applied research, see Newman and Brown 1996; Joint Committee on Standards for Educational Evaluation 1994; Kimmel 1988.)

Informed Consent and Confidentiality

Informed consent protocols and opening statements in interviews typically cover the following issues:

What is the purpose of collecting the information?

Who is the information for? How will it be used?

What will be asked in the interview?

How will responses be handled, including confidentiality?

What risks and/or benefits are involved for person being interviewed?

The interviewer often provides this information in advance of the interview and then again at the beginning of the interview. Providing such information does not, however, require making long and elaborate speeches. Statements of purpose should be simple, straightforward, and understandable. Long statements about what the interview is going to be like and how it will be used, when such statements are made at the beginning of the interview, are usually either boring or produce anxiety. The interviewee will find out soon enough what kinds of questions are going to be asked and, from the nature of the questions, will make judgments about the likely use of such information. The basic messages to be communicated in the opening statement are (1) the information is important, (2) the reasons for that importance, and (3) the willingness of the interviewer to explain the purpose of the interview out of respect for the interviewee. Here's an example of an opening interview statement from an evaluation study:

> I'm a program evaluator brought in to help improve this program. As someone who has been in the program, you are in a unique position to describe what the program does and how it affects people. And that's what the interview is about: your experiences with the program and your thoughts about your experiences.
>
> The answers from all the people we interview, and we're interviewing about 25 people, will be combined for our report. Nothing you say will ever be identified with you personally. As we go through the interview, if you have any questions about why I'm asking something, please feel free to ask. Or if there's anything you don't want to answer, just say so. The purpose of the interview is to get your insights into how the program operates and how it affects people.
>
> Any questions before we begin?

This may seem straightforward enough, but dealing with real people in the real world, all kinds of complications can arise. Moreover,

---

EXHIBIT 7.6	Ethical Issues Checklist

1. *Explaining purpose.* How will you explain the purpose of the inquiry and methods to be used in ways that are accurate and understandable?
   - What language will make sense to participants in the study?
   - What details are critical to share? What can be left out?
   - What's the expected value of your work to society and to the greater good?

2. *Promises and reciprocity.* What's in it for the interviewee?
   - Why should the interviewee participate in the interview?
   - Don't make promises lightly, for example, promising a copy of the tape recording or the report. *If you make promises, keep them.*

3. *Risk assessment.* In what ways, if any, will conducting the interview put people at risk? Psychological stress?
   Legal liabilities?
   In evaluation studies, continued program participation (if certain things become known)?
   Ostracism by peers, program staff, or others for talking?
   Political repercussions?

   - How will you describe these potential risks to interviewees?
   - How will you handle them if they arise?

4. *Confidentiality.* What are reasonable promises of confidentiality that can be fully honored? Know the difference between confidentiality and anonymity. (Confidentiality means you know but won't tell. Anonymity means you don't know, as in a survey returned anonymously.)
   - What things can you *not* promise confidentiality about, for example, illegal activities, evidence of child abuse or neglect?
   - Will names, locations, and other details be changed? Or do participants have the option of being identified? (See discussion of this in the text.)
   - Where will data be stored?
   - How long will data be maintained?

---

some genuine ethical quandaries have arisen in recent years around the ethics of research in general and qualitative inquiry in particular.

HOW MUCH OF AN INTERVIEW MUST BE APPROVED IN ADVANCE?

In the chapter on observation and field-work, I discussed the problems posed by ap-proval protocols aimed at protecting human subjects given the emergent and flexible designs of naturalistic inquiry. Institutional review boards (IRBs) for the protection of human subjects often prefer to approve actual interview questions, which can be done when using the standardized interview format discussed in this chapter, but works less well when using an interview guide, and doesn't work at all for conversational interviewing where the questions emerge at the

5. *Informed consent.* What kind of informed consent, if any, is necessary for mutual protection?
   - What are your local institutional review board (IRB) guidelines and/or requirements, or those of an equivalent committee for protection of human subjects in research?
   - What has to be submitted, under what timelines, for IRB approval, if applicable?

6. *Data access and ownership.* Who will have access to the data? For what purposes?
   - Who owns the data in an evaluation? (Be clear about this in the contract.)
   - Who has right of review before publication? For example, of case studies, by the person or organization depicted in the case; of the whole report, by a funding or sponsoring organization?

7. *Interviewer mental health.* How will you and other interviewers likely be affected by conducting the interviews?
   - What might be heard, seen, or learned that may merit debriefing and processing?
   - Who can you talk to about what you experience without breaching confidentiality?
   - How will you take care of yourself?

8. *Advice.* Who will be the researcher's confidant and counselor on matters of ethics during a study? (Not all issues can be anticipated in advance. Knowing who you will go to in the event of difficulties can save precious time in a crisis and bring much-needed comfort.)

9. *Data collection boundaries.* How hard will you push for data?
   - What lengths will you go to in trying to gain access to data you want? What won't you do?
   - How hard will you push interviewees to respond to questions about which they show some discomfort?

10. *Ethical versus legal.* What ethical framework and philosophy informs your work and ensures respect and sensitivity for those you study, beyond whatever may be required by law?
    - What disciplinary or professional code of ethical conduct will guide you?

moment in context. A compromise is to specify those questions one can anticipate and list other possible topics while treating the conversational component as probes, which are not typically specified in advance. But in a full naturalistic inquiry design, interview questions can and should change as the interviewer understands the situation more fully and discovers new pathways for questioning. The tension between specifying questions in advance for approval and allowing questions to emerge in context in the field led Elliot Eisner (1991) to ask, "Can qualitative studies be informed ... [since] we have such a hard time predicting what we need to get consent about?" (p. 215). An alternative to specifying precise questions for approval in advance is to specify areas of inquiry that will be avoided, that is, to anticipate ways in which respondents might be put at risk and affirm that the interviewer will avoid such areas.

Uninformed consent seeker

Conversational interviewing poses special informed consent problems:

> Whipping out an informed consent statement and asking for a signature can be awkward at best. To the extent that interviews are an extension of a conversation and part of a relationship, the legality and formality of a consent form may be puzzling to your conversational partner or disruptive to the research. On the one hand, you may be offering conversational partners anonymity and confidentiality, and on the other asking them to sign a legal form saying they are participating in the study. How can they later deny they spoke to you—which they may need to do to protect themselves—if you possess a signed form saying they were willing to participate in the study? (Rubin and Rubin 1995:95)

Rubin and Rubin go on to warn that "institutional review boards are not geared for qualitative research. Often the qualitative researcher cannot come up with the detailed proposal the board demands" (p. 96). They then distinguish importantly between legal compliance with human subjects protection requirements and conscientious ethical behavior:

> You cannot achieve ethical research by following a set of preestablished procedures that will always be correct. *Yet, the requirement to behave ethically is just as strong in qualitative interviewing as in other types of research on humans—maybe even stronger.* You must build ethical routines into your work. You should carefully study codes of ethics and cases of unethical behavior to sensitize yourself to situations in which ethical commitments become particularly salient. Throughout your research, keep thinking and judging what are your ethical obligations. (Rubin and Rubin 1995:96)

New Directions in Informed Consent: Confidentiality Versus People Owning Their Own Stories

Confidentiality norms are also being challenged by new directions in qualitative inquiry. Traditionally, researchers have been advised to disguise the locations of their fieldwork and change the names of respondents, usually giving them pseudonyms, as a way of protecting their identities. The presumption has been that the privacy of research subjects should always be protected. This remains the dominant presumption, as well it should. It is being challenged, however, by participants in research who insist on "owning their own stories." Some politically active groups take pride in their identities and refuse to be involved in research that disguises who they are. Some programs that aim at empowering participants emphasize that participants own their stories and should insist on using their real names. I encountered women in a program helping them overcome a history of violence and abuse who were combating the stigma of their past by telling their stories and attaching their real names to their stories as part of healing, empowerment, and pride. Does the researcher, in such cases, have the right to impose confidentiality against the wishes of those involved? Is it patronizing and disempowering for a university-based human subjects committee to insist that these women are incapable of understanding the risks involved if they choose to turn down an offer of confidentiality? On the other hand, by identifying themselves they give up not only their own privacy but perhaps that of their children, other family members, and current or former partners.

A doctoral student studying a local church worked out an elaborate consent form in which the entire congregation de-

PROTECTIVE OR PATRONIZING?

Rita Arditti (1999) interviewed Grand-mothers of Plaza de Mayo who were part of the resistance against the Argentine dicta-torship, women who organized together to find their disappeared grandchildren. The children that the grandmothers sought "were born in captivity in the more than 340 concentration camps where their pregnant mothers were detained and killed after de-livering them, as well as children who were kidnapped and disappeared with their par-ents" (p. 1).

"I sent a detailed description of the [in-terviewing] project to twenty women: three declined the interview, but later another three joined in. Each of the twenty grand-mothers I interviewed expressed their de-sire to go on record with their comments rather than be anonymous" (p. 3).

Arditti's moving book includes bio-graphical sketches of the grandmothers in-terviewed, their photographs, and rich at-tributed quotations. This was part of their commitment to break "the conspiracy of si-lence" that is so "deeply entrenched in Ar-gentina" (p. 5). "The grandmothers want the past to be remembered and speak often about the importance of collective mem-ory" (p. 6).

Many American institutional review boards would deny the grandmothers the option of being identified with their own stories. Are such policies protective or pa-tronizing?

cided whether to let itself be identified in his dissertation. Individual church members also had the option of using their real names or choosing pseudonyms. Another student studying alternative health practitioners of-fered them the option of confidentiality and

pseudonyms or using their real identities in their case studies. Some chose to be identi-fied; some didn't. A study of organizational leaders offered the same option. In all of these cases, the research participants also had the right to review and approve the final versions of their case studies and transcripts before they were made public. In cases of collaborative inquiry where the researcher works with "coresearchers" and data collec-tion involves more of a dialogue than an in-terview, the coresearchers may also become coauthors as they choose to identify them-selves and share in publication. These are ex-amples of how the norms about confidenti-ality are changing and being challenged as tension has emerged between the important ethic of protecting people's privacy and, in some cases, their desire to own their story. Informed consent, in this regard, does not automatically mean confidentiality. In-formed consent can mean that participants understand the risks and benefits of having their real names reported and choose to do so. Protection of human subjects properly insists on informed consent. That does not now automatically mean confidentiality, as these examples illustrate.

Reciprocity: Should Interviewees Be Compensated? If So, How?

The issues of whether and how to com-pensate interviewees involve questions of both ethics and data quality. Will payment, even of small amounts, affect people's re-sponses, increasing acquiescence or, alterna-tively, enhancing the incentive to respond thoughtfully and honestly? Is it somehow better to appeal to people on the basis of the contribution they can make to knowledge or, in the case of evaluation, improving the pro-gram, instead of appealing to their pecuniary interest? Modest payments in surveys can increase response rates to ensure an adequate sample size. Does the same apply to depth interviewing and focus groups? The interviewer is usually getting paid. Shouldn't the time of interviewees be respected, especially the time of low-income people, by offering compensation? What alternatives are there to cash for compensating interviewees? In Western capitalist societies, issues of compensation are arising more and more both because people in economically disadvantaged communities are reacting to being overstudied and undervalued and because private sector marketing firms routinely compensate focus group participants, so this practice has spread to the public and nonprofit sectors. At the time of this writing, a lively discussion of these issues took place on EvalTalk, the American Evaluation Association Internet listserv. Here are a few postings.

- I believe in paying people, particularly in areas of human services. I am thinking of parenting and teen programs where it can be very difficult to get participation in interviews. If their input is valuable, I believe you should put your money where your mouth is. However, I would always make it very clear to the respondent that, although they are being paid for their time, they are NOT being paid for their responses and should be as candid and forthright as possible.

- One inner city project offered parent participants in a focus group vouchers to buy books for their kids, which for some low-income parents proved to be their first experience owning books rather than always borrowing them.

- Cash payment for participation in interviews is considered income and is therefore taxable. This can create problems if the payment comes from a public agency, as our County Attorney has pointed out in the past. Consequently, when we "pay" for participation, we use incentives other than cash, e.g., vouchers or gift certificates donated by local commercial vendors such as a discount store. These seem to be as effective.

- If you are detaining a person with a face-to-face interview, and it isn't a friendly conversation, rather it is a business exercise, it is only appropriate to offer to pay the prospective respondent for their time and effort. This should not preclude, and it would certainly help, to explain the importance of their contribution.

John Reed, owner of TecMRKT Works in Arlington, Virginia, has had extensive experience on this issue and offered the following observations on EvalTalk.

We have paid and not paid incentives for focus groups for low-income folks as well as professionals and corporate CEOs. The bottom line is that in most cases the incentive doesn't make a lot of difference in terms of participation rates, especially if you have well-trained interviewers and well-designed data collection procedures.

One of my concerns is that we are moving in a direction in which it is assumed (with very little substantive foundation) that people will only respond if given incentives. Our studies tell us that one of the most frequently cited reasons why people participate is for the "community good." Sometimes, I think the incentives are really more for the peace of mind of the project and evaluation managers than for increasing participation in programs or research. I am concerned that the research community may go in the direction of substituting incentives for good methods and obtain poorer results for having done so.

We have stopped using incentives for professional and corporate focus groups and interviews except in very special circumstances. This hasn't affected participation rates. We have found that in many instances the incentive creates a dilemma for professionals. Some professionals feel that they are participating in activities as a representative of their companies and that they are getting paid for engaging in such activities as part of their salary. We have had people refuse the incentive because they really don't have any mechanism for turning it over to the company, so they don't know what to do with it and are bothered by the ethics of taking the incentive. Some take it and put it in the office party fund and still others just pocket it. Some of the professionals with whom we work charge several hundred dollars an hour. In these cases, any meaningful incentive for travel and participation in a focus group is likely to be in excess of $1,000. It is not clear what a $100 incentive means in this case. We have come to the position that if we are doing something that professionals feel is important and we are doing it in a professional manner, then they will participate. If not, then we may not be doing something that is perceived as very useful and we may want to examine our own methods and participation in the project. I think this position is easily extended to other communities. If you are doing something that is perceived to be of value and you do it in a professional and respectful way, people will respond.

When we have paid people (low-income or professionals), we haven't seen any evidence that people feel that they are being paid to say what we want to hear. Again, we think this is an issue of balancing the issues, good question design, being credible with the respondents, and giving credible assurances that respondents' responses are confidential.

With respect to low-income populations, incentives make really good sense if you are asking low-income people to come to you and they will have out-of-pocket expenses for transportation, child care, etc. In these circumstances, the incentive is clearly justified to help people cope with a situation in which other resources may not be available. In one recent case, we felt we had to use incentives in a low-income neighborhood because the neighborhood had been surveyed extensively by various firms many of whom had offered incentives. We were told residents had come to expect to be paid for providing information. In the end, given the methods we used, it wasn't clear that we really needed to supply the incentives other than for the reason the client thought we needed to.

A host of issues emerge with respect to paying for interviews in low-income communities. We have run across those who want to count every last dime given to low-income residents, including incentives, as part of low-income residents' incomes. There are also potentially security issues with respect to interviewers carrying cash or checks, or the problem of negotiating checks.

I am not against incentives. In some instances, for example, small well-chosen incentives can make a significant difference. My plea here is that colleagues not fall into the trap of using incentives as a crutch but that they constantly examine and reexamine the whole issue of incentives and not simply assume that they are either needed and/or effective. (Reed 2000)[3]

Alternatives to cash can instill a deeper sense of reciprocity. In doing family history interviews, I found that giving families a copy of the interview was much appreciated and increased the depth of responses because they were speaking not just to me, the interviewer, but to their grandchildren and great-grandchildren in telling the family's story. In one project in rural areas, we carried a tape duplicator in the truck and made copies for them instantly at the end of the interview. Providing complete transcripts of interviews can also be attractive to participants. In an early childhood parenting program where data collection included videotaping parents playing with their children, copies of the videotapes were prized by parents. The basic principle informing these exchanges is reciprocity. Participants in research provide us with something of great value, their stories and their perspectives on their world. We show that we value what they give us by offering something in exchange.

How Hard Should Interviewers Push for Sensitive Information?

Skillful interviewers can get people to talk about things they may later regret having revealed. Or sharing revelations in an interview may unburden people, letting them get something off their chest. Since one can't know for sure, interviewers are often faced with an ethical challenge concerning how hard to push for sensitive information, a matter in which the interviewer has a conflict of interest since the interviewer's predilection is likely to be to push for as much as

possible. Herb and Irene Rubin (1995) tell of interviewing an administrator in Thailand and learning that two months after their fieldwork, he committed suicide, "leaving us wondering if our encouraging him to talk about his problems may have made them more salient to him" (p. 98).

In deciding how hard to push for information, the interviewer must balance the value of a potential response against the potential distress for the respondent. This requires sensitivity, but it is not a burden the interviewer need take on alone. When I see that someone is struggling for an answer, seems hesitant or unsure, or I simply know that an area of inquiry may be painful or uncomfortable, I prefer to make the interviewee a partner in the decision about how deeply to pursue the matter. I would say something like: "I realize this is a difficult thing to talk about. Sometimes people feel better talking about something like this and, of course, sometimes they don't. You decide how much is comfortable for you to share. If you do tell me what happened and how you feel, and later you wish you hadn't, I promise to delete it from the interview. Okay? Obviously I'm very interested in what happened, so please tell me what you're comfortable telling me."

Be Careful. It's Dangerous Out There.

*J*n our teaching and publications we tend to sell students a smooth, almost idealized, model of the research process as neat, tidy, and unproblematic. . . . Perhaps we should be more open and honest about the actual pains and perils of conducting research in order to prepare and forewarn aspiring researchers.

—Maurice Punch (1986:13-14)

In the television show *Hill Street Blues*, the sergeant ended each daily briefing of police officers by saying, "Let's be careful out

there." The same warning applies to qualitative researchers doing fieldwork and interviewing: "Be careful. It's dangerous out there." It's important to protect those who honor us with their stories by participating in our studies. It's also important to protect yourself.

I was once interviewing a young man at a coffee shop for a recidivism study when another man showed up, an exchange took place, and I realized I had been used as a cover for a drug purchase. In doing straightforward outcomes evaluation studies, I have discovered illegal and unethical activities that I would have preferred not to have stumbled across. When our team did the needs assessment of distressed farm families in rural Minnesota, we took the precaution of alerting the sheriffs' offices in the counties where we would be interviewing in case any problems arose. One sheriff called back and said that a scam had been detected in the county that involved a couple in a pickup truck soliciting home improvement work and then absconding with the down payment. Since we were interviewing in couple teams and driving pickup trucks, the sheriff, after assuring himself of the legitimacy of our work, offered to provide us with a letter of introduction, an offer we gratefully accepted.

I supervised a dissertation that involved interviews with young male prostitutes. We made sure to clear that study with the local police and public prosecutors and to get the men's agreement that promises of confidentiality would be respected given the potential contribution of the findings to reducing both prostitution and the spread of AIDS. This, by the way, was a clear case where it would have been inappropriate to pay the interviewees. Instead of cash, the reciprocity incentive the student offered was the results of a personality instrument he administered.

One of the more famous cases of what seemed like straightforward fieldwork that became dangerous involved dissertation research on the culture of a bistro in New York

City. Through in-depth interviews, graduate student Mario Brajuha gathered detailed information from people who worked and ate at the restaurant, information about their lives and their views about others involved with the restaurant. He made the usual promise of confidentiality. In the midst of his fieldwork, the restaurant was burned and the police suspected arson. Learning of his fieldwork, they subpoenaed his interview notes. He decided to honor his promises of confidentiality and ended up going to jail rather than turning over his notes. This case, which dragged on for years disrupting his graduate studies and his life, reaffirmed that researchers lack the protection that clergy and lawyers have when subpoenas are involved, promises of confidentiality notwithstanding. (For details, see Hallowell 1985; Brajuha and Hallowell 1986.)

It helps to think about potential risks and dangers prior to gathering data, but Brajuha could not have anticipated the arson. Anticipation, planning, and ethical reflection in advance only take you so far. As Maurice Punch (1986) has observed, sounding very much like he is talking from experience: "How to cope with a loaded revolver dropped in your lap is something you have to resolve on the spot, however much you may have anticipated it in prior training" (p. 13).

Be careful. It's dangerous out there.

⑤ Personal Reflections on Interviewing

Though there are dangers, there are also rewards.

I find interviewing people invigorating and stimulating—the opportunity for a short period of time to enter another person's world. If participant observation means "walk a mile in my shoes," in-depth interviewing means "walk a mile in my head." New worlds are opened up to the interviewer on these journeys.

I'm personally convinced that to be a good interviewer you must like doing it. This means being interested in what people have to say. You must yourself believe that the thoughts and experiences of the people being interviewed are worth knowing. In short, you must have the utmost respect for these persons who are willing to share with you some of their time to help you understand their world. There is a Sufi story that describes what happens when the interviewer loses this basic sensitivity to and respect for the person being interviewed.

An Interview With the King of the Monkeys

A man once spent years learning the language of monkeys so that he could personally interview the King of the Monkeys. Having completed his studies, he set out on his interviewing adventure. In the course of searching for the king, he talked with a number of monkey underlings. He found that the monkeys he spoke with were generally, to his mind, neither very interesting nor very clever. He began to doubt whether he could learn very much from the King of the Monkeys after all.

Finally, he located the king and arranged for an interview. Because of his doubts, however, he decided to begin with a few basic questions before moving on to the deeper, meaning-of-life questions that had become his obsession.

"What is a tree?" he asked.

"It is what it is," replied the King of the Monkeys. "We swing through trees to move through the jungle."

"And what is the purpose of the banana?"

"Purpose? Why, to eat."

"How do animals find pleasure?"

"By doing things they enjoy."

At this point the man decided that the king's responses were rather shallow and uninteresting, and he went on his way, crushed and cynical. Soon afterward, an owl flew into the tree next to the King of the Monkeys. "What was that man doing here?" the owl asked.

"Oh, he was only another silly human," said the King of the Monkeys. "He asked a bunch of simple and meaningless questions, so I gave him simple and meaningless answers."

Not all interviews are interesting and not all interviews go well. Certainly, there are uncooperative respondents, people who are paranoid, respondents who seem overly sensitive and easily embarrassed, aggressive and hostile interviewees, timid people, and the endlessly verbose who go on at great length about very little. When an interview is going badly, it is easy to call forth one of these stereotypes to explain how the interviewee is ruining the interview. Such blaming of the victim (the interviewee), however, does little to improve the quality of the data. Nor does it improve interviewing skills.

I prefer to believe that there is a way to unlock the internal perspective of every interviewee. My challenge and responsibility as an interviewer involve finding the appropriate and effective interviewing style and question format for a particular respondent. It is my responsibility as the interviewer to establish an interview climate that facilitates open responses. When an interview goes badly, as it sometimes does even after all these years, I look first at my own shortcomings and miscalculations, not the shortcomings of the interviewee. That's how, over the years, I've gotten better and come to value reflexivity, not just as an intellectual concept but as a personal and professional commitment to learning and engaging people with respect.

Halcolm on Interviewing _____

Ask.

Listen and record.

Ask.

Listen and record.

Asking involves a grave responsibility.

Listening is a privilege.

Researchers, listen and observe. Remember that your questions will be studied by those you study. Evaluators, listen and observe. Remember that you shall be evaluated by your questions.

To ask is to seek entry into another's world. Therefore, ask respectfully and with sincerity. Do not waste questions on trivia and tricks, for the value of the answering gift you receive will be a reflection of the value of your question.

Blessed are the skilled questioners, for they shall be given mountains of words to ascend.

Blessed are the wise questioners, for they shall unlock hidden corridors of knowledge.

Blessed are the listening questioners, for they shall gain perspective.

—From Halcolm's *Beautitides*

▣ Notes

1. Radhika Parameswaran, *Qualitative Inquiry* (7, 1 February), pp. 69-103, copyright © 2001 by Sage Publications. Reprinted with permission.

2. Copyright © 1998 Jose Hilario Cedillos. Used with permission.

3. Reprinted with permission of John H. Reed, Owner, TecMRKT Works, Arlington, Virginia.

APPENDIX 7.1

⑤ ⑤ ⑤

Sample of a Detailed Interview Guide

Guidelines for the Descriptive Interview

Spirit of the guidelines. This set of guidelines is not a checklist. If it were, it would defeat the basic strategy of the study—which is to make full use of the observations and thoughts of the teacher and other team members. The guidelines are intended as an index of topics that should be discussed over the course of the year.

Organization and use of the guidelines. The guidelines are divided into three broad categories of topics for discussion:

 I. Salient Observations
 II. General Behavior Topics
 III. Language and Reading Topics

This corresponds roughly to the organization of each interview, though not necessarily in the sequence given above. That is, each interview will begin with the teacher's salient impressions derived from observation—what the teacher thinks is important to report about the child. Depending on what those impressions are, the interviewer will pick up on related topics within the guidelines. For example, if the teacher begins the interview with a description of some interesting work the child has done, the interviewer might pick up his/her end of the conversation by asking questions about the child's method of work. After exploring other related topics that seem pertinent to the sense of the discussion, the interviewer would then move on to talk about some topics in another category. If, on the other hand, the teacher's salient impressions were mainly concerned with reading, the interviewer would move directly to related topics or reading and eventually wind backwards into earlier topics on the outline.

Teachers should strive to be as descriptive as possible throughout the interview, and interviewers should strive to facilitate description by asking for concrete instances and examples.

Coverage of topics in the guidelines. No one interview could possibly aspire to cover all topics in the guidelines. Throughout the course of five interviews over the year, however, we will be able to obtain information relevant to each topic.

Some topics (e.g., Physical/Gestural Characteristics) may only be discussed once, assuming the child does not change. Other topics (e.g., Activities and Reading Competence) will undoubtedly be touched on at every interview to update the child's documentary record. Again, it is the judgment of teacher and interviewer alike that will determine the most relevant topics of discussion for any given interview.

I. Teacher's Salient Observations About Child's Functioning

Basically cover impressions gained through teacher's own observations of the children during the normal course of instruction.

Where appropriate include
—comments about continuities/changes/fluctuations
—comments about child's work samples

Organization of the Day (first interview only)
—any changes in organization (subsequent interviews)

II. General Behavior Topics

A. Physical/Gestural Characteristics
— typical posture, bearing
— pace of movement
— forcefulness/impact of physical presence
— gestural characteristics
— eye contact
— voice qualities (e.g., loud, soft, fluent, halting)
— voice tone/inflection

B. Affective Expression
— characteristic disposition and how expressed
— how is anger expressed, controlled?
— how is affection expressed?
— general level of energy

C. Relationships
— how does child relate to (fit in with) the whole class?
— what social situations does child seek in work/play?
— do other children seek out child?
— relationship to adults
— does approach/interaction vary in different settings? at different times?

D. Activities
- —what does child do in classrooms when there is an opportunity to choose?
- — breadth and depth of activities
- — what are unusual activities for the child to engage in?
- — what are things child has never engaged/attempted in the classroom?

E. Method of Working
- — how does child organize self for work?
- — how does child carry through on work?
- — does child seek feedback about work? when? from whom?
- — does child ask for help with work? when? from whom?
- — does child use help that is offered? how?
- — evidence that child "knows what he or she knows"
- — evidence that child can gauge own capabilities
- — how does child demonstrate capabilities?

F. Summary of Progress in School-Related Work (other than reading)
- — differential/even progress
- — unusual accomplishments, activities
- — unusual difficulties, blockings

(The remaining parts of the guide are omitted because of length.)

SOURCE: My thanks to Ann Bussis and Ted Chittenden of the Educational Testing Service (ETS) for permission to include this guide. See Bussis, Chittenden, and Amarel (1973).
NOTE: This example of the guide approach to interviewing makes it clear that a great deal of preparation, effort, and concentration are required of the interviewer in using the guide. The interviewer must be thoroughly familiar with the details of the outline so that the interview flows smoothly. After any one interview session, the interviewer would compare the data actually obtained in the interview to the data desired as specified in the guide in order to begin planning for the next interview.

APPENDIX 7.2

🖼 🖼 🖼

Examples of Standardized Open-Ended Interviews

Note. The edited interviews below were used in evaluation of an Outward Bound program for the disabled. Outward Bound is an organization that uses the wilderness as an experiential education medium. This particular program consisted of a 10-day experience in the Boundary Waters Canoe Area of Minnesota. The group consisted of half able-bodied participants and half disabled participants including paraplegics; persons with cerebral palsy, epilepsy, or other developmental disabilities; blind or deaf participants; and, on one occasion, a quadriplegic. The first interview was conducted at the beginning of the program, the second interview was used at the end of the ten-day experience, and the third interview took place six months later. To save space, many of the probes and elaboration questions have been deleted and space for writing notes has been eliminated. The overall thrust and format of the interviews have, however, been retained.

Precourse Interview: Minnesota Outward Bound School Course for the Disabled

This interview is being conducted before the course as part of an evaluation process to help us plan future courses. You have received a consent form to sign, which indicates your consent to this interview. The interview will be recorded.

1. First, we'd be interested in knowing how you became involved in the course. How did you find out about it?
   a. What about the course appealed to you?
   b. What previous experiences have you had in the outdoors?

2. Some people have difficulty deciding to participate in an Outward Bound course, and others decide fairly easily. What kind of decision process did you go through in thinking about whether or not to participate?
   a. What particular things were you concerned about?
   b. What is happening in your life right now that stimulated your decision to take the course?

3. Now that you've made the decision to go on the course, how do you feel about it?
   a. How would you describe your feelings right now?

b. What lingering doubts or concerns do you have?

4. What are your expectations about how the course will affect you personally?
    a. What changes in yourself do you hope will result from the experience?
    b. What do you hope to get out of the experience?

5. During the course you'll be with the same group of people for an extended period of time. What feelings do you have about being part of a group like that for nine full days?
    a. Based on your past experience with groups, how do you see yourself fitting into your group at Outward Bound?

For Disabled

6. One of the things we're interested in understanding better as a result of these courses is the everyday experience of disabled people. Some of the things we are interested in are
    a. How does your disability affect the types of activities you engage in?
    b. What are the things that you don't do that you wish you could do?
    c. How does your disability affect the kinds of people you associate with? (Clarification:) Some people find that their disability means that they associate mainly with other disabled persons. Others find that their disability does not affect their contacts with people. What has your experience been along these lines?
    d. Sometimes people with disabilities find that their participation in groups is limited. What has been your experience in this regard?

For Able-Bodied

6. One of the things we're interested in understanding better as a result of these courses is feelings able-bodied people have about being with disabled folks. What kinds of experiences with disabled people have you had in the past?
    a. What do you personally feel you get out of working with disabled people?
    b. In what ways do you find yourself being different from your usual self when you're with disabled people?
    c. What role do you expect to play with disabled people on the Outward Bound course? (Clarification:) Are there any particular things you expect to have to do?
    d. As you think about your participation in this course, what particular feelings do you have about being part of an outdoor course with disabled people?

OPEN-ENDED INTERVIEWS

7. About half of the participants on the course are disabled people and about half are people without disabilities. How would you expect your relationship with the disabled people to be different from your relationship with course participants who are not disabled?

8. We'd like to know something about how you typically face new situations. Some people kind of like to jump into new situations, whether or not some risk may be involved. Other people are more cautious about entering situations until they know more about them. Between these two, how would you describe yourself?

9. Okay, you've been very helpful. Are there other thoughts or feelings you'd like to share with us to help us understand how you're seeing the course right now. Anything at all you'd like to add?

Postcourse Interview

We're conducting this interview right at the end of your course with Minnesota Outward Bound. We hope this will help us better understand what you've experienced so that we can improve future courses. You have signed a form giving your consent for material from this interview to be used in a written evaluation of the course. This interview is being tape-recorded.

1. To what extent was the course what you expected it to be?
   a. How was it different from what you expected?
   b. To what extent did the things you were concerned about before the course come true?
      b-1. Which things came true?
      b-2. Which didn't come true?

2. How did the course affect you personally?
   a. What changes in yourself do you see or feel as a result of the course?
   b. What would you say you got out of the experience?

3. During the last nine days you've been with the same group of people constantly. What kind of feelings do you have about having been a part of the same group for that time?
   a. What feelings do you have about the group?
   b. What role do you feel you played in the group?
   c. How was your experience with this group different from your experiences with other groups?
   d. How did the group affect you?
   e. How did you affect the group?
   f. In what ways did you relate differently to the able-bodied and disabled people in your group?

4. What is it about the course that makes it have the effects it has? What happens on the course that makes a difference?
   a. What do you see as the important parts of the course, that make an Outward Bound course what it is?
   b. What was the high point of the course for you?
   c. What was the low point?

5. How do you think this course will affect you when you return to your home?
   a. Which of the things you experienced this week will carry over to your normal life?
   b. What plans do you have to change anything or do anything differently as a result of this course?

For Disabled

6. We asked you before the course about your experience of being disabled. What are your feelings about what it's like to be disabled now?
   a. How did your disability affect the type of activities you engaged in on the course? (Clarification:) What things didn't you do because of your disability?
   b. How was your participation in the group affected by your disability?

For Able-Bodied

6. We asked you before the course your feelings about being with disabled people. As a result of the experiences of the last nine days, how have your feelings about disabled people changed?
   a. How have your feelings about yourself in relation to disabled persons changed?
   b. What did you personally get out of being/working with disabled people on this course?
   c. What role did you play with the disabled people?
   d. How was this role different from the role you usually play with disabled people?

7. Before the course we asked you how you typically faced a variety of new situations. During the last nine days you have faced a variety of new situations. How would you describe yourself in terms of how you approached these new experiences?
   a. How was this different from the way you usually approach things?
   b. How do you think this experience will affect how you approach new situations in the future?

OPEN-ENDED INTERVIEWS

8. Suppose you were being asked by a government agency whether or not they should sponsor a course like this. What would you say?
   a. What arguments would you give to support your opinion?

9. Okay, you've been very helpful. We'd be very interested in any other feelings and thoughts you'd like to share with us to help us understand your experience of the course and how it affected you.

Six-Month Follow-Up Interview

This interview is being conducted about six months after your Outward Bound course to help us better understand what participants experience so that we can improve future courses.

1. Looking back on your Outward Bound experience, we'd like to ask you to begin by describing for me what you see as the main components of the course. What makes an Outward Bound course what it is?
   a. What do you remember as the highlight of the course for you?
   b. What was the low point?

2. How did the course affect you personally?
   a. What kinds of changes in yourself do you see or feel as a result of your participation in the course?
   b. What would you say you got out of the experience?

3. For nine days you were with the same group of people; how has your experience with the Outward Bound group affected your involvement with groups since then?

For Disabled

(Check previous responses before interview. If person's attitude appears to have changed, ask if they perceive a change in attitude.)

4. We asked you before the course to tell us what it's like to be disabled. What are your feelings now about what it's like to be disabled?
   a. How does your disability affect the types of activities you engage in? (Clarification:) What are some of the things you don't do because you're disabled?
   b. How does your disability affect the kinds of people you associate with? (Clarification:) Some people find that their disability means they associate mainly with other disabled persons. Other people with disabilities find that their disability in no way limits their contacts with people. What has been your experience?
   c. As a result of your participation in Outward Bound, how do you believe you've changed the way you handle your disability?

For Able-Bodied

4. We asked you before the course to tell us what it's like to work with the disabled. What are your feelings now about what it's like to work with the disabled?
   a. What do you personally feel you get out of working with disabled persons?
   b. In what ways do you find yourself being different from your usual self when you are with disabled people?
   c. As you think about your participation in the course, what particular feelings do you have about having been part of a course with disabled people?

5. About half of the people on the course were disabled people and about half were people without disabilities. To what extend did you find yourself acting differently with disabled people compared to the way you acted with able-bodied participants?

6. Before this course we asked you how you typically face new situations. For example, some people kind of like to jump into new situations even if some risks are involved. Other people are more cautious, etc. How would you describe yourself along these lines right now?
   a. To what extent, if at all, has the way you have approached new situations since the course been a result of your Outward Bound experience?

7. Have there been any ways in which the Outward Bound course affected you that we haven't discussed? (If yes:) How? Would you elaborate on that?
   a. What things that you experienced during that week carried over to your life since the course?
   b. What plans have you made, if any, to change anything or do anything differently as a result of the course?

8. Suppose you were being asked by a government agency whether or not they should support a course like this. What would you say?
   a. Who shouldn't take a course like this?

9. Okay, you've been very helpful. Any other thoughts or feelings you might share with us to help us understand your reactions to the course and how it affected you?
   a. Anything at all you'd like to add?

OPEN-ENDED INTERVIEWS

PART 3

Analysis, Interpretation, and Reporting

Halcolm will tell you this:

> *"Because you can name something does not mean you understand it.*
> *Because you understand it does not mean it can be named."*

And this:

> *"What you do not see you cannot describe.*
> *What you cannot describe you cannot interpret.*
> *But because you can describe something does not mean you can interpret it."*

And yet this:

> *"The riddle about the sound of one hand clapping arose from watching the first*
> *decision maker reading the first evaluation report."*

And finally this:

> *"Where the sun shines, there too is shadow.*
> *Be illumined by the light of knowledge no less than by its shadow."*

8

Qualitative Analysis and Interpretation

The Challenge

Qualitative analysis transforms data into findings. No formula exists for that transformation. Guidance, yes. But no recipe. Direction can and will be offered, but the final destination remains unique for each inquirer, known only when—and if—arrived at.

Medieval alchemy aimed to transmute base metals into gold. Modern alchemy aims to transform raw data into knowledge, the coin of the information age. Rarity increases value. Fine qualitative analysis remains rare and difficult—and therefore valuable.

Metaphors abound. Analysis begins during a larval stage that, if fully developed, metamorphoses from caterpillar-like beginnings into the splendor of the mature butterfly. Or this: The inquirer acts as catalyst on raw data, generating an interaction that synthesizes new substance born alive from the catalytic conversion. Or this: Findings emerge like an artistic mural created from collage-like pieces that make sense in new ways when seen and understood as part of a greater whole.

Consider the patterns and themes running through these metaphors. Transformation. Transmutation. Conversion. Synthesis. Whole from parts. Sense-making. Such motifs run through qualitative analysis like golden threads in a royal garment. They decorate the garment and enhance its quality, but they may also distract attention from the basic cloth that gives the garment its strength and shape—the skill, knowledge, experience, creativity, diligence, and work of the garment maker. No abstract processes of analysis, no matter how eloquently named and finely described, can substitute for the skill, knowledge, experience, creativity, diligence, and work of the of the qualitative analyst. Thus, Stake (1995) writes of the

art of case study research. Van Maanen (1988) emphasizes the storytelling motifs of qualitative writing in his ethnographic book on telling tales. Golden-Biddle and Locke (1997) make *story* the central theme in their book *Composing Qualitative Research*. Corrine Glesne (1999), a researcher and a poet, begins with the story analogy, describing qualitative analysis as "finding your story," then later represents the process as "improvising a song of the world." Lawrence-Lightfoot and Davis (1997) call to mind "portraits" in naming their form of qualitative analysis *The Art and Science of Portraiture*. Brady (2000) explores "anthropological poetics." Janesick (2000) evokes dance in "The Choreography of Qualitative Research Design," which suggests that, for warming up, we may need "stretching exercises" (Janesick 1998). Hunt and Benford (1997) call to mind theater as they use "dramaturgy" to examine qualitative inquiry. Richardson (2000b) reminds us that qualitative analysis and writing involve us not just in making sense of the world but also in making sense of our relationship to the world and therefore in discovering things about ourselves even as we discover things about some phenomenon of interest. In this complex and multi- faceted analytical integration of disciplined science, creative artistry, and personal reflexivity, we mold interviews, observations, documents, and field notes into *findings*.

The challenge of qualitative analysis lies in making sense of massive amounts of data. This involves reducing the volume of raw information, sifting trivia from significance, identifying significant patterns, and constructing a framework for communicating the essence of what the data reveal. The problem is that "we have few agreed-on canons for qualitative data analysis, in the sense of shared ground rules for drawing conclu-

Depth and Detail in Qualitative Analysis

Transcriptions

sions and verifying their sturdiness" (Miles and Huberman 1984: 16). There are no formulas for determining significance. No ways exist of perfectly replicating the researcher's analytical thought processes. No straightforward tests can be applied for reliability and validity. In short, no absolute rules exist except perhaps this: Do your very best with your full intellect to fairly represent the data and communicate what the data reveal given the purpose of the study. Appendix 9.1, "A Documenter's Perspective," at the end of the next chapter takes you inside the experience of one novice analyst as she tries to make sense of the voluminous data she had gathered from observations and interviews.

Guidelines for analyzing qualitative data can be found in abundance, and studying examples of qualitative analysis can be especially helpful, as in the Miles and Huberman (1994) sourcebook. But guidelines, procedural suggestions, and exemplars are not rules. Applying guidelines requires judgment and creativity. Because each qualitative study is unique, the analytical approach used will be unique. Because qualitative inquiry depends, at every stage, on the skills, training, insights, and capabilities of the inquirer, qualitative analysis ultimately depends on the analytical intellect and style of the analyst. The human factor is the great strength and the fundamental weakness of qualitative inquiry and analysis—a scientific two-edged sword.

The first chapter presented several examples of qualitative findings:

- Patterns in women's ways of knowing (Belenky et al. 1986)

- Eight characteristics of organizational excellence (Peters and Waterman 1982)

- Seven habits of highly effective people (Covey 1990)

- Case studies illuminating why battered women kill (Browne 1987)

- Three primary processes that contribute to the development of a relationship: Being-In, Being-For, and Being-With (Moustakas 1995)

- Paradigm motifs in tribe-centered initiations compared with modern youth-centered coming-of-age celebrations (Patton 1999a)

- Case examples illustrating the diversity of experiences and outcomes in an adult literacy program (Patton and Stockdill 1987)

- Teachers' reactions to a Kalamazoo school accountability system (Perrone and Patton 1976)

- Observation of a parent education class to illuminate the parent-staff interactive process

Reviewing these examples of qualitative findings from the first chapter will ground this discussion of analytical processes in samples of the real fruit of qualitative inquiry. And this chapter will add many more examples.

The strategies, guidelines, and ideas for analysis offered here are meant to be suggestive and facilitating rather than confining or exhaustive. In actually doing analysis, you will have to adapt what is presented here to fit your specific situation and study. However analysis is done, **analysts have an obligation to monitor and report their own analytical procedures and processes as fully and truthfully as possible.** This means that qualitative analysis is a new stage of field-

work in which analysts must observe their own processes even as they are doing the analysis. The final obligation of analysis is to analyze and report on the analytical process as part of the report of actual findings. The extent of such reporting will depend on the purpose of the study.

🔄 Purpose as Context

Purpose guides analysis. Chapter 5 presented a typology of inquiry purposes: basic research, applied research, summative evaluation research, formative evaluation, and action research. These varying purposes affect analysis because they involve different norms and expectations for what will be concluded and how it will be presented.

Basic qualitative research is typically reported through a scholarly monograph or published article with primary attention to the contribution of the research to social science theory. The theoretical framework within which the study is conducted will heavily shape the analysis. As Chapter 3 made clear, the theoretical framework for an ethnographic study will differ from that for ethnomethodology, heuristics, or hermeneutics.

Applied qualitative research may have a more or less scholarly orientation depending on primary audience. If the primary audience is scholars, then applied research will be judged by the standards of basic research, namely, research rigor and contribution to theory. If the primary audience is policymakers, the relevance, clarity, utility, and applicability of the findings will become most important.

For *scholarly qualitative research*, the published literature on the topic being studied helps bring focus to a particular study. Scholarship involves an ongoing dialogue with colleagues about particular questions of interest within the scholarly community. The analytical focus, therefore, derives in part from what one has learned that will make a contribution to the literature in a field of inquiry. That literature will likely have contributed to the initial design of the study (implicitly or explicitly), so it is appropriate to revisit that literature to help focus the analysis.

Focus in *evaluation research* should derive from questions generated at the very beginning of the evaluation process, ideally through interactions with primary intended users of the findings. Too many times evaluators go through painstaking care, even agony, in the process of working with primary stakeholders to clearly conceptualize and focus evaluation questions before data collection begins. But, then, once the data are collected and analysis begins, they never look back over their notes to review and renew their clarity on the central issues in the evaluation. It is not enough to count on remembering what the evaluation questions were. The early negotiations around the purpose of an evaluation usually involve important nuances. To reestablish those nuances for the purpose of helping focus the analysis, it is important to review notes on decisions that were made during the conceptual part of the evaluation. (This assumes, of course, that the evaluator has treated the conceptual phase of the evaluation as a field experience and has kept detailed notes about the negotiations that went on and the decisions that were made.)

In addition, it may be worth reopening discussions with intended evaluation users to make sure that the original focus of the evaluation remains relevant. This accomplishes two things. First, it allows the evaluator to make sure that the analysis will focus on needed information. Second, it prepares evaluation users for the results. At the point of beginning formal analysis, the evaluator will have a much better perspective on what kinds of questions can be answered with the data that have been collected. It pays to check out which questions should take priority in the final report and to suggest new possibilities that may have emerged during fieldwork.

Summative evaluations will be judged by the extent to which they contribute to making decisions about a program or intervention, usually decisions about overall effectiveness, continuation, expansion, and/or replication in other sites. A full report presenting data, interpretations, and recommendations is required. In contrast, *formative evaluations,* conducted for program improvement, may not even generate a written report. Findings may be reported primarily orally. Summary observations may be listed in outline form or an executive summary may be written, but the timelines for formative feedback and the high costs of formal report writing may make a full, written report unnecessary. Staff and funders often want the insights of an experienced outsider who can interview program participants effectively, observe what goes on in the program, and provide helpful feedback. The methods are qualitative, the purpose is practical, and the analysis is done throughout fieldwork; no written report is expected beyond a final outline of observations and implications. Academic theory takes second place to understanding the program's theory of action as actually practiced and implemented. In addition, formative feedback to program staff may be ongoing rather than simply at the end of the study. However, in some situations, funders may request a carefully documented, fully developed, and formally written formative report. The nature of formative reporting, then, is dictated by user needs rather than scholarly norms.

Action research reporting also varies a great deal. **In much action research, the process is the product,** so no report will be produced for outside consumption. On the other hand, some action research efforts are undertaken to test organizational or community development theory and therefore require fairly scholarly reports and publications. Action research undertaken by a group of people to solve a specific problem may involve the group sharing the analysis process to generate a mutually understood and acceptable solution with no permanent, written record of the analysis.

Students writing *dissertations* will typically be expected to follow very formal and explicit analytical procedures to produce a scholarly monograph with careful attention to methodological rigor. Graduate students will be expected to report in detail on all aspects of methodology, usually in a separate chapter, including thorough discussion of analytical procedures, problems, and limitations.

The point here is that the rigor, duration, and procedures of analysis will vary depending on the study's purpose and audience. Likewise, the reporting format will vary. First and foremost, then, analysis depends on clarity about purpose (as do all other aspects of the study).

When Does Analysis Begin?

Research texts typically make a hard-and-fast distinction between data collection and analysis. For data collection based on surveys, standardized tests, and experimental designs, the lines between data collection and analysis are clear. But the fluid and emergent nature of naturalistic inquiry makes the distinction between data gathering and analysis far less absolute. In the course of fieldwork, ideas about directions for analysis will occur. Patterns take shape. Possible themes spring to mind. Hypotheses emerge that inform subsequent fieldwork. While earlier stages of fieldwork tend to be generative and emergent, following wherever the data lead, later stages bring closure by moving toward confirmatory data collection—deepening insights into and confirming (or disconfirming) patterns that seem to have appeared.

Ideas for making sense of the data that emerge while still in the field constitute the beginning of analysis; they are part of the record of field notes. Sometimes insights emerge almost serendipitously. When I was interviewing recipients of MacArthur Foundation Fellowships, I happened to interview several people in major professional and personal transitions followed by several in quite stable situations. This happenstance of how interviews were scheduled suggested a major distinction that became important in the final analysis—distinguishing the impact of the fellowships on recipients in transition from those in more stable situations, at least comparatively.

Recording and tracking analytical insights that occur during data collection are part of fieldwork *and* the beginning of qualitative analysis. I've heard graduate students instructed to repress all analytical thoughts while in the field and concentrate on data collection. Such advice ignores the emergent nature of qualitative designs and the power of field-based analytical insights. Certainly, this can be overdone. Too much focus on analysis while fieldwork is still going on can interfere with the openness of naturalistic inquiry, which is its strength. Rushing to premature conclusions should be avoided. But repressing analytical insights may mean losing them forever, for there's no guarantee they'll return. And repressing in-the-field insights removes the opportunity to deepen data collection that would test the authenticity of those insights while still in the field and fails to acknowledge the confirmatory possibilities of the closing stages of fieldwork. In the MacArthur Fellowship study, I added transitional cases to the sample near the end of the interviewing to better understand the varieties of transitions fellows were experiencing—an in-the-field form of emergent, purposeful sampling driven by field-based analysis. Such overlapping of data collection and analysis improves both the quality of data collected and the quality of the analysis so long as the fieldworker takes care not to allow these initial interpretations to overly confine analytical possibilities. Indeed, instead of focusing additional data collection entirely on confirming preliminary field hypotheses, the inquiry should become particularly sensitive to looking for alternative explanations and patterns that would invalidate initial insights.

In essence, when data collection has formally ended and it is time to begin the final analysis, the investigator has two primary sources to draw from in organizing the analysis: (1) the questions that were generated during the conceptual and design phases of the study, prior to fieldwork, and (2) analytic insights and interpretations that emerged during data collection.

Even then, once analysis and writing are under way, fieldwork may not be over. On occasion, gaps or ambiguities found during analysis cry out for more data collection, so, where possible, interviewees may be recontacted to clarify or deepen responses, or new observations are made to enrich descriptions. While writing the Grand Canyon-based book that describes modern male coming-of-age issues (Patton 1999a), I returned to the Grand Canyon four times to deepen my understanding of Canyon geology and add descriptive depth, and I conducted several follow-up and clarifying interviews with my two key informants. Each time that I thought, at last, fieldwork was over and I could just concentrate on writing, I came to a point where I simply could not continue without more data collection. Such can be the integrative, iterative, and synergistic processes of data collection and analysis in qualitative inquiry.

A final caveat, however: Perfectionism breeds imperfections. Often additional fieldwork isn't possible, so gaps and unresolved ambiguities are noted as part of the final report. Dissertation and publication deadlines may also obviate additional confirmatory fieldwork. And no amount of additional fieldwork can, or should, be used to force the vagaries of the real world into hard-and-fast conclusions or categories. Such perfectionist and forced analysis ultimately undermines the authenticity of inductive, qualitative analysis. Finding patterns is one result of analysis. Finding vagaries, uncertainties, and ambiguities is another.

🔲 Thick Description

Thick, rich description provides the foundation for qualitative analysis and reporting. Good description takes the reader into the setting being described. In his classic *Street Corner Society*, William Foote Whyte (1943) took us to the "slum" neighborhood where he did his fieldwork and introduced us to the characters there, as did Elliot Liebow in *Tally's Corner* (1967), a description of the lives of unemployed Black men in Washington, D.C., during the 1960s. In Constance Curry's (1995) oral history of school integration in Drew, Mississippi, in the 1960s, she tells the story of African American mother Mae Bertha Carter and her seven children as they faced day-to-day and night-to-night threats and terror from resistant, angry

Whites. Through in-depth case study descriptions, Angela Browne (1987) helps us experience and understand the isolation and fear of being a battered woman whose life is controlled by a rage-filled, violent man. Through detailed description and rich quotations, Alan Peshkin (1986) showed readers the "total world of a fundamentalist Christian school" as Erving Goffman (1961) had done earlier for other "total institutions," closed worlds such as prisons, army camps, boarding schools, nursing homes, and mental hospitals. Howard Becker (1953, 1985) described how one learns to become a marijuana user in such detail that you almost get the scent of the smoke from his writing.

These classic qualitative studies share the capacity to open up a world to the reader through rich, detailed, and concrete descriptions of people and places—"thick description" (Geertz 1973; Denzin 2001)—in such a way that we can understand the phenomenon studied and draw our own interpretations about meanings and significance.

Description forms the bedrock of all qualitative reporting, whether for scholarly inquiry, as in the examples above, or for program evaluation. For evaluation studies, basic descriptive questions include the following: What are the stated goals of the program (including different goals reported by different stakeholders)? What are the primary activities of the program? How do people get into the program? What is the program setting like? What happens to people in the program? What are the effects of the program on participants? Thick evaluation descriptions take those who need to use the evaluation findings *into* the experience and outcomes of the program.

A basic tenet of research admonishes careful separation of description from interpretation. Interpretation involves explain-

ing the findings, answering "why" questions, attaching significance to particular results, and putting patterns into an analytic framework. It is tempting to rush into the creative work of interpreting the data before doing the detailed, hard work of putting together coherent answers to major descriptive questions. But description comes first.

Several options exist for organizing and reporting descriptive findings. Exhibit 8.1 presents several alternatives, depending on whether the primary organizing motif centers on telling the story of what occurred, presenting case studies, or illuminating an analytical framework.

These are not mutually exclusive or exhaustive ways of organizing and reporting qualitative data. Different parts of a report may use different reporting approaches. The point is that one must have some initial framework for organizing and managing the voluminous data collected during fieldwork.

For example, where variations in the experiences of individuals are the primary focus of the study, it is appropriate to begin by writing a case study using all the data for each person. Only then are cross-case analysis and comparative analysis done. For example, if one has studied 10 juvenile delinquents, the analysis would begin by doing a case description of each juvenile before doing cross-case analysis. On the other hand, if the focus is on a criminal justice program serving juveniles, the analysis might begin with description of variations in answers to common questions, for example, what were patterns of major program experiences, what did they like, what did they dislike, how did they think they had changed, and so forth.

Likewise in analyzing interviews, the analyst has the option of beginning with case analysis or cross-case analysis. Beginning

EXHIBIT 8.1	Options for Organizing and Reporting Qualitative Data

Storytelling Approaches

Chronology and history — Describe what happened chronologically, over time, telling the story from beginning to end. This focuses on some development over time to portray the life of a person, the history of an organization or community, or the story of a family.

Flashback — Start at the end, then work backward to describe how the ending emerged. For example, in an evaluation study, a participant case study might begin with the outcome realized (or unrealized) and then present the chronology or story that illuminates that outcome.

Case Study Approaches

People — If individuals or groups are the primary unit of analysis, then case studies of people or groups may be the focus for case studies. In *Respect*, Sara Lawrence-Lightfoot (2000) illustrates different forms of respect through case studies of people who manifest those different forms in the way they live their lives.

Critical incidents — Critical incidents or major events can constitute self-contained descriptive units of analysis, often presented in order of importance rather than in sequence of occurrence. McClure (1989) reported a case study of a university through the critical incidents that shaped it.

Various settings — Describe various places, sites, settings, or locations (doing case studies of each) before doing cross-setting pattern analysis. In an evaluation of multinational efforts to preserve ancient buildings, we reported on cases in Japan, England, and Indonesia before drawing cross-cultural conclusions.

Analytical Framework Approaches

Processes — Qualitative data may be organized to describe important processes. For example, an evaluation of a program may describe recruitment processes, socialization processes, decision-making and communication processes, and so on. Distinguishing important processes becomes the analytical framework for organizing qualitative descriptions.

Issues — An analysis can be organized to illuminate key issues, often the equivalent of the primary evaluation questions, for example, variations in how participants changed as a result of the program. In a study of leadership training, we organized the qualitative report around such key issues as conflict management, negotiation skills, enhancing creativity, and effective communications—all important training issues.

Questions — Responses to interviews can be organized question by question, especially where a standardized interviewing format was used. For example, if an evaluation includes questions about perceived strengths and perceived weaknesses, responses to these questions would be grouped together.

Sensitizing concepts — Where sensitizing concepts such as "leadership" versus "followership" have played an important preordinate role in guiding fieldwork, the data can be organized and described through those sensitizing concepts.

with case analysis means writing a case study for each person interviewed or each unit studied (e.g., each critical event, each group, or each program location). Beginning with cross-case analysis means grouping together answers from different people to common questions, or analyzing different perspectives on central issues. If a standardized open-ended interview has been used, it is fairly easy to do cross-case or cross-interview analysis for each question in the interview. With an interview guide approach, answers from different people can be grouped by topics from the guide, but the relevant data won't be found in the same place in each interview. An interview guide, if it has been carefully conceived, actually constitutes a descriptive analytical framework for analysis.

A qualitative study will often include both kinds of analysis—individual cases and cross-case analyses—but one has to begin somewhere. Trying to do both individual case studies and cross-case analysis at the same time will likely lead to confusion.

🗉 Organizing the Data

*J*t wasn't curiosity that killed the cat.
It was trying to make sense of all the data curiosity generated.

—Halcolm

The data generated by qualitative methods are voluminous. I have found no way of preparing students for the sheer mass of information they will find themselves confronted with when data collection has ended. Sitting down to make sense out of pages of interviews and whole files of field notes can be overwhelming. Organizing and analyzing a mountain of narrative can seem like an impossible task.

How big a mountain? Consider a study of community and scientist perceptions of HIV vaccine trials in the United States done by the Centers for Disease Control. In a large, complex, multisite effort called Project LinCS: Linking Communities and Scientists, the study's 313 interviews generated more than 10,000 pages of transcribed text from 238 participants on a range of topics (MacQueen and Milstein 1999). Now that's an extreme case, but, on average, a one-hour interview will yield 10 to 15 single-spaced pages of text; 10 two-hour interviews will yield roughly 200 to 300 pages of transcripts.

Getting organized for analysis begins with an inventory of what you have. Are the field notes complete? Are there any parts that you put off to write later and never got to but need to be finished, even at this late date, before beginning analysis? Are there any glaring holes in the data that can still be filled by collecting additional data before the analysis begins? Are all the data properly labeled with a notation system that will make retrieval manageable (dates, places, interviewee identifying information, etc.)? Are interview transcriptions complete? Get a sense of the data; check out the quality of the information you have collected. **Get a sense of the whole.**

The problem of incomplete data is illustrated by the experience of a student who had conducted 30 in-depth pre- and post-interviews with participants in a special program. The transcription process took several weeks. She made copies of three transcripts and brought them to our seminar for assistance in doing the analysis. As I read the interviews, I got a terrible sinking feeling in my stomach. While other students were going over the transcriptions, I pulled her aside and asked her what instructions she had given the typist. It was clear from reading just a few pages that she did not have *verbatim* transcriptions—the essential raw data for qualitative analysis. The language in each interview was the same. The sentence structures were the same. The answers were grammatically correct. People in natural conversations simply do not talk that way. The grammar in natural conversations comes out atrocious when transcribed. Sentences hang incomplete, interrupted by new thoughts before the first sentence was completed. Without the knowledge of this student, and certainly without her permission, the typist had decided to summarize the participants' responses because "so much of what they said was just rambling on and on about nothing." All of the interviews had to be transcribed again before analysis could begin.

Earlier I discussed the transition between fieldwork and analysis. Transcribing offers another point of transition between data collection and analysis as part of data management and preparation. Doing all or some of your own interview transcriptions (instead of having them done by a transcriber), for example, provides an opportunity to get immersed in the data, an experience that usually generates emergent insights. Typing and organizing handwritten field notes offer another opportunity to immerse yourself in the data in the transition between fieldwork and full analysis, a chance to get a feel for the cumulative data as a whole. Doing your own

transcriptions, or at least checking them by listening to the tapes as you read them, can be quite different from just working off transcripts done by someone else.

Protecting Data

Thomas Carlyle lent the only copy of his handwritten manuscript on the history of the French Revolution, his master work, to philosopher J. S. Mill, who lent it to a Mrs. Taylor. Mrs. Taylor's illiterate housekeeper thought it was waste paper and burned it. Carlyle behaved with nobility and stoicism, and immediately set about rewriting the book. It was published in 1837 to critical acclaim and consolidated Carlyle's reputation as one of the foremost men of letters of his day. We'll never know how the acclaimed version compared with the original or what else Carlyle might have written in the year lost after the fireplace calamity.

So, it is prudent to make back-up copies of all your data, putting one master copy away someplace secure for safekeeping. Indeed, if data collection has gone on over any long period, it is wise to make copies of the data as they are collected, being certain to put one copy in a safe place where it will not be disturbed and cannot be lost or burned. The data you've collected are unique and precious. The exact observations you've made, the exact words people have spoken in interviews—these can never be recaptured in precisely the same way, even if new observations are undertaken and new interviews are conducted. Moreover, you've likely make promises about protecting confidentiality, so you have an obligation to take care of the data. Field notes and interviews should be treated as the valuable material they are. Protect them.

Beyond Thomas Carlyle's cautionary tale, my advice in this regard comes from two more recent disasters. I was at the University of Wisconsin when antiwar protesters bombed a physics building, destroying the life work of several professors. I also had a psychology doctoral student who carried his dissertation work, including all the raw data, in the trunk of his car. An angry patient from a mental health clinic with whom he was working firebombed his car, destroying all of his work. Tragic stories of lost research, while rare, occur just often enough to remind us about the wisdom of an ounce of prevention.

Once a copy is put away for safekeeping, I like to have one hard copy handy throughout the analysis, one copy for writing on, and one or more copies for cutting and pasting. A great deal of the work of qualitative analysis involves creative cutting and pasting of the data, even if done on a computer, as is now common, rather than by hand. Under no circumstances should one yield to the temptation to begin cutting and pasting the master copy. The master copy or computer file remains a key resource for locating materials and maintaining the context for the raw data.

🖫 Computer-Assisted Qualitative Data Management and Analysis

Computers and software are tools that *assist* analysis. Software doesn't really analyze qualitative data. Qualitative software programs facilitate data storage, coding, retrieval, comparing, and linking—but human beings do the analysis. Software has eased significantly the old drudgery of manually locating a particular coded paragraph. Analysis programs speed up the processes of locating coded themes, grouping data together in categories, and comparing passages in transcripts or incidents from

field notes. But the qualitative analyst doing content analysis must still decide what things go together to form a pattern, what constitutes a theme, what to name it, and what meanings to extract from case studies. The human being, not the software, must decide how to frame a case study, how much and what to include, and how to tell the story. Still, computers can play a role in qualitative analysis as they do in statistical analysis.

Quantitative programs revolutionized that research by making it possible to crunch our numbers, more accurately, more quickly, and in more ways. . . . Much of the tedious, boring, mistake-prone data manipulation has been removed. This makes it possible to spend more time investigating the meaning of their data.

In a similar way, QDA [qualitative data analysis] programs improve our work by removing drudgery in managing qualitative data. Copying, highlighting, cross-referencing, cutting and pasting transcripts and field notes, covering floors with index cards, making multiple copies, sorting and resorting card piles, and finding misplaced cards have never been the highlights of qualitative research. It makes at least as much sense for us to use qualitative programs for tedious tasks as it does for those people down the hall to stop hand-calculating gammas. (Durkin 1997:93)

The analysis of qualitative data involves creativity, intellectual discipline, analytical rigor, and a great deal of hard work. Computer programs can facilitate the work of analysis, but they can't provide the creativity and intelligence that make each qualitative analysis unique. Moreover, since new software is being constantly developed and upgraded, this book can do no more than provide some general guidance about how to undertake computer-assisted analysis.

Most of this chapter will focus on the human thinking processes involved in analysis rather than the mechanical data management challenges that computers help solve. For an excellent review of computer software in relation to various theoretical and practical issues in qualitative analysis, see Fielding and Lee (1998).

Exhibit 8.2 presents examples of major computer-assisted qualitative data analysis software (CAQDAS). What began as distinct software approaches have become more standardized as the various packages converged to offer similar functions, though sometimes with different names for the same functions. They all facilitate marking text, building codebooks, indexing, categorizing, creating memos, and displaying multiple text entries side-by-side. Import and export capabilities vary. Some support teamwork and multiple users more than others. Graphics and matrix capabilities vary but are becoming increasingly sophisticated. All take time to learn to use effectively. The greater the volume of data to be analyzed, the more helpful these software programs are. Moreover, knowing which software program you will use *before* data collection will help you collect and enter data in the way that works best for a particular program.

Fielding (1995, 2000), who has followed qualitative software as diligently as anyone, distinguishes three basic types of qualitative analysis software: text retrievers, code-and-retrieve packages, and theory-builders. He advises that packages vary substantially and that one must use care in picking the right software for a particular set of analysis challenges, for example, whether you'll be engaged in individual or team analysis. Indeed, he cautions that you need to know something about qualitative analysis before choosing a package. He has identified several critical ways in which qualitative analysis software varies (Fielding 1995):

- How you enter your data (typing directly, imported from word processing, scanning; flexible or fixed formatting)

- Storage differences (internal vs. external databases)

- Coding variations (on-screen coding vs. assign the codes first)

- Differences in ease of organizing, reorganizing, and relabeling codes

- Variations in whether memos and annotations can be attached to codes (especially important for team analysis)

- Data-linking mechanisms and ease vary (connecting different data sources or segments during analysis)

- Ease of navigating and browsing

- Ease, speed, and process of search and retrieval

- Important display variations (e.g., with and without context)

- Tracking details (recording what you've done for review)

Qualitative discussion groups on the Internet regularly discuss, rate, compare, and debate the strengths and weaknesses of different software programs (see Exhibit 8.3 for examples of such groups). While preferences vary, these discussions usually end with consensus that any of the major programs will satisfy the needs of most qualitative researchers. Increasingly, distinctions depend on "feel," "style," and "ease of use" —matters of individual taste—more than differences in function. Still, differences exist and new developments can be expected to solve existing limitations.

| EXHIBIT 8.2 | Examples of Software Programs for Qualitative Analysis |

AnSWR (Analysis Software for Word-Based Records):
(freeware from CDC[a])   www.cdc.gov/hiv/software/answr.htm

ATLAS.ti   www.atlasti.de/

C-I-SAID   www.scolari.com
(Code-A-Text)

CDC EZ-Text   www.cdc.gov/hiv/software/ez-text.htm
(freeware from CDC)

Ethnograph   www.qualisresearch.com

HyperRESEARCH   www.researchware.com

QCA   www.nwu.edu/IPR/publications/qca.html
(Qualitative Comparative Analysis)

QSR NVivo   www.qsr-software.com

QSR NUD*IST   www.qsr-software.com
(Non-numerical Unstructured Data With Indexing, Searching, and Theorizing)

TextSmart   www.spss.com

winMAX   www.scolari.com

Computer-assisted qualitative data analysis software (CAQDAS) continues to develop rapidly. See www.scolari.com for the latest versions, prices, and links to home pages of software companies. Most major software marketers have their own Web sites for support and will provide demo disks that allow a user to learn and compare functions. A number of organizations worldwide have developed training workshops to teach use of CAQDAS. These are often posted on qualitative listservs (see Chapter 1, Exhibit 1.5, for a resource list). Software comparisons are also frequently discussed on the Qualitative Internet listservs. Exhibit 8.3 in this chapter lists Internet listserv resources for analysis, including software support discussion lists.

a. Centers for Disease Control, U.S. government: If these URLs have changed, go to the CDC home page (www.cdc.gov). From there, a simple text search should turn up the software.

Data management is a black box in virtually all qualitative software, hidden from view and difficult to access. Programs differ in the specific elements in the underlying database (the design), the way these elements are configured (the architecture), the mechanics of how the user works with the database on-screen (the graphical user interface, or GUI), and the extent to which the database elements can be separated from the software program with their linkages intact (the export capability). (MacQueen and Milstein 1999:30)

One special challenge involves better interfaces between programs. To help solve this problem, MacQueen and Milstein (1999)

EXHIBIT 8.3	**Internet Resources and E-mail Discussion Groups (listservs) on Qualitative Analysis**

1. Qual-software@jiscmail.ac.uk: A list on qualitative analysis computer programs; to subscribe, send this message to jiscmail@jiscmail.ac.uk: join qual-software ourname.

2. ATLAS-TI@atlasti.de: Topics on the text analysis, text management, and theory-building program ATLAS/ti; to subscribe, send a one-line message to listserv@atlasti.DE: SUB ATLAS-TI yourfirstname yourlastname your institution.

3. QSR-Forum@qsr.com.au (Qualitative Solutions and Research), for the qualitative analysis programs NUD*IST and Nvivo. To subscribe, send a message to mailing-list-request@qsr.com.au with the words SUBSCRIBE QSR-FORUM in the main body of the text. If you have any problems, send e-mail to list-master@qsr.com.au.

4. VISCOM@listserv.temple.edu: Visual Communications Discussion List; to subscribe, send this message to listserv@listserv.temple.edu: subscribe viscom ourname.

5. OnlineRsch@onelist.com: Discussion of analysis, methodology, and ethics in online research, including sociology, anthropology, and other related disciplines.

6. Online articles about CAQDAS: http://caqdas.soc.surrey.ac.uk/news.htm.

NOTE: Thanks to Judith Preissle, Aderhold Distinguished Professor, Social Foundations of Education, University of Georgia, for list subscription details. These sites and subscription details may change, and this list is not exhaustive. This list is meant to be suggestive of the qualitative analysis resources available through the Internet. See Chapter 1, Exhibit 1.5, and Chapter 3, Exhibit 3.7, for additional qualitative resources through the Internet.

---

have proposed "a systems approach to qualitative data management and analysis" that focuses on the data elements that are commonly found in a wide range of qualitative approaches in hopes of encouraging the development of common protocols for importing and exporting data between software programs. They note that "with a common foundation, qualitative researchers could work with multiple programs without penalty" (p. 30). Their proposal centers on a database whose elements correspond to the fundamental types of information associated with qualitative research and the processes driving the generation of that information. These four fundamental types of information that contribute to the construc-

tion of a finding or "answer" in qualitative analysis are

(1) characteristics of the sources where information is sought, (2) primary information or objects collected from the sources, (3) secondary information or objects created to aid in the interpretation of primary objects, and (4) characteristics of the coders who construct the secondary objects. (MacQueen and Milstein 1999:31)

Their approach has been encapsulated as the foundation for a public domain software program called AnSWR: Analysis Software for Word-Based Records, sponsored by the Centers for Disease Control (CDC) (see Exhibit 8.2). From a database management perspective, they divide coding activities into two categories: *segmenting activities* and *metadata activities.*

Segmenting activities: Any analytic actions that can be directly mapped onto text or other digitized objects are classified here as segmenting activities. Examples include defining the boundaries of a narrative passage or segment, applying codes to a segment, using tags or other marks to identify points in an object, and creating hyper links between segments or points in an object.

Metadata activities: Metadata activities entail the creation of data about data; here, we extend the meaning of *data* to encompass all symbolic representations of information and meaning. Prompted by meaning discerned in the primary objects, the coder generates metadata in the form of codes, comments, memos, and annotations, as well as graphical summaries of the interpreted objects (e.g., diagrams, networks, clusters, and maps) capable of showing the multidimensional structure of coding patterns.

Segmenting and metadata activities take place in an iterative fashion, with feedback between the two elements. For example, a typical sequence of coder activities may include the highlighting or bracketing of a chunk of text containing semantically related terms (segmenting), the creation of a code to describe the cultural significance of the chunk of text (metadata), the establishment of a link between the code and the chunk in the data base (segmenting), the creation of a memo describing related concepts described in the literature (metadata), the establishment of a link between the memo and the chunk in the data base (segmenting), and incorporation of the code into a diagram describing conceptual links among related codes (metadata). This complex process is the primary focus of most qualitative approaches. (MacQueen and Milstein 1999:35-36)

For more detailed discussion of computer-assisted qualitative data management and analysis, especially graphics and display capabilities, see Ryan and Bernard (2000), Fielding and Lee (1998), and Gahan and Hannibal (1998). In considering whether to use software to assist in analysis, keep in mind that this is partly a matter of individual style, comfort with computers, amount of data to be analyzed, and personal preference. Computer analysis is not necessary and can interfere with the analytic process for those who aren't comfortable spending long hours in front of a screen. Some self-described "concrete" types like to get a physical feel for the data that isn't possible with a computer. Participants on a qualitative listserv posted these responses to a thread on software analysis:

The best advice I ever received about coding was to read the data I collected over and over and over. The more I interacted with the data, the more patterns and categories began to "jump out" at me. I never even bothered to use the software program I installed on the computer because I found it much easier to code it by hand.

I found that hand-coding was easier and more productive than using a computer program. For me, actually seeing the data in concrete form was vital in recognizing emerging themes. I actually printed multiple copies of data and cut it into individual "chunks," color coding as I went along, and actually physically manipulating the data by grouping chunks by apparent themes, filing in colored folders, etc. This technique was especially useful when data seemed to fit more than one theme and facilitated merging of my initial impressions as themes solidified. Messy, but vital for us concrete people.

So although software analysis has become common and many swear by it—it can offer leaps in productivity for those adept at it—it is not a requisite for qualitative inquiry. We turn now to how to think through and actually analyze qualitative data with emphasis on where the real work takes place—in your head.

⑤ Case Studies

> Case study is not a methodological choice but a choice of what is to be studied. . . . We could study it analytically or holistically, entirely by repeated measures or hermeneutically, organically or culturally, and by mixed methods—but we concentrate, at least for the time being, on the case. (Stake 2000:435)

Case analysis involves organizing the data by specific cases for in-depth study and comparison. Well-constructed case studies are *holistic* and *context sensitive,* two of the primary strategic themes of qualitative inquiry discussed in Chapter 2. Cases can be individuals, groups, neighborhoods, programs, organizations, cultures, regions, or nation-states. "In an ethnographic case study, there is exactly one unit of analysis —the community or village or tribe" (Bernard 1995:35-36). Cases can also be critical incidents, stages in the life of a person or program, or anything that can be defined as a "specific, unique, bounded system" (Stake 2000:436). Cases are units of analysis. What constitutes a case, or unit of analysis, is usually determined during the design stage and becomes the basis for purposeful sampling in qualitative inquiry (see Chapter 5, especially Exhibit 5.5). Sometimes, however, new units of analysis, or cases, emerge during fieldwork or from the analysis after data collection. For example, one might have sampled schools as the unit of analysis, expecting to do case studies of three schools, and then, reviewing the fieldwork, decide that

classrooms are a more meaningful unit of analysis and shift to case studies of classrooms instead of schools, or add case studies of particular teachers or students. Contrariwise, one could begin by sampling classrooms and end up doing case studies on schools. This illustrates the critical importance of thinking carefully about the question "What is a case?" (Ragin and Becker 1992).

The case study approach to qualitative analysis constitutes a specific way of collecting, organizing, and analyzing data; in that sense it represents an analysis *process.* The purpose is to gather comprehensive, systematic, and in-depth information about each case of interest. The analysis process results in a *product:* a case study. Thus, the term *case study* can refer to either the process of analysis or the product of analysis, or both.

Case studies may be layered or nested. For example, in evaluation, a single program may be a case study. However, within that single-program case ($N = 1$), one may do case studies of several participants. In such an approach, the analysis would begin with the individual case studies; then the cross-case pattern analysis of the individual cases might be part of the data for the program case study. Likewise, if a national or state program consists of several project sites, the analysis may consist of three layers of case studies: individual participant case studies at project sites combined to make up project site case studies, project site case studies combined to make up state program case studies, and state programs combined to make up a national program case study. Exhibit 8.4 shows this layered case study approach.

This kind of layering recognizes that you can always build larger case units out of smaller ones; that is, you can always combine studies of individuals into studies of a program, but if you only have program-

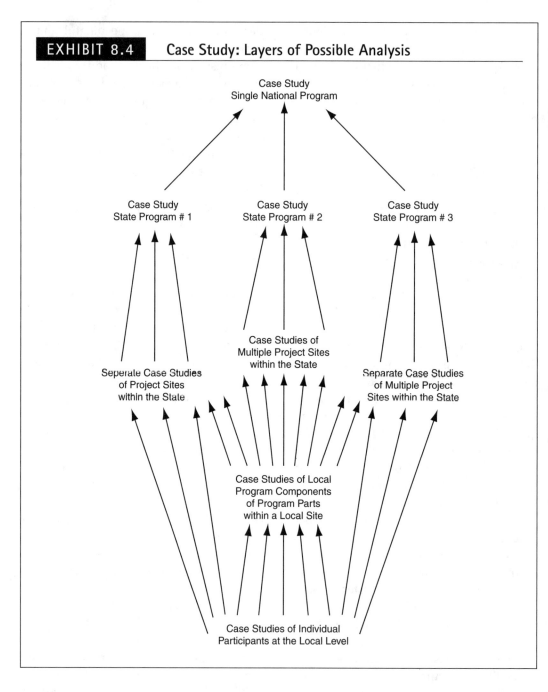

EXHIBIT 8.4   Case Study: Layers of Possible Analysis

level data, you can't disaggregate it to construct individual cases.

Remember this rule: No matter what you are studying, always collect data on the lowest level unit of analysis possible. . . .

Collect data about individuals, for example, rather than about households. If you are interested in issues of production and consumption (things that make sense at the household level), you can always package your data about individuals into data about households during analysis. . . . You can always aggregate data collected on individuals, but you can never disaggregate data collected on groups. (Bernard 1995:37)

Though a scholarly or evaluation project may consist of several cases and include cross-case comparisons, **the analyst's first and foremost responsibility consists of doing justice to each individual case. All else depends on that.**

> Ultimately, we may be interested in a general phenomenon or a population of cases more than in the individual case. And we cannot understand this case without knowing about other cases. But while we are studying it, our meager resources are concentrated on trying to understand its complexities. For the while, we probably will not study comparison cases. We may simultaneously carry on more than one case study, but each case study is a concentrated inquiry into a single case. (Stake 2000:436)

Case data consist of all the information one has about each case: interview data, observations, the documentary data (e.g., program records or files, newspaper clippings), impressions and statements of others about the case, and contextual information—in effect, all the information one has accumulated about each particular case goes into that case study. These diverse sources make up the raw data for case analysis and can amount to a large accumulation of material. For individual people, case data can include interviews with the person and those who know her or him, clinical records, background and statistical information about the person, a life history profile, things the person has produced (diaries, photos, writings, paintings, etc.), and personality or other test results (yes, quantitative data can be part of a qualitative case study). At the program

level, case data can include program documents, statistical profiles, program reports and proposals, interviews with program participants and staff, observations of the program, and program histories.

From Data to Case Study

Once the raw case data have been accumulated, the researcher may write a case record. The case record pulls together and organizes the voluminous case data into a comprehensive, primary resource package. The case record includes all the major information that will be used in doing the final case analysis and writing the case study. Information is edited, redundancies are sorted out, parts are fitted together, and the case record is organized for ready access chronologically and/or topically. The case record must be complete but manageable; it should include all the information needed for subsequent analysis, but it is organized at a level beyond that of the raw case data.

> A case record should make no concessions to the reader in terms of interest or communication. It is a condensation of the case data aspiring to the condition that no interpreter requires to appeal behind it to the raw data to sustain an interpretation. Of course, this criterion cannot be fully met: some case records will be better than others. The case record of a school attempts a portrayal through the organization of data alone, and a portrayal without theoretical aspirations. (Stenhouse 1977:19)

The case record is used to construct a case study appropriate for sharing with an intended audience, for example, scholars, policymakers, program decision makers, or practitioners. The tone, length, form, structure, and format of the final case presentation depend on audience and study purpose. The final case study is what will be

---

EXHIBIT 8.5	The Process of Constructing Case Studies
Step 1	Assemble the raw case data.
	These data consist of all the information collected about the person, program, organization, or setting for which a case study is to be written.
Step 2	Construct a case record.
(optional; depends on complexity of data and case)	This is a condensation of the raw case data organized, classified, and edited into a manageable and accessible file.
Step 3	Write a final case study narrative.
	The case study is a readable, descriptive picture of or story about a person, program, organization, and so forth, making accessible to the reader all the information necessary to understand the case in all its uniqueness. The case story can be told chronologically or presented thematically (sometimes both). The case study offers a holistic portrayal, presented with any context necessary for understanding the case.

---

communicated in a publication or report. The full report may include several case studies that are then compared and contrasted, but the basic unit of analysis of such a comparative study remains the distinct cases and the credibility of the overall findings will depend on the quality of the individual case studies. Exhibit 8.5 shows this sequence of moving from raw case data to the written case study. The second step—converting the raw data to a case record before writing the actual case study—is optional. A case record is constructed only when a great deal of unedited raw data from interviews, observations, and documents must be edited and organized before writing the final case study. In many studies, the analyst will work directly and selectively from raw data to write the final case study.

The case study should take the reader into the case situation and experience—a person's life, a group's life, or a program's life. Each case study in a report stands alone, al-

lowing the reader to understand the case as a unique, holistic entity. At a later point in analysis, it is possible to compare and contrast cases, but initially each case must be represented and understood as an idiosyncratic manifestation of the phenomenon of interest. A case study should be sufficiently detailed and comprehensive to illuminate the focus of inquiry without becoming boring and laden with trivia. A skillfully crafted case reads like a fine weaving. And that, of course, is the trick. How to do the weaving? How to tell the story? How to decide what stays in the final case presentation and what gets deleted along the way? Elmore Leonard (2001:7), the author of *Glitz* and other popular detective thrillers, was once asked how he managed to keep the action in his books moving so quickly. He said, "I leave out the parts that people skip." Not bad advice for writing an engaging case study.

In doing biographical or life history case studies, Denzin (1989b) has found particular value in identifying what he calls "epiphanies"—"existentially problematic moments in the lives of individuals" (p. 129).

It is possible to identify four major structures, or types of existentially problematic moments, or epiphanies, in the lives of individuals. First, there are those moments that are major and touch every fabric of a person's life. Their effects are immediate and long term. Second, there are those epiphanies that represent eruptions, or reactions, to events that have been going on for a long period of time. Third are those events that are minor yet symbolically representative of major problematic moments in a relationship. Fourth, and finally, are those episodes whose effects are immediate, but their meanings are only given later, in retrospection, and in the reliving of the event. I give the following names to these four structures of problematic experience: (1) the major epiphany, (2) the cumulative epiphany, (3) the illuminative, minor epiphany, and (4) the re-lived epiphany. (Of course, any epiphany can be relived and given new retrospective meaning.) These four types may, of course, build upon one another. A given event may, at different phases in a person's or relationship's life, be first, major, then minor, and then later relived. A cumulative epiphany will, of course, erupt into a major event in a person's life. (Denzin 1989b:129)

Programs, organizations, and communities have parallel types of epiphanies, though they're usually called critical incidents, crises, transitions, or organizational lessons learned. For a classic example of an organizational development case study in the business school tradition, see the analysis of the Nut Island sewage treatment plant in Quincy, Massachusetts, the complex story of how an outstanding team—highly competent, deeply committed to excellence, focused on the organizational mission, and working hard—still ended up in a "catastrophic failure" (Levy 2001).

Studying such examples is one of the best ways to learn how to write case studies. The Thick Description section, earlier in this chapter, cited a number of case studies that have become classics in the genre. Chapter 1 presented case vignettes of individuals in an adult literacy program. Chapter 4 (Exhibit 4.2) presented highlights of a participant case study used to illuminate a Vietnamese woman's experience in an employment training program; in addition to describing what a job placement meant to her, the case was constructed to illuminate such hard-to-measure outcomes as "understanding the American workplace culture" and "speaking up for oneself," learnings that can be critical to long-term job success for an emigrant. Another example of a full individual case study is presented as Appendix 8.2 at the end of this chapter. Originally prepared for an evaluation report that included several participant case studies, it tells the story of one person's experiences in a career education program. This case represents an exemplar of how multiple sources of information can be brought together to offer a comprehensive picture of a person's experience, in this instance, a student's changing involvement in the program and changing attitudes and behaviors over time. The case data for each student in the evaluation study included

(a) observations of selected students at employer sites three times during the year,

(b) interviews three times per year with the students' employer-instructors at the time of observation,

(c) parent interviews once a year,

(d) in-depth student interviews four times a year,

(e) informal discussions with program staff,

(f) a review of student projects and other documents, and

(g) 23 records from the files of each student (including employer evaluations of students, student products, test scores, and staff progress evaluations of students).

A set of guide questions was prepared for analyzing and reviewing each source (Fehrenbacher, Owens, and Haehnn 1976: 7-8). Information from all of these sources was integrated to produce a highly readable narrative that could be used by decision makers and funders to better understand what it was like to be in the program (Owens, Haehnn, and Fehrenbacher 1987). The evaluation staff of the Northwest Regional Educational Laboratory took great pains to carefully validate the information in the case studies. Different sources of information were used to cross-validate findings, patterns, and conclusions. Two evaluators reviewed the material in each case study to independently make judgments and interpretations about the content and meaning of the material in the case. In addition, an external evaluator reviewed the raw data to check for biases or unwarranted conclusions. Students were asked to read their own case studies and comment on the accuracy of fact and interpretation in the study. Finally, to guarantee the readability of the case studies, a newspaper journalist was employed to help organize and edit the final versions. Such a rigorous case study approach increases the confidence of readers that the cases are accurate and comprehensive. Both in its content and the process by which it was constructed, the Northwest Lab case study presented at the end of this chapter (Appen-

dix 8.2) exemplifies how an individual case study can be prepared and presented.

The same rigorous process would apply to case study data at the group or program level. For excellent examples of case studies in education, see Brizuela et al. (2000), Stake, Bresler, and Mabry (1991), Perrone (1985), and Alkin, Daillak, and White (1979); for family research see Sussman and Gilgun (1996); for international development see Salmen (1987) and Searle (1985); in government accountability see Kloman (1979); and for a detailed example of conducting and presenting an evaluation case study, see Hébert (1986).

How one compares and contrasts cases will depend on the purpose of the study and how cases were sampled. As discussed in Chapter 5, critical cases, extreme cases, typical cases, and heterogeneous cases serve different purposes. Other excellent resources for qualitative case analysis include Stake (1995), Merriam (1997), Yin (1994), Hamel (1993), and the U.S. General Accounting Office (1987). To pursue case studies as stories that build on and display the elements of good storytelling, see Glesne (1999).

Once case studies have been written, the analytic strategies described in the remainder of this chapter can be used to further analyze, compare, and interpret the cases to generate cross-case themes, patterns and findings.

🔄 Pattern, Theme, and Content Analysis

The ability to use thematic analysis appears to involve a number of underlying abilities, or competencies. One competency can be called *pattern recognition*. It is the ability to see patterns in seemingly random information. (Boyatzis 1998:7)

No precise or agreed-on terms describe varieties and processes of qualitative analysis. Content analysis, for example, sometimes refers to searching text for recurring words or themes. For example, a speech by a politician might be analyzed to see what phrases or concepts predominate, or speeches of two politicians might be compared to see how many times and in what contexts they used a phrase such as "global economy" or "family values." Content analysis usually refers to analyzing text (interview transcripts, diaries, or documents) rather than observation-based field notes. **More generally, however, content analysis is used to refer to any qualitative data reduction and sense-making effort that takes a volume of qualitative material and attempts to identify core consistencies and meanings.** Case studies, for example, can be content analyzed.

The core meanings found through content analysis are often called patterns or themes. Alternatively, the process of searching for patterns or themes may be distinguished, respectively, as pattern analysis or theme analysis. I'm asked frequently about the difference between a pattern and a theme. There's no hard-and-fast distinction. The term *pattern* usually refers to a descriptive finding, for example, "Almost all participants reported feeling fear when they rappelled down the cliff," while a theme takes a more categorical or topical form: *Fear.* Putting these terms together, a report on a wilderness education study might state:

> The *content analysis* revealed a *pattern* of participants reporting being afraid when rappelling down cliffs and running river rapids; many also initially experienced the group process of sharing personal feelings as evoking some fear. Those patterns make "Dealing with fear" a major *theme* of the wilderness education program experience.

Inductive and Deductive Qualitative Analyses

> Francis Bacon is known for his emphasis on *induction, the use of direct observation to confirm ideas and the linking together of observed facts to form theories or explanations of how natural phenomenon work.* Bacon correctly never told us how to get ideas or how to accomplish the linkage of empirical facts. Those activities remain essentially humanistic—you think hard. (Bernard 2000:12)

Bacon (1561-1626) is recognized as one of the founders of scientific thinking, but he also has been awarded "the dubious honor of being the first martyr of empiricism" (Bernard 2000:12). Still pondering the universe at age 65, he got an idea one day while driving his carriage in the snow in a farming area north of London. It occurred to him that cold might delay the biological process of putrefaction, so he stopped, purchased a hen from a farmer, killed it on the spot, and stuffed it with snow. His idea worked. The snow did delay the rotting process, but he caught bronchitis and died a month later. As I noted in Chapter 6, fieldwork can be risky. Engaging in analysis, on the other hand, is seldom life threatening, though you do risk being disputed and sometimes ridiculed by those who arrive at contrary conclusions.

Inductive analysis involves *discovering* patterns, themes, and categories in one's data. Findings emerge out of the data, through the analyst's interactions with the data, in contrast to *deductive analysis* where the data are analyzed according to an existing framework. Qualitative analysis is typically inductive in the early stages, especially when developing a codebook for content analysis or figuring out possible categories, patterns, and themes. This is often called "open coding" (Strauss and Corbin 1998:223) to emphasize the importance of being open to the data. "Grounded theory" (Glaser and Strauss 1967) emphasizes becoming immersed in the data—being *grounded*—so that embedded meanings and relationships can emerge. The French would say of such an immersion process: *Je m'enracine.* "I root myself." The analyst becomes implanted in the data. The resulting analysis grows out of that groundedness.

Once patterns, themes, and/or categories have been established through inductive analysis, the final, confirmatory stage of qualitative analysis may be deductive in testing and affirming the authenticity and appropriateness of the inductive content analysis, including carefully examining deviate cases or data that don't fit the categories developed. Generating theoretical propositions or formal hypotheses after inductively identifying categories is considered deductive analysis by grounded theorists Strauss and Corbin (1998): "Anytime that a researcher derives hypotheses from data, because it involves interpretation, we consider that to be a deductive process" (p. 22). Grounded theorizing, then, involves both inductive and deductive processes: "At the heart of theorizing lies the interplay of making inductions (deriving concepts, their properties, and dimensions from data) and deductions (hypothesizing about the relationships between concepts)" (Strauss and Corbin 1998:22).

Analytic induction, in contrast to grounded theory, begins with an analyst's deduced propositions or theory-derived hypotheses and "is a procedure for verifying theories and propositions based on qualitative data" (Taylor and Bogdan 1984:127). Sometimes, as with analytic induction, qualitative analysis is first deductive or quasi-deductive and then inductive as when, for example, the analyst begins by examining the data in terms of theory-derived sensitizing concepts or applying a theoretical frame-

work developed by someone else (e.g., testing Piaget's developmental theory on case studies of children). After or alongside this deductive phase of analysis, the researcher strives to look at the data afresh for undiscovered patterns and emergent understandings (inductive analysis). I'll discuss both grounded theory and analytic deduction at greater length later in this chapter.

Because, as identified and discussed in Chapter 2, inductive analysis is one of the primary characteristics of qualitative inquiry, we'll focus on strategies for thinking and working inductively. There are two distinct ways of analyzing qualitative data inductively. First, the analyst can identify, define, and elucidate the categories developed and articulated by the people studied to focus analysis. Second, the analyst may also become aware of categories or patterns for which the people studied did not have labels or terms, and the analyst develops terms to describe these inductively generated categories. Each of these approaches is described below.

Indigenous Concepts and Practices

A good place to begin inductive analysis is to inventory and define key phrases, terms, and practices that are special to the people in the setting studied. What are the indigenous categories that the people interviewed have created to make sense of their world? What are practices they engage in that can be understood only within their worldview? Anthropologists call this *emic* analysis and distinguish it from *etic* analysis, which refers to labels imposed by the researcher. (For more on this distinction and its origins, see Chapter 6, which discusses emic and etic perspectives in fieldwork.) "Identifying the categories and terms used by informants themselves is also called *in vivo* coding" (Bernard and Ryan 1998:608).

Consider the practice among traditional Dani women of amputating a finger joint when a relative dies. The Dani people live in the lush Baliem Valley of Irian Java, Indonesia's most remote province on the western half of New Guinea. The joint is removed to honor and placate ancestral ghosts. Missionaries have fought the practice as sinful and the government has banned it as barbaric, but many traditional women still practice it.

> Some women in Dani villages have only four stubs and a thumb on each hand. In tribute to her dead mother and brothers, Soroba, 38, has had the tops of six of her fingers amputated. "The first time was the worst," she said. "The pain was so bad, I thought I would die. But it's worth it to honor my family." (Sims 2001:6)

Analyzing such an indigenous practice begins by understanding it from the perspective of its practitioners, within the indigenous context, in the words of the local people, in their language, within their worldview.

> According to this view, cultural behavior should always be studied and categorized in terms of the inside view—the actors' definition—of human events. That is, the units of conceptualization in anthropological theories should be "discovered" by analyzing the cognitive processes of the people studied rather than "imposed" from cross-cultural (hence, ethnocentric) classifications of behavior. (Pelto and Pelto 1978:54)

Anthropologists, working cross-culturally, have long emphasized the importance of preserving and reporting the indigenous categories of people studied. Franz Boas (1943) was a major influence in this direction: "If it is our serious purpose to under-

stand the thoughts of a people, the whole analysis of experience must be based on their concepts, not ours" (p. 314).

In an intervention program, certain terms may emerge or be created by participants to capture some essence of the program. In the wilderness education program I evaluated, the idea of "detoxification" became a powerful way for participants to share meaning about what being in the wilderness together meant (Patton 1999a:49-52). In the Caribbean Extension Project evaluation, the term *liming* had special meaning to the participants. Not really translatable, it essentially means passing time, hanging out, doing nothing, shooting the breeze—but doing so agreeably, without guilt, stress, or a sense that one ought to be doing something more productive with one's time. *Liming* has positive, desirable connotations because of its social, group meaning—people just enjoying being together with nothing that has to be accomplished. Given that uniquely Caribbean term, what does it mean when participants describe what happened in a training session or instructional field trip as primarily "liming"? How much liming could acceptably be built into training for participant satisfaction and still get something done? How much programmatic liming was acceptable? These became key formative evaluation issues.

In evaluating a leadership training program, we gathered extensive data on what participants and staff meant by the term *leadership.* Pretraining and posttraining exercises involved participants in writing a paragraph on leadership; the writing was part of the program curriculum, not designed for evaluation, but the results provided useful qualitative evaluation data. There were small group discussions on leadership. The training included lectures and group discussions on leadership, which we observed. We participated in and took notes on informal discussions about leadership. Because the very idea of "leadership" was central to the program, it was essential to capture variations in what participants meant when they talked about leadership. The results showed that ongoing confusion about what leadership meant was one of the problematic issues in the program. Leadership was an indigenous concept in that staff and participants throughout the training experience used it extensively, but it was also a *sensitizing concept* because we knew going into the fieldwork that it would be an important notion to study.

Sensitizing Concepts

In contrast to purely indigenous concepts, sensitizing concepts refer to categories that the analyst brings to the data. Experienced observers often use sensitizing concepts to orient fieldwork, an approach discussed in Chapter 6. These sensitizing concepts have their origins in social science theory, the research literature, or evaluation issues identified at the beginning of a study. Sensitizing concepts give the analyst "a general sense of reference" and provide "directions along which to look" (Blumer 1969: 148). Using sensitizing concepts involves examining how the concept is manifest and given meaning in a particular setting or among a particular group of people.

Conroy (1987) used the sensitizing concept "victimization" to study police officers. Innocent citizens are frequently thought of as the victims of police brutality or indifference. Conroy turned the idea of victim around and looked at what it would mean to study police officers as victims of the experiences of law enforcement. He found the sensitizing concept of victimization helpful in understanding the isolation, lack of interpersonal affect, cynicism, repressed anger, and sadness observed among police officers.

He used the idea of victimization to tie together the following quotes from police officers:

> As a police officer and as an individual I think I have lost the ability to feel and to empathize with people. I had a little girl that was run over by a bus and her mother was there and she had her little book bag. It was really sad at the time but I remember feeling absolutely nothing. It was like a mannequin on the street instead of some little girl. I really wanted to be able to cry about it and I really wanted to have some feelings about it, but I couldn't. It's a little frightening for me to be so callous and I have been unable to relax.

> I am paying a price by always being on edge and by being alone. I have become isolated from old friends. We are different. I feel separate from people, different, out of step. It becomes easier to just be with other police officers because they have the same basic understanding of my environment, we speak the same language. The terminology is crude. When I started I didn't want to get into any words like "scumbags" and "scrotes," but it so aptly describes these people.

> I have become isolated from who I was because I have seen many things I wish I had not seen. It's frustrating to see things that other people don't see, won't see, can't see. I wish sometimes, I didn't see the things. I need to be assertive, but don't like it. I have to put on my police mask to do that. But now it is getting harder and harder to take that mask off. I take my work home with me. I don't want my work to invade my personal life but I'm finding I need to be alone more and more. I need time to recharge my batteries. I don't like to be alone, but must. (Conroy 1987:52)

Two additional points are worth making about these quotations. First, by presenting the actual data on which the analysis is based, the readers are able to make their own determination of whether the concept "victimization" helps in making sense of the data. By presenting respondents in their own words and reporting the actual data that was the basis of his interpretation, Conroy invites readers to make their own analysis and interpretation. The analyst's constructs should not dominate the analysis, but rather should facilitate the reader's understanding of the world under study.

Second, these three quotations illustrate the power of qualitative data. The point of analysis is not simply to find a concept or label to neatly tie together the data. What is important is understanding the people studied. Concepts are never a substitute for direct experience with the descriptive data. **What people actually say and the descriptions of events observed remain the essence of qualitative inquiry.** The analytical process is meant to organize and elucidate telling the story of the data. Indeed, the skilled analyst is able to get out of the way of the data to let the data tell their own story. The analyst uses concepts to help make sense of and present the data, but not to the point of straining or forcing the analysis. The reader can usually tell when the analyst is more interested in proving the applicability and validity of a concept than in letting the data reveal the perspectives of the people interviewed and the intricacies of the world studied.

Having suggested how singular concepts can bring focus to inductive analysis, the next level of analysis, constructing typologies, moves us into a somewhat more complex analytical strategy.

Indigenous Typologies

Typologies are classification systems made up of categories that divide some aspect of

the world into parts along a continuum. They differ from *taxonomies*, which completely classify a phenomenon through mutually exclusive and exhaustive categories, like the biological system for classifying species. Typologies, in contrast, are built on ideal-types or illustrative endpoints rather than a complete and discrete set of categories. Well-known and widely used sociological typologies include Redfield's folk-urban continuum (*gemeinschaft/gesellschaft*) and Von Wiese's and Becker's sacred-secular continuum (for details, see Vidich and Lyman 2000:52). Sociologists classically distinguish ascribed from achieved characteristics. Psychologists distinguish degrees of mental illness (neuroses to psychoses). Political scientists classify governmental systems along a democratic-authoritarian continuum. Economists distinguish laissez-faire from centrally planned economic systems. Systems analysts distinguish open from closed systems. In all of these cases, however, the distinctions involves matters of degree and interpretation rather than absolute distinctions. All of these examples have emerged from social science theory and represent theory-based typologies constructed by analysts. We'll examine that approach in greater depth in a moment. First, however, let's look at identifying indigenous typologies as a form of qualitative analysis.

Illuminating indigenous typologies requires an analysis of the continua and distinctions used by people in a setting to break up the complexity of reality into distinguishable parts. The language of a group of people reveals what is important to them in that they name something to separate and distinguish it from other things with other names. Once these labels have been identified from an analysis of what people have said during fieldwork, the next step is to identify the attributes or characteristics that distinguish one thing from another. In describing this kind of analysis, Charles Frake (1962) used the example of a hamburger. Hamburgers can vary a great deal in how they are cooked (rare to well-done) or what is added to them (pickles, mustard, ketchup, lettuce), and they are still called hamburgers. However, when a piece of cheese is added to the meat, it becomes a cheeseburger. The task for the analyst is to discover what it is that separates "hamburger" from "cheeseburger," that is, to discern and report "how people construe their world of experience from the way they talk about it" (Frake 1962:74).

An analysis example of this kind comes from a formative evaluation aimed at reducing the dropout rate among high school students. In observations and interviews at the targeted high school, it became important to understand the ways in which teachers categorized students. With regard to problems of truancy, absenteeism, tardiness, and skipping class, the teachers had come to label students as either "chronics" or "borderlines." One teacher described the chronics as "the ones who are out of school all the time and everything you do to get them in doesn't work." Another teacher said, "You can always pick them out, the chronics. They're usually the same kids." The borderlines, on the other hand, "skip a few classes, waiting for a response, and when it comes they shape up. They're not so different from your typical junior high student, but when they see the chronics getting away with it, they get more brazen in their actions." Another teacher said, "Borderlines are gone a lot but not constantly like the chronics."

Not all teachers used precisely the same criteria to distinguish chronics from borderlines, but all teachers used these labels in talking about students. To understand the program activities directed at reducing high school dropouts and the differential impact of the program on students, it became important to observe differences in how bor-

derlines and chronics were treated. Many teachers, for example, refused even to attempt to deal with chronics. They considered it a waste of their time. Students, it turned out, knew what labels were applied to them and how to manipulate these labels to get more or less attention from teachers. Students who wanted to be left alone called themselves "chronics" and reinforced their "chronic" image with teachers. Students who wanted to graduate, even if only barely and with minimal school attendance, cultivated an image as "borderline."

Another example of an indigenous typology emerged in the wilderness education program I evaluated. During the second year of the project, one subgroup's members started calling themselves the "turtles." They contrasted themselves to the "truckers." On the surface, these labels were aimed at distinguishing different styles of hiking and backpacking, one slow and one fast. Beneath the surface, however, the terms came to represent different approaches to the wilderness and different styles of experience in relation to the wilderness and the program.

Groups, cultures, organizations, and families develop their own language systems to emphasize distinctions they consider important. Every program gives rise to a special vocabulary that staff and participants use to differentiate types of activities, kinds of participants, styles of participation, and variously valued outcomes. These indigenous typologies provide clues to analysts that the phenomena to which the labels refer are important to the people in the setting and that to fully understand the setting it is necessary to understand those terms and their implications.

Analyst-Constructed Typologies

Once indigenous concepts, typologies, and themes have been surfaced, the analyst

---

BEYOND NAMING PROBLEMS: HOLISTIC AND BROADLY GAUGED ANALYSES

Excerpts of Reflections of Philosopher Elizabeth Minnich

United States readers [of critiques of popular culture such as Robert Putnam's Bowling Alone*] tend to respond with enthusiasm to easily grasped analyses of what is wrong with us from whatever left/middle/right stance they come—viz., to pick just a few that otherwise differ radically, the popularity of 50's analyses of "the organization man" and "the ugly American"; of Baldwin's* The Fire Next Time*; Friedan's "the problem that has no name" in* The Feminine Mystique*; Harrington's* The Other America*; Bellah et al.'s* Habits of the Heart*; Bloom's* The Closing of the American Mind*; William Bennett's and Cornel West's politically opposite diagnoses of a moral crisis that is besetting the nation.*

Such analyses give us the relief of names to attach to widespread concerns: they catch on like a new kind of pill for a real social ill that, whether the catchily named pill works or

not, gives us some sense that at least someone knows about our pain. . . .

It is because they come into the vicinity of where we are hurting that we respond so strongly: poke my wound, even to help me heal it, and I will react. But this "poking" is also not as healing as it could be insofar as it remains too narrow in ways that constrain and may misdirect the holistic help we want. Like many analysts before them, what they have done is to focus on where a problem becomes readily evident. But as analyses of wife beating that focus on the victims tend to lead to proposals (often formulated by entirely other people than the analysts) that also focus on the women, excluding from the picture the male perpetrators and the systems that empower them, this won't do. We need other analyses and broader gauge ones. (Minnich 1999:8,11)

---

moves to a different task of induction—looking for patterns, categories, and themes for which the analyst can construct a typology to further elucidate findings. Such constructions must be done with considerable care to avoid creating things that are not really in the data. The advice of biological theorist John Maynard Smith (2000) is informative in this regard: Seek models of the world that make sense and whose consequences can be worked out, for "to replace a world you do not understand by a model of a world you do not understand is no advance" (p. 46).

Constructing ideal-types or alternative paradigms is one simple form of presenting qualitative comparisons. Exhibit 1.3 in

Chapter 1 presented my ideal-typical comparison of coming-of-age paradigms that contrasts tribal initiation themes with contemporary coming-of-age themes (Patton 1999a). A series of patterns is distilled into contrasting themes that create alternative ideal-types. The notion of "ideal-types" makes it explicit that the analyst has constructed and interpreted something that supersedes purely descriptive analysis.

In creating analyst-constructed typologies through inductive analysis, you take on the task of identifying and making explicit patterns that appear to exist but remain unperceived by the people studied. The danger is that analyst-constructed typologies impose a world of meaning on the participants that better reflects the observer's world than the world under study. One way of testing analyst-constructed typologies is to present them to people whose world is being analyzed to find out if the constructions make sense to them.

> The best and most stringent test of observer constructions is their recognizability to the participants themselves. When participants themselves say, "yes, that is there, I'd simply never noticed it before," the observer can be reasonably confident that he has tapped into extant patterns of participation. (Lofland 1971:34)

Exhibit 8.6, using the problem of classifying people's ancestry, shows what can happen when indigenous and official constructions conflict, a matter of some consequence to those affected.

A good example of an analyst-generated typology comes from an evaluation of the National Museum of Natural History, Smithsonian Institution, done by Robert L. Wolf and Barbara L. Tymitz (1978). This has become a classic in the museum studies field. They conducted a naturalistic inquiry of viewers' reactions to the "Ice Age Mammals and Emergence of Man" exhibit. From their observations, they identified four different kinds of visitors to the exhibit. These descriptions are progressive in that each new category identifies a person more serious about the exhibit hall.

- *The Commuter:* This is the person who merely uses the hall as a vehicle to get from the entry point to the exit point. . . .
- *The Nomad:* This is a casual visitor, a person who is wandering through the hall, apparently open to becoming interested in something. The Nomad is not really sure why he or she is in the hall and

not really sure that s/he is going to find anything interesting in this particular exhibit hall. Occasionally the Nomad stops, but it does not appear that the nomadic visitor finds any one thing in the hall more interesting than any other thing.

- *The Cafeteria Type:* This is the interested visitor who wants to get interested in something, and so the entire museum and the hall itself are treated as a cafeteria. Thus, the person walks along, hoping to find something of interest, hoping to "put something on his or her tray" and stopping from time to time in the hall. While it appears that there is something in the hall that spontaneously sparks the person's interest, we perceive this visitor has a predilection to becoming interested, and the exhibit provides the many things from which to choose.
- *The V.I.P.—Very Interested Person:* This visitor comes into the hall with some prior interest in the content area. This person may not have come specifically to the hall, but once there, the hall serves to remind the V.I.P.'s that they were, in fact, interested in something in that hall beforehand. The V.I.P. goes through the hall much more carefully, much slower, much more critically— that is, he or she moves from point to point, stops, examines aspects of the hall with a greater degree of scrutiny and care. (Wolf and Tymitz 1978: 10-11)

This typology of types of visitors became important in the full evaluation because it permitted analysis of different kinds of museum experiences. Moreover, the evaluators recommended that when conducting interviews to get museum visitors' reactions to exhibits, the interview results should be dif-

---

EXHIBIT 8.6   Qualitative Analysis of Ancestry at the U.S. Census

To count different kinds of people—the job of the Census Bureau—you need categories to count them in. The long form of the 2000 census, given to 1 in 6 households, asked an open-ended, fill-in-the-blank question about "ancestry." Analysts then coded the responses into categories, 1 of 604 categories, up from 467 in 1980. The government doesn't ask about religion, so if people respond that they are Jewish, they don't get their ancestry counted. However, those who write in that they are Amish or Mennonite do get counted because those are considered cultural categories.

Ethnic minorities that cross national boundaries, such as French and Spanish Basques, and groups affected by geopolitical change, such as Czechs and Slovaks or groups within the former Yugoslavia, are counted in distinct categories. The Census Bureau, following advice from the U.S. State Department, differentiates Taiwanese Americans from Chinese Americans, a matter of political sensitivity.

Can Assyrians and Chaldeans be lumped together? When the Census Bureau announced that it would combine the two in the same ancestry code, an Assyrian group sued over the issue, but lost the lawsuit. Assyrian Americans trace their roots to a biblical-era empire covering much of what is now Iraq and believe that Chaldeans are a separate religious subgroup. A fieldworker for the Census Bureau did fieldwork on the issue.

"I went into places where there were young people playing games, went into restaurants, and places where older people gathered," says Ms. McKenney. . . . She paid a visit to Assyrian neighborhoods in Chicago, where a large concentration of Assyrian Americans live. At a local community center and later that day at the Assyrian restaurant next door, community leaders presented their case for keeping the ancestry code the same. Over the same period, she visited Detroit to look into the Chaldean matter. . . .

"I found that many of the people, especially the younger people, viewed it as an ethnic group, not a religion," says Ms. McKenney. She and Mr. Reed (Census Bureau ancestry research expert) concurred that enough differences existed that the Chaldeans could potentially qualify as a separate ancestry group.

In a conference call between interested parties, a compromise was struck. Assyrians and Chaldeans would remain under a single ancestry code, but the name would no longer be Assyrian, it would be Assyrian/Chaldean/Syriac—Syriac being the name of the Aramaic dialect that Assyrians and Chaldeans speak. "There was a meeting of the minds between all the representatives, and basically it was a unified decision to say that we're going to go under the same name," says the Chaldean Federation's Mr. Yono. (Kulish 2001:1)

---

ferentially valued depending on the type of person being interviewed—commuter, nomad, cafeteria type, or VIP.

A different typology was developed to distinguish how visitors learn in a museum:

"Museum Encounters of the First, Second, and Third Kind," a take-off on the popular science fiction movie *Close Encounters of the Third Kind,* which referred to direct human contact with visitors from outer space.

- *Museum Encounters of the First Kind:* This encounter occurs in halls that use display cases as the primary approach to specimen presentation. Essentially, the visitor is a passive observer to the "objects of interest." Interaction is visual and may occur only at the awareness level. The visitor is probably not provoked to think or consider ideas beyond the visual display.

- *Museum Encounters of the Second Kind:* This encounter occurs in halls that employ a variety of approaches to engage the visitor's attention and/or learning. The visitor has several choices to become active in his/her participation. . . . The visitor is likely to perceive, question, compare, hypothesize, etc.

- *Museum Encounters of the Third Kind:* This encounter occurs in halls that invite high levels of visitor participation. Such an encounter invites the visitor to observe phenomena in process, to create, to question the experts, to contribute, etc. Interaction is personalized and within the control of the visitor. (Wolf and Tymitz 1978:39)

Here's a sample of a quite different classification scheme, this one developed from fieldwork by sociologist Rob Rosenthal (1994) as "a map of the terrain" of the homeless.

- *Skidders:* Most often women, typically in their 30s, grew up middle or upper class but "skidded" into homelessness as divorced or separated parents.

- *Street people:* Mostly men, often veterans, rarely married; highly visible net and know how to use the resources of the street.

- *Wingnuts:* People with severe mental problems, occasionally due to longterm alcoholism, a visible subgroup.

- *Transitory workers:* People with job skills and a history of full-time work who travel from town to town, staying months or years in a place, and then heading off to greener pastures.

Categories of how homeless people spend their time:

- Hanging out
- Getting by
- Getting ahead

As these examples illustrate, the first purpose of typologies is to distinguish aspects of an observed pattern or phenomenon *descriptively.* Once identified and distinguished, these types can later be used to make interpretations and they can be related to other observations to draw conclusions, but the first purpose is description based on an inductive analysis of the patterns that appear in the data.

⑤ The Intellectual and Mechanical Work of Analysis

Coding Data, Finding Patterns, Labeling Themes, and Developing Category Systems

C lassification is Ariadne's clue through the labyrinth of nature.

—George Sand, *Nouvelles Lettres d'un Voyageur,* 1869

Thus far, I've provided lots of examples of the fruit of qualitative inquiry: patterns, themes, categories, and typologies. Let's back up now to consider how you recognize patterns in qualitative data and turn those patterns into meaningful categories and themes. This chapter could have started with this section, but I think it's helpful to understand what kinds of findings can be generated from qualitative analysis before delving very deeply into the mechanics, especially because the mechanics vary greatly and are undertaken differently by analysts in different disciplines and working from divergent frameworks. That said, some guidance can be offered.

Raw field notes and verbatim transcripts constitute the undigested complexity of reality. Simplifying and making sense out of that complexity constitutes the challenge of content analysis. **Developing some manageable classification or coding scheme is the first step of analysis.** Without classification there is chaos and confusion. Content analysis, then, involves identifying, coding, categorizing, classifying, and labeling the primary patterns in the data. This essentially means analyzing the core *content* of interviews and observations to determine what's significant. In explaining the process, I'll describe it as done traditionally, which is without software, to highlight the thinking and mechanics involved. Software programs provide different tools and formats for coding, but the principles of the analytical process are the same whether doing it manually or with the assistance of a computer program.

I begin by reading through all of my field notes or interviews and making comments in the margins or even attaching pieces of paper or Post-it notes that contain my notions about what I can do with the different parts of the data. This constitutes the first cut at organizing the data into topics and files. Coming up with topics is like constructing an index for a book or labels for a file system: You look at what is there and give it a name, a label. The copy on which these topics and labels are written becomes the indexed copy of the field notes or interviews. Exhibit 8.7 shows a sampling of codes from the field note margins of the evaluation of the wilderness education program I described in the chapter on observation.

The shorthand codes are written directly on the relevant data passages, either in the margins or with an attached tab on the relevant page. Many passages will illustrate more than one theme or pattern. The first reading through the data is aimed at developing the coding categories or classification system. Then a new reading is done to actually start the formal coding in a systematic way. Several readings of the data may be necessary before field notes or interviews can be completely indexed and coded. Some people find it helpful to use colored highlighting pens—color coding different idea or concepts. Using self-adhesive colored dots or Post-it notes offers another option. Some use a color printer to print out transcripts in different colors to make it easy to track the source of a quote when cutting and pasting different quotes into a theme.

> If sensing a pattern or "occurrence" can be called *seeing*, then the encoding of it can be called *seeing as*. That is, you first make the observation that something important or notable is occurring, and then you classify or describe it. . . . [T]he *seeing as* provides us with a link between a new or emergent pattern and any and all patterns that we have observed and considered previously. It also provides a link to any and all patterns that others have observed and considered previously through reading. (Boyatzis 1998:4)

| EXHIBIT 8.7 | First-Cut Coding Examples: Sample Codes From the Field Note Margins |

Code: Ps Re Prog (meaning: participants' reactions to the program)
Code: Ps Re Ps (participants' reactions to other participants)
Code: Ob PP (observations of participants' interactions)
Code: Ob SS (observations of staff's interactions)
Code: Ob SP (observations of staff/participant interactions)
Code: Phil (statements about program philosophy)
Code: Prc (examples of program processes)
Code: P/outs (effects of program on participants/outcomes)
Code: S-G (subgroup formations)
Code: GPrc (group process)
Code: C! (conflicts)
Code: C-PP (conflicts among participants)
Code: C-SP (conflicts between staff and participants)
Code: C-SS (conflicts among staff)

NOTE: P = participants, S = staff. These codes are from the field note margins of the evaluation of the wilderness education program described in the chapter on observation. The shorthand codes (abbreviations) are written in the margins directly on the relevant data passages or quotations. The full labels in parentheses are the designations for separate files that contain all similarly coded passages.

Where more than one person is working on the analysis, it is helpful to have each person (or small teams for large projects) develop the coding scheme independently, then compare and discuss similarities and differences. Important insights can emerge from the different ways in which two people look at the same set of data, a form of analytical triangulation.

Often an elaborate classification system emerges during coding, particularly in large projects where a formal scheme must be developed that can be used by several trained coders. In the study of evaluation use that is the basis for *Utilization-Focused Evaluation* (Patton 1997a), graduate students in the evaluation program at the University of Minnesota conducted lengthy interviews with 60 project officers, evaluators, and federal decision makers. We developed a comprehensive classification system that would

provide easy access to the data by any of the student or faculty researchers. Had only one investigator been intending to use the data, such an elaborate classification scheme would not have been necessary. However, to provide access to several students for different purposes, every paragraph in every interview was coded using a systematic and comprehensive coding scheme made up of 15 general categories with subcategories. Portions of the codebook used to code the utilization of evaluation data appear in Appendix 8.1 at the end of this chapter as an example of one kind of qualitative analysis codebook. This codebook was developed from four sources: (a) the standardized open-ended questions used in interviewing, (b) review of the utilization literature for ideas to be examined and hypotheses to be reviewed, (c) our initial inventory review of the interviews in which two of us read all the data and added categories for coding, and (d) a few additional categories added during coding when passages didn't fit well in the available categories.

Every interview was coded twice by two independent coders. Each individual code, including redundancies, was entered into our qualitative analysis database so that we could retrieve all passages (data) on any subject included in the classification scheme, with brief descriptions of the content of those passages. The analyst could then go directly to the full passages and complete interviews from which passages were extracted to keep quotations in context. In addition, the computer analysis permitted easy cross-classification and cross-comparison of passages for more complex analyses across interviews.

Some such elaborate coding system is routine for very rigorous analysis of a large amount of data. Complex coding systems with multiple coders categorizing every paragraph in every interview constitute a labor-intensive form of coding, one that would not be used for small-scale formative evaluation or action research projects. However, where data are going to be used by several people, or where data are going to be used over a long period of time, including additions to the data set over time, such a comprehensive and computerized system can be well worth the time and effort required.

Kibel (1999) developed a very sophisticated and comprehensive system for coding stories of successful outcomes attainment that he called "results mapping." His system permitted converting individualized stories into standardized categories that permitted aggregation, comparison, and even quantification. However, it required intensive training to use and proved too cumbersome and demanding for most human services and educational programs. As this was being

written, he had gone back to the drawing board and was working on a more usable coding framework to capture and code the stories of program participants in a standardized framework, an approach to be called "journey mapping."

Classifying and coding qualitative data produce a framework for organizing and describing what has been collected during fieldwork. (For published examples of coding schemes, see Bernard 1998:325-28, 387-89, 491-92, 624; Bernard 2000:447-50; Boyatzis 1998; Strauss and Corbin 1998; Miles and Huberman 1994.) This descriptive phase of analysis builds a foundation for the interpretative phase when meanings are extracted from the data, comparisons are made, creative frameworks for interpretation are constructed, conclusions are drawn, significance is determined, and, in some cases, theory is generated.

Convergence and Divergence in Coding and Classifying

In developing codes and categories, a qualitative analyst must first deal with the challenge of *convergence* (Guba 1978)—figuring out what things fit together. Begin by looking for *recurring regularities* in the data. These regularities reveal patterns that can be sorted into categories. Categories should then be judged by two criteria: *internal homogeneity* and *external heterogeneity*. The first criterion concerns the extent to which the data that belong in a certain category hold together or "dovetail" in a meaningful way. The second criterion concerns the extent to which differences among categories are bold and clear. "The existence of a large number of unassignable or overlapping data items is good evidence of some basic fault in the category system" (Guba 1978:53). The analyst then works back and forth between the data and the classification system to verify the meaningfulness and accuracy of the categories and the placement of data in categories. If several different possible classification systems emerge or are developed, some priorities must be established to determine which are more important and illuminative. Prioritizing is done according to the utility, salience, credibility, uniqueness, heuristic value, and feasibility of the classification schemes. Finally, the category system or set of categories is tested for completeness.

1. The set should have internal and external plausibility, a property that might be termed "integratability." Viewed internally, the individual categories should appear to be consistent; viewed externally, the set of categories should seem to comprise a whole picture. . . .

2. The set should be reasonably inclusive of the data and information that do exist. This feature is partly tested by the absence of unassignable cases, but can be further tested by reference to the problem that the inquirer is investigating or by the mandate given the evaluator by his client/sponsor. If the set of categories did not appear to be sufficient, on logical grounds, to cover the facets of the problem or mandate, the set is probably incomplete.

3. The set should be reproducible by another competent judge. . . . The second observer ought to be able to verify that (a) the categories make sense in view of the data which are available, and (b) the data have been appropriately arranged in the category system. . . . The category system auditor may be called upon to attest that the category system "fits" the data and that the data have been properly "fitted into" it.

4. The set should be credible to the persons who provided the information which the set is presumed to assimilate. . . . Who is in a better position to judge whether the categories appropriately reflect their issues and concerns than the people themselves? (Guba 1978:56-57)

After analyzing for convergence, the mirror analytical strategy involves examining *divergence*. By this Guba means the analyst must "flesh out" the patterns or categories. This is done by processes of extension (building on items of information already known), bridging (making connections among different items), and surfacing (proposing new information that ought to fit and then verifying its existence). The analyst brings closure to the process when sources of information have been exhausted, when sets of categories have been saturated so that new sources lead to redundancy, when clear regularities have emerged that feel integrated, and when the analysis begins to "overextend" beyond the boundaries of the issues and concerns guiding the analysis. Divergence also includes careful and thoughtful examination of data that doesn't seem to fit including *deviant cases* that don't fit the dominant identified patterns.

This sequence, convergence then divergence, should not be followed mechanically, linearly, or rigidly. The processes of qualitative analysis involve both technical and creative dimensions. As noted early in this chapter, no abstract processes of analysis, no matter how eloquently named and finely described, can substitute for the skill, knowledge, experience, creativity, diligence, and work of the qualitative analyst. "The task of converting field notes and observations about issues and concerns into systematic categories is a difficult one. No infallible procedure exists for performing it" (Guba 1978:53).

Determining Substantive Significance

In lieu of statistical significance, qualitative findings are judged by their *substantive significance*. The analyst makes an argument for substantive significance in presenting findings and conclusions, but readers and users of the analysis will make their own value judgments about significance. In determining substantive significance, the analyst addresses these kinds of questions:

- How solid, coherent, and consistent is the evidence in support of the findings? (Triangulation, for example, can be used in determining the strength of evidence in support of a finding.)

- To what extent and in what ways do the findings increase and deepen understanding of the phenomenon studied (*Verstehen*)?

- To what extent are the findings consistent with other knowledge? (A finding supported by and supportive of other work has confirmatory significance. A finding that breaks new ground has discovery or innovative significance.)

- To what extent are the findings useful for some intended purpose (e.g., contributing to theory, informing policy, summative or formative evaluation, or problem solving in action research)?

The qualitative analyst's effort at uncovering patterns, themes, and categories includes using both creative and critical faculties in making carefully considered judgments about what is really significant and meaningful in the data. Since qualitative analysts do not have statistical tests to tell them when an observation or pattern is significant, they must rely first on their own intelligence, experience, and judgment; second,

> **INTEROCULAR SIGNIFICANCE**
>
> *"If we are interested in real significance, we ignore little differences.... We ignore them because, although they are very likely real, they are very unlikely to hold up in replications. Fred Mosteller, the great applied statistician, was fond of saying that he did not care much for statistically significant differences, he was more interested in interocular differences, the differences that hit us between the eyes"* (Scriven 1993:71).

they should take seriously the responses of those who were studied or participated in the inquiry; and third, the researcher or evaluator should consider the responses and reactions of those who read and review the results. Where all three—analyst, those studied, and reviewers—agree, one has *consensual validation* of the substantive significance of the findings. Where disagreements emerge, which is the more usual case, you get a more interesting life and the joys of debate.

Determining substantive significance can involve the making of the qualitative analyst's equivalent of Type I and Type II errors from statistics: The analyst may decide that something is not significant when in fact it is, or, conversely, the analyst may attribute significance to something that is meaningless. A story illustrates this problem of making judgments about what is really significant.

Halcolm was approached by a woman who handed him something. Without hesitation, Halcolm returned the object to the woman. The many young disciples who followed Halcolm to learn his wisdom began arguing among themselves about the special meaning of this interchange. A variety of interpretations were offered.

When Halcolm heard of the argument among his young followers, he called them together and asked each one to report on the significance of what they had observed. They offered a variety of interpretations. When they had finished he said, "The real purpose of the exchange was to enable me to show you that you are not yet sufficiently masters of observation to know when you have witnessed a meaningless interaction."

⑤ Logical Analysis

While working inductively, the analyst is looking for emergent patterns in the data. These patterns, as noted in preceding sections, can be represented as dimensions, categories, classification schemes, themes, and categories. Once some dimensions have been constructed, using either participant-generated constructions or analyst-generated constructions, it is sometimes useful to cross-classify different dimensions to generate new insights about how the data can be organized and to look for patterns that may not have been immediately obvious in the initial, inductive analysis. Creating cross-classification matrices is an exercise in logic.

The logical process involves creating potential categories by crossing one dimension or typology with another, and then working back and forth between the data and one's logical constructions, filling in the resulting matrix. This logical system will create a new typology, all parts of which may or may not actually be represented in the data. Thus, the analyst moves back and forth between the logical construction and the actual data in a search for meaningful patterns.

In the high school dropout program described earlier, the focus of the program was reducing absenteeism, skipping of classes, and tardiness. An external team of consul-

tant/change agents worked with teachers in the school to help them develop approaches to the dropout problem. Observations of the program and interviews with the teachers gave rise to two dimensions. The first dimension distinguished *teachers' beliefs about what kind of programmatic intervention was effective* with dropouts, that is, whether they primarily favored maintenance (caretaking or warehousing of kids to just keep the schools running), rehabilitation efforts (helping kids with their problems), or punishment (no longer letting them get away with the infractions they had been committing in the past). *Teachers' behaviors toward dropouts* could be conceptualized along a continuum from taking direct responsibility for doing something about the problem, at one end, to shifting responsibility to others at the opposite end. Exhibit 8.8 shows what happens when these two dimensions are crossed. Six cells are created, each of which represents a different kind of teacher role in response to the program.

The evaluator analyst working with these data had been struggling in the inductive analysis to find the patterns that would express the different kinds of teacher roles manifested in the program. He had tried several constructions, but none of them quite seemed to work. The labels he came up with were not true to the data. When he described to me the other dimensions he had generated, I suggested that he cross them, as shown in Exhibit 8.8. When he did, he said that "the whole thing immediately fell into place." Working back and forth between the matrix and the data, he generated a full descriptive analysis of diverse and conflicting teacher roles.

The description of teacher roles served several purposes. First, it gave teachers a mirror image of their own behaviors and attitudes. It could thus be used to help teach-

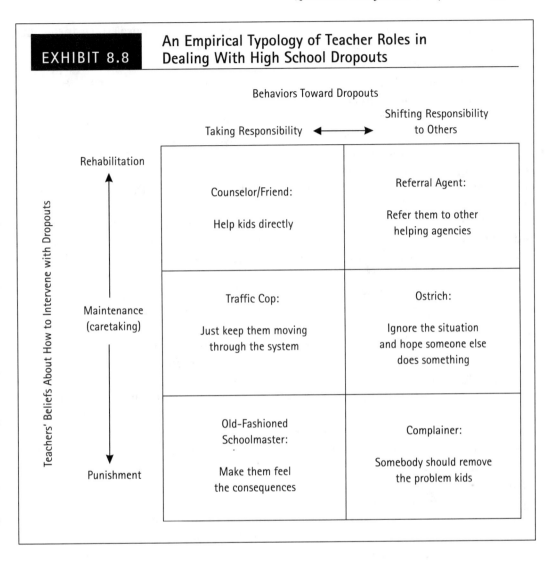

EXHIBIT 8.8 — An Empirical Typology of Teacher Roles in Dealing With High School Dropouts

Behaviors Toward Dropouts

Taking Responsibility ←————→ Shifting Responsibility to Others

Teachers' Beliefs About How to Intervene with Dropouts

Rehabilitation
- Counselor/Friend: Help kids directly
- Referral Agent: Refer them to other helping agencies

Maintenance (caretaking)
- Traffic Cop: Just keep them moving through the system
- Ostrich: Ignore the situation and hope someone else does something

Punishment
- Old-Fashioned Schoolmaster: Make them feel the consequences
- Complainer: Somebody should remove the problem kids

ers make more explicit their own understanding of roles. Second, it could be used by the external team of consultants to more carefully gear their programmatic efforts toward different kinds of teachers who were acting out the different roles. The matrix makes it clear that an omnibus strategy for helping teachers establish a program that would reduce dropouts would not work in this school; teachers manifesting different roles would need to be approached and worked with in different ways. Third, the description of teacher roles provided insights into the nature of the dropout problem. Having identified the various roles, the evaluator analyst had a responsibility to report on the distribution of roles in this school and the observed consequences of that distribution.

One must be careful about this kind of logical analysis. It is easy for a matrix to begin to manipulate the data as the analyst is tempted to force data into categories created by the cross-classification to fill out the matrix and make it work. Logical analysis to generate new sensitizing concepts must be tested out and confirmed by the actual data. **Such logically derived sensitizing concepts provide conceptual hypotheses to test.** Levin-Rozalis (2000), following American philosopher Charles Sanders Pierce of the pragmatic school of thought, suggests labeling the logical generation and discovery of hypotheses and findings *abduction* to distinguish such logical analysis from data-based inductive analysis and theory-derived deductive analysis.

Denzin (1978b) has explained abduction in qualitative analysis as a combination of inductive and deductive thinking with logical underpinnings:

> Naturalists inspect and organize behavior specimens in ways which they hope will permit them to progressively reveal and better understand the underlying problematic features of the social world under study. They seek to ask the question or set of questions which will make that world or social organization understandable. They do not approach that world with a rigid set of preconceived hypotheses. They are initially directed toward an interest in the routine and taken-for-granted features of that world. They ask how it is that the persons in question know about producing orderly patterns of interaction and meaning. . . . They do not use a full-fledged deductive hypothetical scheme in thinking and developing propositions. Nor are they fully inductive, letting the so-called "facts" speak for themselves. Facts do not speak for themselves. They must be interpreted. Previously developed deductive models seldom conform with empirical data that are gathered. The method of abduction combines the deductive and inductive models of proposition development and theory construction. It can be defined as *working from consequence back to cause or antecedent*. The observer records the occurrence of a particular event, and then works back in time in an effort to reconstruct the events (causes) that produced the event (consequence) in question. (pp. 109-10)

Famous fictional detective Sherlock Holmes relied on abduction more than deduction or induction, at least according to a review by William Sanders (1976) of Holmes's analytical thinking in *The Sociologist as Detective*. We've already suggested that the qualitative analyst is part scientist and part artist. Why not add the qualitative analyst as detective? The empty cell of a logically derived matrix (the cell created by crossing two dimensions for which no name or label immediately occurs) creates an intersection of a possible consequence and antecedent that begs for abductive exploration and explanation. Each such intersection of consequence and antecedent sensitizes the analyst to the possibility of a category of activity or behavior that either has been overlooked in the data or is logically a possibility in the setting but has not been manifested. The latter cases are important to note because their importance derives from the fact that they did not occur. The next section will look in detail at a process/outcomes matrix ripe with abductive possibilities.

Nick Smith (1980) used a matrix to draw important distinctions among different kinds of evaluation use by asking if "techniques of effective evaluation utilization differ with regard to audience or entity studied." His matrix crossed a programs/policies dimension (what can be studied?) with a program managers/policymakers distinction (who is to be aided?) to show different kinds of utilization in each case. Exhibit 8.9 shows a matrix for mapping stakeholders' stakes in a program or policy. This matrix can be used to guide data collection as well as analysis. Later this chapter presents a process/outcomes matrix for crossing

MODUS OPERANDI ANALYSIS

Modus operandi (MO) was conceptualized by evaluation theorist Michael Scriven (1976) as a way of inferring causality when experimental designs are impractical or inappropriate. The MO approach, drawing from forensic science, makes the inquirer a detective. Detectives compare clues discovered at a crime scene to known patterns of possible suspects. Those suspects whose MO (method of operating) does not fit the crime scene pattern are eliminated from further investigation.

Translated to research and evaluation, the inquirer/detective observes some pattern and makes a list of possible causes. Evidence from the inquiry is compared to the list of suspects (possible causes). Those possible causes that do not fit the pattern of evidence can be eliminated from further consideration. Following the autopsy-like logic of Occam's razor, as each possible cause is compared to the evidence, that cause supported by the preponderance of evidence and offering the simplest interpretation among competing possibilities is preferred and considered most likely.

nity, district), 10 components of the statewide project (planning, goal-setting, . . . student involvement), and 10 factors affecting utilization (personal factor, political factors, . . .). Exhibit 8.10 again illustrates matrix thinking for both data organization and analytical/conceptual purposes.

Miles and Huberman (1994) have provided a rich source of ideas and illustrations of how to use matrices in qualitative analysis. They include examples of a time-ordered matrix, role-ordered matrix, role-by-time matrix, role-by-group matrix, conceptually clustered matrix, site dynamics matrix, and predictor-outcome matrix, among others. Their *Sourcebook* provides a variety of ideas for analytical approaches to qualitative data including a variety of concept mapping and visual display techniques.

Other ways of graphing and mapping findings include concept mapping and cognitive mapping. For a detailed discussion of concept mapping as a way of visually displaying data to facilitate analytic clarity and depicting relationships in a network or system, see Trochim (1989). For an example of cognitive mapping as a way of displaying qualitative results showing the "structure and content of decision schemas" among senior managers, see Clarke and Mackaness (2001).

program processes with program outcomes as a qualitative analysis framework.

To study how schools used planning and evaluation processes, Campbell (1983) developed a 500-cell matrix (Exhibit 8.10) that begins (but just begins) to reach the outer limits of what one can do in three-dimensional space. Campbell used this matrix to guide data collection and analysis in studying how the mandated, statewide educational planning, evaluation, and reporting system in Minnesota was used. She examined 5 levels of use (high school, . . . community)

▣ A Process/Outcomes Matrix

The linkage between processes and outcomes constitutes such a fundamental issue in many program evaluations that it provides a particularly good focus for illustrating qualitative matrix analysis. As discussed in Chapter 4, qualitative methods can be particularly appropriate for evaluation where program processes, impacts, or both are largely unspecified or difficult to measure. This can be the case because the outcomes are meant to be individualized;

EXHIBIT 8.9	Mapping Stakeholders' Stakes		
	Estimate of Various Stakeholders' Inclination Toward the Program		
How high are the stakes for various primary stakeholders?	Favorable	Neutral or Unknown	Antagonistic
High			
Moderate			
Low			

SOURCE: Patton (1997a:344).

NOTE: Construct illustrative case studies for each cell based on fieldwork.

---

sometimes the program is simply uncertain what its outcomes will be; and, in many programs, neither processes nor impacts have been carefully articulated. Under such conditions, one purpose of the evaluation may be to illuminate program processes, program impacts, and the linkages between the two. This task can be facilitated by constructing a process/outcomes matrix to organize the data.

Exhibit 8.11 (p. 474) shows how such a matrix can be constructed. Major program processes or identified implementation components are listed along the left side. Types or levels of outcomes are listed across the top. The category systems for program processes and outcomes are developed from the data in the same way that other typologies are constructed (see previous sections). The cross-classification of any process with any outcome produces a cell in the matrix; for example, the first cell in Exhibit 8.11 is created by the intersection of process 1 with outcome a. The information that goes in cell 1a (or any other cell in the matrix) describes

linkages, patterns, themes, experiences, content, or actual activities that help us understand the relationships between processes and outcomes. Such relationships may have been identified by participants themselves during interviews or discovered by the evaluator in analyzing the data. In either case, the process/outcomes matrix becomes a way of organizing, thinking about, and presenting the qualitative connections between program implementation dimensions and program impacts.

An example will help make the notion of the process/outcomes matrix more concrete. Suppose we have been evaluating a juvenile justice program that places delinquent youth in foster homes. We have visited several foster homes, observed what the home environments are like, and interviewed the juveniles, the foster home parents, and the probation officers. A *regularly recurring process theme* concerns the importance of "letting kids learn to make their own decisions." A *regularly recurring outcomes theme* involves "keeping the kids

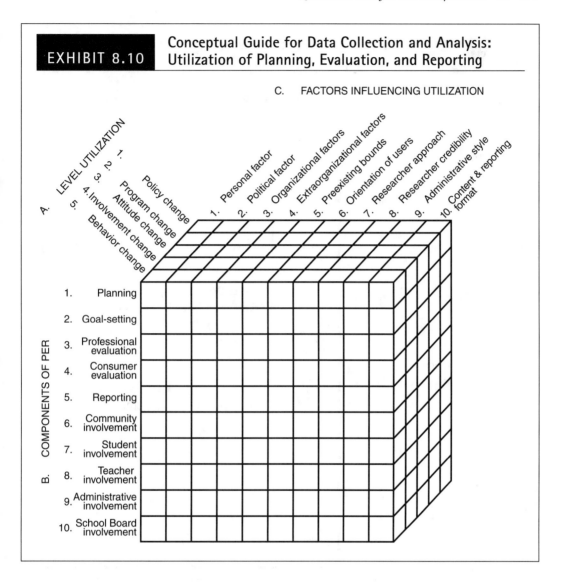

EXHIBIT 8.10 — Conceptual Guide for Data Collection and Analysis: Utilization of Planning, Evaluation, and Reporting

C. FACTORS INFLUENCING UTILIZATION

A. LEVEL UTILIZATION
1. Policy change
2. Program change
3. Attitude change
4. Involvement change
5. Behavior change

C. FACTORS INFLUENCING UTILIZATION
1. Personal factor
2. Political factor
3. Organizational factors
4. Extraorganizational factors
5. Preexisting bounds
6. Orientation of users
7. Researcher approach
8. Researcher credibility
9. Administrative style
10. Content & reporting format

B. COMPONENTS OF PER
1. Planning
2. Goal-setting
3. Professional evaluation
4. Consumer evaluation
5. Reporting
6. Community involvement
7. Student involvement
8. Teacher involvement
9. Administrative involvement
10. School Board involvement

straight" (reduced recidivism). By crossing the program process ("kids making their own decisions") with the program outcome ("keeping kids straight"), we create a data analysis question: What actual decisions do juveniles make that are supposed to lead to reduced recidivism? We then carefully review our field notes and interview quotations looking for data that help us understand how people in the program have answered this question based on their actual behaviors and practices. By describing what decisions juveniles actually make in the program, the decision makers to whom our findings are reported can make their own judgments about the strength or weakness of the linkage between this program process and the desired outcome. Moreover, once the process/outcomes descriptive analysis of linkages has been completed, the evaluator is at liberty to offer interpretations and judgments about the nature and quality of this process/outcomes connection.

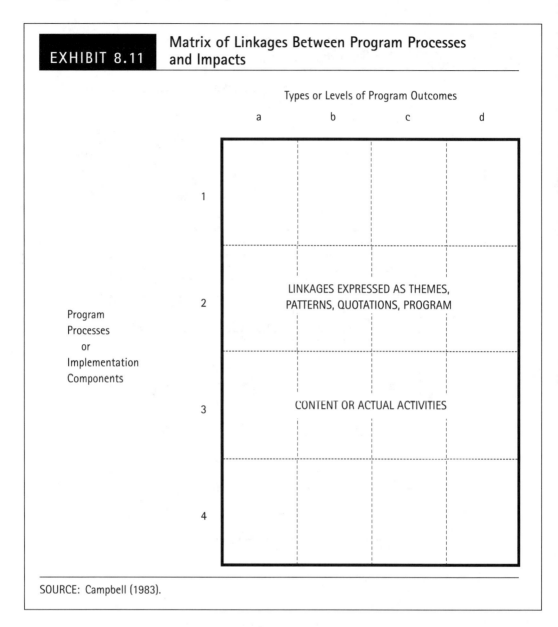

EXHIBIT 8.11   **Matrix of Linkages Between Program Processes and Impacts**

Types or Levels of Program Outcomes

a   b   c   d

Program
Processes
or
Implementation
Components

1

2   LINKAGES EXPRESSED AS THEMES,
           PATTERNS, QUOTATIONS, PROGRAM

3   CONTENT OR ACTUAL ACTIVITIES

4

SOURCE: Campbell (1983).

An Analysis Example: Recognizing Processes, Outcomes, and Linkages in Qualitative Data

Because of the centrality of the sensitizing concepts "program process" and "program outcome" in evaluation research, it may be helpful to provide a more detailed descrip-tion of how these concepts can be used in qualitative analysis. How does one recog-nize a program process? Learning to identify and label program processes is a critical evaluation skill. This sensitizing notion of "process" is a way of talking about the com-mon action that cuts across program activi-ties, observed interactions, and program content. The example I shall use involves data from the wilderness education program I evaluated and discussed throughout the observations chapter (Chapter 6). That program, titled the Southwest Field Training Project, used the wilderness as a training arena for professional educators in the philosophy and methods of experiential education by engaging those educators in their own experiential learning process. Participants went from their normal urban environments into the wilderness for 10 days at a time, spending at least one day and night completely alone in some wilderness spot "on solo." At times, while backpacking, the group was asked to walk silently so as not to be distracted from the wilderness sounds and images by conversation. In group discussions, participants were asked to talk about what they had observed about the wilderness and how they felt about being in the wilderness. Participants were also asked to write about the wilderness environment in journals. *What do these different activities have in common, and how can that commonality be expressed?*

We begin with several different ways of abstracting and labeling the underlying process:

- Experiencing the wilderness

- Learning about the wilderness

- Appreciating the wilderness

- Immersion in the environment

- Developing awareness of the environment

- Becoming conscious of the wilderness

- Developing sensitivity to the environment

Any of these phrases, each of which consists of some verb form (experiencing, learning, developing, and so on) and some noun form (wilderness, environment), captures some

nuance of the process. The qualitative analyst works back and forth between the data (field notes and interviews) and his or her conception of what it is that needs to be expressed to find the most fitting language to describe the process. What language do people in the program use to describe what those activities and experiences have in common? What language comes closest to capturing the essence of this particular process? What level of generality or specificity will be most useful in separating out this particular set of things from other things? How do program participants and staff react to the different terms that could be used to describe the process?

It's not unusual during analysis to go through several different phrases before finally settling on exact language that will go into a final report. In the Southwest Field Training Project, we began with the concept label "Experiencing the wilderness." However, after several revisions, we finally described the process as "developing sensitivity to the environment" because this broader label permitted us to include discussions and activities that were aimed at helping participants understand how they were affected by and acted in their normal institutional environments. "Experiencing the wilderness" became a specific subprocess that was part of the more global process of "developing sensitivity to the environment." Program participants and staff played a major role in determining the final phrasing and description of this process.

Below are other processes identified as important in the implementation of the program:

- Encountering and managing stress

- Sharing in group settings

- Examining professional activities, needs, and commitments

- Assuming responsibility for articulating personal needs

- Exchanging professional ideas and resources

- Formally monitoring experiences, processes, changes, and impacts

As you struggle with finding the right language to communicate themes, patterns, and processes, keep in mind that there is no absolutely "right" way of stating what emerges from the analysis. There are only more and less useful ways of expressing what the data reveal.

Identifying and conceptualizing program outcomes and impacts can involve induction, deduction, and/or logical analysis. *Inductively,* the evaluator analyst looks for changes in participants, expressions of change, program ideology about outcomes and impacts, and ways that people in the program make distinctions between "those who are getting *it*" and "those who aren't getting *it*" (where *it* is the desired outcome). In highly individualized programs, the statements about change that emerge from program participants and staff may be global. Such outcomes as "personal growth," increased "awareness," and "insight into self" are difficult to operationalize and standardize. That is precisely the reason qualitative methods are particularly appropriate for capturing and evaluating such outcomes. The task for the evaluator analyst, then, is to describe what actually happens to people in the program and what they say about what happens to them. Appendix 8.3 at the end of this chapter presents portions of the report describing the effects on participants of their experiences in the wilderness education program. The data come from in-depth, open-ended interviews. This report excerpt shows how descriptive data (direct quotations) are used to support and explain inductive thematic analysis.

Deductively, the evaluator analyst may draw from outcomes identified in similar programs or from goal statements found in program proposals, brochures, and planning documents that were used to guide data collection.

Logically (or abductively), constructing a process/outcomes matrix can suggest additional possibilities. That is, where data on both program processes and participant outcomes have been sorted, analysis can be deepened by organizing the data through a logical scheme that links program processes to participant outcomes. Such a logically derived scheme was used to organize the data in the Southwest Field Training Project. First, a classification scheme that described different types of outcomes was conceptualized:

(a) changes in skills,

(b) changes in attitudes,

(c) changes in feelings,

(d) changes in behaviors, and

(e) changes in knowledge.

These general themes provided the reader of the report with examples of and insights into the kinds of changes that were occurring and how those changes that were perceived by participants to be related to specific program processes. I emphasize that the process/outcomes matrix is merely an organizing tool; the data from participants themselves and from field observations provide the actual linkages between processes and outcomes.

What was the relationship between the program process of "developing sensitivity to the environment" and these individual-level outcomes? Space permits only a few examples from the data.

Skills: "Are you kidding? I learned how to survive without the comforts of civilization. I learned how to read the terrain ahead and pace myself. I learned how to carry a heavy load. I learned how to stay dry when it's raining. I learned how to tie a knot so that it doesn't come apart when pressure is applied. You think those are metaphors for skills I need in my work? You're damn right they are."

Attitudes: "I think it's important to pay attention to the space you're in. I don't want to just keep going through my life oblivious to what's around me and how it affects me and how I affect it."

Feelings: "Being out here, especially on solo, has given me confidence. I know I can handle a lot of things I didn't think I could handle."

Behaviors: "I use my senses in a different way out here. In the city you get so you don't pay much attention to the noise and the sounds. But listening out here I've also begun to listen more back there. I touch more things too, just to experience the different textures."

Knowledge: "I know about how this place was formed, its history, the rock formations,

the effects of the fires on the vegetation, where the river comes from and where it goes."

A different way of thinking about organizing data around outcomes was to think of different levels of impact: effects at the individual level, effects on the group, and effects on the institutions from which participants came into the program. The staff hoped to have impacts at all of these levels. Thus, it also was possible to organize the data by looking at what themes emerged when program processes were crossed with levels of impact. How did "developing sensitivity to the environment" affect individuals? How did the process of "developing sensitivity to the environment" affect the group? What was the effect of "developing sensitivity to the environment" on the institutions to which participants returned after their wilderness experiences? The process/outcomes matrix thus becomes a way of asking questions of the data, an additional source of focus in looking for themes and patterns in hundreds of pages of field notes and interview transcriptions.

🔳 Interpreting Findings

S imply observing and interviewing do not ensure that the research is qualitative; the qualitative researcher must also interpret the beliefs and behaviors of participants.

—Valerie J. Janesick (2000:387)

Interpreting for Meaning

Qualitative interpretation begins with elucidating meanings. The analyst examines a story, a case study, a set of interviews, or a collection of field notes and asks, What does

this mean? What does this tell me about the nature of the phenomenon of interest? In asking these questions, the analyst works back and forth between the data or story (the evidence) and his or her own perspective and understandings to make sense of the evidence. Both the evidence and the perspective brought to bear on the evidence need to be elucidated in this choreography in searching of meaning. Alternative interpretations are tried and tested against the data.

For example, when we analyzed follow-up interviews with participants who had gone through intensive community leadership training, we found a variety of expressions of uncertainty about what they should do with their training. In the final day of a six-day retreat, after learning how to assess community needs, work with diverse groups, communicate clearly, empower people to action, and plan for change, they were cautioned to go easy in transitioning back to their communities and take their time in building community connections before taking action. What program staff meant as a last-day warning about not returning to the community as a bull in a china shop and charging ahead destructively had, in fact, paralyzed the participants and made them afraid to take any action at all. The program, which intended to poise participants for action, had inadvertently left graduates in "action paralysis" for fear of making mistakes. That *meaning*, "action paralysis," emerged from the data analysis through interpretation. No one used that specific phrase. Rather, we interpreted that as the essence of what interviewees were reporting through a haze of uncertainties, ambiguities, worried musings, and wait-and-see-before-acting reflections.

Narrative analysis (see Chapter 3) has focused specifically on how to interpret stories, life history narratives, historical memoirs, and creative nonfiction to reveal cultural and social patterns through the lens of individual experiences. This "biographical turn in social science" (Chamberlayne, Bornat, and Wengraf 2000) or "narrative turn" in qualitative inquiry (Bochner 2001) honors people's stories as data that can

stand on their own as pure description of experience or be analyzed for connections between the psychological, sociological, cultural, political, and dramaturgic dimensions of human experience to reveal larger meanings. Much of the analytical focus in narrative studies concerns the nature of interpretation (Denzin 1989a, 1989b, 1997b). How to interpret stories and, more specifically, the texts that tell the stories is at the heart of narrative analysis (Lieblich, Tuval-Mashiach, and Zilber 1998). Meaning-making also comes from comparing stories and cases and can take the form of inquiring into and interpreting causes, consequences, and relationships.

Comparisons, Causes, Consequences, and Relationships

Thus far, this chapter has emphasized the tasks of organization, description, and linking. Even the matrix analyses just discussed were aimed at organizing and describing the themes, patterns, activities, and content of a study rather than elucidating causal linkages between processes and outcomes. To the extent that you are describing the causal linkages suggested by and believed in by those you've interviewed, you haven't crossed the line from description into causal interpretation. And, indeed, much qualitative inquiry stops with the presentation of case data and cross-case descriptive comparisons aimed at enhancing understanding rather than explaining "why." Stake (1995) has emphasized that "explanations are intended to promote understanding and understanding is sometimes expressed in terms of explanation—but the two aims are epistemologically quite different . . . , a difference important to us, the difference between case studies seeking to identify cause and effect relationships and those seeking

understanding of human experience" (p. 38). Appreciating and respecting this distinction, once case studies have been written and descriptive typologies have been developed and supported, the tasks of organization and description are largely complete and it is appropriate, if desired, to move on to making comparisons and considering causes, consequences, and relationships.

Statements about which things appear to lead to other things, for example, which aspects of a program produce certain effects, and how processes lead to outcomes are natural areas for interpretation and hypothesizing. When careful study of the data gives rise to ideas about causal linkages, there is no reason to deny those interested in the study's results the benefit of those insights. What is important is that such statements be clearly qualified as what they are: interpretation and hypothesizing.

A researcher who has lived in a community for an extensive period of time will likely have insights into why things happen as they do there. A qualitative analyst who has spent hours interviewing people will likely come away from the analysis with possible explanations for how the phenomenon of interest takes the forms and has the effects it does. The evaluator who has studied a program, lived with the data from the field, and reflected at length about the patterns and themes that run through the data is in as good a position as anyone else at that point to speculate about meanings, make conjectures about significance, and offer hypotheses about relationships. Moreover, if decision makers and evaluation users have asked for such information—and in my experience they virtually always welcome these kinds of analyses—there is no reason not to share insights with them to help them think about their own causal presuppositions and hypotheses and to explore what the data do and do not support in the way of interconnections and potential causal relationships.

Lofland's (1971) musings are helpful in clarifying the role of causal speculation in qualitative analysis. He argued that the strong suit of the qualitative researcher is the ability "to provide an orderly description of rich, descriptive detail" (p. 59); the consideration of causes and consequences using qualitative data should be a "tentative, qualified, and subsidiary task" (p. 62).

> It is perfectly appropriate that one be curious about causes, so long as one recognizes that whatever account or explanations he develops is conjecture. In more legitimacy-conferring terms, such conjectures are called hypotheses or theories. It is proper to devote a portion of one's report to conjectured causes of variations so long as one clearly labels his conjectures, hypotheses or theories as being that. (Lofland 1971:62)

Interpretation, by definition, involves going beyond the descriptive data. Interpretation means attaching significance to what was found, making sense of findings, offering explanations, drawing conclusions, extrapolating lessons, making inferences, considering meanings, and otherwise imposing order on an unruly but surely patterned world. The rigors of interpretation and bringing data to bear on explanations include dealing with rival explanations, accounting for disconfirming cases, and accounting for data irregularities as part of testing the viability of an interpretation. All of this is expected—and appropriate—as

long as the researcher owns the interpretation and makes clear the difference between description and interpretation.

Schlechty and Noblit (1982) concluded that an interpretation may take one of three forms:

- Making the obvious obvious
- Making the obvious dubious
- Making the hidden obvious

This captures rather succinctly what research colleagues, policymakers, and evaluation stakeholders expect: (1) Confirm what we know that is supported by data, (2) disabuse us of misconceptions, and (3) illuminate important things that we didn't know but should know. Accomplish these three things and those interested in the findings can take it from there.

A particular limitation as one moves into the arena of interpretations about causes, consequences, and relationships concerns our capacity to escape simplistic linear modeling. We fall back on the linear assumptions of much quantitative analysis and begin to specify isolated independent and dependent variables that are mechanically linked together out of context. In contrast, the challenge of qualitative inquiry involves portraying a *holistic picture* of what the phenomenon, setting, or program is like and struggling to understand the fundamental nature of a particular set of activities and people *in a specific context.* "Particularization is an important aim, coming to know the particularity of the case" (Stake 1995:39). Simple statements of linear relationships may be more distorting than illuminating. The ongoing challenge, paradox, and dilemma of qualitative analysis engage us in constantly moving back and forth between the phenomenon of interest and our abstractions of that phenomenon, between the descriptions of what has occurred and our interpretations of those descriptions, between the complexity of reality and our simplifications of those complexities, between the circularities and interdependencies of human activity and our need for linear, ordered statements of cause-effect.

Gregory Bateson traced at least part of the source of our struggle to the ways we have been taught to think about things. We are told that a *noun* is the "name of a person, place, or thing." We are told that a *verb* is an "action word." These kinds of definitions, Bateson argues, were the beginning of teaching us that "the way to define something is by what it supposedly is in itself—not by its relations to other things."

> Today all that should be changed. Children could be told a noun is a word having a certain relationship to a predicate. A verb has a certain relationship to a noun, its subject, and so on. Relationship could now be used as a basis for definition, and any child could then see that there is something wrong with the sentence, " 'Go' is a verb." . . . We could have been told something about the pattern which connects: that all communication necessitates context, and that without context there is no meaning. (Bateson 1978:13)

Without belaboring this point about the difference between linear causal analysis (*x* causes *y*) and a holistic perspective that describes the interdependence and interrelatedness of complex phenomena, I would simply offer the reader a Sufi story. I suggest trying to analyze the data represented by the story in two ways. First, try to isolate specific variables that are important in the story, deciding which are the independent and which the dependent variables, and then write a statement of the form: These things caused this thing. Then read the story again. For the second analysis, try to distinguish among and label the different meanings of the situation expressed by the characters observed in the story, then write a statement of the form: These things and these things came together to create _____. Don't try to decide that one approach is right and the other is wrong; simply try to experience and understand the two approaches. Here's the case data, otherwise known as a story.

> Walking one evening along a deserted road, Mulla Nasrudin saw a troop of horsemen coming towards him. His imagination started to work; he imagined himself captured and sold as a slave, or robbed by the oncoming horsemen, or conscripted into the army. Fearing for his safety, Nasrudin bolted, climbed a wall into a graveyard, and lay down in an open tomb.
>
> Puzzled at this strange behavior the men —honest travelers—pursued Nasrudin to see if they could help him. They found him stretched out in the grave, tense and quivering.
>
> "What are you doing in that grave? We saw you run away and see that you are in a state of great anxiety and fear. Can we help you?"
>
> Seeing the men up close Nasrudin realized that they were honest travelers who were genuinely interested in his welfare. He didn't want to offend them or embarrass himself by telling them how he had misperceived them, so Nasrudin simply sat up in the grave and said, "You ask what I'm doing in this grave. If you must know, I can tell you only this: *I* am here because of you, and you are here because of me." (adapted from Shah 1972:16)

🖫 Theory-Based Analysis Approaches

Thus far, this chapter has been looking at generic approaches to qualitative analysis.

The next sections examine how certain theoretical and philosophical perspectives affect analysis. Every perspective presented in Chapter 3 on theoretical orientations has implications for analysis in that the fundamental premises articulated in a theoretical framework or philosophy are meant to inform how one makes sense of the world. Likewise, the various applications in Chapter 4 affect analysis in that they shape the questions that guide the inquiry and therefore the analysis. While Chapters 3 and 4 were presented early in this book to help researchers and evaluators select frameworks to guide their inquiry, those chapters also offer frameworks for analyzing data. The two sections that follow contrast two of the major theory-oriented analytical approaches discussed in Chapter 3, but this time focusing on analysis. The two contrasting approaches are phenomenological analysis and grounded theory.

Phenomenological Analysis

P henomenology asks for the very nature of a phenomenon, for that which makes a some-"thing" what it is—and without which it could not be what it is.

—Max Van Manen (1990:10)

Phenomenological analysis seeks to grasp and elucidate the meaning, structure, and essence of the lived experience of a phenomenon for a person or group of people. Before I present the steps of one particular approach to phenomenological analysis, it is important to note that phenomenology has taken on a number of meanings, has a number of forms, and encompasses varying traditions including transcendental phenomenology, existential phenomenology, and hermeneutic phenomenology (Schwandt 2001). Moustakas (1994:13) further distinguishes empirical phenomenological from transcendental phenomenology. Gubrium and Holstein (2000:488) add the label "social phenomenology." Van Manen (1990) prefers "hermeneutical phenomenological reflection." Sonnemann (1954:344) introduced the term "phenomenography" to label phenomenological investigation aimed at "a descriptive recording of immediate subjec-tive experience as reported." Harper (2000: 727) talks of looking at images through "the phenomenological mode," that is, from the perspective of the self: "from the phenomenological perspective, photographs express the artistic, emotional, or experiential intent of the photographer." Add to this confusion of terminology the difficulty of distinguishing phenomenological philosophy from phenomenological methods and phenomenological analysis, all of which adds to tensions and contradictions in qualitative inquiry (Gergen and Gergen 2000).

The use of the term phenomenology in contemporary versions of qualitative inquiry in North America tends to reflect a subjectivist, existentialist, and non-critical emphasis not present in the Continental tradition represented in the work of Husserl and Heidegger. The latter viewed the phenomenological pro-

A PHENOMENOGRAPHY OF ADULT CRITICAL REFLECTION

Phenomenography applied to adult education focuses on exploring and portraying how learners experience and interpret learning. Brookfield (1994) identified five themes related to critical reflection "as an adult capacity"; he examined "the way adults feel their way through critically reflective episodes—to understanding the visceral, emotive dimensions of this process" (p. 203). He found the following five themes in journals, conversations, and autobiographies:

- *Impostership—the sense that participating in critical thought is an act of bad faith*
- *Cultural suicide—the recognition that challenging conventional assumptions risks cutting people off from the cultures that have defined and sustained them up to the that point in their lives*
- *Lost innocence—the move from dualistic certainty toward dialectical and multiplistic modes of reasoning*
- *Roadrunning—the incrementally fluctuating flirtation with new modes of thought and being*
- *Community—the importance of a sustaining support group to those in critical process.*

studying everyday experience from the point of view of the subject, and it shuns critical evaluation of forms of social life. (Schwandt 2001:192)

These distinctions and variations in use make it relatively meaningless to describe "phenomenological analysis" as if it constituted a single approach or perspective. I have chosen to include here the phenomenological approach to analysis taken by Clark Moustakas and Bruce Douglass of The Union Institute Graduate College (Cincinnati, Ohio) and the Center for Humanistic Studies (Detroit, Michigan). More than most approaches, they focus on the analytical process itself (Douglass and Moustakas 1985). Moreover, the extensive writings of Moustakas on phenomenology (1961, 1988, 1990b, 1994, 1995) are readily accessible and highly readable. Finally, they are esteemed colleagues whose work I know, appreciate, and, no small point when dealing with phenomenology, I think I understand. They have developed an outline of phenomenological analysis that they use in graduate seminars. Much of this section is based on their work and that of their students. Before presenting the steps and procedures of phenomenological analysis, let's get deeper into the perspective and language.

> Husserl's transcendental phenomenology is intimately bound up in the concept of intentionality. In Aristotelian philosophy the term *intention* indicates the orientation of the mind to its object; the object exists in the mind in an intentional way. . . .
>
> *Intentionality* refers to consciousness, to the internal experience of being conscious of something; thus the act of consciousness and the object of consciousness are intentionally related. Included in understanding of consciousness are important background factors

ject, so to speak, as an effort to get beneath or behind subjective experience to reveal the genuine, objective nature of things, and as a critique of both taken-for-granted meanings and subjectivism. Phenomenology, as it is commonly discussed in accounts of qualitative research, emphasizes just the opposite: It aims to identify and describe the subjective experiences of respondents. It is a matter of such as stirrings of pleasure, shapings of judgment, or incipient wishes.

Knowledge of intentionality requires that we be present to ourselves and things in the world, that we recognize that self and world are inseparable components of meaning. . . .

Consider the experience of joy on witnessing a beautiful landscape. The landscape is the *matter.* The landscape is also the object of the intentional act, for example, its perception in consciousness. The matter enables the landscape to become manifest as an object rather than merely exist in consciousness.

The *interpretive form* is the perception that enables the landscape to appear; thus the landscape is self-given; my perception creates it and enables it to exist in my consciousness. The *objectifying quality* is the actuality of the landscape's existence, as such, while the *non-objectifying quality* is a joyful feeling evoked in me by the landscape.

Every intentionality is composed of a *nomea* and *noesis.* The nomea is not the real object but the phenomenon, not the tree but the appearance of the tree. The object that appears in perception varies in terms of when it is perceived, from what angle, with what background of experience, with what orientation of wishing, willing, or judging, always from the vantage point of the perceiving individual. . . . The tree is out there present in time and space while the perception of the tree is in consciousness. . . .

Every intentional experience is also noetic. . . .

In considering the nomea-noesis correlate . . . , the "perceived as such" is the nomea; the "perfect self-evidence" is the noesis. Their relationship constitutes the intentionality of consciousness. For every nomea, there is a noesis; for every noesis, there is a nomea. On the noematic side is the uncovering and explication, the unfolding and becoming distinct, the clearing of what is actually presented in consciousness. On the noetic side is an explica-

tion of the intentional processes themselves.
. . .

Summarizing the challenges of intentionality, the following processes stand out:

1. Explicating the sense in which our experiences are directed;

2. Discerning the features of consciousness that are essential for the individuation of objects (real or imaginary) that are before us in consciousness (Noema);

3. Explicating how beliefs about such objects (real or imaginary) may be acquired, how it is that we are experiencing what we are experiencing (Noesis); and

4. Integrating the noematic and noetic correlates of intentionality into meanings and essences of experience. (Moustakas 1994:28-32)

If those are the challenges, what are the steps for meeting them? The first step in phenomenological analysis is called *epoche.*

Epoche is a Greek word meaning to refrain from judgment, to abstain from or stay away from the everyday, ordinary way of perceiving things. In a natural attitude we hold knowledge judgmentally; we presuppose that what we perceive in nature is actually there and remains there as we perceive it. In contrast, Epoche requires a new way of looking at things, a way that requires that we learn *to see* what stands before our eyes, what we can distinguish and describe. . . .

In the Epoche, the everyday understandings, judgments, and knowings are set aside, and the phenomena are revisited, visually, naively, in a wide-open sense, from the vantage point of a pure or transcendental ego. (Moustakas 1994:33)

In taking on the perspective of *epoche*, the researcher looks inside to become aware of personal bias, to eliminate personal involvement with the subject material, that is, eliminate, or at least gain clarity about, preconceptions. Rigor is reinforced by a "phenomenological attitude shift" accomplished through *epoche*.

The researcher examines the phenomenon by attaining an attitudinal shift. This shift is known as the phenomenological attitude. This attitude consists of a different way of looking at the investigated experience. By moving beyond the natural attitude or the more prosaic way phenomena are imbued with meaning, experience gains a deeper meaning. This takes place by gaining access to the constituent elements of the phenomenon and leads to a description of the unique qualities and components that make this phenomenon what it is. In attaining this shift to the phenomenological attitude, *epoche* is a primary and necessary phenomenological procedure.

Epoche is a process that the researcher engages in to remove, or at least become aware of, prejudices, viewpoints or assumptions regarding the phenomenon under investigation. *Epoche* helps enable the researcher to investigate the phenomenon from a fresh and open viewpoint without prejudgment or imposing meaning too soon. This suspension of judgment is critical in phenomenological investigation and requires the setting aside of the researcher's personal viewpoint in order to see the experience for itself. (Katz 1987:36-37)

According to Ihde (1979), *epoche* requires that looking precede judgment and that judgment of what is "real" or "most real" be suspended until all the evidence (or at least sufficient evidence) is in (p. 36). As such, *epoche* is an ongoing analytical process rather than a single fixed event. The process

of *epoche* epitomizes the data-based, evidential, and empirical (vs. empiricist) research orientation of phenomenology.

Following *epoche*, the second step is phenomenological reduction. In this analytical process, the researcher "brackets out" the world and presuppositions to identify the data in pure form, uncontaminated by extraneous intrusions.

Bracketing is Husserl's (1913) term. In bracketing, the researcher holds the phenomenon up for serious inspection. It is taken out of the world where it occurs. It is taken apart and dissected. Its elements and essential structures are uncovered, defined, and analyzed. It is treated as a text or a document; that is, as an instance of the phenomenon that is being studied. It is not interpreted in terms of the standard meanings given to it by the existing literature. Those preconceptions, which were isolated in the deconstruction phase, are suspended and put aside during bracketing. In bracketing, the subject matter is confronted, as much as possible, on its own terms. Bracketing involves the following steps:

1. Locate within the personal experience, or self-story, key phrases and statements that speak directly to the phenomenon in question.

2. Interpret the meanings of these phrases, as an informed reader.

3. Obtain the subject's interpretations of these phrases, if possible.

4. Inspect these meanings for what they reveal about the essential, recurring features of the phenomenon being studied.

5. Offer a tentative statement, or definition, of the phenomenon in terms of the essen-

tial recurring features identified in step 4. (Denzin 1989b:55-56)

Once the data are bracketed, all aspects of the data are treated with equal value, that is, the data are "horizontalized." The data are spread out for examination, with all elements and perspectives having equal weight. The data are then organized into meaningful clusters. Then the analyst undertakes a delimitation process whereby irrelevant, repetitive, or overlapping data are eliminated. The researcher then identifies the invariant themes within the data in order to perform an "imaginative variation" on each theme. Douglass has described this as "moving around the statue" to see the same object from differing views. Through imaginative variation, the researcher develops enhanced or expanded versions of the invariant themes.

Using these enhanced or expanded versions of the invariant themes, the researcher moves to the textural portrayal of each theme—a description of an experience that doesn't contain that experience (i.e., the feelings of vulnerability expressed by rape victims). The textural portrayal is an abstraction of the experience that provides content and illustration, but not yet essence.

Phenomenological analysis then involves a "structural description" that contains the "bones" of the experience for the whole group of people studied, "a way of understanding *how* the coresearchers as a group experience *what* they experience" (Moustakas 1994:142). In the structural synthesis, the phenomenologist looks beneath the affect inherent in the experience to deeper meanings for the individuals who, together, make up the group.

The final step requires "an integration of the composite textual and composite structural descriptions, providing a synthesis of the meanings and essences of the experi-

ence" (Moustakas 1994:144). In summary, the primary steps of the Moustakas transcendental phenomenological model are *epoche*, phenomenological reduction, imaginative variation, and synthesis of texture and structure. Other detailed analytical techniques are used within each of these stages (see Moustakas 1994:180-81).

Heuristic inquiry (Moustakas 1990b) involves a somewhat different analytical process. The heuristic process of phenomenological inquiry is a highly personal process. Moustakas describes five basic phases in the heuristic process of phenomenological analysis: immersion, incubation, illumination, explication, and creative synthesis.

Immersion is the stage of steeping oneself in all that is, of contacting the texture, tone, mood, range, and content of the experience. This state "requires my full presence, to savor, appreciate, smell, touch, taste, feel, know without concrete goal or purpose" (Moustakas 1981:56). The researcher's total life and being are centered in the experience. He or she becomes totally involved in the world of the experience, questioning, mediating, dialoging, daydreaming, and indwelling.

The second state, *incubation*, is a time of "quiet contemplation" where the researcher waits, allowing space for awareness, intuitive or tacit insights, and understanding. In the incubation stage, the researcher deliberately withdraws, permitting meaning and awareness to awaken in their own time. One "must permit the glimmerings and awakenings to form, allow the birth of understanding to take place in its own readiness and completeness" (Moustakas 1981:50). This stage leads the way toward a clear and profound awareness of the experience and its meanings.

In the phase of *illumination*, expanding awareness and deepening meaning bring new clarity of knowing. Critical textures and structures are revealed so that the experience is known in all of its essential parameters. The experience takes on a vividness and understanding grows. Themes and patterns emerge, forming clusters and parallels. New life and new visions appear along with new discoveries.

In the *explication* phase, other dimensions of meanings are added. This phase involves a full unfolding of the experience. Through focusing, self-dialogue, and reflection, the experience is depicted and further delineated. New connections are made through further explorations into universal elements and primary themes of the experience. The heuristic analyst refines emergent patterns and discovered relationships.

> It is an organization of the data for oneself, a clarification of patterns for oneself, a conceptualization of concrete subjective experience for oneself, an integration of generic meanings for oneself, and a refinement of all these results for *oneself.* (Craig 1978:52)

What emerges is a depiction of the experience and a portrayal of the individuals who participated in the study. The researcher is ready now to communicate findings in a creative and meaningful way. *Creative synthesis* is the bringing together of the pieces that have emerged into a total experience, showing patterns and relationships. This phase points the way for new perspectives and meanings, a new vision of the experience. The fundamental richness of the experience and the experiencing participants is captured and communicated in a personal and creative way. In heuristic analysis, the insights and experiences of the analyst are primary, including drawing on "tacit" knowledge that is deeply internal (Polanyi 1967).

These brief outlines of phenomenological and heuristic analysis can do no more than hint at the in-depth *living with the data* that is intended. The purpose of this kind of

disciplined analysis is to elucidate the essence of experience of a phenomenon for an individual or group. The analytical vocabulary of phenomenological analysis is initially alien, and potentially alienating, until the researcher becomes immersed in the holistic perspective, rigorous discipline, and paradigmatic parameters of phenomenology. As much as anything this outline reveals the difficulty of defining and sequencing the internal intellectual processes involved in qualitative analysis more generally.

Grounded Theory

> *Theory denotes a set of well-developed categories (e.g., themes, concepts) that are systematically interrelated through statements of relationship to form a theoretical framework that explains some relevant social, psychological, educational, nursing, or other phenomenon. The statements of relationship* explain who, what, when, where, why, how, and with what consequences an event occurs. Once concepts are related through statements of relationship into an explanatory theoretical framework, the research findings move beyond conceptual ordering to theory. . . . A theory usually is more than a set of findings; it offers an explanation about phenomena. (Strauss and Corbin 1998:22)

Chapter 3 provided an overview of grounded theory in the context of other theoretical perspectives such as ethnography, constructivism, phenomenology, and hermeneutics. Norman K. Denzin, coeditor of the *Handbook of Qualitative Research* and the journal *Qualitative Inquiry,* has called grounded theory "the most influential paradigm for qualitative research in the social sciences today" (1997a:18). As I noted in Chapter 3, grounded theory has opened the door to qualitative inquiry in many traditional academic social science and education

Heuristic inquiry reactivity

departments, especially as a basis for doctoral dissertations, in part, I believe, because of its overt emphasis on the importance of and specific procedures for generating theory. In addition, I suspect its popularity (Glaser 2000) may owe much to the fact that it unabashedly admonishes the researcher to strive for "objectivity." The postmodern attack on objectivity has found its way into qualitative inquiry through constructivism, hermeneutic interpretivism, and the emphasis on subjective experience in phenomenology. Those social scientists and academics who find some value in the methods of qualitative inquiry, namely, in-depth interviewing and observation, but who eschew the philosophical underpinnings of constructivism and interpretivism can find comfort in the attention paid to objectivity in grounded theory.

Fortunately, over the years, researchers have learned that a state of complete objectivity is impossible and that in every piece of research—quantitative or qualitative—there is an element of subjectivity. What is important is to recognize that subjectivity is an issue and researchers should take appropriate measures to minimize its intrusion into their analyses. . . . Over the years, we have wrestled with the problem of objectivity and have developed some techniques to increase our awareness and help us control intrusion of bias into analysis while retaining sensitivity to what is being said in the data. (Strauss and Corbin 1998:43)

Thinking comparatively is one such technique.

> *Theoretical comparisons are tools (a list of properties) for looking at something somewhat objectively rather than naming or classifying without a thorough examination of the object at the property and dimensional levels.* If the properties are evident within the data, then we do not need to rely on these tools. However, because details are not always evident to the "naked" eye, and because we (as human beings) are so fallible in our interpretations despite all attempts to "deconstruct" an event, incident, or interview, there are times when this is not so easy and we have to stand back and ask, "What is this?" In asking this question, we begin, even if unconsciously, to draw on properties from what we do know to make comparisons. (Strauss and Corbin 1998:80-81)

In addition to comfort with striving for objectivity, grounded theory emphasizes systematic rigor and thoroughness from initial design, through data collection and analysis, culminating in theory generation.

> By systematic, I still mean systematic every step of the way; every stage done systematically so the reader knows exactly the process by which the published theory was generated. The bounty of adhering to the whole grounded theory method from data collection through the stages to writing, using the constant comparative method, shows how well grounded theory fits, works and is relevant. Grounded theory produces a core category and continually resolves a main concern, and through sorting the core category organizes the integration of the theory. . . . Grounded theory is a package, a lock-step method that starts the researcher from a "know nothing" to later become a theorist with a publication and with a theory that accounts for most of the action in a substantive area. The researcher becomes an expert in the substantive area. . . . And if an incident comes his way that is new he can humbly through constant comparisons modify his theory to integrate a new property of a category. . . .
>
> Grounded theory methodology leaves nothing to chance by giving you rules for every stage on what to do and what to do next. If the reader skips any of these steps and rules, the theory will not be as worthy as it could be. The typical falling out of the package is to yield to the thrill of developing a few new, capturing categories and then yielding to use them in unending conceptual description and incident tripping rather than analysis by constant comparisons. (Glaser 2001:12)

In their book on techniques and procedures for developing grounded theory, Strauss and Corbin (1998:13) emphasize that analysis is the interplay between researchers and data, so what grounded theory offers as a framework is a set of "coding procedures" to "help provide some standardization and rigor" to the analytical process. Grounded theory is meant to "build theory rather than test theory." It strives to "provide researchers with analytical tools for handling masses of raw data." It seeks to help qualitative analysts "consider alternative meanings of phenomena." It emphasizes being "systematic and creative simultaneously." Finally, it elucidates "the concepts that are the building blocks of theory." Grounded theory operates from a *correspondence perspective* in that it aims to generate explanatory propositions that correspond to real-world phenomena. The characteristics of a grounded theorist, they posit, are these:

1. The ability to step back and critically analyze situations

2. The ability to recognize the tendency toward bias

3. The ability to think abstractly

4. The ability to be flexible and open to helpful criticism

5. Sensitivity to the words and actions of respondents

6. A sense of absorption and devotion to work process. (Strauss and Corbin 1998:7)

Grounded theory begins with *basic description,* moves to *conceptual ordering* (organizing data into discrete categories "according to their properties and dimensions and then using description to elucidate those categories," p. 19), and then *theorizing* ("conceiving or intuiting ideas—concepts—then also formulating them into a logical, systematic, and explanatory scheme," p. 21).

In doing our analyses, we *conceptualize and classify* events, acts, and outcomes. The categories that emerge, along with their relationships, are the foundations for our developing theory. This abstracting, reducing, and relating is what makes the difference between *theoretical and descriptive coding (or theory building and doing description).* Doing line-by-line coding through which categories, their properties, and relationships emerge automatically takes us beyond description and puts us into a *conceptual mode of analysis.* (Strauss and Corbin 1998:66)

Strauss and Corbin (1998) have defined terms and processes in ways that are quite specific to grounded theory. It is informative to compare the language of grounded theory with the language of phenomenological analysis presented in the previous section. Here's a sampling of important terminology.

Microanalysis: "The detailed line-by-line analysis necessary at the beginning of a study to generate initial categories (with their properties and dimensions) and to suggest relationships among categories; a combination of open and axial coding" (p. 57).

Theoretical sampling: "Sampling on the basis of the emerging concepts, with the aim being to explore the dimensional range or varied conditions along which the properties of concepts vary" (p. 73).

Theoretical saturation: "The point in category development at which no new properties, dimensions, or relationships emerge during analysis" (p. 143).

Range of variability: "The degree to which a concept varies dimensionally along its properties, with variation being built into the theory by sampling for diversity and range of properties" (p. 143).

Open coding: "The analytic process through which concepts are identified and their properties and dimensions are discovered in data" (p. 101).

Axial coding: "The process of relating categories to their subcategories, termed 'axial' because coding occurs around the axis of the category, linking categories of the level of properties and dimensions" (p. 123).

Relational statements: "We call these initial hunches about how concepts relate 'hypotheses' because they link two or more concepts, explaining the what, why, where, and how of phenomena" (p. 135).

As noted in introducing this section, comparative analysis constitutes a central feature of grounded theory development. Making *theoretical comparisons*—systematically and creatively—engages the analyst in "raising questions and discovering properties and dimensions that might be in the data by increasing researcher sensitivity" (p. 67). Theoretical comparisons are one of the techniques used when doing microscopic analysis. Such comparisons enable "identification of *variations* in the patterns to be found in the data. It is not just one form of a category or pattern in which we are interested but also how that pattern varies dimensionally, which is discerned through a comparison of properties and dimensions under different conditions" (p. 67). Strauss and Corbin (1998) offer specific techniques to increase the systematic and rigorous processes of comparison, for example, "the flip-flop technique":

> This indicates that a concept is turned "inside out" or "upside down" to obtain a different perspective on the event, object, or actions/interaction. In other words, we look at opposites or extremes to bring out significant properties. (p. 94)

In the course of conducting a grounded theory analysis, one moves from lower-level concepts to higher-level theorizing:

> Data go to concepts, and concepts get transcended to a core variable, which is the underlying pattern. Formal theory is on the fourth level, but the theory can be boundless as the research keeps comparing and trying to figure out what is going on and what the latent patterns are. (Glaser 2000:4)

Glaser (2000) worries that the popularity of grounded theory has led to a preponderance of lower-level theorizing without completing the full job. Too many qualitative analysts, he warns, are satisfied to stop when they've merely generated "theory bits."

> Theory bits are a bit of theory from a substantive theory that a person will use briefly in a sentence or so. . . .

Theory bits come from two sources. First, they come from generating one concept in a study and conjecturing without generating the rest of the theory. With the juicy concept, the conjecture sounds grounded, but it is not; it is only experiential. Second, theory bits come from a generated substantive theory. A theory bit emerges in normal talk when it is impossible to relate the whole theory. So, a bit with grab is related to the listener. The listener can then be referred to an article or a report that describes the whole theory. . . .

Grounded theory is rich in imageric concepts that are easy to apply "on the fly." They are applied intuitively, with no data, with a feeling of "knowing" as a quick analysis of a substantive incident or area. They ring true with great credibility. They empower conceptually and perceptually. They feel theoretically complete ("Yes, that accounts for it"). They are exciting handles of explanation. They can run way ahead of the structural constraints of research. They are simple one or two variable applications, as opposed to being multivariate and complex. . . . They are quick and easy. They invade social and professional conversations as colleagues use them to sound knowledgeable. . . . The danger, of course, is that they might be just plain wrong or irrelevant unless based in a grounded theory. Hopefully, they get corrected as more data come out. The grounded theorist should try to fit, correct, and modify them even as they pass his or her lips.

Unfortunately, theory bits have the ability to stunt further analysis because they can sound so correct. . . . Multivariate thinking stops in favor of a juicy single variable, a quick and sensible explanation. . . . Multivariate thinking can continue these bits to fuller explanations. This is the great benefit of trusting a theory that fits, works, and is relevant as it is continually modified. . . . But a responsible grounded theorist always should finish his or her bit with a statement to the effect that "Of course, these situations are very complex or multivariate, and without more data, I cannot tell what is really going on." (Glaser 2000:7-8)

As noted throughout this chapter in commenting on how to learn qualitative analysis, it is crucial to study examples. Bunch (2001) has published a grounded theory study about people living with HIV/AIDS. Glaser (1993) and Strauss and Corbin (1997) have collected together in edited volumes a range of grounded theory exemplars that include several studies of health (life after heart attacks, emphysema, chronic renal failure, chronically ill men, tuberculosis, Alzheimer's disease), organizational headhunting, abusive relationships, women alone in public places, selfhood in women, prison time, and characteristics of contemporary Japanese society. The journal *Grounded Theory Review* began publication in 2000. (See Exhibit 3.7 in Chapter 3 for the grounded theory Web site.)

Qualitative Comparative Analysis

Another approach that focuses on making comparisons to generate explanations is "qualitative comparative analysis" (QCA) presented by Charles Ragin (1987, 2000). Ragin has taken on the problem of making systematic case comparisons across a number of cases. He uses Boolean algebra to facilitate comparisons of large case units such as nation-states and historical periods, or macro-social phenomena such as social movements. His comparative method involves representing each case as a combination of causal and outcome conditions. These combinations can be compared with each other and then logically simplified through a bottom-up process of paired comparison. Ragin's aim in developing this con-

figurational approach to cross-case pattern analysis was to retain the strength of holism embedded in context-rich individual cases while making possible systematic comparisons of relatively large numbers of cases, for example, 15 to 25, or more. Ragin (2000) draws on fuzzy set theory and calls the result "diversity-oriented research" because it systematically codes and takes into account case variations and uniquenesses as well as commonalities, thereby elucidating both similarities and differences. The analysis involves constructing a "truth table" in which the analyst codes each case for the presence or absence of each attribute of interest (Fielding and Lee 1998:158-59). The information in the truth table displays the different combinations of conditions that produce a specific outcome. To deal with the large number of comparisons needed, QCA is done using a software program (Drass and Ragin 1992; see Exhibit 8.2).

Analysts conducting diversity-oriented research are admonished to assume maximum causal complexity by considering the possibility that no single causal condition may be either necessary or sufficient to explain the outcome of interest. Different combinations of causal conditions might produce the observed result, though singular causes can also be considered, examined, and tested. Despite reducing large amounts of data to broad patterns represented in matrices or some other form of shorthand, Ragin (1987) stresses repeatedly that these representations must ultimately be evaluated by the extent to which they enhance understanding of specific cases. A cause-consequence comparative matrix, then, can be thought of as a map providing guidance through the terrain of multiple cases.

QCA seeks to recover the complexity of particular situations by recognizing the conjunctural and context-specific character of causation. Unlike much qualitative analysis, the method forces researchers to select cases and variables in a systematic manner. This reduces the likelihood that "inconvenient" cases will be dropped from the analysis or data forced into inappropriate theoretical moulds. . . .

QCA clearly has the potential to be used beyond the historical and cross-national contexts originally envisioned by Ragin. (Fielding and Lee 1998:160, 161-62)

In cross-cultural research, the challenge of determining *comparable units of analysis* has created controversy. For example, when definitions of "family" vary dramatically, can one really do systematic comparisons? Are extended families in nonliterate societies and nuclear families in modern societies so different that, beyond the obvious surface differences, they cease to be comparable units for generating theory? "The main problem for ethnologists has been to define and develop adequate and equivalent cultural units for cross-cultural comparison" (De Munck 2000:279). Analytic induction, another comparative approach, which we turn to now, also depends on defining comparable units of analysis.

Analytic Induction

Analytic induction also involves cross-case analysis in an effort to seek explanations. Ragin's QCA formalized and moderated the logic of analytic induction (Ryan and Bernard 2000:787), but it was first articulated as a method of "exhaustive examination of cases in order to prove universal, causal generalizations" (Peter Manning quoted in Vidich and Lyman 2000:57). Norman Denzin, in his sociological methods classic *The Research Act* (1978b), identified analytic induction based on comparisons of

carefully done case studies as one of the three primary strategies available for dealing with and sorting out rival explanations in generating theory; the other two are experiment-based inferences and multivariate analysis. Analytic induction as a comparative case method

was to be the critical foundation of a revitalized qualitative sociology. The claim to universality of the causal generalizations is . . . derived from the examination of a single case studied in light of a preformulated hypothesis that might be reformulated if the hypothesis does not fit the facts. . . . Discovery of a single negative case is held to disprove the hypothesis and to require its reformulation. (Vidich and Lyman 2000:57)

Over time, those using analytic induction have eliminated the emphasis on discovering universal causal generalizations and have instead emphasized it as a strategy for engaging in qualitative inquiry and comparative case analysis that includes examining preconceived hypotheses, that is, without the pretense of the mental blank slate advocated in purer forms of phenomenological inquiry and grounded theory.

In analytic induction, researchers develop hypotheses, sometimes rough and general approximations, prior to entry into the field or, in cases where data already are collected, prior to data analysis. These hypotheses can be based on hunches, assumptions, careful examination of research and theory, or combinations. Hypotheses are revised to fit emerging interpretations of the data over the course of data collection and analysis. Researchers actively seek to disconfirm emerging hypotheses through negative case analysis, that is, analysis of cases that hold promise for disconfirming emerging hypotheses and that add variability to the sample. In this way, the originators of the method sought to examine enough cases to assure the development of universal hypotheses.

Originally developed to produce universal and causal hypotheses, contemporary researchers have de-emphasized universality and causality and have emphasized instead the development of descriptive hypotheses that identify patterns of behaviors, interactions and perceptions. . . . Bogdan and Biklen (1992) have called this approach modified analytic induction. (Gilgun 1995:268-69)

Jane Gilgun used modified analytic induction in a study of incest perpetrators to test hypotheses derived from the literature on care and justice and to modify them to fit in-depth subjective accounts of incest perpetrators. She used the literature-derived concepts to sensitize her throughout the research while remaining open to discovering concepts and hypotheses not accounted for in the original formulations. And she did have new insights:

Most striking about the perpetrators' accounts was that almost all of them defined incest as love and care. The types of love they expressed ranged from sexual and romantic to care and concern for the welfare of the children. These were unanticipated findings. I did not hypothesize that perpetrators would view incest as caring and as romantic love. Rather, I had assumed that incest represented lack of care and, implicitly, an inability to love. It did not occur to me that perpetrators would equate incest and romance, or even incest and feelings of sexualized caring. From previous research, I did assume that incest perpetrators would experience profound sexual gratification through incest. Ironically, their professed love of whatever type was contradicted by many other aspects of their accounts, such as contin

uing the incest when children wanted to stop, withholding permission to do ordinary things until the children submitted sexually, and letting others think the children were lying when the incest was disclosed. These perpetrators, therefore, did not view incest as harmful to victims, did not reflect on how they used their power and authority to coerce children to cooperate, and even interpreted their behavior in many cases as forms of care and romantic love. (Gilgun 1995:270)

Analytic induction reminds us that qualitative inquiry can do more than discover emergent concepts and generate new theory. A mainstay of science has always been examining and reexamining and reexamining yet again those propositions that have become the dominant belief or explanatory paradigm within a discipline or group of practitioners. Modified analytic induction provides a name and guidance for undertaking such qualitative inquiry and analysis.

⑤ Special Analytical Issues and Frameworks

Reflexivity and Voice

In Chapter 2, when presenting the major strategic themes of qualitative inquiry, I included as one of the 12 primary themes that of "voice, perspective, and reflexivity."

The qualitative analyst owns and is reflective about her or his own voice and perspective; a credible voice conveys authenticity and trustworthiness; complete objectivity being impossible and pure subjectivity undermining credibility, the researcher's focus becomes balance—understanding and depicting the world *authentically* in all its complexity while being self-analytical, politically aware, and re-flexive in consciousness. (see Exhibit 2.1)

Analysis and reporting are where these awarenesses come to the fore. Throughout analysis and reporting, as indeed through-out all of qualitative inquiry, questions of re-flexivity and voice must be asked as part of a process of engaging the data and extracting findings. Triangulated reflexive inquiry in-volves three sets of questions (see Exhibit 2.2 in Chapter 2):

1. *Self-reflexivity.* What do I know? How do I know what I know? What shapes and has shaped my perspective? How have my perceptions and my background affected the data I have collected and my analysis of those data? How do I perceive those I have studied? With what voice do I share my per-spective? (See Chapter 3, discussion of autoethnography.) What do I do with what I have found? These questions challenge the researcher to also be a learner, to reflect on our "personal epistemologies"—the ways we understand knowledge and the con-struction of knowledge (Rossman and Rallis 1998:25).

2. *Reflexivity about those studied.* How do those studied know what they know? What shapes and has shaped their worldview? How do they perceive me, the inquirer? Why? How do I know?

3. *Reflexivity about audience.* How do those who receive my findings make sense of what I give them? What perspectives do they bring to the findings I offer? How do they perceive me? How do I perceive them? How do these perceptions affect what I re-port and how I report it?

Self-awareness, even a certain degree of self-analysis, has become a requirement of qualitative inquiry. As these reflexive ques-tions suggest, attention to voice applies not only to intentionality about the voice of the analyst but also to intentionality and con-sciousness about whose voices and what messages are represented in the stories and interviews we report. Qualitative data "can be used to relay dominant voices or can be appropriated to 'give voice' to otherwise si-lenced groups and individuals" (Coffey and Atkinson 1996:78). Eminent qualitative soci-ologist Howard Becker (1967) posed this classically as the question of "Whose side are we on?" Societies, cultures, organizations, programs, and families are stratified. Power, resources, and status are distributed differ-entially. How we sample in the field, and then sample again during analysis in decid-ing who and what to quote, involves deci-sions about whose voices will be heard.

Finally, as we report findings, we need to anticipate how what we report will be heard and understood. We need strategies for thinking about the nature of the reporter-au-dience interaction, for example, under-standing how "six basic tendencies of hu-man behavior come into play in generating a positive response: reciprocation, consis-tency, social validation, liking, authority and scarcity" (Cialdini 2001:76). Some writers es-chew this responsibility, claiming that they write only for themselves. But researchers and evaluators have larger social responsi-bilities to present their findings for peer re-view and, in the cases of applied research, evaluation and action research, to present their findings in ways that are understand-able and useful.

Triangulated reflexive inquiry provides a framework for sorting through these issues during analysis and report writing—and then including in the report how these re-flections informed your findings. For exam-ples of qualitative writings centered on illu-minating issues of reflexivity and voice, see Hertz (1997).

Collaborative and Participatory Analyses

Collaborative and participatory approaches to qualitative inquiry include working with nonresearchers and nonevaluators not only in collecting data but also in analyzing data. This requires special facilitation skills to help those involved adopt analytical thinking. Some of the challenges include the following:

- Deciding how much involvement nonresearchers will have, for example, whether they will simply react and respond to the researcher's analysis or whether they will be involved in the generative phase of analysis. Determining this can be a shared decision. "In participatory research, participants make decisions rather than function as passive subjects" (Reinharz 1992:185).

- Creating an environment in which those collaborating feel that their perspective is genuinely valued and respected.

- Demystifying research.

- Combining training in how to do analysis with the actual work of analysis.

- Managing the difficult mechanics of the process, especially where several people are involved.

- Developing processes for dealing with conflicts in interpretations (e.g., agreeing to report multiple interpretations).

- Maintaining confidentiality with multiple analysts.

A good example of these challenges concerns how to help lay analysts deal with counterintuitive findings and counterfactuals, that is, data that don't fit primary patterns, negative cases, and data that oppose primary preconceptions or predilections. M. W. Morris (2000) found that shared learning, especially the capacity to deal with counterfactuals, was reduced when participants feared judgment by others, especially those in positions of authority.

In analyzing hundreds of open-ended interviews with parents who had participated in early childhood parent education programs throughout the state of Minnesota, I facilitated a process of analysis that involved some 40 program staff. The staff worked in groups of two and three, each analyzing 10 pre and post paired interviews at a time. No staff analyzed interviews with parents from their own programs. The analysis included coding interviews with a framework developed at the beginning of the study as well as inductive, generative coding in which the staff could create their own categories. Following the coding, new and larger groups engaged in interpreting the results and extracting central conclusions. Everyone worked together in a large center for three days. I moved among the groups helping resolve problems. Not only did we get the data coded, but the process, as is intended in collaborative and participatory research processes, proved to be an enormously stimulating and provocative learning experience for the staff participants. The process forced them to engage deeply with parents' perceptions and feedback, as well as to engage each other's reactions, biases, and interpretations. In that regard, the process also facilitated communication among diverse staff members from across the state, another intended outcome of the collaborative analysis process. Finally, the process saved thousands of dollars in research and evaluation costs, while making a staff and program development contribution. The results were intended primarily for internal program improvement use. As would be expected in such a nonresearcher analysis process, external stakeholders placed less value on the results than did those who participated in the process (Program Evaluation Division 2001; Mueller 1996; Mueller and Fitzpatrick 1998).

The Hermeneutic Circle and Interpretation

> Hermes was messenger to the Greek gods. . . . Himself the god of travel, commerce, invention, eloquence, cunning, and thievery, he acquired very early in his life a reputation for being a precocious trickster. (On the day he was born he stole Apollo's cattle, invented the lyre, and made a fire.) His duties as messenger included conducting the souls of the dead to Hades, warning Aeneas to go to Italy, where he founded the Roman race, and commanding the nymph Calypso to send Odysseus away on a raft, despite her love for him. With good reason his name is celebrated in the term "hermeneutics," which refers to the business of interpreting. . . . Since we don't have a godly messenger available to us, we have to interpret things for ourselves. (Packer and Addison 1989:1)

Hermeneutics focuses on interpreting something of interest, traditionally a text or work of art, but in the larger context of qualitative inquiry, it has also come to include interpreting interviews and observed actions. The emphasis throughout concerns the nature of interpretation, and various philosophers have approached the matter differently, some arguing that there is no method of interpretation per se because everything involves interpretation (Schwandt 2000, 2001). For our purposes here, the *hermeneutic circle,* as an analytical process aimed at enhancing understanding, offers a particular emphasis in qualitative analysis, namely, relating parts to wholes, and wholes to parts.

> Construing the meaning of the whole meant making sense of the parts, and grasping the meaning of the parts depended on having some sense of the whole. . . . [T]he hermeneutic circle indicates a necessary condition of interpretation, but the circularity of the process is only temporary—eventually the interpreter can come to something approximating a complete and correct understanding of the meaning of a text in which whole and parts are related in perfect harmony. Said somewhat differently, the interpreter can, in time, get outside of or escape the hermeneutic circle in discovering the "true" meaning of the text. (Schwandt 2001:112)

The *method* involves playing the strange and unfamiliar parts of an action, text, or utterance off against the integrity of the action, narrative, or utterance as whole until the meaning of the strange passages and the meaning of the whole are worked out or accounted for. (Thus, for example, to understand the meaning of the first few lines of a poem, I must have a grasp of the overall meaning of the poem, and vice versa.) In this process of applying the hermeneutic method, the interpreter's self-understanding and sociohistorical location neither affects nor is affected by the effort to interpret the meaning of the text or utterance. In fact, in applying the method, the interpreter abides by a set of procedural rules that help ensure that the interpreter's historical situation does not distort the bid to uncover the actual meaning embedded in the text, act, or utterance, thereby helping to ensure the objectivity of the interpretation. (Schwandt 2001:114)

The circularity and universality of hermeneutics (every interpretation is layered in and dependent on other interpretations, like a series of dolls that fit one inside the other, and then another and another) pose the problem for the qualitative analyst of where to begin. How and where do you break into the hermeneutic circle of interpretation? Packer and Addison (1989), in adapting the hermeneutic circle as an inquiry approach for psychology, suggest beginning with "practical understanding":

> Practical understanding is not an origin for knowledge in the sense of a foundation; it is, instead, the starting place for interpretation. Interpretive inquiry begins not from an absolute origin of unquestionable data or totally consistent logic, but at a place delineated by our everyday participatory understanding of people and events. We begin there in full awareness that this understanding is corrigible, and that it is partial in the twin senses of being incomplete and perspectival. Understanding is always moving forward. Practical activity projects itself forward into the world from its starting place, and shows us the entities we are home among. This means that neither commonsense nor scientific knowledge can be traced back to an origin, a foundation. . . . (p. 23)
>
> The circularity of understanding, then, is that we understand in terms of what we already know. But the circularity is not, Heidegger argues, a "vicious" one where we simply confirm our prejudices, it is an "essential" one without which there would be no understanding at all. And the circle is complete; there is accommodation as well as assimilation. If we are persevering and open, our attention will be drawn to the projective character of our understanding and—in the backward arc, the movements of return—we gain an increased appreciation of what the fore-structure involves, and where it might best be changed. . . . (p. 34).
>
> Hermeneutic inquiry is not oriented toward a grand design. Any final construction that would be a resting point for scientific inquiry represents an illusion that must be resisted. If all knowledge were to be at last collected in some gigantic encyclopedia this would mark not the triumph of science so

much as the loss of our human ability to encounter new concerns and uncover fresh puzzles. So although hermeneutic inquiry proceeds from a starting place, a self-consciously interpretive approach to scientific investigation does not come to an end at some final resting place, but works instead to keep discussion open and alive, to keep inquiry under way. (p. 35)

At a general level and in a global way, hermeneutics reminds us of the interpretive core of qualitative inquiry, the importance of context and the dynamic whole-part interrelations of a holistic perspective. At a specific level and in a particularistic way, the hermeneutic circle offers a process for formally engaging in interpretation.

Analyzing Institutional Documents

Gale Miller (1997) has studied the particular challenges of "contextualizing organizational texts." Written documents of all kinds are pervasive in modern institutions such as hospitals, schools, nursing homes, police departments, courts, clinics, and social welfare agencies. Governments, nonprofit agencies, philanthropic organizations, and private institutions produce massive amounts of files and reports. Miller argues that

> qualitative researchers are uniquely positioned to study these texts by analyzing the practical social contexts of everyday life within which they are constructed and used. Texts are one aspect of the sense-making activities through which we reconstruct, sustain, contest and change our senses of social reality. They are socially constructed realities that warrant study in their own right. (p. 77)

Special challenges in analyzing documents include the following:

- Getting access to documents
- Understanding how and why the documents were produced
- Determining the accuracy of documents
- Linking documents with other sources, including interviews and observations
- Deconstructing and demystifying institutional texts

Miller concludes, "Demystifying institutional texts is one way of demystifying institutional authority" (p. 91).

Dramaturgical Analysis

> Dramaturgy is a perspective that uses a theatrical metaphor to understand social interaction. The approach takes *act* to be its central concept. From a dramaturgical point of view, humans, in a specific social and temporal context, act to create meaning and demonstrate purpose.... [Doing this involves] "impression management," suggesting that individuals present themselves to others so as to foster and maintain particular images or fronts. In their performances, individuals construct some images intentionally and provide others inadvertently. (Hunt and Benford 1997:106)

Dramaturgy puts the concept of "acting" on center stage at the theater of qualitative inquiry. A dramaturgical analysis of human interactions employs theatrical sensitizing concepts:

- Scripting
- Staging
- Dialogue and direction
- Developing dramatis personae

- Confrontations between protagonists and antagonists
- Costumes and props
- Dramaturgical loyalty, which "requires performers to 'act as if they have accepted certain moral obligations'" (p. 113).

Hunt and Benford (1997) argue that "dramaturgy might provide a reflexive sociological method":

> First, our approach presents a conceptual framework for understanding research productions generally and field studies more specifically. Dramaturgical method also illuminates common pitfalls in social science work, implying that researchers might be well-advised to pay particular attention to the details of impression management as well as the problems of securing resources, audiences and the like. The third contribution is that dramaturgical method furnishes a vantage point for social scientists to examine their own research productions critically. By equating research with drama, we have sought to limit the pretentiousness that seems endemic to most social science work. Instead of presenting a window to "reality," a dramaturgical method serves as a constant reminder that researchers are in the business of "reality construction." (Hunt and Benford 1997:116-17)

To appreciate how an interpretive framework such as dramaturgical analysis affects interpretation, it helps to compare data and conclusions using different frameworks. Martha Feldman (1995) has done just that by analyzing her study of a university housing office through the lenses of ethnomethodology (how physical realities such as buildings become institutional realities), semiotics (how written policies become institutional realities with real consequences), deconstruction (of university salaries in relation to hierarchy and power), and dramaturgical analysis (how "backstage" events deep within the institution become manifest for targeted audiences). She compares the strengths and weaknesses of each approach, a useful reminder that all frameworks have both strengths and weaknesses.

Finding Nothing

Students beginning dissertations often ask me, their anxiety palpable and understandable, "What if I don't find out anything?" Bob Stake of responsive evaluation and case study fame said at his retirement:

> Paraphrasing Milton: They also serve who leave the null hypothesis tenable. . . .
>
> It is a sophisticated researcher who beams with pride having, with thoroughness and diligence, found nothing there. (Stake 1998:364, with a nod to Michael Scriven for inspiration)

True enough. But in another sense, it's not possible to find nothing there, at least not in qualitative inquiry. The case study is there. It may not have led to new insights or confirmed one's predictions, but the description of that case at that time and that place is there. That is much more than nothing. The interview responses and observations are there. They, too, may not have led to headline-grabbing insights or confirmed someone's eminent theory, but the thoughts and reflections from those people at that time and that place are there, recorded and reported. That is much more than nothing.

Halcolm will tell you this:

> You can only find nothing if you stare at a vacuum.

> You can only find nothing if you immerse yourself in nothing.
>
> You can only find nothing if you go nowhere.
>
> Go to real places.
>
> Talk to real people.
>
> Observe real things.
>
> You will find something.
>
> Indeed, you will find much, for much is there.
>
> You will find the world.

⑤ Synthesizing Qualitative Studies

Synthesizing research to aggregate and substantiate knowledge has become one of the important challenges of the information age, especially synthesizing applied research to inform policy making (Cooper 1998). As qualitative research has become better understood, more widely used, and more fully reported, a new opportunity —and a new challenge—has emerged: *synthesizing qualitative studies.* In one sense each qualitative study is a case. Synthesis of different qualitative studies on the same subject is a form of cross-case analysis. Such a synthesis is much more than a literature review. Noblit and Hare (1988) describe synthesizing qualitative studies as "meta-ethnography" in which the challenge is to "retain the uniqueness and holism of accounts even as we synthesize them in the translations" (p. 7).

For scholarly inquiry, the qualitative synthesis is a way to build theory through induction and interpretation. For evaluators, a qualitative synthesis can identify and extrapolate *lessons learned.* Evaluators can synthesize lessons from a number of case studies to generate generic factors that contribute to program effectiveness as, for example, Lisbeth Schorr (1988) did for poverty programs in her review and synthesis *Within Our Reach: Breaking the Cycle of Disadvantage*. The U.S. Agency for International Development has supported lessons learned synthesis studies on such subjects as irrigation (Steinberg 1983), rural electrification (Wasserman and Davenport 1983), food for peace (Rogers and Wallerstein 1985), education development efforts (Warren 1984), private sector development (Bremer et al. 1985), contraceptive social marketing (Binnendijk 1986), agriculture and rural development (Johnston et al. 1987), agricultural policy analysis and planning (Tilney and Riordan 1988), and agroforestry (Chew 1989). In synthesizing separate evaluations to identify lessons learned, evaluators build a store of knowledge for future program development, more effective program implementation, and enlightened policy making.

The sample for synthesis studies usually consists of case studies with a common focus, for example, elementary education, health care for the elderly, and so forth. However, one can also learn lessons about effective human intervention processes more generically by synthesizing case studies on quite different subjects. I synthesized three quite different qualitative evaluations conducted for The McKnight Foundation: a major family housing effort, a downtown development endeavor, and a graduate fellowship program for minorities. Before undertaking the synthesis, I knew nothing about these programs, nor did I approach them with any particular preconceptions. I was not looking for any specific similarities and none were suggested to me by either McKnight or program staff. The results were intended to provide insights into The McKnight Foundation's operating philosophy and strategies *as exemplified in practice by real operating programs*. Independent evaluations of each program had already been con-

ducted and presented to The McKnight Foundation showing that these programs had successfully attained and exceeded intended outcomes. But why were they successful? That was the intriguing and complex question on which the synthesis study focused.

The synthesis design included fieldwork (interviews with key players and site visits to each project) as well as extensive review of their independent evaluations. I identified common success factors that were manifest in all three projects. Those were illuminating, but not surprising. The real contribution of the synthesis was in how the success factors fit together, an unanticipated pattern that deepened the implications for understanding effective philanthropy.

The 12 success factors common to all three programs were as follows:

- High-quality people
- Substantial financial resources
- Creative partnerships
- Leverage
- Vision
- A clear values orientation
- Self-sustaining institutions
- Long time frames
- Flexibility
- Cutting edge foresight
- Risk taking
- Leadership

While each of these factors provided insight into an important element of effective philanthropic programming, the unanticipated pattern was how these factors fit together to form a constellation of excellence. I found that I couldn't prioritize these factors because they worked together in such a way that no one factor was primary or sufficient; rather, each made a critical contribution to an integrated, effectively functioning whole. The lesson that emerged for effective philanthropy was not a series of steps to follow, but rather a mosaic to create; that is, effective philanthropy appears to be a process of matching and integrating elements so that the pieces fit together in a meaningful and comprehensive way as a solution to complex problems. This means matching people with resources; bringing vision and values to bear on problems; and nurturing partnerships through leverage, careful planning, community involvement, and shared commitments. And doing all these things in mutually reinforcing ways. The challenge for effective philanthropy, then, is putting all the pieces and factors together to support integrated, holistic, and high-impact efforts and results—and to do so creatively (Storm and Vitt 2000:115-16).

As qualitative evaluation and research proliferate, the opportunities for and importance of synthesizing diverse studies will increase accordingly.

ş Reporting Findings

*A*t one time, one blade of grass is as effective as a sixteen-foot golden statue of Buddha. At another time, a sixteen-foot golden statute of Buddha is as effective as a blade of grass.

—Wu-Men

Some reports are thin as a blade of grass; others feel 16 feet thick. Size, of course, is not the issue. Quality is. But given the volume of data involved in qualitative inquiry and the challenges of data reduction already discussed, reporting qualitative findings is the final step in data reduction and size is a real constraint, especially when writing in forms other than research monographs and book-length studies, such as journal articles and newsletter summaries. Each step in completing a qualitative project presents *quality* challenges (Morse 1997), but the final step is completing a report so that others can know what you've learned and how you learned it. This means finding and writing your story (Glesne 1999). It also means dealing with what Lofland (1971) called the "the agony of omitting"—deciding what material to leave out of the story.

It can happen that an overall structure that organizes a great deal of material happens also to leave out some of one's most favorite material and small pieces of analysis. . . . Unless one decides to write a relatively disconnected report, he must face the hard truth that no overall analytic structure is likely to encompass every small piece of analysis and all the empirical material that one has on hand. . . .

The underlying philosophical point, perhaps, is that everything is related to everything else in a flowing, even organic fashion, making coherence and organization a difficult and problematic human task. But in order to have any kind of understanding, we humans require that some sort of order be imposed upon that flux. No order fits perfectly. All order is provisional and partial. Nonetheless, understanding requires order, provisional and partial as it may be. It is with that philosophical view that one can hopefully bring himself to accept the fact that he cannot write about everything that he has seen (or analyzed) and still write something with overall coherence or overall structure. (Lofland 1971:123)

This chapter opened with the reminder that purpose guides analysis. Purpose also guides report writing and dissemination of findings. The keys to all writing start with (1) knowing your audience and (2) knowing what you want to say to them—a form of strategic communications (Weiss 2001). *Dissertations* have their own formats and requirements (Patton 1996a; Fitzpatrick, Secrist, and Wright 1998; Rudestam and Newton 1992). *Scholarly journals* in various disciplines and applied research fields have their own standards and norms for what they publish. The best way to learn those is to read and study them, and study specialized qualitative methods journals such as *Qualitative Inquiry, Field Methods, Symbolic Interaction, Journal of Contemporary Ethnography*, and *Grounded Theory Review*. Below I'll discuss evaluation and action research reporting.

Balance Between Description and Interpretation

One of the major decisions that has to be made about what to omit in the process of data reduction for reporting involves how much description to include. Description and quotation provide the foundation of qualitative reporting. Sufficient description and direct quotations should be included to allow the reader to enter into the situation and thoughts of the people represented in the report. Description should stop short, however, of becoming trivial and mundane. The reader does not have to know everything that was done or said. Focus comes from having determined what's substan-

tively significant and providing enough detail and evidence to illuminate and make that case.

Yet, the description must not be so "thin" as to remove context or meaning. Qualitative analysis, remember, is grounded in "thick description."

A thick description does more than record what a person is doing. It goes beyond mere fact and surface appearances. It presents detail, context, emotion, and the webs of social relationships that join persons to one another. Thick description evokes emotionality and self-feelings. It inserts history into experience. It establishes the significance of an experience, or the sequence of events, for the person or persons in question. In thick description, the voices, feelings, actions, and meanings of interacting individuals are heard. (Denzin 1989b:83)

Thick description sets up and makes possible interpretation. "It contains the necessary ingredients for thick interpretation" (Denzin 1989b:83). By "thick interpretation" Denzin means, in part, connecting individual cases to larger public issues and to the programs that serve as the linkage between individual troubles and public concerns. "The perspectives and experiences of those persons who are served by applied programs must be grasped, interpreted, and understood if solid, effective, applied programs are to be put into place" (p. 105).

Description is thus balanced by analysis and interpretation. Endless description becomes its own muddle. The purpose of analysis is to organize the description so that it is manageable. Description provides the skeletal frame for analysis that leads into interpretation. An interesting and readable report provides sufficient description to allow the reader to understand the basis for an interpretation, and sufficient interpretation to allow the reader to appreciate the description.

Details of verification and validation processes (topics of the next chapter) are typically placed in a separate methods section of a report, but parenthetical remarks throughout the text about findings that have been validated can help readers value what they are reading. For example, if I describe some program process and then speculate on the relationship between that process and client outcomes, I may mention that (1) staff and clients agreed with this analysis when they read it, (2) I experienced this linkage personally in my own participant-observation experience in the program, and (3) this connection was independently arrived at by two analysts looking at the data separately.

The analyst should help readers understand different degrees of significance of various findings, if these exist. Because qualitative analysis lacks the parsimonious statistical significance tests of statistics, the qualitative analyst must make judgments that provide clues for the reader as to the writer's belief about variations in the credibility of different findings: When are patterns "clear"? When are they "strongly supported by the data"? When are the patterns "merely suggestive"? Readers will ultimately make their own decisions and judgments about these matters based on the evidence you've provided, but your analysis-based opinions and speculations deserve to be reported and are usually of interest to readers given that you've struggled with the data and know the data better than anyone else.

Appendix 8.3 at the end of this chapter presents portions of a report describing the effects on participants of their experiences in the wilderness education program. The data come from in-depth, open-ended interviews. This excerpt illustrates the centrality of quotations in supporting and explaining thematic findings.

Communicating With Metaphors and Analogies

A ll perception of truth is the detection of an analogy.

—Henry David Thoreau (1817-1862)

The museum study reported earlier in the discussion of analyst-generated typologies differentiated different kinds of visitors by using metaphors: the "commuter," the "nomad," the "cafeteria type," and the "V.I.P." and an analogy between visitors to Earth from outer space and visitors to a museum. In the dropout study, we relied on metaphors to depict the different roles we observed teachers playing in interacting with truants: the "cop," the "old-fashioned school master," and the "ostrich." Language not only supports communication but also serves as a form of representation, shaping how we perceive the world (Chatterjee 2001; Patton 2000; Smith 1981).

Metaphors and analogies can be powerful ways of connecting with readers of qualitative studies, but some analogies offend certain audiences. Thus, metaphors and analogies must be selected with some sensitivity to how those being described would feel and how intended audiences will respond. At a meeting of the Midwest Sociological Society, distinguished sociologist Morris Janowitz was asked to participate in a panel on the question "What is the cutting edge of sociology?" Janowitz, having written extensively on the sociology of the military, took offense at the "cutting edge" metaphor. He explained:

> Paul Russell, the humanist, has prepared a powerful and brilliant sociological study of the literary works of the great wars of the 20th century which he entitled *The Great War and Modern Memory*. It is a work which all sociologists should read. His conclusion is that World War I and World War II, Korea and Vietnam have militarized our language. I agree and therefore do not like the question "Where is the cutting edge of sociology?" "Cutting Edge"is a military term. I am put off by the very term cutting edge. Cutting edge, like the parallel term breakthrough, are slogans which intellectuals have inherited from the managers of violence. Even if they apply to the physical sciences, I do not believe that they apply to the social sciences, especially sociology, which grows by gradual accretion. (Janowitz 1979:591)

"Strategic planning" has military origins and connotations as does "rapid reconnaissance," a phrase used to describe certain short-term, intensive fieldwork efforts (see Chapter 4). Some stakeholder groups will object to such associations. Of particular importance, in this regard, is avoiding metaphors with possible racist and sexist connotations, for instance, "It's black and white." At the Educational Evaluation and Public Policy Conference sponsored by the Far West Laboratory for Educational Research and Development, the women's caucus expressed concern about the analogies used in evaluation and went on to suggest some alternatives.

To deal with diversity is to look for new metaphors. We need no new weapons of assess-

ment—the violence has already been done! How about brooms to sweep away the attic-y cobwebs of our male/female stereotypes? The tests and assessment techniques we frequently use are full of them. How about knives, forks, and spoons to sample the feast of human diversity in all its richness and color. Where are the techniques that assess the delicious-ness of response variety, independence of thought, originality, uniqueness? (And lest you think those are female metaphors, let me do away with that myth—at our house everybody sweeps and everybody eats!) Our workgroup talked about another metaphor —the cafeteria line versus the smorgasbord banquet of styles of teaching/learning/assessing. Many new metaphors are needed as we seek clarity in our search for better ways of evaluating. To deal with diversity is to look for new metaphors. (Hurty 1976)

Metaphors can be powerful and clever ways of communicating findings. A great deal of meaning can be conveyed in a single phrase with a powerful metaphor. Moreover, developing and using metaphors can be fun, both for the analyst and for the reader. It is important, however, to make sure that the metaphor serves the data and not vice versa. The creative analyst who finds a powerful metaphor may be tempted to manipulate the data to fit the metaphor. Moreover, because metaphors carry implicit connotations, it is important to make sure that the data fit the most prominent of those connotations so that what is communicated is what the analyst wants to communicate. Finally, one must avoid reifying metaphors and acting as if the world were really the way the metaphor suggests it is.

> The metaphor is chiefly a tool for revealing special properties of an object or event. Frequently, theorists forget this and make their metaphors a real entity in the empirical world.

It is legitimate, for example, to say that a social system is like an organism, but this does not mean that a social system is an organism. When metaphors, or concepts, are reified, they lose their explanatory value and become tautologies. A careful line must be followed in the use of metaphors, so that they remain a powerful means of illumination. (Denzin 1978b:46)

Drawing Conclusions

In his practical monograph *Writing Up Qualitative Research*, Wolcott (1990) considers the challenge of how to conclude a qualitative study. Purpose again rules in answering this question. Scholarly articles, dissertations, and evaluation reports have different norms for drawing conclusions. But Wolcott goes further by questioning the very idea of conclusions:

Give serious thought to dropping the idea that your final chapter must lead to a conclusion or that the account must build toward a dramatic climax. . . . In reporting qualitative work, I avoid the term *conclusion*. I do not want to work toward a grand flourish that might tempt me beyond the boundaries of the material I have been presenting or detract from the power (and exceed the limitations) of an individual case. (p. 55)

This admonition reminds us not to take anything for granted or fall into following some recipe for writing. Asking yourself, "When all is said and done, what conclusions do I draw from all this work?" can be a focusing question that forces you to get at essence. Or, as Wolcott suggests, it can be an unnecessary and inappropriate burden.

Or it can be a chance to look to the future. The Spanish-born philosopher and poet George Santayana concluded thusly when he retired from Harvard. Students and colleagues packed his classroom for his final appearance. He gave an inspiring lecture and was about to conclude when, in mid-sentence, he cut the head of a forsythia beginning to blossom in melting snow outside the window. He stopped abruptly, picked up his coat, hat, and gloves, and headed for the door. He turned at the door and said gently, "Gentlemen, I should not be able to finish that sentence. I have just discovered that I have an appointment with April."

Or as Halcolm would say, **Not concluding is its own conclusion.**

⧉ Special Issues in Evaluation Reporting and an Example

A dialectic among several mindsets is essential to good evaluation.

—Robert Stake (1998:370)

Feedback and Analysis

Evaluation poses special challenges when, as is typical, intended users (especially program staff and administrators) want preliminary feedback while fieldwork is still under way or as soon as data collection is over. Providing preliminary feedback provides an opportunity to reaffirm with intended users the final focus of the analysis and nurture their interest in findings. Academic social scientists have a tendency to want to withhold their findings until they have polished their presentation. Use of evaluation findings, however, does not necessarily center on the final report, which should be viewed as one element in a total utilization process, sometimes a minor element, especially in formative evaluation.

Evaluators who prefer to work diligently in the solitude of their offices until they can spring a final report on a waiting world may find that the world has passed them by. Feedback can inform ongoing thinking about a program rather than serve only as a one-shot information input for a single decision point. However, sessions devoted to reestablishing the focus of the evaluation analysis and providing initial feedback need to be handled with care. The evaluator will need to explain that analysis of qualitative data involves a painstaking process requiring long hours of careful work, going over notes, organizing the data, looking for patterns, checking emergent patterns against the data, cross-validating data sources and findings, and making linkages among the various parts of the data and the emergent dimensions of the analysis. Thus, any early discussion of findings can only be preliminary, directed at the most general issues and the most striking, obvious results. If, in the course of conducting the more detailed and complete analysis of the data, the evaluator finds that statements made or feedback given during a preliminary session were inaccurate, evaluation users should be informed about the discrepancy at once.

Evaluative Feedback Using Indigenous Typologies

Identifying indigenous typologies as part of a program evaluation can facilitate increased understanding when providing feedback. A good example comes from feedback we provided after evaluating the leadership development program described earlier. After six days of intense (and sometimes tense) participant observation in a retreat setting, we needed a framework for providing formative, descriptive feedback to program staff *in a way that could be heard.* We knew that staff were heavily ego-involved in the program and would be very sensitive to an approach that might appear to substitute *our* concept of the program for theirs. Yet, a major purpose of the evaluation was to help them identify and make explicit their operating assumptions as evidenced in what actually happened during the six-day retreat. As our team of three accumulated more and more data, debriefing each night what we were finding, we became increasingly worried about how to focus feedback. The problem was solved the fifth night when we realized that we could use *their* frameworks for describing to them what we were finding. For example, a major component of the program was having participants work with the Myers-Briggs Type Indicator, an instrument that measures individual personality type based on the work of Carl Jung (cf. Berens and Nardi 1999; Myers 1995; Krueger and Thuesen 1988; Hirsh and Kummerow 1987). The Myers-Briggs Type Indicator gives individuals scores on four bipolar scales:

(E)	Extraversion-Introversion	(I)
(S)	Sensing-Intuition	(N)
(T)	Thinking-Feeling	(F)
(J)	Judgment-Perception	(P)

In the feedback session, we began by asking the six staff members to characterize the overall retreat culture using the Myers-Briggs framework. Staff members shared their separate ratings, on which there was not consensus, and then we shared our perceptions. We spent the whole morning discussing the data for and implications of each scale as a manifestation of the program's culture. We ended the session by discussing where the staff wanted the program to be on each dimension. Staff members were able to hear what we said, without becoming defensive, because we used *their* framework, a framework they had defined as nonjudgmental, facilitative, and developmental.

We formatted our presentation to staff using a distinction between "observations" and "perceived impacts" that program participants were taught as part of the leadership training. Observation: "You interrupted me in midsentence." Perceived impact: "I felt cut-off and didn't contribute after that." This simple distinction, aimed at enhancing interpersonal communications, served as a comfortable, familiar format for program staff to receive formative evaluation feedback. Our report, then, followed this format. Three of 20 observations from the report are reproduced in Exhibit 8.12.

The critical point here is that we presented the findings using their categories and their frameworks. This greatly facilitated the feedback and enhanced the subsequent formative, developmental discussions. Capturing and using indigenous typologies can be a powerful analytical approach for making sense of and reporting qualitative data.

For evaluators, the inductive search for patterns is guided by the evaluation questions identified at the beginning of the study and a focus on how the findings are intended to be used by intended users (Patton 1997a). This utilization focus keeps findings from becoming too abstract, esoteric, or theoretical. For example, I was asked by The McKnight Foundation to review The McKnight Programs in Higher Education in Florida, a minority fellowship program en-

dowed with $15 million ($10 million from The McKnight Foundation and $5 million from the state of Florida). The program had conducted its own evaluations, which showed they were successfully attaining intended outcomes. The question posed to me by The McKnight Foundation decision makers was, What factors explain the high level of success achieved by this program? I observed the program's annual conference for all 92 doctoral fellows; made site visits; reviewed program records and documents; interviewed a purposeful sample of participants, key knowledgeables, and the program's executive director; and asked all participants to write responses to some questions. The analysis of all that data reduced to 10 major success factors (which later became part of the synthesis reported earlier, p. 501):

1. *Strong leadership* through a bold initiative from The McKnight Foundation that mobilized educational leaders in Florida.

2. A *sizable amount of money* ($15 million) able to attract attention and generate support.

3. Effective use of *leverage* at every level of program operation. (McKnight insisted on major matching funds and use of local in-kind resources from participating universities.)

4. A *long-term perspective* on and commitment to a sustainable program with cumulative impact over time—in perpetuity. (The program was finally converted to an endowment.)

5. A carefully melded *public-private partnership*.

6. A program based on a *vision* made real through a carefully designed model that was true to the vision.

EXHIBIT 8.12	Distinguishing Observations From Perceived Impacts

Observations	Perceived Impacts
1. The retreat setting, away from the world, is introverted.	1. There is deep bonding among group members; there is a sense of the group as separate from the "real" world, though participants are expected to engage the "real" world after the retreat.
2. The retreat is more conceptual and abstract in content than fact and skill oriented. It is primarily intuitive (as opposed to step-by-step and practical).	2. Participants are conceptually stimulated and exposed to a variety of ideas. Some express uncertainty about what to do with the ideas (lack of practical applications).
3. Retreat culture is heavily affective, feelings oriented, not thinking oriented.	3a. Highly emotional connections are made among participants.
	b. Participants are sensitized to how they feel about what they are experiencing, explicitly encouraged to share feelings.
	c. Participants are affirmed as important; they feel special, cared about, and valued; it is a safe environment for learning.
	d. Participants are not stretched intellectually; logical distinctions are not made, key concepts remain ambiguous. Affirming participants is clearly more important than challenging them; harmony is valued over clarity.

7. Taking the time and effort to carefully *plan* in a process that generated *broad-based community and political support* throughout the state.

8. The careful structuring of *local board control* so that responsibility and ownership resided in Florida among key influentials.

9. Taking advantage of the right *timing* and climate for this kind of program.

10. Clear *accountability and evaluation* so that problems could be corrected and accomplishments could be recognized.

These patterns are straightforward and understandable. The themes above answer a focused evaluation question. The report presented data supporting each success factor and explaining in greater detail what each one meant and how it operated. But the list

represents *the* 10 major patterns in the data. There is no presentation of an elegant theory or carefully conceptualized typology. These 10 factors were the qualitative evaluation findings. They answered the intended users' primary evaluation question. Such an analysis is an example of practical, utilization-focused evaluation.

To Write a Report or Not to Write a Report?

I find in my own work that final reports frequently have less impact than the direct, face-to-face interactions I have with primary evaluation users to provide them with feedback about evaluation findings and to share with them the nature of the data. Making oral briefings is an increasingly important evaluation competence (Hendricks 1982). Final reports often serve an important dissemination function to audiences beyond immediate decision makers and information users, but they are not automatically and necessarily the primary source of information for those who are expected to actually use evaluation findings. I have done evaluations that involved no polished, final report because certain formative situations don't justify putting a lot of scarce resources into the production of a polished final report that will sit on a shelf somewhere. Eyebrows may be raised when evaluators ask, "Is there any reason to produce a final, written report for this evaluation?" But it's a question worth asking, and, in my opinion, the burden of proof lies with the evaluation users to justify production of a full report in cases of formative evaluation and informal action research.

Normally, of course, a full report will be produced. The contents, length, and nature of the report are partly a matter for negotiation between evaluators and primary users (Patton 1997a). While individual style will and should affect what a final report looks like, following some basic principles can enhance the presentation of qualitative evaluation data.

Focus

Even a comprehensive report will have to omit a great deal of information collected by the evaluator. **Focus is essential.** Evaluators who try to include everything risk losing their readers in the sheer volume of the presentation. To enhance a report's impact, the evaluation should address clearly each major evaluation question, that is, present the descriptive findings, analysis, and interpretation of each focused issue together succinctly. An evaluation report should be readable, understandable, and relatively free of academic jargon. The data should impress the reader, not the academic training of the evaluator.

The advice I find myself repeating most often to students when they are writing reports is, *Focus, focus, focus!* The agony on the part of the evaluator of having omitted things is matched only by the readers' agony in having to read those things that were not omitted but should have been. (See illustration of utilization-focused reporting in Exhibit 8.13 [p. 512].)

The Executive Summary and Research Abstract

*T*he executive summary is a fiction.

—Robert Stake (1998:370)

The fact that qualitative reports tend to be relatively lengthy can be a major problem when busy decision makers do not have the time (*or, more likely, will not take the time*) to read a lengthy report. Stake's preference for insisting on telling the whole story notwithstanding (a preference I share, by the way), my pragmatic, living-in-the-real-world side leads me to conclude that evaluators must develop the ability to produce an executive summary of one or two pages that presents the essential findings, conclusions, and rea-

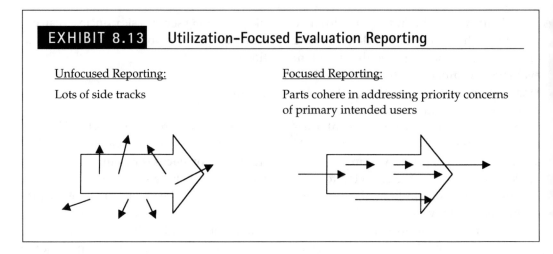

EXHIBIT 8.13   Utilization–Focused Evaluation Reporting

Unfocused Reporting:

Lots of side tracks

Focused Reporting:

Parts cohere in addressing priority concerns of primary intended users

---

sons for confidence in the summary. The executive summary is a dissemination document, a political instrument, and cannot be—nor is it meant to be—a full and fair representation of the study. An executive summary or abstract should be written in plain language, be highly focused, and state the core findings and conclusions. Keep in mind, when writing the executive summary or research abstract, that more people are likely to read the summary than any other document you produce.

Carpe Diem Briefings

As the hymnbook is to the sound of music, the executive summary is to the oral briefing. Legendary are the stories of having spent a year of one's life gathering data, pouring over it, and writing a rigorous and conscientious evaluation report, then encountering some "decision" maker (I use the term here lightly) who says, "Well, now, I know that you put a lot of work into this. I'm anxious to hear all about what you've learned. I've got about 10 minutes before my next appointment."

Should you turn heel and show him your back side? Not if you want your findings to make a difference. Use that 10 minutes well! Be prepared to make it count. *Carpe diem.*

⑤ The Creativity of Qualitative Inquiry

*C*reativity will dominate our time after the concepts of work and fun have been blurred by technology.

—Isaac Asimov (1983:42)

I have commented throughout this book that the human element in qualitative inquiry is both its strength and weakness—its strength in allowing human insight and experience to blossom into new understandings and ways of seeing the world, its potential weakness in being so heavily dependent on the inquirer's skills, training, intellect, discipline, and creativity. Because the researcher is the instrument of qualitative inquiry, the quality of the result depends heavily on the qualities of that human being. Nowhere does this ring more true than in analysis. Being an empathic interviewer or astute observer does not necessarily make one an insightful analyst—or a creative one. Creativity seems to be one of those special human qualities that plays an especially important part in qualitative analysis, interpretation, and reporting. Therefore, I close this chapter with some observations on creativity in qualitative inquiry.

I opened this chapter by commenting on qualitative inquiry as both science and art, especially qualitative analysis. The scientific part demands systematic and disciplined intellectual work, rigorous attention to details within a holistic context, and a critical perspective in questioning emergent patterns even while bringing evidence to bear in support of them. The artistic part invites exploration, metaphorical flourishes, risk taking, insightful sense-making, and creative connection-making. While both science and art involve critical analysis and creative expression, science emphasizes *critical* faculties more, especially in analysis, while art encourages creativity. The critical thinker assumes a stance of doubt and skepticism; things have to be proven; faulty logic, slippery linkages, tautological theories, and unsupported deductions are targets of the criti-

cal mind. The critical thinker studies details and looks beyond appearances to find out what is really happening. Evaluators are trained to be rigorous and unyielding in critically thinking about and analyzing programs. Indeed, evaluation is built on the foundation of critical analysis.

Critical thinkers, however, tend not to be very creative. The creative mind generates new possibilities; the critical mind analyzes those possibilities looking for inadequacies and imperfections. In summarizing research on critical and creative thinking, Barry Anderson (1980) warned that the centrality of doubt in critical thinking can lead to a narrow, skeptical focus that hampers the creative ability to come up with innovative linkages or new insights.

> The critical attitude and the creative attitude seem to be poles apart. . . . On the one hand, there are those who are always telling you why ideas won't work but who never seem able to come up with alternatives of their own; and, on the other hand, there are those who are constantly coming up with ideas but seem unable to tell good from the bad.
>
> There are people in whom both attitudes are developed to a high degree . . . , but even these people say they assume only one of these attitudes at a time. When new ideas are needed, they put on their creative caps, and when ideas need to be evaluated, they put on their critical caps. (Anderson 1980:66)

Qualitative inquiry draws on both critical and creative thinking—both the science and art of analysis. But the technical, procedural, and scientific side of analysis is easier to present and teach. Creativity, while easy to prescribe, is harder to teach, and perhaps harder to learn, but here's some guidance derived from research and training on creative thinking (Kelley and Littman 2001; De Bono 1999; Von Oech 1998; Patton 1987a: 247-48).

1. *Be open.* Creativity begins with openness to multiple possibilities.

2. *Generate options.* There's always more than one way to think about or do something.

3. *Diverge-converge-integrate.* Begin by exploring a variety of directions and possibilities before focusing on the details. Branch out, go on mental excursions and brainstorm multiple perspectives before converging on the most promising.

4. *Use multiple stimuli.* Creativity training often includes exposure to many different avenues of expression: drawing, music, role-playing, story-boarding, metaphors, improvisation, playing with toys, and constructing futuristic scenarios. Synthesizing through triangulation (see Chapter 9) promotes creative integration of multiple stimuli.

5. *Side-track, zigzag, and circumnavigate.* Creativity is seldom a result of purely linear and logical induction or deduction. The creative person explores back and forth, round and about, in and out, over and under.

6. *Change patterns.* Habits, standard operating procedures, and patterned thinking pose barriers to creativity. Become aware of and change your patterned ways of thinking and behaving.

7. *Make linkages.* Many creative exercises include practice in learning how to connect the seemingly unconnected. Matrix approaches presented in this chapter push linkages. Explore linking qualitative and quantitative data.

8. *Trust yourself.* Self-doubt short-circuits creative impulses. If you say to yourself, "I'm not creative," you won't be. Trust the process.

9. *Work at it.* Creativity is not all fun. It takes hard work, background research, and mental preparation.

10. *Play at it.* Creativity is not all work. It can and should be play and fun.

I close this chapter with a practical reminder that both the science and art of qualitative analysis are constrained by limited time. Some people thrive under intense time pressure and their creativity blossoms. Others don't. The way in which any particular analyst combines critical and creative thinking becomes partly a matter of style, partly a function of the situation, and often is dependent on how much time can be found to

play with creative possibilities. But exploring possibilities can also become an excuse for not finishing. There comes a time for bringing closure to analysis (or a book chapter) and getting on with other things. Taking too much time to contemplate creative possibilities may involve certain risks, a point made by the following story (to which you can apply both your critical and creative faculties).

The Past and the Future:
Deciding in Which Direction to Look _____

A spirit appeared to a man walking along a narrow road. "You may know with certainty what has happened in the past, or you may know with certainty what will happen in the future, but you cannot know both. Which do you choose?"

The startled man sat down in the middle of the road to contemplate his choices. "If I know with certainty what will happen in the future," he reasoned to himself, "then the future will soon enough become the past and I will also know with certainty what has happened in the past. On the other hand, it is said that the past is prologue to the future, so if I know with certainty what has happened in the past I will know much about what will happen in the future without losing the elements of surprise and spontaneity."

Deeply lost to the present in the reverie of his calculations about the past and future he was unaware of the sound of a truck approaching at great speed. Just as he came out of his trance to tell the spirit that he had chosen to know with certainty the future, he looked up and saw the truck bearing down on him, unable to stop its present momentum.

—From Halcolm's *Evaluation Parables*

APPENDIX 8.1

🔲 🔲 🔲

Excerpts From a Codebook for Use by Multiple Coders

Characteristics of Program Evaluated
   0101 nature or kind of program
   0102 program relationship to government hierarchy
   0103 funding (source, amount, determination of, etc.)
   0104 purpose of program
   0105 history of program (duration, changes, termination, etc.)
   0106 program effectiveness
Evaluator's Role in Specific Study
   0201 evaluator's role in initiation and planning stage
   0203 evaluator's role in data collection stage
   0204 evaluator's role in final report and dissemination
   0205 relationship of evaluator to program (internal/external)
   0206 evaluator's organization (type, size, staff, etc.)
   0207 opinions/feelings about role in specific study
   0208 evaluator's background
   0209 comments on evaluator, evaluator process
Decision Maker's Role in Specific Study
   0301 decision maker's role in initiation and planning stage
   0302 decision maker's role in data-collection stage
   0303 decision maker's role in final report and dissemination
   0304 relationship of decision maker to program
   0305 relationship of decision maker to other people or units in government
   0306 comments on decision maker and decision-making process
          (opinions, feelings, facts, knowledge, etc.)
Stakeholder Interactions
   0501 stakeholder characteristics
   0502 interactions during or about initiation of study
   0503 interactions during or about design of study
   0504 interactions during or about data collection
   0505 interactions during or about final report/findings
   0506 interactions during or about dissemination
Planning and Initiation Process of This Study (how and who started)
   0601 initiator
   0602 interested groups or individuals
   0603 circumstances surrounding initiation
Purpose of Study (why)
   0701 description of purpose
   0702 changes in purpose

Political Context
    0801 description of political context
    0802 effects on study
Expectations for Utilization
    0901 description of expectations
    0902 holders of expectations
    0903 effect of expectations on study
    0904 relationship of expectations to specific decisions
    0905 reasons for lack of expectations
    0906 people mentioned as not having expectations
    0907 effect of lack of expectations on study
Data Collection, Analysis, Methodology
    1001 methodological quality
    1002 methodological appropriateness
    1003 factors affecting data collection and methodology
Findings, Final Report
    1101 description of findings/recommendations
    1102 reception of findings/recommendations
    1103 comments on final report (forms, problems, quality)
    1104 comments and description of dissemination
Impact of Specific Study
    1201 description of impacts on program
    1202 description of nonprogram impacts
    1203 impact of specific recommendations
Factors and Effects on Utilization
    1301 lateness
    1302 methodological quality
    1303 methodological appropriateness
    1304 positive/negative findings
    1305 surprise findings
    1306 central/peripheral objectives
    1307 point in life of program
    1308 presence/absence of other studies
    1309 political factors
    1310 interaction with evaluators
    1311 resources
    1312 most important factor

NOTE: This codebook was for use by multiple coders of interviews with decision makers and evaluators about their utilization of evaluation research.

APPENDIX 8.2

⑤ ⑤ ⑤

Mike: An Illustrative Case Study

Background: Sitting in a classroom at Metro City High School was difficult for Mike. In some classes he was way behind. In math he was always the first to finish a test. "I loved math and could always finish a test in about ten minutes, but I wasn't doing well in my other classes," Mike explained.

He first heard about Experience-Based Career Education (EBCE) when he was a sophomore. "I really only went to the assembly to get out of one of the classes I didn't like," Mike confessed.

But after listening to the EBCE explanation, Mike was quickly sold on the idea. He not only liked the notion of learning on the job, but also thought the program might allow him to work at his own speed. The notion of no grades and no teachers also appealed to him.

Mike took some descriptive materials home to his parents and they joined him for an evening session at the EBCE learning center to find out more about the program. Now, after two years in the program, Mike is a senior and his parents want his younger brother to get into the program.

Early EBCE testing sessions last year verified the inconsistency of Mike's experiences in school. While his reading and language scores were well below the average scored by a randomly selected group of juniors at his school, he showed above average abilities in study skills and demonstrated superior ability in math.

On a less tangible level, EBCE staff members early last school year described Mike as being hyperactive, submissive, lacking in self-confidence and unconcerned about his health and physical appearance when he started the EBCE program. He was also judged to have severe writing deficiencies. Consequently, Mike's EBCE learning manager devised a learning plan that would build his communication skills (in both writing and interpersonal relations) while encouraging him to explore several career possibilities. Mike's job experiences and projects were designed to capitalize on his existing interests and to broaden them.

First-year EBCE experiences.   A typical day for Mike started at 8:00 a.m., just as in any other high school, but the hours in between varied considerably. When he first arrived at the EBCE learning center, Mike said he usually spent some time "fooling around" with the computer before he worked on projects underway at the center.

On his original application, Mike indicated his career preference would be computer operator. This led to an opportunity in the EBCE program to further explore that area and to learn more about the job. During April and May, Mike's second learning level experience took place in the computer department of City

Bank Services. He broke up his time there each day into morning and afternoon blocks, often arriving before his employer instructor did for the morning period. Mike usually spent that time going through computer workbooks. When his employer instructor arrived they went over flow charts together and worked on computer language.

Mike returned to the high school for lunch and a German class he selected as a project. EBCE students seldom take classes at the high school but Mike had a special interest in German since his grandparents speak the language.

Following German class, Mike returned to the learning center for an hour of work on other learning activities and then went to City Bank. "I often stayed there until 5:00 p.m.," Mike said, even though high school hours ended at three.

Mike's activities and interests widened after that first year in the EBCE program but his goal of becoming a computer programmer was reinforced by the learning experience at City Bank. The start of a new hobby—collection of computer materials—also occurred during the time he spent at City Bank. "My employer instructor gave me some books to read that actually started the collection," Mike said.

Mike's interests in animals also was enhanced by his EBCE experience. Mike has always liked animals and his family has owned a horse since he was 12 years old. By picking blueberries Mike was able to save enough to buy his own colt two years ago. One of Mike's favorite projects during the year related to his horse. The project was designed to help Mike with Basic Skills and to improve his critical thinking skills. Mike read about breeds of horses and how to train them. He then joined a 4-H group with hopes of training his horse for show.

Several months later, Mike again focused on animals for another EBCE project. This time he used the local zoo as a resource, interviewing the zoo manager and doing a thorough study of the Alaskan brown bear. Mike also joined an Explorer Scouting Club of volunteers to help at the zoo on a regular basis. "I really like working with the bears," Mike reflected. "They were really playful. Did you know when they rub their hair against the bars it sounds like a violin?" Evaluation of the zoo project, one of the last Mike completed during the year, showed much improvement. The learning manager commented to Mike, "You are getting your projects done faster, and I think you are taking more time than you did at first to do a better job."

Mike got off to a slow start in the area of Life Skills development. Like some of his peers, he went through a period described by one of the learning managers as "freedom shock" when removed from the more rigid structure normally experienced in a typical school setting. Mike tended to avoid his responsibility to the more "academic" side of his learning program. At first, Mike seldom followed up on commitments and often did not let the staff know what he was doing. By the end of the year, he had improved remarkably in both of these behavior areas.

Through the weekly writing required in maintaining his journal, Mike demonstrated a significant improvement in written communications, both in terms of presenting ideas and feelings and in the mechanics of writing. Mike also

CASE STUDY

noted an interesting change in his behavior. "I used to watch a lot of TV and never did any reading." At the beginning of the following year, Mike said: "I read two books last year and have completed eight more this summer. Now I go to the book instead of the television" Mike's favorite reading materials are science fiction.

Mike also observed a difference in his attitude about homework. "After going to school for six hours I wouldn't sit down and do homework. But in the EBCE program I wasn't sitting in a classroom, so I didn't mind going home with some more work on my journal or projects."

Mike's personal development was also undergoing change. Much of this change was attributed to one of his employer instructors, an elementary school teacher, who told him how important it is in the work world to wash and wear clean clothes. Both she and the project staff gave Mike much positive reinforcement when his dress improved. That same employer also told Mike that she was really interested in what he had to say and therefore wanted him to speak slower so he could be understood.

Mike's school attendance improved while in the EBCE program. During the year, Mike missed only six days. This was better than the average absence for others in the program, which was found to be 12.3 days missed during the year, and much improved over his high school attendance.

Like a number of other EBCE students in his class, Mike went out on exploration level experiences but completed relatively few other program requirements during the first three months of the school year. By April, however, he was simultaneously working on eight different projects and pursuing a learning experience at City Bank. By the time Mike completed his junior year he had finished nine of the required thirteen competencies, explored nine business sites, completed two learning levels and carried through on eleven projects. Two other projects were dropped during the year and one is uncompleted but could be finished in the coming year.

On a more specific level, Mike's competencies included transacting business on a credit basis, maintaining a checking account, designing a comprehensive insurance program, filing taxes, budgeting, developing physical fitness, learning to cope with emergency situations, studying public agencies and operating an automobile.

Mike did not achieve the same level of success on all of his job sites. However, his performance consistently improved throughout the year. Mike criticized the exploration packages when he started them in the first months of the program and, although he couldn't pinpoint how, said they could be better. His own reliance on the questions provided in the package was noted by the EBCE staff with a comment that he rarely followed up on any cues provided by the person he interviewed. The packets reflected Mike's disinterest in the exploration portion of EBCE work. They showed little effort and a certain sameness of remarks about his impressions at the various sites.

Mike explored career possibilities at an automobile dealer, an audiovisual repair shop, a supermarket, an air control manufacturer, an elementary school, a housing development corporation, a city public works, a junior high school and a bank services company.

Mike's first learning level experience was at the elementary school. At the end of three and one-half months the two teachers serving as his employer instructors indicated concern about attendance, punctuality, initiative in learning and amount of supervision needed to see that Mike's time was used constructively. Mike did show significant improvement in appropriate dress, personal grooming and quality of work on assignments.

Reports from the second learning level experience—at the computer department of the bank services company—showed a marked improvement. The employer instructor there rated Mike satisfactory in all aspects and by the time of the final evaluation gave excellent ratings in ten categories—attendance/punctuality, adhering to time schedules, understanding and accepting responsibility, observing employer rules, showing interest and enthusiasm, poise and self-confidence, using initiative in seeking opportunities to learn, using employer site learning resources, beginning assigned tasks promptly and completing tasks assigned.

During the latter part of the school year, Mike worked on several projects at once. He worked on a project on basic electricity and took a course on "Beginning Guitar" for project credit.

To improve his communication skills Mike also worked on an intergroup relations project. This project grew out of an awareness by the staff that Mike liked other students but seemed to lack social interaction with his peers and the staff. Reports at the beginning of the year indicated that he appeared dependent and submissive and was an immature conversationalist. In response to these observations, Mike's learning manager negotiated project objectives and activities with him that would help improve his communication skills and help him solve some of his interpersonal problems. At the end of the year Mike noted a positive change related to his communication skills. "I can now speak up in groups," he said.

Mike's unfinished project related to his own experience and interests. He had moved to the Portland area from Canada ten years previously and frequently returns to see relatives. The project was on immigration laws and regulations in the functional citizenship area. At the same time, it will help Mike improve his grammar and spelling. Since students have the option of completing a project started during their junior year when they are a senior, Mike had a chance to finish the project this year. Of the year Mike said, "It turned out even better than I thought." Things he liked best about the new experience in EBCE were working at his own speed, going to a job and having more freedom.

At the end of the year, Mike's tests showed significant increases in both reading and language skills. In the math and study skills areas where he was already above average, only slight increases were indicated.

Tests on attitudes, given both at the beginning and the end of the year, indicated positive gains in self-reliance, understanding of roles in society, tolerance for people with differences in background and ideas than his, and openness to change.

Aspirations did not change for Mike. He still wants to go into computer programming after finishing college. "When I started the year I really didn't know too much about computers. I feel now that I know a lot and want even more to make it my career."

(The description of Mike's second year in EBCE is omitted. We pick up the case study after the second-year description.)

Mike's views of EBCE. Mike reported that his EBCE experiences, especially the learning levels, had improved all of his basic skills. He felt he had the freedom to do the kinds of things he wanted to do while at employer sites. These experiences, according to Mike, have strengthened his vocational choice in the field he wanted to enter and have caused him to look at educational and training requirements plus some other alternatives. For instance, Mike tried to enter the military, figuring it would be a good source of training in the field of computers, but was unable to because of a medical problem.

By going directly to job sites Mike has gotten a feel for the "real world" of work. He said his work at computer repair-oriented sites furthered his conceptions of the patience necessary when dealing with customers and fine degree of precision needed in the repair of equipment. He also discovered how a customer engineer takes a problem, evaluates it and solves it.

When asked about his work values Mike replied, "I figure if I get the right job, I'd work at it and try to do my best . . . in fact, I'm sure that even though I didn't like the job I'd still do more than I was asked to. . . . I'd work as hard as I could." Although he has always been a responsible person, he feels that his experiences in EBCE have made him more trustworthy. Mike also feels that he is now treated more like an adult because of his own attitudes. In fact, he feels he understands himself a lot more now.

Mike's future plans concern trying to get a job in computer programming at an automobile dealership or computer services company. He had previously done some computer work at the automobile dealership in relation to a project in Explorer Scouts. He also wants more training in computer programming and has discussed these plans with the student coordinator and an EBCE secretary. His attitude towards learning is that it may not be fun, but it is important, important to his future.

When asked in which areas he made less growth than he had hoped to, Mike responded, "I really made a lot of growth in all areas." He credits the EBCE program for this, finding it more helpful than high school. It gives you the opportunity to "get out and meet more people and get to be able to communicate better with people out in the community."

Most of Mike's experiences at the high school were not too personally rewarding. He did start a geometry class there this year, but had to drop it as he had started late and could not catch up. Although he got along all right with the staff at the high school, in the past he felt the teachers there had a "barrier be-tween them and the students." The EBCE staff "treat you on a more individual type circumstance . . . have the time to talk to you." In EBCE you can "work at your own speed . . . don't have to be in the classroom."

Mike recommends the program to most of his friends, although some of his friends had already dropped out of school. He stated, "I would have paid to come into EBCE, I think it's really that good of a program. . . . In fact, I've learned more in these two years in EBCE than I have in the last four years at the high school." He did not even ask for reimbursement for travel expenses be-cause he said he liked the program so much.

The views of his parents. When Mike first told his parents about the program they were concerned about what was going to be involved and whether it was a good program and educational. When interviewed in March, they felt that EBCE had helped Mike to be more mature and know where he is going.

Mike's parents said they were well-informed by the EBCE staff in all areas. Mike tended to talk to them about his activities in EBCE, while the only thing he ever talked about at the high school was photography. Mike's career plans have not really changed since he entered EBCE and his parents have not tried to in-fluence him, but EBCE has helped him to rule out mechanic and truck driving as possible careers.

Since beginning the EBCE program his parents have found Mike to be more mature, dependable and enthusiastic. He also became more reflective and con-cerned about the future. His writing improved and he read more.

There are no areas where his parents felt that EBCE did not help him and they rated the EBCE program highly in all areas.

Test progress measures on Mike. Although Mike showed a great improvement in almost all areas of the Comprehensive Test of Basic Skills during the first year of participation, his scores decline considerably during the second year. Espe-cially significant were the declines in Mike's arithmetic applications and study skills scores.

Mike's attitudinal scores all showed a positive gain over the two-year total period, but also tended to decline during the second year of participation. On the semantic differential, Mike scored significantly below the EBCE mean at FY 75 posttest on the community resources, adults, learning and work scales.

Mike showed continued growth over the two-year period on the work, self-reliance, communication, role, and trust scales of the Psychosocial Matu-rity Scale. He was significantly above the EBCE posttest means on the work, role, and social commitment scales and below average on only the openness to change scale. The openness to change score also showed a significant decline over the year.

The staff rated Mike on seven student behaviors. At the beginning of the year he was significantly above the EBCE mean on "applies knowledge of his/her own aptitudes, interests, and abilities to potential career interests" and below the mean on "understands another person's message and feelings." At posttest time he was still below the EBCE mean on this latter behavior as well as on "demonstrates willingness to apply Basic Skills to work tasks and to vocational interests."

Over the course of the two years in the EBCE program Mike's scores on the Self-Directed Search (SDS) showed little change in pattern, although the number of interests and competencies did expand. Overall, realistic (R) occupations decreased and enterprising (E) occupations increased as his code changed from RCI (where C is conventional and I is investigative occupations) at pretest FY 74 to ICR at pretest FY 75 (a classification which includes computer operators and equipment repairers) to CEI at posttest FY 75. However, the I was only one point stronger than the R and the CER classification includes data processing workers. Thus, Mike's SDS codes appeared very representative of his desired occupational future.

Evaluators' reflections. Mike's dramatic declines in attitudes and basic skill scores reflect behavior changes which occurred during the second half of his second year of the program and were detected by a number of people. In February at a student staffing meeting his learning manager reported of Mike that "no progress is seen in this zone with projects . . . still elusive . . . coasting right now . . . may end up in trouble." The prescription was to "watch him—make him produce . . . find out where he is." However, at the end of the next to last zone in mid-May the report was still "the elusive butterfly! (Mike) needs to get himself in high gear to get everything completed on time!!!" Since the posttesting was completed before this time, Mike probably coasted through the posttesting as well.

Other data suggesting his lack of concern and involvement during the second half of his senior year was attendance. Although he missed only two days the first half of the year, he missed thirteen days during the second half.

Mike showed a definite change in some of his personality characteristics over the two years he spent in the EBCE program. In the beginning of the program he was totally lacking in social skills and self-confidence. By the time he graduated, he had made great strides in his social skills (although there was still much room for improvement). However, his self-confidence had grown to the point of overconfidence. Indeed the employer instructor on his last learning level spent a good deal of time trying to get Mike to make a realistic appraisal of his own capabilities.

When interviewed after graduation, Mike was working six evenings a week at a restaurant where he worked part-time for the last year. He hopes to work there for about a year, working his way up to cook, and then go to a business college for a year to study computers.

SOURCE: Fehrenbacher, Owens, and Haehnn (1976). Used by permission of Northwest Regional Educational Laboratory.

APPENDIX 8.3

🔄 🔄 🔄

Excerpts From an Illustrative Interview Analysis:
Reflections on Outcomes From Participants
in a Wilderness Education Program

Experiences affect people in different ways. This experiential education truism means that the individual outcomes, impacts, and changes that result from participation in some set of activities are seldom predictable with any certainty. Moreover, the meaning and meaningfulness of such changes as do occur are likely to be highly specific to particular people in particular circumstances. While the individualized nature of learning is a fundamental tenet of experiential education, it is still important to stand back from those individual experiences in order to look at the patterns of change that cut across the specifics of person and circumstances. One of the purposes of the evaluation of the Learninghouse Southwest Field Training Project was to do just that—to document the experiences of individuals and then to look for the patterns that help provide an overview of the project and its impacts.

A major method for accomplishing this kind of reflective evaluation was the conduct of follow-up interviews with the 11 project participants. The first interviews were conducted at the end of October 1977, three weeks following the first field conference in the Gila wilderness of New Mexico. The second interviews were conducted during the third week of February, three weeks after the wilderness experience in the Kofa Mountains of Arizona. The third and final interviews were conducted in early May following the San Juan River conference in southern Utah. All interviews were conducted by telephone. The average interview took 20 minutes with a range from 15 to 35 minutes. Interviews were tape-recorded and transcribed for analysis.

The interviews focus on three central issues: (1) How has your participation in the Learninghouse Project affected you personally? (2) How has your participation in the project affected you professionally? (3) How has your participation in the Learninghouse Project affected your institution?

In the pages that follow, participant responses to these questions are presented and analyzed. The major purpose of the analysis was to organize participant responses in such a way that overall patterns would become clear. The emphasis throughout is on letting participants speak for themselves. The challenge for the evaluators was to present participant responses in a cogent fashion that integrates the great variety of experiences and impacts recorded during the interviews.

Personal Change

"How has your participation in the Learninghouse Project affected you personally? What has been the impact of the project on you as a person?"

Questions about personal change generated more reactions from participants than subsequent questions about professional and institutional change. There is an intensity to these responses about individual change that makes it clear just how significant these experiences were in stimulating personal growth and development. Participants attempted throughout the interviews to indicate that they felt differently about themselves as persons because of their Learninghouse experiences. While such personal changes are often difficult to articulate, the interviews reflect a variety of personal impacts.

Confidence: A Sense of Self

During the three weeks in the wilderness, participants encountered a number of opportunities to test themselves. Can I carry a full pack day after day, uphill and downhill? Can I make it up that mountain? Do I have anything to contribute to the group? As participants encountered and managed stress, they learned things about themselves. The result was often an increase in personal confidence and a greater sense of self.

It's really hard to say that LH did one thing or another. I think increased self-confidence has helped me do some things that I was thinking about doing. And I think that came, self-confidence came about largely because of the field experiences. I, right after we got back, I had my annual merit evaluation meeting with my boss, and at that I requested that I get a, have a change in title or a different title, and another title really is what it amounts to, and that I be given the chance for some other responsibilities that are outside the area that I work in. I want to get some individual counseling experience, and up to this point I have been kind of hesitant to ask for that, but I feel like I have a better sense of what I need to do for myself and that I have a right to ask for it at least. (Cliff, post-Kofas)

I guess something that has been important to me in the last couple of trips and will be important in the next one is just the outdoor peace of it. Doing things that perhaps I'd not been willing to attempt before for whatever reason. And finding I'm better at it than expected. Before I was afraid. (Charlene, post-Kofas)

The interviews indicate that increased confidence came not only from physical accomplishments but also—and especially—from interpersonal accomplishments.

After the Kofas I achieved several things that I've been working on for two years. Basically, the central struggle of the last two years of my life has been to no longer try to please people. No matter what my own feelings and needs are I try to please you. And in the past I had done whatever another person wanted me to do in spite of my own feelings and needs. And to have arrived at a point where I could tend to my own feelings and take care of what I needed to do for me is by far the most important victory I've won . . . a major one.

In the Kofas, I amazed myself that I didn't more than temporarily buy into how . . . I was being described . . . when I didn't recognize myself yet. And that's new for me. In the past I'd accept others' criticisms of me as if they were indeed describing me . . . and get sucked into that. And I felt that was an achievement for me to hold onto my sense of myself in the face of criticisms has long been one of my monsters I've been struggling with, so to hold onto me is, especially as I did, was definitely an achievement. (Billie, post-Kofas)

I've been paying a lot of attention to not looking for validation from other people. Just sticking with whatever kinds of feelings I have and not trying to go outside of myself . . . and lay myself on a platter for approval. I think the project did have a lot to do with that, especially this second trip in the Kofas. (Greg, post-Kofas)

I would say the most important thing that happened to me was being able to talk to other people quite honestly about, I think really about their problems more than mine. That's very interesting in that I think that I had, I think I had an effect upon Billie and Charlene both. As a result of that it gave me a lot more confidence and positive feelings. Do you follow that? Where rather than saying I had this problem and I talked to somebody and they solved it for me, it was more my helping other people to feel good about themselves that made me feel more adequate and better about myself. (Rod, post-Gila)

Another element of confidence concerns the extent to which one believes in one's own ideas—a kind of intellectual confidence.

I think if I take the whole project into consideration, I think that I've gained a lot of confidence myself in some of the ideas that I have tried to use, both personally and let's say professionally. Especially in my teaching aspects, especially teaching at a woman's college where I think one of our roles is not only to teach women subject matter, but also to teach them to be more assertive. I think that's a greater component of our mission than normally would have it at most colleges. I think that a lot of the ideas that I had about personal growth and about my own interactions with people were maybe reinforced by the LH experience, so that I felt more confident about them, and as a result they have come out more in my dealings with people. I would say specifically in respect to a sort of a more humanistic approach to things. (Rod, post-Kofas)

Increased confidence for participants was often an outcome of learning that they could do something new and difficult. At other times, however, increased confidence emerged as a result of finding new ways to handle old and difficult situations, for example, learning how to recognize and manage stress.

> A change I've noticed most recently and most strongly is the ability to recognize stress. And also the ability to recognize that I can do a task without needing to make it stressful, which is something I didn't know I did. So what I find I wind up doing, for example, is when I've had a number of things happen during the day and I begin to feel myself keying up I find myself very willing to say both to close friends and to people I don't know very well, I can't deal with this that you're bringing me. Can we talk about it tomorrow? This is an issue that really needs a lot of time and a lot of attention. I don't want to deal with it today, can we talk later, . . . etc. So I'm finding myself really able to do that. And I'm absolutely delighted about it.
> (Whereas before you just piled it on?)
> Exactly. I'd pile it and pile it until I wouldn't understand why I was going in circles. (Charlene, post-Kofas)

Personal Change—Overview

The personal outcomes cited by Learninghouse participants are all difficult to measure. What we have in the interviews are personal perceptions about personal change. The evidence, in total, indicates that participants felt differently and, in many cases, behaved differently as a result of their project participation. Different participants were affected in different ways and to varying extents. One participant reported virtually no personal effects from the experiences.

> And as far as the effect it had on me personally, which was the original question, okay, to be honest with you, to a large degree it had very little effect, and that's not a dig on the program, because at some point in people's lives I think things start to have smaller effect, but they still have effect. So I think that for me, what it did have an effect on was tolerance. Because there were a lot of things that occurred on the trip that I didn't agree with. And still don't agree, but I don't find myself to be viciously in disagreement any longer, just plainly in disagreement. So it was kind of like before, I didn't want to listen to the disagreement, or I wanted to listen to it but resolve it. Now, you know, there's a third option, that I can listen to it, continue to disagree with it, and not mind continuing to listen to it. (Cory, post-San Juan)

The more common reaction, however, was surprise at just how much personal change occurred.

> My expected outcome was increase the number of contacts in the Southwest, and every one of my expected outcomes were professional. That, you know, much more talk about potential innovations in education and directions to go, and you know, field-based education, what that's about, and I didn't expect at all, which

may not be realistic on my part, but at least I didn't expect at all—the personal impact. (Charlene, post-Gila)

For others the year's participation in Learninghouse was among the most important learning experiences of a lifetime, precisely because the project embraced personal as well as professional growth.

I've been involved in institutions and in projects as an educator, let's say, for 20 years. I started out teaching in high school, going to the NSF institutions during the summertime and I've gone to a lot of Chautauqua things and a lot of conferences, you know, of various natures. And I really think that this project has by far the greatest . . . has had by far the greatest impact on me. And I think that the reason is that in all the projects that I've had in the past . . . they've been all very specifically oriented toward one subject or toward one . . . more of a, I guess, more of a science, more of a subject matter orientation to them. Whereas this having a process orientation has a longer effect. I mean a lot of the things I learn in these instances is out of date by now and you keep up with the literature, for example, and all that and maybe that stimulates you to keep up . . . but in reality as far as a growth thing on my part, I think on the part of other participants, I think that this has been phenomenal. And I just think that this is the kind of thing that we should be looking towards funding on any level, federal, or any level. (Rod, post-San Juan)

We come now to a transition point in this report. Having reported participants' perceptions about personal change, we want to report the professional outcomes of the Learninghouse Project. The problem is that in the context of a holistic experience like the Southwest Field Training Project, the personal-professional distinction becomes arbitrary. A major theme running throughout discussions during the conferences was the importance of reducing the personal-professional schism, the desirability of living an integrated life and being an integrated self. This theme is reflected in the interviews, as many participants had difficulty responding separately to questions about personal versus professional change.

Personal/Professional Change

Analytically, there is at least a connotative difference between personal and professional change. For evaluation purposes, we tried to distinguish one from the other as follows: personal changes concern the thoughts, feelings, behaviors, intentions, and knowledge people have about themselves; professional changes concern the skills, competences, ideas, techniques, and processes people use in their work. There is, however, a middle ground. How does one categorize changes in thoughts, feelings, and intentions about competences, skills, and processes? There are changes in the person that affect that person's work. This section is a tribute to the complexity of human beings in defying the neat categories of social scientists and evaluators. This section reports changes that, for lack of a better nomenclature, we have called simply personal/professional impacts.

The most central and most common impact in this regard concerned changes in personal perspective that affected fundamental notions about and approaches to the world of work. The wilderness experiences and accompanying group processes permitted and/or forced many participants to stand back and take a look at themselves in relation to their work. The result was a changed perspective. The following four quotations are from interviews conducted after the first field conference in the Gila, a time when the contrasts provided by the first wilderness experience seemed to be felt most intensely.

> The trip came at a real opportune time. I've been on this new job about 4-5 weeks and was really getting pretty thoroughly mired in it, kind of overwhelmed by it, and so it came after a particularly hellish week, so in that sense it was just a critical, really helpful time to get away. To feel that I had, to remember that I had some choices, both in terms of whether I stayed here or went elsewhere, get some perspective of what it was I actually wanted to accomplish in higher education rather than just surviving to keep my sanity. And it gave me some, it renewed some of my ability to think of doing what I wanted to do here at the University, or trying to, that there were things that were important for me to do rather than just handling the stuff that poured across my desk. (Henry, post-Gila)

> I think it's helped make me become more creative, and just, and that's kind of tied in with the whole idea of the theory of experiential education. And the way we approached it on these trips. And so for instance I'm talking with my wife the other night, after I got Laura's paper that she'd given in Colorado, and I said you oughta read this because you can go out and teach history and you know, experientially. Then I gave her an idea of how I would teach frontier history for instance, and I don't know beans about frontier history. But it was an idea which, then she told another friend about it, and this friend says oh, you can get a grant for that. You know. So that was just a real vivid example, and I feel like, it's, I've been able to apply, or be creative in a number of different situations, I think just because I give myself a certain freedom, I don't know, I can't quite pinpoint what brought it about, but I just feel more creative in my work. (Cliff, post-San Juan)

> You know my biggest problem is I've been trying to save the world, and what I'm doing is pulling back. Because, perhaps the way I've been going about it has been wrong or whatever, but at least my motives are clearer and I know much more directly what I need and what I don't need and so I'm more open but less, yeah, as I said, I've been in a let's save the world kind of thing, now I feel more realistic and honest. (Charlene, post-Gila)

> I've been thinking about myself and my relationship to men and my boss, and especially to ideas about fear and risk . . . I decided that I needed to become a little

more visible at the department. After the October experience, I just said I was a bit more ready to become visible at the department level. And I volunteered then to work on developing a department training policy and develop the plan and went down to the department and talked to the assistant about it and put myself in a consulting role while another person was assigned the actual job of doing it. And I think that I was ready to make that decision and act on it after I first of all got clear that I was working on male-female relationships. My department has a man, again, not a terribly easy one to know, so it's a risk for me to go talk with him and yet I did it. I was relatively comfortable and felt very good and very pleased with myself that I had done that and I think that's also connected. (Billie, post-Kofas)

The connection between personal changes and professional activities was an important theme throughout the Learninghouse Project. The passages reported in this section illustrate how that connection took hold in the minds and lives of project participants. As we turn now to more explicit professional impacts, it is helpful to keep in mind the somewhat artificial and arbitrary nature of the personal-professional distinction.

(Omitted are sections on changed professional knowledge about experiential education, use of journals, group facilitation skills, individual professional skills, personal insights regarding work and professional life, and the specific projects participants undertook professionally. Also omitted are sections on institutional impacts. We pick up the report in the concluding section.)

Final Reflections

Personal change . . . professional change . . . institutional change. . . . Evaluation categories aim at making sense out of an enormously complex reality. The reflections by participants throughout the interviews make it clear that most of them came away from the Learninghouse program feeling changes in themselves. Something had touched them. Sometimes it meant a change in perspective that would show up in completely unexpected ways.

For one thing, I just finished the purchase of my house. First of all, that's a new experience for me. I've never done it before. I've never owned a home and never even wanted to. It seemed odd to me that my desire to "settle down" or make this type of commitment to a place occurred just right after the Gila trip. Just sort of one of those things that I woke up and went, "Wow, I want to stay here. I like this place. I want to buy it." And I had never in my life lived in a house or a place that I felt that way about. I thought that was kind of strange. And I do see that as a function of personal growth and stability. At least some kind of stability.

Other areas of personal growth: one has been, and this kind of crosses over I think into the professional areas, and that would be an ability to gain perspective. Certainly the trips I think . . . incredibly valuable for gaining perspective on what's happening in my home situation, my personal life, my professional life . . . the whole thing. And it has allowed me to focus on some priority types of things for me. And deal with some issues that I've been kind of dragging on for years and years and not really wanting to face up with them or deal with them. And I have been able to move on and move through those kinds of things in the last 6 or 9 months or so to a much greater extent than ever before. (Tom, post-San Juan)

Other participants came away from the wilderness experiences with a more concrete orientation that they could apply to work, play, and life.

The thing that I realized as I was trying to make some connections between the river and raft trip, was that in some ways I can see the parallels of my life being kind of like our raft trip was, and the rapids, or the thrill ride, and they're a lot of fun, but it's nice to get out of them for a while and dry off. It's nice sometimes to be able to just drift along and not worry about things. But a lot of it also is just hard work. A lot of times I wish I could get out of it and go a different way, and that's been kind of a nice thing for me to think about and kind of a viewpoint to have whenever I see things in a lull or in a real high speed pace, that I can say, "Okay, I'm going to be in this for a while, but I'm going to come out of it and go into something else." And so that's kind of a metaphor that I use as somewhat of a philosophy or point of view that's helpful as I go from day to day. (Cliff, post-San Juan)

A common theme that emerged as participants reflected on their year's involvement with Learninghouse was a new awareness of options, alternatives, and possibilities.

I would say that if I have one overall comment, the effect of the first week overall, is to renew my sense of the broader possibilities in my job and in my life. Opens things to me. I realize that I have a choice to be here and be myself. And since I have a choice, there are responsibilities. Which is a good feeling. (Henry, post-Gila)

I guess to me what sticks out overall is that the experience was an opportunity for me to step out of the rest of my life and focus on it and evaluate it, both my personal life and my work, professional life aspect. (Michael, post-San Juan)

As participants stood back and examined themselves and their work they seemed to discover a clarity that had previously been missing. Perspective, awareness, clarity . . . stuff of which personal/professional/institutional change is made.

I think I had a real opportunity to explore some issues of my own worth with a group of people who were willing to allow me to explore those. And it may have come later, but it happened then. On the Learninghouse, through the Learninghouse . . . and I think it speeded up the process of growing for me in that way, accepting my own worth, my own ideas about education, about what I was doing, and in terms of being a teacher it really aided my discussions of people and my interactions. It really gave me a lot of focus on what I was doing. I think I would've muddled around a long time with some issues that I was able to, I think, gain some clarity on pretty quickly by talking to people who were sharing their experience and were working towards the same goals, self-directed learning, and experiential education. (Greg, post-San Juan)

I think what happened is that for me it served as a catalyst for some personal changes, you know, the personal, institutional, they're all wound up, bound up together. I think I was really wrestling with jobs and career and so on. For me the whole project was a catalyst, a kind of permission to look at things that I hadn't looked at before. One of the realizations, one of the insights that I had in the process was, kind of neat on my part, to become concrete, specific in my actions in my life, no matter whether that was writing that I was doing, or if it was in my job, or whatever it was. But to really pay attention to that. I think that's one of the things that happened to me. (Peter, post-San Juan)

These statements from interviews do not represent a final assessment of the impacts of the Learninghouse Southwest Field Training Project. Several participants resisted the request to make summary statements about the effects and outcomes of their participation in the program because they didn't want to force premature closure.

(Can you summarize the overall significance of participation in the project?)
I do want to make a summary, and I don't again. . . . It feels like the words aren't easy and for me being very much a words person, that's unusual. It's not necessarily that the impact hasn't been in the cognitive areas. There have been some. But what they've been, where the impact has been absolutely overwhelming is in the affective areas. Appreciation of other people, appreciation of this kind of education. Though I work in it, *I haven't done it before!* A real valuing of people, the profession, of my colleagues in a sense that I never had before. . . .

The impact feels like it's been dramatic, and I'm not sure that I can say exactly how. I'm my whole . . . it all can be summarized perhaps by saying I'm much more in control. In a good kind of sense. In accepting risk and being willing to take it; accepting challenge and being willing to push myself on that; accepting and understanding more about working at the edge of my capabilities . . . what that means to me. Recognizing very comfortably what I can do and feeling good about that confidence, and recognizing that what I haven't yet done, and feeling okay about trying it. The whole perception of confidence has changed. (Charlene, post-San Juan)

The Learninghouse program was many things—the wilderness, a model of experiential education, stress, professional development—but most of all, the project was the people who participated. In response after response participants talked about the importance of the people to everything that happened. Because of the dominance of that motif throughout the interviews, we want to end this report with that highly personal emphasis.

I said before I think that to know some people, that meant a lot to me, people who were also caring. And people who were also involved, very involved in some issues, philosophical and educational, that were pretty basic not only to education, but to living. Knowing these people has been really important to me. It's given me a kind of continuity and something to hold onto in the midst of a really frustrating, really difficult situation where I didn't have people where I could get much feedback from, or that I could share much thinking about, talking about, and working with. It's just kind of basic issues. That kind of continuity is real important to just my feelings, important to myself. Feeling like I have someplace to go. . . . Sometimes I feel funny about placing so much emphasis on the people. . . . But the people have really meant a lot to me as far as putting things together for myself. Being able to have my hands in something that might, that really offers me a way to go. (Greg, post-San Juan)

SOURCE: By Jeanne Campbell and Michael Patton.

Between-Chapters Interlude

Riddles of Qualitative Inquiry
Who Am I?

Gary D. Shank

Lately, I have been thinking about riddles. Riddles are one of those things that we used for millennia to build inquiry around and then conveniently mislaid or trivialized. Riddles were once powerful and heady things. Now we have riddles that are nothing but child's word play. Word play was certainly important in riddles, but they were anything but simply child's fare.

We have discarded the riddle in favor of the puzzle. Scientists and other empirical inquirers "puzzle" over the meaning of their data and seek to solve the "puzzles" of life and creation. This is all well and good, but why can't we reclaim the riddle as well? Each of the following four riddles seeks to highlight and illuminate some overlooked or covert or murky aspect of a qualitative research skill.[1] Since most riddles are in verse, I decided to preserve the form—for these riddles I used Petrarchian sonnet structure. (Note: As a reminder of the imperfect patterns found in the real world, the last line of Riddle Four violates the sonnet rules; instead of abbaabba cdecde it is abbaabba cdecdc.)

The question is: Can you solve the riddles?

Riddle Number One

When I have fears that I have found a place
Where I have never chanced to be before
And where the odds are great, that never-
more
Will I again be out there, face to face;
How then should I begin to set the chase?
When wonder's great and familiarity poor
How then should my tired eyes keep up
the score
When all things strange are ordinary
grace?

Where is my ear, when eyes run fast
ahead?
What do my fingertips alone reveal?
What is the pulse and pace of this strange
land?
And by whose claim are things mundane
instead,
Like some dried tangerine stripped of its
peel,
An hourglass sucked dry of all its sand?

Who am I?

Riddle Number Two

Your hands rest lightly on your chin,
because
You cannot always find the words you
need.
Life races past our thoughts, both trapped
and freed
Of solid form, like sheets of film and gauze
Whose shifting shapes cause us to halt and
pause.
We find ourselves belonging to a breed

Of ordinary folk, like some strange creed
Who seek out yet another staged applause.

What do you say, that I have never said?
What brave new world can you make me
believe?
Are you this calm, or are you filled with
spite?
These ragged thoughts take root, and then
my head
Seeks any path of rest. You may relieve
My fright, or plunge me deeper in the
night.

Who am I?

Riddle Number Three

Suppose your home looks like a subway
station
Where geeks and pimps roll out their
tattered wares
And teenage mothers linger on the stairs,
Framed once more in hollow
consternation.
Refugees who know both love and
Haitian
Size up easy marks, doled out in pairs
You feel like turning circles into squares—
Two moves away from last year's
conflagration.

How could there be no peace in Paradise?
Where children and their parents all excel?
With levees standing high above the flood.
How can you rage, if everything is nice?
Down here inside the Nineteenth hole
of Hell
Where school kids lie in puddles of their
blood?

Who am I?

Riddle Number Four

I see the rats somewhere inside the cheese.
Cheddar, or Brie, or Swiss with all its
    holes?
Rats burrowing inside, like long-tailed
    moles
Or ghostly galleons tossed on stormy seas?
How do these metaphors lock up and seize
My brain, like glaciers marching from the
    Poles
Or fiery furnaces with red-hot coals
That simultaneously burn and freeze?

Things are themselves, as much as they are
    not
I want to put my hand upon their flank
And with a mighty yank to reel them in.

But they seek me as much as they are
    sought,
They bind my hands and make me walk
    the plank
And night is broken down without a shot.

Who am I?

> Answers are at the end of
> Chapter 9, page 598.

🔄 Note

1. Riddles composed by Gary D. Shank, author of *Qualitative Research: A Personal Skills Approach* (2002). Used by permission.

9

Enhancing the Quality and Credibility of Qualitative Analysis

Interpreting Truth _____

A young man traveling through a new country heard that a great Mulla, a Sufi guru with unequaled insight into the mysteries of the world, was also traveling in that region. The young man was determined to become his disciple. He found his way to the wise man and said, "I wish to place my education in your hands that I might learn to interpret what I see as I travel through the world."

After six months of traveling from village to village with the great teacher, the young man was confused and disheartened. He decided to reveal his frustration to the Mulla.

"For six months I have observed the services you provide to the people along our route. In one village you tell the hungry that they must work harder in their fields. In another village you tell the hungry to give up their preoccupation with food. In yet another village you tell the people to pray for a richer harvest. In each village the problem is the same, but always your message is different. I can find no pattern of Truth in your teachings."

The Mulla looked piercingly at the young man.

"Truth? When you came here you did not tell me you wanted to learn Truth. Truth is like the Buddha. When met on the road it should be killed. If there were only one Truth to be applied to all villages there would be no need of Mullahs to travel from village to village.

"When you first came to me you said you wanted to 'learn how to interpret' what you see as you travel through the world. Your confusion is simple. To interpret and to state Truths are two quite different things."

Having finished his story Halcolm smiled at the attentive youths. "Go, my children. Seek what you will, do what you must."

—From Halcolm's *Evaluation Parables*

🖻 Alternative Criteria for Judging Quality

*E*very way of seeing is also a way of not seeing.

—David Silverman (2000:825)

It all depends on criteria. Judging quality requires criteria. Credibility flows from those judgments. Quality and credibility are connected in that judgments of quality constitute the foundation for perceptions of credibility.

Diverse approaches to qualitative inquiry —phenomenology, ethnomethodology, ethnography, hermeneutics, symbolic interaction, heuristics, critical theory, realism, grounded theory, and feminist inquiry, to name but a few—remind us that issues of quality and credibility intersect with audience and intended inquiry purposes. Research directed to an audience of independent feminist scholars, for example, may be judged by somewhat different criteria from research addressed to an audience of government economic policy makers. Formative research or action inquiry for program improvement involves different purposes and therefore different criteria of quality compared with summative evaluation aimed at making fundamental continuation decisions about a program or policy. Thus, it is important to acknowledge at the outset

that particular philosophical underpinnings or theoretical orientations and special purposes for qualitative inquiry will generate different criteria for judging quality and credibility.

In broad terms, I have identified five contrasting sets of criteria for judging the quality of qualitative inquiry from different perspectives and within different philosophical frameworks. Some of the criteria within these frameworks overlap, but even then subtle differences in nuances of meaning can be distinguished. The five contrasting, and to some extent competing, sets of criteria flow from the following:

- Traditional scientific research criteria
- Social construction and constructivist criteria
- Artistic and evocative criteria
- Critical change criteria
- Evaluation standards and principles

Exhibit 9.1 lists the criteria that flow from each of these perspectives or frameworks.

The *traditional scientific research criteria* are embedded in and derived from what I discussed in Chapter 3 in the Truth and Reality-Oriented Correspondence Theory section that included postpositivist and realist approaches to qualitative inquiry. The *social construction and constructivist criteria* highlight elements of the detailed discussion of those perspectives in the section by that name in Chapter 3. The *artistic and evocative criteria* are derived from the Autoethnography and Evocative Forms of Inquiry section in Chapter 3, especially the criteria suggested by Richardson (2000b) for "creative analytic practice ethnography." The fourth set of criteria, *critical change criteria*, flow from critical theory, feminist inquiry, activist research, and participatory research processes aimed at empowerment; these were discussed in Chapter 3 as Orientational Qualitative Inquiry (done from a particular values-based perspective) and in Chapter 4 as participatory and collaborative strategies. The final set of criteria, *evaluation standards and principles*, are from *The Standards for Program Evaluation* (Joint Committee 1994) and "Guiding Principles for Evaluators" (AEA Task Force 1995); they provide the foundation for the extended discussion of qualitative evaluation applications in Chapter 4.

To some extent, all of the theoretical, philosophical, and applied orientations reviewed in Chapters 3 and 4 provide somewhat distinct criteria, or at least priorities and emphases, for what constitutes a quality contribution within those particular perspectives and concerns. I've chosen these five broader sets of criteria to correspond roughly with major stages in the development of qualitative research (Denzin and Lincoln 2000b), to capture the primary debates that differentiate qualitative approaches and, more specifically, to highlight what seem to differentiate *reactions* to quali-

tative inquiry. In this chapter, we are primarily concerned with how others respond to our work. With what perspectives and by what criteria will our work be judged by those who encounter and engage it?

Some of the confusion that people have in assessing qualitative research stems from thinking it represents a uniform perspective, especially in contrast to quantitative research. This makes it hard for them to make sense of the competing approaches within qualitative inquiry. By understanding the criteria that others bring to bear on our work, we can anticipate their reactions and help them position our intentions and criteria in relation to their own expectations and criteria. In terms of the reflexive triangulated inquiry model presented in Chapter 2 as Exhibit 2.2, we're dealing here with the intersection between the inquirer's perspective and those receiving the study (the audiences).

Different perspectives about such things as truth and the nature of reality constitute paradigms or worldviews based on alternatve epistemologies and ontologies. People viewing qualitative findings through different paradigmatic lenses will react differently just as we, as researchers and evaluators, vary in how we think about what we do when we study the world. These differences are nicely illustrated by the classic story of three baseball umpires who, having retired after a game to a local establishment for the dispensing of reality-distorting but truth- enhancing libations, are discussing how they call balls and strikes.

"I call them as I see them," says the first.

"I call them as they are," says the second.

"They ain't nothing until I call them," says the third.

EXHIBIT 9.1 | Alternative Sets of Criteria for Judging the Quality and Credibility of Qualitative Inquiry

Traditional Scientific Research Criteria

Objectivity of the inquirer (attempts to minimize bias)
Validity of the data
Systematic rigor of fieldwork procedures
Triangulation (consistency of findings across methods and data sources)
Reliability of codings and pattern analyses
Correspondence of findings to reality
Generalizability (external validity)
Strength of evidence supporting causal hypotheses
Contributions to theory

Social Construction and Constructivist Criteria

Subjectivity acknowledged (discusses and takes into account biases)
Trustworthiness
Authenticity
Triangulation (capturing and respecting multiple perspectives)
Reflexivity
Praxis
Particularity (doing justice to the integrity of unique cases)
Enhanced and deepened understanding (*Verstehen*)
Contributions to dialogue

Artistic and Evocative Criteria

Opens the world to us in some way
Creativity
Aesthetic quality
Interpretive vitality
Flows from self; embedded in lived experience

As an exercise in distinguishing paradigms, try matching the three umpires' perspectives to the frameworks in Exhibit 9.1. (Hint: All four of the other perspectives can be found within evaluation, so treating the umpires as evaluators reduces your matching options to the remaining four.) The short sections that follow elaborate the five alternative sets of criteria for judging the quality of qualitative work.

Traditional Scientific Research Criteria

One way to increase the credibility and legitimacy of qualitative inquiry among those who place priority on traditional scientific research criteria is to emphasize those criteria that have priority within that tradition. Science has traditionally emphasized objec-

Stimulating
Provocative
Connects with and moves the audience
Voice distinct, expressive
Feels "true" or "authentic" or "real"

Critical Change Criteria

Critical perspective: Increases consciousness about injustices
Identifies nature and sources of inequalities and injustices
Represents the perspective of the less powerful
Makes visible the ways in which those with more power exercise
   and benefit from power
Engages those with less power respectfully and collaboratively
Builds the capacity of those involved to take action
Identifies potential change-making strategies
Praxis
Clear historical and values context
Consequential validity

Evaluation Standards and Principles

Utility
Feasibility
Propriety
Accuracy (balance)
Systematic inquiry
Evaluator competence
Integrity/honesty
Respect for people (fairness)
Responsibility to the general public welfare
   (taking into account diversity of interests and values)

tivity, so qualitative inquiry within this tradition emphasizes procedures for minimizing investigator bias. Those working within this tradition will emphasize rigorous and systematic data collection procedures, for example, cross-checking and cross-validating sources during fieldwork. In analysis it means, whenever possible, using multiple coders and calculating intercoder consistency to establish the validity and reliability of pattern and theme analysis. Qualitative researchers working in this tradition are comfortable using the language of "variables" and "hypothesis testing" and striving for causal explanations and generalizability, especially in combination with quantitative data. Qualitative approaches that manifest some or all of these characteristics include grounded theory (Glaser 2000: 200), qualitative comparative analysis (Ragin 1987,

VARYING CRITERIA FOR DETERMINING TRUTH

"Each society has its regime of truth, its 'general politics' of truth; that is, the types of discourse which it accepts and makes function as true; the mechanisms in instances which enable one to distinguish true and false statements, the means by which each is sanctioned; the techniques and procedures accorded value in the acquisition of truth; the status of those who are charged with saying what counts as true" (Foucault 1972:131).

2000), realists such as Miles and Huberman (1994), and some aspects of analytic induction (see Chapter 8). Their common aim is to use qualitative methods to describe and explain phenomena as accurately and completely as possible so that their descriptions and explanations correspond as closely as possible to the way the world is and actually operates. Government agencies supporting qualitative research (e.g., the U.S. General Accounting Office, the National Science Foundation, and the National Institutes of Health) usually operate within this traditional scientific framework.

Social Construction and Constructivist Criteria

Social construction, constructivist, and "interpretivist" perspectives have generated new language and concepts to distinguish quality in qualitative research (e.g., Glesne 1999:5-6). Lincoln and Guba (1986) proposed that constructivist inquiry demanded different criteria from those inherited from traditional social science. They suggested "credibility as an analog to internal validity, transferability as an analog to external validity, dependability as an analog to reliability, and confirmability as an analog to objectivity." In combination, they viewed these criteria as addressing "trustworthiness (itself a parallel to the term *rigor*)" (pp. 76-77). They went on to emphasize that naturalistic inquiry should be judged by dependability (a systematic process systematically followed) and authenticity (reflexive consciousness about one's own perspective, appreciation for the perspectives of others, and fairness in depicting constructions in the values that undergird them). They view the social world (as opposed to the physical world) as socially, politically, and psychologically constructed, as are human understandings and explanations of the physical world. They triangulate to capture and report multiple perspectives rather than seek a singular truth. Constructivists embrace subjectivity as a pathway deeper into understanding the human dimensions of the world in general as well as whatever specific phenomena they are examining (Peshkin 1985, 1988, 2000a). They're more interested in deeply understanding specific cases within a particular context than in hypothesizing about generalizations and causes across time and space. Indeed, they are suspicious of causal explanations and empirical generalizations applied to complex human interactions and cultural systems. They offer perspective and encourage dialogue among perspectives rather than aiming at singular truth and linear prediction. Social constructivists' case studies, findings, and reports are explicitly informed by attention to praxis and reflexivity, that is, understanding how one's own experiences and background affect what one understands and how one acts in the world, including acts of inquiry. Guba and Lincoln (1989, 1990), Lincoln and Guba (1986), Smith (1991), Denzin (1997a,

A realist views a constructivist proposal.

2001), Neimeyer (1993), and Potter (1996) have articulated and work within the tradition of social constructionism and constructivism. (See Chapter 3 for a much lengthier discussion of constructionism and constructivism.)

Artistic and Evocative Criteria

In the last chapter, I discussed qualitative analysis as both science and art. Researchers and audiences operating from the perspective of traditional scientific research criteria emphasize the scientific nature of qualitative inquiry. Researchers and audiences that view the world through the lens of social construction emphasize qualitative inquiry as both science and art, and mix the two motifs. That brings us to this third alternative, which emphasizes the artistic and evocative aspects of qualitative inquiry, or what is sometimes called "the narrative turn" in social science (Bochner 2001). Keep in mind that these are matters of emphasis drawn here to highlight contrasts, and not mutually exclusive or pure types. Artistic criteria focus on aesthetics, creativity, interpretive vitality, and expressive voice. Case studies become literary works. Poetry or performance art may be used to enhance the audience's direct experience of the essence that emerges from analysis. Artistically oriented qualitative analysts seek to engage those receiving the work, to connect with them, move them, provoke and stimulate. Creative nonfiction and fictional forms of representation blur the boundaries between what is "real" and what has been created to represent the essence of a reality, at least as it is perceived, without a literal presentation of that perceived reality. The results may be called creative syntheses, ideal-typical case constructions, scientific poetics, or any number of phrases that suggest the artistic emphasis. (See Exhibit 3.3 in Chapter 3, Varieties of Autoethnography: A Partial Lexicology.) Artistic expressions of qualitative analysis strive to provide an experience with the findings where "truth" or "reality" is understood to have a *feeling dimension* that is every bit as important as the cognitive dimension. The performance art of *The Vagina Monologues* (Ensler 2001), based on interviews with women but presented as theater, offers a prominent example. The audience feels as much as knows the truth of the presentation because of the essence it reveals. In the artistic tradition, the analyst's interpretive and expressive voice, experience, and perspective may become as central to the work as depictions of others or the phenomenon of interest. Qualitative inquiry illustrative of this emergent approach includes the works of Bochner and Ellis (2001), Goodall (2000), Richardson (2000b), Barone (2000), Ellis and Bochner (1996, 2000), Glesne (1997), Patton (1999a), and Denzin (2000b).

Critical Change Criteria

Those engaged in qualitative inquiry as a form of critical analysis aimed at social and political change eschew any pretense of open-mindedness or objectivity; they take an activist stance. For example, consequential validity as a criterion for judging a research design or instrument makes the social consequences of its use a value basis for assessing its credibility and utility. Thus, standardized achievement tests are criticized because of the discriminatory consequences for minority groups of educational decisions made with "culturally biased" tests. Consequential validity asks for assessments of who benefits and who is harmed by an inquiry, measurement, or method (Messick 1989; Shepard 1993; Brandon, Lindberg, and Wang 1993). As an example of the critical change orientation, *critical theory* approaches fieldwork and analysis with an explicit agenda of elucidating power, economic, and social inequalities. The "critical" nature of critical theory flows from a commitment to go beyond just studying society for the sake of increased understanding. Critical theorists set out to use research to critique society, raise consciousness, and change the balance of power in favor of those less powerful. Influenced by Marxism, informed by the presumption of the centrality of class conflict in understanding community and societal structures, and updated in the radical struggles of the 1960s, critical theory provides both philosophy and methods for approaching research and evaluation as fundamental and explicit manifestations of political praxis (connecting theory and action) and as change-oriented forms of engagement.

Likewise, *feminist inquiry* often includes an explicit agenda of bringing about social change (e.g., Benmayor 1991). *Liberation research* and *empowerment evaluation* derive, in part, from Paulo Freire's philosophy of praxis and liberation education articulated in his classics *Pedagogy of the Oppressed* (1970) and *Education for Critical Consciousness* (1973), still sources of influence and debate (e.g., Glass 2001). Barone (2000:247) aspires to "emancipatory educational storysharing." Qualitative studies informed by critical change criteria range from largely intellectual and research-oriented approaches that aim to expose injustices to more activist forms of inquiry that actually engage in bringing about social change. This category can include *collaborative and participatory approaches* to fieldwork that are conducted in ways that build the capacity of those involved to better understand their own situations, raise consciousness, and support future action aimed at political change. Examples of a range of critical change approaches to qualitative inquiry can be found in work on feminist methods (Reinharz 1992; Harding 1991; Fonow and Cook 1991; Gluck and Patai 1991), critical theory (Fonte 2001; Lather 1986; Comstock 1982), and critical ethnography (Thomas 1993; Simon and Dippo 1986).

Evaluation Standards and Principles

The evaluation profession has adopted standards that call for evaluations to be useful, practical, ethical, and accurate (Joint Committee 1994). In 1995, the American Evaluation Association (AEA Task Force 1995) added the following principles: systematic inquiry, evaluator competence, integrity/honesty, respect for people (fairness), and responsibility to the general public welfare (taking into account diversity of interests and values). The complete and specific standards and principles are available through the AEA Web site (see Exhibit 4.9 in Chapter 4).

In the 1970s, as evaluation was just emerging as a field of professional practice, many evaluators took the position of traditional researchers that their responsibility was merely to design studies, collect data, and publish findings; what decision makers did with those findings was not their problem. This stance removed from the evaluator any responsibility for fostering use and placed all the "blame" for nonuse or underutilization on decision makers. Moreover, before the field of evaluation identified and adopted its own standards, criteria for judging evaluations could scarcely be differentiated from criteria for judging research in the traditional social and behavioral sciences, namely, technical quality and methodological rigor. Utility was largely ignored. Methods decisions dominated the evaluation design process. Validity, reliability, measurability, and generalizability were the dimensions that received the greatest attention in judging evaluation research proposals and reports. Indeed, evaluators concerned about increasing a study's usefulness often called for ever more methodologically rigorous evaluations to increase the validity of findings, thereby supposedly compelling decision makers to take findings seriously.

By the late 1970s, however, program staff and funders were becoming openly skeptical about spending scarce funds on evaluations they couldn't understand and/or found irrelevant. Evaluators were being asked to be "accountable" just as program staff were supposed to be accountable. The questions emerged with uncomfortable directness: Who will evaluate the evaluators? How will evaluation be evaluated? It was in this context that professional evaluators began discussing standards.

The most comprehensive effort at developing standards was hammered out over five years by a 17-member committee appointed by 12 professional organizations with input from hundreds of practicing evaluation professionals. Just prior to publication, Dan Stufflebeam (1980), chair of the committee, summarized the results as follows:

> The standards that will be published essentially call for evaluations that have four features. These are *utility, feasibility, propriety* and *accuracy*. And I think it is interesting that the Joint Committee decided on that particular order. Their rationale is that an evaluation should not be done at all if there is no prospect for its being useful to some audience. Second, it should not be done if it is not feasible to conduct it in political terms, or practicality terms, or cost effectiveness terms. Third, they do not think it should be done if we cannot demonstrate that it will be conducted fairly and ethically. Finally, if we can demonstrate that an evaluation will have utility, will be feasible and will be proper in its conduct, then they said we could turn to the difficult matters of the technical adequacy of the evaluation. (p. 90)

In 1994, revised standards were published following an extensive review spanning several years (Joint Committee 1994). While some changes were made in the 30 individual standards, the overarching framework of four primary criteria remained unchanged: utility, feasibility, propriety, and accuracy. Taking the standards seriously has meant looking at the world quite differently.

Unlike the traditionally aloof stance of basic researchers, evaluators are challenged to take responsibility for use. Implementation of a utility-focused, feasibility-conscious, propriety-oriented, and accuracy-based evaluation requires situational responsiveness, methodological flexibility, multiple evaluator roles, political sophistication, and substantial doses of creativity (Patton 1997a).

While the standards and principles offer a generic set of criteria for judging the quality of evaluations, many different models and viewpoints coexist under this broad umbrella (Stufflebeam, Madeus, and Kellaghan 2000; Greene 2000; Patton 1997a; Worthen, Sanders, and Fitzpatrick 1996). Indeed, one can find in evaluation examples of evaluators applying any of the four sets of criteria already reviewed. The traditional scientific research criteria are the basis for evaluation research as represented by Rossi, Freeman, and Lipsey (1999) and Huey-Tsyh Chen and Peter H. Rossi (1987). Constructivist criteria applied to evaluation provide the foundation for *Fourth Generation Evaluation* (Guba and Lincoln 1989) and sensitivity to multiple stakeholder perspectives (Greene 1998a, 1998b, 2000). The artistic and evocative criteria inform "connoisseurship evaluation" (Eisner 1985, 1991). Critical change criteria undergird empowerment evaluation (Fetterman 2000a), diversity-inclusive evaluation (Mertens 1998), and aspects of deliberative democratic evaluation that involve values-based advocating for democracy (House and Howe 2000). Spanning this diversity and variety of practice is a general understanding that those who use evaluations apply both "truth tests" (Are the findings accurate and valid?) and "utility tests" (Are the findings relevant and useful?) (Weiss and Bucuvalas 1980). This involves attending to and balancing legitimate concerns about both technical quality and utility of findings (Greene 1990). Stufflebeam (2001) has prepared the Evaluation Values and Criteria Checklist to help evaluators and their clients consider an appropriate range of generic values and criteria as they identify those that will undergird particular evaluations.

Clouds and Cotton: Mixing and Changing Perspectives

The five frameworks just reviewed show the range of criteria that can be brought to bear in judging a qualitative study. They can also be viewed as "angles of vision" or "alternative lenses" for expanding the possibilities available, not only for critiquing inquiry but also for undertaking it (Peshkin 2001). While each set of criteria manifests a certain coherence, many researchers mix and match approaches. The work of Tom Barone (2000), for example, combines aesthetic, political (critical change), and constructivist elements. As an evaluator, I have worked with and mixed criteria from all five frameworks to match particular designs to the needs and interests of specific stakeholders and clients (Patton 1997a). But any particular evaluation study has tended to be dominated by one set of criteria with a second set as possibly secondary.

Mixing and combining criteria mean dealing with tensions between them. After reviewing the tensions between traditional social science criteria and postmodern constructivist criteria, narrative researchers Lieblich, Tuval-Mashiach, and Zilber (1998) assert "a middle course," but that middle course reveals the very tensions they are trying to supersede as they work with one leg in each camp.

> We do not advocate total relativism that treats all narratives as texts of fiction. On the other hand, we do not take narratives at face value, as complete and accurate representations of reality. We believe that stories are usually constructed around a core of facts or life events, yet allow a wide periphery for freedom of individuality and creativity in selection, addition to, emphasis on, and interpretation of these "remembered facts."
>
> Life stories are subjective, as is one's self or identity. They contain "narrative truth" which may be closely linked, loosely similar, or far removed from "historical truth." Consequently, our stand is that life stories, when properly used, may provide researchers with a key to discovering identity and understanding it—both in its "real" or "historical" core, and as narrative construction. (p. 8)

The remainder of this chapter will elaborate some of the most prominent of these competing criteria that affect judgments about the quality and credibility of qualitative inquiry and analysis. Which criteria you choose to emphasize in your work will depend on the purpose of your inquiry, the values and perspectives of the audiences for your work, and your own philosophical and methodological orientation. Operating within any particular framework and using any specific set of criteria will invite criticism from those who judge your work from a different framework and with different criteria. (For examples of the vehemence of such criticisms between those using traditional social science criteria and those using artistic narrative criteria, see Bochner 2001 or English 2000.) Understanding that criticisms (or praise) flow from criteria can help you anticipate how to position your inquiry and make explicit what criteria to apply to your own work as well as what criteria to offer others given the purpose and orientation of your work.

But it's not always easy to tell whether someone is operating from a realist, con-

CROSSING BORDERS AND GENRES

The borders between sets of criteria for evaluating the quality of qualitative work will necessarily remain fluid as qualitative inquirers move back and forth among genres ignoring the boundaries much as birds ignore human fences—except to use them occasionally as convenient places to rest. Consider the reflections on genre of self-described "critical educators" Patricia Burdell and Beth Blue Swadener (1999). They note the importance of research that blurs genres by combining autobiographical narratives with a variety of theoretical perspectives, including critical, dialogic, phenomenological, feminist, and semiotic perspectives. They speculate that "it is perhaps both the intent and effect of many of these texts to broaden the 'acceptable' or give voice to the intellectual contradictions and tensions in everyday lives of scholar-teachers and researchers" (p. 23).

Our research has used narrative inquiry, collaborative ethnography, and applied

semiotics. Between us, we share an identity and scholarship in critical and feminist curriculum theory. . . . We are frequent border-crossers. . . . We seek texts that allow us to enter the world of others in ways that have us more present in their experience, while better understanding our own. (Burdell and Swadener 1999:23)

They call this border-crossing genre "critical personal narrative and autoethnography," an approach that combines elements of three sets of criteria identified here: social construction and constructivist criteria, artistic and evocative criteria, and critical change criteria. Thanks to border-crossers, the real world of practice is not a very neat and orderly place. Nor, thankfully, is it likely to become so, for without border-crossers the world of research would quickly become stagnant.

structionist, artistic, activist, or evaluative framework. Indeed, the criteria can shift quickly. Consider this example. My six-year-old son, Brandon, was explaining to me a geography science project he had done for school. He had created an ecological display out of egg cartons, ribbons, cotton, bottle caps, and styrofoam beads. "These are three mountains and these are four valleys," he said, pointing to the egg cup arrangement. "And is that a cloud?" I asked, pointing to the big hunk of cotton. He looked at me, disgusted, as though I'd said just about the dumbest thing he'd ever heard. "That's a piece of cotton, Dad."

🔄 Credibility

The credibility of qualitative inquiry depends on three distinct but related inquiry elements:

- *rigorous methods* for doing fieldwork that yield high-quality data that are systematically analyzed with attention to issues of credibility;

- the *credibility of the researcher,* which is dependent on training, experience, track record, status, and presentation of self; and

- *philosophical belief in the value of qualitative inquiry,* that is, a fundamental appreciation of naturalistic inquiry, qualitative methods, inductive analysis, purposeful sampling, and holistic thinking.

🖳 Rigor: Strategies for Enhancing the Quality of Analysis

Chapters 6 and 7 focused on rigorous techniques for increasing the quality of data collected during fieldwork (observing, interviewing, and document gathering), while Chapter 8 reviewed systematic analysis strategies. However, at the heart of much controversy about qualitative findings are doubts about the nature of the analysis. Statistical analysis follows formulas and rules, while, at the core, qualitative analysis depends on the insights and conceptual capabilities of the analyst. Qualitative analysis depends from the beginning on astute pattern recognition, a process epitomized in health research by the scientist working on one problem who suddenly notices a pattern related to a quite different problem —and thus discovers Viagra. As Pasteur posited, "Chance favors the prepared mind." Here, then, are some techniques that prepare the mind for insight while also enhancing the credibility of the resulting analysis.

Integrity in Analysis: Generating and Assessing Rival Conclusions

One barrier to credible qualitative findings stems from the suspicion that the analyst has shaped findings according to predispositions and biases. Whether this may have happened unconsciously, inadvertently, or intentionally (with malice aforethought) is not the issue. The issue is how to counter such a suspicion before it takes root. One strategy involves discussing one's predispositions, making biases explicit, to the extent possible, and engaging in mental cleansing processes (e.g., *epoche* in phenomenological analysis; see Chapter 8). Or one may simply acknowledge one's orientation as a feminist researcher or critical theorist and move on from there.

However one approaches the issue, being able to report that you engaged in a systematic search for alternative themes, divergent patterns, and rival explanations enhances credibility. This can be done both inductively and logically. Inductively it involves looking for other ways of organizing the data that might lead to different findings. Logically it means thinking about other logical possibilities and then seeing if those possibilities can be supported by the data. When considering rival organizing schemes and competing explanations, your mind-set shouldn't be focused on attempting to disprove the alternatives; rather, you *look for data that support alternative explanations.* Failure to find strong supporting evidence for alternative ways of presenting the data or contrary explanations helps increase confidence in the original, principal explanation you generated. Comparing alternative patterns will not typically lead to clear-cut "yes there is support" versus "no there is not support" kinds of conclusions. You're searching for the *best fit.* This requires assessing the weight of evidence and looking for those patterns and conclusions that fit the preponderance of data. Keep track of and report alternative classification systems, themes, and explanations that you considered and "tested" during data analysis. This demonstrates intellectual integrity and lends considerable credibility to the final set of findings offered, especially if explanations are proffered. As Yin (1999a) has observed, analysis of rival explanations in case studies constitutes a form of rigor in qualitative analysis parallel to the rigor of experimental designs aimed at eliminating rival explanations.

A formal and forced approach to engaging rival conclusions draws on the legal system's reliance on opposing perspectives battling it out in the courtroom. The advocacy-adversary model suggested by Wolf (1975) developed in response to concerns that evaluators could be biased in their conclusions. So, to balance biases, two teams engage in the evaluation. The *advocacy team* gathers and presents information that supports the proposition that the program is effective; the *adversary team* gathers information that supports the conclusion that the program ought to be changed or terminated. A variation of this strategy would be to arbitrarily create advocacy and adversary teams *only* during the analysis stage so that both teams work with the same set of data but each team organizes and interprets those data to support different and opposite conclusions. Another variation would be for a lone analyst to organize data systematically into *pro* and *con* sets to see what each yielded. The weakness of the advocacy-adversary approach is that it emphasizes contrasts and opposite conclusions to the detriment of synthesis and integration. It forces data sets into combat with each other. Such oversimplification of complex and multifaceted findings is a primary reason that advocacy-adversary evaluation is rarely used (in addition to being expensive and time-consuming). Still, it highlights the importance of engaging in some systematic analysis of alternative and rival conclusions.

Negative Cases

Closely related to testing alternative constructs is the search for and analysis of *negative cases*. Where patterns and trends have been identified, our understanding of those patterns and trends is increased by considering the instances and cases that do not fit within the pattern. These may be exceptions that prove the rule. They may also broaden the "rule," change the "rule," or cast doubt on the "rule" altogether. Analytic induction (see Chapter 8) makes analysis of negative cases a centerpiece of its analytical strategy for revising and fine tuning hypotheses and conclusions (Denzin 1989c).

In the Southwest Field Training Project involving wilderness education, virtually all participants reported significant "personal growth" as a result of their participation in the wilderness experiences; however, the two people who reported "no change" provided particularly useful insights into how the program operated and affected participants. These two had crises going on back home that limited their capacity to "get into" the wilderness experiences. The project staff treated the wilderness experiences as fairly self-contained, closed-system experiences. The two negative cases opened up thinking about "baggage carried in from the outside world," "learning-oriented mindsets," and a "readiness" factor that subsequently affected participant selection and preparation.

No specific guidelines can tell you how and how long to search for negative cases or how to find alternative constructs and hypotheses in qualitative data. Your obligation is to make an "assiduous search . . . until no further negative cases are found" (Lincoln and Guba 1986:77). You then report the basis for the conclusions you reach about the significance of negative or deviant cases.

Negative cases also provide instructive opportunities for new learning in formative evaluations. For example, in a health education program for teenage mothers where the large majority of participants complete the program and show knowledge gains, an important component of the analysis should include examination of reactions from dropouts, even if the sample is small for the dropout group. While the small proportion of dropouts may not be large enough to make a difference in a statistical analysis, qualitatively the dropout feedback may provide critical information about a niche group, specific subculture, and/or clues to program improvement.

Readers of a qualitative study will make their own decisions about the plausibility of alternate explanations and the reasons why deviant cases do not fit within dominant patterns. But I would note that the section of the report that involves exploration of alternative explanations and consideration of why certain cases do not fall into the main pattern can be among the most interesting sections of a report to read. When well written, this section of a report reads something like a detective study in which the analyst (detective) looks for clues that lead in different directions and tries to sort out which direction makes the most sense given the clues (data) that are available. Such writing adds credibility by showing the analyst's authentic search for what makes most sense rather than marshaling all the data toward a single conclusion. Indeed, the whole tone of a report feels different when the researcher is willing to openly consider possibilities other than those finally settled on as most reasonable. Compare the approach of weighing alternatives to the report where all the data lead in a single-minded fashion, in a rising crescendo, toward an overwhelming presentation of a single point of view. Perfect patterns and omniscient explanations are likely to be greeted skeptically—and for good reason: The human world is not perfectly ordered and human researchers are not omniscient. Humility can do more than certainty to enhance credibility. Dealing openly with the complexities and dilemmas posed by negative cases is both intellectually honest and politically strategic.

Triangulation

By combining multiple observers, theories, methods, and data sources, [researchers] can hope to overcome the intrinsic bias that comes from single-methods, single-observer, and single-theory studies.

—Norman K. Denzin (1989c:307)

Chapter 5 on design discussed the benefits of using multiple data collection techniques, a form of triangulation, to study the same setting, issue, or program. You may recall from that discussion that the term *triangulation* is taken from land surveying. Knowing a single landmark only locates you somewhere along a line in a direction from the landmark, whereas with two landmarks you can take bearings in two directions and locate yourself at their intersection. The notion of triangulating also works metaphorically to call to mind the world's strongest geometric shape—the triangle. The logic of triangulation is based on the premise that no single method ever adequately solves the problem of rival explanations. Because each method reveals different aspects of empirical reality, multiple methods of data collection and analysis provide more grist for the research mill. Combinations of interviewing, observation, and document analysis are expected in much fieldwork. Studies that use only one method are more vulnerable to errors linked to that particular method (e.g., loaded interview questions, biased or untrue responses) than studies that use multiple methods in which different types of data provide cross-data consistency checks.

It is in data analysis that the strategy of triangulation really pays off, not only in providing diverse ways of looking at the same phenomenon but in adding to credibility by strengthening confidence in whatever conclusions are drawn. Four kinds of triangulation can contribute to verification and validation of qualitative analysis:

1. *Methods triangulation:* Checking out the consistency of findings generated by different data collection methods

2. *Triangulation of sources:* Checking out the consistency of different data sources within the same method

3. *Analyst triangulation:* Using multiple analysts to review findings

4. *Theory/perspective triangulation:* Using multiple perspectives or theories to interpret the data

By triangulating with multiple data sources, observers, methods, and/or theories, researchers can make substantial strides in overcoming the skepticism that greets singular methods, lone analysts, and single-perspective interpretations.

However, a common misconception about triangulation involves thinking that the purpose is to demonstrate that different data sources or inquiry approaches yield es-

sentially the same result. The point is to *test for* such consistency. Different kinds of data may yield somewhat different results because different types of inquiry are sensitive to different real-world nuances. Thus, **understanding inconsistencies in findings across different kinds of data can be illuminative and important.** Finding such inconsistencies ought not be viewed as weakening the credibility of results, but rather as offering opportunities for deeper insight into the relationship between inquiry approach and the phenomenon under study. I'll comment briefly on each of these types of triangulation.

METHODS TRIANGULATION: RECONCILING QUALITATIVE AND QUANTITATIVE DATA

Methods triangulation often involves comparing and integrating data collected through some kind of qualitative methods with data collected through some kind of quantitative methods. Such efforts flow from a pragmatic approach to mixed methods analysis that assumes potential *compatibility* and seeks to discover the degree and nature of such compatibility (Tashakkori and Teddlie 1998:12). This is seldom straightforward because certain kinds of questions lend themselves to qualitative methods (e.g., developing hypotheses or theory in the early stages of an inquiry, understanding particular cases in depth and detail, getting at meanings in context, capturing changes in a dynamic environment), while other kinds of questions lend themselves to quantitative approaches (e.g., generalizing from a sample to a population, testing hypotheses, making systematic comparisons on standardized criteria). Thus, it is common that quantitative methods and qualitative methods are used in a complementary fashion to answer different questions that do not easily come together to provide a single, well-integrated picture of the situation.

Given the varying strengths and weaknesses of qualitative versus quantitative approaches, the researcher using different methods to investigate the same phenomenon should not expect that the findings generated by those different methods will automatically come together to produce some nicely integrated whole. Indeed, the evidence is that one ought to expect initial conflicts in findings from qualitative and quantitative data and expect those findings to be received with varying degrees of credibility. It is important, then, to consider carefully what each kind of analysis yields and give different interpretations the chance to arise and be considered on their merits before favoring one result over the other based on methodological biases.

Shapiro (1973) has described in detail her struggle to resolve basic differences between qualitative data and quantitative data in her study of Follow Through classrooms; she eventually concluded that some of the conflicts between the two kinds of data were a result of measuring different things, although the ways in which different things were measured were not immediately apparent until she worked to sort out the conflicting findings. She began with greater trust in the data derived from quantitative methods and ended by believing that the most useful information came from the qualitative data.

An article by M. G. Trend (1978) of ABT Associates has become required reading for anyone becoming involved in a team project that will involve collecting and analyzing both qualitative and quantitative data and where different members of the team have

responsibilities for different kinds of data. The Trend study involved an analysis of three social experiments designed to test the concept of using direct cash housing allowance payments to help low-income families obtain decent housing on the open market. The analysis of qualitative data from a participant observation study produced results that were at variance with those generated by analysis of quantitative data. The credibility of the qualitative data became a central issue in the analysis.

> The difficulty lay in conflicting explanations or accounts, each based largely upon a different kind of data. The problems we faced involved not only the nature of observational versus statistical inferences, but two sets of preferences and biases within the entire research team. . . .
>
> Though qualitative/quantitative tension is not the only problem which may arise in research, I suggest that it is a likely one. Few researchers are equally comfortable with both types of data, and the procedures for using the two together are not well developed. The tendency is to relegate one type of analysis or the other to a secondary role, according to the nature of the research and the predilections of the investigators. . . . Commonly, however, observational data are used for "generating hypotheses," or "describing process." Quantitative data are used to "analyze outcomes," or "verify hypotheses." I feel that this division of labor is rigid and limiting. (Trend 1978:352)

The 1980 meeting of the Society of Applied Anthropology in Denver included a symposium on the problems encountered by anthropologists participating in teams in which both quantitative and qualitative data were being collected. The problems they shared were stark evidence that qualitative methods were typically perceived as

exploratory and secondary when used in conjunction with quantitative/experimental approaches. When qualitative data supported quantitative findings, that was icing on the cake. When qualitative data conflicted with quantitative data, the qualitative data have often been dismissed or ignored. A strategy of methods triangulation, then, doesn't magically put everyone on the same page. While valuing and endorsing triangulation, Trend (1978) suggested that "we give different viewpoints the chance to arise, and postpone the immediate rejection of information or hypotheses that seem out of joint with the majority viewpoint. Observationally derived explanations are particularly vulnerable to dismissal without a fair trial" (pp. 352-53).

Qualitative and quantitative data can be fruitfully combined to elucidate complementary aspects of the same phenomenon. For example, a community health indicator (e.g., teenage pregnancy rate) can provide a general and generalizable picture of an issue, while case studies of a few pregnant teenagers can put faces on the numbers and illuminate the stories behind the quantitative data. This becomes even more powerful when the indicator is broken into categories (e.g., those under age 15, those 16 and older) with case studies illustrating the implications of and rationale for such categorization.

In essence, triangulation of qualitative and quantitative data constitutes a form of comparative analysis. The question is, What

EXHIBIT 9.2	A Story of Triangulation: Testing Conclusions With More Fieldwork

Economists Lawrence Katz and Jeffrey Liebman of Harvard and Jeffrey R. Kling of Princeton were trying to interpret data from a federal housing experiment that involved randomly assigning people to a program that would help them get out of the slums. The evaluation focused on the usual outcomes of improved school and job performance. However, to get beyond the purely statistical data, they decided to conduct face-to-face interviews with residents in an inner-city poor community after studying the results of a preliminary survey with the people who were participating in this program.

Professor Liebman commented to a *New York Times* reporter: "I thought they were going to say they wanted access to better jobs and schools, and what we came to understand was their consuming fear of random crime; the need the mothers felt to spend every minute of their day making sure their children were safe" (Uchitelle 2001:4).

By adding qualitative, field-based interview data to their study, Kling, Liebman, and Katz (2001) came to a new and different understanding of the program's impacts and participants' motivations based on interviewing the people directly affected, listening to their perspectives, and including those perspectives in their analysis.

does each analysis contribute to our understanding? Areas of convergence increase confidence in findings. Areas of divergence open windows to better understanding the multifaceted, complex nature of a phenomenon. Deciding whether results have converged remains a delicate exercise subject to both disciplined and creative interpretation. Focusing on the *degree of convergence* rather than forcing a dichotomous choice—that the different kinds of data do or not converge —yields a more balanced overall result.

TRIANGULATION OF QUALITATIVE DATA SOURCES

The second type of triangulation involves triangulating data sources. This means comparing and cross-checking the consistency of information derived at different times and by different means *within qualitative methods*. It means

- comparing observations with interviews;

- comparing what people say in public with what they say in private;

- checking for the consistency of what people say about the same thing over time;

- comparing the perspectives of people from different points of view, for example, in an evaluation, triangulating staff views, client views, funder views, and views expressed by people outside the program; and

- checking interviews against program documents and other written evidence that can corroborate what interview respondents report.

Quite different kinds of data can be brought together in a case study to illuminate various aspects of a phenomenon.

Smith and Kleine (1986) triangulated historical analyses, life history interviews, and ethnographic participant observations to illuminate the roles of powerful actors in evaluating an innovative educational project.

As we found with methods triangulation, triangulation of data sources within qualitative methods may not lead to a single, totally consistent picture. The point is to study and understand when and why these differences appear. The fact that observational data produce different results than interview data does not mean that either or both kinds of data are "invalid," although that may be the case. More likely, it means that different kinds of data have captured different things and so the analyst attempts to understand the reasons for the differences. Either consistency in overall patterns of data from different sources or reasonable explanations for differences in data from divergent sources can contribute significantly to the overall credibility of findings.

TRIANGULATION WITH MULTIPLE ANALYSTS

A third kind of triangulation is investigator or analyst triangulation, that is, using multiple as opposed to singular observers or analysts. Triangulating observers or using several interviewers helps reduce the potential bias that comes from a single person doing all the data collection and provides means of more directly assessing the consistency of the data obtained. Triangulating observers provides a check on bias in data collection. A related strategy is *triangulating analysts*—that is, having two or more persons independently analyze the same qualitative data and compare their findings.

In evaluation, an interesting form of team triangulation has been used. Michael Scriven (1972b) used two separate teams, one that conducted a traditional goals-based evaluation (assessing the stated outcomes of the program) and a second that undertook a "goal-free" evaluation in which the evaluators assess clients' needs and program outcomes without focusing on stated goals (see Chapter 4). Comparing the results of the goals-based team with those of the goal-free team provides a form of analytical triangulation for determining program effectiveness.

REVIEW BY INQUIRY PARTICIPANTS

Having those who were studied review the findings offers another approach to analytical triangulation. Researchers and evaluators can learn a great deal about the accuracy, completeness, fairness, and perceived validity of their data analysis by having the people described in that analysis react to what is described and concluded. To the extent that participants in the study are unable to relate to and confirm the description and analysis in a qualitative report, questions are raised about the credibility of the findings. Alkin, Daillak, and White (1979), in studying how evaluations were used, presented each case study to the people in the setting described and asked them for both verbal and written reactions. They then included those written reactions in the report.

> Obtaining the reactions of respondents to your working drafts is time-consuming, but respondents may (1) verify that you have reflected their perspectives; (2) inform you of sections that, if published, could be problematic for either personal or political reasons; and (3) help you to develop new ideas and interpretations. (Glesne 1999:152)

How important can participant feedback be, not only to confirm findings but to make sure the right questions are being asked?

Massachusetts Institute of Technology researcher Eric Von Hipple reported that 77% of the innovations in equipment used to make semiconductor and printed circuit boards and 67% of the breakthroughs reported in four major types of scientific instruments came from customers (Gladwell 1997:47). In phenomenological terms, the real-world lived experience of customers is driving technological innovation among those able to hear it.

Collaborative and participatory inquiry builds in participants' review of findings as a matter of course. However, investigative inquiry (Douglas 1976) aims at exposing what goes on beyond the public eye and is often antagonistic to those in power, so their responses would not typically be used to revise conclusions but might be used to at least offer them an opportunity to provide context and an alternative interpretation. Some researchers worry that sharing findings with participants for their reactions will undermine the independence of their analysis. Others view it as an important form of triangulation. In an Internet listserv discussion of this issue, one researcher reported this experience:

I gave both transcripts and a late draft of findings to participants in my study. I wondered what they would object to. I had not promised to alter my conclusions based on their feedback, but I had assured them that my aim was being sure not to do them harm. My findings included some significant criticisms of their efforts that I feared/expected they might object to. Instead, their review brought forth some new information about initiatives that had not previously been mentioned. And their primary objection was to my not giving the credit for their successes to a wider group in the community. What I learned was not to make assumptions about participants' thinking.

AUDIENCE REVIEW AS CREDIBILITY TRIANGULATION

Reflexive triangulation (Exhibit 2.2 in Chapter 2) adds the audience's reactions to the triangulation mix. Evaluation constitutes a particular challenge in establishing credibility because the ultimate test of the credibility of an evaluation report is the response of primary intended users and readers of that report. Their reactions revolve around *face validity*. On the face of it, is the report believable? Are the data reasonable? Do the results connect to how people understand the world? In seriously soliciting users' reactions, the evaluator's perspective is joined to the perspective of the people who must use the findings. House (1977) suggests that the more "naturalistic" the evaluation, the more it relies on its audiences to reach their own conclusions, draw their own generalizations, and make their own interpretations:

Unless an evaluation provides an explanation for a particular audience, and enhances the understanding of that audience by the content and form of the argument it presents, it is not an adequate evaluation for that audience, even though the facts on which it is based are verifiable by other procedures. One indicator of the explanatory power of evaluation data is the degree to which the audience is persuaded. Hence, an evaluation may be "true" in the conventional sense but not persuasive to a particular audience for whom it does not serve as an explanation. *In the fullest sense, then, an evaluation is dependent both on the person who makes the evaluative statement and on the person who receives it.* (p. 42, emphasis added)

Understanding the interaction and mutuality between the evaluator and the people who use the evaluation, as well as relationships with participants in the program, is critical to understanding the human side of evaluation. This is part of what gives evaluation—and the evaluator—situational and interpersonal "authenticity" (Lincoln and Guba 1986). Appendix 9.1 at the end of this chapter provides an experiential account from an evaluator dealing with issues of credibility while building relationships with program participants and evaluation users; her reflections provide a personal, in-depth description of what authenticity is like from the perspective of one participant observer.

EXPERT AUDIT REVIEW

A final review alternative involves using experts to assess the quality of analysis or, where the stakes for external credibility are especially high, performing a metaevaluation or process audit. An external audit by a disinterested expert can render judgment about the quality of data collection and analysis. "That part of the audit that examines the process results in a *dependability judgment*, while that part concerned with the product (data and reconstructions) results in a *confirmability judgment*" (Lincoln and Guba 1986:77, emphasis added). Such an audit would need to be conducted according to appropriate criteria. For example, it would not be fair to audit an aesthetic and evocative qualitative presentation by traditional social science standards, or vice versa. But within a particular framework, expert reviews can increase credibility for those who are unsure how to distinguish high-quality work. That, of course, is the role of the doctoral committee for graduate students and peer reviewers for scholarly journals. Problems arise when peer reviewers apply traditional scientific criteria to constructivist submissions, and vice versa. In such cases, the review or audit itself lacks credibility. The challenge of getting the right expert, one who can apply an appropriately critical eye,

is nicely illustrated by a story about the great artist Pablo Picasso.

Marketing of fakes of his paintings plagued Picasso. His friends became involved in helping check out the authenticity of supposed genuine originals. One friend in particular became active in this regard and brought several paintings to Picasso, all of which he identified as fake. A poor artist who hoped to profit from having obtained a Picasso before the great artist's works had become so valuable sent his painting for inspection via the friend. Again Picasso pronounced it a forgery.

"But I saw you paint this one with my very own eyes," protested the friend.

"I can paint false Picassos as well as anyone," retorted Picasso.

THEORY TRIANGULATION

A fourth kind of triangulation involves using different theoretical perspectives to look at the same data. Chapter 3 presented a number of general theoretical frameworks derived from divergent intellectual and disciplinary traditions. More concretely, multiple theoretical perspectives can be brought to bear on specialized substantive issues. For example, one might examine interviews with therapy clients from different psychological perspectives: psychotherapy, Gestalt, Adlerian, and behavioral psychology. Observations of a group, community, or organization can be examined from a Marxian or Weberian perspective, a conflict or functionalist point of view. The point of theory triangulation is to understand how differing assumptions and premises affect findings and interpretations.

A concrete version of theory triangulation for evaluation would involve examining the data from the perspectives of various stakeholder positions. It is common for divergent stakeholders to disagree about program purposes, goals, and means of attaining goals. These differences represent different "theories of action" (Patton 1997a) that can cast the same findings in different perspective-based lights.

THOUGHTFUL, SYSTEMATIC TRIANGULATION

All of these different types of triangulation—methods triangulation, triangulation of data sources, analyst triangulation, and theory or perspective triangulation—offer strategies for reducing systematic bias and distortion during data analysis. In each case, the strategy involves checking findings against other sources and perspectives. Triangulation, in whatever form, increases credibility and quality by countering the concern (or accusation) that a study's findings are simply an artifact of a single method, a single source, or a single investigator's blinders.

Design Checks: Keeping Methods and Data in Context

One possible source of distortion in qualitative findings concerns how design decisions affect results. For example, purposeful sampling strategies provide a limited number of cases for examination. When interpreting findings, then, it becomes important to reconsider how design constraints may have affected the data available for analysis. This means considering the rival methodological hypothesis that the findings are due to methodological idiosyncrasies.

By their nature, qualitative findings are highly context and case dependent. Three kinds of sampling limitations typically arise in qualitative research designs:

- Limitations in the situations (critical events or cases) that are sampled for ob-

servation (because it is rarely possible to observe all situations even within a single setting)

- Limitations from the time periods during which observations took place, that is, constraints of temporal sampling

- Limitations based on selectivity in the people who were sampled either for observations or interviews, or selectivity in document sampling

In reporting how purposeful sampling strategies affect findings, the analyst returns to the reasons for having made initial design decisions. Purposeful sampling involves studying information-rich cases in depth and detail to understand and illuminate important cases rather than generalizing from a sample to a population (see Chapter 5). For instance, sampling and studying highly successful and unsuccessful cases in an intervention yield quite different results than studying a typical case or a mix of cases. People unfamiliar with purposeful samples may think of small samples as "biased," a perception that undermines credibility in their minds. In communicating findings, then, it becomes important to emphasize that the issue is not one of dealing with a distorted or biased sample, but rather one of clearly delineating the purpose and limitations of the sample studied—and therefore being careful about extrapolating (much less generalizing) the findings to other situations, other time periods, and other people. Reporting both methods and results in their proper contexts will avoid many controversies that result from yielding to the temptation to overgeneralize from purposeful samples. **Keeping findings in context is a cardinal principle of qualitative analysis.**

Mulla Nasrudin was once called upon to make this point to his monarch. Although he was supposed to be a wise and holy man,

Nasrudin was accused of being almost illiterate. One day the ruler of his country decided to put this to the test.

"Write something for me, Nasrudin," said he.

"I would willingly do so, but I have taken an oath never to write so much as a single letter again," replied Nasrudin.

"Well, write something in the way in which you used to write before you decided not to write, so that I can see what it was like."

"I cannot do that, because every time you write something, your writing changes slightly through practice. If I wrote now, it would be something written for now."

"Then bring me an example of his writing, anyone who has one," ordered the ruler.

Someone brought a terrible scrawl that the Mulla had once written to him.

"Is this your writing?" asked the monarch.

"No," said Nasrudin. "Not only does writing change with time, but reasons for writing change. You are now showing a piece of writing done by me to demonstrate to someone how he should *not* write" (Shah 1973:92).

High-Quality Lessons Learned

The notions of identifying and articulating "lessons learned" and "best practices" have become popular purposes of cross-case analyses in multisite organizational studies and cluster evaluations that aim to build knowledge comparatively. Rather than being stated in the form of traditional scientific empirical generalizations, lessons learned and best practices more often take the form of *principles of practice* that must be adapted to particular settings in which the principle is to be applied. For example, a lesson learned from research on evaluation use is that evaluation use will likely be enhanced by designing an evaluation to answer the focused questions of specific primary intended users (Patton 1997a). However, as we looked at examples of lessons learned being included as conclusions in a variety of cluster evaluation reports, Ricardo Millett, former director of evaluation at the W. K. Kellogg Foundation, and I began discussing the deteriorating meaningfulness of the phrases "lessons learned" and "best practices." As these phrases became widely used, they began to be applied to any kind of insight, evidentially based or not. We began thinking about what would constitute a "high-quality lessons learned" and decided that one's confidence in the transferability or extrapolated relevance of a supposed lesson learned would increase to the extent that it was supported by multiple sources and types of learnings. Exhibit 9.3 presents a list of kinds of evidence that could be accumulated to support a proposed lesson learned, making it more worthy of application and adaptation to new settings if it has independent triangulated support from a variety of perspectives. Questions for generating lessons learned are also listed. Thus, for example, the lesson that designing an evaluation to answer the focused questions of specific primary intended users enhances evaluation use is supported by research on use, theories about diffusion of innovation and change, practitioner wisdom, cross-case analyses of use, the profession's articulation of standards, and expert testimony. For example, House's reflections about generalizability in *The Logic of Evaluative Argument* (1977) constitute an example of expert testimony in support of the lesson learned about evaluation use:

> In evaluation, the social and psychological contexts become particularly relevant and the knowledge less certain. Under those conditions argumentation aimed at gaining the ad-

---

EXHIBIT 9.3   High-Quality Lessons Learned

High-quality lessons learned: Knowledge that can be applied to future action and derived from screening according to specific criteria:

- Evaluation findings—patterns across programs
- Basic and applied research
- Practice wisdom and experience of practitioners
- Experiences reported by program participants/clients/intended beneficiaries
- Expert opinion
- Cross-disciplinary connections and patterns
- Assessment of the importance of the lesson learned
- Strength of the connection to outcomes attainment

The idea is that the greater the number of supporting sources for a "lesson learned," the more rigorous the supporting evidence, and the greater the *triangulation of supporting sources,* the more confidence one has in the significance and meaningfulness of a lesson learned. Lessons learned with only one type of supporting evidence would be considered a "lessons learned hypothesis." Nested within and cross-referenced to lessons learned should be the actual cases from which practice wisdom and evaluation findings have been drawn. A critical principle here is to maintain the contextual frame for lessons learned, that is, to keep lessons learned grounded in their context. For ongoing learning, the trick is to follow future supposed applications of lessons learned to test their wisdom and relevance over time in action in new settings.

Questions for generating high-quality lessons learned

1. What is meant by a "lesson"?
2. What is meant by "learned"?
3. By whom was the lesson learned?
4. What is the evidence supporting each lesson?
5. What is the evidence the lesson was learned?
6. What are the contextual boundaries around the lesson (i.e., under what conditions does it apply)?
7. Is the lesson specific, substantive, and meaningful enough to guide practice in some concrete way?
8. Who else is likely to care about this lesson?
9. What evidence will they want to see?
10. How does this lesson connect with other lessons?

---

herence and increasing the understanding of particular audiences is more appropriate. Persuasion claims validity only for particular audiences and the intensity with which particular audiences accept the evaluation findings is a measure of this effectiveness. The evaluator does not aim at convincing a univer-

sal audience of all rational men with the necessity of his conclusions.

Persuasion is directly related to action. Even though evaluation information is less certain than scientific information addressed to a universal audience, persuasion is effective in promoting action because it focuses on a particular audience and musters information with which this audience is concerned. (p. 6)

High-quality lessons learned, then, represent principles extrapolated from multiple sources and independently triangulated to increase transferability as cumulative knowledge working hypotheses that can be adapted and applied to new situations, a form of pragmatic utilitarian generalizability, if you will. The pragmatic bias in this approach reflects the wisdom (dare one say lesson learned) of Samuel Johnson: "As gold which he cannot spend will make no man rich, so knowledge which he cannot apply will make no man wise."

🆂 The Credibility of the Researcher

The previous sections have reviewed strategies for enhancing the quality and credibility of qualitative analysis, searching for rival explanations, explaining negative cases, triangulation, and keeping data in context. Technical rigor in analysis is a major factor in the credibility of qualitative findings. This section now takes up the issue of how the credibility of the inquirer affects the way findings are received.

Because the researcher is the instrument in qualitative inquiry, a qualitative report should include some information about the researcher. What experience, training, and perspective does the researcher bring to the field? Who funded the study and under what arrangements with the researcher? How did the researcher gain access to the study site? What prior knowledge did the researcher bring to the research topic and study site? What personal connections does the researcher have to the people, program, or topic studied? For example, suppose the observer of an Alcoholics Anonymous pro-

gram is a recovering alcoholic. This can either enhance or reduce credibility depending on how it has enhanced or detracted from data gathering and analysis. Either way, the analyst needs to deal with it in reporting findings. In a similar vein, it is only honest to report that the evaluator of a family counseling program was going through a difficult divorce at the time of fieldwork.

No definitive list of questions must be addressed to establish investigator credibility. **The principle is to report any personal and professional information that may have affected data collection, analysis, and interpretation**—either negatively or positively—in the minds of users of the findings. For example, health status should be reported if it affected one's stamina in the field. (Were you sick part of the time? The fieldwork for evaluation of an African health project was conducted over three weeks during which time the evaluator had severe diarrhea. Did that affect the highly negative tone of the report? The evaluator said it didn't, but I'd want to have the issue out in the open to make my own judgment.) Background characteristics of the researcher (e.g., gender, age, race, ethnicity) may be relevant to report in that such characteristics can affect how the researcher was received in the setting under study and what sensitivities the inquirer brings to the issues under study.

In preparing to interview farm families in Minnesota, I began building up my tolerance for strong coffee a month before the fieldwork. Being ordinarily a non-coffee drinker, I knew my body would be jolted by 10 to 12 cups of coffee a day doing interviews in farm kitchens. In the Caribbean, when interviewing farmers, I had to increase my tolerance for rum because some interviews took place in rum shops. These are matters of personal preparation—both mental and physical—that affect perceptions about the quality of the study. Preparation and training for fieldwork, discussed at the beginning of Chapter 6, should be reported as part of the study's methodology.

Considering Investigator Effects: Varieties of Reactivity

Another factor to consider and report concerns how the presence of an observer or evaluator may have affected what was observed. There are four primary ways in which the presence of an outside observer, or the fact that an evaluation is taking place, can distort the findings of a study:

1. reactions of those in the setting (e.g., program participants and staff) to the presence of the qualitative fieldworker;

2. changes in the fieldworker (the measuring instrument) during the course of the data collection or analysis, that is, what has traditionally been called instrumentation effects;

3. the predispositions, selective perceptions, and/or biases of the inquirer; and

4. researcher incompetence (including lack of sufficient training or preparation).

Problems of reactivity are well documented in the anthropological literature, which is one of the prime reasons why qualitative methodologists advocate long-term observations that permit an initial period during which observers and the people in the setting being observed get a chance to get used to each other. This increases trustworthiness and that supports credibility both within and outside the study setting.

The credibility of your findings and interpretations depends upon your careful attention to establishing trustworthiness. . . . Time is a major factor in the acquisition of trustworthy data. Time at your research site, time spent interviewing, and time building sound relationships with respondents all contribute to trustworthy data. When a large amount of time is spent with your research participants, they less readily feign behavior or feel the need to do so; moreover, they are more likely to be frank and comprehensive about what they tell you. (Glesne 1999:151)

On the other hand, prolonged engagement may actually increase reactivity as the researcher becomes more a part of the setting and begins to affect what goes on through prolonged engagement. Thus, whatever the length of inquiry or method of data collection, researchers have an obligation to examine how their presence affects what goes on and what is observed.

It is axiomatic that observers must record what they perceive to be their own reactive effects. They may treat this reactivity as bad and attempt to avoid it (which is impossible), or they may accept the fact that they will have a reactive effect and attempt to use it to advantage. . . . The reactive effect will be measured by daily field notes, perhaps by interviews in which the problem is pointedly inquired about, and also in daily observations. (Denzin 1978b:200)

Anxieties that surround an evaluation can exacerbate reactivity. The presence of an evaluator can affect how a program operates as well as its outcomes. The evaluator's presence may, for example, create a halo effect so that staff performs in an exemplary fashion and participants are motivated to "show off." On the other hand, the presence of the evaluator may create so much tension and anxiety that performances are below par. Some forms of program evaluation, especially "empowerment evaluation" and "intervention-oriented evaluation" (Patton 1997a: Chapter 5) turn this traditional threat to validity into an asset by designing data collection to enhance achievement of the desired program outcomes. For example, at the simplest level, the observation that "what gets measured gets done" suggests the power of data collection to affect outcomes attainment. A leadership program, for example, that includes in-depth interviewing and participant journal writing as ongoing forms of evaluation data collection may find that participating in the interviewing and writing reflectively have effects on participants and program outcomes. Likewise, a community-based AIDS awareness intervention can be enhanced by having community participants actively engaged in identifying and doing case studies of critical community incidents. In short, a variety of reactive responses are possible, some that support program processes, some that interfere, and many that have implications for interpreting findings. Thus, the evaluator has a responsibility to think about the problem, make a decision about how to handle it in the field, attempt to monitor evaluator/observer effects, and reflect on how reactivities may have affected findings.

Evaluator effects are often considerably overrated, particularly by evaluators. There is more than a slight touch of self-importance in some concerns about reactivity. Lillian Weber, director of the Workshop Center for Open Education, City College School of Education, New York, once set me straight on this issue, and I pass her wisdom on to my colleagues. In doing observations of open classrooms, I was concerned that my presence, particularly the way kids flocked around me as soon as I entered the classroom, was distorting the situation to the point where it was impossible to do good observations. Lillian laughed and suggested to me that what I was experiencing was the way those classrooms actually were. She went on to note that this was common among visitors to schools; they were always concerned that the teacher, knowing visitors were coming, whipped the kids into shape for those visitors. She suggested that under the best of circumstances a teacher might get kids to move out of habitual patterns into some model mode of behavior for as much as 10 or 15 minutes, but that, habitual patterns being what they were, kids would rapidly revert to normal behaviors and whatever artificiality might have been introduced by the presence of the visitor would likely become apparent.

Evaluators and researchers should strive to neither overestimate nor underestimate their effects but to take seriously their responsibility to describe and study what those effects are.

A second concern about evaluator effects arises from the possibility that the evaluator changes during the course of the evaluation. In Chapter 7 on interviewing I offered several examples including how, in a study of child sexual abuse, those involved were deeply affected by what they heard. One of the ways this sometimes happens in anthropological research is when participant observers "go native" and become absorbed into the local culture. The epitome of this in a shorter-term observation is the story of the observers who became converted to Christianity while observing a Billy Graham crusade (Lang and Lang 1960). Evaluators sometimes become personally involved with program participants or staff and therefore lose their sensitivity to the full range of events occurring in the setting.

Johnson (1975) and Glazer (1972) have reflected on how they and others have been changed by doing field research. The consensus of advice on how to deal with the problem of changes in the observers as a result of involvement in research is similar to advice about how to deal with the reactive effects created by the presence of observers.

> It is central to the method of participant observation that changes will occur in the observer; the important point, of course, is to record these changes. Field notes, introspection, and conversations with informants and colleagues provide the major means of measuring this dimension, . . . for to be insensitive to shifts in one's own attitudes opens the way for placing naive interpretations on the complex set of events under analysis. (Denzin 1978b:200)

The third concern about inquirer effects has to do with the extent to which the predispositions or biases of the evaluator may affect data analysis and interpretations. This issue carries mixed messages because, on the one hand, rigorous data collection and analytical procedures, like triangulation, are aimed at substantiating the validity of the data and minimizing inquirer biases; on the other hand, the interpretative and constructivist perspectives remind us that data from and about humans inevitably represent some degree of perspective rather than absolute truth. Getting close enough to the situation observed to experience it firsthand means that researchers can learn from their experiences, thereby generating personal insights, but that closeness makes their objectivity suspect. "For social scientists to refuse to treat their own behavior as data from which one can learn is really tragic" (Scriven 1972a:99). In effect, all of the procedures for validating and verifying analysis that have been presented in this chapter are aimed at reducing distortions introduced by inquirer predisposition. Still, people who use different criteria in determining evidential credibility will come at this issue from

difference stances and end up with different conclusions.

Consider the interviewing stance of *empathic neutrality* introduced in Chapter 2 and elaborated in Chapter 7. An empathically neutral inquirer will be perceived as caring about and interested in the people being studied, but neutral about the content of what they reveal. House (1977) balances the caring, interested stance against independence and impartiality for evaluators, a stance that also applies to those working according to the standards of traditional science.

> The evaluator must be seen as caring, as interested, as responsive to the relevant arguments. He must be impartial rather than simply objective. The impartiality of the evaluator must be seen as that of an actor in events, one who is responsive to the appropriate arguments but in whom the contending forces are balanced rather than non-existent. The evaluator must be seen as not having previously decided in favor of one position or the other. (House 1977:45-46)

But neutrality and impartiality are not easy stances to achieve. Denzin (1989b) cites a number of scholars who have concluded, as he does, that every researcher brings preconceptions and interpretations to the problem being studied, regardless of methods used.

> All researchers take sides, or are partisans for one point of view or another. Value-free interpretive research is impossible. This is the case because every researcher brings preconceptions and interpretations to the problem being studied. The term *hermeneutical circle or situation* refers to this basic fact of research. All scholars are caught in the circle of interpretation. They can never be free of the hermeneutical situation. This means that scholars

must state beforehand their prior interpretations of the phenomenon being investigated. Unless these meanings and values are clarified, their effects on subsequent interpretations remain clouded and often misunderstood. (Denzin 1989b:23)

Earlier (Exhibit 9.1) I presented five sets of criteria for judging the quality of qualitative inquiry. Those varying frameworks offer different perspectives on how inquirers should deal with concerns about bias. Neutrality and impartiality are expected when qualitative work is being judged by traditional scientific criteria or by evaluation standards, thus the source of House's admonition quoted above. In contrast, constructivist analysts are expected to deal with these issues through conscious and committed reflexivity—entering the *hermeneutical circle of interpretation* and therein reflecting on and analyzing how their perspective interacts with the perspectives they encounter. Artistic inquirers often deal with issues of how they personally relate to their work by invoking aesthetic criteria: Judge the work on its artistic merits. When critical change criteria are applied in judging reactivity, the issue becomes whether, how, and to what extent the inquiry furthered the cause or enhanced the well-being of those involved and studied; neutrality is eschewed in favor of explicitly using the inquiry process to facilitate change, or at least illuminate the conditions needed for change.

The politics of evaluation mean that individual evaluators must make their own peace with how they are going to describe what they do. The meaning and connotations of words such as *objectivity, subjectivity, neutrality,* and *impartiality* will have to be worked out with particular stakeholders in specific evaluation settings. Essentially, these are all concerns about the extent to which the evaluator's findings can be trusted; that is, trustworthiness can be understood as one dimension of perceived methodological rigor (Lincoln and Guba 1986; Glesne 1999). For better or worse, the trustworthiness of the data is tied directly to the trustworthiness of the person who collects and analyzes the data—and his or her demonstrated competence. Competence is demonstrated by using the verification and validation procedures necessary to establish the quality of analysis and thereby building a "track record" of quality work.

Intellectual Rigor

The thread that runs through this discussion of credibility is the importance of intellectual rigor, professional integrity, and methodological competence. There are no simple formulas or clear-cut rules about how to do a credible, high-quality analysis. The task is to do one's best to make sense of things. A qualitative analyst returns to the data over and over again to see if the constructs, categories, explanations, and interpretations make sense, if they really reflect the nature of the phenomena. Creativity, intellectual rigor, perseverance, insight—these are the intangibles that go beyond the routine application of scientific procedures. As Nobel prize-winning physicist Percy Bridgman put it: "There is no scientific method as such, but the vital feature of a scientist's procedure has been merely to do his utmost with his mind, *no holds barred*" (quoted in Mills 1961:58).

▣ The Paradigms Debate and Credibility

We come now to the third leg of the credibility triangle, the first two having been (1) *rigorous methods* for doing fieldwork that yield

GUIDELINES FOR QUALITY IN AUTOBIOGRAPHICAL FORMS OF SELF-STUDY RESEARCH

- Autobiographical self-studies should ring true and enable connection.
- Self-studies should promote insight and interpretation.
- Autobiographical self-study research must engage history forthrightly and the author must take an honest stand.
- Authentic voice is a necessary but not sufficient condition for the scholarly standing of a biographical self-study.
- The autobiographical self-study researcher has an ineluctable obligation to seek to improve the learning situation not only for the self but for the other.
- Powerful autobiographical self-studies portray character development and include dramatic action: Something genuine is at stake in the story.
- Quality autobiographical self-studies attend carefully to persons in context or setting.
- Quality autobiographical self-studies offer fresh perspectives on established truths.
- To be scholarship, edited conversation or correspondence must not only have coherence and structure, but that coherence and structure should provide argumentation and convincing evidence.
- Interpretations made of self-study data should not only reveal but also interrogate the relationships, contradictions, and limits of the views presented. (adapted from Bullogh and Pinnegar 2001:13-21)

high-quality data that are systematically analyzed with attention to issues of credibility and (2) the *credibility of the researcher,* which is dependent on training, experience, track record, status, and presentation of self. We take up now the issue of *philosophical belief in the value of qualitative inquiry,* that is, a fundamental appreciation of naturalistic inquiry, qualitative methods, inductive analysis, purposeful sampling, and holistic thinking.

The use of qualitative methods can be quite controversial. The controversy stems from the long-standing debate in science over how best to study and understand the world. As discussed in earlier chapters, the debate sometimes takes the form of qualitative versus quantitative methods, or science versus phenomenology, or positivism versus constructivism, or realism versus interpretivism. How the debate is framed depends on the perspectives that people bring to it and the language available to them to talk about it. The debate is rooted in philosophical differences about the nature of reality and epistemological differences about what constitutes knowledge and how it is created. This has come to be called "the paradigms debate," a paradigm in this case being a particular worldview where philosophy and methods intersect to determine what kinds of evidence one finds acceptable. The literature on the paradigms debate is extensive (cf. Denzin and Lincoln 2000b; Tashakkori and Teddlie 1998; Patton 1997a: Chapter 12; Shadish 1995a, 1995b, 1995c; Guba 1991; Fetterman 1988a, 1988b; Lincoln and Guba 1985, 1986, 2000; Cronbach 1975; Guba and Lincoln 1981; Reichardt and Cook 1979; Rist 1977; Campbell 1974, 1999a,

1999b). The point here is to alert those new to the debate that it has been and can be intense, divisive, emotional, and rancorous. **Both scientists and nonscientists often hold strong opinions about what constitutes credible evidence.** These opinions are paradigm derived and paradigm dependent because a paradigm constitutes a worldview built on implicit assumptions, accepted definitions, comfortable habits, values defended as truths, and beliefs projected as reality. As such, paradigms are deeply embedded in the socialization of adherents and practitioners telling them what is important, legitimate, and reasonable. Paradigms are also normative, telling the practitioner what to do without the necessity of long existential or epistemological consideration. But it is this aspect of paradigms that constitutes both their strength and their weakness— their strength in that it makes action possible, their weakness in that the very reason for action is hidden in the unquestioned assumptions of the paradigm.

Given the often controversial nature of qualitative findings and the necessity, on occasion, to be able to explain and even defend the value and appropriateness of qualitative approaches, the sections that follow will briefly discuss the most common concerns. I'll then tell you how to make the case that *the debate is over,* or as my teenage daughter says, "That's so 10 minutes ago."

First, however, to set the context and acknowledge that the debate continues for many, let me share a story to illustrate the antagonisms that sometimes undergird (and undermine) the debate. A former student sent me the following story, which she had received as an e-mail chain letter, a matter of interest only because it suggests widespread distribution.

Once upon a time, not so very long ago, a group of statisticians (hereafter known as "quants") and a party of qualitative methodologists (hereafter known as "quals") found themselves together on a train traveling to the same professional meeting. The quals, all of whom had tickets, observed that the quants had only one ticket for their whole group.

"How can you all travel on one ticket?" asked a qual.

"We have our methods," replied a quant.

Later, when the conductor came to punch tickets, all the quants slipped quickly behind the door of the toilet. When the conductor knocked on the door, the head quant slipped their one ticket under the door, thoroughly fooling the conductor.

On their return from the conference, the two groups again found themselves on the same train. The qualitative researchers, having learned from the quants, had schemed to share a single ticket. They were chagrined, therefore, to learn that, this time, the statisticians had boarded with no tickets.

"We know how you traveled together with one ticket," revealed a qual, "but how can you possibly get away with no tickets?"

"We have new methods," replied a quant.

Later, when the conductor approached, all the quals crowded into the toilet. The head statistician followed them and knocked authoritatively on the toilet door. The quals slipped their one and only ticket under the door. The head quant took the ticket and joined the other quants in a different toilet. The quals were subsequently discovered without tickets, publicly humiliated, and tossed off the train at its next stop.

Beyond the Numbers Game

Philosopher of science Thomas H. Kuhn (1970), having studied extensively the value systems of scientists, observed that "the most deeply held values concern predictions" and "quantitative predictions are preferable to qualitative ones" (pp. 184-85).

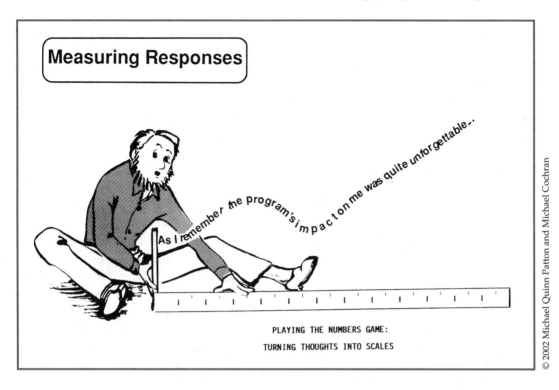

Measuring Responses

As I remember the program's impact on me was quite unforgettable...

PLAYING THE NUMBERS GAME:
TURNING THOUGHTS INTO SCALES

The methodological status hierarchy in science ranks "hard data" above "soft data" where "hardness" refers to the precision of statistics. Qualitative data, then, carry the stigma of "being soft." This carries over into the public arena, especially in the media and among policymakers, creating what has been called "the tyranny of numbers" (Eberstadt, Eberstadt, and Moynihan 1995).

How can one deal with a lingering bias against qualitative methods?

The starting point is understanding and being able to communicate the particular strengths of qualitative methods (Chapters 1 and 2) and the kinds of evaluation and other applications for which qualitative data are especially appropriate (Chapter 4). It is also helpful to understand the special seductiveness of numbers in modern society. Numbers convey a sense of precision and accuracy even if the measurements that yielded the numbers are relatively unreliable, in-

valid, and meaningless (for examples, see Hausman 2000; Huff and Geis 1993). Indeed, Gephart (1988) has designated "ethnostatistics" as a form of ethnographic study of groups that routinely produce statistics, focusing on the technical and operational assumptions involved in the production of statistics and deconstructing statistics as a rhetorical device in research and the public arena.

The point, however, is not to be anti-numbers. The point is to be *pro-meaningful-ness*. Thus, by knowing the strengths and weaknesses of both quantitative and qualitative data, you can help those with whom you dialogue focus on really important questions rather than, as sometimes happens, focusing primarily on how to generate numbers. The really important questions are, What's worth knowing? What data will be most illuminative? Most useful? How can the design be appropriately matched to the inquiry purpose? In evaluation, what design is most appropriate for the type of evaluation needed (formative, developmental, summative), the stage of program development, and the priority information needs of primary stakeholders? In policy formulation, one must understand where, how, and when qualitative data can inform and influence policy processes, a matter examined in depth by experienced policy analyst Ray Rist (2000).

Moreover, as noted in discussing the value of methods triangulation, the issue need not be quantitative *versus* qualitative methods, but rather how to combine the strengths of each in a multimethods approach to research and evaluation. Qualitative methods are not weaker or softer than quantitative approaches. Qualitative methods are *different*. Furthermore, "we no longer need to regard qualitative research as provisional, because qualitative studies have already assembled a usable, cumulative body of knowledge" (Silverman 1997:1). Given that context, let's examine some ways of reframing old quantitative-qualitative debate issues.

Beyond Objectivity and Subjectivity: New Concepts, New Language

Science places great value on objectivity. Often the primary reason decision makers commission an evaluation is to get objective data from an independent and objective source external to the program being evaluated. The charge that qualitative methods are inevitably "subjective" casts an aspersion connoting the very antithesis of scientific inquiry. Objectivity is traditionally considered the sine qua non of the scientific method. To be subjective means to be biased, unreliable, and irrational. Subjective data

imply opinion rather than fact, intuition rather than logic, impression rather than confirmation. Chapter 2 briefly discussed concerns about objectivity versus subjectivity, but I return to the issue here to address how these concerns affect the credibility and utility of qualitative analysis.

Social scientists are exhorted to eschew subjectivity and make sure that their work is "objective." The conventional means for controlling subjectivity and maintaining objectivity are the methods of quantitative social science: distance from the setting and people being studied, formal operationalism and quantitative measurement, manipulation of isolated variables, and experimental designs. Yet, the ways in which measures are constructed in psychological tests, questionnaires, cost-benefit indicators, and routine management information systems are no less open to the intrusion of biases than making observations in the field or asking questions in interviews. Numbers do not protect against bias; they merely disguise it. All statistical data are based on *someone's* definition of what to measure and how to measure it. An "objective" statistic such as the consumer price index is really made up of very subjective decisions about what consumer items to include in the index. Periodically, government economists change the basis and definition of such indices.

Scriven (1972a) has insisted that quantitative methods are no more synonymous with objectivity than qualitative methods are synonymous with subjectivity:

> Errors like this are too simple to be explicit. They are inferred confusions in the ideological foundations of research, its interpretations, its application. . . . It is increasingly clear that the influence of ideology on methodology and of the latter on the training and behavior of researchers and on the identification and dis-

bursement of support is staggeringly powerful. Ideology is to research what Marx suggested the economic factor was to politics and what Freud took sex to be for psychology. (p. 94)

Scriven's lengthy discussion of objectivity and subjectivity in educational research deserves careful reading by students and others concerned by this distinction. He skillfully detaches the notions of objectivity and subjectivity from their traditionally narrow associations with quantitative and qualitative methodology, respectively. He presents a clear explanation of how objectivity has been confused with consensual validation of something by multiple observers. Yet, a little research will yield many instances of "scientific blunders" (Youngson 1998) where the majority of scientists (or other people) were factually wrong while *one* dissenting observer described things as they actually were (Kuhn 1970).

Qualitative rigor has to do with the quality of the observations made by an evaluator. Scriven emphasizes the importance of being factual about observations rather than being distant from the phenomenon being studied. **Distance does not guarantee objectivity; it merely guarantees distance.** Nevertheless, in the end, Scriven (1998) still finds the ideal of objectivity worth striving for as a counter to bias, and he continues to find the language of objectivity serviceable.

In contrast, Lincoln and Guba (1986), as noted earlier, have suggested replacing the traditional mandate to be objective with an emphasis on *trustworthiness* and *authenticity* by being balanced, fair, and conscientious in taking account of multiple perspectives, multiple interests, and multiple realities. They have suggested that researchers and evaluators can learn something about these attributes from the stance of investigative journalists.

Journalism in general and investigative journalism in particular are moving away from the criterion of objectivity to an emergent criterion usually labeled "fairness." . . . Objectivity assumes a single reality to which the story or evaluation must be isomorphic; it is in this sense a one-perspective criterion. It assumes that an agent can deal with an objective (or another person) in a nonreactive and noninteractive. It is an absolute criterion.

Journalists are coming to feel that objectivity in that sense is unattainable. . . .

Enter "fairness" as a substitute criterion. In contrast to objectivity, fairness has these features:

- It assumes multiple realities or truths— hence a test of fairness is whether or not "both" sides of the case are presented, and there may even be multiple sides.

- It is adversarial rather than one-perspective in nature. Rather than trying to hew the line with the truth, as the objective reporter does, the fair reporter seeks to present each side of the case in the manner of an advocate—as, for example, attorneys do in making a case in court. The presumption is that the public, like a jury, is more likely to reach an equitable decision after having heard each side presented with as much vigor and commitment as possible.

- It is assumed that the subject's reaction to the reporter and interactions between them heavily determines what the reporter perceives. Hence one test of fairness is the length to which the reporter will go to test his own biases and rule them out.

- It is a relative criterion that is measured by *balance* rather than by isomorphism to enduring truth.

Clearly, evaluators have a great deal to learn from this development. (Guba 1981:76-77)

Earlier in this chapter, I discussed the credibility of the inquirer and noted that trustworthiness of the inquirer is one dimension of rigor. The issue, then, is not really about objectivity in the abstract, but about researcher credibility and trustworthiness, about fairness and balance. How, then, does one deal with concerns about objectivity?

It is helpful to know that scholarly philosophers of science now typically doubt the possibility of anyone or any method being totally "objective." But subjectivity, even if acknowledged as inevitable (Peshkin 1988), carries negative connotations at such a deep level and for so many people that the very term can be an impediment to mutual understanding. For this and other reasons, as a way of elaborating with any insight the nature of the research process, the notion of subjectivity may have become as useless as the notion of objectivity.

> The death of the notion that objective truth is attainable in projects of social inquiry has been generally recognized and widely accepted by scholars who spend time thinking about such matters. . . . I will take this recognition as a starting point in calling attention to a second corpse in our midst, an entity to which many refer as if it were still alive. Instead of exploring the meaning of subjectivity in qualitative educational research, I want to advance the notion that following the failure of the objectivists to maintain the viability of their epistemology, the concept of subjectivity has been likewise drained of its usefulness and therefore no longer has any meaning. Subjectivity, I feel obliged to report, is also dead. (Barone 2000:161)

Barone (2000:169-70) goes on to argue in favor of the "criterion of critical persuasiveness" based on "neopragmatisim," essentially elevating a search for utility above the

futile search for truth, the topic we consider in the next section. As this is written we are still searching for language and terminology to transcend the old and outdated divisions of objective versus subjective. No consensus about new terminology has emerged, and given the five different sets of criteria for judging qualitative inquiry I identified at the beginning of this chapter, it seems unlikely that a consensus is on the horizon. This can be liberating because it opens up the possibility of getting beyond the meaningless abstractions of objectivity and subjectivity and moving instead to carefully selecting *descriptive* methodological language that best describes your own inquiry processes and procedures. That is, don't label those processes as "objective," "subjective," "trustworthy," "neutral," "authentic," or "artistic." Describe them and what you bring to them and how you've reflected on them, and then let the reader be persuaded, or not, by the intellectual and methodological rigor, meaningfulness, value, and utility of the result. In the meantime, be very careful how you use particular terms in specific contexts, a point made nicely by the following cautionary tale.

During a tour of America, former British Prime Minister Winston Churchill attended a buffet luncheon at which chicken was served. As he returned to the buffet for a second helping he asked, "May I have some more breast?"

His hostess, looking embarrassed, explained that "in this country we ask for white meat or dark meat."

Churchill, taking the white meat he was offered, apologized and returned to his table.

The next morning the hostess received a beautiful orchid from Churchill with the following card: "I would be most obliged if you would wear this on your white meat."

© 2002 Michael Quinn Patton and Michael Cochran

Reflections on Truth and Utility as Criteria of Quality

L ady, I do not make up things. That is lies. Lies are not true. But the truth
could be made up if you know how. And that's the truth.

—Lily Tomlin

One paradigm-related belief that affects how people react to qualitative data involves how they think about the idea of "Truth." "Do you, as a qualitative researcher, swear to tell the truth, the whole truth and nothing but the truth?" I was once asked this very question by a hostile school researcher at a public meeting who sought to embarrass me in front of a school board in a debate about standardized tests. I knew from previous discussion that he had read, in a previous edition of this book, this very section expressing doubt about the utility of truth as a criterion of quality and I suspected that he hoped to lure me into an academic-

sounding, arrogant, and philosophical discourse on the question "What is truth?" in the expectation that the public officials present would be alienated and dismiss my testimony. So I did *not* reply, "That depends on what *truth* means." I said simply: "Certainly I promise to respond honestly." Notice the shift from truth to honesty.

Lancelot Andrews, a 17th-century priest, observed that Pontius Pilate is recorded to have asked Jesus at his trial, "What is Truth?" Pilate asked his question, Andrews observed, "and then some other matter took him in the head, and so he rose and went his way before he had his answer." While the question "What is truth?" may be intrinsically rhetorical and unanswerable, beliefs about the nature of truth affect how one views the findings of research and evaluations. So the question remains: "Do you, as a qualitative researcher, swear to tell the truth, the whole truth and nothing but the truth?"

The researcher applying traditional social science criteria might respond, "I can show you truth insofar as it is revealed by the data."

The constructivist might answer: "I can show you multiple truths."

The artistically inclined might suggest that "fiction gets at truth better than nonfiction" and that "beauty is truth."

The critical theorist could explain that "truth depends on one's consciousness" or the activist might say, "I offer you praxis. Here is where I take my stand. This is true for me."

The pragmatic evaluator might reply, "I can show you what is useful. What is useful is true."

Finding Truth can be a heavy burden. I once had a student who was virtually paralyzed in writing an evaluation report because he wasn't sure if the patterns he thought he had uncovered were really true. I suggested that he not try to convince himself or others that his findings were true in any absolute sense but, rather, that he had done the best job he could in describing the patterns that appeared to him to be present in the data and that he present those patterns as *his* perspective based on his analysis and interpretation of the data he had collected. Even if he believed that what he eventually produced was Truth, sophisticated people reading the report would know that what he presented was no more than his perspective, and they would judge that perspective by their own commonsense understandings and use the information according to how it contributed to their own needs.

The entire October 2000 issue of the technology and business magazine *Forbes ASAP* was devoted to writings on "what is true?" with contributions from 50 people drawn from history, science, media, religion, business, technology, and popular culture. Surprise. They didn't agree.

Earlier I cited the research of Weiss and Bucuvalas (1980) that decision makers apply both truth tests and utility tests to evaluation. *Truth,* in this case, however, means reasonably accurate and believable data rather than data that are true in some absolute sense. Savvy policymakers know better than most the context- and perspective-laden nature of competing truths. Qualitative inquiry can present accurate data on various perspectives, including the evaluator's perspective, without the burden of determining that only one perspective must be true. Smith (1978), pondering these questions, has noted that in order to act in the world we often accept either approximations to truth or even untruths:

> For example, when one drives from city to city, one acts as if the earth is flat and does not try to calculate the earth's curvature in planning the trip, even though acting as if the earth is flat means acting on an untruth. Therefore, in our study of evaluation methodology, two criteria replace exact truth as paramount: practical utility and level of certainty. The level of certainty required to make an adequate judgment under the law differs depending on whether one is considering an administrative hearing, an inquest, or a criminal case. Although it seems obvious that much greater certainty about the nature of things is required when legislators set national and educational policy than when a district superintendent decides whether to continue a local program, the rhetoric in evaluation implies that the same high level of certainty is required of both cases. If we were to first determine the level of cer-

TRUTH VERSUS RELATIVISM

"Postmodern work is often accused of being relativistic (and evil) since it does not advocate a universal, independent standard of truth. In fact, relativism is only an issue for those who believe there is a foundation, a structure against which other positions can be objectively judged. In effect, this position implies that there is no alternative between objectivism and relativism. Postmodernists dispute the assumptions that produce the objectivism/relativism binary since they think of truth as multiple, historical, contextual, contingent, political, and bound up in power relations. Refusing the binary does not lead to the abandonment of truth, however, as Foucault (1988) emphasizes when he says, 'I believe too much in truth not to suppose that there are different truths and different ways of speaking the truth' (p. 51).

"Furthermore, postmodernism does not imply that one does not discriminate among multiple truths, that 'anything goes.'... If there is no absolute truth to which every instance can be compared for its truth-value, if truth is instead multiple and contextual, then the call for ethical practice shifts from grand, sweeping statements about truth and justice to engagements with specific, complex problems that do not have generalizable solutions. This different state of affairs is not irresponsible, irrational, or nihilistic.... As with truth, postmodern critiques argue for multiple and historically specific forms of reason" (St. Pierre 2000:25).

tainty desired in a specific case, we could then more easily choose appropriate methods. Naturalistic descriptions give us greater certainty in our understanding of the nature of an educational process than randomized, controlled experiments do, but less certainty in our knowledge of the strength of a particular effect.... [O]ur first concern should be the practical utility of our knowledge, not its ultimate truthfulness. (p. 17)

In studying evaluation use (Patton 1997a), I found that decision makers did not expect evaluation reports to produce "Truth" in any fundamental sense. Rather, they viewed evaluation findings as additional information that they could and did combine with other information (political, experiential, other research, colleague opinions, etc.), all of which fed into a slow, evolutionary process of incremental decision making. Kvale (1987) echoed this interactive

and contextual approach to truth in emphasizing the "pragmatic validation" of findings in which the results of qualitative analysis are judged by their relevance to and use by those to whom findings are presented. This *criterion of utility* can be applied not only to evaluation but also to qualitative analyses of all kinds, including textual analysis. Barone (2000), having rejected objectivity and subjectivity as meaningless criteria in the postmodern age, makes the case for pragmatic utility as follows:

If all discourse is culturally contextual, how do we decide which deserves our attention and respect? The pragmatists offer the criterion of usefulness for this purpose.... An idea, like a tool, has no intrinsic value and is "true" only in its capacity to perform a desired service for its handler within a given situation. When the criterion of usefulness is applied to context-bound, historically situated transactions between itself and a text, it helps us to judge which textual experiences are to be valued. . . . The gates are opened for textual encounters, in any inquiry genre or tradition, that serve to fulfill an important human purpose. (pp. 169-70)

Focusing on the connection between truth tests and utility tests shifts attention back to credibility and quality, not as absolute generalizable judgments but as contextually dependent on the needs and interests of those receiving our analysis. This obliges researchers and evaluators to consider carefully how they present their work to others, with attention to the purpose to be fulfilled. That presentation should include reflections on how your perspective affected the questions you pursued in fieldwork, careful documentation of all procedures used so that others can review your methods for bias, and being open in describing the limitations of the perspective presented. Appendix 9.1 contains an in-depth description of how one qualitative inquirer, engaged in program "documentation," dealt with these issues in a long-term participant observer relationship. This excerpt, titled "A Documenter's Perspective," is based on the documenter's research journal and field notes. It moves the discussion from abstract philosophizing to day-to-day, in-the-trenches fieldwork encounters aimed at sorting out what is true (small *t*) and useful.

As one additional source of reflection on these issues, perhaps the following Sufi story will provide some guidance about the difference between truth and perspective. Sagely, in this encounter, Nasrudin gathers data to support his proposition about the nature of truth. Here's the story.

Mulla Nasrudin was on trial for his life. He was accused of no less a crime than treason by the king's ministers, wise men charged with advising on matters of great import. Nasrudin was charged with going from village to village inciting the people by saying, "The king's wise men do not speak truth. They do not even know what truth is. They are confused." Nasrudin was brought before the king and the court. "How do you plead, guilty or not guilty?"

"I am both guilty and not guilty," replied Nasrudin.

"What, then, is your defense?"

Nasrudin turned and pointed to the nine wise men who were assembled in the court. "Have each sage write an answer to the following question: 'What is water?' "

The king commanded the sages to do as they were asked. The answers were handed to the king, who read to the court what each sage had written.

The first wrote: "Water is to remove thirst."

The second: "It is the essence of life."

The third: "Rain."

The fourth: "A clear, liquid substance."

The fifth: "A compound of hydrogen and oxygen."

The sixth: "Water was given to us by God to use in cleansing and purifying ourselves before prayer."

The seventh: "It is many different things—rivers, wells, ice, lakes, so it depends."

The eighth: "A marvelous mystery that defies definition."

The ninth: "The poor man's wine."

Nasrudin turned to the court and the king, "I am guilty of saying that the wise men are confused. I am not, however, guilty of treason because, as you see, the wise men are confused. How can they know if I have committed treason if they cannot even decide what water is? If the sages cannot agree on the truth about water, something they consume every day, how can one expect that they can know the truth about other things?"

The king ordered that Nasrudin be set free.

From Generalizations to Extrapolations and Transferability

*T*he trouble with generalizations is that they don't apply to particulars.

—Yvonna S. Lincoln and Egon G. Guba (1985:110)

The pragmatic criterion of utility leads to the question of what one can do with qualitative findings. Certainly, the results illuminate a particular situation or small number of cases. But what of utility beyond the limited case or cases studied? Can qualitative findings be generalized?

Chapter 5 discussed the logic and value of purposeful sampling with small, but carefully selected, information-rich cases. Certain kinds of small samples, for example, a critical case, are selected and studied precisely because they have broader relevance. Other sampling strategies, for example, extreme cases (exemplars of excellence or failure), are selected for their potential to yield insights about principles that might be applied elsewhere. However, purposeful sampling is not widely understood. Thus, qualitative inquirers may encounter a predisposition toward large, random samples and disbelief in (or ignorance about) the value of small, purposeful samples. It is important in responding to such concerns that one fully understands the relative strengths and weaknesses of different sampling strategies. Nor are qualitative and quantitative samples incompatible. Chapter 5 discusses several mutually reinforcing combinations.

Shadish (1995a) argued that the core principles of generalization apply to both experiments and ethnographies (or qualitative methods generally). Both experiments and

case studies share the problem of being highly localized. Findings from a study, experimental or naturalistic in design, can be generalized according to five principles:

1. *The Principle of Proximal Similarity.* We generalize most confidently to applications where treatments, settings, populations, outcomes, and times are most similar to those in the original research. . . .

2. *The Principle of Heterogeneity of Irrelevancies.* We generalize most confidently when a research finding continues to hold over variations in persons, settings, treatments, outcome measures, and times that are presumed to be conceptually irrelevant. The strategy here is identifying irrelevancies, and where possible including a diverse array of them in the research so as to demonstrate generalization over them. . . .

3. *The Principle of Discriminant Validity.* We generalize most confidently when we can show that it is the target construct, and not something else, that is necessary to produce a research finding. . . .

4. *The Principle of Empirical Interpolation and Extrapolation.* We generalize most

confidently when we can specify the range of persons, settings, treatments, outcomes, and times over which the finding holds more strongly, less strongly, or not all. The strategy here is empirical exploration of the existing range of instances to discover how that range might generate variability in the finding for instances not studied. . . .

5. *The Principle of Explanation.* We generalize most confidently when we can specify completely and exactly (a) which parts of one variable (b) are related to which parts of another variable (c) through which mediating processes (d) with which salient interactions, for then we can transfer only those essential components to the new application to which we wish to generalize. The strategy here is breaking down the finding into component parts and processes so as to identify the essential ones. (Shadish 1995a: 424-26)

Still, deeper philosophical and epistemological issues are embedded in concerns about generalizing. What's desirable or hoped for in science (generalizations across time and space) runs into considerations about what's possible. Lee J. Cronbach (1975), one of the major figures in psychometrics and research methodology, has given considerable attention to the issue of generalizations. He has concluded that social phenomena are too variable and context bound to permit very significant empirical generalizations. Cronbach also compared generalizations in natural sciences with what was likely to be possible in behavioral and social sciences. His conclusion is that "generalizations decay. At one time a conclusion describes the existing situation well, at a later time it accounts for rather little variance, and ultimately is valid only as history" (p. 122).

In suggesting that generalizations have not stood up well in the sciences, Cronbach (1975) offered an alternative strategy that constitutes excellent advice for the qualitative analyst:

Instead of making generalization the ruling consideration in our research, I suggest that we reverse our priorities. An observer collecting data in a particular situation is in a position to appraise a practice or proposition in that setting, observing effects in context. In trying to describe and account for what happened, he will give attention to whatever variables were controlled, but he will give equally careful attention to uncontrolled conditions, to personal characteristics, and to events that occurred during treatment and measurement. As he goes from situation to situation, his first task is to describe and interpret the effect anew in each locale, perhaps taking into account factors unique to that locale or series of events. . . . When we give proper weight to local conditions, any generalization is a working hypothesis, not a conclusion. (pp. 124-25)

Robert Stake (1978, 1995, 2000), master of case methods, concurs with Cronbach that the first priority is to do justice to the specific case, to do a good job of "particularization" before looking for patterns across cases. He quotes William Blake on the subject: "To generalize is to be an idiot. To particularize is the lone distinction of merit. General knowledges are those that idiots possess." Stake (1978) continued:

Generalization may not be all that despicable, but particularization does deserve praise. To know particulars fleetingly, of course, is to know next to nothing. What becomes useful understanding is a full and thorough knowledge of the particular, recognizing it also in new and foreign contexts. That knowledge is a form of generalization too, not scientific induction but naturalistic generalization, arrived at by recognizing the similarities of objects and issues in and out of context and by sensing the natural covariations of happenings. To generalize this way is to be both intuitive and empirical, and not idiotic. (p. 6)

Stake extends "naturalistic generalizations" to include the kind of learning that readers take from their encounters with specific case studies. The "vicarious experience" that comes from reading a rich case account can contribute to the social construction of knowledge that, in a cumulative sense, builds general, if not necessarily generalizable, knowledge.

Readers assimilate certain descriptions and assertions into memory. When a researcher's narrative provides opportunity for vicarious experience, readers extend their memories of happenings. Naturalistic, ethnographic case materials, to some extent, parallel actual experience, feeding into the most fundamental processes of awareness and understanding . . . [to permit] *naturalistic generalizations.* The reader comes to know some things told, as if he or she had experienced it. Enduring meanings come from encounter, and are modified and reinforced by repeated encounter.

In life itself, this occurs seldom to the individual alone but in the presence of others. In a social process, together they bend, spin, consolidate, and enrich their understandings. We come to know what has happened partly in terms of what others reveal as their experience. The case researcher emerges from one social experience, the observation, to choreograph another, the report. Knowledge is socially constructed, so we constructivists believe, and, in their experiential and contextual accounts, case study researchers assist readers in the construction of knowledge. (Stake 2000:442)

Guba (1978) considered three alternative positions that might be taken in regard to the generalizability of naturalistic inquiry findings:

1. Generalizability is a chimera; it is impossible to generalize in a scientific sense at all. . . .

2. Generalizability continues to be important, and efforts should be made to meet normal scientific criteria that pertain to it. . . .

3. Generalizability is a fragile concept whose meaning is ambiguous and whose power is variable. (pp. 68-70)

Having reviewed these three positions, Guba proposed a resolution that recognizes the diminished value and changed meaning of generalizations and echoes Cronbach's emphasis, cited above, on treating conclusions as hypotheses for future applicability and testing rather than as definitive.

The evaluator should do what he can to establish the generalizability of his findings. . . . Often naturalistic inquiry can establish at least the "limiting cases" relevant to a given situation. But in the spirit of naturalistic inquiry he should regard each possible generalization only as a working hypothesis, to be tested again in the next encounter and again in the encounter after that. For the naturalistic inquiry evaluator, premature closure is a cardinal sin, and tolerance of ambiguity a virtue. (Guba 1978:70)

Guba and Lincoln (1981) emphasized appreciation of and attention to context as a natural limit to naturalistic generalizations. They ask, "What can a generalization be except an assertion that is context free? [Yet] *it is virtually impossible to imagine any human behavior that is not heavily mediated by the context* in which it occurs" (p. 62). They proposed substituting the concepts "transferability" and "fittingness" for generalization when dealing with qualitative findings:

> The degree of *transferability* is a direct function of the *similarity* between the two contexts, what we shall call *"fittingness."* Fittingness is defined as degree of congruence between sending and receiving contexts. If context A and context B are "sufficiently" congruent, then working hypotheses from the sending originating context may be applicable in the receiving context. (Lincoln and Guba 1985:124)

Cronbach and Associates (1980) have offered a middle ground in the methodological paradigms debate over generalizability. They found little value in experimental designs that are so focused on carefully controlling cause and effect (internal validity) that the findings are largely irrelevant beyond that highly controlled experimental situation (external validity). On the other hand, they were equally concerned about entirely idiosyncratic case studies that yield little of use beyond the case study setting. They were also skeptical that highly specific empirical findings would be meaningful under new conditions. They suggested instead that designs balance depth and breadth, realism and control so as to permit reasonable "extrapolation" (pp. 231-35).

Unlike the usual meaning of the term *generalization,* an *extrapolation* clearly connotes that one has gone beyond the narrow confines of the data to think about other applications of the findings. Extrapolations are modest speculations on the likely applicability of findings to other situations under similar, but not identical, conditions. Extrapolations are logical, thoughtful, case derived, and problem oriented rather than statistical and probabilistic. Extrapolations can

be particularly useful when based on information-rich samples and designs, that is, studies that produce relevant information carefully targeted to specific concerns about both the present and the future. Users of evaluation, for example, will usually expect evaluators to thoughtfully extrapolate from their findings in the sense of pointing out lessons learned and potential applications to future efforts. Sampling strategies in qualitative evaluations can be planned with the stakeholders' desire for extrapolation in mind.

⑤ The Credibility Issue in Retrospect: Increased Legitimacy for Qualitative Methods

Beyond the Qualitative-Quantitative Debate

This chapter has reviewed ways of enhancing the quality and credibility of qualitative analysis by dealing with three distinct but related inquiry concerns:

- *rigorous methods* for doing fieldwork that yield high-quality data that are systematically analyzed with attention to issues of credibility;

- the *credibility of the researcher,* which is dependent on training, experience, track record, status, and presentation of self; and

- *philosophical belief in the value of qualitative inquiry,* that is, a fundamental appreciation of naturalistic inquiry, qualitative methods, inductive analysis, purposeful sampling, and holistic thinking.

The debate between qualitative and quantitative methodologists has often been strident. In recent years, the debate has softened. A consensus has gradually emerged that the important challenge is to appropriately match methods to purposes, questions, and issues and not to universally advocate any single methodological approach for all inquiry situations. Indeed, eminent methodologist Thomas Cook, one of evaluation's luminaries, pronounced in his keynote address to the 1995 International Evaluation Conference in Vancouver that "qualitative researchers have won the qualitative-quantitative debate."

Won in what sense?

Won acceptance.

The validity of experimental methods and quantitative measurement, appropriately used, was never in doubt. Now, qualitative methods have ascended to a level of parallel respectability. I have found increased interest in and acceptance of qualitative methods in particular and multiple methods in general. Especially in evaluation, a consensus has emerged that researchers and evaluators need to know and use a variety of methods to be responsive to the nuances of particular empirical questions and the idiosyncrasies of specific stakeholder needs.

The credibility and respectability of qualitative methods vary across disciplines, university departments, professions, time periods, and countries. In the field I know best, program evaluation, the increased legitimacy of qualitative methods is a function of more examples of useful, high-quality evaluations employing qualitative methods and an increased commitment to providing useful and understandable information based on stakeholders' concerns. Other factors that contribute to increased credibility include more and higher-quality training in qualitative methods and the publication of a substantial qualitative literature.

The history of the paradigms debate parallels the history of evaluation. The earliest evaluations focused largely on quantitative measurement of clear, specific goals and objectives. With the widespread social and educational experimentation of the 1960s and early 1970s, evaluation designs were aimed at comparing the effectiveness of different programs and treatments through rigorous controls and experiments. This was the period when the quantitative/experimental paradigm dominated. By the middle 1970s, the paradigms debate had become a major focus of evaluation discussions and writings. By the late 1970s, the alternative qualitative/naturalistic paradigm had been fully articulated (Guba 1978; Patton 1978; Stake 1975, 1978). During this period, concern about finding ways to increase use became predominant in evaluation, and evaluators began discussing standards. A period of pragmatism and dialogue followed, during which calls for and experiences with multiple methods and a synthesis of paradigms became more common. The advice of Cronbach and Associates (1980), in their important book on reform of program evaluation, was widely taken to heart: "The evaluator will be wise not to declare allegiance to either a quantitative-scientific-summative methodology or a qualitative-naturalistic-descriptive methodology" (p. 7).

Signs of détente and pragmatism now abound. Methodological tolerance, flexibility, eclecticism, and concern for appropriateness rather than orthodoxy now characterize the practice, literature, and discussions of evaluation. Several developments seem to me to explain the withering of the methodological paradigms debate.

1. The articulation of professional standards has emphasized methodological appropriateness rather than paradigm orthodoxy (Joint Committee 1994). Within the standards as context, the focus on conducting evaluations that are useful, practical,

ethical, and accurate, and accumulation of practical evaluation experience during the past two decades, has reduced paradigms polarization.

2. The strengths and weaknesses of both quantitative/experimental methods and qualitative/naturalistic methods are now better understood. In the original debate, quantitative methodologists tended to attack some of the worst examples of qualitative evaluations while the qualitative evaluators tended to hold up for critique the worst examples of quantitative/experimental approaches. With the accumulation of experience and confidence, exemplars of both qualitative and quantitative approaches have emerged with corresponding analyses of the strengths and weaknesses of each. This has permitted more balance and a better understanding of the situations for which various methods are most appropriate as well as grounded experience in how to combine methods.

3. A broader conceptualization of evaluation, and of evaluator training, has directed attention to the relation of methods to other aspects of evaluation, such as use, and has therefore reduced the intensity of the methods debate as a topic unto itself. Methods decisions are now framed in a broader context of use that, I believe, has reduced the intensity of the paradigms debate, a debate that often went on in absolute, context-free terms.

4. Advances in methodological sophistication and diversity within both paradigms have strengthened diverse applications to evaluation problems. The proliferation of books and journals in evaluation, including but not limited to methods contributions, has converted the field into a rich mosaic that cannot be reduced to quantitative versus qualitative in primary orientation.

Moreover, the upshot of all the developmental work in qualitative methods is that, as documented in Chapter 3, today there is as much variation among qualitative researchers as there is between qualitatively and quantitatively oriented scholars.

5. Support for methodological eclecticism from major figures and institutions in evaluation increased methodological tolerance. When eminent measurement and methods scholars such as Donald Campbell and Lee J. Cronbach began publicly recognizing the contributions that qualitative methods could make, the acceptability of qualitative/naturalistic approaches was greatly enhanced. Another important endorsement of multiple methods came from the Program Evaluation and Methodology Division of the U.S. General Accounting Office (GAO), which arguably did the most important and influential evaluation work at the national level. Under the leadership of Assistant Comptroller General and former American Evaluation Association president (1995) Eleanor Chelimsky, the GAO published a series of methods manuals including *Case Study Evaluations* (1987), *Prospective Methods* (1989), and *The Evaluation Synthesis* (1992). The GAO manual *Designing Evaluations* (1991) puts the paradigms debate to rest as it describes what constitutes a "strong evaluation":

> Strength is not judged by adherence to a particular paradigm. It is determined by use and technical adequacy, whatever the method, within the context of purpose, time and resources.
>
> Strong evaluations employ methods of analysis that are appropriate to the question, support the answer with evidence, document the assumptions, procedures, and modes of analysis, and rule out the competing evidence. Strong studies pose questions clearly, address

them appropriately, and draw inferences commensurate with the power of the design and the availability, validity, and reliability of the data. Strength should not be equated with complexity. Nor should strength be equated with the degree of statistical manipulation of data. Neither infatuation with complexity nor statistical incantation makes an evaluation stronger.

The strength of an evaluation is not defined by a particular method. Longitudinal, experimental, quasi-experimental, before-and-after, and case study evaluations can be either strong or weak. . . . That is, the strength of an evaluation has to be judged within the context of the question, the time and cost constraints, the design, the technical adequacy of the data collection and analysis, and the presentation of the findings. A strong study is technically adequate and useful—in short, it is high in quality. (pp. 15-16)

6. Evaluation professional societies have supported exchanges of views and high-quality professional practice in an environment of tolerance and eclecticism. The evaluation professional societies and journals serve a variety of people from different disciplines who operate in different kinds of organizations at different levels, in and out of the public sector, and in and out of universities. This diversity, and opportunities to exchange views and perspectives, has contributed to the emergent pragmatism, eclecticism, and tolerance in the field. A good example is the volume of *New Directions for Program Evaluation* titled "The Qualitative-Quantitative Debate: New Perspectives" (Reichardt and Rallis 1994). The tone of the eight distinguished contributions in that volume is captured by such phrases as "peaceful coexistence," "each tradition can learn from the other," "compromise solution," "important shared characteristics," and "a call for a new partnership."

7. There is increased advocacy of and experience in combining qualitative and quantitative approaches. The Reichardt and Rallis (1994) volume *The Qualitative-Quantitative Debate: New Perspectives* just cited also included these themes: "blended approaches," "integrating the qualitative and quantitative," "possibilities for integration," "qualitative plus quantitative," and "working together." (For elaboration of these reasons for the withering of the paradigms debate, see Patton 1997a: 290-99.)

Matching Claims and Criteria

The withering of the methodological paradigms debate holds out the hope that studies of all kinds can be judged on their merits according to the claims they make and the evidence marshaled in support of those claims. The thing that distinguished the five sets of criteria introduced at the beginning of this chapter is that they support different kinds of claims. Traditional scientific claims, constructivist claims, artistic claims, critical change claims, and evaluation claims will tend to emphasize different kinds of conclusions with varying implications. In judging claims and conclusions, validity of the claims made is only partly related to the methods used in the process.

Validity is a property of knowledge, not methods. No matter whether knowledge comes from an ethnography or an experiment, we may still ask the same kind of questions about the ways in which that knowledge is valid. To use an overly simplistic example, if someone claims to have nailed together two boards, we do not ask if their hammer is valid, but rather whether the two boards are now nailed together, and whether the claimant was, in fact, responsible for that result. In fact, this particular claim may be valid whether the nail was set

REALITY IS AMBIGUOUS

Excerpts of a speech by President Václav Havel upon receiving the Open Society Prize awarded by the Central European University in Budapest in 1999; translated by Paul Wilson (1999):

I have to admit that Hegel ... was probably right about one thing: reality is ambiguous. ... Where does patriotism end and nationalism and chauvinism begin? Where does civic solidarity end and tribal passion begin? Where does the spontaneous and thoroughly respectable delight in the remarkable athletic achievement of one's fellow citizens end, and the expropriation of someone else's achievement by a mob with no ideas and no personal sense of responsibility begin?

Reality, after all, is ambiguous and it is immensely difficult to have to continually distinguish among its different faces and to recognize immediately the point at which the good-natured jubilation of sports fans suddenly becomes the raging of deprived and inferior souls. ... How do we make such distinctions?

There are no exact guidelines. There are probably no guidelines at all. The only thing I can recommend at this stage is a sense of humor, and ability to see things in their ridiculous and absurd dimensions, to laugh at others and at ourselves, a sense of irony regarding everything that calls out for parody in this world. In other words, I can only recommend perspective and distance. Awareness of all the most dangerous kinds of vanity, both in others and in ourselves. A good mind. A modest certainty about the meaning of things. Gratitude for the gift of life and the courage to take responsibility for it. Vigilance of spirit.

in place by a hammer, an airgun, or the butt of a screwdriver. A hammer does not guarantee successful nailing, successful nailing does not require a hammer, and the validity of the claim is in principle separate from which tool was used. The same is true of methods in the social behavioral sciences. (Shadish 1995a:421)

This brings us back to a pragmatic focus on the utility of findings as a point of entry for determining what's at stake in the claims made in a study and therefore what criteria to use in assessing those claims. As I noted in opening this chapter, judgments about credibility and quality depend on criteria. And though this chapter has been devoted to ways of enhancing quality and credibility, all such efforts ultimately depend on the willingness of the inquirer to weigh the evidence carefully and be open to the possibility that what has been learned most from a particular inquiry is how to do it better next time. Canadian-born bacteriologist Oswald Avery, discoverer of DNA as the basic genetic material of the cell, worked for years in a small laboratory at the hospital of the Rockefeller Institute in New York City. Many of his initial hypotheses and research conclusions turned out, upon further investigation, to be wrong. His colleagues marveled that he never turned argumentative when findings countered his predictions and he never became discouraged. He was committed to learning and was often heard telling his students: "Whenever you fall, pick up something."

APPENDIX 9.1

兒 兒 兒

Case Study: A Documenter's Perspective

Introduction. This appendix provides a reflective case study, by Beth Alberty, of the struggle experienced by one internal, formative program evaluator of an innovative school art program as she tried to figure out how to provide useful information to program staff from the voluminous qualitative data she collected. Beth begins by describing what she means by "documentation" and then shares her experiences as a novice in analyzing the data, a process of moving from a mass of documentary material to a unified, holistic document.

Documentation

Documentation, as the word is commonly used, may refer to "slice of life" recordings in various media or to the marshaling of evidence in support of a position or point of view. We are familiar with "documentary" films; we require lawyers or journalists to "document" their cases. Both meanings contribute to my view of what documentation is, but they are far from describing it fully. Documentation, to my mind, is the interpretive reconstitution of a focal event, setting, project, or other phenomenon, based on observation and on descriptive records set in the context of guiding purposes and commitments.

I have always been a staff member of the situations I have documented, rather than a consultant or an employee of an evaluation organization. At first this was by accident, but now it is by conviction: My experience urges that the most meaningful evaluation of a program's goals and commitments is one that is planned and carried out by the staff and that such an evaluation contributes to the program as well as to external needs for information. As a staff member, I participate in staff meetings and contribute to decisions. My relationships with other staff members are close and reciprocal. Sometimes I provide services or perform functions that directly fulfill the purposes of the program—for example, working with children or adults, answering visitors' questions, writing proposals and reports. Most of my time, however, is spent planning, collecting, reporting, and analyzing documentation.

First Perceptions

With this context in mind, let me turn to the beginning plunge. Observing is the heart of documenting and it was into observing that I plunged, coming up delighted at the apparent ease and swiftness with which I could fish insight and ideas from the ceaseless ocean of activity around me. Indeed, the fact that observing (and record-keeping) does generate questions, insight, and matters for discussion is one of many reasons why records for any documentation should be gathered by those who actually work in the setting.

My observing took many forms, each offering a different way of releasing questions and ideas—interactive and noninteractive observations were transcribed or discussed with other staff members, and thereby rethought; children's writing was typed out, the attention to every detail involving me in what the child was saying; notes of meetings and other events were rewritten for the record; and so on. Handling such detail with attention, I found, enabled me to see into the incident or piece of work in a way I hadn't on first look. Connections with other things I knew, with other observations I made, or questions I was puzzling over seemed to proliferate during these processes; new perceptions and new questions began to form.

I have heard others describe similarly their delighted discovery of the provocativeness of record-keeping processes. The teacher who begins to collect children's art, without perhaps even having a particular reason for the collecting, will, just by gathering the work together, begin to notice things about them that he or she had not seen before—how one child's work influences another's, how really different (or similar) are the trees they make, and so on. The in-school advisor or resource teacher who reviews all his or her contacts with teachers—as they are recorded or in a special meeting with his or her colleagues—may begin, for example, to see patterns of similar interest in the requests he or she is getting and thus become aware of new possibilities for relationships within the school.

My own delight in this apparently easy access to a first level of insight made me eager to collect more and more, and I also found the sheer bulk of what I could collect satisfying. As I collected more records, however, my enthusiasm gradually changed to alarm and frustration. There were so many things that could be observed and recorded, so many perspectives, such a complicated history! My feelings of wanting more changed to a feeling of needing to get everything. It wasn't enough for me to know how the program worked now—I felt I needed to know how it got started and how the present workings had evolved. It wasn't enough to know how the central part of the program worked—I felt I had to know about all its spinoff activities and from all points of view. I was quickly drawn into a fear of losing something significant, something I might need later on. Likewise, in my early observations of class sessions, I sought to write down everything I saw. I have had this experience of wanting to get everything in every setting in which I have documented, and I think it is not unique.

I was fortunate enough to be able to indulge these feelings and to learn from where they led me. It did become clear to me after a while that my early ambitions for documenting everything far exceeded my time and, indeed, the needs of the program. Nevertheless, there was a sense to them. Collecting so much was a way of getting to know a new setting, of orienting myself. And, not knowing the setting, I couldn't know what would turn out to be important in "reconstituting" it; also, the purpose of "reconstituting" it was sufficiently broad to include any number of possibilities from which I had not yet selected. In fact, I found that the first insights, the first connections that came from gathering the records were a significant part of the process of determining what would be important and what were the possibilities most suited to the purposes of the documentation. The process of gathering everything at first turned out to be important and, I think, needs to be allowed for at the beginning of any documenting effort. Even though much of the material so gathered may remain apparently unused, as it was in my documenting, in fact it has served its purpose just in being collected. A similar process may be required even when the documenter is already familiar with the setting, since the new role entails a new perspective.

The first connections, the first patterns emerging from the accumulating records were thus a valuable aspect of the documenting process. There came a moment, however, when the data I had collected seemed more massive than was justified by any thought I'd had as a result of the collecting. I was ill at ease because the first patterns were still fairly unformed and were not automatically turning into a documentation in the full sense I gave earlier, even though I recognized them as part of the documentary data. Particularly, they did not function as "evaluation." Some further development was needed, but what? "What do I do with them now?" is a cry I have heard regularly since then from teachers and others who have been collecting records for a while.

I began with the relatively simple procedure of rereading everything I had gathered. Then I returned to rethink what my purposes were, and sought out my original resources on documentation. Rereading qualitative references, talking with the staff of the school and with my staff colleagues, I began to imagine a shape I could give to my records that would make a coherent representation of the program to an outside audience.

At the same time I began to rethink how I could make what I had collected more useful to the staff. Conceiving an audience was very important at this stage. I will be returning to this moment of transition from initial collecting to rethinking later, to analyze the entry into interpretation that it entails. Descriptively, however, what occurred was that I began to see my observations and records as a body with its own configurations, interrelationships, and possibilities, rather than simply as excerpts of the larger program that related only to the program. Obviously, the observations and records continued to have meaning through their primary relationship to the setting in which they were made, but they also began to have meaning through their secondary relationships to each other.

These secondary relationships also emerge from observation as a process of reflecting. Here, however, the focus of observation is the setting as it appears in and through the observations and records that have accumulated, with all their representation of multiple perspectives and longitudinal dimensions. These observations in and through records—"thickened observations"—are of course confirmed and added to by continuing direct observation of the setting.

Beginning to see the records as a body and the setting through thickened observation is a process of integrating data. The process occurs gradually and requires a broad base of observation about many aspects of the program over some period of time. It then requires concentrated and systematic efforts to find connections within the data and weave them into patterns, to notice changes in what is reported, and find the relationship of changes to what remains constant. This process is supported by juxtaposing the observations and records in various ways, as well as by continual return to reobserve the original phenomenon. There is, in my opinion, no way to speed up the process of documenting. Reflectiveness takes time.

In retrospect I can identify my own approach to an integration of the data as the time when I began to give my opinions on long-range decisions and interpretations of daily events with the ease of any other staff member. Up to the moment of transition, I shared specific observations from the records and talked them over as a way of gathering yet more perspectives on what was happening. I was aware, however, that my opinions or interpretations were still personal. They did not yet represent the material I was collecting.

Thus, it may be that integration of the documentary material becomes apparent when the documenter begins to evince a broad perspective about what is being documented, a perspective that makes what has been gathered available to others without precluding their own perceptions. This perspective is not a fixed-point view of a finished picture, both the view and the picture constructed somehow by the documenter in private and then unveiled with a flourish. It is also not a personal opinion; nor does it arise from placing a predetermined interpretive structure or standard on the observations. The perspective results from the documenter's own current best integration of the many aspects of the phenomenon, of the teachers' or staff's aims, ideas, and current struggles, and of their historical development as these have been conveyed in the actions that have been observed and the records that have been collected.

As documenter, my perspective of a program or a classroom is like my perspective of a landscape. The longer I am in it, the sharper defined become its features, its hills and valleys, forests and fields, and the folds of distance; the more colorful and yet deeply shaded and nuanced in tone it appears; the more my memory of how it looks in other weather, under other skies, and in other seasons, and my knowledge of its living parts, its minute detail, and its history deepen my viewing and valuing of it at any moment. This landscape has constancy in its basic configurations, but is also always changing as circumstances move it and as my perceptions gather. The perspective the documenter offers to others must evoke the constancy, coherence, and integrity of the landscape, and its possibilities for changing its appearance. Without such a perspective, an organization or integration that is both personal and informed by all that has been gathered by myself and by others in the setting—others could not share what I have seen—could not locate familiar landmarks and reflect on them as they exhibit new relationships to one another and to less familiar aspects. All that material, all those observations and records, would be a lifeless and undoubtedly dusty pile.

The process of forming a perspective in which the data gathered are integrated into an organic configuration is obviously a process of interpretation. I had begun documenting, however, without an articulated framework for interpretation or a format for representation of the body of records, like the theoretical framework researchers bring to their data. Of course, there was a framework. Conceptions of artistic process, of learning and development, were inherent in the program, but these were not explicit in its goals as a program to provide certain kinds of service. The plan of the documentation had called for certain results, but there was no specified format for presentation of results. Therefore, my entry into interpretation became a struggle with myself over what I was supposed to be doing. It was a long internal debate about my responsibilities and commitments.

When I began documenting this particular school's art program, for example, I had priorities based on my experience and personal commitments. It seemed to me self-evidently important to provide art activities for children and to try and connect these to other areas of their learning. I knew that art was not something that could be "learned" or even experienced on a once-a-week basis, so I thought it was important to help teachers find various ways of integrating art and other activities into their classrooms. I had already made a personal estimate that what I was documenting was worthwhile and honest. I had found points of congruence between my priorities and the program. I could see how the various structures of the program specified ways of approaching the goals that seemed possible and that also enabled the elaboration of the goals.

This initial commitment was diffuse; I felt a kind of general enthusiasm and interest for the efforts I observed and a desire to explore and be helpful to the teachers. In retrospect, however, the commitment was sufficiently energizing to sustain me through the early phases of collecting observations and records, when I was not sure what these would lead to. Rather than restricting me, the commitment freed me to look openly at everything (as reflected in the early enthusiasm for collecting everything). Obviously, it is possible to begin documenting from many other positions of relative interest and investment, but I suspect that even if there is no particular involvement in program content on the part of the documenter, there must be at least some idea of being helpful to its staff. (Remember, this was a formative evaluation.) Otherwise, for example, the process of gathering data may be circumscribed.

At the point of beginning to "do something" with the observations and records, I was forced to specify the original commitment, to rethink my purposes and goals. Rereading the observations and records as a preliminary step in reworking to address different audiences, I found myself at first reading with an idea of "balancing" success and failure, an idea that constricted and trivialized the work I had observed and recorded. Thankfully, it was immediately evident from the data itself that such balance was not possible. If, during ten days of observation, a child's experience was intense one day and characterized by rowdy socializing the other nine, a simple weigh-off would not establish the success or failure of the child's experience. The idea was ludicrous. Similarly, the staff might be thorough in its planning and follow-through on one day and disorganized on another day, but organization and planning were clearly not the totality of the experience for children.

Such trade-offs implied an external, stereotyped audience awaiting some kind of quantitative proof, which I was supposed to provide in a disinterested way, like an external, summative evaluator. The "balanced view" phase was also like my early record-gathering of everything. What I was documenting was still in fragments for me, and my approach was to the particulars, to every detail.

A second approach to interpreting, also brief, took a slightly broader view of the data, a view that acknowledged my original estimate of program value and attempted to specify it. Perceiving through the data the landscape-like configurations of program strengths, I made assessments that included statements of past mistakes or inadequacies like minor "flaws" in the landscape (a few odd billboards and a garbage dump in one of Poussin's dreams of classical Italy, for example) rather than debits on a balance sheet. Here again, the implication was of an external audience, expecting some absolute of accomplishment. The "flaws" could be "minor" only by reference to an implied major flaw—that of failing to carry out the program goals altogether.

The formulation of strength subsuming weakness could not withstand the vitality of the records I was reading. The reality the data portrayed became clearer as the inadequacy of my first formulations of how to interpret the documentary material was revealed. Similarly, the implications of external audience expectations were not justified by the actuality of my relationship to the program and staff. My stated goal as documenter had been originally to set up record-keeping procedures that would preserve and make available to staff and to other interested persons aspects of the beginnings and workings of the program, and to collect and analyze some of the material as an assessment of what further possibilities for development actually existed. My goals had not been to evaluate in the sense of an external judgment of success or failure.

Thinking over what other approaches to interpretation were possible, I recalled that I had gathered documentary materials quite straightforwardly as a participant, whose engagement was initially through recognition of shared convictions and points of congruence with the program. Perhaps, I decided, I could share my viewpoint of the observations just as straightforwardly, as a participant with a particular point of view. In examining this possibility, I came to a view of interpreting observational data as a process of "rendering," much as a performer renders a piece of classical music. The interpretation follows a text closely—as a scientist might say, it sticks closely to the facts. But it also reflects the performer, specifically the performer's particular manner of engagement in the enterprise shared by text and performer, the enterprise of music. The same relationship could exist, it seemed to me, between a body of observations and records gathered participatively and as documenter. The relationship would allow my personal experience and viewpoint to enhance rather than distort the data. Indeed, I would become their voice.

Through this relationship I could make the observations available to staff and to other audiences in a way that was flexible and responsive to *their* needs, purposes, and standards. In so doing, of course, the framework of inherent conceptions underlying the work of the program would be incorporated. Thus, to interpret the observational data I had gathered, I had to reaffirm and clarify my relationship, my attachment to and participation in the program.

My initial engagement, with its strong coloring of prior interests and ideas, had never meant that I understood or was sympathetic with every goal or practice of every participant of the program all the time. In any joint enterprise, such as a school or program, there are diverse and multiple goals and practices. Part of the task of documenting is to describe and make these various understandings, points of view, and practices visible so that participants can reflectively consider them as the basis for planning. No participant agrees on all issues and points of practice. Part of being a participant is exploring differences and how these illuminate issues or contribute to practice. My participation allowed me to examine and extend the interests and ideas I came with as well as observing and recording those other people brought. In this process my engagement was deepened, enabling me to make assessments closer to the data than my first readings brought. These assessments are evaluation in its original sense of "drawing-value-from," an interactive process of valuing, of giving weight and meaning.

In the context of renewed engagement and deepened participation, assessments of mistakes or inadequacies are construed as discrepancies between a particular practice and the intent behind it, between immediate and long-range purposes. The discrepancy is not a flaw in an otherwise perfect surface, but—like the discrepancy in a child's understanding that stimulates new learning—is the occasion for growth. It is a sign of life and possibility. The burden of the discrepancy can lie either with the practice or with the intent, and that is the point for further examination. Assessment can also occur through the observation of and search for underlying themes of continuity between present and past intent and practice, and the point of change or transformation in continuity. Whereas discrepancy will usually be a more immediate trigger to evaluation, occasions for the consideration of continuity may tend to be longer-range—planning for the coming year, contemplating changes in staff and function, or commemorating an anniversary.

I have located the documenter as participant, internal to the program or setting, gathering and shaping data in ways that make them available to participants and potentially to an external audience. Returning to the image of a landscape, let me comment on the different forms availability assumes for these different audiences.

Participant access to the landscape through the documenter's perspective cannot be achieved through ponderous written descriptions and reports on what has been observed but must be concentrated in interaction. Sometimes this may require the development of special or regular structures—a series of short-term meetings on a particular issue or problem; an occasional event that sums up and looks ahead; a regular meeting for another kind of planning. But many times the need is addressed in very slight forms, such as a comment in passing about something a child or adult user is doing, or about the appearance of a display, or the recounting of another staff member's observation. I do not mean that injecting documentation into the self-assessment process is a juggling act or some feat of manipulation; merely that the documenter must be aware that his or her role is to keep things open and that, while the observations and records are a resource for doing this, a sense of the whole they create is also essential. The landscape is, of course, changed by the new observations offered by fellow viewers.

The external audience places different requirements on the documenter who seeks to represent to it the documentary perspective. By external audience I refer to funding agencies, supervisors, school boards, institutional hierarchies, and researchers. Proposals, accounts, and reports to these audiences are generally required. They can be burdensome because they may not be organically related to the process of internal self-reflection and because the external audience has its own standards, purposes, and questions; it is unfamiliar with the setting and with the documenter, and it needs the time offered by written accounts to return and review the material. The external audience will need more history and formal description of the broad aspects than the internal audience, with commentary that indicates the significance of recent developments. This need can be met in the overall organization, arrangement, and introduction of documents, which also convey the detail and vividness of daily activity.

To limit the report to conventional format and expectations would probably misrepresent the quality of thought, of relating, of self-assessment that goes into developing the work. If there is intent to use the occasion of a report for reflection—for example, by including staff in the development of the report—the reporting process can become meaningful internally while fulfilling the legitimate external demands for accounting. Naturally, such a comment engages the external audience in its own evaluative reflections by evoking the phenomenon rather than reducing it.

In closing, I return to what I see as the necessary engaged participation of the documenter in the setting being documented, not only for data-gathering but for interpretation. Whatever authenticity and power my perspective as documenter has had has come, I believe, from my commitment to the development of the setting I was documenting and from the opportunities in it for me to pursue my own understanding, to assess and reassess my role, and to come to terms with issues as they arose.

We come to new settings with prior knowledge, experience, and ways of understanding, and our new perceptions and understandings build on these. We do not simply look at things as if we had never seen anything like them before. When we look at a cluster of light and dark greens with interstices of blue and some of deeper browns and purples, what we identify is a tree against the sky. Similarly, in a classroom we do not think twice when we see, for example, a child scratching his head, yet the same phenomenon might be more strictly described as a particular combination of forms and movements. Our daily functioning depends on this kind of apparently obvious and mundane interpretation of the world. These interpretations are not simply personal opinion—though they certainly may be unique—nor are they made up. They are instead organizations of our perceptions as "tree" or "child scratching" and they correspond at many points with the phenomena so described.

It is these organizations of perception that convey to someone else what we have seen and that make objects available for discussion and reflection. Such organizations need not exclude our awareness that the tree is also a cluster of colors or that the child scratching his head is also a small human form raising its hand in a particular way. Indeed, we know that there could be many other ways to describe the same phenomena, including some that would be completely numerical—but not necessarily more accurate, more truthful, or more useful! After all, we organize our perceptions in the context of immediate purposes and relationships. The organizations must correspond to the context as well as to the phenomenon.

Facts do not organize themselves into concepts and theories just by being looked at; indeed, except within the framework of concepts and theories, there are no scientific facts but only chaos. There is an inescapable a priori element in all scientific work. Questions must be asked before answers can be given. The questions are all expressions of our interest in the world; they are at bottom valuations. Valuations are thus necessarily involved already at the stage when we observe facts and carry on theoretical analysis and not only at the stage when we draw political inferences from facts and valuations (Myrdal 1969:9).

My experience suggests that the situation in documenting is essentially the same as what I have been describing with the tree and the child scratching and what Myrdal describes as the process of scientific research. Documentation is based on observation, which is always an individual response both to the phenomena observed and to the broad purposes of observation. In documentation observation occurs both at the primary level of seeing and recording phenomena and at secondary levels of reobserving the phenomena through a volume of records and directly, at later moments. Since documentation has as its purpose to offer these observations for reflections and evaluation in such a way as to keep alive and open the potential of the setting, it is essential that observations at both primary and secondary levels be interpreted by those who have made them. The usefulness of the observations to others depends on the documenter's rendering them as finely as he or she is able, with as many points of correspondence to both the phenomena and the context of interpretation as possible. Such a rendering will be an interpretation that preserves the phenomena and so does not exclude but rather invites other perspective.

Of course, there is a role for the experienced observer from outside who can see phenomena freshly; who can suggest ways of obtaining new kinds of information about it, or, perhaps more important, point to the significance of already existing procedures or data; who can advise on technical problems that have arisen within a documentation; and who can even guide efforts to interpret and integrate documentary information. I am stressing, however, that the outside observer in these instances provides support, not judgment or the criteria for judgment.

The documenter's obligation to interpret his or her observations and those reflected in the records being collected becomes increasingly urgent, and the interpretations become increasingly significant, as all the observers in the setting become more knowledgeable about it and thus more capable of bringing range and depth to the interpretation. Speaking of the weight of her observations of the Manus over a period of some 40 years to great change, Margaret Mead clarifies the responsibility of the participant-observer to contribute to both people studied and to a wider audience the rich individual interpretation of his or her own observations:

> Uniqueness, now, in a study like this (of people who have come under the continuing influence of contemporary world culture), lies in the relationships between the fieldworker and the material. I still have the responsibility and incentives that come from the fact that because of my long acquaintance with this village I can perceive and record aspects of this people's life that no one else can. But even so, this knowledge has a new edge. This material will be valuable only if I myself can organize it. In traditional fieldwork, another anthropologist familiar with the area can take over one's notes and make them meaningful. But here it is my individual consciousness that provides the ground on which the lives of these people are figures. (Mead 1977:282-83)

In documenting it seems to me the contribution is all the greater, and all the more demanded, because what is studied is one's own setting and commitment.

SOURCE: Used with permission of Beth Alberty.

Answers to riddles presented on pages 538-9.		
Riddle Number One:	Who Am I?	*Observer*
Riddle Number Two:	Who Am I?	*Interviewer*
Riddle Number Three:	Who Am I?	*Participant in field settings*
Riddle Number Four:	Who Am I?	*Interpreter*

References

Abbey, Edward. 1968. *Desert Solitaire: A Season in the Wilderness.* New York: Ballantine.

Ackoff, Russell. 1999a. *Ackoff's Best: His Classic Writings on Management.* New York: John Wiley.

———. 1999b. *Re-Creating the Corporation: A Design of Organizations for the 21st Century.* Oxford, UK: Oxford University Press.

———. 1987. *The Art of Problem Solving Accompanied by Ackoff's Fables.* New York: John Wiley.

Ackoff, Russell and Fred Emery. 1982. *On Purposeful Systems.* Salinas, CA: Intersystems.

Academy for Educational Development (AED). 1989. *Handbook for Excellence in Focus Group Research.* Washington, DC: Academy for Educational Development.

AEA Task Force on Guiding Principles for Evaluators. 1995. "Guiding Principles for Evaluators." *New Directions for Program Evaluation* 66 (summer): 19-34, *Guiding Principles for Evaluators,* edited by William R. Shadish, D. L. Newman, M. A. Scheirer, and C. Wye. San Francisco: Jossey-Bass.

Agar, Michael. 2000. "Border Lessons: Linguistic 'Rich Points' and Evaluative Understanding." *New Directions for Evaluation* 86 (summer): 93-109. San Francisco: Jossey-Bass.

———. 1999. "Complexity Theory: An Exploration and Overview." *Field Methods* 11 (2, November): 99-120.

———. 1986. *Speaking of Ethnography.* Qualitative Research Methods Series, Vol. 2. Beverly Hills, CA: Sage.

Agar, Michael H. and H. S. Reisinger. 1999. "Numbers and Patterns: Heroin Indicators and What They Represent." *Human Organization* 58 (4, winter): 365-74.

Alasuutari, Pertti. 1995. *Researching Culture.* Thousand Oaks, CA: Sage.

Alkin, M. 1997. "Stakeholder Concepts in Program Evaluation." In *Evaluation for Educational Productivity,* edited by A. Reynolds and H. Walberg. Greenwich, CT: JAI.

Alkin, Marvin C. 1972. "Wider Context Goals and Goals-Based Evaluators." In *Evaluation Comment: The Journal of Educational Evaluation*. Center for the Study of Evaluation, UCLA, 3 (4, December): 10-11.

Alkin, Marvin C., Mary Andrews, G. L. Lewis, H. Manhertz, L. Sandmann, and J. West. 1989. *External Evaluation of the Caribbean Agricultural Extension Project*. Bridgetown, Barbados: U.S. Agency for International Development.

Alkin, Marvin C., Richard Daillak, and Peter White. 1979. *Using Evaluations: Does Evaluation Make a Difference?* Beverly Hills, CA: Sage.

Alkin, Marvin C. and Michael Q. Patton. 1987. "Working Both Sides of the Street." *New Directions for Program Evaluation* 36 (winter): 19-32, *The Client Perspective on Evaluation*, edited by Jeri Nowakowski. San Francisco: Jossey-Bass.

Allen, Charlotte. 1997. "Spies Like Us: When Sociologists Deceive Their Subjects." *Lingua Franca* (November): 31-38.

Allison, Mary Ann. 2000. "Enriching Your Practice With Complex Systems Thinking." *OD Practitioner* 32 (3): 11-22.

Anderson, Barry. 1980. *The Complete Thinker*. Englewood Cliffs, NJ: Prentice Hall.

Anderson, Richard B. 1977. "The Effectiveness of Follow Through: What Have We Learned?" Presented at the annual meeting of the American Educational Research Association, New York City, April 5.

Anderson, Virginia and Lauren Johnson. 1997. *Systems Thinking Basics: From Concepts to Causal Loops*. Williston, VT: Pegasus Communications.

Arcana, Judith. 1983. *Every Mother's Son: The Role of Mothers in the Making of Men*. London: The Women's Press.

———. 1981. *Our Mothers' Daughters*. London: The Women's Press.

Arditti, Rita. 1999. *Searching for Life: The Grandmothers of the Plaza de Mayo and the Disappeared Children of Argentina*. Berkeley: University of California Press.

Arendt, Hannah. 1968. *Between Past and Future: Eight Exercises in Political Thought*. New York: Viking.

Argyris, Chris. 1982. *Reasoning, Learning and Action: Individual and Organizational*. San Francisco: Jossey-Bass.

Argyris, Chris, Robert Putnam, and Diana M. Smith. 1985. *Action Science*. San Francisco: Jossey-Bass.

Argyris, Chris and Donald Schon. 1978. *Organizational Learning: A Theory of Action Perspective*. Reading, MA: Addison-Wesley.

Armstrong, David. 1992. *Managing by Storying Around*. New York: Doubleday.

Asimov, Isaac. 1983. "Creativity Will Dominate Our Time After the Concepts of Work and Fun Have Been Blurred by Technology." *Personnel Administrator* 28 (2): 42-46.

Atkinson, Paul. 1992. *Understanding Ethnographic Texts*. Qualitative Research Methods Series, Vol. 25. Newbury Park, CA: Sage.

Atkinson, Robert. 1998. *The Life Story Interview*. Qualitative Research Methods Series, Vol. 44. Thousand Oaks, CA: Sage.

Aubel, Judi. 1993. *Participatory Program Evaluation: A Manual for Involving Stakeholders in the Evaluation Process*. Dakar, Senegal: Catholic Relief Services, under a U.S. AID grant.

Aubrey, Robert and Paul Cohen. 1995. *Working Wisdom: Learning Organizations*. San Francisco: Jossey-Bass.

Azumi, Koya and Jerald Hage. 1972. "Towards a Synthesis: A Systems Perspective." Pp. 511-22 in *Organizational Systems*, edited by Koya Azumi and Jerald Hage. Lexington, MA: D. C. Heath.

Baert, Patrick. 1998. *Social Theory in the Twentieth Century*. New York: New York University Press.

Baldwin, James. 1990. *Notes of a Native Son*. Boston: Beacon.

Ball, Michael S. and Gregory W. H. Smith. 1992. *Analyzing Visual Data.* Qualitative Research Methods Series, Vol. 24. Newbury Park, CA: Sage.

Bandler, Richard and John Grinder. 1975a. *Patterns of the Hypnotic Techniques of Milton H. Erikson, M.D.* Vol. 1. Cupertino, CA: Meta Publications.

———. 1975b. *The Structure of Magic.* Vols. 1 and 2. Palo Alto, CA: Science and Behavior Books.

Barker, Roger G. 1968. *Ecological Psychology.* Stanford, CA: Stanford University Press.

Barker, Roger G. and P. Schoggen. 1973. *Qualities of Community Life: Methods of Measuring Environment and Behavior Applied to an American and an English Town.* San Francisco: Jossey-Bass.

Barker, Roger G. and H. F. Wright. 1955. *Midwest and Its Children.* New York: Harper & Row.

Barker, Roger G., H. F. Wright, M. F. Schoggen, and L. S. Barker. 1978. *Habitats, Environments, and Human Behavior.* San Francisco: Jossey-Bass.

Barone, Tom. 2000. *Aesthetics, Politics, and Educational Inquiry: Essays and Examples.* New York: Peter Lang.

Barton, David, Mary Hamilton, and Roz Ivanic. 1999. *Situated Literacies: Reading and Writing in Context.* New York: Routledge.

Bartunek, Jean M. and Meryl Reis Louis. 1996. *Insider/Outsider Team Research.* Qualitative Research Methods Series, Vol. 40. Thousand Oaks, CA: Sage.

Bateson, Gregory. 1978. "The Pattern Which Connects." *CoEvolution Quarterly* (summer): 5-15. Originally a speech for the Lindisfarne Association, October 17, 1977, at the Cathedral of St. John the Divine, Manhattan, NY.

Bateson, Mary Catherine. 2000. *Full Circles, Overlapping Lives: Culture and Generation in Transition.* New York: Random House.

Bawden, R. J. and R. G. Packham. 1998. "Systemic Praxis in the Education of the Agricultural Systems Practitioner." *Systems Research And Behavioral* 15 (5, September-October): 403-12.

Becker, Howard S. 1985. *Outsiders: Studies in the Sociology of Deviance.* New York: Free Press.

———. 1970. *Sociological Work: Method and Substance.* Chicago: Aldine.

———. 1967. "Whose Side Are We On?" *Social Problems* 14:239-248.

———. 1953. "Becoming a Marijuana User." *American Journal of Sociology* 59:235-42.

Becker, Howard and Blanche Geer. 1970. "Participant Observation and Interviewing: A Comparison." In *Qualitative Methodology,* edited by W. J. Filstead. Chicago: Markham.

Beebe, James. 2001. *Rapid Assessment Process.* Walnut Creek, CA: AltaMira.

Belenky, M. F., B. M. Clinchy, N. R. Goldberger, and J. M. Tarule. 1986. *Women's Way of Knowing: The Development of Self, Voice, and Mind.* New York: Basic Books.

Benko, S. and A. Sarvimaki. 2000. "Evaluation of Patient-Focused Health Care From a Systems Perspective." *Systems Research and Behavioral Science* 17 (6, November-December): 513-25.

Benmayor, Rina. 1991. "Testimony, Action Research, and Empowerment: Puerto Rican Women and Popular Education." Pp. 159-74 in *Women's Words: The Feminist Practice of Oral History,* edited by Sherna Berger Gluck and Daphne Patai. New York: Routledge.

Benson, Alexis P., D. Michelle Hinn, and Claire Lloyd, eds. 2001. *Visions of Quality: How Evaluators Define, Understand, and Represent Program Quality.* Advances in Program Evaluation Vol. 7. Amsterdam, the Netherlands: Elsevier Science.

Bentz, Valerie Malhotra and Jeremy J. Shapiro. 1998. *Mindful Inquiry in Social Research.* Thousand Oaks, CA: Sage.

Berens, Linda V. and Dario Nardi. 1999. *The 16 Personality Types: Description for Self Discovery.* New York: Telos.

Berger, Peter and T. Luckmann. 1967. *The Social Construction of Reality: A Treatise in the Sociology of Knowledge.* Garden City, NY: Anchor.

Berland, Jody. 1997. "Nationalism and the Modernist Legacy: Dialogues With Innis." *Culture and Policy* 8 (3): 9-39.

Bernard, H. Russell. 2000. *Social Research Methods: Qualitative and Quantitative Approaches.* Thousand Oaks, CA: Sage.

———, ed. 1998. *Handbook of Methods in Cultural Anthropology.* Walnut Creek, CA: AltaMira.

———. 1995. *Research Methods in Anthropology: Qualitative and Quantitative Approaches.* Walnut Creek, CA: AltaMira.

Bernard, H. Russell and Gery W. Ryan. 1998. "Textual Analysis: Qualitative and Quantitative Methods." Pp. 595-646 in *Handbook of Methods in Cultural Anthropology,* edited by H. Russell Bernard. Walnut Creek, CA: AltaMira.

Bernthal, N. 1990. *Motherhood Lost and Found: The Experience of Becoming an Adoptive Mother to a Foreign Born Child.* Unpublished doctoral dissertation, Graduate College, The Union Institute, Cincinnati, OH.

Bhaskar, R. A. 1975. *A Realist Theory of Science.* Leeds, UK: Leeds Books.

Bierce, Ambrose. [1906] 1999. *The Devil's Dictionary.* New York: Oxford University Press.

Binnendijk, Annette L. 1986. *AID's Experience With Contraceptive Social Marketing: A Synthesis of Project Evaluation Findings.* A.I.D. Evaluation Special Study No. 40. Washington, DC: U.S. Agency for International Development.

Blumer, Herbert. 1978. "Methodological Principles of Empirical Science." In *Sociological Methods: A Sourcebook,* edited by Norman K. Denzin. New York: McGraw-Hill.

———. 1969. *Symbolic Interactionism.* Englewood Cliffs, NJ: Prentice Hall.

———. 1954. "What Is Wrong With Social Theory?" *American Sociological Review* 19:3-10.

Boas, Franz. 1943. "Recent Anthropology." *Science* 98:311-14, 334-37.

Bochner, Arthur P. 2001. "Narrative's Virtues." *Qualitative Inquiry* 7 (2): 131-57.

Bochner, Arthur P. and Carolyn Ellis. 2001. *Ethnographically Speaking.* Oxford, UK: Rowman & Littlefield.

Bochner, Arthur P., Carolyn Ellis, and L. Tillman-Healy. 1997. "Relationships as Stories." Pp. 307-24 in *Handbook of Personal Relationships: Theory, Research, and Interventions.* 2d ed., edited by S. Dick. New York: John Wiley.

Bogdan, R. C. and S. K. Biklen. 1992. *Qualitative Research for Education.* Boston: Allyn & Bacon.

Boring, E. G. 1942. *Sensation and Perception in the History of Psychology.* Bloomington, IN: Appleton Century.

Borman, Kathryn M. and Judith P. Goetz. 1986. "Ethnographic and Qualitative Research Design and Why It Doesn't Work." *American Behavioral Scientist* 30 (1, September-October): 42-57.

Boruch, R. and D. Rindskopf. 1984. "Data Analysis." Pp. 121-58 in *Evaluation Research Methods.* 2d ed., edited by L. Rutman. Beverly Hills, CA: Sage.

Boston Women's Teachers' Group. 1986. *The Effect of Teaching on Teachers.* North Dakota Study Group on Evaluation monograph series. Grand Forks: Center for Teaching and Learning, University of North Dakota.

Boulding, Kenneth E. 1985. *Human Betterment.* Beverly Hills, CA: Sage.

Boxill, Nancy A. 1990. *Homeless Children: The Watchers and the Waiters.* New York: Haworth.

Boyatzis, Richard E. 1998. *Transforming Qualitative Information: Thematic Analysis and Code Development.* Thousand Oaks, CA: Sage.

Brady, Ivan. 2000. "Anthropological Poetics." Pp. 949-79 in *Handbook of Qualitative Research.* 2d ed., edited by Norman K. Denzin and Yvonna S. Lincoln. Thousand Oaks, CA: Sage.

———. 1998. "A Gift of the Journey." *Qualitative Inquiry* 4 (4, December): 463.

Brajuha, Mario and L. Hallowell. 1986. "Legal Intrusion and the Politics of Fieldwork: The Impact of the Brajuha Case." *Urban Life* 1 (4): 454-78.

Brandon, Paul R., Marlene A. Lindberg, and Zhigand Wang. 1993. "Involving Program Beneficiaries in the Early Stages of Evaluation: Issues of Consequential Validity and Influence." *Educational Evaluation and Policy Analysis* 15 (4): 420-28.

Braud, William and Rosemarie Anderson. 1998. *Transpersonal Research Methods for the Social Sciences: Honoring Human Experience*. Thousand Oaks, CA: Sage.

Bremer, J., E. Cole, W. Irelan, and P. Rourk. 1985. *A Review of AID's Experience in Private Sector Development*. A.I.D. Program Evaluation Report No. 14. Washington, DC: U.S. Agency for International Development.

Brewer, J. and A. Hunter. 1989. *Multimethod Research: A Synthesis of Styles*. Newbury Park, CA: Sage.

Brinkley, David. 1968. "Public Broadcasting Laboratory." Interview on Public Broadcasting Service, December 2.

Brislin, Richard W., K. Cushner, C. Cherrie, and Mahealani Yong. 1986. *Intercultural Interactions: A Practical Guide*. Beverly Hills, CA: Sage.

Brizuela, B. M., J. P. Stewart, R. G. Carrillo, and J. G. Berger. 2000. *Acts of Inquiry in Qualitative Research*. Reprint Series No. 34. Cambridge, MA: Harvard Educational Review.

Brock, James, Richard Schwaller, and R. L. Smith. 1985. "The Social and Local Government Impacts of the Abandonment of the Milwaukee Railroad in Montana." *Evaluation Review* 9 (2): 127-43.

Brookfield, Stephen. 1994. "Tales From the Dark Side: A Phenomenography of Adult Critical Reflection." *International Journal of Lifelong Education* 13 (3): 203-16.

Brown, John Seely, Alan Collins, and Paul Duguid. 1989. "Situated Cognition and the Culture of Learning." *Educational Researcher* 18 (1, January-February): 32-42.

Brown, Judith R. 1996. *The I in Science: Training to Utilize Subjectivity in Research*. Oslo, Norway: Scandinavian University Press.

Browne, Angela. 1987. *When Battered Women Kill*. New York: Free Press.

Bruce, Christine and Rod Gerber. 1997. *Phenomenographic Research: An Annotated Bibliography*. Occasional Paper 95.2. Centre for Applied Environmental and Social Education Research. Brisbane, Australia: QUT Publications.

Bruner, Edward M. 1996. "My Life in an Ashram." *Qualitative Inquiry* 2 (3, September): 300-19.

Bruyn, Severyn. 1966. *The Human Perspective in Sociology: The Methodology of Participant Observation*. Englewood Cliffs, NJ: Prentice Hall.

———. 1963. "The Methodology of Participant Observation." *Human Organization* 21:224-35.

Buber, Martin. 1923. *I and Thou*. New York: Macmillan Library.

Buckholt, Marcia. 2001. *Women's Voices of Resilience: Female Adult Abuse Survivors Define the Phenomenon*. Unpublished doctoral dissertation, Graduate College, The Union Institute, Cincinnati, OH.

Bullogh, Robert V., Jr. and Stefinee Pinnegar. 2001. "Guidelines for Quality in Autobiographical Forms of Self-Study Research." *Educational Researcher* 30 (3): 13-21.

Bunch, Eli Haugen. 2001. "Quality of Life of People With Advanced HIV/AIDS in Norway." *Grounded Theory Review* 2:30-42.

Bunge, Mario. 1959. *Causality*. Cambridge, MA: Harvard University Press.

Burdell, Patricia and Beth Blue Swadener. 1999. "Critical Personal Narrative and Autoethnography in Education: Reflections on a Genre." *Educational Researcher* 28 (6): 21-26.

Burns, Tom and G. M. Stalker. 1972. "Models of Mechanistic and Organic Structure." Pp. 240-55 in *Organizational Systems*, edited by Koya Azumi and Jerald Hage. Lexington, MA: D. C. Heath.

Bussis, Anne, Edward A. Chittenden, and Marianne Amarel. 1973. *Methodology in Educational Evaluation and Research.* Princeton, NJ: Educational Testing Service.

Buxton, Amity. 1982. *Children's Journals: Further Dimensions of Assessing Language Development.* North Dakota Study Group on Evaluation monograph series. Grand Forks: Center for Teaching and Learning, University of North Dakota.

Cambel, Ali Bulent. 1992. *Applied Chaos Theory: A Paradigm for Complexity.* New York: Academic Press.

Campbell, Donald T. 1999a. "Legacies of Logical Positivism and Beyond." Pp. 131-44 in *Social Experimentation,* by Donald T. Campbell and M. Jean Russo. Thousand Oaks, CA: Sage.

————. 1999b. "On the Rhetorical Use of Experiments." Pp. 149-58 in *Social Experimentation,* by Donald T. Campbell and M. Jean Russo. Thousand Oaks, CA: Sage.

————. 1974. "Qualitative Knowing in Action Research." Presented at the annual meeting of the American Psychological Association, New Orleans, LA.

Campbell, Donald T. and M. Jean Russo. 1999. *Social Experimentation.* Thousand Oaks, CA: Sage.

Campbell, Jeanne L. 1983. *Factors and Conditions Influencing Usefulness of Planning, Evaluation and Reporting in Schools.* Unpublished doctoral dissertation, University of Minnesota.

Carchedi, G. 1983. "Class Analysis and the Study of Social Forms." Pp. 347-67 in *Beyond Method,* edited by Gareth Morgan. Beverly Hills, CA: Sage.

Carini, Patricia F. 1979. *The Art of Seeing and the Visibility of the Person.* North Dakota Study Group on Evaluation monograph series. Grand Forks: Center for Teaching and Learning, University of North Dakota.

————. 1975. *Observation and Description: An Alternative Method for the Investigation of Human Phenomena.* North Dakota Study Group on Evaluation monograph series. Grand Forks: Center for Teaching and Learning, University of North Dakota.

Carlin, George. 1997. *Brain Droppings.* New York: Hyperion.

Casse, Pierre and Surinder Deol. 1985. *Managing Intercultural Negotiations: Guidelines for Trainers and Negotiators.* Washington, DC: SIETAR International.

Castaneda, Carlos. 1973. *Journey to Ixtlan.* New York: Pocket Books.

Cedillos, Jose Hilario. 1998. "Mayan Fragments and Bricolage: Roots of Layered Consciousness." Unpublished manuscript.

————. Forthcoming. *The Bricolage Arts: The Postmodernist Search for Shamanic Jazz.*

Cernea, Michael, ed. 1991. *Putting People First: Sociological Variables in Rural Development.* 2d ed. New York: Oxford University Press.

Cernea, Michael M. and Scott E. Guggenheim. 1985. "Is Anthropology Superfluous in Farming Systems Research?" World Bank Reprint Series No. 367. Washington, DC: World Bank.

Cervantes Saavedra, Miguel de. 1964. *Don Quixote.* New York: Signet Classics.

Chagnon, Napoleon. 1992. *Yanomamo: The Last Days of Eden.* New York: Harcourt Brace.

Chamberlayne, P., J. Bornat, and T. Wengraf. 2000. *The Turn to Biographical Methods in Social Science.* London: Routledge.

Chambers, Erve. 2000. "Applied Ethnography." Pp. 851-69 in *Handbook of Qualitative Research.* 2d ed., edited by Norman K. Denzin and Yvonna S. Lincoln. Thousand Oaks, CA: Sage.

Charmaz, Kathy. 2000. "Grounded Theory: Objectivist and Constructivist Methods." Pp. 509-35 in *Handbook of Qualitative Research.* 2d ed., edited by Norman K. Denzin and Yvonna S. Lincoln. Thousand Oaks, CA: Sage.

Charon, Rita, M. G. Greene, and R. D. Adelman. 1998. "Qualitative Research in Medicine and Health Care: Questions and Controversy, a Response. *Journal of General Internal Medicine* 13 (January): 67-68.

Chatterjee, A. 2001. "Language and Space: Some Interactions." *Trends in Cognitive Sciences* 5 (2): 55-61.

Checkland, Peter. 1999. *Systems Thinking, Systems Practice: A 30-Year Retrospective.* New York: John Wiley.

Chen, Huey-Tsyh and Peter H. Rossi. 1987. "The Theory-Driven Approach to Validity" *Evaluation and Program Planning* 10:95-103.

Chew, Siew Tuan. 1989. *Agroforestry Projects for Small Farmers.* A.I.D. Evaluation Special Study No. 59. Washington, DC: U.S. Agency for International Development.

Cheyne, V. 1988. *Growing Up in a Fatherless Home: The Female Experience.* Ann Arbor, MI: University Microfilms International. Unpublished doctoral thesis, Graduate College, The Union Institute, Cincinnati, OH.

Chibnik, M. 2000. "The Evolution of Market Niches in Oaxacan Woodcarving." *Ethnology* 39 (3, summer): 225-42.

Christians, Clifford G. 2000. "Ethics and Politics in Qualitative Research." Pp. 133-55 in *Handbook of Qualitative Research.* 2d ed., edited by Norman K. Denzin and Yvonna S. Lincoln. Thousand Oaks, CA: Sage.

Church, Kathryn. 1995. *Forbidden Narratives: Critical Autobiography as Social Science.* Toronto, Ontario, Canada: University of Toronto Press.

Cialdini, Robert B. 2001. "The Science of Persuasion." *Scientific American* 284 (2): 76-81.

Clark, J. 1988. *The Experience of the Psychologically Androgynous Male.* Unpublished doctoral dissertation, Graduate College, The Union Institute, Cincinnati, OH.

Clarke, I. and W. Mackaness. 2001. "Management 'Intuition': An Interpretative Account of Structure and Content of Decision Schemas Using Cognitive Maps." *Journal of Management Studies* 38 (2): 147-72.

Cleveland, Harlan. 1989. *The Knowledge Executive: Leadership in an Information Society.* New York: E. P. Dutton.

Coffey, Amanda and Paul Atkinson. 1996. *Making Sense of Qualitative Data: Complementary Research Strategies.* Thousand Oaks, CA: Sage.

Cole, Andra L. and J. Gary Knowles. 2000. *Doing Reflexive Life History Research.* Walnut Creek, CA: AltaMira.

Coles, Robert. 1990. *The Spiritual Life of Children.* Boston: Houghton Mifflin.

———. 1989. *The Call of Stories: Teaching and the Moral Imagination.* Boston: Houghton Mifflin.

Collins, Jim. 2001. "Level 5 Leadership: The Triumph of Humility and Fierce Resolve." *Harvard Business Review* 79 (1, January): 67-76, 175.

Comstock, D. E. 1982. "A Method for Critical Research." Pp. 370-90 in *Knowledge and Values in Social and Educational Research,* edited by E. Bredo and W. Feinberg. Philadelphia: Temple University Press.

Connolly, Deborah R. 2000. *Homeless Mothers: Face to Face With Women and Poverty.* Minneapolis: University of Minnesota Press.

Connor, Ross. 1985. "International and Domestic Evaluation: Comparisons and Insights." Pp. 19-28 in *Culture and Evaluation,* edited by Michael Quinn Patton. San Francisco: Jossey-Bass.

Conrad, Joseph. 1960. *Heart of Darkness.* New York: Dell.

Conroy, Dennis L. 1987. *A Phenomenological Study of Police Officers as Victims.* Unpublished doctoral thesis, Graduate College, The Union Institute, Cincinnati, OH.

Constas, M. A. 1998. "Deciphering Postmodern Educational Research." *Educational Researcher* 27 (9): 36-42.

Cook, Thomas D. 1995. "Evaluation Lessons Learned." Plenary address at the International Evaluation Conference "Evaluation '95," November 4, Vancouver, BC.

Cook, Thomas D., Laura C. Leviton, and William R. Shadish, Jr. 1985. "Program Evaluation." Pp. 699-777 in *Handbook of Social Psychology, Theory and Method.* Vol. 1. 3d ed., edited by G. Lindzey and E. Aronson. New York: Random House.

Cook, Thomas D. and Charles S. Reichardt, eds. 1979. *Qualitative and Quantitative Methods in Evaluation Research.* Beverly Hills, CA: Sage.

Cooke, N. J. 1994. "Varieties of Knowledge Elicitation Techniques." *International Journal of Human-Computer Studies* 41 (6): 801-49.

Cooper, Harris. 1998. *Synthesizing Research.* Thousand Oaks, CA: Sage.

Coulon, Alain. 1995. *Ethnomethodology.* Qualitative Research Methods Series, Vol. 36. Thousand Oaks, CA: Sage.

Cousins, J. Bradley and Lorna M. Earl, eds. 1995. *Participatory Evaluation in Education: Studies in Evaluation Use and Organizational Learning.* London: Falmer.

———. 1992. "The Case for Participatory Evaluation." *Educational Evaluation and Policy Analysis* 14:397-418.

Covey, Stephen R. 1990. *The 7 Habits of Highly Effective People: Powerful Lessons in Personal Change.* New York: Fireside.

Cox, Gary B. 1982. "Program Evaluation." Pp. 338-51 in *Handbook on Mental Health Administration,* edited by Michael S. Austin and William E. Hersley. San Francisco: Jossey-Bass.

Craig, P. 1978. *The Heart of a Teacher: A Heuristic Study of the Inner World of Teaching.* Ann Arbor, MI: University Microfilms International.

Creswell, John W. 1998. *Qualitative Inquiry and Research Design: Choosing Among Five Traditions.* Thousand Oaks, CA: Sage.

Cronbach, Lee J. 1988. "Playing With Chaos." *Educational Researcher* 17 (6, August-September): 46-49.

———. 1982. *Designing Evaluations of Educational and Social Programs.* San Francisco: Jossey-Bass.

———. 1975. "Beyond the Two Disciplines of Scientific Psychology." *American Psychologist* 30:116-27.

Cronbach, Lee J. and Associates. 1980. *Toward Reform of Program Evaluation.* San Francisco: Jossey-Bass.

Crosby, Philip B. 1979. *Quality Is Free: The Art of Making Quality Certain.* New York: McGraw-Hill.

Crotty, Michael. 1998. *The Foundations of Social Research: Meaning and Perspective in the Research Process.* London: Sage.

Curry, Constance. 1995. *Silver Rights.* Chapel Hill, NC: Algonquin.

Czarniawska, Barbara. 1998. *A Narrative Approach to Organization Studies.* Qualitative Research Methods Series, Vol. 43. Thousand Oaks, CA: Sage.

Cziko, Gary A. 1989. "Unpredictability and Indeterminism in Human Behavior: Arguments and Implications for Educational Research." *Educational Researcher* 18 (3, April): 17-25.

Dalgaard, K. A., M. Brazzel, R. T. Liles, D. Sanderson, and E. Taylor-Powell. 1988. *Issues Programming in Extension.* Washington, DC: Extension Service, U.S. Department of Agriculture.

Dart, Jessica. 2000. Personal e-mail communication. For more information online about the "most significant changes" monitoring system, go to http://www.egroups.com/group/MostSignificantChanges.

Dart, J. J., G. Drysdale, D. Cole, and M. Saddington. 2000. "The Most Significant Change Approach for Monitoring an Australian Extension Project." *PLA Notes* 38:47-53. London: International Institute for Environment and Development.

Davies, Rick J. 1996. "An Evolutionary Approach to Facilitating Organisational Learning: An Experiment by the Christian Commission for Development in Bangladesh." Swansea, UK: Centre for Development Studies.

Davis, Kingsley. 1947. "Final Note on a Case of Extreme Social Isolation." *American Journal of Sociology* 52 (March): 432-37.

————. 1940. "Extreme Social Isolation of a Child." *American Journal of Sociology* 45 (January): 554-65.

De Bono, Edward. 1999. *Six Thinking Hats*. New York: Little, Brown.

DeCramer, Gary. 1997. *Minnesota's District/Area Transportation Partnership Process*. Vol. 1, *Cross-Case Analysis*. Vol. 2, *Case Studies and Other Perspectives*. Minneapolis: Center for Transportation Studies, University of Minnesota.

De Munck, V. 2000. "Introduction: Units for Describing and Analyzing Culture and Society." *Ethnology* 39 (4): 279-92.

Denning, Stephen. 2001. *The Springboard: How Storytelling Ignites Action in Knowledge-Era Organizations*. Portsmouth, NH: Butterworth-Heinemann.

Denny, Terry. 1978. "Storytelling and Educational Understanding." Occasional Paper No. 12, Evaluation Center. Kalamazoo: Western Michigan University.

Denzin, Norman K. 2001. *Interpretive Interactionism*. 2d ed. Thousand Oaks, CA: Sage.

————. 2000a. "Aesthetics and the Practices of Qualitative Inquiry." *Qualitative Inquiry* 6 (2): 256-65.

————. 2000b. "Rock Creek History." *Symbolic Interaction* 23 (1): 71-81.

————. 1997a. "Coffee With Anselm." *Qualitative Family Research* 11 (1, 2 November): 16-18.

————. 1997b. *Interpretive Ethnography: Ethnographic Practices for the 21st Century*. Thousand Oaks, CA: Sage.

————. 1991. *Images of Postmodern Society: Social Theory and Contemporary Cinema*. London: Sage.

————. 1989a. *Interpretive Biography*. Qualitative Research Methods Series, Vol. 17. Newbury Park, CA: Sage.

————. 1989b. *Interpretive Interactionism*. Newbury Park, CA: Sage.

————. 1989c. *The Research Act: A Theoretical Introduction to Sociological Methods*. 3d ed. Englewood Cliffs, NJ: Prentice Hall.

————. 1978a. "The Logic of Naturalistic Inquiry." In *Sociological Methods: A Sourcebook*, edited by Norman K. Denzin. New York: McGraw-Hill.

————. 1978b. *The Research Act: A Theoretical Introduction to Sociological Methods*. 2d ed. New York: McGraw-Hill.

Denzin, Norman K. and Yvonna S. Lincoln, eds. 2000a. *Handbook of Qualitative Research*. 2d ed. Thousand Oaks, CA: Sage.

————. 2000b. "Introduction: The Discipline and Practice of Qualitative Research." Pp. 1-28 in *Handbook of Qualitative Research*. 2d ed., edited by Norman K. Denzin and Yvonna S. Lincoln. Thousand Oaks, CA: Sage.

Deutsch, Claudia H. 1998. "The Guru of Doing It Right Still Sees Much Work to Do." *New York Times*, November 15, p. B5.

Deutscher, Irwin. 1970. "Words and Deeds: Social Science and Social Policy." Pp. 27-51 in *Qualitative Methodology*, edited by W. J. Filstead. Chicago: Markham.

Dewey, John. 1956. *The Child and the Curriculum*. Chicago: University of Chicago Press.

Dobbert, Marion L. 1982. *Ethnographic Research: Theory and Application for Modern Schools and Societies*. New York: Praeger.

Domaingue, Robert. 1989. "Community Development Through Ethnographic Futures Research." *Journal of Extension* (summer): 22-23.

Douglas, Jack D. 1976. *Investigative Social Research: Individual and Team Field Research*. Beverly Hills, CA: Sage.

Douglass, Bruce and Clark Moustakas. 1985. "Heuristic Inquiry: The Internal Search to Know." *Journal of Humanistic Psychology* 25 (3, summer): 39-55.

Douglass, W. A. 2000. "In Search of Juan de Onate: Confessions of a Crypto-essentialist." *Journal of Anthropological Research* 56 (2): 137-62.

Drass, Kriss and Charles Ragin. 1992. *QCA: Qualitative Comparative Analysis*. A DOD software program distributed by the Publications Office, Institute for Public Policy,

Northwestern University. Evanston, IL: Northwestern University.

Duckworth, Eleanor. 1978. *The African Primary Science Program: An Evaluation and Extended Thoughts.* North Dakota Study Group on Evaluation monograph series. Grand Forks: Center for Teaching and Learning, University of North Dakota.

Dunn, Stephen. 2000. "Empathy." *The New Yorker,* April 10, p. 62.

Durkin, Tom. 1997. "Using Computers in Strategic Qualitative Research." Pp. 92-105 in *Context and Method in Qualitative Research,* edited by Gale Miller and Robert Dingwall. Thousand Oaks, CA: Sage.

Durrenberger, E. P. and S. Erem. 1999. "The Weak Suffer What They Must: A Natural Experiment in Thought and Structure." *American Anthropologist* 101 (4): 783-93.

Eberstadt, Nicholas, Nicolas Eberstadt, and Daniel Patrick Moynihan. 1995. *The Tyranny of Numbers: Mismeasurement and Misrule.* Washington, DC: American Enterprise Institute Press.

Edmunds, Stahrl W. 1978. *Alternative U.S. Futures: A Policy Analysis of Individual Choices in a Political Economy.* Santa Monica, CA: Goodyear.

Edwards, Ward, Marcia Guttentag, and Kurt Snapper. 1975. "A Decision-Theoretic Approach to Evaluation Research." In *Handbook of Evaluation Research.* Vol. 1, edited by E. L. Struening and M. Guttentag. Beverly Hills, CA: Sage.

Eichelberger, R. Tony. 1989. *Disciplined Inquiry: Understanding and Doing Educational Research.* White Plains, NY: Longman.

Eichenbaum, Luise and Susie Orbach. 1983. *Understanding Women: A Feminist Psychoanalytic Approach.* New York: Basic Books.

Eisner, Elliot W. 1997. "The New Frontier in Qualitative Research Methodology." *Qualitative Inquiry* 3 (3, September): 259-73.

————. 1996. "Should a Novel Count as a Dissertation in Education?" *Research in the Teaching of English* 30 (4): 403-27.

————. 1991. *The Enlightened Eye: Qualitative Inquiry and the Enhancement of Educational Practice.* New York: Macmillan.

————. 1988. "The Primacy of Experience and the Politics of Method." *Educational Researchers* (June/July): 15-20.

————. 1985. *The Art of Educational Evaluation: A Personal View.* London: Falmer.

Elliott, John. 1976. *Developing Hypotheses About Classrooms From Teachers Practical Constructs.* North Dakota Study Group on Evaluation monograph series. Grand Forks: Center for Teaching and Learning, University of North Dakota.

Ellis, Carolyn. 1986. *Fisher Folk: Two Communities on Chesapeake Bay.* Lexington: University Press of Kentucky.

Ellis, Carolyn and Arthur P. Bochner. 2000. "Autoethnography, Personal Narrative, Reflexivity: Researcher as Subject." Pp. 733-68 in *Handbook of Qualitative Research.* 2d ed., edited by Norman K. Denzin and Yvonna S. Lincoln. Thousand Oaks, CA: Sage.

————. 1996. *Composing Ethnography: Alternative Forms of Qualitative Writing.* Walnut Creek, CA: AltaMira.

Elmore, Richard F. 1976. "Follow Through Planned Variation." In *Social Program Implementation,* edited by Walter Williams and Richard F. Elmore. New York: Academic Press.

English, Fenwick W. 2000. "A Critical Appraisal of Sara Lawrence-Lightfoot's *Portraiture* as a Method of Educational Research." *Educational Researcher* 29 (7): 21-26.

Ensler, Eve. 2001. *The Vagina Monologues: The V-Day Edition.* New York: Villard.

Eoyang, Glenda H. 1997. *Coping With Chaos: Seven Simple Tools.* Cheyenne, WY: Lagumo.

Erickson, Fred. 1973. "What Makes School Ethnography 'Ethnographic'?" *Anthropology and Education Quarterly* 4 (2): 10-19.

Erickson, Ken and Donald Stull. 1998. *Doing Team Ethnography: Warnings and Advice.* Qualitative Research Methods Series, Vol. 42. Thousand Oaks, CA: Sage.

Ericsson, K. Anders and Herbert Alexander Simon. 1993. *Protocol Analysis: Verbal Reports as Data.* Cambridge: MIT Press.

Fadiman, Clifton, ed. 1985. *The Little, Brown Book of Anecdotes.* Boston: Little, Brown.

Farming Systems Support Project (FSSP). 1987. *Bibliography of Readings in Farming Systems.* Gainesville: University of Florida Institute of Food and Agricultural Sciences.

—————. 1986. *Diagnosis in Farming Systems Research and Extension.* Vol. 1. Gainesville: University of Florida Institute of Food and Agricultural Sciences.

Fehrenbacher, Harry L., Thomas R. Owens, and Joseph F. Haehnn. 1976. *The Use of Student Case Study Methodology in Program Evaluation.* Research Evaluation Development Paper Series No. 10. Portland, OR: Northwest Regional Educational Laboratory.

Feiman, Sharon. 1977. "Evaluating Teacher Centers." *School Review* 8:395-411.

Feldman, Martha S. 1995. *Strategies for Interpreting Qualitative Data.* Qualitative Research Methods Series, Vol. 33. Thousand Oaks, CA: Sage.

Ferguson, Cecile. 1989. *The Use and Impact of Evaluation by Decision Makers: Four Australian Case Studies.* Unpublished doctoral thesis, Macquarie University, Australia.

Festinger, Leon. 1956. *When Prophecy Fails: A Social and Psychological Study.* New York: HarperCollins College Division.

Fetterman, David M. 2000a. *Foundations of Empowerment Evaluation: Step by Step.* Thousand Oaks, CA: Sage.

—————. 2000b. "Summary of the STEP Evaluation and Dialogue." *American Journal of Evaluation* 21 (2, spring-summer): 239-259.

—————. 1989. *Ethnography: Step by Step.* Newbury Park, CA: Sage.

—————. 1988a. "Qualitative Approaches to Evaluating Education." *Educational Researcher* 17 (8, November): 17-23.

—————. 1988b. *Qualitative Approaches to Evaluation in Education: The Silent Scientific Revolution.* New York: Praeger.

—————, ed. 1984. *Ethnography in Educational Evaluation.* Beverly Hills, CA: Sage.

Fetterman, David M., A. J. Kaftarian, and A. Wandersman, eds. 1996. *Empowerment Evaluation: Knowledge and Tools for Self-Assessment and Accountability.* Thousand Oaks, CA: Sage.

Fielding, Nigel G. 2000. "The Shared Fate of Two Innovations in Qualitative Methodology: The Relationship of Qualitative Software and Secondary Analysis of Archived Qualitative Data." *Qualitative Social Research* [Online] 1 (3, December). Available from http://caqdas.soc.surrey.ac.uk/news.

—————. 1995. "Choosing the Right Qualitative Software Package." *Data Archive Bulletin* [Online] 58. Available from http://caqdas.soc.surrey.ac.uk/choose.htm.

Fielding, Nigel G. and Jane L. Fielding. 1986. *Linking Data.* Qualitative Research Methods Series, Vol. 4. Beverly Hills, CA: Sage.

Fielding, Nigel G. and Raymond M. Lee. 1998. *Computer Analysis and Qualitative Research.* Thousand Oaks, CA: Sage.

Filstead, William J., ed. 1970. *Qualitative Methodology.* Chicago: Markham.

Fitz-Gibbon, Carol Taylor and Lynn Lyons Morris. 1987. *How to Design a Program Evaluation.* Newbury Park, CA: Sage.

Fitzpatrick, Jacqueline, Jan Secrist, and Debra J. Wright. 1998. *Secrets for a Successful Dissertation.* Thousand Oaks, CA: Sage.

Fitzsimmons, Ellen L. 1989. "Alternative Extension Scenarios." *Journal of Extension* 28 (3, fall): 13-15.

Fonow, Mary Margaret and Judith A. Cook. 1991. *Beyond Methodology: Feminist Scholarship as Lived Research.* Bloomington: Indiana University Press.

Fontana, Andrea and James H. Frey. 2000. "The Interview: From Structured Questions to Negotiated Text." Pp. 645-72 in *Handbook of Qualitative Research.* 2d ed., edited by Norman K. Denzin and Yvonna S. Lincoln. Thousand Oaks, CA: Sage.

Fonte, John. 2001. "Why There Is a Culture War: Gramsci and Tocqueville in America." *Policy Review* 104 (January): 14-23.

Foucault, Michel. 1988. "The Aesthetics of Existence." In *Politics, Philosophy, Culture: Interviews and Other Writings 1977-1984*, edited by L. D. Kritzman. New York: Routledge.

———. 1972. *The Archaeology of Knowledge and the Discourse on Language.* New York: Pantheon.

Frake, Charles. 1962. "The Ethnographic Study of Cognitive Systems." In *Anthropology and Human Behavior*, edited by T. Gladwin and W. H. Sturtlevant. Washington, DC: Anthropology Society of Washington.

Frank, A. 2000. "Illness and Autobiographical Work." *Qualitative Sociology* 23:135-56.

———. 1995. *The Wounded Storyteller: Body, Illness, and Ethics.* Chicago: University of Chicago Press

Freire, Paulo. 1973. *Education for Critical Consciousness.* New York: Seabury.

Fricke, John G. and Raj Gill. 1989. "Participative Evaluations." *Canadian Journal of Evaluation* 4 (1, April/May): 11-26.

———. 1970. *Pedagogy of the Oppressed.* New York: Seabury.

Frow, John and Meaghan Morris. 2000. "Cultural Studies." Pp. 315-46 in *Handbook of Qualitative Research.* 2d ed., edited by Norman K. Denzin and Yvonna S. Lincoln. Thousand Oaks, CA: Sage.

Fuller, Steve. 2000. *Thomas Kuhn: A Philosophical History of Our Times.* Chicago: University of Chicago Press.

Gahan, Celia and Mike Hannibal. 1998. *Doing Qualitative Research Using QSR.NUD.IST.* Thousand Oaks, CA: Sage.

Gallucci, M. and M. Perugini 2000. "An Experimental Test of a Game-Theoretical Model of Reciprocity." *Journal of Behavioral Decision Making* 13 (4): 367-89.

Galt, D. L. and S. B. Mathema. 1987. "Farmer Participation in Farming Systems Research." In *Farming Systems Support Project Newsletter*, Vol. 5, No. 7. Gainesville: University of Florida Institute of Food and Agricultural Sciences.

Gamson, Joshua. 2000. "Sexualities, Queer Theory, and Qualitative Research." Pp. 347-65 in *Handbook of Qualitative Research.* 2d ed., edited by Norman K. Denzin and Yvonna S. Lincoln. Thousand Oaks, CA: Sage.

Garcia, Samuel E. 1984. *Alexander the Great: A Strategy Review.* Report No. 84-0960, Maxwell Air Force Base. Montgomery, Alabama: Air Command and Staff College.

Garfinkel, Harold. 1967. *Studies in Ethnomethodology.* Englewood Cliffs, NJ: Prentice Hall.

Geertz, Clifford. 2001. "Life Among the Anthros." *The New York Review of Books* 48 (2, February 8): 18-22.

———. 1973. "Deep Play: Notes on the Balinese Cockfight." Pp. 412-53 in *The Interpretation of Cultures.* New York: Basic Books.

Gentile, J. Ronald. 1994. "Inaction Research: A Superior and Cheaper Alternative for Educational Researchers." *Educational Researcher* 23 (2): 30-32.

Gephart, Robert P., Jr. 1988. *Ethnostatistics: Qualitative Foundations for Quantitative Research.* Qualitative Research Methods Series, Vol. 12. Newbury Park, CA: Sage.

Gergen, Mary M. and Kenneth J. Gergen. 2000. "Qualitative Inquiry: Tensions and Transformation." Pp. 1025-46 in *Handbook of Qualitative Research.* 2d ed., edited by Norman K. Denzin and Yvonna S. Lincoln. Thousand Oaks, CA: Sage.

Gharajedaghi, Jamshid. 1985. *Toward a Systems Theory of Organization.* Salinas, CA: Intersystems.

Gharajedaghi, Jamshid and Russell L. Ackoff. 1985. "Toward Systemic Education of Systems Scientists." *Systems Research* 2 (1): 21-27.

Gilgun, Jane. 1999. "Fingernails Painted Red: A Feminist Semiotic Analysis of a 'Hot' Text." *Qualitative Inquiry* 5 (2): 181-207.

———. 1996. "Human Development and Adversity in Ecological Perspective, Part 2, Three Patterns." *Families in Society* 77:459-576.

———. 1995. "We Shared Something Special: The Moral Discourse of Incest Perpetrators." *Journal of Marriage and the Family* 57:265-81.

———. 1994. "Avengers, Conquerors, Playmates, and Lovers: A Continuum of Roles Played by Perpetrators of Child Sexual Abuse." *Families in Society* 75:467-80.

———. 1991. "Resilience and the Intergenerational Transmission of Child Sexual Abuse." Pp. 93-105 in *Family Sexual Abuse: Frontline Research and Evaluation*, edited by Michael Quinn Patton. Newbury Park, CA: Sage.

Gilgun, Jane and Laura McLeod. 1999. "Gendering Violence." *Studies in Symbolic Interaction* 22:167-93.

Gilligan, Carol. 1982. *In a Different Voice: Psychological Theory and Women's Development.* Cambridge, MA: Harvard University Press.

Giorgi, A. 1971. "Phenomenology and Experimental Psychology." In *Duquesne Studies in Phenomenological Psychology*, edited by A. Giorgi, W. Fischner, and R. Von Eckartsberg. Pittsburgh, PA: Duquesne University Press.

Gladwell, Malcolm. 2000. "Annals of Medicine." *The New Yorker*, March 13, pp. 55-56.

———. 1997. "Just Ask for It: The Real Key to Technological Innovation." *The New Yorker*, April 7, pp. 45-49.

Gladwin, Christina H. 1989. *Ethnographic Decision Tree Modeling.* Qualitative Research Methods Series, Vol. 19. Newbury Park, CA: Sage.

Glaser, Barney G. 2001. "Doing Grounded Theory." *Grounded Theory Review* 2:1-18.

———. 2000. "The Future of Grounded Theory." *Grounded Theory Review* 1:1-8.

———, ed. 1993. *Examples of Grounded Theory: A Reader.* Mill Valley, CA: Sociology Press.

———. 1978. *Theoretical Sensitivity: Advances in the Methodology of Grounded Theory.* Mill Valley, CA: Sociology Press.

Glaser, Barney G. and Anselm L. Strauss. 1967. *Discovery of Grounded Theory: Strategies for Qualitative Research.* Chicago: Aldine.

Glass, Ronald David. 2001. "On Paulo Freire's Philosophy of Praxis and the Foundations of Liberation Education." *Educational Researcher* 30 (2): 15-25.

Glazer, Myron. 1972. *The Research Adventure: Promise and Problems of Fieldwork.* New York: Random House.

Gleick, James. 1987. *Chaos: Making a New Science.* New York: Penguin.

Glennon, Lynda M. 1983. "Synthesism: A Case of Feminist Methodology." Pp. 260-71 in *Beyond Method*, edited by Gareth Morgan. Beverly Hills, CA: Sage.

Glesne, Corrine. 1999. *Becoming Qualitative Researchers: An Introduction.* 2d ed. New York: Longman.

———. 1997. "That Rare Feeling: Representing Research Through Poetic Transcription." *Qualitative Inquiry* 3 (2, June): 202-21.

Gluck, Sherna Berger and Daphne Patai, eds. 1991. *Women's Words: The Feminist Practice of Oral History.* New York: Routledge.

Godet, Michel. 1987. *Scenarios and Strategic Management.* London: Butterworths.

Goffman, Erving. 1961. *Asylums: Essays on the Social Situation of Mental Patients and Other Inmates.* Garden City, NY: Anchor.

Golden-Biddle, Karen and Karen D. Locke. 1997. *Composing Qualitative Research.* Thousand Oaks, CA: Sage.

Golembiewski, Bob. 2000. "Three Perspectives on Appreciative Inquiry." *OD Practitioner* 32 (1): 53-58.

Goodall, H. L., Jr. 2000. *Writing the New Ethnography.* Walnut Creek, CA: AltaMira.

Goodenough, W. 1971. *Culture, Language, and Society.* Reading, MA: Addison-Wesley.

Goodson, Ivor and Martha Foote. 2001. "Testing Times: A School Case Study." *Education Policy Analysis Archives* 9 (2, January 15): 1-10.

Gore, Jennifer M. and Kenneth M. Zeichner. 1995. *Connecting Action Research to Genuine Teacher Development.* Pp. 203-14 in *Critical Discourses on Teacher Development,* edited by John Smyth. London: Cassell.

Graham, Robert J. 1993. "Decoding Teaching: The Rhetoric and Politics of Narrative Form." *Journal of Natural Inquiry* 8 (1, fall): 30-37.

Graue, M. Elizabeth and Daniel J. Walsh. 1998. *Studying Children in Context: Theories, Methods, and Ethics of Studying Children.* Thousand Oaks, CA: Sage.

Grbich, Carol. 1998. *Qualitative Research in Health: An Introduction.* Thousand Oaks, CA: Sage.

Greenbaum, Thomas L. 1997. *The Handbook for Focus Group Research.* 2d ed. Thousand Oaks, CA: Sage.

Greene, Jennifer C. 2000. "Understanding Social Programs through Evaluation." Pp. 981-99 in *Handbook of Qualitative Research.* 2d ed., edited by Norman K. Denzin and Yvonna S. Lincoln. Thousand Oaks, CA: Sage.

———. 1998a. "Balancing Philosophy and Practicality in Qualitative Evaluation." Pp. 35-49 in *Proceedings of the Stake Symposium on Educational Evaluation,* edited by Rita Davis. Champaign/Urbana: University of Illinois.

———. 1998b. "Qualitative Interpretive Interviewing." Pp. 135-54 in *Educational Research for Educational Productivity.* Advances in Educational Productivity, Vol. 7, edited by A. J. Reynolds and H. J. Walberg. Greenwich, CT: JAI.

———. 1990. "Technical Quality Versus User Responsiveness in Evaluation Practice." *Evaluation and Program Planning* 13 (3): 267-74.

Greig, Anne and Jayne Taylor. 1998. *Doing Research With Children.* Thousand Oaks, CA: Sage.

Grinder, John, J. DeLozier, and R. Bandler. 1977. *Patterns of the Hypnotic Techniques of Milton Erickson, M.D.* Vol. 2. Cupertino, CA: Meta Publications.

Guba, Egon G., ed. 1991. *The Paradigm Dialog.* Newbury Park, CA: Sage.

———. 1981. "Investigative Reporting." Pp. 67-86 in *Metaphors for Evaluation,* edited by Nick L. Smith. Beverly Hills, CA: Sage.

———. 1978. *Toward a Methodology of Naturalistic Inquiry in Educational Evaluation.* CSE Monograph Series in Evaluation No. 8. Los Angeles: Center for the Study of Evaluation, University of California, Los Angeles.

Guba, Egon G. and Yvonna S. Lincoln. 1990. "Can There Be a Human Science?" *Person-Centered Review* 5 (2): 130-54.

———. 1989. *Fourth Generation Evaluation.* Newbury Park, CA: Sage.

———. 1988. "Do Inquiry Paradigms Imply Inquiry Methodologies?" Pp. 89-115 in *Qualitative Approaches to Evaluation in Education: The Silent Scientific Revolution,* edited by D. Fetterman. New York: Praeger.

———. 1981. *Effective Evaluation: Improving the Usefulness of Evaluation Results Through Responsive and Naturalistic Approaches.* San Francisco: Jossey-Bass.

Gubrium, Jaber F. and James Holstein. 2000. "Analyzing Interpretive Practice." Pp. 487-508 in *Handbook of Qualitative Research.* 2d ed., edited by Norman K. Denzin and Yvonna S. Lincoln. Thousand Oaks, CA: Sage.

Gubrium, Jaber F. and Andrea Sankar. 1993. *Qualitative Methods in Aging.* Newbury Park, CA: Sage.

Guerrero, Sylvia H., ed. 1999a. *Gender-Sensitive & Feminist Methodologies: A Handbook for Health and Social Researchers.* Quezon City: University of the Philippines Center for Women's Studies.

———, ed. 1999b. *Selected Readings on Health and Feminist Research: A Sourcebook.* Quezon City: University of the Philippines Center for Women's Studies.

Guerrero-Manalo, Stella. 1999. Child Sensitive Interviewing: Pointers in Interviewing Child Victims of Abuse." Pp. 195-203 in *Gender-Sensitive & Feminist Methodologies: A Handbook for Health and Social Researchers,* edited by S. H. Guerrero. Quezon City:

University of the Philippines Center for Women's Studies.

Hacking, Ian. 2000. *The Social Construction of What.* Cambridge, MA: Harvard University Press.

Hall, Nina, ed. 1993. *Exploring Chaos: A Guide to the New Science of Disorder.* New York: Norton.

Hallowell, L. 1985. "The Outcome of the Brajuha Case: Legal Implications for Sociologists." *Footnotes, American Sociological Association* 13 (1): 13.

Hamel, Jacques with S. Dufour and D. Fortin. 1993. *Case Study Methods.* Qualitative Research Methods Series, Vol. 32. Newbury Park, CA: Sage.

Hamon, Raeann R. 1996. "Bahamian Life as Depicted by Wives' Tales and Other Old Sayings." Pp. 57-88 in *The Methods and Methodologies of Qualitative Family Research,* edited by Marvin B. Sussman and Jane F. Gilgun. New York: Haworth.

Handwerker, W. Penn. 2001. *Quick Ethnography.* Walnut Creek, CA: AltaMira.

Harding, Sandra. 1991. *Whose Science? Whose Knowledge? Thinking From Women's Lives.* Ithaca, NY: Cornell University Press.

Harkreader, Steve A. and Gary T. Henry. 2000. "Using Performance Measurement Systems for Assessing the Merit and Worth of Reforms." *American Journal of Evaluation* 21 (2, spring-summer): 151-70.

Harper, Douglas. 2000. "Reimagining Visual Methods. Pp. 717-32 in *Handbook of Qualitative Research.* 2d ed., edited by Norman K. Denzin and Yvonna S. Lincoln. Thousand Oaks, CA: Sage.

Harris, P. R. and R. T. Moran. 1979. *Managing Cultural Differences.* Houston, TX: Gulf.

Hart, L.K. 1999. "Culture, Civilization, and Demarcation at the Northwest Borders of Greece." *American Ethnologist* 26 (1, February): 196-220.

Harvey, C. and J. Denton. 1999. "To Come of Age: The Antecedents of Organizational Learning." *Journal of Management Studies* 36 (7, December): 897-918.

Harwood, Richard R. 1979. *Small Farm Development: Understanding and Improving Farming Systems in the Humid Tropics.* Boulder, CO: Westview.

Hausman, Carl. 2000. *Lies We Live By.* New York: Routledge.

Hawka, S. 1986. *The Experience of Feeling Unconditionally Loved.* Ann Arbor, MI: University of Microfilms International. Doctoral thesis, Graduate College, The Union Institute, Cincinnati, OH.

Hayano, D. M. 1979. "Autoethnography: Paradigms, Problems, and Prospects." *Human Organization* 38:113-20.

Hayes, T. A. 2000. "Stigmatizing Indebtedness: Implications for Labeling Theory. *Symbolic Interaction* 23 (1): 29-46.

Headland, T., Kenneth Pike, and M. Harris, eds. 1990. "Emics and Etics: The Insider/Outsider Debate." *Frontiers of Anthropology* 7.

Heap, James L. 1995. "Constructionism in the Rhetoric and Practice of Fourth-Generation Evaluation." *Evaluation and Program Planning* 18 (1): 51-61.

Hébert, Yvonne M. 1986. "Naturalistic Evaluation in Practice: A Case Study." *New Directions for Program Evaluation* 30 (March): 3-22, *Naturalistic Evaluation,* edited by David D. Williams. San Francisco: Jossey-Bass.

Heilein, Robert A. 1973. The Notebooks of Lazarus Long. New York: G.P.Putnam's Sons.

Helmer, Olaf. 1983. *Looking Forward: A Guide to Futures Research.* Beverly Hills, CA: Sage.

Hendricks, Michael. 1982. "Oral Policy Briefings." Pp. 249-58 in *Communication Strategies in Evaluation,* edited by N. L. Smith. Beverly Hills, CA: Sage.

Heron, John. 1996. *Cooperative Inquiry: Research Into the Human Condition.* Thousand Oaks, CA: Sage.

Hertz, Rosanna, ed. 1997. *Reflexivity and Voice.* Thousand Oaks, CA: Sage.

Heydebrand, Wolf V. 1983. "Organization and Praxis." Pp. 306-20 in *Beyond Method,* edited by Gareth Morgan. Beverly Hills, CA: Sage.

Higginbotham, J. B. and K. K. Cox. 1979. *Focus Group Interviews.* Chicago: American Marketing Association.

Hill, Michael R. 1993. *Archival Strategies and Techniques: Analytical Field Research.* Qualitative Research Methods Series, Vol. 31. Newbury Park, CA: Sage.

Hirsh, Sandra K. and Jean M. Kummerow. 1987. *Introduction to Type in Organizational Settings.* Palo Alto, CA: Consulting Psychologists Press.

Hodder, Ian. 2000. "The Interpretation of Documents and Material Culture." Pp. 703-15 in *Handbook of Qualitative Research.* 2d ed., edited by Norman K. Denzin and Yvonna S. Lincoln. Thousand Oaks, CA: Sage.

Hoffman, Lynn. 1981. *Foundations of Family Therapy: A Conceptual Framework for Systems Theory.* New York: Basic Books.

Holbrook, Terry L. 1996. "Document Analysis: The Contrast Between Official Case Records and the Journal Woman on Welfare." Pp. 41-56 in *The Methods and Methodologies of Qualitative Family Research,* edited by Marvin B. Sussman and Jane F. Gilgun. New York: Haworth.

Holland, J. H. 1998. *Emergence: From Chaos to Order.* Reading, MA: Helix.

———. 1995. *Hidden Order: How Adaptation Builds Complexity.* Reading, MA: Perseus.

Holley, Heather and Julio Arboleda-Florez. 1988. "Utilization Isn't Everything." *Canadian Journal of Program Evaluation* 3 (2, October/November): 93-102.

Hollinger, David. A. 2000. "Paradigms Lost." *The New York Times Book Review,* May 28, p. 23.

Holmes, Robyn M. 1998. *Fieldwork With Children.* Thousand Oaks, CA: Sage.

Holstein, James A. and Jaber F. Gubrium. 1995. *The Active Interview.* Qualitative Research Methods Series, Vol. 37. Thousand Oaks, CA: Sage.

Holte, John, ed. 1993. *Chaos: The New Science.* Nobel Conference 26. Saint Peter, MN: Gustavus Adolphus College.

Holtzman, John S. 1986. "Rapid Reconnaissance Guidelines for Agricultural Marketing and Food Systems Research in Developing Countries." Working Paper No. 30, Department of Agricultural Economics, Michigan State University, Lansing.

Hopson, Rodney, ed. 2000. *How and Why Language Matters in Evaluation. New Directions for Evaluation* 86 (summer). San Francisco: Jossey-Bass.

House, Ernest. 1991. "Confessions of a Responsive Goal-Free Evaluation." *Evaluation Practice* 12 (1, February): 109-13.

———. 1978. "Assumptions Underlying Evaluation Models." *Educational Researcher* 7:4-12.

———. 1977. *The Logic of Evaluative Argument.* CSE Monograph Series in Evaluation No. 7. Los Angeles: Center for the Study of Evaluation, University of California, Los Angeles.

House, E. R. and K. R. Howe. 2000. "Deliberative Democratic Evaluation." *New Directions for Evaluation* 85 (spring): 3-12, *Evaluation as a Democratic Process: Promoting Inclusion, Dialogue, and Deliberation,* edited by Katherine E. Ryan and Lizanne DeStefano. San Francisco: Jossey-Bass.

Huff, Darrell and Irving Geis. 1993. *How to Lie With Statistics.* New York: Norton.

Hull, Bill. 1978. *Teachers' Seminars on Children's Thinking.* North Dakota Study Group on Evaluation monograph series. Grand Forks: Center for Teaching and Learning, University of North Dakota.

Human Services Research Institute. 1984. *Assessing and Enhancing the Quality of Human Services.* Boston: Human Service Research Institute.

Humphrey, Derek. 1991. *Final Exit.* Eugene, OR: Hemlock Society.

Humphreys, Laud. 1970. *Tearoom Trade: Impersonal Sex in Public Places.* New York: Aldine de Gruyter.

Hunt, Scott A. and Robert D. Benford. 1997. "Dramaturgy and Methodology." Pp. 106-18 in *Context and Method in Qualitative Research,* edited by Gale Miller and Robert

Dingwall. Thousand Oaks, CA: Sage.

Hurty, Kathleen. 1976. "Report by the Women's Caucus." *Proceedings: Educational Evaluation and Public Policy, A Conference.* San Francisco: Far West Laboratory for Educational Research and Development.

Husserl, Edmund. 1967. "The Thesis of the Natural Standpoint and Its Suspension. " Pp. 68-79 in *Phenomenology,* edited by J. J. Kockelmans. Garden City, NY: Doubleday.

———. 1913. *Ideas.* London: George Allen and Unwin. Republished 1962, New York: Collier.

Ihde, D. 1977. *Experimental Phenomenology.* New York: Putnam.

Ivanic, Roz. 1998. *Writing and Identity: The Discoursal Construction of Identity in Academic Writing.* Studies in Written Language and Literacy, Vol. 5. Amsterdam: John Benjamins.

Jacob, Evelyn. 1988. "Clarifying Qualitative Research: A Focus on Traditions." *Educational Research* 17 (1, January-February): 16-24.

———. 1987. "Qualitative Research Traditions: A Review." *Review of Educational Research* 57 (1): 1-50.

James, William. [1902] 1999. *The Varieties of Religious Experience.* New York: Random House.

Janesick, Valerie J. 2000. "The Choreography of Qualitative Research Design: Minuets Improvisations, and Crystalization. Pp. 379-99 in *Handbook of Qualitative Research.* 2d ed., edited by Norman K. Denzin and Yvonna S. Lincoln. Thousand Oaks, CA: Sage.

———. 1998. *"Stretching" Exercises for Qualitative Researchers.* Thousand Oaks, CA: Sage.

Janowitz, Morris. 1979. "Where Is the Cutting Edge of Sociology?" *Sociological Quarterly* 20: 591-93.

Jarvis, Sara. 2000. *Getting the Log Out of Our Own Eyes: An Exploration of Individual and Team Learning in a Public Human Services Agency.* Unpublished doctoral dissertation, Graduate College, The Union Institute, Cincinnati, OH.

Jervis, Kathe. 1999. *Between Home and School: Cultural Interchange in an Elementary Classroom.* Teacher's College, Columbia University. New York: National Center for Restructuring Education, Schools and Teaching.

Johnson, Allen and Ross Sackett, 1998. "Direct Systematic Observation of Behavior." Pp. 301-31 in *Handbook of Methods in Cultural Anthropology,* edited by H. Russell Bernard. Walnut Creek, CA: AltaMira.

Johnson, Jeffrey C. 1990. *Selecting Ethnographic Informants.* Qualitative Research Methods Series, Vol. 22. Newbury Park, CA: Sage.

Johnson, John M. 1975. *Doing Field Research.* Beverly Hills, CA: Sage.

Johnston, Bruce F., Allen Hoben, D. W. Dijkerman, and W. K. Jaeger. 1987. *An Assessment of A.I.D. Activities to Promote Agricultural and Rural Development in Sub-Saharan Africa.* A.I.D. Evaluation Special Study No. 54. Washington, DC: U.S. Agency for International Development.

Johnstone, B. 2000. "The Individual Voice in Language." *Annual Review of Anthropology* 29:405-24.

Joint Committee on Standards for Educational Evaluation. 1994. *The Standards for Program Evaluation.* Thousand Oaks, CA: Sage.

Jones, James H. 1993. *Bad Blood: The Tuskegee Syphilis Experiment.* New York: Free Press.

Jones, Michael Owen. 1996. *Studying Organizational Symbolism.* Qualitative Research Methods Series, Vol. 39. Thousand Oaks, CA: Sage.

Jorgensen, Danny L. 1989. *Participant Observation: A Methodology for Human Studies.* Newbury Park, CA: Sage.

Junker, Buford H. 1960. *Field Work: An Introduction to the Social Sciences.* Chicago: University of Chicago Press.

Juran, Joseph M. 1951. *Quality Control Handbook.* New York: McGraw-Hill.

"Kalamazoo Schools." 1974. *American School Board Journal* (April): 32-40.

Kanter, Rosabeth Moss. 1983. *The Change Masters: Innovation for Productivity in the American Corporation.* New York: Simon & Schuster.

Kaplowitz, M. D. 2000. "Statistical Analysis of Sensitive Topics in Group and Individual Interviews." *Quality & Quantity* 34 (4, November): 419-31.

Kartunnen, Lauri. 1973. "Remarks on Presuppositions." Presented at the Texas conference Performances, Conversational Implicature and Presuppositions, March.

Katz, Louis. 1987. *The Experience of Personal Change.* Unpublished doctoral dissertation, Graduate College, The Union Institute, Cincinnati, OH.

Katzer, Jeffrey, Kenneth H. Cook, and Wayne W. Crouch. 1978. *Evaluating Information: A Guide for Users of Social Science Research.* Reading, MA: Addison-Wesley.

Kegan, Jerome. 1982. *The Evolving Self: Problem and Process in Human Development.* Cambridge, MA: Harvard University Press.

Kelley, Tom and Jonathan Littman. 2001. *The Art of Innovation: Lessons in Creativity From Ideo, America's Leading Design Firm.* Garden City, NY: Doubleday.

Kemmis, Stephen and Robin McTaggart. 2000. "Participatory Action Research." Pp. 567-606 in *Handbook of Qualitative Research.* 2d ed., edited by Norman K. Denzin and Yvonna S. Lincoln. Thousand Oaks, CA: Sage.

Kenny, M. L. 1999. "No Visible Means of Support: Child Labor in Urban Northeast Brazil." *Human Organization* 58 (4, winter): 375-86.

Kibel, Barry M. 1999. *Success Stories as Hard Data: An Introduction to Results Mapping.* New York: Kluwer Academic/Plenum.

Kim, Daniel H. 1999. *Introduction to Systems Thinking.* Williston, VT: Pegasus Communications.

———. 1994. *Systems Archetypes II: Using Systems Archetypes to Take Effective Action.* Williston, VT: Pegasus Communications.

———. 1993. *Systems Archetypes I.* Williston, VT: Pegasus Communications.

Kimmel, Allan J. 1988. *Ethnics and Values in Applied Social Research.* Newbury Park, CA: Sage.

Kincheloe, Joe L. and Peter McLaren. 2000. "Rethinking Critical Theory and Qualitative Research." Pp. 279-313 in *Handbook of Qualitative Research.* 2d ed., edited by Norman K. Denzin and Yvonna S. Lincoln. Thousand Oaks, CA: Sage.

King, Jean A. 1995. "Involving Practitioners in Evaluation Studies: How Viable Is Collaborative Evaluation in Schools." Pp. 86-102 in *Participatory Evaluation in Education: Studies in Evaluation Use and Organizational Learning,* edited by J. Bradley Cousins and Lorna Earl. London: Falmer.

King, Jean A. and M. Peg Lonnquist. 1994a. "The Future of Collaborative Action Research: Promises, Problems and Prospects." Unpublished paper, College of Education, University of Minnesota, Minneapolis, based on a presentation at the annual meeting of the American Educational Research Association, Atlanta, GA, 1993.

———. 1994b. "A Review of Writing on Action Research: 1944-Present." Unpublished paper, Center for Applied Research and Educational Improvement, University of Minnesota, Minneapolis.

King, Jean A., Lynn L. Morris, and Carol T. Fitz-Gibbon. 1987. *How to Assess Program Implementation.* Newbury Park, CA: Sage.

King, Jean A. and Ellen Pechman. 1982. *Improving Evaluation Use in Local Schools.* Washington, DC: National Institute of Education.

Kirk, Jerome and M. L. Miller. 1986. *Reliability and Validity in Qualitative Research.* Beverly Hills, CA: Sage.

Kleining, Gerhard and Harald Witt. 2000. "The Qualitative Heuristic Approach: A Methodology for Discovery in Psychology and the Social Sciences. Rediscovering the Method of Introspection as an Example." *Forum: Qualitative Social Research* [Online] 1 (1, January). Available from http://qualitative-research.net/fqs.

Kling, Jeffrey R., Jeffrey B. Liebman, and Lawrence F. Katz. 2001. "Bullets Don't Got No Name: Consequences of Fear in the Ghetto." Paper presented at the conference Mixed Methods sponsored by the MacArthur Network on Successful Pathways Through Middle Childhood, January 25, Santa Monica, CA.

Kloman, Erasmus H., ed. 1979. *Cases in Accountability: The Work of GAO.* Boulder, CO: Westview.

Kneller, G. F. 1984. *Movements of Thought in Modern Education.* New York: John Wiley.

Kopala, Mary and Lisa A. Suzuki. 1999. *Using Qualitative Methods in Psychology.* Thousand Oaks, CA: Sage.

Kramer, Peter D. 1993. *Listening to Prozac.* New York: Penguin.

Krenz, Claudia and Gilbert Sax. 1986. "What Quantitative Research Is and Why It Doesn't Work." *American Behavioral Scientist* 30 (1, September-October): 58-69.

Krishnamurti, J. 1964. *Think on These Things.* New York: Harper & Row.

Krueger, Otto and Janet M. Thuesen. 1988. *Type Talk.* New York: Delacorte.

Krueger, Richard A. 1997a. *Analyzing and Reporting Focus Group Results.* The Focus Group Kit, Vol. 6. Thousand Oaks, CA: Sage.

———. 1997b. *Developing Questions for Focus Groups.* The Focus Group Kit, Vol. 3. Thousand Oaks, CA: Sage.

———. 1997c. *Moderating Focus Groups.* The Focus Group Kit, Vol. 5. Thousand Oaks, CA: Sage.

———. 1994. *Focus Group Interviews: A Practical Guide for Applied Research.* 2d ed. Thousand Oaks, CA: Sage.

Krueger, Richard A. and Mary Anne Casey. 2000. *Focus Group Interviews: A Practical Guide for Applied Research.* 3d ed. Thousand Oaks, CA: Sage.

Krueger, Richard A. and Jean A. King. 1997. *Involving Community Members in Focus Groups.* The Focus Group Kit, Vol. 4. Thousand Oaks, CA: Sage.

Kuhn, Thomas. 1970. *The Structure of Scientific Revolutions.* Chicago: University of Chicago Press.

Kuhns, Eileen and S. V. Martorana, eds. 1982. *Qualitative Methods for Institutional Research.* San Francisco: Jossey-Bass.

Kulish, Nicholas. 2001. "Ancient Split of Assyrians and Chaldeans Leads to Modern-Day Battle Over Census." *Wall Street Journal,* March 12, p. 1.

Kushner, Saville. 2000. *Personalizing Evaluation.* London: Sage.

Kvale, Steinar. 1996. *InterViews: An Introduction to Qualitative Research Interviewing.* Thousand Oaks, CA: Sage.

———. 1987. "Validity in the Qualitative Research Interview." *Methods: A Journal for Human Science* 1 (2, winter): 37-72.

Ladson-Billings, Gloria. 2000. "Racialized Discourses and Ethnic Epistemologies." Pp. 257-77 in *Handbook of Qualitative Research.* 2d ed., edited by Norman K. Denzin and Yvonna S. Lincoln. Thousand Oaks, CA: Sage.

Lahey, Lisa, E. Souvaine, R. Kegan, R. Goodman, and S. Felix. n.d. (about 1988). "A Guide to the Subject-Object Interview: Its Administration and Interpretation." Cambridge, MA: Subject-Object Research Groups, Harvard Graduate School of Education. Mimeo.

Lalonde, Bernadette I. D. 1982. "Quality Assurance." Pp. 352-75 in *Handbook on Mental Health Administration,* edited by Michael J. Austin and William E. Hershey. San Francisco: Jossey-Bass.

Lang, K. and G. E. Lang. 1960. "Decisions for Christ: Billy Graham in New York City." In *Identity and Anxiety,* edited by M. Stein, A. J. Vidich, and D. M. White. New York: Free Press.

Lather, P. 1986. "Research as Praxis." *Harvard Educational Review* 56 (3): 257-77.

Lawrence-Lightfoot, Sara. 2000. *Respect: An Exploration.* Cambridge, MA: Perseus.

————. 1997. "Illumination: Framing the Terrain." Pp. 41-59 in *The Art and Science of Portraiture*, by S. Lawrence-Lightfoot and J. H. Davis. San Francisco: Jossey-Bass.

Lawrence-Lightfoot, Sara and Jessica Hoffman Davis. 1997. *The Art and Science of Portraiture*. San Francisco: Jossey-Bass.

LeCompte, Margaret D. and Jean Schensul. 1999. *Designing and Conducting Ethnographic Research*. Ethnographer's Toolkit, Vol. 1. Walnut Creek, CA: AltaMira.

Lee, Penny. 1996. *The Whorf Theory Complex: A Critical Reconstruction. Amsterdam Studies in Theory and History of Linguistic Science, Series 3, Studies in History of Language*. Vol. 81. Philadelphia: John Benjamins.

Lee, Thomas W. 1998. *Using Qualitative Methods in Organizational Research*. Thousand Oaks, CA: Sage.

Leeuw F., R. Rist, and R. Sonnichsen, eds. 1993. *Comparative Perspectives on Evaluation and Organizational Learning*. New Brunswick, NJ: Transaction.

Leonard, Elmore. 2001. "Anecdotes." Week in Review. *New York Times*, March 11, p. 7.

Levin, B. 1993. "Collaborative Research in and With Organizations." *Qualitative Studies in Education* 6 (4): 331-40.

Levin-Rozalis, Miri. 2000. "Abduction: A Logical Criterion for Programme and Project Evaluation." *Evaluation* 6 (4): 415-32.

Levi-Strauss, Claude. 1966. *The Savage Mind*. 2d ed. Chicago: University of Chicago Press.

Levitt, Norman. 1998. "Why Professors Believe Weird Things." *Skeptic* 6 (3): 28-35.

Levy, P. F. 2001. "The Nut Island Effect: When Good Teams Go Wrong." *Harvard Business Review* 79 (3): 51-59, 163.

Lewis, P. J. 2001. "The Story of I and the Death of a Subject." *Qualitative Inquiry* 7 (1, February): 109-28.

Lieblich, Amia, Rivka Tuval-Mashiach, and Tamar Zilber. 1998. *Narrative Research: Reading, Analysis, and Interpretation*. Thousand Oaks, CA: Sage.

Liebow, Elliot. 1967. *Tally's Corner*. Boston: Little, Brown.

Lincoln, Yvonna S. 1990. "Toward a Categorical Imperative for Qualitative Research." Pp. 277-95 in *Qualitative Inquiry in Education: The Continuing Debate*, edited by Elliot Eisner and Alan Peshkin. New York: Teachers College Press.

————. 1985. *Organizational Theory and Inquiry: The Paradigm Revolution*. Beverly Hills, CA: Sage.

Lincoln, Yvonna S. and Egon G. Guba. 2000. "Paradigmatic Controversies, Contradictions, and Emerging Confluences." Pp. 163-88 in *Handbook of Qualitative Research*. 2d ed., edited by Norman K. Denzin and Yvonna S. Lincoln. Thousand Oaks, CA: Sage.

————. 1986. "But Is It Rigorous? Trustworthiness and Authenticity in Naturalistic Evaluation." *New Directions for Program Evaluation* 30 (summer): 73-84, *Naturalistic Evaluation*, edited by David D. Williams. San Francisco: Jossey-Bass.

————. 1985. *Naturalistic Inquiry*. Beverly Hills, CA: Sage.

Lofland, John. 1971. *Analyzing Social Settings*. Belmont, CA: Wadsworth.

Lofland, John and L. H. Lofland. 1984. *Analyzing Social Settings*. Belmont, CA: Wadsworth.

Lonner, Walter J. and John W. Berry. 1986. *Field Methods in Cross-Cultural Research*. Beverly Hills, CA: Sage.

Louis, M. R. 1983. "Organizations as Culture Bearing Milieux." In *Organizational Symbolism*, edited by L. R. Pondy, G. Morgan, P. J. Frost, Samuel B. Bacharach, & T. C. Dandridge. Greenwich, CT: JAI.

Love, Arnold J. 1991. *Internal Evaluation: Building Organizations From Within*. Newbury Park, CA: Sage.

Mabry, L., ed. 1997. *Evaluation and the Postmodern Dilemma*. Advances in Program Evaluation, Vol. 3. Greenwich, CT: JAI.

MacBeth, Douglas. 2001. On Reflexivity in Qualitative Research." *Qualitative Inquiry* 7(1): 35-68.

MacDonald, B. 1987. "Evaluation and Control of Education." In *Issues and Methods in Evaluation,* edited by R. Murphy and H. Torrance. London: Paul Chapman.

MacQueen, Kathleen M. and Bobby Milstein. 1999. "A Systems Approach to Qualitative Data Management and Analysis." *Field Methods* 11 (1): 27-39.

Madriz, Esther. 2000. "Focus Groups in Feminist Research." Pp. 835-50 in *Handbook of Qualitative Research.* 2d ed., edited by Norman K. Denzin and Yvonna S. Lincoln. Thousand Oaks, CA: Sage.

Maguire, Patricia. 1996. "Considering More Feminist Participatory Research: What's Congruency Got to Do With It?" *Qualitative Inquiry* 2 (1, March): 106-18.

Mairs, Nancy. 1997. *Voice Lessons: On Becoming a (Woman) Writer.* Boston: Beacon.

Manning, Peter K. 1987. *Semiotics and Fieldwork.* Qualitative Research Methods Series, Vol. 7. Newbury Park, CA: Sage.

Marino, Rocco A. 1985. *How Adolescent Sons Perceive and Describe the Impact of the Father-Son Relationship on Their Own Sense of Self-Identity.* Doctoral dissertation, Graduate College, The Union Institute, Cincinnati, OH.

Mark, M. M., G. T. Henry, and G. Julnes. 2000. *Evaluation: An Integrated Framework for Understanding, Guiding, and Improving Public and Nonprofit Policies and Programs.* San Francisco: Jossey-Bass.

Marshall, Catherine and Gretchen Rossman. 1989. *Designing Qualitative Research.* Newbury Park, CA: Sage.

Marx, Leo. 1999. "The Struggle Over Thoreau." *The New York Review of Books* 46 (11): 60-64.

Maslow, Abraham H. 1966. *The Psychology of Science.* New York: Harper & Row.

———. 1956. "Toward a Humanistic Psychology." *Etc.* 13:10-22.

Mathews, Ruth, J. K. Matthews, and Kathleen Speltz. 1989. *Female Sexual Offenders.* Orwell, VT: Safer Society Press.

Matthews, Jane K., Jodie Raymaker, and Kathleen Speltz. 1991. "Effects of Reunification on Sexually Abusive Families." Pp. 147-61 in *Family Sexual Abuse: Frontline Research and Evaluation,* edited by Michael Quinn Patton. Newbury Park, CA: Sage.

Maxwell, Joseph A., Philip G. Bashook, and Leslie J. Sandlow. 1987. "Combining Ethnographic and Experimental Methods in Educational Evaluation: A Case Study." Pp. 568-90 in *Evaluation Studies Review Annual,* No. 12, edited by William R. Shadish, Jr. and Charles S. Reichardt. Newbury Park, CA: Sage.

McClure, Gail. 1989. *Organizational Culture as Manifest in Critical Incidents: A Case Study of the Faculty of Agriculture, University of the West Indies.* Unpublished doctoral dissertation, University of Minnesota, Minneapolis.

McCracken, Grant. 1988. *The Long Interview.* Qualitative Research Methods Series, Vol. 13. Newbury Park, CA: Sage.

McGuigan, Jim. 1998. *Cultural Methodologies.* Thousand Oaks, CA: Sage.

McLaughlin, Milbrey. 1976. "Implementation as Mutual Adaptation." In *Social Program Implementation,* edited by Walter Williams and Richard F. Elmore. New York: Academic Press.

McNamara, Carter. 1996. *Evaluation of a Group-Managed, Multi-Technique Management Development Program That Includes Action Learning.* Unpublished doctoral dissertation, Graduate College, The Union Institute, Cincinnati, OH.

Mead, George H. 1934. *Mind, Self and Society.* Chicago: University of Chicago Press.

Mead, Margaret. 1977. *Letters From the Field, 1925-1975.* New York: Harper & Row.

Meeker, Joseph W. 1980. *The Comedy of Survival: In Search of an Environmental Ethic.* Los Angeles: Guild of Tutors Press. Reprinted 1997, University of Arizona Press.

Merleau-Ponty, Maurice. 1962. *The Phenomenology of Perception.* London: Routledge & Kegan Paul.

Merriam, John E. and Joel Makower. 1988. *Trend Watching: How the Media Create Trends and How to Be the First to Uncover Them.* New York: Tilden Press, American Management Association (AMACOM).

Merriam, Sharon. 1997. *Qualitative Research and Case Study Applications in Education.* San Francisco: Jossey-Bass.

Mertens, Donna M. 1999. "Inclusive Evaluation: Implications of Transformative Theory for Evaluation. *American Journal of Evaluation* 20 (1, winter): 1-14.

———. 1998. *Research Methods in Education and Psychology: Integrating Diversity With Quantitative and Qualitative Approaches.* Thousand Oaks, CA: Sage.

Merton, R., M. Riske, and P. L. Kendall. 1956. *The Focused Interview.* New York: Free Press.

Messick, S. 1989. "Validity." Pp. 13-103 in *Educational Measurement.* 3d ed., edited by R. L. Linn. New York: American Council on Education/Macmillan.

Meyers, William R. 1981. *The Evaluation Enterprise.* San Francisco: Jossey-Bass.

Miles, Matthew B. and A. M. Huberman. 1994. *Qualitative Data Analysis: An Expanded Sourcebook.* 2d ed. Newbury Park, CA: Sage.

———. 1984. *Qualitative Data Analysis: A Sourcebook of New Methods.* Beverly Hills, CA: Sage.

Milgram, Stanley. 1974. *Obedience to Authority.* New York: Harper & Row.

Milius, Susan. 1998. "When Worlds Collide." *Science* 154 (6): 92-93.

Miller, Gale. 1997. "Contextualizing Texts: Studying Organizational Texts." Pp. 77-91 in *Context and Method in Qualitative Research,* edited by Gale Miller and Robert Dingwall. Thousand Oaks, CA: Sage.

Miller, Sally and Patricia Winstead-Fry. 1982. *Family Systems Theory and Nursing Practice.* East Norwalk, CT: Appleton & Lange.

Miller, William L. and Benjamin F. Crabtree. 2000. "Clinical Research." Pp. 607-32 in *Handbook of Qualitative Research.* 2d ed., edited by Norman K. Denzin and Yvonna S. Lincoln. Thousand Oaks, CA: Sage.

Mills, C. Wright. 1961. *The Sociological Imagination.* New York: Oxford University Press.

Minnich, Elizabeth. Forthcoming. *Transforming Knowledge.* 2d ed. Philadelphia: Temple University Press.

———. 1999. "What's Wrong With Civic Life? Remembering Political Wellsprings of U.S. Democratic Action." *The Good Society* 9 (2): 7-14.

———. 1990. *Transforming Knowledge.* Philadelphia: Temple University Press.

Mitchell, Richard. 1979. *Less Than Words Can Say: The Underground Grammarian.* Boston: Little, Brown.

Mitchell, Richard G., Jr. 1993. *Secrecy and Fieldwork.* Qualitative Research Methods Series, Vol. 29. Newbury Park, CA: Sage.

Montgomery, Jason and Willard Fewer. 1988. *Family Systems and Beyond.* New York: Human Science Press.

Moos, Rudolf. 1975. *Evaluating Correctional and Community Settings.* New York: Wiley Interscience.

Morgan, David L. 1997a. *The Focus Group Guidebook.* The Focus Group Kit, Vol. 1. Thousand Oaks, CA: Sage.

———. 1997b. *Planning Focus Groups.* The Focus Group Kit, Vol. 2. Thousand Oaks, CA: Sage.

———. 1988. *Focus Groups as Qualitative Research.* Qualitative Research Methods Series, Vol. 16. Newbury Park, CA: Sage.

Morgan, Gareth. 1989. *Creative Organizational Theory: A Resourcebook.* Newbury Park, CA: Sage.

———. 1986. *Images of Organization.* Beverly Hills, CA: Sage.

———, ed. 1983. *Beyond Methods: Strategies for Social Research.* Beverly Hills, CA: Sage.

Morris, Edmund. 2000. *Dutch: A Memoir of Ronald Reagan.* New York: Random House.

Morris, M. W. 2000. "The Lessons We (Don't) Learn: Counterfactual Thinking and Organizational Accountability After a Close Call." *Administrative Science Quarterly* 45 (4): 737-65.

Morrison, David. 1999. "The Role of Observation." *Skeptical Briefs* 9 (1): 8.

Morse, Janice M., ed. 1997. *Completing a Qualitative Project.* Thousand Oaks, CA: Sage.

———. 1991. *Qualitative Nursing Research.* Newbury Park, CA: Sage.

Morse, Janice M. and Peggy Anne Field. 1995. *Qualitative Research Methods for Health Professionals.* Thousand Oaks, CA: Sage.

Morse, Janice M., Janice Penrod, and Judith Hupcey. 2000. "Qualitative Outcome Analysis: Evaluating Nursing Interventions for Complex Clinical Phenomena." *Journal of Nursing Scholarship* 32 (2): 125-30.

Moustakas, Clark. 1997. *Relationship Play Therapy.* Northvale, NJ: Jason Aronson.

———. 1995. *Being-In, Being-For, Being-With.* Northvale, NJ: Jason Aronson.

———. 1994. *Phenomenological Research Methods.* Thousand Oaks, CA: Sage.

———. 1990a. "Heuristic Research: Design and Methodology." *Person-Centered Review* 5 (2): 170-90.

———. 1990b. *Heuristic Research: Design, Methodology, and Applications.* Newbury Park, CA: Sage.

———. 1988. *Phenomenology, Science and Psychotherapy.* Sydney, Nova Scotia, Canada: Family Life Institute, University College of Cape Breton.

———. 1981. *Rhythms, Rituals and Relationships.* Detroit, MI: Center for Humanistic Studies.

———. 1975. *The Touch of Loneliness.* Englewood Cliffs, NJ: Prentice Hall.

———. 1972. *Loneliness and Love.* Englewood Cliffs, NJ: Prentice Hall.

———. 1961. *Loneliness.* Englewood Cliffs, NJ: Prentice Hall.

Mueller, Marsha R. 1996. *Immediate Outcomes of Lower-Income Participants in Minnesota's Universal Access Early Childhood Fairly Education.* St. Paul, MN: Department of Children, Families, and Learning.

Mueller, Marsha R. and Jody Fitzpatrick. 1998. "Dialogue With Marsha Mueller." *American Journal of Evaluation* 19 (1): 97-98.

Murali, M. Lakshmanan, ed. 1995. *Chaos in Nonlinear Oscillators: Controlling and Synchronization.* World Scientific Series on Nonlinear Science, Series A: Monographs and Treatises. New York: World Scientific.

Murray, Michael and Kerry Chamberlain. 1999. *Qualitative Health Psychology: Theories and Methods.* Thousand Oaks, CA: Sage.

Mwaluko G. S. and T. B. Ryan. 2000. "The Systemic Nature of Action Learning Programmes." *Systems Research and Behavioral Science* 17 (4, July-August): 393-401.

Myers, Isabel Briggs with Peter Meyers. 1995. *Gifts Differing.* Palo Alto, CA: Consulting Psychologists Press.

Myrdal, Gunnar. 1969. *Objectivity in Social Research.* New York: Random House/Pantheon.

Nadel, Lynn and Daniel Stein, eds. 1995. *The 1993 Lectures in Complex Systems.* Santa Fe Institute Studies in the Sciences of Complexity. Lectures, Vol. 6. Boulder, CO: Perseus.

Nagel, Ernest. 1961. *The Structure of Science.* New York: Harcourt, Brace and World.

Naisbitt, John. 1982. *Megatrends: Ten New Directions Transforming Our Lives.* New York: Warner Books.

Naisbitt, John and Patricia Aburdene. 1990: *Megatrends 2000: Ten New Directions for the 1990s.* New York: William Morrow.

Nash, Roderick. 1986. *Wilderness and the American Mind.* New Haven, CT: Yale University Press.

Neimeyer, Greg J., ed. 1993. *Constructivist Assessment: A Casebook.* Newbury Park, CA: Sage.

Newman, Diana and Robert Brown. 1996. *Applied Ethics for Program Evaluation.* Thousand Oaks, CA: Sage.

Noblit, George W. and R. Dwight Hare. 1988. *Meta-Ethnography: Synthesizing Qualitative Studies.* Newbury Park, CA: Sage.

Nussbaum, Martha. 2001. "Disabled Lives: Who Cares?" *The New York Review of Books* 48 (1, January 11): 34-37.

Oakley, A. 1981. "Interviewing Women: A Contradiction in Terms." Pp. 30-61 in *Doing Feminist Research,* edited by H. Roberts. London: Routledge & Kegan Paul.

Ogbor, J. O. 2000. "Mythicizing and Reification in Entrepreneurial Discourse: Ideology-Critique of Entrepreneurial Studies." *Journal of Management Studies* 37 (5, July): 605-35.

Olesen, Virginia L. 2000. "Feminisms and Qualitative Research At and Into the Millennium." Pp. 215-56 in *Handbook of Qualitative Research.* 2d ed., edited by Norman K. Denzin and Yvonna S. Lincoln. Thousand Oaks, CA: Sage.

Olson, Ruth Anne. 1974. "A Value Perspective on Evaluation." Marcy Open School, Minneapolis Public Schools. Mimeo.

Ormerod, Paul. 2001. *Butterfly Economics: A New General Theory of Social and Economic Behavior.* New York: Basic Books.

Owens, Thomas, Joseph F. Haehnn, and Harry L. Fehrenbacher. 1976. *The Use of Multiple Strategies in the Evaluation of an Experience-Based Career Education Program.* Research Evaluation Development Paper Series No. 9. Portland, OR: Northwest Regional Educational Laboratory.

Packer, Martin and Richard Addison. 1989. *Entering the Circle: Hermeneutic Investigation in Psychology.* Albany: State University of New York Press.

Padgett, Deborah K. 1998. *Qualitative Methods in Social Work Research: Challenges and Rewards.* Thousand Oaks, CA: Sage.

Page, Reba N. 2000. "The Turn Inward in Qualitative Research." Pp. 3-16 in *Acts of Inquiry in Qualitative Research,* edited by B. M. Brizuela, J. P. Stewart, R. G. Carrillo, and J. G. Berger. Reprint Series No. 34. Cambridge, MA: Harvard Educational Review.

Palmer, Laura. 1988. *Shrapnel in the Heart.* New York: Vintage.

Palmer, R. E. 1969. *Hermeneutics.* Evanston, IL: Northwestern University Press.

Palumbo, Dennis J., ed. 1987. *The Politics of Program Evaluation.* Newbury Park, CA: Sage.

Panati, Charles. 1987. *Extraordinary Origins of Everyday Things.* New York: Harper & Row.

Parameswaran, Radhika. 2001. "Feminist Media Ethnography in India: Exploring Power, Gender, and Culture in the Field." *Qualitative Inquiry* 7 (1, February): 69-103.

Park, Clair Claiborne with Oliver Sacks. 2001. *Exiting Nirvana: A Daughter's Life With Autism.* Boston: Little, Brown.

Parlett, Malcolm and David Hamilton. 1976. "Evaluation as Illumination: A New Approach to the Study of Innovatory Programs." In *Evaluation Studies Review Annual,* Vol. 1, edited by G. V. Glass. Beverly Hills, CA: Sage.

Partnow, Elaine. 1978. *The Quotable Woman, 1800-On.* Garden City, NY: Anchor.

Patton, Michael Quinn. 2000. "Language Matters." *New Directions for Evaluation* 86 (summer): 5-16, *How and Why Language Matters in Evaluation,* edited by Rodney Hopson. San Francisco: Jossey-Bass.

———. 1999a. *Grand Canyon Celebration: A Father-Son Journey of Discovery.* Amherst, NY: Prometheus.

———. 1999b. "On Enhancing the Quality and Credibility of Qualitative Analysis." *Health Services Research* 34 (5, Part 2, December): 1189-208.

———. 1999c. "Organizational Development and Evaluation." Special issue of *Canadian Journal of Program Evaluation,* pp. 93-113.

———. 1999d. "Some Framing Questions About Racism and Evaluation." *American Journal of Evaluation* 20 (3, fall): 437-51.

———. 1998. "Discovering Process Use." *Evaluation* 4 (2): 225-33.

———. 1997a. *Utilization-Focused Evaluation: The New Century Text.* 3d ed. Thousand Oaks, CA: Sage.

———. 1997b. "View Toward Distinguishing Empowerment Evaluation and Placing It in a Larger Context." *Evaluation Practice* 18 (2): 147-63.

———. 1996a. *Inside the Doctoral Dissertation.* 2-hr. videotape. Cincinnati, OH: The Union Institute. Online at www.tui.edu.

———. 1996b. "A World Larger Than Formative and Summative." *Evaluation Practice* 17 (2): 131-44.

———. 1994. "Developmental Evaluation." *Evaluation Practice* 15 (3): 311-20.

———, ed. 1991. *Family Sexual Abuse: Frontline Research and Evaluation.* Newbury Park, CA: Sage.

———. 1990. "Humanistic Psychology and Qualitative Research: Shared Principles and Processes." *Person-Centered Review* 5 (2): 191-202.

———. 1988a. "Extension's Future: Beyond Technology Transfer." *Knowledge* 1 (4, June): 476-91.

———. 1988b. "Integrating Evaluations Into a Program for Increased Utility and Cost-Effectiveness." *New Directions for Program Evaluation* 39 (fall), *Evaluation Utilization,* edited by John A. McLaughlin, Larry J. Weber, Robert W. Covert, and Robert B. Ingle. San Francisco: Jossey-Bass.

———. 1988c. "Paradigms and Pragmatism." Pp. 116-37 in *Qualitative Approaches to Evaluation in Education: The Silent Scientific Revolution,* edited by David M. Fetterman. New York: Praeger.

———. 1988d. "Query: The Future and Evaluation." *Evaluation Practice* 9 (4): 90-93.

———. 1987a. *Creative Evaluation.* 2d ed. Newbury Park, CA: Sage.

———. 1987b. "The Extension Organization of the Future." *Journal of Extension* 15 (spring): 22-24.

———, ed. 1985. *Culture and Evaluation. New Directions for Program Evaluation* 25 (March). San Francisco: Jossey-Bass.

———. 1981. *Practical Evaluation.* Beverly Hills, CA: Sage.

———. 1978. *Utilization-Focused Evaluation.* Beverly Hills, CA: Sage.

———. 1975. *Alternative Evaluation Research Paradigms.* North Dakota Study Group on Evaluation monograph series. Grand Forks: Center for Teaching and Learning, University of North Dakota.

Patton, Michael Quinn with Brandon Q. T. Patton. 2001. "What's in a Name? Heroic Nomenclature in the Grand Canyon." *Plateau Journal* 4 (2, winter): 16-29.

Patton, Michael Quinn and Stacey Stockdill. 1987. "Summative Evaluation of the Technology for Literacy Center." St. Paul, MN: Saint Paul Foundation.

Paul, Jim. 1994. *What I Learned Losing a Million Dollars.* Chicago: Infrared.

Pawson, R. and N. Tilley. 1997. *Realistic Evaluation.* London: Sage.

Payne, Stanley L. 1951. *The Art of Asking Questions.* Princeton, NJ: Princeton University Press.

Pedler, M., ed. 1991. *Action Learning in Practice.* Aldershot Hauts, UK: Gower.

Pelto, Pertti J. and Gretel H. Pelto. 1978. *Anthropological Research: The Structure of Inquiry.* Cambridge, UK: Cambridge University Press.

Peräkylä, Anssi. 1997. "Reliability and Validity in Research Based on Transcripts." Pp. 201-20 in *Qualitative Research: Theory, Method and Practice,* edited by David Silverman. London: Sage.

Percy, Walker. 1990. *The Message in the Bottle.* New York: Noonday.

Perls, Fritz. 1973. *The Gestalt Approach and Eye Witness to Therapy.* Palo Alto, CA: Science and Behavior Books.

Perrone, Vito, ed. 1985. *Portraits of High Schools.* Carnegie Foundation for the Advancement of Teaching. Lawrenceville, NJ: Princeton University Press.

———. 1977. *The Abuses of Standardized Testing.* Bloomington, IN: Phi Delta Kappa Educational Foundation.

Perrone, Vito and Michael Quinn Patton with Barbara French. 1976. *Does Accountability Count Without Teacher Support?* Minneapolis: Minnesota Center for Social Research, University of Minnesota.

Peshkin, Alan. 2001. "Angles of the Vision: Enhancing Perception in Qualitative Research." *Qualitative Inquiry* 7 (2): 238-53.

———. 2000a. "The Nature of Interpretation in Qualitative Research." *Educational Researcher* 17 (7, October): 17-22.

———. 2000b. *Permissible Advantage? The Moral Consequences of Elite Schooling.* Mahwah, NJ: Lawrence Erlbaum.

———. 1997. *Places of Memory: Whiteman's Schools and Native American Communities.* Sociocultural, Political, and Historical Studies in Education. Mahwah, NJ: Lawrence Erlbaum.

———. 1988. "In Search of Subjectivity—One's Own." *Educational Researcher* 29 (9, December): 5-9.

———. 1986. *God's Choice: The Total World of a Fundamentalist Christian School.* Chicago: University of Chicago Press.

———. 1985. "Virtuous Subjectivity: In the Participant-Observer's I's." Pp. 267-68 in *Exploring Clinical Methods for Social Research,* edited by David N. Berg and Kenwyn K. Smith. Beverly Hills, CA: Sage.

Peters, Thomas J. 1987. *Thriving on Chaos: Handbook for a Management Revolution.* New York: Knopf.

Peters, Thomas J. and Robert H. Waterman, Jr. 1982. *In Search of Excellence: Lessons From America's Best-Run Companies.* New York: Harper & Row.

Pettigrew, Andrew M. 1983. "On Studying Organizational Cultures." Pp. 87-104 in *Qualitative Methodology,* edited by John Van Maanen. Beverly Hills, CA: Sage.

Philliber, Susan. 1989. Workshop on Evaluating Adolescent Pregnancy Prevention Programs, Children's Defense Fund Conference, Washington, DC, March 10.

Pietro, Daniel Santo. 1983. *Evaluation Sourcebook For Private and Voluntary Organizations.* New York: American Council of Voluntary Agencies for Foreign Service.

Pike, Kenneth. 1954. *Language in Relation to a Unified Theory of the Structure of Human Behavior.* Vol. 1. University of California: Summer Institute of Linguistics. Republished in 1967, The Hague, the Netherlands: Mouton.

Pillow, Wanda S. 2000. "Deciphering Attempts to Decipher Postmodern Educational Research." *Educational Researcher* 29 (5, June-July): 21-24.

Pirsig, Robert M. 1991. *Lila: An Inquiry Into Morals.* New York: Bantam.

———. 1984. *Zen and the Art of Motorcycle Maintenance: An Inquiry Into Values.* New York: Bantam.

Polanyi, Michael. 1967. *The Tacit Dimension.* Reprinted 1983. Magnolia, MA: Peter Smith.

———. 1962. *Personal Knowledge.* Chicago: University of Chicago Press.

Porter, Michael E. and Mark R. Kramer. 1999. "Philanthropy's New Agenda: Creating Value." *Harvard Business Review* 78 (6, November-December): 121-30.

Potter, J. 1996. *Representing Reality: Discourse, Rhetoric and Social Construction.* London: Sage.

Powdermaker, Hortense. 1966. *Stranger and Friend.* New York: Norton.

Preskill, Hallie and R. T. Torres. 1999. *Evaluative Inquiry for Learning in Organizations.* Thousand Oaks, CA: Sage.

Preskill, Stephen and Robin Smith Jacobvitz. 2000. *Stories of Teaching: A Foundation for Educational Renewal.* Englewood Cliffs, NJ: Prentice Hall.

Preskill, Stephen L. and Hallie Preskill. 1997. "Meeting the Postmodern Challenge: Pragmatism and Evaluative Inquiry for Organizational Learning." Pp. 155-69 in *Evaluation and the Postmodern Dilemma.* Advances in Program Evaluation, Vol. 3, edited by L. Mabry. Greenwich, CT: JAI.

Pressley, Michael and Peter Afflerbach. 1995. *Verbal Protocols of Reading: The Nature of Constructively Responsive Reading.* Mahwah, NJ: Lawrence Erlbaum.

Private Agencies Collaborating Together (PACT). 1986. *Participatory Evaluation.* New York: Private Agencies Collaborating Together.

Program Evaluation Division (PED). 2001. *Early Childhood Education Programs: Program Evaluation Report.* Report No. 01-01. St. Paul, MN: Office of the Legislative Auditor.

Punch, Maurice. 1997. *Dirty Business: Exploring Corporate Misconduct.* London: Sage.

———. 1989. "Researching Police Deviance: A Personal Encounter With the Limitations and Liabilities of Fieldwork." *British Journal of Sociology* 40 (2): 177-204.

———. 1986. *The Politics and Ethics of Fieldwork.* Qualitative Research Methods Series, Vol. 3. London: Sage.

———. 1985. *Conduct Unbecoming: Police Deviance and Control.* London: Tavistock.

Putnam, H. 1990. *Realism With a Human Face.* Cambridge, MA: Harvard University Press.

———. 1987. *The Many Faces of Realism.* LaSalle, IL: Open Court.

Radavich, David. 2001. "On Poetry and Pain." *A View From the Loft* 24 (6, January): 3-6, 17.

Ragin, Charles C. 2000. *Fuzzy-Set Social Science.* Chicago: University of Chicago Press.

———. 1987. *The Comparative Method: Moving Beyond Qualitative and Quantitative Strategies.* Berkeley: University of California Press.

Ragin, Charles C. and Howard S. Becker, eds. 1992. *What Is a Case? Exploring the Foundations of Social Inquiry.* Cambridge, UK: Cambridge University Press.

Raia, Anthony and Newton Margulies. 1985. "Organizational Development: Issues, Trends, and Prospects." Pp. 246-72 in *Human Systems Development,* edited by R. Tannenbaum, N. Margulies, and F. Massarik. San Francisco: Jossey-Bass.

Ramachandran, V. S. and Sandra Blakeslee. 1998. *Phantoms in the Brain: Probing the Mysteries of the Human Mind.* New York: William Morrow.

Reed, John H. 2000. "Paying for Interviews." Posting on EvalTalk Internet listserv of the American Evaluation Association, September 1. Posted from Arlington, VA: TecMRKT Works.

Reichardt, Charles S. and Thomas D. Cook. 1979. "Beyond Qualitative Versus Quantitative Methods." Pp. 7-32 in *Qualitative and Quantitative Methods in Evaluation Research,* edited by Thomas D. Cook and Charles S. Reichardt. Beverly Hills, CA: Sage.

Reichardt, Charles S. and Sharon F. Rallis, eds. 1994. *The Qualitative-Quantitative Debate: New Perspectives. New Directions for Program Evaluation* 61 (spring). San Francisco: Jossey-Bass.

Reinharz, Shulamit. 1992. *Feminist Methods in Social Research.* New York: Oxford University Press.

Rettig, Kathryn, Vicky Chiu-Wan Tam, and Beth Maddock Magistad. 1996. "Using Pattern Matching and Modified Analytic Induction in Examining Justice Principles in Child Support Guidelines." Pp. 193-222 in *The Methods and Methodologies of Qualitative Family Research,* edited by Marvin B. Sussman and Jane F. Gilgun. New York: Haworth.

Rhee, Y. 2000. "Complex Systems Approach to the Study of Politics." *Systems Research and Behavioral Science* 17 (6, November-December): 487-91.

Rheingold, Howard. 2000. *They Have a Word for It: A Lighthearted Lexicon of Untranslatable Words and Phrases.* 2d ed. Louisville, KY: Sarabande.

———. 1988. *They Have a Word for It: A Lighthearted Lexicon of Untranslatable Words and Phrases.* Los Angeles: Tarcher.

Ribbens, Jane and Rosalind Edwards. 1998. *Feminist Dilemmas in Qualitative Research: Public Knowledge and Private Lives.* London: Sage.

Richardson, Laurel. 2000a. "Evaluating Ethnography." *Qualitative Inquiry* 6 (2, June): 253-55.

———. 2000b. "Writing: A Method of Inquiry." Pp. 923-48 in *Handbook of Qualitative Research.* 2d ed., edited by Norman K. Denzin and Yvonna S. Lincoln. Thousand Oaks, CA: Sage.

Richardson, Miles. 1998. "Poetics in the Field and on the Page." *Qualitative Inquiry* 4 (4, December): 451-62.

Riessman, Catherine Kohler. 1993. *Narrative Analysis.* Newbury Park, CA: Sage.

Rist, Ray C. 2000. "Influencing a Policy Process With Qualitative Research." Pp. 1000-17 in *Handbook of Qualitative Research.* 2d ed., edited by Norman K. Denzin and Yvonna S. Lincoln. Thousand Oaks, CA: Sage.

———. 1977. "On the Relations Between Educational Research Paradigms: From Disdain to Detente." *Anthropology and Education Quarterly* 8:42-49.

Robinson, C. A., Jr. 1949. *Alexander the Great, the Meeting of East and West in World Government and Brotherhood.* New York: Dutton.

Rog, Deborah. 1985. *A Methodological Analysis of Evaluability Assessment.* Unpublished doctoral dissertation, Vanderbilt University, Nashville, TN.

Rogers, B. L. and M. B. Wallerstein. 1985. *PL 480 Title I: Impact Evaluation Results and Recommendations.* A.I.D. Program Evaluation Report No. 13. Washington, DC: U.S. Agency for International Development.

Rogers, Carl. 1977. *On Personal Power.* New York: Delacorte.

———. 1969. "Toward a Science of the Person." In *Readings in Humanistic Psychology,* edited by A. Sutich and M. Vich. New York: Free Press.

———. 1961. *On Becoming a Person.* Boston: Houghton Mifflin.

Rogers, Everett. 1962. *Diffusion of Innovations.* New York: Free Press.

Rogers, Patricia J., Timothy A. Hacsi, Anthony Petrosino, and Tracy A. Huebner, eds. 2000. *Program Theory in Evaluation: Challenges and Opportunities. New Directions for Evaluation* 87 (fall). San Francisco: Jossey-Bass.

Ronai, Carol Rambo. 1999. "The Next Night *Sous Rature*: Wrestling With Derrida's Mimesis." *Qualitative Inquiry* 5 (1, March): 114-29.

Rorty, Richard. 1994. "Method, Social Science, and Social Hope." In *The Postmodern Turn: New Perspectives on Social Theory,* edited by Stephen Seidman. Cambridge, UK: Cambridge University Press.

Rose, Dan. 1990. *Living the Ethnographic Life.* Qualitative Research Methods Series, Vol. 23. Newbury Park, CA: Sage.

Roseanne. 2001. "What I've Learned." *Esquire* (March): 194.

Rosenblatt, Paul C. 1985. *The Family in Business.* San Francisco: Jossey-Bass.

Rosenthal, Rob. 1994. *Homeless in Paradise: A Map of the Terrain.* Philadelphia: Temple University Press.

Rossi, Peter H., Howard E. Freeman, and Mark W. Lipsey. 1999. *Evaluation: A Systematic Approach.* 6th ed. Thousand Oaks, CA: Sage.

Rossi, Peter H. and W. Williams, eds. 1972. *Evaluating Social Programs: Theory, Practice, and Politics.* New York: Seminar Press.

Rossman, Gretchen B. and Sharon F. Rallis. 1998. *Learning in the Field: An Introduction to Qualitative Research.* Thousand Oaks, CA: Sage.

Rubin, Herbert J. and Irene S. Rubin. 1995. *Qualitative Interviewing: The Art of Hearing Data.* Thousand Oaks, CA: Sage.

Rudestam, Kjell E. and Rae R. Newton. 1992. *Surviving Your Dissertation.* Newbury Park, CA: Sage.

Ruhleder, Karen. 2000. "The Virtual Ethnographer: Fieldwork in Distributed Electronic Environments." *Field Methods* 12 (1, February): 3-17.

Ryan, Gery W. and H. Russell Bernard. 2000. "Data Management and Analysis Methods." Pp. 769-802 in *Handbook of Qualitative Research*. 2d ed., edited by Norman K. Denzin and Yvonna S. Lincoln. Thousand Oaks, CA: Sage.

Sacks, Oliver. 1985. *The Man Who Mistook His Wife for a Hat*. New York: Summit.

———. 1973. *Awakenings*. New York: Harper & Row.

Safire, William and Leonard Safire. 1991. *Leadership*. New York: Fireside.

Salmen, Lawrence F. 1987. *Listen to the People: Participant-Observer Evaluation of Development Projects*. New York: Oxford University Press for the World Bank.

Sanday, Peggy Reeves. 1983. "The Ethnographic Paradigm." Pp. 19-36 in *Qualitative Methodology*, edited by John Van Maanen. Beverly Hills, CA: Sage.

Sanders, William. 1976. *The Sociologist as Detective*. 2d ed. New York: Praeger.

Sandmann, Lorilee R. 1989. *Educational Program Development Approaches Associated With Eastern Caribbean Extension Programs*. Unpublished doctoral dissertation, University of Wisconsin–Madison.

Sands, Deborah M. 1986. "Farming Systems Research: Clarification of Terms and Concepts." Pp. 87-104 in *Experimental Agriculture, Farming Systems Series*. Vol. 22. Cambridge, UK: Cambridge University Press.

Sands, G. 2000. *A Principal at Work: A Story of Leadership for Building Sustainable Capacity of a School*. Unpublished Ed.D thesis, Centre for Leadership, Management and Policy, Faculty of Education, Queensland University of Technology, Brisbane, Australia.

Schein, Edgar H. 1985. *Organizational Culture and Leadership*. San Francisco: Jossey-Bass.

Schensul, Jean and Margaret D. LeCompte, eds. 1999. *Ethnographer's Toolkit*. 7 vols. Walnut Creek, CA: AltaMira.

Schlechty, P. and G. Noblit. 1982. "Some Uses of Sociological Theory in Educational Evaluation." In *Policy Research*, edited by Ron Corwin. Greenwich, CT: JAI.

Schmidt, Mary R. 1993. "Alternative Kinds of Knowledge and Why They Are Ignored." *Public Administration Review* 53 (6): 526-31.

Schoggen, P. 1978. "Ecological Psychology and Mental Retardation." Pp. 33-62 in *Observing Behavior*. Vol. 1, *Theory and Applications in Mental Retardation*, edited by G. Sackett. Baltimore: University Park Press.

Schon, D. A. 1987. *Educating the Reflective Practitioner: Toward a New Design for Teaching and Learning in the Professions*. San Francisco: Jossey-Bass.

———. 1983. *The Reflective Practitioner: How Professionals Think in Action*. New York: Basic Books.

Schorr, Lisbeth B. 1988. *Within Our Reach: Breaking the Cycle of Disadvantage*. New York: Doubleday.

Schultz, Emily, ed. 1991. *Dialogue at the Margins: Whorf, Bakhtin, and Linguistic Relativity*. Madison: University of Wisconsin Press.

Schultz, Stephen J. 1984. *Family Systems Therapy: An Integration*. Northvale, NJ: Jason Aronson.

Schutz, Alfred. 1977. "Concepts and Theory Formation in the Social Sciences." In *Understanding and Social Inquiry*, edited by F. R. Pallmayr and T. A. McCarthy. Notre Dame, IN: University of Notre Dame Press.

———. 1970. *On Phenomenology and Social Relations*. Chicago: University of Chicago Press.

———. 1967. *The Phenomenology of the Social World*. Evanston, IL: Northwestern University Press.

Schwandt, Thomas A. 2001. *Dictionary of Qualitative Inquiry*. 2d rev. ed. Thousand Oaks, CA: Sage.

———. 2000. "Three Epistemological Stances for Qualitative Inquiry: Interpretivism, Hermeneutics, and Social Constructivism. Pp. 189-214 in *Handbook of Qualitative Research*. 2d ed., edited by Norman K. Denzin and Yvonna S. Lincoln. Thousand Oaks, CA: Sage.

———. 1997a. *Qualitative Inquiry: A Dictionary of Terms.* Thousand Oaks, CA: Sage.

———. 1997b. "Whose Interests Are Being Served? Program Evaluation as a Conceptual Practice of Power." Pp. 89-104 in *Evaluation and the Postmodern Dilemma.* Advances in Program Evaluation, Vol. 3, edited by L. Mabry. Greenwich, CT: JAI.

———. 1989. "Recapturing Moral Discourse in Evaluation." *Educational Researcher* 18 (8): 11-16, 34.

Schwartzman, Helen B. 1993. *Ethnography in Organizations.* Qualitative Research Methods Series, Vol. 27. Newbury Park, CA: Sage.

Scott, Myrtle and Susan J. Eklund. 1979. "Ecological Methods in the Study of Administrative Behavior." Presented at the 1979 American Educational Research meetings, San Francisco.

Scriven, Michael. 1998. "The Meaning of Bias." In *Stake Symposium on Educational Evaluation.* Urbana: CIRCE, University of Illinois.

———. 1993. *Hard-Won Lessons in Program Evaluation. New Directions for Program Evaluation* 58. San Francisco: Jossey-Bass.

———. 1976. "Maximizing the Power of Causal Investigation: The Modus Operandi Method." Pp. 120-39 in *Evaluation Studies Annual Review 1,* edited by G. V. Glass. Beverly Hills, CA: Sage.

———. 1972a. "Objectivity and Subjectivity in Educational Research." In *Philosophical Redirection of Educational Research: The Seventy-First Yearbook of the National Society for the Study of Education,* edited by L. G. Thomas. Chicago: University of Chicago Press.

———. 1972b. "Prose and Cons About Goal-Free Evaluation." *Evaluation Comment* 3:1-7.

Scudder, T. 1999. "The Emerging Global Crisis and Development Anthropology: Can We Have an Impact?" The 1999 Malinowski Award Lecture. *Human Organization* 58 (4, winter): 351-64.

Searle, Barbara, ed. 1985. *Evaluation in World Bank Education Projects: Lessons From Three Case Studies.* Report No. EDT 5. Washington, DC: World Bank.

Senge, Peter M. 1990. *The Fifth Disciple: The Art and Practice of the Learning Organization.* New York: Doubleday.

Shadish, William R. 1995a. "The Logic of Generalization: Five Principles Common to Experiments and Ethnographies." *American Journal of Community Psychology* 23 (3): 419-28.

———. 1995b. "Philosophy of Science and the Quantitative-Qualitative Debates: Thirteen Common Errors." *Evaluation and Program Planning* 18 (1): 63-75.

———. 1995c. The Quantitative-Qualitative Debates: "DeKuhnifying the Conceptual Context." *Evaluation and Program Planning* 18 (1): 47-49.

Shah, Idries. 1973. *The Subtleties of the Inimitable Mulla Nasrudin.* New York: Dutton.

———. 1972. *The Exploits of the Incomparable Mullah Nasrudin.* New York: Dutton.

Shaner, W. W., P. F. Philipp, and W. R. Schmehl. 1982a. *Farming Systems Research and Development: Guidelines for Developing Countries.* Boulder, CO: Westview.

———. 1982b. *Readings in Farming Systems Research and Development.* Boulder, CO: Westview.

Shank, Gary D. 2002. *Qualitative Research: A Personal Skills Approach.* Englewood Cliffs, NJ: Prentice Hall.

Shapiro, Edna. 1973. "Educational Evaluation: Rethinking the Criteria of Competence." *School Review* 81 (August): 523-49.

Shaw, Gordon, Robert Brown, and Philip Bromiley. 1998. "Strategic Stories: How 3M Is Rewriting Business Planning." *Harvard Business Review* 76 (3, May-June): 41-50.

Shepard, L. 1993. "Evaluating Test Validity." *Review of Research in Education* 19:405-50.

Shils, Edward A. 1959. "Social Inquiry and the Autonomy of the Individual." In *The Human Meaning of the Social Sciences,* edited by D. Lerner. Cleveland, OH: Meridian.

Silverman, David. 2000. "Analyzing Talk and Text." Pp. 821-34 in *Handbook of Qualitative Research.* 2d ed., edited by Norman K. Denzin and Yvonna S. Lincoln. Thousand Oaks, CA: Sage.

———, ed. 1997. *Qualitative Research: Theory, Method and Practice.* London: Sage.

Silverzweig, Stan and Robert F. Allen. 1976. "Changing the Corporate Culture." *Sloan Management Review* 17 (3): 33-49.

Simic, Charles. 2000. "Tragicomic Soup." *The New York Review of Books* 47 (9): 8-11.

Simmons, Richard. 1985. *Farming Systems Research: A Review.* World Bank Technical Paper No. 43. Washington, DC: World Bank.

Simon, R. I. and D. Dippo. 1986. "On Critical Ethnographic Work." *Anthropology and Education Quarterly* 17 (4): 195-202.

Sims, Calvin. 2001. "Stone Age Ways Surviving, Barely: Indonesian Village Is Caught Between Worlds Very Far Apart." *New York Times,* March 11, p. 6.

Smith, Dorothy. 1979. "A Sociology for Women." In *The Prism of Sex,* edited by J. A. Sherman and E. T. Beck. Madison: University of Wisconsin Press.

Smith, John K. 1991. "Goodness Criteria: Alternative Research Paradigms and the Problem of Criteria." Pp. 167-87 in *The Paradigm Dialogue,* edited by Egon Guba. Newbury Park, CA: Sage.

Smith, John Maynard. 2000. "The Cheshire Cat's DNA: Review of the Century of the Gene." *New York Review of Books* 47 (20, December 21): 43-46.

Smith, Louis M. and Paul F. Kleine. 1986. "Qualitative Research and Evaluation: Triangulation and Multimethods Reconsidered." *New Directions for Program Evaluation* 30 (summer): 55-72, *Naturalistic Evaluation,* edited by David D. Williams. San Francisco: Jossey-Bass.

Smith, Midge F. 1989. *Evaluability Assessment: A Practical Approach.* Norwell, MA: Kluwer-Nijhoff.

Smith, Nick, ed. 1981. *Metaphors for Evaluation: Sources of New Methods.* Beverly Hills, CA: Sage.

———. 1980. "Evaluation Utilization: Some Needed Distinctions." *Evaluation Network Newsletter* 16:24-25.

———. 1978. "Truth, Complementarity, Utility, and Certainty." *CEDR Quarterly* 11:16-17.

Snow, D. A. 1980. "The Disengagement Process: A Neglected Problem in Participant Observation Research." *Qualitative Sociology* 3 (2): 100-22.

Sociometrics. 1989. *Evaluating Programs Aimed at Preventing Teenage Pregnancies.* Palo Alto, CA: Sociometrics.

Sonnemann, Ulrich. 1954. *Existence and Therapy: An Introduction to Phenomenological Psychology & Existential Analysis.* New York: Grune & Stratton.

Sonnichsen, Richard C. 2000. *High Impact Internal Evaluation.* Thousand Oaks, CA: Sage.

———. 1993. "Can Governments Lean?" In *Comparative Perspectives on Evaluation and Organizational Learning,* edited by F. Leeuw, R. Rist, and R. Sonnichsen. New Brunswick, NJ: Transaction.

Sorensen, Peter F., Therese F. Yaeger, and Dave Nicoll. 2000. "Appreciative Inquiry: Fad or Important Focus for OD?" *OD Practitioner* 32 (1): 3-5.

Spindler, George and Lorie Hammond. 2000. "The Use of Anthropological Methods in Educational Research." Pp. 17-25 in *Acts of Inquiry in Qualitative Research,* edited by B. M. Brizuela, J. P. Stewart, R. G. Carrillo, and J. G. Berger. Reprint Series No. 34. Cambridge, MA: Harvard Educational Review.

Stake, Robert E. 2000. "Case Studies." Pp. 435-54 in *Handbook of Qualitative Research.* 2d ed., edited by Norman K. Denzin and Yvonna S. Lincoln. Thousand Oaks, CA: Sage.

———. 1998. "Hoax?" In *Stake Symposium on Educational Evaluation.* Urbana: CIRCE, University of Illinois.

————. 1995. *The Art of Case Study Research.* Thousand Oaks, CA: Sage.

————. 1978. "The Case Study Method in a Social Inquiry." *Educational Researcher* 7:5-8.

————. 1975. *Evaluating the Arts in Education: A Responsive Approach.* Columbus, OH: Charles E. Merrill.

Stake, Robert E., L. Bresler, and L. Mabry. 1991. *Custom and Cherishing: The Arts in Elementary Schools.* Urbana: Council for Research in Music Education, University of Illinois.

Stanfield, J. H. 1999. "Slipping Through the Front Door: Relevant Social Sciences in the People of Color Century." *American Journal of Evaluation* 20 (3, fall): 415-35.

Steinberg, D. I. 1983. *Irrigation and AIDs Experience: A Consideration Based on Evaluation.* A.I.D. Program Evaluation Report No. 8. Washington, DC: U.S. Agency for International Development.

Stenhouse, Lawrence. 1977. *Case Study as a Basis for Research in a Theoretical Contemporary History of Education.* East Anglia, UK: Centre for Applied Research in Education, University of East Anglia.

Stewart, Alex. 1998. *The Ethnographer's Method.* Qualitative Research Methods Series, Vol. 46. Thousand Oaks, CA: Sage.

Stewart, Edward C. 1985. *American Cultural Patterns: A Cross-Cultural Perspective.* Yarmouth, ME: Intercultural Press.

Stockdill, S. H., R. M. Duhon-Sells, R. A. Olson, and M. Q. Patton. 1992. "Voices in the Design and Evaluation of a Multicultural Education Program: A Developmental Approach." *New Directions for Program Evaluation* 53 (spring): 17-34, *Minority Issues in Program Evaluation,* edited by Anna-Marie Madison. San Francisco: Jossey-Bass.

Stoecker, R. 1999. "Are Academics Irrelevant? Roles for Scholars in Participatory Research." *American Behavioral Scientist* 542 (5): 840-54.

Storm, Jim and Michael Vitt. 2000. *Master of Creative Philanthropy: The Story of Russ Ewald.* Minneapolis, MN: Philanthropoid.

St. Pierre, Elizabeth Adams. 2000. "The Call for Intelligibility in Postmodern Educational Research." *Educational Researcher* 29 (5): 25-28.

Strauss, Anselm and Juliet Corbin. 1998. *Basics of Qualitative Research: Techniques and Procedures for Developing Grounded Theory.* 2d ed. Thousand Oaks, CA: Sage.

————, eds. 1997. *Grounded Theory in Practice.* Thousand Oaks, CA: Sage.

————. 1990. *Basics of Qualitative Research: Grounded Theory Procedures and Techniques.* Newbury Park, CA: Sage.

Strike, Kenneth. 1972. "Explaining and Understanding: The Impact of Science on Our Concept of Man." In *Philosophical Redirection of Educational Research: The Seventy-First Yearbook of the National Society for the Study of Education,* edited by L. G. Thomas. Chicago: University of Chicago Press.

Stringer, Ernest T. 1996. *Action Research: A Handbook for Practitioners.* Thousand Oaks, CA: Sage.

Stufflebeam, Daniel L. 2001. "Evaluation Values and Criteria Checklist." Posted online at the Western Michigan University's Evaluation Center's Evaluation Checklists Web site: www.wmich.edu/evalctr/checklists.

————. 1980. "An Interview With Daniel L. Stufflebeam." *Educational Evaluation and Policy Analysis* 2 (4): 90-92.

Stufflebeam, Daniel L., George F. Madeus, and Thomas Kellaghan, eds. 2000. *Evaluation Models: Viewpoints on Educational and Human Services Evaluation.* 2d ed. Boston: Kluwer.

Suchman, Edward. 1967. *Evaluation Research: Principles and Practice in Public Service and Social Action Programs.* New York: Russell Sage.

Sussman, Marvin B. and Jane F. Gilgun, eds. 1996. *The Methods and Methodologies of Qualitative Family Research.* New York: Haworth.

Symon, Gillian and Catherine Cassell. 1998. *Qualitative Methods and Analysis in Organizational Research: A Practical Guide.* Thousand Oaks, CA: Sage.

Tallmadge, John. 1997. *Meeting the Tree of Life.* Salt Lake City: University of Utah Press.

Tashakkori, Abbas and Charles Teddlie. 1998. *Mixed Methodology: Combining Qualitative and Quantitative Approaches.* Thousand Oaks, CA: Sage.

Taylor, Steven J. and Robert Bogdan. 1984. *Introduction to Qualitative Research Methods: The Search for Meaning.* 2d ed. New York: John Wiley.

Tedlock, Barbara. 2000. "Ethnography and Ethnographic Representation." Pp. 455-86 in *Handbook of Qualitative Research.* 2d ed., edited by Norman K. Denzin and Yvonna S. Lincoln. Thousand Oaks, CA: Sage.

Tesch, R. 1990. *Qualitative Research: Analysis Types and Software Tools.* New York: Falmer.

Textor, Robert. 1980. *A Handbook on Ethnographic Futures Research.* Stanford, CA: Stanford University Cultural and Educational Future Research Project.

Thomas, Jim. 1993. *Doing Critical Ethnography.* Qualitative Research Methods Series, Vol. 26. Newbury Park, CA: Sage.

Thomas, W. I. and D. Thomas. 1928. *The Child in America.* New York: Knopf.

Thompson, Linda. 1992. "Feminist Methodology for Family Studies." *Journal of Marriage and the Family* 54 (1): 3-18.

Tierney, Patrick. 2000a. *Darkness in El Dorado: How Scientists and Journalists Devastated the Amazon.* New York: Norton.

——. 2000b. "The Fierce Anthropologist." *The New Yorker,* October 9, pp. 50-61.

Tierney, William. 2000. "Undaunted Courage: Life History and the Postmodern Challenge." Pp. 537-65 in *Handbook of Qualitative Research.* 2d ed., edited by Norman K. Denzin and Yvonna S. Lincoln. Thousand Oaks, CA: Sage.

Tikunoff, William with B. Ward. 1980. *Interactive Research and Development on Teaching.* San Francisco: Far West Laboratory for Educational Research and Development.

Tilney, John S., Jr. and James Riordan. 1988. *Agricultural Policy Analysis and Planning: A Summary of Two Recent Analyses of A.I.D.-Supported Projects Worldwide.* A.I.D. Evaluation Special Study No. 55. Washington, DC: U.S. Agency for International Development.

Torres, Rosalie, Hallie Preskill, and Mary Piontek. 1996. *Evaluation Strategies for Communicating and Reporting: Enhancing Learning in Organizations.* Thousand Oaks, CA: Sage.

Travisano, Richard. 1998. "On Becoming Italian American: An Autobiography of an Ethnic Identity." *Qualitative Inquiry* 4 (4, December): 540-63.

Tremmel, Robert. 1993. "Zen and the Art of Reflective Practice in Teacher Education." *Harvard Educational Review* 63 (4): 434-58.

Trend, M. G. 1978. "On the Reconciliation of Qualitative and Quantitative Analyses: A Case Study." *Human Organization* 37:345-54.

Trochim, William M. K., ed. 1989. "Concept Mapping for Evaluation and Planning." Special issue of *Evaluation and Program Planning* 12 (1).

Trow, Martin. 1970. Comment on "Participant Observation and Interviewing: A Comparison." In *Qualitative Methodology,* edited by W. J. Filstead. Chicago: Markham.

Tucker, Eugene. 1977. "The Follow Through Planned Variation Experiment: What Is the Pay-Off?" Presented at the annual meeting of the American Educational Research Association, New York City, April 5.

Turksever, A. and G. Atalik. 2001. "Possibilities and Limitations for the Measurement of the Quality of Life in Urban Areas." *Social Indicators Research* 53 (2, February): 163-87.

Turner, Aaron. 2000. "Embodied Ethnography: Doing Culture." *Social Anthropology* 8 (1): 51-60.

Turner, Jonathan H. 1998. *The Structure of Sociological Theory.* Belmont, CA: Wadsworth.

Turner, Roy, ed. 1974. *Ethnomethodology: Selected Readings.* Baltimore: Penguin.

Turpin, Robin. 1989. "What Is and Is Not Politics in Evaluation?" *Evaluation Practice* 10, 1 (February): 54-57.

Uchitelle, Louis. 2001. "By Listening, Three Economists Show Slums Hurt the Poor." *New York Times,* February 18, p. B4.

U.S. General Accounting Office (GAO). 1998. *Emerging Drug Problems.* Washington, DC: General Accounting Office.

———. 1992. *The Evaluation Synthesis.* Washington, DC: General Accounting Office.

———. 1991. *Designing Evaluations.* Washington, DC: General Accounting Office.

———. 1989. *Prospective Methods: The Prospective Evaluation Synthesis.* Washington, DC: General Accounting Office.

———. 1987. *Case Study Evaluations.* Transfer Paper 9. Washington, DC: General Accounting Office.

United Way of America. 1996. *Measuring Program Outcomes: A Practical Approach.* Alexandria, VA: Effective Practices and Measuring Impact for United Way of America.

Uphoff, Norman. 1991. "A Field Guide for Participatory Self-Evaluation." Special issue, *Evaluation of Social Development Projects. Community Development Journal* 26 (4): 271-85.

van den Hoonaard, Will C. 1997. *Working With Synthesizing Concepts: Analytical Field Research.* Qualitative Research Methods Series, Vol. 41. Thousand Oaks, CA: Sage.

Van Maanen, John, ed. 1998. *Qualitative Studies in Organizations.* Thousand Oaks, CA: Sage.

———. 1988. *Tales of the Field: On Writing Ethnography.* Chicago: University of Chicago Press.

Van Manen, Max. 1990. *Researching Lived Experience: Human Science for an Action Sensitive Pedagogy.* New York: State University of New York.

Vesneski, W. and Kemp, S. 2000. "Families as Resources: Exploring Washington's Family Group Conferencing Project." Pp. 312-23 in *Family Group Conferencing: New Directions in Community-Centered Child and Family Practice,* edited by G. Burford and J. Hudson. New York: Aldine de Gruyter.

Vidich, Arthur J. and Standford M. Lyman. 2000. "Qualitative Methods: Their History in Sociology and Anthropology" Pp. 37-84 in *Handbook of Qualitative Research.* 2d ed., edited by Norman K. Denzin and Yvonna S. Lincoln. Thousand Oaks, CA: Sage.

Von Bertalanffy, Ludwig. 1976. *General System Theory: Foundations, Development, Applications.* New York: George Braziller.

Von Oech, Roger. 1998. *A Whack on the Side of the Head: How You Can Be More Creative.* New York: Warner.

Wadsworth, Yoland. 1993a. *How Can Professionals Help Groups Do Their Own Participatory Action Research?* Melbourne, Australia: Action Research Issues Association.

———. 1993b. *What Is Participatory Action Research?* Melbourne, Australia: Action Research Issues Association.

———. 1984. *Do It Yourself Social Research.* Melbourne, Australia: Victorian Council of Social Service and Melbourne Family Care Organization in association with Allen and Unwin.

Wagoner, David. 1999. "Lost." *Traveling Light: Collected and New Poems.* Champaign: University of Illinois Press.

Waldrop, M. M. 1992. *Complexity: The Emerging Science at the Edge of Order and Chaos.* New York: Simon & Schuster.

Walker, Joyce. 1996. "Letters in the Attic: Private Reflections of Women, Wives and Mothers." Pp. 9-40 in *The Methods and Methodologies of Qualitative Family Research,* edited by Marvin B. Sussman and Jane F. Gilgun. New York: Haworth.

Wallace, Ruth A. and Alison Wolf. 1980. *Contemporary Sociological Theory.* Englewood Cliffs, NJ: Prentice Hall.

Wallerstein, Immanuel. 1980. *The Modern World System.* San Diego, CA: Academic Press.

Walston, J. T. and R. W. Lissitz. 2000. "Computer-Mediated Focus Groups." *Evaluation Review* (5, October): 457-83.

Walters, Jonathan. 1992. "The Cult of Total Quality." *Governing: The Magazine of States and Localities*, May, pp. 38-42.

Warren, Marion K. 1984. *AID and Education: A Sector Report on Lessons Learned*. A.I.D. Program Evaluation Report No. 12. Washington, DC: U.S. Agency for International Development.

Waskul, D., M. Douglass, and C. Edgley. 2000. "Cybersex: Outercourse and the Enselfment of the Body." *Symbolic Interaction* 23 (4): 375-97.

Wasserman, Gary and Alice Davenport. 1983. *Power to the People: Rural Electrification Sector Summary Report*. A.I.D. Program Evaluation Report No. 11. Washington, DC: U.S. Agency for International Development.

Wasson, C. 2000. "Ethnography in the Field of Design." *Human Organization* 59 (4, winter): 377-88.

Watkins, Jane Magruder and David Cooperrider. 2000. "Appreciative Inquiry: A Transformative Paradigm." *OD Practitioner* 32 (1): 6-12.

Watkins, K. E. and V. J. Marsick. 1993. *Sculpting the Learning Organization*. San Francisco: Jossey-Bass.

Watson, Graham and Jean-Guy Goulet. 1998. "What Can Ethnomethodology Say About Power?" *Qualitative Inquiry* 4 (1, March): 96-113.

Wax, Rosalie H. 1971. *Doing Fieldwork: Warnings and Advice*. Chicago: University of Chicago Press.

Webb, Eugene J., Donald T. Campbell, Richard Schwartz, and Lee Sechrest. 1966. *Unobtrusive Measures: Nonreactive Research in the Social Sciences*. Chicago: Rand McNally.

Webb, Eugene J. and Karl E. Weick. 1983. "Unobtrusive Measures in Organizational Theory: A Reminder." Pp. 209-24 in *Qualitative Methodology*, edited by John Van Maanen. Beverly Hills, CA: Sage.

Weidman, Emmaline. 1985. *Dancing With a Demon: A Heuristic Investigation of Jealousy*. Unpublished doctoral dissertation, Graduate College, The Union Institute, Cincinnati, OH.

Weiss, Carol. 1972. *Evaluation Research: Methods of Assessing Program Effectiveness*. Englewood Cliffs, NJ: Prentice Hall.

Weiss, Carol H. and Michael Bucuvalas. 1980. "Truth Test and Utility Test: Decision Makers' Frame of Reference for Social Science Research." *American Sociological Review* (April): 302-13.

Weiss, Heather B. 2001. "Strategic Communications: From the Director's Desk." *The Evaluation Exchange* 7 (1): 1.

Weiss, Heather B. and Jennifer C. Greene. 1992. "An Empowerment Partnership for Family Support and Education Programs and Evaluations." *Family Science Review* 5 (1, 2, February/May): 145-63.

Wheatley, Margaret. 1992. *Leadership in the New Science*. San Francisco: Berrett-Koehler.

White, Michael and David Epston. 1990. *Narrative Means to Therapeutic Ends*. New York: Norton.

Whitehead, Alfred N. 1958. *Modes of Thought*. New York: Capricorn.

Whiting, Robert. 1990. *You Gotta Have Wa*. New York: Vintage.

Wholey, Joseph S. 1994. "Assessing the Feasibility and Likely Usefulness of Evaluation." Pp. 15-39 in *Handbook of Practical Program Evaluation*, edited by J. Wholey, H. Hatry, and K. Newcomer. San Francisco: Jossey-Bass.

———. 1979. *Evaluation: Promise and Performance*. Washington, DC: Urban Institute.

Whyte, William Foote, ed. 1989. *Action Research for the Twenty-First Century: Participation, Reflection, and Practice*. Special issue of *American Behavioral Scientist* 32 (5, May/June).

———. 1984. *Learning From the Field: A Guide From Experience*. Beverly Hills, CA: Sage.

———. 1943. *Street Corner Society*. Chicago: University of Chicago Press.

Wildavsky, A. 1985. "The Self-Evaluating Organization." Pp. 246-65 in *Program Evaluation: Patterns and Directions*, edited by E. Chelimsky. Washington, DC: American Society for Public Administration.

Wilkinson, Alec. 1999. "Notes Left Behind." *The New Yorker*, February 15, pp. 44-49.

Williams, Brackette F. 1991. *Stains on My Name, War in My Veins: Guyana and the Politics of Cultural Struggle*. Durham, NC: Duke University Press.

Williams, Walter. 1976. "Implementation Analysis and Assessment." In *Social Program Implementation*, edited by Walter Williams and Richard F. Elmore. New York: Academic Press.

Wilson, E. O. 1998. "Back to the Enlightenment: We Must Know, We Will Know." *Free Inquiry* 18 (4): 21-22.

Wilson, Paul. 1999. "The First Laugh." Translation of a speech by President Václav Havel upon receiving the Open Society Prize awarded by the Central European University in Budapest in 1999. *The New York Review of Books* 46 (20): 59.

Wilson, Stacy. 2000. "Construct Validity and Reliability of a Performance Assessment Rubric to Measure Student Understanding and Problem Solving in College Physics: Implications for Public Accountability in Higher Education." Doctoral dissertation, University of San Francisco. *Dissertation Abstracts International* AAT 9970526.

Wirth, Louis. 1949. "Preface." In *Ideology and Utopia*, by K. Mannheim. New York: Harcourt Brace Jovanovich.

Wispé, L. 1986. "The Distinction Between Sympathy and Empathy: To Call Forth a Concept, a Word Is Needed." *Journal of Personality and Social Psychology* 50:314-21.

Wolcott, Harry F. 1992. "Posturing in Qualitative Inquiry." Pp. 3-52 in *The Handbook of Qualitative Research in Education*, edited by M. D. LeCompte, W. L. Milroy, and J. Preissle. New York: Academic Press.

———. 1990. *Writing Up Qualitative Research*. Qualitative Research Methods Series, Vol. 20. Newbury Park, CA: Sage.

———. 1980. "How to Look Like an Anthropologist Without Really Being One." *Practicing Anthropology* 3 (2): 56-59.

Wolf, Robert L. 1975. "Trial by Jury: A New Evaluation Method." *Phi Delta Kappan*, November.

Wolf, Robert L. and Barbara L. Tymitz. 1978. "Whatever Happened to the Giant Wombat: An Investigation of the Impact of the Ice Age Mammals and Emergence of Man Exhibit." Washington, DC: National Museum of Natural History, Smithsonian Institute.

Worthen, Blaine R., James R. Sanders, & Jody L. Fitzpatrick. 1996. *Program Evaluation: Alternative Approaches and Practical Guidelines*. Reading, MA: Addison-Wesley.

Wright, H. F. 1967. *Recording and Analyzing Child Behavior*. New York: Harper & Row.

Yin, Robert K. 1999a. "Rival Explanations as an Alternative to 'Reforms as Experiments.' " In *Validity and Social Experimentation: Donald Campbell's Legacy*, edited by Leonard Bickman. Thousand Oaks, CA: Sage.

———. 1999b. "Strategies for Enhancing the Quality of Case Studies." Presentation at Health Sciences Research conference, Qualitative Methods in Health Sciences Research. Bethesda, MD: Cosmos.

———. 1994. *Case Study Research: Design and Methods*. Applied Social Research Methods, Vol. 5. Thousand Oaks, CA: Sage.

———. 1989. *Case Study Research: Design and Methods*. Rev. ed. Newbury Park, CA: Sage.

Youngson, Robert. 1998. *Scientific Blunders: A Brief History of How Wrong Scientists Can Sometimes Be*. New York: Caroll & Graf.

Zaner, R. M. 1970. *The Way of Phenomenology: Criticism as a Philosophical Discipline*. New York: Pegasus.

Author Index

Subject Index

About the Author

Michael Quinn Patton lives in Minnesota where, according to the state's poet laureate, Garrison Keillor, "all the women are strong, all the men are good-looking, and all the children are above average." It was this interesting lack of statistical variation in Minnesota that led him to qualitative inquiry despite the strong quantitative orientation of his doctoral studies in sociology at the University of Wisconsin. He serves on the graduate faculty of The Union Institute, a nontraditional, interdisciplinary, nonresidential, and individually designed doctoral program. He was on the faculty of the University of Minnesota for 18 years, including 5 years as Director of the Minnesota Center for Social Research, where he was awarded the Morse-Amoco Award for innovative teaching. Readers of this book will not be surprised to learn that he has also won the University of Minnesota storytelling competition.

He has authored five other Sage books: *Utilization-Focused Evaluation, Creative Evaluation, Practical Evaluation, How to Use Qualitative Methods in Evaluation,* and *Family Sexual Abuse: Frontline Research and Evaluation.* He edited *Culture and Evaluation* for the journal *New Direction in Program Evaluation.* His creative nonfiction book, *Grand Canyon Celebration: A Father-Son Journey of Discovery,* was a finalist for 1999 Minnesota Book of the Year.

He is former President of the American Evaluation Association and the only recipient of both the Alva and Gunnar Myrdal Award for Outstanding Contributions to Useful and Practical Evaluation from the Evaluation Research Society and the Paul F. Lazarsfeld Award for Lifelong Contributions to Evaluation Theory from the American Evaluation Association. The Society for Applied Sociology awarded him the 2001 Lester F. Ward Award for Outstanding Contributions to Applied Sociology

Halcolm made his debut in the first edition of this book (1980) as a qualitative inquiry muse and Sufi-Zen teaching master who offered stories that probed the deeper philosophical underpinnings of how we come to know what we know—or think we know. Halcolm's musings, like his name (pronounced slowly), lead us to ponder "how come?" Halcolm was inspired by a combination of the character Mulla Nasrudin from Sufi stories (Shah, 1972, 1973) and science fiction writer Robert Heinlein's (1973) immortal character Lazarus Long, the oldest living member of the human race, who travels through time and space offering wisdom to mere mortals. Part muse and part alter ego, part literary character and part scholarly inquirer, Halcolm's occasional appearances in this research and evaluation text remind us to ponder what we think is real, question what we think we know, and inquire into *how come* we think we know it.